T0389452

Cover image: The first pages of one of the draft constitutions of 119 articles, Başbakanlık Osmanlı Arşivleri, Istanbul, Y.EE 71/33.

NEGOTIATING THE OTTOMAN CONSTITUTION
1839-1876

COLLECTION TURCICA
VOL. XXIV

Negotiating the Ottoman Constitution 1839-1876

Aylin KOÇUNYAN

PEETERS
PARIS - LOUVAIN - BRISTOL, CT
2018

This publication is a revised version of the EUI PhD thesis submitted for assessment with a view to obtaining the degree of Doctor of History and Civilisation of the European University Institute, Florence: it was defended in June 2013.

A catalogue record for this book is available from the Library of Congress.

ISBN 978-90-429-3506-8 (Peeters Leuven)
ISBN 978-2-7584-0282-4 (Peeters France)
D/2018/0602/34

TABLE OF CONTENTS

LIST OF APPENDICES

FOREWORD

The research and writing of this book, which is based on the dissertation I defended in June 2013 at the Department of History and Civilisation at the European University Institute, Florence, were completed with the support of various people. I would like to begin by expressing my special gratitude to my thesis advisor Prof. Anthony Molho, whose critical approach, advice, and continuous support greatly contributed to the maturation of the dissertation. His seminar on modern Jewish history in European perspective was an enriching experience for rethinking the transnational dimension of the issue of religious communities in general. I must also express my deepest gratitude to my external advisor Prof. Edhem Eldem for his valuable feedback on different aspects of the dissertation and his continuous support for my adventure in the Ottoman constitutional process, which started under his supervision during my master's studies at Bogaziçi University.

I also wish to express my special thanks to the other members of the jury, Prof. Antonella Romano, director of the Centre Alexandre Koyré at the Ecole des Hautes Etudes en Sciences Sociales, and Prof. Gilles Pécout, president of the Académie de Paris. Prof. Romano's seminars on space, science, and claims to European domination were a good experience for finding a balance between Eurocentric approaches and domestic instrumentality in the dissertation. I am also grateful to Prof. Pécout for his valuable advice and support for the avenues that the dissertation took. Equally, I owe special thanks to Prof. Sebastian Conrad, my former second reader at the EUI before he left for the Freie Universität, for the interesting questions he raised. Prof. Conrad's seminar on global history, held together with Prof. Steve Smith, inspired me to reconsider the interaction between the global and the local, for which I am grateful.

I owe special gratitude to Prof. Nathalie Clayer, director of studies at the Ecole des Hautes Etudes en Sciences Sociales and director of the CETOBAC (Centre d'Etudes turques, ottomanes, balkaniques et centrasiatiques), and to Prof. François Georgeon, former director of studies at the Ecole des Hautes Etudes en Sciences Sociales: both offered valuable advice and criticism for the final reshaping of this book. My special thanks also go to Prof. Bernard Heyberger, director of studies at the Ecole des Hautes Etudes en Sciences Sociales and faculty member at the Centre d'Etudes en Sciences Sociales du Religieux, with whom I had the opportunity and honour to discuss my research during his seminars.

Many thanks also go to Prof. Selim Deringil, my former professor of intellectual history at Boğaziçi University. It was a great pleasure to experience the first year of my studies at the EUI in the presence of Prof. Deringil, who joined the institute as a Fernand Braudel fellow. He participated in my presentations and gave valuable advice and feedback on the general structure of my dissertation.

Special thanks are due to Prof. Ali Akyıldız, professor of Ottoman history at Marmara University, for his helpful guidance within the Ottoman archives of the Prime Ministry. His advice completely changed the course of my research in the archives. I am also very grateful to Prof. Mustafa Kaçar, chair of the history of science at Fatih Sultan Mehmet University and my professor of Ottoman palaeography for many years, for his continuous support and assistance when deciphering Ottoman documents. His office was my usual stop after research in the Ottoman archives. I also thank him for sharing in the enthusiasm and the ups and downs of the research period.

There are also a number of professors who shared their coffee breaks or lunch times with me to discuss the various stages of my dissertation. I would thus like to take the opportunity to thank Anaide der Minassian, former *maître de conférence* at the Université Paris-I Panthéon-Sorbonne, and Kevork Bardakjian, professor of Armenian language and literature at the University of Michigan. I would also like to thank Claire Mouradian, director of research at the Ecole des Hautes Etudes en Sciences Sociales in Paris, for drawing my attention to the constitutional experience of Indian Armenians and to Saténig Toufanian, who works on the Madras movement, for our productive discussions and their hospitality during my visits to Paris.

I would also like to thank the staff of various libraries and archives who facilitated the research process: the Ottoman archives of the Prime Ministry (Istanbul), Public Record Office (London), archives of the French and Italian foreign ministries (Paris and Rome), Salt Research Library, Library of Koç University Research Centre for Anatolian Civilisations and Boğaziçi University Library (Istanbul), Bibliothèque Noubar, Bibliothèque du Musée d'Art et d'Histoire du Judaïsme, Bibliothèque de l'Alliance israélite universelle, Bibliothèque de la Société de l'Histoire du Protestantisme français, Archives du Consistoire central israélite de France (Paris), British Library (London), and the EUI Library (Florence).

Special thanks are due to His Excellency Sergio Romano, former diplomat and historian, for his helpful guidance with regards to the archives of the Italian Foreign Ministry in Rome.

Research and writing also overlapped with the convention of productive working groups and conferences the frameworks of which greatly contributed to the maturation of this book. In this respect I cannot fail to mention the inspiration proffered by the working group on constitutions and the legitimation of power, sponsored by the European Research Council within the research project *Europe 1815-1914* at the University of Helsinki. My special thanks go to the directors of the project, Prof. Bo Stråth, chair in Nordic, European, and World History at the Department of World Cultures, and Prof. Martti Koskenniemi, director of the Erik Castrén Institute of International Law and Human Rights at the University of Helsinki, for inviting me to join their working group. I also thank the project organisers Dr. Kelly Grotke and Dr. Markus Prutsch for the productive discussions during our meetings in Helsinki. Our contributions to the working group were collected in a collaborative volume *Constitutionalism, Legitimacy, and Power: Nineteenth-Century Experiences*: an earlier version of my reflections on the Armenian National Constitution and other community regulations was already published there under the title *Long Live Sultan Abdülaziz, Long Live the Nation, Long Live the Constitution!* before being further developed in this book.[1]

I greatly benefited from the general framework of the conference "Well-Connected Domains: Intersections of Asia and Europe in the Ottoman Empire", organised by the Karl Jaspers Centre at the University of Heidelberg in November 2011, which sought to reconsider the nature of transcultural encounters in the Ottoman Empire and the linkages between the latter and Europe. I am grateful to Prof. Thomas Maissen, professor of early modern Europe, and Prof. Michael Ursinus, chair of Islamic Studies at the University of Heidelberg, for inviting me to the conference, as well as to the other organising members of the conference, Pascal Firges, Tobias Graf, Christian Roth, and Gülay Tulasoğlu, for the productive debates in the conference and in the collective volume, *Well-Connected Domains: towards an Entangled Ottoman History*. My earlier thoughts on the transnational aspect of the Ottoman Constitution

---

[1] "Long Live Sultan Abdülaziz, Long Live the Nation, Long Live the Constitution!," in Kelly Grotke and Markus Prutsch (eds.), *Constitutionalism, Legitimacy, and Power: Nineteenth-Century Experiences* (Oxford: Oxford University Press, 2014), pp. 189-210.

and the interaction between non-Muslim community regulations and the first *Kanun-i Esasi* were initially published in this volume under the title *The Transcultural Dimension of the Ottoman Constitution* before being developed with additional archival research in this book.[2]

The revisions to my PhD thesis were made possible by generous grants. I would like to express my deepest gratitude to the Italian Foreign Ministry, which financed the first three years of my studies at the European University Institute, and to the institute itself for its fourth-year grant. This book has been published with a financial subsidy from the European University Institute, to which I am grateful as a former researcher. The revision process of the book was partially made possible through financial support from the French National Research Agency (Agence Nationale de la Recherche) within the programme "Trans-acting Matters: Areas and Eras of a (post-) ottoman Globalisation" (Matières à transfaire. Espaces-temps d'une globalisation (post-) Ottomane, (ANR-12-GLOB-003), and I am sincerely grateful to my colleague Dr. Marc Aymes, coordinator of the project and a member of the CETOBAC.

My stay in Florence was an enriching experience. Looking out from the hill in Fiesole, I discovered new approaches to life in general. The writing of this book saw many familial pains during which I could not always support my parents, as I was absent from Istanbul for research. I thank my husband Ara for replacing me in Istanbul during these difficult moments and for shortening the distance between Florence, Istanbul, and the other cities I visited for research missions.

Last but not least, I thank my corrector, Dr. James White. My ideas could not have been expressed so clearly without his help.

---

[2] "The Transcultural Dimension of the Ottoman Constitution," in Pascal Firges, Tobias Graf, Christian Roth, and Gülay Tulasoğlu (eds.), *Well-Connected Domains: towards an Entangled Ottoman History* (Leiden: Brill, 2014), pp. 235-258. See also Aylin Koçunyan, "The *Millet* System and the Challenge of Other Confessional Models, 1856-1865,", *Ab Imperio*, 1/2017, pp. 59-85.

NOTES ON TRANSLITERATION AND DATES

The book respects the rules of IJMES Translation and Transliteration Guide for Ottoman Turkish. The modern Turkish orthography is used for the transliteration of Ottoman words and personal names, including those of non-Muslims: the only exception is for names or words ending with *d*, which is replaced by *t* in modern Turkish. Consequently, Mahmud is used instead of Mahmut. The online Armenian translit converter, available at http://am.translit.cc/, with a western Armenian option, is used for the transliteration of Armenian words. The online date converter of the Turkish Historical Society, available at http://www.ttk.gov.tr/, is used when converting Hegirian dates into the Gregorian calendar.

To Nadia and Kevork, my two angels

INTRODUCTION

This book is about the genesis of the Ottoman Constitution, which was promulgated on December 23, 1876. The main objective is to reconstruct the nineteenth-century Ottoman constitutional movement in relation to Europe and international politics without neglecting the internal administrative developments that affected the process. Consequently, the study contextualises the Ottoman Constitution within earlier legal reforms, namely the 1839 Imperial Rescript and the 1856 Reform Edict, which initiated a constitutional debate in the empire.

The comparative presentation of the historiographical context together with my understanding of the Ottoman constitutional process will be the first step of my introductory remarks. My observations will be accompanied by a critical overview of scholarly narratives dealing with Ottoman constitutional history and new approaches and methodological tools with which the Ottoman constitutional reforms may be alternatively conceptualised from 1839 to 1876. In what follows, I will describe the logic according to which the chapters are organised, define the limits of the book together with deficiencies and asymmetries and present the primary sources that enabled me to reconstruct the main argument. In addition to these structural concerns, the introduction provides an overview of the historical context in which the Ottoman Empire was situated in the first half of the nineteenth century, together with the state apparatus and the social, economic and legal orders that characterised society in general.

1. Historiographical Narratives and New Approaches

My general impression of the historiographical framework is that the idea of reforms emerged in the Ottoman context with the frustrations of military defeats in the seventeenth century. Consequently, military reforms acquired priority in state policy from the early eighteenth century. Awareness of the need to borrow European techniques and knowledge was thus a phenomenon that preceded the nineteenth century.[1] It is

[1] M. Şükrü Hanioğlu, *A Brief History of the Late Ottoman Empire* (Princeton & Oxford: Princeton University Press, 2008), p. 43.

possible to imagine the Ottoman Empire as non-European before the late 1400s:[2] "Although the two entities already shared much, their ideological, political, military, economic, and historical dissimilarities remained overwhelming".[3] Over the next centuries, although differences persisted in the ideological realm, the two entities came closer in terms of contacts and interaction.[4] At the end of the seventeenth century, the Ottoman Empire was integrated into Europe.[5] Ottoman military reforms necessitated more revenue, and more revenue required more efficient government. The "plans" and "regulations" that constituted Selim III's "New Order" also inaugurated the "Enlightenment's systematising spirit" (*esprit de système*) in the Ottoman realm. In Weberian terms, this spirit of planning announced the transition from "traditional" to "rational-legal authority".[6]

If the military was the first realm of Ottoman administrative westernisation, the extension of the idea of reforms to governmental spheres followed soon after. The Tanzimat-*ı Hayriyye* (literally meaning "auspicious reorganisation" and metaphorically designating the sultan's 1839 Rescript) announced a period of "sustained legislation" and "reform", and reshaped both the Ottoman state and society between 1839 and 1876. The roots of the Tanzimat movement lay in the "passion" for "ordering" (*nizam*), which shaped the eighteenth century and regulated all aspects of life during the nineteenth century through the establishment of new institutions.[7]

The historiographical understanding of Ottoman constitutionalism considers the movement a gradual process. Tanzimat reforms cumulatively evolved towards the creation of the Ottoman Constitution in 1876. Mention is made of the principal stipulations of the Gülhane Rescript, which intended to introduce complete security of life, property and honour for individuals, to extend these guarantees to non-Muslims, to establish a

---

[2] Daniel Goffman, *The Ottoman Empire and Early Modern Europe* (Cambridge: Cambridge University Press, 2002), p. 19.

[3] Goffman, p. 19.

[4] Goffman, p. 19.

[5] Goffman, p. 224.

[6] Carter Vaughn Findley, "The Tanzimat," in Reşat Kasaba (ed.), *The Cambridge History of Turkey: Turkey in the Modern World* (Cambridge: Cambridge University Press, 2008), v. 4, p. 12.

[7] Stanford J. Shaw & Ezel Kural Shaw, *History of the Ottoman Empire and Modern Turkey: Reform, Revolution and Republic. The Rise of Modern Turkey, 1808-1975* (Cambridge: Cambridge University Press, 2002), v. 2, p. 55.

lawful mode of the collection for taxes and to reform military recruitment and the judicial procedure: it also promised the promulgation of new laws for the application of these reforms.[8] Contrary to general opinion, the Rescript did not put Ottoman Muslims and non-Muslims on equal footing, something that would contradict the shari'a.[9] "The decree did declare that the privileges it granted applied without exception to all subjects of the Sultanate, both 'Muslims and members of other communities' (ehl-i İslam ve milel-i saire), as the state's law (kanun) could do".[10] In an interview with Palmerston, Reşid Pasha also complained about the mistreatment to which Ottoman ministers were subject when they incited the sultan's anger.[11] When drafting the document, Reşid Pasha probably aimed to guarantee the lives and honour of the bureaucratic elite and to enable Ottoman bureaucrats to take advantage of the protection of organic laws.[12]

The internalist conventional historiography thus goes for a grand narrative of Ottoman political maturation by describing a continuous process of democratisation from the 1808 Sened-i İttifak (Deed of Agreement) to the 1876 Ottoman Constitution through the 1839 Imperial Rescript and the 1856 Reform Edict. This grand narrative profiles a quasi-unilinear development without taking into consideration the ups and downs of the political processes that resulted in these textual productions.[13] In order to put emphasis on the maturation of internal political traditions, conventional historiography cannot entirely relinquish the importance of Europe as a model. The Deed of Agreement is compared to the Magna Carta,[14] the 1839 Imperial Rescript to the French Declaration of the Rights of Man or to a constitutional charter, etc.[15] These approaches, while they aim to construct a "grand narrative of Ottoman

---

[8] Nicolas Milev, "Réchid Pacha et la Réforme ottomane," Zeitschrift für Osteuropaische Geschichte (1912), II, 382-398; here 388. Cited in Şerif Mardin, The Genesis of Young Ottoman Thought: a Study in the Modernisation of Turkish Political Ideas (Syracuse NY: Syracuse University, 2000), p. 157; Findley, "The Tanzimat", p. 18.

[9] Findley, "The Tanzimat", p. 18.

[10] Findley, "The Tanzimat", p. 18.

[11] For the text of the interview see Frank Edgar Bailey, British Policy and the Turkish Reform Movement: a Study in Anglo-Turkish Relations, 1826-1853 (Cambridge: Harvard University Press, 1942), Appendix IV, 271-276. Cited in Mardin, p. 158.

[12] Mardin, p. 157.

[13] See for instance, Bülent Tanör, Osmanlı-Türk Anayasal Gelişmeler (Ottoman-Turkish Constitutional Developments), (İstanbul: Afa Yayınları, 1996), pp. 24-127 where the author mentions the approaches of internalist conventional historiography.

[14] Tanör, pp. 40-47 for different approaches to the Magna Carta.

[15] Tanör, pp. 69-70 for different views on the issue.

political maturation" to show the extent to which Ottomans created the equivalents of European institutions, and thus escape a Eurocentric view of Ottoman constitutional history, in fact overshadow the authenticity of the circumstances that engendered these texts and orient Ottoman historiography towards simplistic comparisons between Europe and the Ottoman Empire.

Internalist approaches that aim to question externalist conventional historiography, according to which nineteenth-century Ottoman political maturation was only the result of institutional inputs from Europe, try to demonstrate that some constitutional developments resembling those of Europe occurred in the Ottoman Empire before the process of westernisation. As Hüseyin Yılmaz mentions, "[m]odern constitutionalism of the nineteenth century was thus as much a continuation of the existing constitutional traditions of the Ottoman experience in government as it was a result of Westernisation".[16] In Yılmaz's view, the military, financial and religious institutions that progressively developed to challenge each other's power and, more importantly, the rule of the sultan could be considered "constitutional checks".[17] This scholar also argues that textual agreements such as *Hüccet-i Şeriyye* and the Deed of Agreement in 1808 between social groups (Janissaries in the first case and rural notables in the other) and the political authorities,[18] and consultative assemblies (*meclis-i meşveret*), which were instituted as an administrative obligation from the seventeenth century and gradually transformed into "regular decision-making bodies" in the eighteenth century under Selim III's rule,[19] forced the sultan to concede some rights and privileges, thus paving the way to an Ottoman constitutional process and providing traditional grounds for the legitimation of a parliamentary system in the Ottoman Empire.[20] Yılmaz considers the *Hüccet-i Şeriyye* to be the first contract between the ruler and a military institution, namely the Janissaries, while the Deed of Agreement is viewed as the first contract between the ruler and rural notables, symbolically representing Ottoman subjects and their integration into the political process.[21]

---

[16] Hüseyin Yılmaz, "Osmanlı Devleti'nde Batılılaşma Öncesi Meşrutiyetçi Gelişmeler," (Constitutionalist Developments in the Ottoman Empire before Westernisation) *Divan*, vol. 13, no. 24 (2008), p. 30.
[17] Yılmaz, p. 30; pp. 1-20.
[18] Yılmaz, pp. 19-23.
[19] Yılmaz, pp. 25-27, 30.
[20] Yılmaz, pp. 2-4.
[21] Yılmaz, p. 23.

However, as Yılmaz himself demonstrates, the non-delimitation by a legal framework of the alternative sources of power (the grand vizier, sheikh ül-Islam and Janissaries) challenging the authority of the sultan engendered permanent tensions.[22] These alternative powers sometimes shaped political authority on behalf of their collective aspirations and interests and not always in the name of the public good.[23] Moreover, there was no clear legal rule to determine the borders of sultanic power; qualifying a sultan as cruel or equitable was a matter of propaganda for opponent groups. This flexibility of the shariʿa framework engendered rivalry between various powerful groups for the tools to legitimise resistance or obedience. The Janissaries, who held physical power in their hands, often allied themselves with the ulema and took advantage of the gap left by the flexibility of the shariʿa to dominate state politics.[24] Any share of or challenge to sultanic power did not necessarily bring about the democratisation of the Ottoman Empire: the dethronement of two sultans, Abdülaziz I and Murad V, did not establish a constitutional government in 1876. These domestic mechanisms of challenging political authority would have undoubtedly oriented the Ottoman Empire towards an alternative mode of legitimate governance if the Ottomans, inspired by the charisma of a global and powerful wave of constitutionalism, had not chosen to invest in a global/universal/external solution wherein the constitution was a response to their internal quest for legitimacy.

The quest for "legitimate opposition"[25] also preoccupies Baki Tezcan's work, which focuses on the period from 1580 to 1826: the author conceives of this era as a second Ottoman Empire, where patrimonial, dynastic and medieval institutions evolved, in his view, towards a limited monarchy together with the development of administrative, cultural, economic and monetary components.[26] Tezcan draws attention to the fact that, from the nine sultans who reigned from 1603 to 1703, six were subject to dethronements. Although conventional historiography has interpreted these depositions as the expression of Ottoman decline and corruption, Tezcan challenges this paradigm, arguing that the latter, accompanied by military rebellions, may be interpreted as limitations on monarchical

---

[22] Yılmaz, pp. 4-19.

[23] Yılmaz, p. 16.

[24] Yılmaz, pp. 12-14.

[25] This is the terminology that Tezcan uses; see Baki Tezcan, *The Second Ottoman Empire* (Cambridge: Cambridge University Press, 2010), p. 7.

[26] Tezcan, p. 10.

absolutism.[27] "How have we been led to believe that the English Civil War, which led to the execution of Charles I in 1649, and the 'Glorious' Revolution of 1688, which dethroned Charles I's son James II, were advances in the history of limited government, whereas the regicide of the Ottoman Sultan İbrahim in 1648 and the deposition of İbrahim son's Mehmed IV in 1687, for instance, were simply signs of decline?"[28] He also underlines that the Janissaries, who played a major role along with the jurisconsults in the depositions, were defending the people against absolute power:[29] the Janissaries were "identified with the nation", acted under the influence of public opinion and partially represented popular sovereignty.[30] Tezcan also refers to Namık Kemal, a major representative of Young Ottoman thought, who stated that the Janissaries were the "armed consultative assembly of the nation" before their abolition in 1826.[31]

Considering the limitation of political authority as an essential condition for "proto-democratisation" and the "victory for the constitutionalist cause",[32] Tezcan explains how the monetisation of the Ottoman economy in the sixteenth and seventeenth centuries assured the formation of socio-economic groups such as merchants and financiers and the enlargement of the "political nation", which also included jurists, Janissaries and local notables, *ayan*s.[33] Tezcan relates how the economic empowerment of these groups allowed them to challenge the sultan's *kanun* or *kanun-name*s, a compilation of administrative, financial, and penal customs,[34] and paved the way to the consolidation of the jurists' law, based on the shari'a.[35]

Thus, the Second Ottoman Empire experienced early modernity due to the development of a polity in the course of its economic empowerment and cooperation in limiting sultanic authority.[36] However, as Tezcan

---

[27] Tezcan, pp. 1-5.

[28] Tezcan, p. 5.

[29] Victor Fontanier, *Voyages en Orient, entrepris par ordre du gouvernement français: Turquie d'Asie* (Paris: Mongie aîné, 1829), vol. 1, p. 322. Cited in Tezcan, p. 6.

[30] Antoine de Juchereau de Saint-Denys, *Histoire de l'Empire ottoman depuis 1792 jusqu'en 1844* (Paris: Comptoir des Imprimeurs Réunis, 1844), vol. 1, 349, 355. Cited in Tezcan, p. 6.

[31] Mehmet Kaplan, *Namık Kemal: Hayatı ve Eserleri* (Namık Kemal: His Life and Works), (Istanbul: İbrahim Horoz Basımevi, 1948), p. 107. Cited in Tezcan, p. 6.

[32] Tezcan, p. 77.

[33] Tezcan, p. 11, 197.

[34] Tezcan, p. 19, 23, 24.

[35] Tezcan, p. 11.

[36] Tezcan, p. 13.

underlines, the monetisation of the Ottoman economy did not happen independently of the spreading of a wide network of markets over Asia, Europe and Africa.[37] As Cemal Cafadar argues, the coalition between the jurists and the army corps did not have a "common ideological commitment".[38] Moreover, Tezcan himself adds that not all the jurists belonged to what may be called the "constitutionalist camp", "nor was jurists' law inherently opposed to absolutism".[39] "Yet at the end of this transformation, these institutions were no longer able to fulfil their original functions properly, which left the Ottomans vulnerable in the face of European imperialism".[40]

As for Ali Yaycıoğlu, he contextualises the Deed of Agreement within a different narrative of discontinuity in subsequent periods and singles it out from other developments in the Tanzimat period. Yaycıoğlu underlines that the latter followed a series of revolutions in September 1808, which brought Sultan Mahmud II, the Grand Vizier Bayraktar Alemdar Mustafa Pasha, high-ranking Ottoman officials and the representatives of the leading dynasties of the provinces together in a consultative assembly. The aim was to respond to the political crisis in a spirit of agreement between the representatives of the Ottoman centre and the leading notables of the provinces. It was also emphasised that the financial and military reforms, interrupted by Janissary revolutions in May 1807, would continue and that notables would contribute to the continuity of this process. The Deed of Agreement came into existence in a period when the Ottoman Empire was experiencing difficulties in preserving its territorial integrity following the eighteenth-century Russo-Turkish wars that continued into the early nineteenth century. The unexpected occupation of Egypt in 1798 by Napoleon I pushed the Ottomans to find a new direction in an international political order shaken by the French Revolution. Rebellions in the Balkans, some provoked by the Russians, completed the chaotic context of wars and revolutions. The existing administrative and financial mechanisms were unable to remedy these impasses. However, the agreement necessitated a new way of sharing of power between the central authorities and the provincial dynasties. The central government agreed to delegate its provincial prerogatives to the local elites.

---

[37] Tezcan, p. 17.
[38] Cemal Kafadar, "Yeniçeri-*Esnaf* Relations: Solidarity and Conflict" (Unpublished Master's Thesis, McGill University, 1981), p. 90. Cited in Tezcan, p. 171.
[39] Tezcan, p. 77.
[40] Tezcan, p. 13.

More importantly, the Ottoman political structure was redefined by both the centre and the power holders of the provinces in such a way that the provincial elites were included in this structural fabric together with the central bureaucracy. Starting from the second half of the eighteenth century, these local elites had already succeeded in monopolising administrative and financial positions in the provinces and marginalising Ottoman bureaucrats sent from the centre. They also had access to governerships: Bayraktar Mustafa Pasha rose to power from such a background. These provincial powers, which also wielded local knowledge and economic resources, also possessed considerable military forces. In other words, the Deed of Agreement was a strategic and pragmatic negotiation of the Ottoman centre with local elites for security reasons and in order to guarantee a safe transfer of financial resources to the central government. The agreement placed them at the centre of the provincial administration through their prerogatives of collecting taxes and organising military forces in case of territorial threats or rebellions.[41] The application of the Deed of Agreement was interrupted by a new Janissary revolution in which the provincial dynasties could not intervene to protect the empire as they promised and during which the architect of the Deed, Grand Vizier Bayraktar Alemdar Mustapha Pasha, lost his life.[42] Yaycıoğlu emphasises that the dynamics of the Deed of Agreement did not directly shape nineteenth-century Ottoman modernisation, although many historians and jurists consider the document a milestone in Ottoman constitutional history. Furthermore, the circle of agreement (*daire-i ittifak*), which bound the signatories around the concepts of promise (*ahd*), deed (*sened*), guarantee (*kefalet*) and mutual trust (*emniyet*), was not generalised so as to include the whole empire in the subsequent periods.[43]

My conceptualisation of Ottoman constitutional history goes beyond the sole consideration of internal legal improvements, since it also contextualises the movement within the framework of international politics. One reason for this is the emergence of Ottoman reforms against the background of the dismantlement of the empire and the rivalry of the Great Powers in establishing a sphere of influence over south-eastern

---

[41] Ali Yaycıoğlu, "Sened-i İttifak (1808): Osmanlı İmparatorluğu'nda Bir Ortaklık ve Entegrasyon Denemesi," in Seyfi Kenan (ed.), *Nizam-ı Kadim'den Nizam-ı Cedid'e III. Selim ve Dönemi* (Selim III and His Era from the *Ancien Régime* to a New Order), (Istanbul: ISAM, 2010), pp. 667-676, 702.

[42] Yaycıoğlu, pp. 667-671.

[43] Yaycıoğlu, pp. 669, 705-708.

Europe, the eastern Mediterranean (up to the Persian Gulf and the Indian Ocean) and its southern shores. The rivalry was shared between the five Great Powers, namely Russia, France, Great Britain, Prussia and Austria:[44] "The catastrophes that alerted Ottomans to the menace of European imperialism began with the Russo-Ottoman War of 1768-74, ending with the disastrous Treaty of Küçük Kaynarca. That treaty launched the series of crises known to Europeans as the 'Eastern Question', over how to dispose of the lands under Ottoman rule".[45]

Likewise, the beginning of the Tanzimat period (1839-1878) coincided with the second Egyptian crisis when the Imperial Rescript was promulgated on November 3, 1839. It was probably not a coincidence that the 1839 Imperial Rescript immediately followed the 1838 Anglo-Ottoman Commercial Treaty. The second international conflict was the Crimean War (1853-56), which broke out due to a dispute between Catholic and Orthodox clergy over control of the Holy Places in Palestine.[46] The fact that the 1856 Reform Edict was issued one month before the Treaty of Paris shows the close relationship between "international recognition" and "domestic reform".[47] The 1876 Ottoman Constitution was promulgated in an atmosphere of rebellions, first in Bosnia and Herzegovina and then in Bulgaria. Following the crisis in the Balkans, the delegates of the Great Powers convened in the Ottoman capital to find a solution to the Eastern Question. The Ottoman Constitution was promulgated on the first day of their meeting in Istanbul, in the Admiralty Building beside the Golden Horn, on December 23, 1876 for the Conference of Constantinople. During the Conference, the Ottoman delegates Safved and Edhem Pashas solemnly declared that the meeting had lost its raison d'être, as the Ottoman Constitution granted the whole empire the reforms that the Powers required only for the Balkans.[48] The fact that international crises and diplomatic arrangements formed the backdrop for the Ottoman constitutional process leads one to consider the close connection between the promulgation of Ottoman reforms and European pressure.

[44] Robert Mantran, "Les Débuts de la Question d'Orient (1774-1839)," in *Histoire de l'Empire Ottoman* (Paris: Fayard, 1989), p. 421.

[45] Findley, "The Tanzimat", p. 11.

[46] Paul Dumont, "La Période des Tanzimat," in Robert Mantran (ed.), *Histoire de l'Empire ottoman* (Paris: Fayard, 1989), pp. 505-509. Cited in Findley, "The Tanzimat", p. 16.

[47] Hanioğlu, pp. 84-85.

[48] Robert Devereux, *The First Ottoman Constitutional Period: a Study of the Midhad Constitution and Parliament* (Baltimore: Johns Hopkins Press, 1963), p. 92.

Unlike the internalist approach, another extreme of conventional historiography lies in the sole consideration of external dynamics, which puts Europe at the centre of the Ottoman reforms, within the framework of the paradigms of westernisation and Ottoman decline. It would be erroneous to argue that Ottoman reforms were only undertaken to overcome European pressure. The reform movement was also envisaged as a response to domestic needs.[49] Although this book seems to align itself with the externalist conventional historiography by placing the issue of Great Power politics at the centre (or at least at the beginning) of the debate, it does not neglect to demonstrate how the Ottoman state challenged these politics in its diplomatic responses and the extent to which the state was strong even in the period of decline. There was a threshold beyond which the Great Powers could not interfere with the priorities of the Ottoman state apparatus. However, the reason for associating an internal movement with European developments inherently derives from the ambitions or aspirations of local actors, the men of the Tanzimat, who themselves desired to equalise the Ottoman Empire with Europe (or at least Europe as it existed in their discourse). There is no denying that Europe emerges from the documents of the Ottoman archives as a model. The draftsmen of the Ottoman Constitution themselves identified their legal text with European counterparts and referred to Europe as a source of inspiration. In a letter addressed to the Ottoman ambassador in Paris on December 26, 1876, the Ottoman Minister of Foreign Affairs Safved Pasha proudly declared that the general principles of freedom and equality, mentioned at the head of the Ottoman Constitution, were borrowed from the most liberal European public laws.[50] Moreover, the external influences on local productions show how domestic actors could formulate a particular reading of global movements. The historicisation of an internal process in relation to global developments also sheds light on the ways in which local agents responded to the use of constitutions as "instruments of cultural imperialism"[51] by the Great Powers throughout the nineteenth century. The novelty of this book lies perhaps in its effort to question the limits of this externalist conventional historiography.

---

[49] Cf. Shaw & Shaw, *Ottoman Empire and Modern Turkey*, v. 2, p. 59.

[50] Başbakanlık Osmanlı Arşivi, İstanbul (The Ottoman archives of the Prime Ministry, Istanbul; hereafter BOA). HR. SFR. 4 299/96, 26 December 1876.

[51] I am inspired by the statement of the "Research Project Europe, 1815-1914: Constitutions and the Legitimisation of Power", conducted by the University of Helsinki and available at http://www.helsinki.fi/erere/pages_workinggroups/constitutions_statement.html (accessed 26 April 2013).

Although historiographical approaches to the Ottoman constitutional movement generally treat the phenomenon within the decline paradigm as the result of a gradual process of westernisation from 1839 to 1876, this book is an attempt to go beyond this one-sided paradigm, which reduces Ottoman constitutional history to a simplistic process of adoption of western models without taking into consideration the selective control that dominant local groups exercised over westernisation: "The Tanzimat was both a time of crises, which implied impending collapse, and of accelerating reforms, which signified renewal".[52] The Ottoman Constitution was the outcome of a period of intense recodification in the western style. This process of recodification extended from the redefinition of the *millet* system to the limitation of the influence of the shariʿa, from the regulation of the state apparatus to control of economic resources. Although the new law codes were supposed to harmonise the Ottoman legal system with its European counterparts, the main intention of the Ottoman government was to orchestrate the inevitable process of westernisation under the selective control of the state. This power of control makes the Tanzimat era into something other than a period of mere decline and blind westernisation. Instead of reducing local actors, including the Ottoman state, to the status of passive receptors, the ambition of this book is, in this respect, to show the resistance the state and local intermediaries displayed in the adoption of European constitutional models; to reflect the dynamic atmosphere of conflict and negotiation, and the phases of circulation, translation, adaptation and adoption that characterised the constitutionalisation of the Ottoman Empire; and to grasp some moments of westernisation through the specific case study of the Ottoman Constitution in all its complexities.

Moreover, the westernisation paradigm overshadows the multiple facets of the process. My research shows that the Great Powers and the Ottoman state assigned different meanings to the idea of a constitution. The achievement of administrative reforms in the Ottoman Empire meant better commercial, financial and political penetration appropriate to the interests of the Great Powers. Since European public law was not a homogeneous entity, each of the Powers intended to shape the Ottoman reforms according to their own interests, legal traditions and the manoeuvring of their rivals. The common point was, however, that none of the Great Powers formulated any wish to replace the existing political

---

[52] Findley, "The Tanzimat", p. 14.

regime in the Ottoman Empire with a constitutional framework in the European sense. They rather proposed administrative or pro-Christian reforms without mentioning the term "constitution". For the Powers, the making of Ottoman reforms was a way of interfering in the internal affairs of the Ottoman state in order to dominate this sphere of rivalry.

As for the Ottoman side, the Constitution had a connotation of national sovereignty and territorial integrity. It was not a coincidence that the first article of the Ottoman Constitution was dedicated to territorial integrity: "The Ottoman Empire comprises the actual Countries and possessions and privileged provinces. It forms an indivisible whole from which no part can ever be detached for any motive whatever".[53] The Constitution also served as a western-style legal instrument that would help Ottomans to break the vicious circle of interdependency when facing external pressure from Europe for administrative improvements and put them on equal footing at the negotiation table. Likewise, the Powers and the Ottoman state attributed different meanings to the process of westernisation. For the Great Powers, the westernisation of the Ottoman Empire was the "Eastern Question", while, for the Ottoman side, the Eastern Question represented a "Western question".[54] In that respect, Ottomans also made pragmatic and strategic use of westernisation in order to "preserve the integrity and independence of the Ottoman Empire" and "prevent foreign intervention".[55] This two-sided perception shows that westernisation has many facets and goes beyond the simplistic transformation of the Ottoman Empire into a western-style state.

My concerns are also about the normative dimension of the existing historiographical narratives in Ottoman constitutional history. The normative comparison of the Ottoman Constitution with its European counterparts is a dominant pattern. The 1876 Ottoman Constitution is either compared to the 1831 Belgian Constitution or to the 1850 Prussian Constitution.[56] However, constitutional knowledge circulated from one context to the other in such a fluid way that it is quite difficult to map

---

[53] "The Ottoman Constitution, Promulgated the 7th Zilbridje, 1293 (11/23 December, 1876)," *The American Journal of International Law*, vol. 2, No. 4, Supplement: Official Documents (Oct., 1908), pp. 367-387. Here, p. 367.

[54] Cf. Roderic H. Davison, *Nineteenth-Century Ottoman Diplomacy and Reforms* (Istanbul: Isis, 1999), p. 169.

[55] Cf. Davison, *Ottoman Diplomacy and Reforms*, p. 169.

[56] Roderic Davison, *Reform in the Ottoman Empire, 1856-1876* (Princeton & New Jersey: Princeton University Press, 1963), p. 388; Bernard Lewis, "Turkey," in *Dustur: a Survey of the Constitutions of the Arab and Muslim States* (Leiden: Brill, 1966), p. 11.

the original producer of a constitution only by looking at the final constitutional texts. For instance, the 1831 Belgian Constitution itself is said to be inspired by the 1830 French Constitution.[57] Unlike other narratives, the novelty of my book lies in the emphasis put on the flow of ideas penetrating the empire rather than the comparison of finished constitutional products.[58] My ambition is to reconstruct the intellectual trajectories and political intentions of different actors involved in the making of Ottoman constitutional reforms through their ability to dominate the public debate. The reconstruction of these trajectories, full of tensions, encounters and negotiations, is more productive for echoing multiple human voices than the anachronistic comparative reading of final constitutional texts. This constructivist approach depicts much more clearly how the provisions of Ottoman legal arrangements might have been shaped one after the other from 1839 to 1876.

I also criticise the historiographical approach wherein the Ottoman constitutional process is conceptualised as the initiative of some leading Ottoman bureaucrats, the "western-educated men of the Tanzimat", and as an outcome of their close relationship with foreign statesmen for the accomplishment of reforms: here, Tanzimat reforms are described as initiatives imposed on Ottoman society by reformist bureaucrats who judged them necessary or because they were forced to act in that direction by the representatives of the European Powers.[59] The principal role has been especially attributed to Stratford Canning (from 1852 Lord Stratford de Redcliffe), the British ambassador in Istanbul from 1841 to 1858 in permanent contact with the leading Ottoman reformers, including Reşid Pasha.[60] The 1856 Reform Edict seemed to result from discussions held in early 1856 between Lord Stratford de Redcliffe, the French Ambassador Thouvenel, the Austrian Internuncio Prokesch, Ali and Fuad Pashas (grand vizier and foreign minister respectively), and the Ottoman Greek Prince Kallimaki.[61] Similarly, Midhad Pasha, the

---

[57] *La Grande Encyclopédie: Inventaire raisonné des Sciences, des Lettres et des Arts par une Société de Savants et de Gens de Lettres* (Paris: Lamirault, [s.d.]), v. 12, pp. 692-693.

[58] Cf. Norman Fairclough, *Discourse and Social Change* (Cambridge: Polity Press, 2007), pp. 2, 35, 71.

[59] Erik J. Zürcher, *Turkey: a Modern History* (London & New York, 1998), pp. 69-70; Davison, *Reform in the Ottoman Empire*, pp. 7-8; Hanioğlu, p. 73.

[60] Zürcher, pp. 52-53.

[61] Davison, *Reform, 1856-1876*, pp. 53-59.

author of the 1876 Ottoman Constitution, was described as being very close to Sir Henry Elliot, the British ambassador to the Porte.[62]

Although the interaction between foreign diplomats and local bureaucrats is frequently mentioned, the reason why it started is the missing piece of the puzzle in such historiographical narratives. My interpretation of this relational dependency lies, at first sight, in the ideological fragmentation of the Ottoman state as well as of its European counterparts "into rival segments pursuing contradictory strategies"[63] in the matter of reforms. In this context of ideological rivalry, the linkage of local bureaucrats to transnational networks for legitimacy and support was inevitable if a Constitutional Revolution in the Ottoman Empire was to be realised. This linkage also permitted reformist actors to challenge the power of their conservative rivals. "High officials struggled constantly to build up their networks of supporters and dependents–whence the political importance of the great official households and the patron-client networks formed around them–and to destroy their rivals".[64] Moreover, the search for global models in the resolution of local tensions and the investment of domestic bureaucrats in global solutions, of which the Ottoman Constitution was an example, necessitated dependence on transnational networks for expertise or advice.[65] On the other side of the coin, the collaboration of foreign diplomats with local bureaucrats meant better political penetration into the Ottoman governmental apparatus. The more a foreign diplomat could dominate the making of Ottoman reforms within the framework of the respective interests of his state and through his connection to local associates, the more the ascendency of other rival Powers in Ottoman politics could be slowed down or eliminated. This book thus intends to shed light on the motivations that led to fraternisation between Ottoman bureaucrats and their European counterparts.

---

[62] Davison, *Ottoman Diplomacy and Reforms*, p. 112.

[63] William Genieys and Marc Smyrl, *Elites, Ideas, and the Evolution of Public Policy* (New York: Palgrave, 2008), p. 23.

[64] Carter Vaughn Findley, *Ottoman Civil Officialdom: a Social History* (Princeton & New Jersey: Princeton University Press, 1989), p. 69.

[65] Cf. Nader Sohrabi, "Global Waves, Local Actors: What the Young Turks Knew about Other Revolutions and Why It Mattered?," *Comparative Studies in Society and History*, no. 44 (January, 2002), pp. 45-79. Here, pp. 45-46.

2. Methodological Tools

Since the reforms of the nineteenth century were inaugurated by state agents, the idea of modernity was located around the state. However, another perspective of modernity was born by the internal social dynamics of the Ottoman Empire.[66] My working hypothesis is that the Ottoman constitutional movement, which apparently started as a state initiative, developed beyond the control of Ottoman bureaucracy and through a web of relations that transcended the boundaries of Ottoman territory. From local authorities to foreign powers, the project incorporated a plurality of formal and informal actors of different ethno-religious and cultural origins and representing different ideologies and legal norms.[67] My research question is how the state authorities, who had the final say in the making of the Ottoman constitutional reforms, synthesised different legal traditions imported from the West into the Ottoman context through various human channels and how the Ottoman constitutional initiative was shaped by the encounter of European constitutional models with local political culture.

The book offers a constructivist conceptualisation of the Ottoman constitutional movement in order to reconstruct the process in a context of contestation and negotiation[68] and in relation to social actors. My approach thus offers a "dynamic process of movement, networks and mobilities" rather than a "static view" of laws and legislation[69] when investigating how the drafting of a constitution was mediated between different actors of various norms, values and interests. Within the framework of this constructivist approach, the first unit of analysis is the process of negotiation.[70] In this respect, the Ottoman Empire itself is conceptualised as a "negotiated enterprise" like its counterparts.[71] The approach of negotiation necessitates a focus on differences in the

---

[66] Karen Barkey, *Empire of Difference: The Ottomans in Comparative Perspective* (Cambridge: Cambridge University Press, 2008), pp. 256-257.

[67] Cf. Francesca Trivellato, *The Familiarity of Strangers: the Sephardic Diaspora, Livorno, and Cross-Cultural Trade in the Early Modern Period* (New Heaven & London: Yale University Press, 2009), pp. 2- 3, 5, 7-9, 18, 99, 155, 157, 163-164, 271.

[68] Gerard Delanty & Chris Rumford, *Rethinking Europe: Social Theory and the Implications of Europeanization* (New York: Routledge, 2005), p. 16.

[69] Cf. Delanty & Rumford, p. 15.

[70] Cf. Roderick M. Kramer & David M. Messick (eds.), *Negotiation as a Social Process* (Thousand Oaks: Sage Publications, 1995), p. 1.

[71] Cf. Barkey, *Empire of Difference*, pp. X, 1, 4.

reasoning of various actors.[72] Consequently, the book focuses on the different angles and interests through which various actors perceived and negotiated the administrative reforms which gradually led to the first Ottoman Constitution.

The issue of negotiation goes together with the concept of agency. Agency is associated in this work with a large spectrum of actions, instrumentalities and discourses targeting different objectives, from strategic gains and state interests to the transfer of European institutions to the Ottoman territory for emancipation and progress. As regards the Powers' agency, the situation was best explained by Palmerston, foreign secretary (1830-34, 1835-41 and 1846-51) and prime minister (1855-58 and 1859-65), who played a fundamental role in the determination of British foreign policy.[73] His famous statement that England has no eternal allies and no permanent enemies and only British interests are eternal[74] reflects the volatility of international politics. In such an atmosphere of fleeting policies, rivalries and interests, one may question the extent to which we can talk about British and French agencies in the making of constitutional reforms in the Ottoman Empire. Nevertheless, the agency of the major European Powers lies in their way of provoking Ottoman incentives for institutional change or, in other terms, harassing the empire's sovereignty through ceaseless ultimatums requiring administrative improvements.

For the agents of the Great Powers, the source of legitimacy when conceptualising Ottoman reforms was apparently based on the standards of civilisation and human rights. However, the implicit criteria were rather the European balance of power on the one side, and the particular interests of individual states on the other. The relation between legitimacy and the Ottoman constitutional reforms was conceptualised in a completely different manner by the sultan. On August 2, 1876, when inviting the Ottoman ministers to deliberate the principles on which the government should be based for a constitutional regime, the sultan emphasised

---

[72] Cf. Deborah M. Kolb, "Negotiation Theory through the Looking Glass of Gender," *ICAR (Institute for Conflict Analysis & Resolution) Working Papers* (George Mason University, 1994), pp. 1-32. Here pp. 4-5. Available online at http://scar.gmu.edu/working_papers.html (accessed 9 November 2012).

[73] Arman J. Kirakossian, *British Diplomacy and the Armenian Question, from the 1830s to 1914* (Princeton & London: Gomidas Institute Books, 2003), p. 3.

[74] Hansard Parliamentary Debates. 3rd Series. Vol. 97, London, 1848, p. 123. Cited in Kirakossian, p. 3.

that the administrative reforms would be examined in relation to the foundations of shariʻa and the manners, habits and capacity of the population.[75] Religion and social customs were the central parameters of legitimacy for the Ottoman government. This book questions the agency of some of the Great Powers, the Ottoman state apparatus, individual actors, the Young Ottomans and non-Muslim communities in the making of the Ottoman constitutional reforms.

Based on the writings of Namık Kemal, who was a member of the Drafting Commission of the Ottoman Constitution, Tarık Zafer Tunaya claims that the commission made a comparative study of all the monarchical constitutions of the world and examined about 1,000 books.[76] The Ottoman Minister of Foreign Affairs Safved Pasha himself stressed that the general principles of the Ottoman Constitution were borrowed from the most liberal European public laws.[77] The assumption can be made, therefore, that a process of negotiation overlapped with a phase of cultural translation during the drafting of the Ottoman Constitution. Local draftsmen probably consulted various foreign constitutions, partially translated them into Ottoman Turkish and adapted them to the political culture of the empire. The book uses Burke's definition of adaptation as a tool of analysis: there, adaptation is a "common response to an encounter with another culture, or items from another culture [...] in order to incorporate the pieces into a traditional structure".[78] Cultural adaptation is a "movement" of "de-contextualization" and "re-contextualization" in the sense that an item is detached from its "original setting" and modified according to a new geographical and social environment.[79] The encounter between European constitutional models and the Ottoman legal tradition was not a harmonious relationship, and Ottoman draftsmen exercised selective control over the transfer of European constitutional thoughts. Which European constitutional models were attractive for the Drafting Commission of the Ottoman Constitution? What did the Commission

---

[75] Public Record Office (hereafter PRO), FO 198/42. Turkey no. 1 (1877). Correspondence respecting the affairs of Turkey, presented to both Houses of Parliament by Command of Her Majesty, 1877. From Constantinople, August 2, 1876.

[76] Tarık Zafer Tunaya, *Türkiye'de Siyasal Gelişmeler, 1876-1938: Kanun-ı Esasi ve Meşrutiyet Dönemi, 1876-1918* (Political Developments in Turkey, 1876-1938: The Ottoman Constitution and the Constitutional Period, 1876-1918), (İstanbul: İstanbul Bilgi Üniversitesi Yayınları, 2003), v. 1, pp. 7-8.

[77] BOA, HR. SFR. 4 299/96, 26 December 1876.

[78] Peter Burke, *Cultural Hybridity* (Cambridge: Polity Press, 2009), p. 93.

[79] Burke, *Cultural Hybridity*, pp. 93-94.

select or reject from these models? Which standards of political culture did the Commission refer to during the processes of selection and rejection? Which cultural domains did draftsmen intend to defend against the penetration of foreign political cultures?[80] In other words, what were the parameters of cultural translation? These are the questions to which the content of the book intends to respond.

3. THE OTTOMAN EMPIRE AS A "NEGOTIATED ENTERPRISE"

"An empire is a large composite and differentiated polity linked to a central power by a variety of direct and indirect relations, where the centre exercises political control through hierarchical and quasi-monopolistic relations over groups ethnically different from itself".[81] Given the variety of ethnic and religious groups within its borders, the Ottoman Empire was one of the most heterogeneous states in the world in the nineteenth century.[82] The power relations between the Ottoman "centre" and the "pieces of the imperial domain" were mediated by "intermediate bodies", "networks", and "elites".[83] The Ottoman centre itself was fragmented and challenged the sultanic power on various occasions.

The Ottoman Centre

The Ottoman state was considered a patrimonial household of which the sultan was the head, the dynasty was the family, the territory was the dynastic patrimony, the ruling class were the sultan's slaves and the subject peoples were the flocks (the raya) entrusted by God to the sultan's care.[84] Together with the sultan and his palace, in the classical period the Ottoman state system roughly included the palace school and the child levy; the *divan* or councils, which deliberated on state affairs, dealt with complaints and received ambassadors; the qadi court system; the hierarchy of religious colleges; the Janissary infantry corps; the timar system

---

[80] Burke, *Cultural Hybridity*, p. 82.

[81] Barkey, *Empire of Difference*, p. 9.

[82] Hanioğlu, pp. 24-25.

[83] Cf. Barkey, *Empire of Difference*, p. 10.

[84] Carter Vaughn Findley, "Political Culture and the Great Households," in Suraiya Faroqhi (ed.), *The Cambridge History of Turkey: The Later Ottoman Empire, 1603-1839* (Cambridge: Cambridge University Press, 2006), v. 3, p. 66.

of landholding, the function of which was to conduct revenue collection and support the cavalry corps; the system of land survey and registration for the maintenance of the timar system; and the administrative apparatus of the Sublime Porte.[85] In other words, the Ottoman centre was composed of the sultan and his family, the imperial cultural tradition, the administrative apparatus and the ruling class.[86]

The Ottoman palace itself was divided into inside and outside services. Before the decline of the empire, the inside (*enderun*) service, which included the immediate personnel of the sultan, was the real centre of the government and organised the sultan's relations with the outside world. It was also the centre of the military-administrative establishment, which, until the sixteenth century, dominated the Grand Vizierate, a part of the outside service at that time.[87] The Ottoman ruling class was divided into a number of different sections: the military establishment (*seyfiye*); the religious establishment (*ilmiye*); the palace service; and the scribal service (*kalemiye*), which later evolved into a civil bureaucracy (*mülkiye*). The religious establishment consisted of born Muslims trained in religious colleges (madrasas) and was headed by the sheikh ül-Islam.[88]

Opposition Groups within the Centre

Although there were no higher institutions that could question the responsibility of the sultan, the latter always encountered resistance from different groups[89] and negotiated his power. When challenging political authority, opposition groups knew how to produce their legal tools of legitimation together with the expression of their demands.

The Ottoman governmental system may be classified as an Islamic patrimonial monarchy in which the state was perceived as an extended household. Before the reform era, the legitimacy of the state was based on the legal priority of the shari'a. The decrees of the sultan and custom successively occupied places in the hierarchy of legal sources.[90] The opposition groups legitimised resistance or disobedience to the sultan on

---

[85] Carter V. Findley, *Bureaucratic Reform in the Ottoman Empire: The Sublime Porte, 1789-1922* (Princeton & New Jersey: Princeton University Press, 1980), p. 12.

[86] Findley, *Bureaucratic Reform*, p. 18.

[87] Findley, *Bureaucratic Reform*, pp. 48-51.

[88] Findley, *Bureaucratic Reform*, pp. 43-47.

[89] Yılmaz, p. 10.

[90] Findley, *Bureaucratic Reform*, pp. 6-7.

the grounds that the shari'a had been transgressed.[91] Since the sixteenth century, one of the administrative practices that limited the arbitrary power of the sultan lay in the partial transfer of sultanic authority to two high-ranking bureaucrats, namely the grand vizier and the sheikh ül-Islam, recognised as the head of the ulema in the fifteenth century. When these two authoritative entities cooperated, they counterbalanced sultanic power. Even in the case of mutual conflict, they operated as a system of checks and balances against one another and tried to limit their respective spheres of influence.[92] Although the sheikh ül-Islam was not a permanent member of the Imperial *Divan* and that his superiority to the grand vizier was only honorary, the former used his authority to obtain more power, thereby succeeding in dominating the administration of educational and judiciary institutions during the sixteenth and seventeenth centuries. This domination limited the sphere of influence of the grand vizier over the administrative apparatus.[93]

As there was no procedure for the dethronement of the sultan, the fatwa represented the instrument of legitimation that the opposition needed to dethrone him or to manifest their resistance. The fatwa of the sheikh ül-Islam, who represented sultanic power in matters regarding the shari'a but who could also act independently, was the condition *sine qua non* for the success of political actions against sultanic authority. Parallel to the rise of the sheikh ül-Islam's authority, his fatwa also acquired a more official status. The latter's attitude was considered the official view of the highest legal authority of the state rather than a personal stance. In that respect, the fatwa served, in many cases, as a legal tool of legitimation to justify sultanic practices, to dethrone the existing sultan or to enthrone another one. It acquired the character of an official decision for the transfer of political authority from one sultan to the other. It assured that opposition groups realised the transfer of authority without threatening the continuity of the state or the legitimacy of the Ottoman dynasty. It also guaranteed that the political authority of the sultan was limited by the resistance of opposing groups.[94] As Ottoman political thought and textual sources of Islam institutionalised the ulema as a mediator of justice which prevented political authority from experiencing persecution and oriented society as well as the ruler towards goodness,

---

[91] Yılmaz, p. 10.
[92] Yılmaz, pp. 4-7.
[93] Yılmaz, pp. 7-8.
[94] Yılmaz, pp. 12-15.

the ulema considered itself not only the representative of religious law in front of and over the state, but also the representative of society, of the ruled as well as the oppressed. As the heirs of the Prophet and spokesmen of religion, the Ottoman ulema thus used its moral prestige to prevent the accumulation of excessive power in the person of the Ottoman ruler.[95] During the seventeenth and eighteenth centuries, Janissaries emerged as another opposition group and often cooperated with the ulema to limit sultanic power.[96] If the ulema represented legal legitimacy, the Janissaries monopolised physical power to become key actors in Ottoman politics.[97]

The Imperial Political Tradition

Ottoman political culture cemented the different pieces of the imperial domain to one another. The Ottomans made Islam one of the strongest components of legitimacy in addition to dynastic legitimation.[98] Islam as a "system of beliefs" and as a "world view", a "set of ideas", "institutions" and "practices", united in the "person of the judge", provided a framework for the functioning of everyday life.[99] As a local magistrate, the qadi was an intermediary body between "state" and "folk", between "high culture" and "folk culture", between "literate society" and an "illiterate understanding of religion": he was entrusted with the preservation of "basic moral and cultural unity" through the application of the shari'a:[100] "The court was among the most important source of linkage between the state and religion because it functioned parallel to the mosque and the Sufi lodges, and worked to satisfy the spiritual needs of the people while administering them".[101] There were in fact two categories of ulema in the Ottoman Empire. The muftis were those who interpreted Islamic law while the qadis were those who executed Islamic and other laws (*kanun*). The muftis had relative independence from the government and operated

---

[95] Yılmaz, pp. 17-18.

[96] Yılmaz, p. 16.

[97] For Hüccet-i Şeriyye, see Kemal Beydilli, "Kabakçı İsyanı Akabinde hazırlanan Hüccet-i Şeriyye," (Hüccet-i Şeriyye prepared in the aftermath of the Kabakçı Revolt) *Türk Kültürü İncelemeleri Dergisi* 4, İstanbul (2001), pp. 33-48. Cited in Yılmaz, p. 19. See also Cemal Kafadar, "Janissaries and other Riffraff of Ottoman Istanbul: Rebels without a Cause?," *International Journal of Turkish Studies*, vol. 13, nos. 1 & 2 (2007), pp. 113-134. Cited in Yılmaz, p. 13.

[98] Barkey, *Empire of Difference*, p. 104.

[99] Barkey, *Empire of Difference*, p. 105.

[100] Barkey, *Empire of Difference*, p. 106.

[101] Barkey, *Empire of Difference*, p. 107.

as a centre of opposition, while the qadis were appointees of the state. Two *kazasker*s, one for Rumelia (European provinces) and the other for Anatolia (Asian provinces), were at the top of the hierarchy. The two *kazasker*s and the sheikh ül-Islam had seats in the sultan's imperial council.[102]

Ottoman law was based on two main sources: the shari'a and sultanic law. The shari'a served as a basis for the settlement of issues regarding individual rights, family law, inheritance, commerce and the rights of foreign subjects. The fatwas promulgated by the highest judicial authority entrusted the sultan with the authority to legislate on the grounds of public interest.[103] The sultan's decree was a major source of law complementing the shari'a and custom.[104] The shari'a was applicable to all issues involving Muslims. Although the sultan maintained control over the *kanun* (sultanic law) and the shari'a, the state did not reject "alternative legal and institutional frames".[105] Non-Muslims could submit their cases to their own religious institutions (the courts of the patriarchates or Jewish rabbinical courts) or to shari'a courts.[106] Nevertheless, the hearing of cross-communal cases in the shari'a courts meant that the Islamic judicial system would have priority over the others.[107] Cases between foreign nationals were settled according to the laws of their own countries within the courts of embassies and consulates. Legal conflicts between a non-Muslim foreigner and a Muslim were heard in shari'a courts in front of dragomans.[108]

The Periphery of the "Imperial Domain"

Provincial Notables and Administration

The *ayan*s (provincial notables) were another social category which acquired alternative power in the provinces. The Ottoman state tolerated the rise of the *ayan*s in order to slow down the independence of provincial

---

[102] Goffman, pp. 70, 72.

[103] Halil İnalcık, "Osmanlı Hukukuna Giriş: Örfi-Sultani Hukuk ve Fatih'in Kanunları," *Ankara Üniversitesi Siyasal Bilgiler Fakültesi Dergisi*, vol. 13, no. 2 (1958), pp. 104ff. Cited in Hanioğlu, p. 18.

[104] Findley, "Political Culture", p. 66.

[105] Barkey, *Empire of Difference*, p. 105.

[106] Hanioğlu, p. 19.

[107] Goffman, p. 73.

[108] Hanioğlu, p. 19.

governors[109] and used them as tax farmers. The practice was based on a short-term contract accessible to state officials, who hired tax farmers as revenue collectors. As the tax farmers intended to maximise their profits, the system engendered the abuse of the peasantry. Tax farming deviated from its initial form after 1650 and was transformed into a life-term contract (*malikane*) by providing a large amount of cash to the Ottoman treasury. Life-term tax farming engendered many enterprises of different sizes, and the *malikane* became one of the most important financial instruments for the eighteenth-century Ottoman Empire. The *malikane* owners were at first members of the military class. The practice was then extended to bureaucrats, ulema, members of the dynastic family and *ayan*s. The *malikane* system contributed to the evolution of the idea of ownership and paved the way to the privatisation of land.[110]

Although the central elites obtained the "lion's share" from the contracts, the extension of rights to local provincials was also the result of their importance as a group. Both central and provincial groups were permitted to appropriate surpluses in exchange of their financial help to the state. The unintended result of this extension of rights was the empowerment of notables, which created regional networks and modernities. "Among these, a Balkan, a western Anatolian, and a central Anatolian mode can be clearly discerned".[111] These notables invested in land and real estate in the cities and constructed local political networks.[112] The state was conscious of the resulting transfer of authority to notables but used the influence of one *ayan* family against another in regional conflicts.[113] "Hence, to a significant degree the state 'made' provincial power elites, as much as provincial power holders 'made' the state at the local level. Provincial elites 'localised' the hegemony of the state".[114] The *ayan*s pushed the state into modernity by forcing open the doors of private property and developing an alternative understanding of the notion of "state control of resources".[115]

---

[109] Halil İnalcık, "Centralization and Decentralization in Ottoman Administration," in Thomas Naff and Roger Owen (ed.), *Studies in Eighteenth Century Islamic Society* (Carbondale: Southern Illinois University Press, 1977), pp. 27-53. Cited in Yılmaz, p. 21.

[110] Barkey, *Empire of Difference*, pp. 231-233.

[111] Barkey, *Empire of Difference*, pp. 234-236; p. 243.

[112] Barkey, *Empire of Difference*, p. 244.

[113] Barkey, *Empire of Difference*, p. 251.

[114] Dina Rizk Khoury, "The Ottoman Centre versus Provincial Power-Holders," in Faroqhi (ed.), *The Cambridge History of Turkey*, v. 3, p. 136.

[115] Barkey, *Empire of Difference*, pp. 258-259.

A single administrative policy for the Ottoman frontiers was not realistic, and the state had to count on local elites of different religions in the remote provinces. Although the Ottoman Empire made efforts to establish more centralised control throughout the nineteenth century, "compromise" and "pragmatism" secured Ottoman sovereignty. Similarly, the Ottoman programme of modernisation varied from province to province.[116] "On sensitive frontiers with a religiously mixed population, the reforms aimed at reducing inter-communal tensions and increasing administrative efficiency would be introduced, but elsewhere, in strongly Muslim areas, the Ottomans were prepared to allow local elites to remain in control until the twentieth century".[117]

The comparison of the south-western Balkan frontier of 1787-1820 with that of eastern Arabia in 1870-1915 shows a policy of continuity in the Ottoman mentality with regards to the settlement of centre-periphery relations. In some provinces, the central government interfered only to a limited extent in the local affairs of some regions as long as its "security goals" were fulfilled and permitted local intermediaries to operate in the achievement of these goals. Nineteenth-century reforms were carried out more ambitiously in core provinces than in others. The application of reforms encountered opposition, anti-Tanzimat feelings, inter-communal violence, etc. On each such occasion, the government made a choice between the application of reforms on the one hand and the mobilisation of resources, the settlement of inter-communal tensions and security risks on the other. All this leads to the idea that the reforms affected the empire unequally:[118] "Where conditions dictated, as in relatively rich border areas, those with significant Christian populations or on land frontiers most vulnerable to attack from a strong enemy, the centre did apply reforms".[119] In other regions, such as Arabia, Jordan and parts of eastern Anatolia and Iraq, the frontier embraced reforms later and to a more limited degree, as the population was "overwhelmingly Muslim" and faced less threat.[120]

---

[116] A. C. S. Peacock, "Introduction: The Ottoman Empire and Its Frontiers," in A. C. S. Peacock (ed.), *The Frontiers of the Ottoman World* (Oxford & New York: Oxford University Press, 2009), pp. 21-22.

[117] Peacock, p. 22.

[118] Frederick Anscombe, "Continuities in Ottoman Centre-Periphery Relations, 1787-1915," in Peacock (ed.), *The Frontiers of the Ottoman World*, pp. 250-251.

[119] Anscombe, p. 251.

[120] Anscombe, p. 251.

The Millet System

Ottoman territory at the turn of the nineteenth century covered a vast area inhabited by 30 million people.[121] Ottoman society in general was organised according to religious affiliations, the principal division being between Muslims and non-Muslims. Approximately 80 per cent of the population was rural, and the Muslim community, which was not a monolithic bloc, formed a majority over the non-Muslim population of the empire. Various forms of eastern Christianity constituted almost one-third of the subjects. The Jewish population was small in number but prominent.[122]

The *millet* system was an intermediate body that regulated the relations between the Ottoman centre and the non-Muslim periphery. The combination of secular and religious authority held by the patriarch suited the Ottomans, who themselves united the *kanun* (sultanic/secular law) and the shari'a in the person of the sultan.[123] The church was an "umbrella organisation" whose administration and networks extended from the Ottoman capital to villages. However, in addition to local clergymen and notables, the guild leaders in urban centres organised the diversity of Ottoman society.[124] The power of the church was counterbalanced by the presence of local secular leaders who assured "linkages to the regional Ottoman officials and their superiors at the centre" through tax collecting. In the Muslim community, *ayan*s accomplished the same tasks for provincial leaders.[125] The *millet* system offered a more or less "normative order" that could engender "concrete" and "reproducible relations" between the sovereign and his subjects.[126] Equally, it enabled non-Muslim communities to preserve their religious, cultural and ethnic continuity while providing for their integration into the Ottoman administrative, economic and political systems through their ties of subjection.[127] Religion provided

---

[121] Charles Issawi, "Population and Resources in the Ottoman Empire and Iran," in Thomas Naff and Roger Owen (ed.), *Studies in Eighteenth Century Islamic History*, pp. 155-6. Cited in Hanioğlu, p. 7.

[122] Hanioğlu, pp. 24-25.

[123] Barkey, *Empire of Difference*, pp. 130, 134.

[124] Barkey, *Empire of Difference*, p. 143.

[125] Barkey, *Empire of Difference*, p. 144.

[126] Cf. Barkey, *Empire of Difference*, p. 68.

[127] Kemal H. Karpat, "*Millets* and Nationality: The Roots of the Incongruity of Nation and State in the Post-Ottoman Era," in Benjamin Braude and Bernard Lewis (eds.), *Christians and Jews in the Ottoman Empire* (New York: Holmes & Meier Publishers, 1982), vol. 1, pp. 141-142.

a universal framework of beliefs despite the ethnic and linguistic differences between each communal structure[128] and legitimated the authority of community leaders and, indirectly, that of the sultan.[129] Thus, individual identity was the outcome of a fusion of religion with ethnicity.[130] Although Muslims in other parts of the world, for example in Russia, India and Indonesia, developed community organisations resembling the *millet*s in the Ottoman Empire, Ottoman Turks, in contrast, did not have any communal organisation outside the state apparatus.[131]

Separate religious identities evolved towards national consciousness and nationalism in the 1860s through the reform of the *millet* structures.[132] The changes which affected the *millet* system emanated primarily from the rise of rural notables, new entrepreneurial-commercial elites and a secular intelligentsia. The economic and political claims of these secular groups were in conflict with the structure of the *millet*s, their churches and the "traditional Ottoman concepts of authority".[133] Merchants belonging to various non-Muslim *millet*s were involved in new businesses, such as insurance, transportation agencies, and banking, and acquired influential positions within their communities due to their wealth. Their contacts with international markets and Europe inspired them with new ideas about administration and justice. This interaction led to the development of secular and enlightened views on how to organise the relations between the church, the community and the Ottoman government. The merchants, the craftsmen (to a lesser degree) and the intellectuals differentiated themselves educationally, philosophically and socially from the clergy and combined their forces to urge the *millet* structure to reform. The new intelligentsia, mostly educated in Europe and influenced by French secularism, anticipated the future of their community on more "secular-national" grounds and expressed their demand for *millet* reform.[134] In that respect, faith ceased to serve as a universal framework for the Christian *millet*, which experienced a process of nationalisation and ethno-linguistic

---

[128] Karpat, "*Millet*s and Nationality", pp. 141-142, 144.

[129] Karpat, "*Millet*s and Nationality", pp. 142-144.

[130] Hanioğlu, pp. 24-25.

[131] Niyazi Berkes, *The Development of Secularism in Turkey* (London: Hurst, 1998), p. 159.

[132] Cf. Roderic Davison, "The *Millet*s as Agents of Change in the Nineteenth-Century Ottoman Empire," in Braude & Lewis (eds.), *Christians and Jews in the Ottoman Empire*, vol. 1, p. 333.

[133] Cf. Karpat, "*Millet*s and Nationality", p. 152.

[134] Cf. Karpat, "*Millet*s and Nationality", pp. 158-159.

scission. After the 1856 Reform Decree, Bulgarian merchants for instance attempted to found an exarchate in the 1860s, which was officially recognised in 1870 by imperial decree.[135]

The Enlargement of the Ottoman Centre

The gradual rise of the scribal service by the sixteenth century was due to the state's need to deal with foreign Powers through diplomatic relations.[136] The most evident change in the scribal service was the transfer of its several departments to new locations outside the palace, and especially the development of the new grand vizierial headquarters known as the Sublime Porte in the second half of the seventeenth century. "At the beginning of the nineteenth century, the Sublime Porte in the stricter sense was a distinct complex, which was adjacent to the Imperial Palace and contained the household and office of the grand vizier, the offices of several officials immediately subordinate to him, and the meeting place of the grand vizier's *divan* or council".[137] His council started to become the real centre of governmental affairs while the function of the imperial *divan* at the palace progressively declined. As the diplomatic business of the Ottoman Empire grew in volume, the chief scribe began to perform the role of foreign minister and acquired influence within the scribal service.[138] During the Tanzimat period, it was common for a foreign minister to also serve as grand vizier. Mustafa Reşid (1800-58), Keçecizade Fuad (1815-69) and Mehmed Emin Ali Pashas dominated "this combination of posts". "Their associates formed a revolving interministerial elite, rotating among ministries and provincial governorships".[139]

Political authority extended from the sultan and the inner palace circles to other state departments and opposition groups after the classical era. The opening of permanent embassies in Europe in the eighteenth century was followed by the inauguration of the Foreign Ministry under Mahmud II, who transformed the chief scribe into a foreign minister in 1836.[140] The emergence of the Foreign Ministry established a kind of interaction

---

[135] Karpat, "*Millet*s and Nationality", p. 161.
[136] Findley, *Bureaucratic Reform,* p. 67.
[137] Findley, *Bureaucratic Reform*, p. 5.
[138] Findley, *Bureaucratic Reform*, pp. 51-56.
[139] Findley, "The Tanzimat", p. 13.
[140] Findley, *Bureaucratic Reform*, pp. 126-141.

between the empire and the outside world.[141] Ottoman diplomats did not only play the role of representatives in European states but also transmitted the demands of the European Powers to their own people: "Thus, in representing the West to the Ottomans, more than the other way round, they quickly acquired an influence that extended in Ottoman official circles far beyond the field of foreign affairs as narrowly defined".[142] Men such as Mustafa Reşid, Sadık Rıfat, Ali and Fuad grew in number, expertise and influence and produced cultural patterns only marginally related to the classical norms of the scribal service.[143]

The trio of Mustafa Reşid, Fuad and Ali Pashas were recognised as the pioneers of the Tanzimat initiative. The drafting of the Gülhane Rescript was generally attributed to Mustafa Reşid Pasha, Ottoman foreign minister.[144] In the 1830s, Mustafa Reşid served as ambassador to Paris and London. This ambassadorship permitted him to get in touch with the leading statesmen of Europe and to witness the functioning of European political systems.[145] He "acquired the French language" noted Henry Layard,[146] attaché of the British embassy in Istanbul in the 1840s, "and through it had studied much of the political literature of Europe".[147] During and after the Crimean War, the new civil-bureaucratic elite created a kind of monopoly on the most important positions at the Porte. For instance, Mustafa Reşid held the Grand Vizierate from 1846 to 1852. He returned to the Foreign Ministry in 1852. Mustafa Reşid became grand vizier three more times between 1854 and 1858.[148]

Keçecizade Mehmed Fuad Pasha (1815-69), five-time Ottoman foreign minister and twice grand vizier, was born in Istanbul as the son of the poet

[141] Findley, *Bureaucratic Reform*, p. 148.

[142] Findley, *Bureaucratic Reform*, p. 137.

[143] Findley, *Bureaucratic Reform*, pp. 138-139.

[144] On Mustafa Reşid Pasha, see Reşat Kaynar, *Mustafa Reşid Paşa ve Tanzimat* (Ankara: Türk Tarih Kurumu, 1954); Ali Fuat Türkgeldi, *Rical-i Mühimme-i Siyasiye* (İstanbul: s.n., 1928); Abdurrahman Şeref, *Tarih Musahabeleri* (İstanbul: Matbaa-i Amire, 1339), pp. 75-87; Cavid Baysun "Mustafa Reşid Paşa," in *Tanzimat* (Ankara: Maarif 1940), 723-746; F. E. Bailey, *British Policy and the Turkish Reform Movement* (Cambridge, Mass., 1942), pp. 179ff. Cited in Butrus Abu-Manneh, *Studies on Islam and the Ottoman Empire in the 19th Century (1826-1876)*, (Istanbul: Isis, 2001), p. 73.

[145] Cf. Ahmed Lütfi Effendi, *Tarih*, vol. 6 (Istanbul: Sabah Matbaası, 1290-1328/1873-1911), pp. 55, 59-60. Cited in Abu-Manneh, p. 73.

[146] On Henry Layard, see *Dictionary of National Biography*, Supplement III (London: Smith, Elder and Co, 1901), pp. 82-84. Cited in Abu-Manneh, p. 73.

[147] Quoted in Albert Habib Hourani, *Arabic Thought in the Liberal Age*, 2nd imp. (Oxford: Oxford University Press, 1969), p. 44. Cited in Abu-Manneh, p. 73.

[148] Findley, *Bureaucratic Reform*, pp. 153-154.

İzzet Molla. He studied in the new medical school, where he learnt French. He spent three years as an army doctor in Tripoli, Africa. He was appointed to the Translation Bureau in November 1837. Like his colleague Mehmed Emin Ali Pasha, he was Reşid Pasha's protégé. Dragoman of the Porte (1839-40), secretary of the Ottoman embassy in London (1841-44), and entrusted with a special mission to Spain (1844), he worked for a special commission of the *Meclis-i Vala* in April 1850 to examine Christian complaints from Vidin and went to Egypt in 1852 to see the application of the Tanzimat decrees. In 1852, he was appointed foreign minister just after Ali Pasha's accession as grand vizier. Thus Reşid's two disciples worked together in the highest offices. Fuad Pasha contributed to the elaboration of the Reform Edict of February 18, 1856 but did not attend the Paris Peace Congress, as Ali Pasha was the Ottoman plenipotentiary. From 1855 to 1857 and in 1863, he was also appointed president of the Tanzimat Council, with some interruptions. Fuad Pasha's Foreign Ministry again alternated with Ali Pasha's Grand Vizierate in 1858 after Reşid Pasha's death. In 1863, he was appointed grand vizier in charge of the war ministry as well. He contributed with Midhad Pasha in the elaboration of the 1864 *vilayet* (province) law first experimented with in Bulgaria. When Ali became grand vizier in 1867, Fuad became foreign minister again. Fuad Pasha also prepared plans for the Council of State and the Galatasaray Lycée, both inaugurated in 1868, before his death in 1869. Fuad Pasha's main objective was the promotion of the Ottoman Empire through diplomacy and reforms.[149]

Compared to Fuad Pasha, Mehmed Emin Ali Pasha (1815-71), born in Istanbul as the son of a shopkeeper in the Egyptian Market, was more or less self-educated and received a madrasa education. He started his career in the translation department of the Imperial Divan. He accompanied Mustafa Reşid Pasha to London as counsellor when the latter was appointed ambassador. In 1841, he was himself appointed ambassador in London.[150] Ali became foreign minister in 1846 and grand vizier in 1852. He was followed by Fuad some years later in the same positions. After the death of Mustafa Reşid Pasha, Ali and Fuad worked with a small circle of civil-bureaucratic associates (Kıbrıslı Mehmed Emin, Mütercim Mehmed Rüşdi and Yusuf Kâmil Pashas) and shared the Foreign Ministry

---

[149] Davison, *Ottoman Diplomacy and Reforms*, pp. 13-15.
[150] H. Bowen, "Ali Pasha Muhammad Amin," in *The Encyclopaedia of Islam*, new edition (Leiden: Brill, 1986), v. 1, pp. 396-398.

from 1846 onwards with a few other diplomats such as Sadık Rıfat Pasha; between them, they monopolised the post from 1857 to the death of Fuad Pasha in 1869.[151] Ali Pasha mastered French and, after the Paris Peace Conference, acquired a "European reputation" as a successful diplomat. In 1859, Ali was dismissed for having proposed a cut in palace expenditures to remedy the financial crisis.[152] During his final Grand Vizierate, Abdülaziz I would also have preferred to dismiss him but he recognised "Ali's standing in Europe to be such that he could not afford to".[153] After Fuad Pasha's death in 1869, Ali Pasha combined the posts of foreign minister and grand vizier until his own demise in 1871. Since the position of minister of the interior did not exist until 1868, Ali wielded an oligarchic influence over the most important positions of the Porte and dominated the entire administrative system.[154] In 1867 and 1868, Ali and Fuad Pashas were criticised for orienting the Ottoman Empire towards a "secular westernisation" by the Young Ottomans.[155]

In the era of reforms, the Foreign Ministry was the most evolved branch of the Ottoman civil bureaucracy.[156] The legacy of Ottoman diplomacy took shape in the nineteenth and early twentieth centuries within a period of territorial losses. The Ottoman sultan, unlike his European counterparts, did not create any diplomatic establishment abroad in the sixteenth century or after. If he entrusted envoys for special missions, the latter did not have any permanent character. However, other sovereigns sent resident and permanent envoys to the Ottoman capital. This lack of "reciprocity" emanated from the "Ottoman assumption" that the Ottoman sultan was the "preeminent ruler".[157] By 1871, the Ottoman consular and diplomatic services included embassies in Paris, London, Vienna and St Petersburg and legations in Berlin, Washington, Rome, Athens and Tehran.[158] The typical representatives of reformist groups with western-type education were concentrated in the Translation Bureau of the Foreign Ministry and were acquainted with European currents of thought,

---

[151] Findley, *Bureaucratic Reform*, p. 154.
[152] Bowen, pp. 396-398.
[153] Bowen, p. 397.
[154] Findley, *Bureaucratic Reform*, p. 154.
[155] Mardin, pp. 118-121; Davison, *Reform, 1856-1876*, pp. 212-228. Cited in Davison, *Ottoman Diplomacy and Reforms*, p. 19.
[156] Findley, *Bureaucratic Reform,* p. 168.
[157] Davison, *Ottoman Diplomacy and Reforms*, p. 329.
[158] Findley, *Bureaucratic Reform*, pp. 186-189.

especially liberalism and nationalism.[159] The Translation Bureau was "Turkey's open window to the West".[160]

As a state principle, the Ottoman ruling class was always composed of Muslim members.[161] Non-Muslims could not be part of the Ottoman ruling class without conversion to Islam and cultural assimilation. In different periods, some non-Muslims, few in number, played influential roles in the margins of the Ottoman ruling class but their status was not entirely official. The non-Muslim presence had been particularly influential in the local administration of some provinces or tributary regions, such as the vassal principalities of Moldavia and Wallachia. However, these individuals pursued "career patterns exclusive to themselves" and had not been entirely incorporated into the ruling class.[162] Between the 1821 and 1856, a small number of non-Muslims held official or quasi-official positions as translators, engineers in the Imperial Powder Works, architects, physicians and financiers (*sarrafs*).[163] The 1856 Reform Edict extended political power to non-Muslims with their admission into the civil service. From 1856 onwards, the presence of non-Muslims grew in the Ottoman bureaucracy.[164] Given their ethno-religious identification and their educational background, the non-Muslim civil bureaucracy occupied two categories of official posts in the Ottoman Empire. They held administrative positions in various regions of the empire that had an important non-Muslim population or emerged as translators, consuls and diplomats in the Ottoman Foreign Ministry. There were, however, limits to the integration and the promotion of non-Muslims to higher offices.[165] "This is clear from Fuad Paşa's statement, made to the British ambassador at the time of the first appointment of a non-Muslim minister, that some positions, including the ministries of war and foreign affairs and the Grand Vizierate, would have to remain in Muslim hands".[166] In that period,

---

[159] Zürcher, p. 70.

[160] Bernard Lewis, *Islam in History: Ideas, People, and Events in the Middle East* (Illinois: Open Court, 2001), p. 130.

[161] Carter Findley, "The Acid Test of Ottomanism: The Acceptance of non-Muslims in the late Ottoman Bureaucracy," in Braude and Lewis (eds.), *Christians and Jews in the Ottoman Empire*, vol. 1, p. 339.

[162] Findley, *Bureaucratic Reform*, pp. 22-23.

[163] Findley, *Bureaucratic Reform*, pp. 205-206.

[164] Cf. Findley, *Bureaucratic Reform*, pp. 23-24.

[165] Findley, *Bureaucratic Reform*, pp. 206-207.

[166] FO 78/2019, Elliot to Stanley, 10 March, 1868, commenting on appointment of Agathon Effendi, an Armenian, as minister of public works. Cited in Findley, *Bureaucratic Reform*, pp. 207-208.

non-Muslim officials passed from an "ambiguous status" to the "legal recognition" of their position on the grounds of "egalitarian principles", but only occupied intermediate posts.[167]

After 1856, the non-Muslim presence increased in the Ottoman Foreign Ministry: most were Armenians, while other groups such as Jews, Syro-Lebanese Christian Arabs, and westerners remained in the minority.[168] Ottoman Jews benefited from egalitarian principles of recruitment in the Hamidian era.[169] Posts at the Ministry of Foreign Affairs were appropriate for non-Muslims, who worked as translators, consuls, diplomats or representatives of the Porte to the western states.[170] Although Findley argues that the outbreak of the Greek revolution in 1821 created suspicions about the Phanariot elite in official service,[171] Neo-Phanariots still occupied key diplomatic positions in the constitutional process of the Ottoman Empire. The grand dragoman of the Porte, the highest public office open to non-Muslim subjects of the Ottoman Empire, was exclusively held for more than one and a half centuries by the Phanariot elites of the Greek Orthodox community. This was due to their linguistic capabilities and their knowledge of the Ottoman literary language.[172] The Phanariot elite were fluent in European languages (Italian and French) in addition to the *elsine-i selase*, the three languages (Arabic, Persian and Turkish) which formed Ottoman Turkish.[173]

"Phanariot" refers to the Phanar quarter of Istanbul, where the Greek Orthodox Patriarchate was and is located and where Phanariot elites used to live. Phanar was their base of power as they dominated the lay and sometimes ecclesiastical offices of the patriarchal institutions. Involved in commercial activities, they accumulated knowledge of medicine and European languages. In the course of the eighteenth century, they were involved in several sectors of Ottoman governance, holding the positions of imperial dragoman, dragoman of the fleet, *voyvoda*s of Wallachia and Moldavia. These two *voyvoda*s were responsible for tax collection and provincial administration and conducted foreign relations

---

[167] Findley, "Acid Test of Ottomanism", p. 365.

[168] Findley, *Bureaucratic Reform*, pp. 202-207.

[169] Findley, *Ottoman Civil Officialdom*, pp. 93-96.

[170] Findley, *Bureaucratic Reform*, p. 207

[171] Findley, *Bureaucratic Reform*, pp. 132-133.

[172] Johann Strauss, "The *Millet*s and the Ottoman Language: the Contribution of Ottoman Greeks to Ottoman Letters (19th-20th Centuries)," *Die Welt des Islams*, New Series, vol. 35, issue 2 (Nov., 1995), pp. 189-249. Here pp. 190-191, 192.

[173] Strauss, "The *Millet*s and the Ottoman Language", p. 192.

with the Russian and Austrian borders. The dragoman of the court was the link between European envoys and the sultan as well as the Orthodox patriarch and the court. The dragoman of the fleet was *de facto* the second authority after the Ottoman admiral (*kapudan pasha*) and the administrator of many of the Aegean islands and Anatolian coasts.[174] Phanariots were thus Ottoman Christian elites who had ascended to power between the 1660s and 1821.[175] They were instrumental in the rise of "ethnic nationalism" and inspired the Greek "cultural revival".[176] "Taken together, a picture emerges of leading Phanariot dignitaries and their client-retinues as links between, first, the Orthodox Christian Church and subject populations, and second, several aspects of Ottoman governance, including Court politics, the Sublime Porte, foreign relations, military administration, provincial administration, tax farming, and even guild affairs".[177]

The civil bureaucracy grew from roughly 2,000 scribes between 1770 and 1790 to 35,000-70,000 civil officials under Abdülhamid II. The different branches of civil officialdom benefited from reforms, and this sharpened "inter-service rivalries".[178] "Civil officials differed in their degree of westernisation, mastery of French serving as the distinguishing trait".[179] Compared to the civil and military elites, the ulema lost influence but still acted as the "guardians of Islamic values" and as the "masters of the old religious courts and schools". However, the reforms curbed their domination in the fields of justice and education and their control of revenues from charitable foundations (*evkaf*s).[180] Tanzimat reforms also developed an educational policy targeted at the formation of state elites. Military engineering schools were founded for the navy (1773) and the army (1793). Mahmud II founded the Military Medical School (1827) and the Military Academy (1834). Students were sent to Europe and an Ottoman school briefly operated in Paris (1857-64). The Translation Office of the Sublime Porte, founded in 1821, the Galatasaray Lycée

---

[174] Christine Philliou, "Communities on the Verge: Unravelling the Phanariot Ascendency in Ottoman Governance," *Comparative Studies in Society and History*, vol. 51, issue no. 1 (January 2009), pp. 154-156.

[175] Philliou, p. 151.

[176] Philliou, p. 152.

[177] Philliou, p. 174.

[178] Findley, *Bureaucratic Reform*, pp. 22-23, 212-218. Cited in Findley, "The Tanzimat", p. 21.

[179] Findley, "The Tanzimat", p. 22.

[180] Findley, "The Tanzimat", p. 22.

(1868) and the School of Civil Administration (Mülkiye Mektebi, founded in 1859 and upgraded in 1876) sought to train civil officials.[181] "For if Ottoman Sultans sought to train new elites to serve them personally, the ideas these men discovered at school led them to transfer their loyalty from the Sultan to their own ideal of the state, a fact with consequences enduring to the present".[182]

The physical expansion of the governmental body was apparent in Istanbul. Civil, military and religious services were provided by their respective headquarters at the Sublime Porte (*Bab-ı Ali*), the Ministry of War (*Bab-ı Seraskeri*) and the office of the sheikh ül-Islam (*Bab-ı Meşihat*). In 1871, the Sublime Porte included the offices of the grand vizier and the Council of Ministers, the foreign and interior ministries and the conciliar bodies. The ministries of finance, charitable foundations (*evkaf*), education, trade and agriculture, customs and land registry were situated outside the Sublime Porte.[183]

From Flexibility towards Rigidity

The longevity and success of the Ottoman imperial project were the results of "flexible state-society arrangements" and "pragmatic decision-making".[184]"It [the Ottoman Empire] fashioned a society defined by diversity (although certainly not equality) of population and flexibility in governance".[185] The eighteenth century was, however, a transitional period in which state and social reorganisation evolved towards "new patterns of imperial formation" and shifted from the "key aspects of empire" (negotiation, diversity and legitimacy) to "less negotiation", "more uniformity" and "standardised rules and regulations".[186]

In the early decades of the nineteenth century, non-state actors or opposition groups formed political alliances to claim participation in

---

[181] Findley, "The Tanzimat", pp. 22-23.

[182] Fatma Müge Göçek, *Rise of the Bourgeoisie, Demise of Empire: Ottoman Westernisation and Social Change* (New York: Oxford University Press, 1996), pp. 45-46. Cited in Findley, "The Tanzimat", p. 23.

[183] Findley, *Bureaucratic Reform*, pp. 167-190. Coşkun Çakır, *Tanzimat Dönemi Osmanlı Maliyesi* (İstanbul: Küre, 2001), pp. 35-76; Musa Çadırcı, *Tanzimat Döneminde Anadolu Kentlerinin Sosyal ve Ekonomik Yapısı* (Ankara: Türk Tarih Kurumu, 1997), pp. 185-90. Cited in Findley, "The Tanzimat", p. 23.

[184] Barkey, *Empire of Difference*, pp. 193-194.

[185] Goffman, p. 92.

[186] Barkey, *Empire of Difference*, p. 26.

politics, challenged political authority and engendered "a local indige-
nous modernity that provided the new counterweight to traditional state
society arrangements"[187] through the "politicisation of their demands".[188]
Their modernity lay in the fact that they struggled in the "political
arena".[189] However, nineteenth-century Ottoman state policy evolved
towards more centralisation. The suppression of the Janissaries in 1826,
the abolition of timars as the last remnants of Ottoman feudalism, the end
of the "provincial magistracy" of the *ayan*s, the control of the *vakıf*s
(pious foundations) and the attachment of the educational system to a
newly-founded Ministry of Education to financially and administratively
weaken the ulema and the establishment of new ministries were all examples of the state's attempt to centralise the Ottoman administration.[190]
Following the growth of "central power", the ulema were deprived of
their administrative and financial authority. The appointment of teachers
as well as the control of schools passed to the Ministry of Education. The
appointment of judges and the administration of law became the realms
of the Ministry of Justice. Fatwas would be issued by a committee of
legal specialists in the chief mufti's office. The mufti himself became a
government official with some "consultative" and "advisory" functions.[191]

It is evident from the historical context that a number of developments
frustrated the Ottoman centre and curbed Ottoman flexibility. The first
frustration came from territorial retreats. The Treaty of Karlowitz in 1699
marked the end of Ottoman expansion and the empire entered the eighteenth century with unprecedented territorial losses. A new disappointment came with the Treaty of Küçük Kaynarca in 1774, by which the
sultan ceased to exercise his suzerainty over the Khanate of the Crimea
and the Russian Empire obtained rights of protection over the Orthodox
subjects of the Ottoman Empire. The Danubian principalities, Wallachia
and Moldavia, gradually evolved into independent Rumania.[192] The 1815
Serbian Revolution forced the Ottoman state to allow the Serbs to establish their own national assembly and army, which slowly led to complete

---

[187] Barkey, *Empire of Difference*, p. 26.
[188] Barkey, *Empire of Difference*, p. 206.
[189] S. N. Eisenstadt, "Multiples Modernities," *Deadalus* 129 (Winter 2000): 6. Cited
in Barkey, *Empire of Difference*, p. 206.
[190] Bernard Lewis, *The Emergence of Modern Turkey* (London: Oxford University
Press, 1968), pp. 78-98, 134.
[191] Lewis, *Modern Turkey*, p. 97.
[192] Lewis, *Modern Turkey*, pp. 36-37; Hanioğlu, pp. 7-9.

autonomy under Ottoman suzerainty through the Treaty of Edirne (September 29, 1829).[193] In 1830, the Great Powers forced Mahmud II to accept full Greek independence.[194] But worst of all, the sultan faced an attack from his Governor of Egypt Mehmed Ali, who had been left without compensation for his support to the Ottoman army during the Greek Revolution.[195] Mehmed Ali emerged from this struggle with profit. He became the hereditary governor of Egypt, which remained under "nominal Ottoman sovereignty until 1914".[196] But Egypt progressively gained autonomy from Istanbul and became economically dependent on Europe. The construction of the Suez Canal (1869) increased the investment and interest of the European Powers in the country. The British occupied Egypt in 1882.[197]

Proto-nationalist ideas spread in the early nineteenth century. Rigas Velestinlis-Pheraios (1797) developed a new constitutional project envisioning a Pan-Balkan government based on the principles of the French Revolution for the subject peoples of European Turkey.[198] Constitutional regimes and representative bodies emerged in the areas which gained autonomy or semi-independence from the Ottoman Empire in the nineteenth century. Serbia proclaimed its *Skupština* in 1805, Rumania declared a bicameral legislature in 1866, Mount Lebanon had a mixed assembly in 1864 and Crete was granted a general assembly in 1868 by imperial edict.[199] The Lebanese crisis urged the Ottomans to promulgate a special regulation under which Mount Lebanon would be headed by a Christian governor.[200] These developments were not only restricted to the Christian-dominated areas of the Ottoman Empire. The first constitution in the Muslim world was proclaimed in Tunis in 1861. Khedive İsmail founded his *Majlis Shūrā al-Nuwwāb* in Egypt in 1866.[201] Ethnic consciousness progressively emerged in the nineteenth century within various non-Muslim communities. Bulgarian nationalists, for instance, revolted

---

[193] Shaw & Shaw, *Ottoman Empire and Modern Turkey*, v. 2, pp. 14-15.
[194] Shaw & Shaw, *Ottoman Empire and Modern Turkey*, v. 2, p. 32.
[195] Shaw & Shaw, *Ottoman Empire and Modern Turkey*, v. 2, p. 32.
[196] Findley, "The Tanzimat", p. 14.
[197] Findley, "The Tanzimat", p. 14.
[198] Hanioğlu, p. 26.
[199] Hanioğlu, pp. 113-114.
[200] Findley, "The Tanzimat", p. 15.
[201] Hanioğlu, pp. 113-114.

against the domination of the Greek Orthodox Patriarchate in order to found an autocephalous Bulgarian Exarchate in 1870.[202]

Territorial losses aside, the shadow of modernity in the immediate neighbourhood pushed the Ottoman state to readjust the imperial mode of governance to contemporary developments. The European model of military and political modernisation inspired the Ottoman ruling class to construct a certain vision of administrative centralisation targeting national interests.[203] The acceptance of western norms of political legitimisation contradicted the initial objectives of centralisation by offering new arguments for autonomy or even secession to peripheral regions or groups. Consequently, it became more difficult for the Ottoman state to apply the previous flexible norms of plurality and diversity. The Ottoman Empire inevitably took a constitutional course for the sake of homogenisation.[204] Thus claims for plurality and diversity could become more manageable with more homogeneous entities. The Constitution of 1876 seemed to be a "logical response" to the "organic regulatory acts" proclaimed for the various units of the "Ottoman polity".[205] All these developments led Ottoman internal policy in a more centralising direction. The most apparent sign of this politics of centralisation was the new law codes that emerged after the Crimean War. Although the codes were supposed to harmonise the Ottoman legal system with its European counterparts, the main intention of the government was to orchestrate this inevitable process of harmonisation in relation to Ottoman political culture. This process also affected the *millet* system, which, before the nineteenth century, was a blurred administrative "set of central-local arrangements" and was not fully codified.[206] Although the promulgation of new communal statute laws from 1862 to 1865 was launched as an effort to harmonise the Ottoman communal spheres with European standards of progress and secularism, the implicit intention was to integrate these "blurred" administrative structures into the Ottoman legal system. Accordingly, these statute laws became communal laws as well as part of Ottoman legislation[207] and went

---

[202] Hanioğlu, pp. 24-25.
[203] Cf. Eldem, "Istanbul", p. 197.
[204] Cf. Eldem, "Istanbul", p. 197.
[205] Findley, "The Tanzimat", p. 19.
[206] Barkey, *Empire of Difference*, p. 130.
[207] Saro'wxan, *Hah'gagan Xntirn ew Azkah'in Sahmanatro'wt'iwny T'o'wrqiah'o'wm, 1863-1910* (The Armenian Question and the National Constitution in Turkey, 1863-1910), (Tiflis: E'boxa, 1912), page indicated with the Armenian equivalent of the letter "p" in the introduction.

beyond the spontaneous set of arrangements of the previous centuries. The process of secularisation within the *millet*s also assured "a degree of formal institutionalisation they had never had in the classical Ottoman Empire".[208] According to the statesmen of the Tanzimat, the *millet* privileges of a religious nature would be preserved, as they were related to freedom of conscience, but those of civil and judicial nature would be eliminated because of their incompatibility with the uniform application of reforms. Then the shari'a would cease to be the basic legal reference and would instead become the private law of the Muslims. The state would be administered according to administrative, procedural, criminal, civil and commercial codes.[209]

Third, the political, social and administrative reforms of the Tanzimat period coincided with the opening of the Ottoman economy to foreign trade and investment. The 1839 Imperial Rescript followed the 1838 Free Trade Agreement with Britain; the 1856 Reform Edict followed the 1854 foreign borrowing; the 1876 Ottoman Constitution followed the 1875 Ottoman financial moratorium.[210] From the 1850s until 1876, the incorporation of the Ottoman Empire into world capitalism was followed by the penetration of foreign capital through state borrowing and direct investments.[211] Ottoman foreign borrowing was the result of the inability of the central bureaucracy to find a solution to its fiscal crisis and budget deficits by developing an efficient mode of tax collection. Until the second quarter of the nineteenth century, if successive debasing of coinage created additional revenues for the state, the gold equivalent of Ottoman currency declined in a parallel manner.[212] With the high rates of inflation, crisis of confidence and the depreciation of tax revenues which followed this process, the state became aware of the social and political limits of debasing the coinage. In the 1840s, European financiers, merchants and governments encouraged the central bureaucracy to borrow from European bankers. The Ottoman government started its first formal long-term borrowing in European financial markets in 1854 when

---

[208] Zürcher, pp. 64-65.

[209] Berkes, p. 154.

[210] Şevket Pamuk, *The Ottoman Empire and European Capitalism, 1820-1913: Trade, Investment and Production* (Cambridge: Cambridge University Press, 1987), pp. 12-13.

[211] Pamuk, *European Capitalism*, pp. 12-13.

[212] Lewis, *Modern Turkey*, pp. 110-111; Charles Issawi, *The Economic History of Turkey, 1800-1914* (Chicago, 1980), pp. 329-331. Cited in Pamuk, *European Capitalism*, p. 56.

encountering considerable fiscal difficulties due to the Crimean War. The most important characteristic of the period from 1854 to 1876 was the large amounts of borrowing under unfavourable terms.[213]

Economic interaction ended up with a parallel and simultaneous political integration so as to stimulate a constitutional turn in the Ottoman Empire. The periodisation of economic developments thus corresponded to the momenta of political restructuring.[214] In Wallersteinian terms, one would say that Ottoman "governance units" started to meet the requirements of the political superstructure of the capitalist world-economy.[215] Following the 1838 Commercial Treaty, the codification of a commercial law was put on the agenda. The first commercial code, borrowed from the French code of 1807, was promulgated in 1850[216] and then revised in 1860.[217] The direct translation of the French civil code was promoted by the Minister of Trade Kabuli Pasha, who was supported by France.[218] After two attempts at the modernisation of the penal provisions of the shari'a in 1840 and in 1851, a new penal code, an adaptation of the French Penal code of 1810, was promulgated in 1858.[219] Although the third penal code of 1858 was based on the 1810 French model and overshadowed Islamic principles, shari'a courts were not abolished until the collapse of the empire.[220] The land law of 1858 recognised land ownership, inheritance law and the issue of deeds. Private ownership thus acquired legal status.[221] After the proclamation of the Imperial Rescript, the resolution of penal conflicts was transferred from shari'a courts to civil tribunals. The foundation of the Ottoman Ministry of Commerce in 1839 brought a system of mixed commercial courts, which heard cases

[213] Pamuk, *European Capitalism*, pp. 57, 59.

[214] Cf. Pamuk, *European Capitalism*, p. 13.

[215] Immanuel Wallerstein, *The Modern World-System: The Second Era of Great Expansion of the Capitalist World-Economy, 1730-1840s* (San Diego: Academic Press, 1989), v. 3, pp. 131, 170.

[216] See A. Ubicini, *Letters on Turkey*, English trans. Lady Easthope (London, 1856), v. 1, p. 166; Hıfzı Veldet, "Kanunlaştırma Hareketleri ve Tanzimat," *Tanzimat* (İstanbul, 1940), v. 1, pp. 196-197. Cited in Berkes, pp. 161-162.

[217] Berkes, p. 162.

[218] Murat Çizakça, *A Comparative Evolution of Business Partnerships* (Leiden: Brill, 1996), p. 56.

[219] Berkes, pp. 163-164.

[220] Hanioğlu, p. 74.

[221] Ömer Lütfi Barkan, "Türk Toprak Hukuku Tarihinde Tanzimat ve 1274 (1858) Tarihli Arazi Kanunnamesi," *Tanzimat I* (İstanbul: Maarif Vekaleti, 1940), pp. 321-421. Cited in Hanioğlu, p. 90.

arising between European traders and Ottoman merchants. The 1856 Reform Edict stipulated the hearing of commercial and penal cases between Muslims and non-Muslims in mixed courts as well. Consequently, the Tanzimat period limited the sphere of competence of shariʿa courts to religious issues and to matters of succession. The Ottoman Commercial Court, initially founded in 1839 to hear cases between European traders and Ottoman merchants, gradually began to hear all commercial cases. The foundation of *nizamiye* tribunals in the Ottoman Empire, in addition to the existing shariʿa courts, prepared the grounds for the foundation of the Ministry of Justice in 1876.[222]

The *nizamiye* court system was established in the late 1860s with the purpose of dealing with civil, commercial, and criminal cases, thus limiting the sphere of shariʿa courts to individual cases and those of pious foundations. Moreover, in the years 1868-76, the Ottoman jurist Ahmed Cevded Pasha headed the project of compiling a civil code for the Ottoman Empire, known as the *Mecelle*. The latter consisted of the organisation of Hanefi religious law into numbered articles. In other words, although the content was based on Islamic law, the format was European. The *Mecelle* brought a certain legal standard to *nizamiye* courts as well as to shariʿa courts, in which the judge had previously possessed a degree of freedom to choose this or that legal source for the case under consideration. Moreover, the *Code of Civil Procedure*, the *Code of Criminal Procedure*, and the *Law of the Nizamiye Judicial Organisation*, all published in 1879, were a transplantation of their French counterparts, although the process of legal borrowing was quite selective. The proceduralisation of judicial proceedings in *nizamiye* courts engendered the professionalisation of personnel and brought legal formalism and rationality to judicial discourse and practice.[223]

"Throughout the century, the central bureaucracy tried, on the one hand, to curb the power of the provincial groups and, on the other hand, to create some room to manoeuvre for itself by playing one European power off against another".[224] This margin of manoeuvre was the outcome of the changing shares of major European Powers in Ottoman foreign

---

[222] Fatmagül Demirel, *Adliye Nezareti: Kuruluşu ve Faaliyetleri (1876-1914)* (The Ministry of Justice: Its Foundation and Activities, 1876-1914), (İstanbul: Boğaziçi Üniversitesi Yayınevi, 2007), pp. 1-40.

[223] Avi Rubin, *Ottoman Nizamiye Courts: Law and Modernity* (New York: Palgrave Macmillan, 2011), pp. 1-2, 8, 16, 30-32, 102-111.

[224] "For the political history of the relations between the Ottoman Empire and the European Powers and the rivalry amongst the latter," see M. S. Anderson, *The Eastern*

trade.[225] The same margin prevented the Ottoman Empire from entirely penetrating into the sphere of influence of one European power.[226] Throughout the nineteenth century, the Ottoman Empire did not totally lose its political independence and did not become a colony by developing strategies of resistance against attempts of the European world economy to dominate the imperial territory.[227] The manoeuvring margin between European Powers, however, should not be exaggerated. This margin was particularly narrow during the early years of the Pax Britannica. Moreover, political and fiscal crises offered European Powers the opportunity to obtain concessions in favour of their penetration into Ottoman economy.[228] In that sense, "[...] military, political and especially fiscal crises of the central government were one of the key determinants of the timing and rhythms of European penetration".[229]

Even if the signing of the *Sened-i İttifak* in 1808 looked like a victory in terms of power for the provincial *ayan*, a process of state recentralisation started under Mahmud II in the 1820s and 30s and was followed by the administrative reforms of the Tanzimat. The properties of great landlords were expropriated and the state took control of tax collection. The penetration of European capitalism into Ottoman lands, Pamuk says, suited the interests of provincial *ayan*s, merchants and big landowners, who could challenge state power by integrating their activities into the rules of the European world economy. Nevertheless, the Ottoman case differed from other countries of the European periphery. When world capitalism penetrated the Ottoman Empire during the nineteenth century, European economic agents had to deal with a relatively strong central bureaucracy, which had the "upper hand".[230] Although the land code of 1858 recognised private ownership and the Land Law of 1867 granted the right of land ownership to foreign citizens, the state pursued a policy that confiscated the large properties of tribal lords in order to distribute them to the minor peasantry.[231] Although the tax farming system could

---

Question 1774-1923 (London and New York, 1966); Shaw and Shaw, *Ottoman Empire and Modern Turkey*. Cited in Pamuk, *European Capitalism*, p. 10.

[225] Pamuk, *European Capitalism*, p. 77.

[226] Pamuk, *European Capitalism*, p. 77.

[227] Pamuk, *European Capitalism*, p. 53.

[228] Pamuk, *European Capitalism*, p. 133.

[229] Pamuk, *European Capitalism*, p. 134.

[230] Pamuk, *European Capitalism*, pp. 9-10, 77.

[231] Lewis, *Modern Turkey*, 90-92; Charles Issawi, *The Economic History of Turkey, 1800-1914* (Chicago, 1980), p. 202. Cited in Pamuk, *European Capitalism*, p. 87.

not be abolished until World War I,[232] the Ottoman state tried to prevent the strengthening of a powerful class of landlords that could appropriate the agricultural surplus at the expense of the state and challenge the rule of the central bureaucracy.[233]

The period just preceding the proclamation of the Ottoman Constitution was a difficult period for the empire. In 1875, a war with Serbia and Montenegro followed the revolt in Bosnia and Herzegovina.[234] European public opinion generally aligned with the rebels.[235] The Ottoman government suspended the payment of its foreign debt and experienced a financial crisis without European support in 1876.[236] The same year also saw the deposition of two sultans (Abdülaziz I and Murad V), the accession of Abdülhamid II to the throne, the Bulgarian crisis, the Andrassy Note and the Conference of Constantinople.[237] In 1876, an official communiqué alerted the police and the Press Office to forbid all public discussion or private meetings connected to constitutional reforms.[238] People involved in such discussions should be arrested and accused of high treason. This severe measure was taken on the grounds that administrative reforms needed to be examined in the light of "deep studies" and "research" in order to ensure its consistency with the principles of sacred law as well as with the customs, usages and fitness of the people for these institutions. Although Ottoman writers and thinkers were interested in the constitutional debate, the matter was entirely and exclusively left in the hands of the government.[239] The decree regarding the prohibition of all public discussion of the constitution reveals the preponderance of the conservative wing in the Cabinet.[240] The Ottoman Constitution was

---

[232] S. J. Shaw, "The Nineteenth Century Ottoman Tax Reforms and Revenue System," *International Journal of Middle Eastern Studies*, vol. 6, no. 4 (Oct., 1975), pp. 421-459; Donald Quataert, "Ottoman Reform and Agriculture in Anatolia, 1876-1908" (Unpublished PhD dissertation, Los Angeles: University of California, 1973), chapter I. Cited in Pamuk, *European Capitalism*, p. 89.

[233] Pamuk, *European Capitalism*, p. 89.

[234] Devereux, pp. 15-16.

[235] Davison, *Reform, 1856-1876*, p. 311.

[236] Şevket Pamuk, *A Monetary History of the Ottoman Empire* (Cambridge: Cambridge University Press, 2000), p. 217; François Georgeon, *Abdülhamid II: le Sultan calife, 1876-1909* (Paris: Fayard, 2003), pp. 71-78. Cited in Findley, "The Tanzimat", p. 16.

[237] Devereux, pp. 15-16.

[238] *The Times*, August 8, 1876; MAEF (Archives du Ministère des Affaires étrangères français, Paris, La Courneuve, hereafter MAEF), CP (Correspondance politique, hereafter CP), Juillet-Août 1876, Tome 405. From Bourgoing to Decazes. August 9, 1876.

[239] *The Times*, August 8, 1876.

[240] *The Times*, August 8, 1876.

thus promulgated on December 23, 1876 in a context of various internal and external tensions. The months that followed its enactment were also the beginning of new political crises. After Midhad's banishment in February 1877, the Ottoman Parliament opened on March 19, 1877 with 130 deputies (80 Muslims and 50 non-Muslims) and functioned until February 14, 1878.[241] In the meanwhile, the Russo-Turkish war broke out in April 1877. Upon the advice of the Grand Vizier Ahmed Vefik Pasha, Abdülhamid II did not dissolve the Ottoman Parliament but only suspended it. The text of the 1876 Ottoman Constitution continued to appear in the first pages of yearbooks from 1878 to 1908.[242]

4. Organisation of the Chapters

The chapters of the book have been organised in a manner that shifts from external dynamics to internal processes from 1839 to 1876 on the grounds that the Ottoman Constitution was the local dimension of a global movement that originated in Europe and that the incorporation of the Ottoman Empire into the Concert of Europe in 1856, in the aftermath of the Treaty of Paris, accelerated the interaction between European public law and the Ottoman legal edifice. **Chapter I** moves from introductory remarks to a specific focus on three major moments: 1839 (to a lesser extent), 1856 and the 1860s. Such a temporal focus also enables us to observe that law is a process rather than a static text and that all national laws take shape in interaction with dynamics other than local ones, since international factors inevitably affect domestic actors. The chapter examines the mediation of reform issues between international diplomacy and the Ottoman state, and between the Ottoman state and domestic groups such as the Young Ottomans and non-Muslim communities.

The rise of Britain as a "hegemonic power" made Her Majesty's Government, compared to other European states, the most influential in the mediation of Ottoman reforms. The main asset of France was, however, the global impact of Napoleonic codes: the French judicial system was conceived as an ideal type in the nineteenth century not only in the

---

[241] Tunaya, *Siyasal Gelişmeler*, v. 1, pp. 15-16.
[242] Tunaya, *Siyasal Gelişmeler*, v. 1, pp. 15-16.

Ottoman Empire but also on the world stage.[243] France thus shared British hegemony in the matter of legal reforms. Russia challenged their power through Pan-Slavic policies. The Powers differed from one another in terms of their economic and political weight. This asymmetry of power inevitably influenced the degree to which they could intervene in the mediation of Ottoman reforms. The chapter indirectly sheds light on Russian and Austrian interference when positioning Britain and France in relation to the rest of the Great Powers. Although the latter formulated continuous demands for pro-Christian emancipation, their real ambition was not to support a consistent policy of reforms in a broader sense. In fact, when claiming the protection of religious and civil rights of Ottoman non-Muslims, the European Powers never cared about their emancipation in the real sense of the term. Non-Muslims were just human instruments through which they could intervene in the internal affairs of the Ottoman Empire.

The 1856 Reform Edict secularised the administrative fabric of Ottoman non-Muslims. The organic laws which the Greek, Armenian and Jewish communities promulgated from 1862 to 1865 had been the first to apply some principles of western constitutionalism to their communal administration before the Ottoman state proclaimed a general constitution for the whole empire. They served as the first constitutional laboratories for the separation of power between religious and temporal authorities as well as between different bodies of communal administration: the institution of lay assemblies that operated on the basis of representative principles and electoral rules also made them trailblazers. The organic laws also developed a certain idea of communal sovereignty and legality that bound the behaviour of their administrators not only with religious values and canons but also with loyalty to secular laws: equally, they based the election of their administrators on the popular vote and general rules. Thus, ideas of constitutionalism and popular representation started to circulate in the Ottoman context through communal "filters" in the 1860s.[244] While describing the preparatory phase of these constitutions, the book also intends to reflect the fragmentation of these communities between tradition and modernity and their quest for new tools of legitimacy beyond

---

[243] Avi Rubin, "Legal Borrowing and its Impact on Ottoman Legal Culture in the Late Nineteenth Century," *Continuity and Change* 22 (2), 2007, pp. 280-281.

[244] Cf. Mardin, pp. 19-20; The term "filter" was used by Davison, *Ottoman Diplomacy and Reforms*, pp. 422-423.

religion, the various expectations of their different social layers from communal governance and how they perceived the complex relationship between community, state and law. The requests addressed by the Armenian National Assembly to the Ottoman state partially reflect such perceptions, or more precisely the ways in which Armenian community leaders perceived this triple relationship. Non-Muslims expected from the constitutionalisation of the Ottoman Empire an independent democratic legal framework which would enable them to defend their rights without any dependency on the European Powers. The non-application of Ottoman reforms was, however, an obstacle in breaking the vicious circle of dependency on international politics and obliged non-Muslims to internationalise their local grievances and to call the attention of Europe to their local problems. The mediation of some Jewish lobby groups and networks on behalf of their co-religionists in the Ottoman Empire during and in the aftermath of the Crimean War was thus intended to yield their emancipation on equal footing with other non-Muslims and called the attention of major European Powers to the unequal circumstances of Ottoman Jewry.

Modern print media facilitated the formation of new elites and the spread of new ideas in the Tanzimat era. The rise of print media also contributed to the development of a "modern opposition intelligentsia".[245] The Ottoman decree prohibiting any discussion of the constitutional reforms in the public sphere by ordinary people leads us to imagine the existence of a lively but coercive atmosphere of debate among the various segments of Ottoman society.[246] Although the book gives priority to bureaucratic debates rather than to the controversies of Ottoman society as a whole around the constitutional issue, it takes into account one of these opposition groups, the Young Ottomans, who operated through the intermediary of a secret society, *İttifak-ı Hamiyet* (the Patriotic Alliance).[247] The members of the society were mostly former members of the Translation Bureau of the Ottoman Foreign Ministry. Their ideology took shape under the flow of ideas infiltrating into the Foreign Ministry from various external channels. They were thus acquainted with European political systems. The alternative policy of the Young Ottomans was to transform the absolute rule of the sultan into a constitutional regime.[248] The society

---

[245] Findley, "The Tanzimat", p. 14.

[246] *The Times*, August 8, 1876.

[247] See also Christiane Czygan, "Reflections on Justice: A Young Ottoman View of the Tanzimat," *Middle Eastern Studies*, vol. 46, no. 6 (November 2010), pp. 943-956.

[248] Mardin, pp. 10-13; pp. 134-140.

of the Young Ottomans, founded in 1865, was forbidden and some members were exiled. It would be interesting to map the intellectual trajectories of the Young Ottomans through the press they produced in Paris, London and Geneva during their exile, far from governmental pressure and censorship, and to trace the ways in which they conceptualised an alternative reform project. The most eminent members of the Young Ottoman movement were Namık Kemal, Ali Suavi and Ziya Pasha. All three praised the creation of a constitutional monarchy in the Ottoman Empire.[249] The shape of the Patriotic Alliance was inspired by the organisation of the Carbonari, the secret society which fought against the restoration in France and Italy at the beginning of the nineteenth century.[250] The name of the Patriotic Alliance itself recalled earlier European revolutionary societies, such as the Tugendbund and the Giovine Italia. The Alliance also studied Italian liberal movements. In 1866, Mustafa Fazıl Pasha, who became their leader, mentioned the king of Italy as an example for the sultan while Namık Kemal referred to Garibaldi and to Silvio Pellico.[251] Ali Suavi stated that the organisations Young Spain, Young France and Young Italy served as models for the secret society of 1865.[252]

Nevertheless, taking into account the colossal dimension of this intellectual movement is far beyond the scope of this work. I assume that the involvement of the Young Ottomans in shaping the legal mind of the country operated in a much more complex way and that this complexity should constitute the research ambitions of another book. For the sake of specific focus, the book concentrates rather on bureaucratic elites who had the power to shape Ottoman constitutional reforms thanks to the seat they occupied in the state apparatus, or the formal and informal networks which had the ability to penetrate state circles in order to dictate their own perception of reforms. Consequently, although the book does not delineate the ideological profile of the Young Ottoman movement in the

[249] Hagop Cololyan, *Bo 'lis ew ir Tery* (Istanbul and Its Role), (Beyrut: Mesrob, 1987), v. 3, pp. 19-20.

[250] Ebüzziya Tevfik, "Yeni Osmanlılar," *Yeni Tasvir-i Efkar*, June 7, 1909. Cited in Mardin, p. 21.

[251] Mithat Cemal Kuntay, *Namık Kemal: Devrinin İnsanları ve Olayları Arasında* (Namık Kemal: Among The Men and Events of His Time), (İstanbul: Maarif Basımevi, 1956), vol. 2, p. 485. Cited in Mardin, p. 21. According to Mardin's footnote, Silvio Pellico (1789-1854) was an Italian nationalist in touch with the Carbonari and was imprisoned in 1820.

[252] Ali Suavi, "Civan Türk Tarihi," *Ulum*, 15 Zilkade 1286/February 16, 1870, p. 793. Cited in Mardin, p. 22.

matter of reforms, it does deal with the agency of Şinasi Effendi and Mustafa Fazıl Pasha on the one hand and with that of Namık Kemal and Ziya Pasha on the other, since they were informal representatives of the ideology of the Young Ottomans who could infiltrate the state apparatus and occupy seats in the Drafting Commission of the first *Kanun-i Esasi*.

The Ottoman Constitution was elaborated in a process of contestation: language thus played a role "in framing the terms of the debate". The discursive contexts in which the Ottoman Constitution emerged were the indicator of the political perceptions of various actors and draftsmen.[253] **Chapter I** therefore conducts a discourse analysis of the 1839 Imperial Rescript and the 1856 Reform Edict and compares their Ottoman Turkish version with their translations into French and Armenian in order to examine the extent to which the political jargon and concepts the various texts developed differed from one another. Considering that language is not a "neutral" device and is the indicator of a certain "cultural baggage"[254], the chapter intends to investigate the targeted audience of various versions, the political significance of their conceptual differences[255] and the intermediary language(s) in which they were first drafted.[256] Something was always 'lost' in translation. The investigation of what is lost is an efficient way of distinguishing differences between cultures.[257] Some terms were not fully translatable because something was missing in the search for equivalents. What resists translation and which elements are lost because of translation?[258] These are the major questions to which the linguistic survey of the chapter intends to respond.

Chapter II focuses on the political landscape and negotiations that preceded the preparatory phase and promulgation of the first Ottoman Constitution. The chapter draws attention to the expertise of the Ottoman Foreign Ministry in formulating Ottoman concessions in the form of reform projects and to the difficulty that this state unit had in navigating

---

[253] Delanty & Rumford, pp. 16, 18, 19.

[254] Peter Burke, "Translations into Latin in Early Modern Europe," in Peter Burke & R. Po-Chia Hsia (eds.), *Cultural Translation in Early Modern Europe* (Cambridge University Press, 2007), p. 80.

[255] Cf. Burke, "Cultures of Translation in Early Modern Europe," in Burke & Hsia (eds.), *Cultural Translation*, pp. 21-22.

[256] Cf. Burke, "Cultures of Translation in Early Modern Europe," in Burke & Hsia (eds.), *Cultural Translation*, p. 27.

[257] Cf. Burke, "Cultures of Translation in Early Modern Europe," in Burke & Hsia (eds.), *Cultural Translation*, p. 38.

[258] Burke, *Cultural Hybridity*, p. 60.

between European diplomatic pressure and Ottoman political tradition. Consultation of the archives shows that the Ottoman Foreign Ministry was a depository of major recipes of institutional change and reforms that emanated from various local and foreign channels. When the Ottoman Chamber of Deputies was involved in publishing a book about the history of constitutional monarchy in the Ottoman Empire in 1916, it was not a coincidence that the Grand Vizierate appealed to the Foreign Ministry for all the documents related to the 1876 Ottoman Constitution and the 1876-77 sessions of the Chamber of Deputies.[259] In addition to the Ottoman Foreign Ministry's role of institutional continuity in the matter of reforms, the chapter demonstrates that Ottoman foreign policy was in fact intermingled with domestic policy[260] and that important internal administrative reforms were not treated within the sphere of a different authority, such as the Ministry of the Interior.

Chapter II enables us to observe how the Ottoman Constitution emerged from a long process of internal and external confrontations and aimed to overshadow the reform proposals of the Great Powers, which never formulated any wish to replace the existing political regime in the Ottoman Empire with a constitutional framework: these finally material-ised in various schemes such as the Andrassy Note and the autonomy of Bulgaria from 1875 to 1876. The establishment of a constitutional regime was undoubtedly an idea previously cultivated in Ottoman intellectual and bureaucratic circles. The Ottoman Foreign Minister Reşid Pasha had thought about it when proclaiming the 1839 Imperial Rescript but avoided putting it into practice, believing that Ottoman society was not ready for such a regime.[261] Two years after the proclamation of the Rescript, Reşid Pasha himself did not find education in the Ottoman Empire widespread enough to make constitutionalism possible.[262] When Ali and Fuad Pashas undertook the elaboration of a new provincial law in the 1860s through the mediation of Midhad Pasha, they thought that the law would pave the

---

[259] BOA, HR. SYS. 1864. From the Grand Vizierate to the Ottoman Foreign Ministry, September 26, 1916.

[260] Davison, *Ottoman Diplomacy and Reforms*, p. 335.

[261] Frank Edgar Bailey, *British Policy and the Turkish Reform Movement: A Study in Anglo-Turkish Relations, 1826-1853* (Cambridge: Harvard University Press, 1942), p. 193. Cited in Devereux, p. 28.

[262] Nicolas Milev, "Réchid Pacha et la Réforme ottomane," *Zeitschrift für Osteuropaische Geschichte* (1912), II, 388. Cited in Mardin, p. 157.

way for the future Chamber of Deputies.[263] The idea of a constitution had occupied Midhad's mind since his governorship of the Danube.[264] The promulgation of the Ottoman Constitution emerged as a logical and pragmatic response to the demands of the Great Powers in the political circumstances of 1876 in order to enable the empire to survive on the basis of national sovereignty and territorial integrity and to break the vicious circle of external pressures and dependency. The chapter additionally develops another vision of diplomatic history in the sense that it focuses on the informal relations and individual initiatives of foreign or local statesmen, who went beyond their official state policy. The interaction between the Grand Vizier Midhad Pasha and the British Ambassador to the Porte Henry Elliot illustrates the human tools of this new diplomatic history.

The chapter shifts from external negotiations to internal debates by turning the focus to the Drafting Commission and to the centre of the Ottoman government and to their mutual struggles. Here the issue of negotiation gets more complicated: the central government, which was not a monolithic entity, negotiated the nature of the reform project with its domestic actors of different legal norms, ethnic backgrounds and professional specialisation. Like the asymmetry among the European Powers in dominating the Ottoman reform processes, domestic actors had unequal powers in shaping the process. It is debatable the extent to which the Drafting Commission reflected the expectations of wider Ottoman society in the sense that it was not a constituent assembly but rather a commission appointed by the sultan and responsible only to him.[265] However, the composition of the Drafting Commission, its calendar and agenda are worthy of analysis so that we can observe the extent to which it operated as a platform of tensions, how the antagonisms between its members shaped the writing process of a legal text and how law-making is a political process determined by power relations. Some of the non-Muslim bureaucrats who drafted their community regulations took seats in the Drafting Commission of the Ottoman Constitution in 1876. The book also tries to investigate the contribution of these non-Muslim draftsmen in terms of the transmission of their "constitutional" experience of

---

[263] Midhad Paşa, *Tabsıra-i İbret* (My Life as a Lesson), vol. 1 of *Midhad Paşa'nın Hatıraları*, ed. Osman Selim Kocahanoğlu (İstanbul: Temel Yayınları, 1997), p. 44.

[264] Midhad Paşa, *Tabsıra-i İbret*, v. 1, p. 191.

[265] Devereux, p. 61.

the communal level to the Ottoman public administration, an issue less investigated in the historiographical framework. These non-Muslim members were still both community administrators and state officials. The chapter thus inquires how this double identity may have influenced their membership as well as their role and responsibilities within the Drafting Commission and how their status of in-betweenness may have urged them to consider a larger spectrum of interests in the light of limited documentation. The special mission of Odyan Effendi partially satisfies our curiosity on the matter. The chapter also questions the power of non-Muslim diasporas and of ethno-religious ties and solidarity beyond diasporas to democratise the political and social circumstances of their co-religionists in the Ottoman Empire. While finally focusing on the potential reasons behind the banishment of Midhad Pasha and the suspension of the Ottoman Constitution, **Chapter II** simultaneously highlights the entanglement of internal and external dynamics that determined the fate of legal processes through the specific example of the 1876 *Kanun-i Esasi*.

Compared to the previous ones, **Chapter III** is a more conceptual section for turning our attention from the contentious world of actors and negotiations to the mere analysis of texts. The evolution of the constitutional debate from the first drafts to the final text of the Ottoman Constitution is worthy of analysis in order to observe the ideological fragmentation of the Drafting Commission and to follow the intellectual trajectories of the draftsmen. The novelty that the book brings to older narratives of Ottoman constitutional history is perhaps in its use of the pile of draft constitutions that emerged from the Ottoman archives as a new analytical tool for showing how the debate evolved within the Drafting Commission. These draft constitutions were previously studied by Selda Kaya Kılıç,[266] but this book suggests a different reading of the documents, which, if examined carefully in the light of information emerging from various sources of the time, reconstruct the diverse forms

---

[266] Selda Kaya Kılıç, "1876 Kanun-ı Esasi'nin Hazırlanması ve Meclis-i Mebusan'ın Toplanması" [The Elaboration of the 1876 Ottoman Constitution and the Convention of the Chamber of Deputies], Unpublished Master's Thesis (Ankara Üniversitesi Sosyal Bilimler Enstitüsü: Ankara, 1991), pp. 128-213. Selda Kaya Kılıç, "1876 Anayasası'nın Bilinmeyen İki Tasarısı," (The Two Unknown Drafts of the 1876 Ottoman Constitution) *OTAM* (Ankara Üniversitesi Osmanlı Tarihi Araştırma Merkezi Dergisi) 4 (1993), pp. 557-635. Selda Kaya Kılıç, *Osmanlı Devleti'nde Meşrutiyet'e Geçiş: İlk Anayasa'nın Hazırlanması* (The Transition to Constitutional Monarchy in the Ottoman Empire: the Elaboration of the First Constitution), (Ankara: Berikan Yayınevi, 2010), pp. 139-183.

that the constitutional text took, in the midst of controversies and antagonisms between various members, from almost its initial phase until its
evolution into the Ottoman Constitution. These documents lack proper
seals, signatures or other emblematic signs that denote the official minutes of the Drafting Commission. Although the drafts are undated,
matching their content with contextual evidence helps us to roughly
determine a constitutional calendar and distinguish the collective constitutional text authored by the Drafting Commission from initial and subsequent draft constitutions: these were subjected to amendments after
the intervention of the Council of Ministers and therefore shed light on
the power struggles between the palace, the Drafting Commission and
the Council of Ministers. The various constitutional drafts invite us to
reflect on how draftsmen conceptualised the relationship between the
state on the one side and the sultanate, the dynasty, Islam and the shariʿa
on the other, and how they perceived the respective weight of the sultan,
Parliament and the Senate, the Council of State and the Cabinet in the
state apparatus and hierarchy. The evolution of the provisions from initial drafts to the final text of the Ottoman Constitution enables us to
determine the most contested issues during the preparatory phase, to
inquire into the extent to which European constitutions served as models
and to investigate whether the draftsmen of the first Ottoman Constitution themselves saw a linear continuity between 1808 to 1876 as argued
in the conventional historiography. A selection of articles from constitutional drafts offers a case study on the various drafts displayed in the
appendices and indicates the tentative trajectories according to which the
comparative table showing the evolution of provisions from the incep-
tion until the final text of the Ottoman Constitution is constituted in the
book. A reflection on what was adopted from European constitutional
frameworks and how it was adapted to the Ottoman context invites us
to question the cultural parameters of Ottoman law-making and the limits of cultural translation. This reflection also evokes Iza Hussin's argument that "each project of translation is also a project of political
transformation".[267] These transformations also reflect, as we will see, the
political interests of various actors and their intentional misreading of
other existing constitutional models.[268]

---

[267] Iza Hussin, "Misreading and Mobility in Constitutional Texts: A Nineteenth-Century
Case," *Indiana Journal of Global Legal Studies*, vol. 21 no. # 1 (Winter 2014), p. 145.
[268] Cf. Hussin, p. 156.

5. SOURCES, APPROACHES AND LIMITS

The point of departure that guided my selection of primary sources was the idea that the two signatories of the 1856 Paris Treaty, Great Britain and France, occupied the central position in Ottoman internal politics from 1856 to 1876. Consequently, the book uses as main archival sources the records of three foreign ministries: British, French and Ottoman. Foreign ministries incorporated a complex set of networks from foreign ministers to ambassadors, from consuls to dragomans, and included an administrative centre as well as decentralised channels mostly represented by consuls. As regards British and French diplomatic agency, the book takes into consideration the political correspondence exchanged between the three foreign ministries and their ambassadorial networks together with the private papers of ambassadors and generally excludes their consular channels. Foreign ambassadorial narratives have been criticised for leading to the reproduction of a biased and Orientalist perception of the Ottoman Empire. However, the legitimacy and success of ambassadors in the eyes of their governments depended on the reliability of the information they provided and on their ability to interact with local networks in order to collect information. As long as their narratives are viewed with caution, they are able to complete the missing connections of local sources.

As for Ottoman diplomatic records, my research focused on five different categories: the papers of the Head Scribal Service (HR. MKT), which was responsible for the elaboration of correspondence on behalf of the foreign minister with different local and foreign interlocutors; those of the Legal Consultancy Office (HR. HMŞ. ISO), which compiled reports on legal matters; those of the Legal Section (HR.H), which housed the correspondences of Ottoman embassies with the Foreign Ministry; the series of the Political Section (HR. SYS), which included the correspondence of the Ottoman Foreign Ministry on internal and external political issues; and the papers of the Translation Office (HR. TO), which provided translations of documents emanating from Ottoman and foreign embassies, institutions or individuals.[269] The research on the three foreign ministries considers the documents of the diplomatic centre rather than the consular and provincial adjuncts of the diplomatic body.

---

[269] *Başbakanlık Osmanlı Arşivi Rehberi* (The Guide of the Prime Ministry Archives), (Ankara: Başbakanlık Devlet Arşivleri, 2010), pp. 380-386.

Bureaucrats' memoirs are used to fill in the gaps left by the Ottoman, British and French state archives. Although memoirs present a subjective perception of the historical context, they constitute an alternative to state documents, which only reconstruct the administrative, legal and economic dimensions of constitutional reforms without lingering on their psychological and relational aspects. Memoirs go beyond the structural dimension of the state apparatus and show its human aspect together with the overlapping or clash of inter-individual motivations, tensions, harmonies and antagonisms which, as a whole, also determine state behaviour, which is not only a complex set of formal structures but also an amalgamation of human relations. In contrast to memoirs, the production of discourse in state documents is selected, organised and redistributed by a certain number of constraints,[270] which we might call "formality". Finally memoirs shed light on informal relations and dimensions which do not emerge from state documents. This may be considered the "kitchen" of the state apparatus. The consultation of local and foreign newspapers from 1856 to 1876, together with memoirs, will reconstruct the pieces of the nineteenth-century contextual puzzle.

In addition to the records of the Ottoman Foreign Ministry, the material used includes other sections of the Ottoman archives of the Prime Ministry in order to reflect the internal debate that the constitutional process initiated within the various segments of the Ottoman state apparatus. The research incorporates the records of the Yıldız Palace, where Abdülhamid II resided after his investiture. The Yıldız Palace section includes the private papers of some Ottoman bureaucrats and those of the palace secretariat, the requests or petitions addressed by the Sublime Porte and the various Ottoman ministries to the Yıldız Palace.[271] I reconstructed the internal tensions between the palace circles and the other segments of Ottoman bureaucracy through such documents. My research also concentrated on the *Irade* section, which consists of imperial orders grouped according to thematic issues or the state department they concerned.[272]

The difficulties encountered in the Ottoman archives result from the inherent complexity of the Ottoman constitutional process. Although a commission was instituted for drafting the Ottoman Constitution, many

---

[270] Cf. Michel Foucault, *L'Ordre du Discours: Leçon inaugurale au Collège de France prononcée le 2 décembre 1970* (Gallimard, 1971), pp. 10-11.

[271] *Arşivi Rehberi*, p. 336.

[272] *Arşivi Rehberi*, pp. 299-308.

state departments, the Council of State, the Foreign Ministry, the Cabinet, the palace's inner circle and finally the sultan himself intervened in the process. Consequently, the documents concerning the drafting process are disseminated in various sections of the Ottoman archives. This creates a colossal workload for any scholar, particularly those working under the constraints of time limits.

The second difficulty comes from the classification system of the Ottoman archives and their catalogues, which do not indicate the specific section in which the documents of the Drafting Commission of the 1876 Ottoman Constitution can be found. Consequently, the researcher is forced to move from one archival section to another in order to locate the necessary documents. It is only with the superposition or comparison of Ottoman archival documents with various other sources (newspapers, memoirs, foreign archives, etc.) that one can unveil the significance of some of the undated draft constitutions available in the Ottoman archives in terms of authorship and time frame. Interestingly, some draft constitutions bear the seal of the Commission for the Examination of the Documents of the Yıldız Palace, the responsibilities of which are discussed in the last chapter. The other misleading dimension is that the date on their seal refers to 1909, even though they concern the drafting process in the first constitutional period. If one fails to consider the significance of this Commission, one might omit the said documents on the basis of the mistaken assumption that they concern the second constitutional regime.

The Yıldız Palace section seems to be the most likely part of the Ottoman archives to contain the minutes of the Drafting Commission since the latter was instituted by imperial order and the Commission's work was approved by imperial sanction in the final stage. Nevertheless, the section only provides some draft constitutions without date and signature. Further research was required in order to clarify whether or not these documents concerned the first constitutional era (1876) or the second constitutional regime (1908).

The minutes of the Armenian *Millet* Assembly, institutionalised by the Armenian National Constitution, shed light on inter-communal relations in the Ottoman Empire and on the perceptions of Ottoman Armenian elites on reform, constitutionalism and the state-community relationship. My research on the records of the *Alliance israélite universelle*, the *Consistoire central israélite de France* and the French national archives enabled me to better highlight the human channels, connections and interactions between the Napoleonic consistorial system and the changing *millet* structure as ways of managing the diversity of faiths through the case study of the Ottoman Jewish community. Non-Muslim communities are examined in this book through their separate constitutions or regulations for the administration of their communal sphere. The book does not pretend to provide an exhaustive historiography of non-Muslim agency in the making of Ottoman reforms but rather offers some asymmetrical snapshots. Thus, more space is granted to Ottoman Armenians and Jews than Ottoman Greeks because of the limitations of my linguistic abilities.

Although the book includes a broader diversity of actors, I mainly focus on the agency of elite circles. However, the limits of this book, established for the sake of a specific focus, do not mean that the Ottoman constitutional movement was completely devoid of popular involvement. Even this elitist approach does not pretend to exhaust all the issues related to the upper classes, since it remains limited to state elites and their immediate networks. For the sake of reflecting the voices of a plurality of actors, the research of the book has been conducted in various national and international archives. I should confess that the equilibrium between the use of Ottoman archival sources and international archives is more suited to describing the preparatory phase of the 1876 *Kanun-i Esasi* than the 1839 and the 1856 processes. Moreover, the book prioritises the period between 1856 and 1876: although it considers the 1839 Imperial Rescript to be the beginning of the process of negotiations, I have paid this period less attention.

CHAPTER I

THREE PRECEDING MOMENTS:
ACTORS, INTERACTIONS AND CONCEPTS

After the Napoleonic wars of 1804-15, five Powers dominated the affairs of Europe. Unlike Austria and Prussia, which remained within their territorial borders, Great Britain, France and Russia followed expansionist policies.[1] While Austria's policy was to not tolerate anarchy on its borders,[2] Russia aimed to dominate the Balkans in order to protect the Orthodox and Slavic populations and gain access to the open seas. Britain's objective was to protect the routes to India. France sometimes opposed Russia and sometimes Britain as it endeavoured to defend its commercial and cultural interests in relation to the Christians of the Levant. Austria tried to raise a barrier against the expansion of Russian influence in the Balkans.[3]

The Ottoman Empire could no longer threaten any of the Great Powers in the nineteenth century. However, the idea of its capitulation to one Great Power was the nightmare of the competing European states. Furthermore, the Russian menace to Ottoman sovereignty and territorial integrity endangered British, Austrian and French strategic interests in the nineteenth century. The common concern about the alteration of the European balance of power as a result of Ottoman dismantlement was the empire's strongest diplomatic asset in the final period of its existence: "It provided Ottoman statesmen with an entry ticket into the European diplomatic arena, and gave them crucial leverage over foreign powers seeking territorial, strategic, or economic advantages at Ottoman expense".[4]

The growing awareness in both the Ottoman Empire and Europe that the future survival of the empire depended not only on its military power, but also on its ability to develop diplomatic relations with the major states of Europe prepared the grounds for the rise of the Ottoman Foreign

---

[1] Davison, *Ottoman Diplomacy and Reforms*, pp. 149-150.
[2] *The Times*, January 19, 1876. Cited in MAEF, CP, Janvier-Avril, 1876, Tome 403.
[3] Mantran, "Question d'Orient", p. 421.
[4] Hanioğlu, p. 207.

Ministry.[5] Two disastrous experiences with Mehmed Ali, the khedive of
Egypt, demonstrated in 1839 that the collective intervention of Europe
could save the Ottoman Empire.[6] The Paris Treaty, which ended the
Crimean War in 1856, enabled the Ottoman Empire to enter the Concert
of Nations. This was the formal inclusion of the empire into the European
state system.[7] The Earl of Clarendon, the British foreign secretary, was
already shouting in early 1855 that "[i]f Turkey is to gain the great and
important advantage of being deemed part of the European family of
nations, she must by necessity adapt her laws and practices so as to make
them compatible with her association with the community of States into
which she desires to be admitted".[8] The admittance of the Ottoman
Empire to the European family thus developed a relationship of dependency between the two state systems.

     Foreign advice was expressed from 1839 to 1876 for the efficient use
of financial resources, the emancipation of the position of non-Muslims
in the empire, the admission of Christian evidence in Ottoman courts, the
revision of the court system, the establishment of fair taxes and of a new
system of tax collection, the amelioration of the Ottoman provincial
structure, guarantees related to the right of ownership, etc. The Foreign
Ministry acquired experience in the development of counter-responses
and negotiation strategies to the ceaseless demands for administrative
improvements emanating from European foreign offices. The major
intention of these requirements was not to initiate reforms in the real
sense of the term or a constitutional turn in the Ottoman Empire but to
dominate Ottoman internal politics for the sake of the balance of power
in Europe. In an atmosphere of European interference and pressure, the
Ottoman Foreign Ministry not only dealt with foreign affairs but also
undertook initiatives to formulate internal administrative, judicial and
educational reforms. Its dominant role resulted from the concentration of
expertise (knowledge of European languages, experience of European
societies, etc.) and the close relationship between foreign diplomatic

---

[5] Findley, *Bureaucratic Reform*, p. 60.

[6] Findley, *Bureaucratic Reform*, p. 60.

[7] Donald Quataert, *The Ottoman Empire, 1700-1922* (Cambridge University Press, 2000), p. 85.

[8] PRO, FO 78/2436. Instructions Addressed to Her Majesty's Embassy at Constantinople Respecting Administrative and Financial Reforms in Turkey: 1856-1872. The Earl of Clarendon to Lord Stratford de Redcliffe, February 18, 1856 # no. 193.

pressure and the proclamation of new reforms.[9] Ottoman diplomats tried to use the rules of the European balance of power to their advantage and to manoeuvre between the "ceaseless demands for pro-Christian reform". "The attempt to minimise the impact of these demands, to stave off the pressure for such reform, to stall and twist, deflect and renege, is the story of late Ottoman diplomacy".[10] Ali Pasha himself wrote once that if one had a look at the archives of the Ottoman Foreign Ministry, one would see that nine-tenths of the correspondence with the exterior was related to internal affairs.[11]

First of all, the objective of this chapter is to deconstruct the turning points in the negotiation prior to the promulgation of the 1876 Ottoman Constitution, namely the 1839 Imperial Rescript and the 1856 Reform Edict. The Ottoman Foreign Ministry developed western-style diplomatic responses to external pressure and consequently emerged as a new centre of power within the state. The elements of foreign pressure accumulated after 1839, pushing the Ottoman Foreign Ministry to become accustomed to the production of counter-responses and counter-projects prior to 1876. The Ottoman Foreign Ministry was the visible, if not the principal, inter-locutor of negotiation with the Great Powers in the matter of reform. Unlike the proposals of the Powers, which focused on local autonomy, the Ottoman Constitution aimed to conclusively centralise all vital structures such as finance, justice and provincial administration in the hands of the state.

Secondly, this chapter investigates how the Ottoman state responded to foreign pressure regarding the guarantee of equal treatment of non-Muslims in matters of life and honour, religious freedom, education, military service, administration of justice, taxation, appointment to public posts, property and non-Muslim representation in the governmental apparatus. By considering the 1839 Imperial Rescript the starting point of the Ottoman constitutional process, the chapter examines how the Ottoman idea of a constitution progressed until 1876 through a conceptual and textual analysis of the 1839 and 1856 reform decrees together with their translations into local or foreign languages. While concentrating on the conceptual differences that emerged upon the official translation of the

---

[9] Zürcher, pp. 60-61.
[10] Hanioğlu, p. 207.
[11] Ali Pasha, *Testament politique* (extrait de la Revue de Paris des 1er avril et 1er Mai 1910), (Coulommiers: Imprimerie Paul Brodard, 1910), p. 8.

reform decrees, the book invites us to better reflect on grey areas, contested questions and the pressures felt by the Ottoman state when placing the reform issue before various audiences. This allows us to better highlight the changing definitions of law and its components in accordance with particular cultural landscapes and the variety and ambiguity of expectations that crystallised in the ideas of reform and constitution. Finally, it helps us to experience the extent to which the state used language as a political vehicle to connect these various cultural landscapes to one Ottomanist ideal while advertising the reform through various discursive strategies and linguistic delicacy. The multiplicity of versions and audiences also shows, as Hussin suggests, that "a single reading of law is neither possible nor productive".[12] In such a vast empire, inhabited by various populations, conceptual divergences allowed the state to speak and appeal to multiple audiences and to make itself legitimate in their own words and expectations.

After a detailed focus on the negotiations of the Ottoman state with the Great Powers in the context of the 1839 Imperial Rescript and the 1856 Reform Edict, the chapter shifts to the 1860s, when new administrative trends for the governance of non-Muslim *millet*s were discussed in the aftermath of the Crimean War. The chapter thus examines the non-Muslim *millet*s as structural entities and the process of their institutionalisation in the years following the 1856 Reform Edict. It questions the impact of the emerging community constitutions from 1862 to 1865 on the initiation of a constitutional debate in the Ottoman context and explores how the institutional legacy of these ethno-religious groups was transferred to the Ottoman public sphere.[13] The chapter thus retraces the various direct or indirect ways in which non-Muslim communities contributed to the democratisation and secularisation of the Ottoman Empire through their institutional rearrangements or claims of self-recognition.[14] Before 1876, non-Muslim communities were attached to the Ottoman Foreign Ministry, for which this hierarchical attachment comprised a vast area of responsibilities including the administration and codification of

---

[12] Hussin, p. 158.

[13] Cf. Davison, *Ottoman Diplomacy and Reforms*, pp. 411-412.

[14] Cf. Ninth Mediterranean Research Meeting, Florence & Montecatini Terme, 12-15 March 2008, organised by the Mediterranean Program of the Robert Schuman Centre for Advanced Studies at the European University Institute. Workshop no. 12 on *Secularisation, Secularism, Secular: Democracy and Religious Minorities* organised by Sandrine Bertaux and Murat Akan.

their communal sphere. The earlier sections of Chapter I already show that this codification process did not evolve independently of the interference of European foreign ministries after the admission of the Ottoman Empire to the Concert of Europe. Ottoman non-Muslims consequently became an object and a subject of negotiation and preoccupation between the Sublime Porte on the one side, and European foreign ministries on the other. Non-Muslim actors knew how to turn this negotiation in their favour and to use the new manoeuvring room it created to succeed in their efforts for emancipation and self-recognition. The chapter also shows the extent to which the community sphere was a transnational space and the extent to which it included the interaction of various communal actors with their co-religionists in other competing imperial contexts. The term "space" refers here not only to the "physical/geographical place" but also to the "links between actors in different places".[15] The focus of the chapter on three major non-Muslim communities, Orthodox Greeks, Armenians and Jews, does not intend to favour these communities over others. Instead, these limitations aim to provide the basis for a specific focus. The book does not pretend to provide a definitive and comprehensive history of non-Muslim agency even within this limited focus. Although this study draws a kind of general profile of their structure and strategies of emancipation, my approach is *par essence* exemplary. My intention is rather to enrich the social panorama by giving voice to the multiple actors of three religious communities instead of one and convey the plurality of Ottoman reality as much as possible.

1. THE 1839 IMPERIAL RESCRIPT:
THE BEGINNING OF NEGOTIATIONS WITH THE GREAT POWERS?[16]

The rise of Britain as a "hegemonic power" in the nineteenth century distinguishes Her Majesty's Government from the rest of the European Powers in terms of its weight in negotiating the form and content of Ottoman reforms. For the sake of specific inquiry, the chapter mainly focuses on British and French agencies but also deals with the impact of

---

[15] Cf. Thomas Faist, "The Border-Crossing Expansion of Social Space: Concepts, Questions and Topics," in Thomas Faist & Eyüp Özveren (eds.), *Transnational Social Spaces: Agents, Networks and Institutions* (Aldershot: Ashgate, 2004), p. 4.

[16] For an earlier analysis framing the general debate before 1876, see also Koçunyan, "The Transcultural Dimension of the Ottoman Constitution", pp. 235-258.

other Great Powers within the framework of their relation to Britain. What we may question is the extent to which these agencies were successful in implanting a constitutional debate and tradition in the Ottoman context behind calculations, rivalries and interests. For that purpose, this section intends to deconstruct the elements of these various demands from 1839 to 1876 together with continuities and ruptures in order to question the imprint they may have left in the memory of the Ottoman government. Although foreign agency was not as substantial as the humanitarian discourses of the demands proved to be, the Ottoman counter-response will show that these discourses echoed both in sultanic decrees and the reform policies of the Ottoman Foreign Ministry, albeit with changes.

Britain remained indifferent towards the Ottoman Empire in the eighteenth century. After Russian territorial expansion in the wake of the Russo-Turkish wars of the eighteenth century and after the Russian success in the 1828-29 Russo-Turkish War and the 1833 Russo-Ottoman Treaty of Hünkar İskelesi, Britain started to consider Russia as a new power that could endanger the European balance of power and the British domination of India.[17] The "dogma of territorial integrity" of the Ottoman Empire became an element of British policy in the 1830s.[18] The rise of Britain from the Industrial Revolution and the Napoleonic Wars "without rivals" and as a "hegemonic power" in international markets on the one hand, and protectionist measures in Continental Europe against the penetration of British manufactures on the other, urged England to seek markets and raw materials on the periphery. The Free Trade Treaty of 1838 was thus the result of British efforts to gain markets.[19] Britain was aware that the signing of the 1838 Free Trade Treaty would have a harmful impact on Ottoman handicrafts.[20] Consequently, British diplomacy waited for a difficult political conjuncture to break the resistance of the Ottoman central bureaucracy to signing the treaty. This "favourable" political development was the outbreak of the Egyptian crisis,[21] during

[17] J. H. Gleason, *The Genesis of Russophobia in Great Britain* (Cambridge: Harvard University Press, 1950), p. 12. Cited in Kirakossian, pp. 2-3.

[18] Harold Temperley, "British Policy towards Parliamentary Rule and Constitutionalism in Turkey (1830-1914)," *Cambridge Historical Journal*, vol. 4, no. 2 (1933), pp. 156-191, here p. 156.

[19] Pamuk, *European Capitalism*, pp. 11, 19.

[20] See, for example, David Urquhart, *Turkey and Its Resources* (London: Saunders and Otley, 1833). Cited in Pamuk, *European Capitalism*, p. 19.

[21] Pamuk, *European Capitalism*, pp. 19-20.

which the sultan faced an attack from his Governor of Egypt Mehmed Ali. The British-Ottoman Commercial Treaty of 1838 was a turning point for the development of relations between Britain and the Ottoman Empire and for the future of reforms. While France was the principal commercial partner of the Ottoman Empire at the turn of the eighteenth century, Britain became the main trade partner and source of imports in the 1820s.[22] The Free Trade Treaty of 1838 should also be treated in the context of British efforts to open the Ottoman economy to foreign trade.[23]

Based on British archival sources, Edgar Bailey noted that in the 1830s the British Foreign Minister Palmerston suggested through his Ambassador Ponsonby that Turkey required improvements in its civil service, army and navy: most important was the amelioration of the financial administration.[24] Bailey then remarks that of all English statesmen, Palmerston was the closest to Reşid Pasha in the 1830s. Although their solutions to Ottoman problems did not always overlap and Palmerston did not encourage Reşid's constitutional ideas, they agreed on the main difficulties of the Ottoman state. Bailey also drew attention to the similarity of the ideas in the memorandum in Palmerston's handwriting and the Imperial Rescript of November 3.[25] Similarly, Sadık Rıfat Pasha, Ottoman ambassador in Vienna, a year and a half before the proclamation of the Gülhane Rescript, sent a series of despatches which included proposals for governmental reform in the Ottoman Empire. Parallels existed between the ideas of the despatches and the principles proclaimed in the Gülhane Rescript.[26] This leads us to interrogate the potential impact of Metternich on Sadık Rıfat Pasha's reform policy.[27] In fact, Metternich distinguished himself from other European statesmen through the emphasis he put on the consideration of local political culture when transferring foreign institutions from one country to another. In his correspondence

---

[22] I. L. Fadeeva, *Osmanskaya Imperiya i Anglo-Turetskie Otnoskeniya v Seredine XIX v* (Moskow: Nauka, 1982), p. 37. Cited in Kirakossian, p. 5.

[23] Pamuk, *European Capitalism*, pp. 11, 19.

[24] See for examples, Observations on the supposed views of Russia, etc., by James Brant, vice-consul at Trebizond, dated March 26, 1833, enclosed into FO 78/223, Ponsonby to Palmerston # I, May 22, 1833; FO 78/234, Palmerston to Ponsonby # 24, June 1, 1834. Cited in Bailey, *British Policy*, pp. 139, 151.

[25] Cf. Appendices III and IV in Bailey, *British Policy*. Cf. also P. Imbert, *La Rénovation de l'Empire ottoman, affaires de Turquie* (Paris, 1909), 190. Cited in Bailey, *British Policy*, p. 188.

[26] Mardin, p. 177.

[27] Cf. Mardin, pp. 178-179.

with the Ottoman Foreign Ministry, Metternich underlined the insufficiency of legislative initiatives as the main danger for the Ottoman Empire. The second danger was the Ottoman effort to equalise itself with the Great Powers of Europe. Social needs, climate, customs, religion and creeds varied from one country to another. Metternich considered it natural for one state to borrow useful institutions so long as they did not harm its sublime elements.[28] Sadık Rıfat Pasha, the Ottoman ambassador to Vienna, responded to Metternich's concerns on the grounds of "continuity of security" in the Ottoman Empire. Once the danger of the Egyptian question had been overcome, Rıfat Pasha put the elaboration of a regulation for the empire's security on the agenda. Like his Austrian counterpart Metternich, Rıfat Pasha considered the scope of the forthcoming regulation (which would be the 1839 Imperial Rescript) in terms of its suitability for the natural characteristics of the Ottoman state and *millet*, and did not see the benefit to the Ottoman Empire of applying European systems in their entirety.[29]

This exchange of opinions between Metternich and Rıfat Pasha shows that the reform parameters in the 1830s and 40s were based on a precarious balance between European institutional models on the one hand, and Ottoman interests, territorial security, cultural authenticity for the preservation of local customs, religious beliefs and creeds and the elimination of "harmful" foreign components on the other. Considering the stronger emphasis put on the shariʿa in the Gülhane Rescript compared to the Reform Decree that followed it, we may assume that the text was drafted in a conservative spirit respecting "traditional state philosophy".[30] In fact, Abu-Manneh proves in his work the close connection between the "Sunni-Orthodox outlook" of the Imperial Rescript's text and the rise of the *Nakşibendi-Müceddidiye* teachings among the public in Istanbul as well as in governmental circles and among the close entourage of Abülmecid. The order preached the regeneration of the Muslim community and state through shariʿa rules, an idea present throughout the Imperial Rescript.[31]

---

[28] BOA, HR.SYS, 1869 B-1. From Metternich to the Ottoman Foreign Ministry, April 20 [2 May], [1255/1839].

[29] BOA, HR.SYS, 1869 B-1. The statements of Sadık Rıfat Pasha to Metternich during his audience, 28 Şaban 1255/6 November 1839.

[30] H. İnalcık, "The Nature of Traditional Society: Turkey," in R. E. Ward and D. A. Rustow (eds.), *Political Modernisation in Japan and Turkey* (Princeton, 1964), pp. 56-57. Cited in Butrus Abu-Manneh, *Studies on Islam and the Ottoman Empire in the 19th Century (1826-1876)*, (Istanbul: Isis, 2001), p. 74.

[31] Abu-Maneh, *Studies on Islam*, pp. 63-84.

The Imperial Rescript of 1839 and its Foundations: Textual Analysis

The Imperial Rescript was proclaimed on November 3, 1839.[32] The text of the Rescript stated that because the sublime provisions of the Qur'an (*ahkam-ı celile-i Kur'aniye*) and the laws of the shari'a (*kavanin-i şeriye*) had been duly respected since the foundation of the Ottoman state, the sultanate had acquired strength and all its subjects had reached the highest level of prosperity (*refah*) and development (*mamuriyet*). The French translation of the text only mentioned the glorious precepts of the Qur'an (*les préceptes glorieux du Coran*) and the laws of the empire (*les lois de l'empire*) without referring to the shari'a. Unlike the Ottoman version, the French text put emphasis on mentioning "all the subjects" (*bilcümle tebea*) by adding the expression "without exception" (*tous les sujets sans exception*). Over the last 150 years, the text continued, as a result of successive troubles and for various reasons, neither the shari'a (*şer-i şerife*) nor the sublime legislation (*kavanin-i münife*) had been respected, which meant that the former strength and level of development of the empire had transformed into weakness and poverty. The French translation referred in this sentence to the sacred code of laws (*code sacré des lois*) and the regulations which emanated from this code (*règlements qui en découlent*) without directly mentioning the shari'a. The document expresses the observation that countries lose their solidity if they are not governed by the laws of the shari'a (*kavanin-i şeriye*). The French translation mentions the loss of stability in the empire because of the non-observance of its laws (*ses lois*) without referring to the shari'a. The difference in tone and degree between the direct mention of the shari'a in the Ottoman text of the 1839 Gülhane Charter and its indirect mention in the French text, which only referred to the sacred laws of the empire including the Qur'an, was, in my view, due to the different audiences that the Ottoman and French texts targeted.

Since his accession to the throne, the charter continued, the idea of the goodness of the sovereign (*efkar-ı hayriyet-asar-ı mülukanemiz*) was only

---

[32] See the Ottoman text, BOA. I. Mesail-i Mühimme 24. Also cited in Cevat Ekinci (ed.), *Gökkube Altında Birlikte Yaşamak: Belgelerin Diliyle Osmanlı Hoşgörüsü* (Living together under the Same Sky: the Land of Tolerance), (Ankara: Başbakanlık Devlet Arşivleri, 2006), pp. 128-129. For the official French version see BOA, HR. SYS. 1869 A-2, 1839.11.6 & "Hatti-Schérif ou Loi du Tanzimat du 3 Novembre 1839 (26 Saban 1255)," in Aristarchi Bey, *Législation ottomane ou Recueil des Lois, Règlements, Ordonnances, Traités, Capitulations et Autres Documents Officiels de l'Empire ottoman* (Constantinople: Bureau du Journal Thraky, 1874), pp. 7-14.

oriented towards the development of Ottoman countries (*imar-ı mema-lik*), the prosperity of the people (*terfih-i ahali*) and the improvement of the poor ([*terfih-i*] *fukara kaziyye-i nafiası*). Unlike the Ottoman text, the French translation talks about the idea of public good (*la pensée du bien public*), the amelioration of the state of the provinces (*l'amelioration de l'état des provinces*) and the relief of the people (*soulagement des peuples*). Given the geographical position of the Ottoman state, the fertility of its land and the skills of its people, the document expresses the hope that, within a period of five to ten years, and with the assistance of God and the Prophet, some new laws (*kavanin-i cedide*) would be established for the good administration of the Ottoman state and protected countries. The French translation talks about new institutions (*institutions nouvelles*) instead of new laws for the good administration of the provinces of the empire. The emphasis put on the provinces in the French text should be understood as the indirect announcement of provincial reforms and as a response to the Powers urging the empire to ameliorate well-being in the Ottoman provinces. The relief of the people (*soulagement des peuples*) may be read as the result of the cessation of inter-communal conflict in the provinces.

The document stipulated that the new laws would be based on the security of life (*emniyet-i can*), the protection of honour (*mahfuziyet-i ırz u namus*) and property (*mahfuziyet-i mal*) and the determination of taxation and the mode of conscription as well as of the duration of military service. The French translation refers to a similar scope of "new laws", with the only exception being that it uses the term "regularisation" for issues of tax collection and military recruitment (*un mode régulier d'asseoir et de prélever des impôts* & *un mode également régulier pour la levée des soldats et la durée de leur service*). The French text uses the terms "citizen" (*le citoyen*) and "fatherland" (*la patrie*): "if, on the contrary, the citizen possesses confidence in his property of all kinds, then he will be full of fervour for his business and will try to broaden its scope in order to extend that of his enjoyments. He will feel every day in his heart the intensification of his love for the prince and the fatherland and of his devotion to his country" (*Si au contraire le citoyen possède avec confiance ses propriétés de toute nature, alors, plein d'ardeur pour ses affaires, dont il cherche à élargir le cercle afin d'étendre celui de ses jouissances, il sent chaque jour redoubler en son cœur l'amour du Prince et de la patrie, le dévouement à son pays*). The Ottoman text replaces the word "citizen" with "everybody" (*herkes*) while keeping "fatherland" (*vatan*). The simultaneous use of the concepts "state" (*devlet*), "nation" (*millet*) and "fatherland" (*vatan*) in the same sentence gives the impression that the word "*millet*" slightly shifts from its classical connotation of a religious entity to slowly acquire a flavour of national coverage: "On the contrary, if everybody has complete security in his property, he will deal with his business and its enlargement and his devotion to the state and the nation and his love for the fatherland will increase in him from day to day. Thus, he will undoubtedly act with good intentions" (*[herkes]*[33] [...] *aksi takdirde yani emval ü emlakinden emniyet-i kamilesi olduğu halde dahi heman kendi işiyle ve tevsi-i daire-i taayüşüyle uğraşıp kendisinde gün be-gün devlet ve millet gayreti ve vatan muhabbeti artıp ana göre hüsn-i harekete çalışacağı şüpheden azadedir* [...]).

The document confessed that the Ottoman people faced disasters in terms of tax collection because of the system of tax farming and condemned the latter for subjecting the political and financial affairs of a locality to the arbitrary authority of rulers. The document stipulated that every individual in the Ottoman country (*ahali-i memalikeden her fert*) would pay a tax according to his wealth and means (*emlak ve kudretine göre*). The French translation uses the same concepts regarding taxation but refers to each member of the Ottoman society (*chaque membre de la société ottomane*), instead of "the people", as units of taxpayers. The document recognised that the irregularities regarding the mode of military recruitment were harmful to the development of agriculture and commerce and that laws would be established for the regulation of the number of soldiers on national service each locality would provide according to the necessities of the moment and for the reduction of the duration of the military service.

Strength (*tahsil-i kuvvet*), development (*mamuriyet*), security (*asayiş*) and tranquillity (*istirahat*) were impossible, the Rescript stated, without the establishment of regular laws (*kavanin-i nizamiye*). The French translation refers to the same concepts but also included happiness (*bonheur*) and wealth (*richesse*) instead of "development" and talks about new laws (*lois nouvelles*). The Rescript stipulated that the trial of each defendant would be heard publicly in accordance with the laws of the shari'a (*kavanin-i şeriye*) and that nobody would be punished, openly or secretly, without investigation and judgement. The French translation does not

---

[33] Although the word "herkes" (everybody) is used in the previous sentence, it continues to be the subject of this one as well.

mention the laws of the shari'a but refers to conformity with divine law (*loi divine*). The Rescript granted without exception these imperial authorisations (*müsaadat-ı şahane*) regarding the complete security of life, honour and property to the Islamic community (*ehl-i İslam*) and to the other *millet*s (*milel-i saire*) according to the provisions of the shari'a (*hükm-i şeri*). In both the French and the Ottoman texts, being the empire's subject was the precondition for the enjoyment of these authorisations or concessions. The French translation talks about imperial concessions (*concessions impériales*) instead of authorisations, which are extended to all subjects whatever their religion or sect (*ces concessions impériales s'étendant à tous nos sujets, de quelque religion ou secte qu'ils puissent être, ils en jouiront sans exception*). Instead of conformity with the shari'a, the French translation talks about complete security of life, honour and property granted to all the inhabitants of the empire as required by the sacred text of the their law (*ainsi que l'exige le texte sacré de notre loi*).

The Imperial Rescript is an incomplete legal text. It stipulates that the Council of Judicial Ordinances (*Meclis-i Ahkam-ı Adliye*), together with Ottoman ministers and bureaucrats, would discuss the legislation regarding the security of life and property and the issue of taxation, and decide with unanimity of votes: it does not offer completed legislation regarding these spheres of everyday life. The case was similar to the regularisation of the military service, whose principles would be discussed within the Military Council of the Ministry of War. In that way, the Imperial Rescript stipulated that a complete guarantee was granted to the Ottoman people on their life, honour and property and that other issues would be discussed and decided unanimously (*ittifak-ı ârâ*) among ministers, high-ranking officials, the ulema and the military before approval by the sultan. These actors would thus be involved in the law-making process; equally, the idea of agreement ("ittifak"), initiated by the 1808 Deed of Agreement, would be conserved in 1839. In the French text, the Rescript explained that the aim of these new institutions was to regenerate religion, the government, the nation and the empire (*…ces présentes institutions n'ont pour but que de refleurir la religion, le gouvernement, la nation et l'empire…*). The Ottoman text refers to the laws of the shari'a (*kavanin-i şeriye*) and the regeneration of religion, the state and the nation (*din ü devlet ve mülk ü millet*). It condemned the mechanism of bribery, which was considered to be against the shari'a and one of the principal causes of destruction of the Ottoman state. Due to the novelty of its provisions, the charter would be officially communicated to the ambassadors of friendly Powers residing in Istanbul as it was communicated to all the people of Istanbul and of protected Ottoman countries. This communication was, in fact, a part of Ottoman policy to advertise the reform process to the West and to create, through legal texts, a liberal image of the Ottoman Empire. The differences between the French text and its Ottoman counterpart were also a part of this image-making.

The restoration of the supremacy of the shari'a was considered the best guarantee for a virtuous government according to the ideals of Orthodox Islam.[34] "Indeed, the main theme of the Rescript is the state and the community not the rights and liberties of the individual subject. In other words it is not a 'Bill of Rights' but a declaration to abide by a just government according to the precepts of the shari'a, which is a basic duty of a Muslim ruler in Islam".[35] However, equality between Muslims and the other communities on issues regarding security of life, honour, property, taxation and military service does not entail civil and political equality.[36] Legally, non-Muslims continued to be regarded as *zimmi*s (protected non-Muslims) and to pay the *cizye* (poll tax). "In no way could the Gülhane Rescript be claimed to have granted equality to the non-Muslim subjects of the Ottoman Sultan".[37] Reference to Islam, the shari'a, the hadiths or any other Islamic terminology was a "strategy of justification" and a "source of legitimisation" for the draftsmen of the 1839 Imperial Rescript as well as for other constitutional texts.[38] "This strategy in turn is part of the larger discursive strategy of deriving justification from Islam, which was the main pattern in the secularisation process in the Middle East".[39] The French text opened a door to western concepts of political economy. If we keep in mind that the Imperial Rescript followed the signing of the Commercial Treaty between the Ottoman Empire and Britain in 1838, we may consider the entry of these concepts as the beginning of negotiations with the western Powers over the new foundations of the state in the period of reform.

---

[34] Abu-Manneh, p. 89.

[35] Abu-Manneh, p. 96.

[36] Abu-Manneh, p. 96.

[37] Abu-Manneh, p. 96.

[38] Cf. Nurullah Ardıç, "Islam, Modernity and the 1876 Constitution," in Christoph Herzog & Malek Sharif (eds.), *The First Ottoman Experiment in Democracy* (Istanbul: Orient Institut, 2010), pp. 90-92.

[39] Ardıç, p. 90.

2. The 1856 Reform Edict and New Negotiations

In 1842, Canning, British ambassador to the Porte, received instructions
from the British Foreign Secretary Aberdeen on the position of Christian
populations in the Ottoman Empire. The ambassador was asked to push
forward the rights of the Christian population guaranteed by the 1839
Gülhane Decree. In Aberdeen's view, the neglect of Ottoman Christians'
rights could endanger the integrity and survival of the empire. The British
government would adopt an egalitarian attitude towards the Christians of
the Ottoman Empire.[40] Unlike France, which had protected the Catholics
since 1740, and Russia, which protected the Orthodox after 1774, Britain
did not choose any single religious group and followed its commercial
interests through a "variety of faiths".[41] The British government later
moved from its egalitarian policy to the protection of Protestants.[42] One
of Canning's objectives was the recognition of Protestants (and especially
of converted Armenians) as a separate *millet*. This recognition would
allow Britain to claim diplomatic rights comparable to those of Austria,
Russia and France. In 1850, the Protestants of the Ottoman Empire were
granted the status of a distinct *millet*.[43] Canning's second objective was to
extend the principle of *laisser-passer* of the 1838 Anglo-Turkish Commercial Convention to the religious realm and make the Ottoman government abolish the prohibition on apostasy. The Greek and Armenian
churches upheld the prohibition on apostasy because of increasing num-
bers of conversions to Protestantism after missionary propaganda in the
1830s.[44] In January 1844, Canning also urged the Ottoman government to
abolish the death penalty for religious conversion.[45] Although an official
declaration on March 21, 1844 announced that the Sublime Porte would
take measures to prevent the execution of apostates,[46] the sultan did not

[40] M. Todorova, *Angliya, Rossiya i Tanzimat* (Moscow, 1983), p. 77. Cited in Kirakossian, p. 10.

[41] Kirakossian, p. 10.

[42] V. I. Sheremet, *Osmanskaya Imperiya i Zapadnaya Yevropa. Vtoraya Tret' XIX v.*
(Moscow, 1986), pp. 85-86. Cited in Kirakossian, p. 10.

[43] See H. G. O. Dwight, *Christianity in Turkey: A Narrative of the Protestant Reformation in the Armenian Church* (London: J. Nisbet, 1854), pp. 340-341. Cited in Berkes,
p. 150.

[44] Berkes, p. 150.

[45] Eastern Papers, Part XVIII. Correspondence Respecting Christian Privileges in
Turkey (London, 1856), p. 15. Cited in Kirakossian, p. 11.

[46] Eastern Papers, Part XVIII. Correspondence respecting Christian Privileges in
Turkey (London, 1856), p. 15. Cited in Kirakossian, p. 11.

abolish the laws related to the death penalty for those who converted from Islam to other religious faiths.[47] Despite the repeal of the decree on apostasy in 1847, Canning insisted on his interventions.[48] In 1848, he drafted a programme targeting religious freedom and equality of rights and privileges between Ottoman Christians and Muslims, the establishment of immunities for the Christian clergy, the abolition of special taxes on non-Muslims, their admission to military posts and consideration of their testimony against Muslims in Ottoman courts.[49] Canning's programme intended to compete with the Russian protectionist policy on behalf of the Orthodox populations of the empire.[50]

British policy took a more strategic turn in order to ensure better competition with Russia in the 1850s.[51] The work of the British embassy in Istanbul, "measured by the simple statistic of the number of despatches that the embassy sent to the Foreign Office, increased two and a half times between 1850 and 1855 (from 400 to 1000)".[52] This increase was probably due to the Crimean War but also to the involvement of the British government in the internal affairs of the Ottoman Empire. Consular representation in the Ottoman Empire was limited in 1825 to commercial affairs and was situated in the main trade ports of Istanbul, Izmir, and Alexandria.[53] Consular representation was extended in the 1850s to some centres in the Balkans and European Turkey, such as Jassy, Bucharest, Bosnia, Belgrade, Monastir, Yanina, Edirne, Rustchuk, etc. All these consulates functioned under the directives of the British embassy in Istanbul.[54] In the 1850s, the British Foreign Service only maintained two embassies for the sake of economy: Istanbul was one of them (the other was in France).[55]

The Crimean War offered a great opportunity for Britain to gain the upper hand in shaping Ottoman pro-Christian reforms in accordance with

---

[47] Kirakossian, p. 11.

[48] Harold Temperley, "The Last Phase of Stratford de Redcliffe, 1855-1858," *English Historical Review* 47 (1932), p. 230. See also Engelhardt, *La Turquie*, v. 1, p. 133. Cited in Berkes, p. 152.

[49] Sheremet, *Osmanskaya imperiya*, p. 136. Cited in Kirakossian, p. 12.

[50] Kirakossian, p. 12.

[51] Kirakossian, pp. 12-13.

[52] Raymond A. Jones, *The British Diplomatic Service, 1815-1914* (Gerrards Cross: Colin Smythe, 1983), p. 86.

[53] Jones, p. 87.

[54] Jones, p. 87.

[55] Jones, pp. 99, 172.

its interests. Russian claims of protection over the Greek Orthodox Church in the Ottoman Empire during the war threatened the British "dogma of territorial integrity" and endangered the sovereignty and legitimacy of the sultan. In order to not justify Russian claims over Ottoman Christians, the European Powers extended the protection of religious privileges to subjects of all classes and made the Ottoman Empire promulgate the Reform Edict before the Paris Treaty as if it emanated directly from the generosity of the Ottoman sultan.[56]

For the British, any collective or single demand of the Five Powers regarding the emancipation of Ottoman Christian subjects would constitute the same "infringement" of the empire's sovereign rights as the Russian challenge. A better solution was for the sultan to ameliorate the status of Christian populations according to his own sovereign will and then communicate all his accomplishments to the allies. Britain's main objective was to eliminate Russia from the discussions of the 1856 Reform Edict.[57] "This would be a moral guarantee that would not derogate from the Sultan's independent authority".[58] Before the Paris Congress, the British government thus proposed that the Ottoman government on its own initiative extend the privileges of non-Muslim subjects and accept international control over these privileges.[59] Thus, the formal way in which the Reform Edict would take shape was determined by the Powers, especially Britain, which aimed to challenge Russia. In other words, both the form and the content of the reform programmes suggested either by Britain or the rest of the Powers hid strategic calculations, especially Russian defeat, behind their humanitarian coverage. On August 25, 1855, Musurus, Ottoman ambassador to London, communicated to Fuad Pasha, the Ottoman minister of foreign affairs, the opinion of Lord Palmerston regarding certain reforms relating to the condition of Ottoman Christian subjects and the ameliorations that should be introduced in provincial administration. Palmerston's

---

[56] Cf. Mahmud Celaleddin Paşa, *Mirat-ı Hakikat*, prep. by İ. Miroğlu et al. (İstanbul: Tercüman Gazetesi, 1979), v. 1, pp. 35-36.

[57] *Mémoires et Documents*, vol. 51. Turquie, 1854-56. Eastern Papers, Part XVIII, Correspondence respecting Christian privileges in Turkey. From Foreign Office to Lord Stratford de Redcliffe, May 1855. See also Kirakossian, p. 23

[58] *Mémoires et Documents*, vol. 51. Turquie, 1854-56. Eastern Papers, Part XVIII, Correspondence respecting Christian privileges in Turkey. From Foreign Office to Lord Stratford de Redcliffe, May 1855.

[59] Temperley, "The Last Phase of Stratford de Redcliffe", p. 230. See also Engelhardt, *La Turquie*, v. 1, p. 133. Cited in Berkes, p. 152.

view was that the Ottoman Empire could not avoid carrying out reforms on behalf of Ottoman Christian subjects. Finally, the Sublime Porte should take into consideration the fact that the independence and sovereign authority of the Ottoman Empire would be endangered if these reforms were incorporated into an international treaty. Palmerston also emphasised that if Russia and Austria were the parties of a similar treaty, they would surely threaten the independence and integrity of the Ottoman Empire.[60] In turn, Grand Vizier Ali Pasha responded that the insertion of an explicit guarantee in an international treaty would be an attempt against the dignity of the imperial government, as this would constitute the intervention of foreign will and initiative in the exercise of the sovereign authority of the sultan. This could have engendered a paralysis of administrative authority in the eyes of Ottoman populations by establishing that Christian privileges would be due, in future, to foreign interventions. Ali Pasha was conscious that the moral dismantlement of sovereignty was more dangerous than the loss of the most important territories. Prestige and integrity of command were at the heart of any legitimate and solid administrative authority and social unity.[61]

After the communication by Musurus of Ali Pasha's memorandum on the subject of the religious privileges of the Christians of the Ottoman Empire,[62] the British government thus found an intermediate formula which would cause fewer embarrassments to the Porte. The true way to settle the matter would be if the sultan did, through his own sovereign power, all that was required for the Christians and communicate his accomplishments to the allies. In that way, non-Muslims would owe their privileges and advantages not to Russia but to their own sovereign and to the good offices of Britain and France.[63] Thus any decision made by the Sublime Porte regarding Christian subjects would look like an act emanating from the initiative and spontaneous will of the sovereign,

---

[60] BOA, HR. SYS. 1869 B-3.

[61] MAEF, Mémoires et Documents, vol. 51. Turquie, 1854-56. Réformes de l'Empire ottoman. Mémoire d'Ali Pasha aux Cabinets de Paris et de Londres (May 1855), et projet de réformes du Gouvernement britannique.

[62] For the details of the memorandum, see MAEF, Mémoires et Documents, vol. 51. Turquie, 1854-56. Part XVIII, Eastern Papers, Correspondence respecting Christian privileges in Turkey, presented to both Houses of Parliament by Command of Her Majesty (London: Harrison and Sons, 1856). Mémorandum d'Ali Pasha, from Musurus to Clarendon, May 13, 1855.

[63] MAEF, Mémoires et Documents, vol. 51. Turquie, 1854-56. To Lord Stratford de Redcliffe, May 1855.

accomplished independently of any external pressure which could not be the subject of any international negotiations. Britain and France could not enter into new negotiations before having obtained these conditions for the conclusion of peace.[64]

The negotiations ending the Crimean War were opened in Istanbul in January 1856 between the representatives of the Porte, Ali and Fuad Pashas and the French, Austrian and British ambassadors.[65] Before the peace negotiations which would be undertaken by the Congress of Paris, a certain number of issues regarding religious persecutions in the Ottoman Empire were a matter of preoccupation between European foreign ministries. Although the Porte took diplomatic action to abolish the death penalty in 1844 and prevent the execution of Christians who were apostates from Islam, British sources referred to two cases reported by the Committee of the Turkish Missions Aid Society in Aleppo (in 1852) and in Adrianople (1853).[66] The memorialists drew attention to the Ottoman code which condemned a born Muslim to death for the practice of any creed other than that of the Qur'an. Although the mission's account reported the reason behind the two capital punishments as apostasy from Islam, the fact that they were condemned for blaspheming the Prophet was also under consideration. The committee insisted, however, that the execution was for apostasy and not blasphemy.[67] This raised at the Foreign Office the question whether the former law of death for apostasy was still in force and was recently carried into effect.[68] Redcliffe also confirmed the existence of blasphemy according to the information he collected, although he did not leave aside the doubt that blasphemy might

---

[64] BOA, HR. SYS. 1869 B-3.

[65] BOA, HR. SYS. 1869 B-3.

[66] MAEF, Mémoires et Documents, vol. 51. Turquie, 1854-56. Part XVIII, Eastern Papers, Correspondence respecting Christian privileges in Turkey, presented to both Houses of Parliament by Command of Her Majesty (London: Harrison and Sons, 1856). From Shaftesbury, President, Memorial addressed to the Earl of Clarendon by the Committee of the Turkish Missions Aid Society, July 27, 1855; From Mr. Hammond to the Earl of Shaftesbury, July 31, 1855; From Mr. Young to the Earl of Clarendon, August 7, 1855.

[67] Mémoires et Documents, vol. 51. Turquie, 1854-56. Eastern Papers, Part XVIII, Correspondence respecting Christian privileges in Turkey. From Mr. Young to the Earl of Clarendon, August 7, 1855. From Mr. Young to the Earl of Clarendon, September 15, 1855.

[68] Mémoires et Documents, vol. 51. Turquie, 1854-56. Eastern Papers, Part XVIII, Correspondence respecting Christian privileges in Turkey. From Mr. Hammond to the Earl of Shaftesbury, July 31, 1855.

have been used to mask the application of the old law.[69] Moreover, certifying that no clear case of execution had come to his knowledge after the official declaration of the Porte except for the cases cited by the Turkish Missions Aid Society, Redcliffe offered his own interpretation of the Sublime Porte's declaration relinquishing the practice of executions for apostasy. He called his minister's attention to the use of equivocal words in this declaration: "The Sublime Porte engages to take effectual measures to prevent henceforward the execution and the putting to death of the Christian who is an apostate". Redcliffe stated that this might imply the restriction of the law to those who were originally Christian and then apostatised from Islam after having professed it.[70] The ambassador to the Porte also reported a conversation he had with Fuad Pasha, who confirmed that the Ottoman government was opposed to such orders of execution and that the only punishment in the matter of religion was inflicted on people guilty of blasphemy. He also mentioned the visit he paid to the Grand Vizier Ali Pasha, who repeated that blasphemy was subject to capital punishment. The latter also pointed out that the penal laws remained intact but that in practice the state prevented their application in cases of apostasy regarding Christians.[71]

The British government also tried to obtain the support of the French state regarding the recommendations to be made to the Porte in favour of its Christian subjects and the repeal of persecutions and punishments inflicted on apostates.[72] There was apparently no material difference between the approaches of the British and French governments when it came to negotiating religious questions with the Sublime Porte, but Count

[69] Mémoires et Documents, vol. 51. Turquie, 1854-56. Eastern Papers, Part XVIII, Correspondence respecting Christian privileges in Turkey. From Stratford de Redcliffe to the Earl of Clarendon, August 21, 1855.

[70] Mémoires et Documents, vol. 51. Turquie, 1854-56. Eastern Papers, Part XVIII, Correspondence respecting Christian privileges in Turkey. From Stratford de Redcliffe to the Earl of Clarendon, August 21, 1855. See also in the same file the English translation of the official declaration of the Sublime Porte relinquishing the practice of executions for apostasy, from Stratford de Redcliffe to the Earl of Aberdeen, March 23, 1844.

[71] Mémoires et Documents, vol. 51. Turquie, 1854-56. Eastern Papers, Part XVIII, Correspondence respecting Christian privileges in Turkey. From Lord Stratford de Redcliffe to the Earl of Clarendon, October 16, 1855.

[72] MAEF, Mémoires et Documents, vol. 51. Turquie, 1854-56. Part XVIII, Eastern Papers, Correspondence respecting Christian privileges in Turkey, presented to both Houses of Parliament by Command of Her Majesty (London: Harrison and Sons, 1856). From the Earl of Clarendon to Lord Stratford de Redcliffe, June 13, 1855; From the Earl of Clarendon to Lord Cowley, September 17, 1855; From Lord Stratford de Redcliffe to the Earl of Clarendon, October 18, 1855.

Walewski suggested laying down general rules for the future protection of the sultan's subjects of all denominations rather than obtaining the open repeal of the existing law on apostasy.[73] Walewski was also of the opinion that the question regarding the renegates, either Christian or Muslim, should not be discussed before the settlement of the fourth point.[74] Redcliffe's impression was that the Ottoman ministers were little disposed to meet the requirements of the British government on the subject of religious persecutions, since they feared provoking popular discontent among Muslims.[75]

France, Britain and Austria together developed the basis of the Congress of Paris that ended the Crimean War and advanced as one of the essential conditions of peace the consecration of immunities of the non-Muslim subjects of the Porte.[76] This consecration of immunities should not be interpreted, however, as a real preoccupation with the humanitarian conditions of Ottoman non-Muslims. Negotiations regarding these immunities or privileges, entitled the "fourth guarantee", were opened in Istanbul on January 9, 1856 with the participation of three ambassadors to the Porte: Stratford de Redcliffe (Britain), Baron Prokesch (Austria) and Thouvenel (France). The three diplomats were received in Ali Pasha's residence, together with the Ottoman Foreign Minister Fuad Pasha and Prince Kallimaki, the newly nominated Ottoman ambassador to Vienna. Within the framework of these negotiations, Fuad Pasha was expected to finalise a memorandum about the civil and religious conditions of Ottoman Christians.[77] The idea of opening negotiations on the fourth point came

[73] Mémoires et Documents, vol. 51. Turquie, 1854-56. Eastern Papers, Part XVIII, Correspondence respecting Christian privileges in Turkey. From Lord Cowley to the Earl of Clarendon, November 5, 1855.

[74] Mémoires et Documents, vol. 51. Turquie, 1854-56. Eastern Papers, Part XVIII, Correspondence respecting Christian privileges in Turkey. From Stratford de Redcliffe to the Earl of Clarendon, November 13, 1855.

[75] Mémoires et Documents, vol. 51. Turquie, 1854-56. Eastern Papers, Part XVIII, Correspondence respecting Christian Privileges in Turkey. From Stratford de Redcliffe to the Earl of Clarendon, December 3, 1855.

[76] MAEF, CP, January-April 1876, Tome 403. From Decazes to Bourgoing. January 9, 1876.

[77] MAEF, CP, January-February 1856, vol. 324. January 10, 1856. From Thouvenel to Walewski; CP, January-February 1856, vol. 324. January 10, 1856. From Thouvenel to Bourqueney. See also Mémoires et Documents, vol. 51. Turquie, 1854-56. Eastern Papers, Part XVIII, Correspondence respecting Christian Privileges in Turkey. From Stratford de Redcliffe to the Earl of Clarendon, January 9, 1856.

from Clarendon.[78] The objective of the negotiations over the fourth point was to find a balance between the immunities of the rayas and any attempt against the independence and dignity of the sultan made through the deliberations of Austria, France and Britain.[79] The negotiations regarding the privileges of the sultan's non-Muslim subjects were connected to the broader question of administrative reforms. Stratford de Redcliffe reported that all the participants during this meeting agreed that the main issue was a good system of administration granting equality to all classes rather than the extension of privileges to Christian subjects. The idea was that any initiative on future improvements belonged to the sultan and not to Russia, and that a new firman would be shaped for that purpose. The meeting was closed upon agreement that Ottoman ministers would present a statement of existing privileges, spiritual and civil, together with additional proposals.[80] It was the proposal of Count Walewski, the French foreign minister, to incorporate the content of the fourth point into the Paris Treaty in the form of a firman communicated by the sultan. Austria, Britain and the Sublime Porte supported this proposal.[81]

The morning of January 16 was devoted by Thouvenel, Prokesch and Redcliffe to the question of privileges and administrative reforms. They met at the French embassy. The memorandum which Redcliffe drew up in French and transmitted to Clarendon on the 14th for a final check was read and approved by his colleagues.[82] Long before this meeting, Clarendon had already addressed to Redcliffe a draft of instructions regarding the recommendations to be made to the Porte in favour of its Christian subjects. The points he raised essentially comprised the eligibility of Christians to all places in the administration, whether in the capital

---

[78] MAEF, Mémoires et Documents, vol. 51. Turquie, 1854-56. G. A. Mano, *Religion et politique. Examen du Quatrième Point de Garantie* (Paris: Amyot, 1856), p. 16.

[79] MAEF, Mémoires et Documents, vol. 87. Turquie, 1855-59. Congrès et Conférences de Paris. Notes préparatoires pour les négociations de Paris.

[80] MAEF, Mémoires et Documents, vol. 51. Turquie, 1854-56. Part XVIII, Eastern Papers, Correspondence respecting Christian privileges in Turkey, presented to both Houses of Parliament by Command of Her Majesty (London: Harrison and Sons, 1856). From Stratford de Redcliffe to the Earl of Clarendon, Constantinople, January 9, 1856.

[81] MAEF, Mémoires et Documents, vol. 87. Turquie, 1855-59. Congrès et Conférences de Paris. Notes préparatoires pour les négociations de Paris.

[82] MAEF, Mémoires et Documents, vol. 51. Turquie, 1854-56. Part XVIII, Eastern Papers, Correspondence respecting Christian privileges in Turkey, presented to both Houses of Parliament by Command of Her Majesty (London: Harrison and Sons, 1856). From Lord Stratford de Redcliffe to the Earl of Clarendon, Constantinople, January 16, 1856.

or in the provinces, and the appointment of Christians to some places of
trust, civil and military; the admission of non-Muslim evidence in civil
as well as in criminal cases; the establishment of mixed courts of justice
for all cases in which Muslims and non-Muslims were parties; and the
appointment of a Christian officer as assessor to every governor of a
province when that governor was a Muslim (such assessor having full
liberty to appeal to Constantinople against any act of the governor, unjust,
oppressive or corrupt). Furthermore, Her Majesty's Government argued
that there should not only be complete toleration of non-Muslim religion,
but also that all punishments on converts from Islam, whether natives or
foreigners, ought to be abolished.[83]

Redcliffe's memorandum resembled the 1856 Reform Edict's text from
the standpoints of the admission of the Ottoman Empire and dynasty into
the European system; the admission of Christians to military ranks
and public offices; the adaptation of Ottoman institutions to the progress
and necessities of society; the solemn confirmation of ancient privileges
and firmans granted to non-Muslim communities by the Porte in terms
of religious freedom and toleration; the completion of civil, commercial
and penal codes; the regularisation of the tax system; the revision of
the concrete administrative structures of non-Muslims and their representation in the Grand Council as well as in provincial councils; the confirmation of guarantees recognised by the 1839 Imperial Rescript; the
prohibition of humiliating expressions towards any subjects on account
of religion, race or language; permission to open public community
schools under the supervision of the state; the establishment of mixed
tribunals to hear cases between Christian and Muslim subjects; and the
amelioration of the conditions of prisons and the organisation of the
police.[84] This memorandum was read and approved by the Austrian and
French representatives. At the suggestion of his colleagues, Redcliffe
introduced a clause for extending the privilege of holding land in the
Ottoman Empire to foreigners. Stratford de Redcliffe reported that they

---

[83] Mémoires et Documents, vol. 51. Turquie, 1854-56. Eastern Papers, Part XVIII,
Correspondence respecting Christian privileges in Turkey. From the Earl of Clarendon to
Lord Stratford de Redcliffe, May 1855.

[84] See the text of Redcliffe's memorandum. MAEF, Mémoires et Documents, vol. 51.
Turquie, 1854-56. Part XVIII, Eastern Papers, Correspondence respecting Christian Privi-
leges in Turkey, presented to both Houses of Parliament by Command of Her Majesty
(London: Harrison and Sons, 1856). From Stratford de Redcliffe to the Earl of Clarendon,
January 14, 1856. Redcliffe's Memorandum, Inclosure in no. 36.

went to the grand vizier's house after their meeting at the French embassy and met Prince Kallimaki in addition to Ali and Fuad Pashas. The latter presented his memorandum as to *privileges granted ab antiquo to the Christian subjects of the Porte with reference to spiritual affairs.*[85] The representatives of the three Powers found Fuad Pasha's memorandum regarding the religious privileges of Christian subjects more liberal than they expected. Two things were striking, however: the degree of power attributed to the patriarchs and other dignitaries of Christian churches, particularly the Greek patriarch, over their dependents and the lack of provision made for preventing the latter from abusive exercise of authority.[86]

Fuad Pasha's memorandum gives us an idea about the structure of the *millet* system just before the promulgation of the Reform Edict and the community regulations. With non-Muslim communities complaining about the abuses of the clergy, the idea of the Powers in 1856 was to help the Porte extirpate the corruption of the Christian ecclesiastical class.[87] According to Fuad Pasha's memorandum, when the Patriarchate was vacant, archbishops whose sees were located in the neighbourhood of the Ottoman capital together with the Holy Synod, also composed of lay members, were considered responsible for the electoral process of the Greek patriarch, while the clergy together with civil communal notables was charged with the election of Catholic and Apostolic Armenian patriarchs. Responsibilities regarding the direction of religious affairs and the settlement of administrative issues (income, expenditure and other business) were shared between the patriarch, the Synod and archbishops. The jurisdiction of the patriarchs was quite broad in some areas and covered a large spectrum of prerogatives concerning the nomination or dismissal of clergymen without hindrance, the application of ecclesiastical law,

---

[85] MAEF, Mémoires et Documents, vol. 51. Turquie, 1854-56. Part XVIII, Eastern Papers, Correspondence respecting Christian privileges in Turkey, presented to both Houses of Parliament by Command of Her Majesty (London: Harrison and Sons, 1856). From Stratford de Redcliffe to the Earl of Clarendon, January 16, 1856. Redcliffe's Memorandum, Inclosure in no. 37: Memorandum as *to Privileges granted ab antiquo to the Christian Subjects of the Porte with reference to Spiritual Affairs.*

[86] MAEF, Mémoires et Documents, vol. 51. Turquie, 1854-56. Part XVIII, Eastern Papers, Correspondence respecting Christian privileges in Turkey, presented to both Houses of Parliament by Command of Her Majesty (London: Harrison and Sons, 1856). From Lord Stratford de Redcliffe to the Earl of Clarendon, Constantinople, January 16, 1856.

[87] MAEF, Mémoires et Documents, vol. 116. Turquie, Documents divers, 1859-67.

prohibition of some communal publications, the punishment and exile of
individuals who acted contrary to the rites of their sect without trial, etc.
One observes that the management of communal affairs was the sphere
of responsibility of a *millet* assembly and of the patriarch together in
other Christian communities: this probably referred to Catholic and
Apostolic Armenians, as they were the two other Christian entities cited
in the beginning of the text. The rest of the provisions were comprised
of the practice of the rites without molestation, the repair of churches
without hindrance so long as the ancient plan was respected, the guarantee of church properties, the sphere of influence of ecclesiastical law and
patriarchal jurisdiction in affairs concerning marriage, divorce, burial and
succession and the management of properties bequeathed to churches,
patriarchates or the poor. The memorandum also had a section entitled
concessions accorded to non-Muslim subjects since the Tanzimat, in
which the establishment of an assembly within the patriarchates for the
settlement of special affairs such as the control of hospitals, schools, etc.
was presented as the outcome of Tanzimat practices.[88]

The French, British and Austrian representatives criticised the memorandum on the grounds that the powers of the Greek patriarch were
exaggerated. They argued that nobody would be able to control and
oppose the sovereign authority of the patriarch in the political and civil
spheres of everyday life. The three representatives recommended the
constitution of a commission of clerics and laymen under the presidency
of the Greek patriarch and the establishment of foundations for the separation of spiritual and temporal spheres within the Greek Patriarchate.[89]
The Powers sought rather the reform of non-Muslims by weakening the
clergy that represented them and strengthening the secular dynamics of
communal structures. The Armenian historian Alboyacıyan pointed out
that it could not have been only the European diplomats who suggested
the provisions of the 1856 Reform Edict concerning the functioning of

---

[88] MAEF, CP, January-February 1856, vol. 324. Memorandum of Fuad Pasha annexed
to the political despatch of January 17, 1856. See also MAEF, Mémoires et Documents,
vol. 51. Turquie, 1854-56. Part XVIII, Eastern Papers, Correspondence respecting Christian privileges in Turkey, presented to both Houses of Parliament by Command of Her
Majesty (London: Harrison and Sons, 1856). From Stratford de Redcliffe to the Earl of
Clarendon, January 16, 1856. Redcliffe's Memorandum, Inclosure in no. 37: *Memorandum
as to Privileges granted ab antiquo to the Christian Subjects of the Porte with reference
to Spiritual Affairs*.

[89] MAEF, CP, January-February 1856, vol. 324. January 17, 1856. From Thouvenel to
Walewski.

the patriarchates; Ottoman Christian bureaucrats must have played a role by transmitting the internal conflicts of the patriarchates to state circles.[90] However, no mention is made in the archival sources I consulted of any non-Muslim intermediary urging the three Powers' representatives to reshape Fuad Pasha's memorandum in order to limit ecclesiastical power within communal administrations. The question of whether Prince Kallimaki acted as an Ottoman bureaucrat or informally represented the will of the Greek Patriarchate or of the larger Greek community remains ambiguous because of the lack of evidence. However, considering Thouvenel's ideas on the fourth point which he communicated to Count Walewski, one may question whether Kallimaki was instrumental in the development of his vision on patriarchal issues. If Neo-Phanariots were pro-western and favoured reform in community administration, one may find parallels between Thouvenel's suggestions and Neo-Phanariot ideology. The Porte should encourage, Thouvenel stated, the measures that the Greek community required: the constant change of patriarchs in the ecumenical see of Istanbul, he said, was simultaneously a scandal for Christianity and a burden for the populations. In his view, the immovability of these clerics should be assured in exchange for guarantees of their loyalty to the sultan as well as to their Church. Thouvenel also put emphasis on tax problems: prelates should not be allowed to collect taxes from their dioceses as they did in the past. The tax for each diocese should be voted by councils of notables in order to sponsor the maintenance of worship and should be collected by individuals specially nominated *ad hoc* for that purpose.[91]

In response to their criticisms, Fuad Pasha advanced the argument that the Greek clergy would be the principal obstacle to the restriction of the powers of the Greek patriarch, although these reforms were required by the community itself.[92] In 1856, the question of the consolidation of the Orthodox Church was considered by the Porte as one of the essential

[90] Arşak Alboyacıyan, "Azkah'in Sahmanatro'wt'iwny o'w ir Dzako'wmy ew Girar'o'wt'iwny," (The National Constitution, Its Origin and Application) Y*ntartzag Oraco'h'c So'wrp P'rgichean Hiwantano'ci Hah'o'c* (Istanbul: Surp Pırgiç, 1910), pp. 357-358.

[91] MAEF, CP, January-February 1856, vol. 324. January 17, 1856. From Thouvenel to Walewski. CP, January-February 1856, vol. 324. Memorandum on the 4th guarantee. Annexed to the telegraphic despatch dated 7 January 1856.

[92] MAEF, CP, January-February 1856, vol. 324. January 17, 1856. From Thouvenel to Walewski.

questions regarding the consolidation of the Ottoman Empire.[93] In the
Ottoman ministers' minds, the question of the emancipation of Ottoman
Christians was associated with a barrier that could be raised against
Russian intervention.[94] The Porte probably aimed to put an end to Russian
claims of protection over the Greek Orthodox Church. Consequently, the
Ottoman government understood from consolidation the strengthening of
the ecclesiastical apparatus. Fuad Pasha's inclination to prioritise the prerogatives of the Greek patriarch should be interpreted from this perspective. Moreover, the Ottoman administrative system avoided governing
non-Muslim subjects directly, having preferred to create an intermediary
body between the subject and the state for centuries. The patriarchs were
among the main negotiators for the settlement of communal affairs. The
Porte probably preferred to institutionalise former practices accumulated
over time between the Ottoman state and the communal administration
of non-Muslims when revising their structures in the aftermath of the
Crimean War on behalf of the clergy.

Being more familiar with the state of affairs in the Armenian community, but supposing that the process of transition to new communal establishments was more or less similar in other religious communities in
the aftermath of the Crimean War, I would rather consider Fuad Pasha's
argument as a state pretext to preserve the religious fabric of the *millet*
structure. It was true that the traditional elites of religious communities
raised barriers against the loss of ecclesiastical prerogatives, but their
initiatives were not completely devoid of state support. Ottoman Armenians, for instance, drafted three communal regulations regarding their
religious and political rights from 1857 to 1863, and the changes made
prior to the ratification of the final draft in 1863 reflect this governmental state of mind.

To give some examples, the 1860 draft of the said regulation, which
was never ratified by the Ottoman government, turned the communal
administration into an authorised interlocutor that would represent the
Armenian community before the Sublime Porte. The National General
Assembly, instituted within the Armenian Patriarchate to represent the
will of the community, is the first authority of communal administration
in the 1860 text while the Armenian patriarch of Istanbul is elevated to

---

[93] MAEF, Mémoires et Documents, vol. 116. Turquie, Documents divers, 1859-67.

[94] Cf. G. A. Mano, *Examen du Quatrième Point de Garantie* (Paris: Amyot, 1856),
p. 9. Cited in MAEF, Mémoires et Documents, vol. 51. Turquie, 1854-56.

the first authority of community administration in the 1863 text. On the basis of these institutional differences, one may conclude that instead of institutionalising a secular authority, the Ottoman government preferred the mediation of a religious authority, the patriarch of Istanbul, who was the medium for the execution of the orders of the Ottoman government, in particular circumstances. This mediation in fact strengthened the position of the Ottoman state in relation to the autonomous sphere of the community, since the patriarch is considered an intermediary in order to determine the limits of that autonomy.

The study of peace negotiations in the aftermath of the Crimean War reveals the extent to which France was concerned with the shaping of the fourth point on secular principles. If the maintenance of religious privileges regarding Christian subjects of the Porte was the main issue during the Crimean War, the Ottoman government was expected to solemnly reiterate its previous declarations regarding these privileges and could even do more by encouraging the reform of the Greek Orthodox Patriarchate. This reform could be possible with the assignment of a bigger part to laymen in the temporal administration of the Patriarchate.[95] The French in particular argued that Ottoman Christians needed more guarantees against the abuses of power of their own clergy.[96] Thouvenel also suggested that the memorandum on the fourth guarantee should take into consideration not only the exclusive interests of the "conquering class" but also the interests of diverse nations subjected to Ottoman rule. Instead of leaving the Ottoman Empire in a state of isolation, Thouvenel's suggestion was to prepare the empire to become a union of the nationalities of which it was composed and to try to make a homogeneous nation through the juxtaposition of diverse elements.[97] In addition to their religious privileges, Thouvenel also put emphasis on the social dimension of non-Muslim existence. He stated that the rayas should become Ottoman citizens with their rights and obligations. Even if religion, from many standpoints, regulated civil life in the Ottoman Empire, Thouvenel stated, there should be a legal dimension that

[95] MAEF, CP, January-February 1856, vol. 324. From Thouvenel to Walewski, January 7, 1856. Memorandum on the 4th guarantee. Annexed to the telegraphic despatch dated 7 January 1856.

[96] MAEF, Mémoires et Documents, vol. 116. Turquie, Documents divers, 1859-67. The observations of the Marquis de Moustier, French foreign minister, on the 1856 Reform Edict, 1859.

[97] MAEF, CP, January-February 1856, vol. 324. From Thouvenel to Walewski, January 7, 1856.Memorandum on the 4th guarantee. Annexed to the telegraphic despatch dated 7 January 1856.

could be regulated by common legislation and mixed tribunals wherein non-Muslim judges would take their seats together with Muslim colleagues. Except for marriages, lawsuits regarding commerce, issues of land ownership or succession should be regulated by common principles.[98] Mention was made by Thouvenel of the accessibility of civil and military posts to non-Muslim subjects as the only efficient way of facilitating moral fusion as well as the fusion of interests, the formation of a public spirit and the softening of Ottoman customs. The foundation of a university to which Muslims and non-Muslims would be equally admitted and where not only medicine but also other sciences, such as history, administration and law, would be taught was a necessity for overcoming the difficulties of creating an Ottoman magistrature.[99]

The provincial assemblies, or majlises, also required complete reform as far as the French were concerned. Although the proportional participation of different religious communities had been achieved, their representatives to these assemblies were not well selected. There should be a law which would permit Muslims and Christians the right to directly elect their representatives, since it was held to be abnormal that the governors-general designated the members of the administrative bodies that would control them. The same reform, Thouvenel suggested, should be introduced in the communal councils of villages where Christians suffered from the tax extractions of their primates.[100]

The Powers expected the extension of new legal arrangements regarding Ottoman non-Muslims to their nationals as well. If the French considered codifying the right of ownership for Ottoman subjects as well as the suppression of barriers which prevented Muslims from selling their lands or houses to Christians and foreigners, it was because France aimed to allow its own citizens to enjoy these guarantees.[101] Similarly, Thouvenel

---

[98] MAEF, CP, January-February 1856, vol. 324. Memorandum on the 4th guarantee. Annexed to the telegraphic despatch dated 7 January 1856.

[99] MAEF, Mémoires et Documents, vol. 116. Turquie, Documents divers, 1859-67. The observations of the Marquis de Moustier, French foreign minister, on the 1856 Reform Edict, 1859 & Mémoires et Documents, vol. 51. Turquie, 1854-56. Memoire, January 1854. Note sur les réformes à opérer en Turquie. Mémoire présenté au ministre. Réponse de M. Cor à ce mémoire; MAEF, CP, January-February 1856, vol. 324. Memorandum on the 4th guarantee. Annexed to the telegraphic despatch dated 7 January 1856.

[100] MAEF, CP, January-February 1856, vol. 324. Memorandum on the 4th guarantee. Annexed to the telegraphic despatch dated 7 January 1856.

[101] MAEF, Mémoires et Documents, vol. 116. Turquie, Documents divers, 1859-67. The observations of the Marquis de Moustier, French foreign minister, on the 1856 Reform Edict, 1859.

continued, the barriers which did not allow foreigners to exploit Ottoman land and natural resources should be abolished.[102] The French also developed a vision of capitalism and industrialisation within Ottoman lands by requiring the suppression of internal customs, taxes on consumption, and fiscal measures harmful to local industries which impoverish local populations. They also proposed the creation of a budget for public works that would cover the construction of railways, harbours and communication routes: equally, the establishment of municipalities in the capital and big cities and the assignment of special budgets to each ministry were considered necessary. This capitalist vision also aimed to promote French commercial interests through the exploitation of natural resources (mines, forests, etc.) and the management of railways and routes of communication of the first order: this would require not only the cooperation of domestic private industry but also the contribution of foreign industrialists who would be guaranteed a framework of security and profits to operate within Ottoman territories.[103]

Before the promulgation of the Reform Edict on February 18, 1856, the whole of January was dedicated by the ambassadors of Austria, France and Britain to encounters related to this charter. The edict was partially based on Redcliffe's initial memorandum, which was developed through a series of encounters and exchanges with the Austrian and French colleagues as well as the Ottoman state representatives.[104] The equality of Ottoman subjects of all classes in terms of taxation and admission of evidence in the courts had been accepted since the 1839 Imperial Rescript. However, when Redcliffe defended the abolition of the *haraç* (poll tax) for non-Muslims and the admission of the testimony of Christians in Ottoman courts during the negotiations of the fourth point, Ottoman ministers declined responsibility if these proposals were not accepted by the sheikh ül-Islam and the high clergy.[105] Although there was some kind of consensus on the most

[102] MAEF, CP, January-February 1856, vol. 324. Memorandum on the 4th guarantee. Annexed to the telegraphic despatch dated 7 January 1856.

[103] MAEF, Mémoires et Documents, vol. 116. Turquie, Documents divers, 1859-67. The observations of the Marquis de Moustier, French foreign minister, on the 1856 Reform Edict, 1859.

[104] MAEF, Papiers d'agents, Duc Decazes (Louis-Charles), agents spéciaux, Vienne, Rome, Berlin, Constantinople, 1873-77, vol. 5. Here Constantinople, November 10, 1876. Account of Ignatieff. MAEF, CP, January-February 1856, vol. 324. From Thouvenel to Walewski. February 12, 1856.

[105] G. A. Mano, *Religion et Politique. Examen du Quatrième Point de Garantie* (Paris: Amyot, 1856), p. 130. Cited in MAEF, Mémoires et Documents, vol. 51. Turquie, 1854-56.

important elements of the fourth point between the European representatives and the Ottoman delegates, the Turkish ministers argued that they had encountered objections from their colleagues in the Grand Council with regard to the points on religious persecutions, equal admissibility to office and the possession of landed property by foreigners, and thus hesitated to accept the proposals regarding these issues.[106] Redcliffe reminded them, however, of the case of an Armenian executed in Istanbul for having renounced Islam and reconverted to Christianity, and called attention to the cessation of religious persecutions by mentioning the cases of Catholic and Protestant converts.[107]

The negotiations of the fourth point almost produced the provisions of the 1856 Reform Edict. Redcliffe played a dominant role in the negotiation process. His initial memorandum was combined with the text of another one, again drafted in French, as a collective work accomplished with the participation of his French and Austrian colleagues and the contributions of the Ottoman ministers Ali and Fuad Pashas and Prince Kallimaki.[108] The provisions of the second memorandum offered an advanced version of the dispositions, already developed by Redcliffe's memorandum while creating additional clauses regarding the conditions of construction of new religious buildings by non-Muslim communities, the circumstances of remuneration for their religious heads, their temporal administration, the tax system, etc. Unlike the ideas developed in Redcliffe's memorandum, the Ottoman ministers succeeded in insisting that the administrative improvement of the Ottoman Empire was a question independent of the issue of Christian privileges, which constituted the subject matter of the fourth point; nonetheless, they accepted the necessity of thorough administrative reform in the Ottoman Empire.[109]

---

[106] MAEF, Mémoires et Documents, vol. 51. Turquie, 1854-56. Part XVIII, Eastern Papers, Correspondence respecting Christian privileges in Turkey, presented to both Houses of Parliament by Command of Her Majesty (London: Harrison and Sons, 1856). From Stratford de Redcliffe to the Earl of Clarendon, January 28, 1856.

[107] MAEF, Mémoires et Documents, vol. 51. Turquie, 1854-56. Note from From Stratford de Redcliffe to the Porte. Inclosure 2 in no. 43.

[108] For the text of the second memorandum, see MAEF, Mémoires et Documents, vol. 51. Turquie, 1854-56. Part XVIII, Eastern Papers, Correspondence respecting Christian privileges in Turkey, presented to both Houses of Parliament by Command of Her Majesty (London: Harrison and Sons, 1856). From Redcliffe to Clarendon, January 19, 1856. Inclosure in No. 38. See also the entire text of this collective memorandum in Appendix I in comparison with amendements made by the Ottoman state together with the final text of the 1856 Reform Edict in French.

[109] MAEF, Mémoires et Documents, vol. 51. Turquie, 1854-56. Part XVIII, Eastern Papers, Correspondence respecting Christian privileges in Turkey, presented to both

Redcliffe then received information that the Turkish ministers had encountered difficulties in the Grand Council with regards to the acceptance of the propositions in the second collective memorandum. The points they were most inclined to recede were those of religious persecution, equal admissibility to office, the possession of landed property by foreigners and the procedure in civil courts. Redcliffe made new amendments regarding these points in order to accelerate the negotiations on the fourth point and sent a note to the Turkish ministers through Pisani. In this note, he made a few amendements on the provision regarding religious persecutions by which sedition under religious pretences would be repressed in Turkey and blasphemy might be kept on the list of punishable offences. He also made it understood that he was convinced, like his Austrian and French colleagues, that the concession of a right to foreigners to possess real property of every kind was an essential step for the maintenance of the Ottoman Empire and its rapprochement with Europe. Redcliffe also emphasised the necessity of admitting all classes to councils and public offices in order to internally strengthen the Ottoman Empire.[110] He insisted that Muslims who turned Christian should be as free from every kind of punishment as the Christian who embraced the Muslim faith.[111] Clarendon's message to Redcliffe after the Porte's objections to some of the provisions of the collective memorandum shows the extent to which the British government considered the privilege of holding land to be of vast importance for British nationals. In its view, a large amount of capital was ready for investment when guarantees on land tenure were granted after the settlement of peace.[112]

Houses of Parliament by Command of Her Majesty (London: Harrison and Sons, 1856). From Stratford de Redcliffe to the Earl of Clarendon, January 19, 1856.

[110] Mémoires et Documents, vol. 51. Turquie, 1854-56. Eastern Papers, Part XVIII, Correspondence respecting Christian privileges in Turkey. From Stratford de Redcliffe to the Earl of Clarendon, January 28, 1856.

[111] Mémoires et Documents, vol. 51. Turquie, 1854-56. Eastern Papers, Part XVIII, Correspondence respecting Christian privileges in Turkey. Note addressed to the Porte by Lord Stratford de Redcliffe. Inclosure 2 in no. 43 of Stratford de Redcliffe's message to the Earl of Clarendon, January 28, 1856.

[112] PRO, FO 78/1160. Lord Stratford de Redcliffe, Drafts, February 7-March 8, 1856. Foreign Office to Lord Stratford, February 13, 1856 # No. 171 & No. 174. MAEF, Mémoires et Documents, vol. 51. Turquie, 1854-56. Part XVIII, Eastern Papers, Correspondence respecting Christian privileges in Turkey, presented to both Houses of Parliament by Command of Her Majesty (London: Harrison and Sons, 1856). From the Earl of Clarendon to Redcliffe, February 13, 1856.

The Porte succeeded in changing the provisions regarding land ownership for foreigners and religious persecutions.[113] A long meeting took
place between Ottoman ministers and the three European representatives
on 29 January at the British embassy. Ottoman ministers referred to the
reservations of their ministerial council in the matter of religious rights
and land ownership. The ministers alleged that the Porte had promised
there would be no more persecutions due to religious opinions in Turkey
but thought that it was impossible for the sultan to either abrogate the
existing law stipulating punishments for apostasy from Islam or make
any public declaration equivalent to abrogation. Consequently, Redcliffe
accepted the Porte's slightly amended version of the provision regarding
religious freedoms. The initial provision stipulated that "No subject of
His Majesty the Sultan, to whatever faith he may belong, shall be insulted
or molested, much less persecuted or punished, on account of his religious opinions."[114] After the intervention of the Ottoman ministers, the
provision was changed to "All forms of religion are and shall be freely
exercised in the Ottoman dominions, no subject of His Majesty the Sultan
shall be hindered in the exercise of the religion that he professes, nor
shall be in any way disquieted on this account. No one shall be compelled
to change their religion".[115] The term "persecution" was removed from
the provision. Finally, the law of the Qur'an regarding Muslim apostates
was not abolished; Ottoman ministers affirmed that "such a stretch of
authority would exceed even His Majesty's legal power".[116] The Porte

[113] MAEF, Mémoires et Documents, vol. 51. Turquie, 1854-56. Part XVIII, Eastern
Papers, Correspondence respecting Christian privileges in Turkey, presented to both
Houses of Parliament by Command of Her Majesty (London: Harrison and Sons, 1856).
From Stratford de Redcliffe to the Earl of Clarendon, January 28, 1856.
[114] MAEF, Mémoires et Documents, vol. 51. Turquie, 1854-56. Part XVIII, Eastern
Papers, Correspondence respecting Christian Privileges in Turkey, presented to both
Houses of Parliament by Command of Her Majesty (London: Harrison and Sons, 1856).
From Stratford de Redcliffe to the Earl of Clarendon, January 30, 1856. Inclosure I in
No. 45.
[115] MAEF, Mémoires et Documents, vol. 51. Turquie, 1854-56. Part XVIII, Eastern
Papers, Correspondence respecting Christian privileges in Turkey, presented to both
Houses of Parliament by Command of Her Majesty (London: Harrison and Sons, 1856).
From Stratford de Redcliffe to the Earl of Clarendon, January 30, 1856. Inclosure II in
No. 45.
[116] MAEF, Mémoires et Documents, vol. 51. Turquie, 1854-56. Part XVIII, Eastern
Papers, Correspondence respecting Christian privileges in Turkey, presented to both
Houses of Parliament by Command of Her Majesty (London: Harrison and Sons, 1856).
From Stratford de Redcliffe to the Earl of Clarendon, February 12, 1856. Fuad Pasha's
note in French, Inclosure in no. 52, February 12, 1856.

only confirmed its former declaration on apostates and extended it expressly to Muslims through an official note signed by the secretary of state.[117]

The clause of the Porte respecting religious freedom was thus accepted by the European representatives despite the fact that their initial concerns were not totally taken into consideration.[118] With respect to the possession of land by foreigners, the Porte avoided making a great concession without any guarantee against the interference of foreign protection through the Capitulations.[119] It was finally permitted for foreigners to possess landed properties by conforming to the laws of the country and local police regulations. However, the right of land ownership for foreigners would be conditional upon arrangements that would take place between the Porte and the Powers.

A third memorandum was drafted, again in French, as a collective work taking into consideration the concerns of the Porte with regards to the new formulation of religious freedom and the possession of landed property by foreigners. Redcliffe's idea that various communities would have a separate police force according to the needs of various localities and subordinated to the general police was probably rejected by the Porte, as it did not appear among the provisions of the third memorandum. Moreover, the revision of the immunities granted to non-Muslim communities by an *ad hoc* commission, comprised of their communal members, was put under the Porte's supervision in the third memorandum. Despite the differences, the third memorandum was the closest to the 1856 Reform Decree.[120] The final text of the Reform Edict also

---

[117] MAEF, Mémoires et Documents, vol. 51. Turquie, 1854-56. Part XVIII, Eastern Papers, Correspondence respecting Christian privileges in Turkey, presented to both Houses of Parliament by Command of Her Majesty (London: Harrison and Sons, 1856). From Lord Stratford de Redcliffe to the Earl of Clarendon, February 12, 1856. Inclosure in no. 52. From Fuad Pasha to Redcliffe, February 12, 1856.

[118] MAEF, Mémoires et Documents, vol. 51. Turquie, 1854-56. Part XVIII, Eastern Papers, Correspondence respecting Christian privileges in Turkey, presented to both Houses of Parliament by Command of Her Majesty (London: Harrison and Sons, 1856). From Stratford de Redcliffe to the Earl of Clarendon, January 30, 1856.

[119] MAEF, Mémoires et Documents, vol. 51. Turquie, 1854-56. Part XVIII, Eastern Papers, Correspondence respecting Christian privileges in Turkey, presented to both Houses of Parliament by Command of Her Majesty (London: Harrison and Sons, 1856). From Stratford de Redcliffe to the Earl of Clarendon, January 30, 1856.

[120] MAEF, Mémoires et Documents, vol. 51. Turquie, 1854-56. Part XVIII, Eastern Papers, Correspondence respecting Christian privileges in Turkey, presented to both Houses of Parliament by Command of Her Majesty (London: Harrison and Sons, 1856). From Redcliffe to Clarendon, February 13, 1856. Inclosure in No. 51: Memorandum

included a provision at the end regarding the development of national resources in the Ottoman Empire with the aid of foreign capital, science and know-how.[121]

As an Ottoman bureaucrat, Kallimaki did not neglect to defend the interests of the Ottoman government during the negotiations. An ardent debate over terminology broke out between the Ottoman side and the foreign representatives when shaping Article 9 of the Paris Treaty, which stipulated that the sultan, "in his constant solicitude for the welfare of his subjects", would issue a firman which would ameliorate the condition of the Ottoman Christian population "without distinction of religion or of race". The article added that the sultan "wishing to give further proof of his sentiments in that respect", communicated the firman in question to the contracting parties. The parties recognised the high value of this communication. The phrase "recognised the high value" was initially formulated with the expression "take note" (*prendre acte*) in the drafts of the treaty. A council convened in the *Seraskerat* (Ottoman Ministry of War) to discuss the terminology. During the examination of the expression, many dictionaries were consulted, including that of Handjéri, in which the expression corresponded to *sened* (written agreement) in Ottoman Turkish:[122] "For 'acte' meant to the Turks something formal, official, a registering of a document, with the implication that here was a guaranty or contract which might allow the Powers a claim to oversee its enforcement".[123] The pretentions of Prince Menshikoff came to the minds of the Ottomans.[124] Menshikoff's idea was to regulate the religious rights, privileges and immunities of the Greek Orthodox Church by a *sened* between the Russian and Ottoman governments during the Crimean crisis. The Porte responded that such an obligatory act was an

agreed upon relative to the Fourth Point. See the Appendix I for the amendements made to the second memorandum. The parts scored out on the second memorandum in Appendix I show the removals and the parts in red the additions made by the third memorandum.

[121] Cf. MAEF, Mémoires et Documents, vol. 51. Turquie, 1854-56. Part XVIII, Eastern Papers, Correspondence respecting Christian privileges in Turkey, presented to both Houses of Parliament by Command of Her Majesty (London: Harrison and Sons, 1856). From Redcliffe to Clarendon, February 4, 1856.

[122] MAEF, CP, March-May 1856, vol. 325. March 1856. Report by Schefer to the ambassador of France (Thouvenel), pp. 148-149.

[123] Davison, *Ottoman Diplomacy and Reforms*, p. 172.

[124] MAEF, CP, March-May 1856, vol. 325. March 1856. Report by Schefer to the ambassador of France (Thouvenel), pp. 148-149.

attempt to undermine the independence of the Ottoman Empire.[125] During the terminological debate, Kallimaki also confirmed that he found a frightening significance in the expression *"acte"* in Handjéri's dictionary, which he consulted.[126] I maintain that the appointment of Kallimaki as an intervener during the discussion was not coincidental. Prince Kallimaki gained at that time the reputation of having mastered the *elsine-i selase* better than any other Phanariot diplomat.[127] Thus the stipulation *La communication dont les puissances alliées prennent acte* was changed into *dont elles constatent la haute valeur*. In exchange for his efforts, Kallimaki was promoted from the mission of Vienna to the position of Ottoman commissioner in the principalities of Moldavia and Wallachia.[128]

Kostaki Musurus Pasha was another Phanariot diplomat who contributed to the negotiations of the Paris Treaty. He held the office of Ottoman ambassador to London from 1851 to 1885. According to Kuneralp, it is difficult to find a satisfactory explanation for the exceptionally long tenure of Musurus Pasha. Nineteenth-century British policy with respect to the Ottoman Empire and the place occupied by Britain in the Ottoman Foreign Ministry should both be taken into account when considering the exceptional position of Musurus as an Ottoman ambassador to London. Similarly, Stratford de Redcliffe, one of the most powerful representatives of British politics, remained British ambassador to the Porte for around 30 years and acquired great influence. Tanzimat bureaucrats probably expected that Musurus would be able to acquire the same influence through his long stay in London.[129] Musurus acted as a channel of transmission between Britain and the Ottoman Empire and expressed the possibility of negotiating the issues

---

[125] Note de Réchid-pacha aux représentants d'Angleterre, d'Autriche, de France et de Prusse à Constantinople, en date du 26 mai 1853 (17 châban 1269). Cited in Baron I. de Testa, *Recueil des Traités de la Porte ottomane avec les Puissances étrangères* (Paris: Amyot, 1876), v. 4, 1ère partie pp. 255-256.

[126] MAEF, CP, March-May 1856, vol. 325. March 23, 1856. Report by Schefer to the ambassador of France (Thouvenel).

[127] Sinan Kuneralp, "Les Grecs en Stambouline," in Semih Vaner (ed.), *Le Différend greco-turc* (Paris: l'Harmattan, 1988), p. 43. Cited in Strauss, "The *Millets* and the Ottoman Language", pp. 209-210.

[128] MAEF, CP, March-May 1856, vol. 325. March 27, 1856. From Thouvenel to Walewski.

[129] Sinan Kuneralp, "Bir Osmanlı Diplomatı Kostaki Musurus Pasha, 1807-1891," (An Ottoman Diplomat: Kostaki Musurus Pasha, 1807-1891) *Belleten*, vol. 34, no. 135 (July 1970), pp. 421-422.

of reform confidentially and definitively with the two friendly Powers (Britain and France). After examining the reform project indicated by the British government in accordance with the political interests of the Ottoman Empire, the state could communicate to the two governments the reforms that would be adopted with any modifications that the Porte might judge necessary.[130]

The main concern of the Ottoman diplomatic apparatus was to defend the empire's independence and integrity as a response to European intervention.[131] During the Crimean War, Ali Pasha drafted a treaty article that would constitute the defence of Ottoman foreign policy: "The Contracting Powers, wishing to demonstrate the importance they attach to assuring that the Ottoman Empire participate in the advantages of the Concert established by public law among the different European States, declare that they henceforth consider that empire as an integral part of the Concert and engage themselves to respect its territorial integrity and its independence as an essential condition of the general balance of power".[132] In Article 7 of the Treaty of Paris, Ali's expectations, except those regarding the balance of power, were satisfied.[133] Article 9 of the Paris Treaty stipulated that the sultan's communication of the Reform Edict "cannot, in any case, give to the said Powers the right to interfere, either collectively or separately, in the relations of His Majesty the Sultan with his subjects, nor in the internal administration of his Empire".[134] In the following years, the Ottoman state would respond to European intervention by referring to the treaty on the basis of respect of international law and non-interference in the internal affairs of other states, thus creating the legal principles of its foreign policy.[135]

[130] BOA, HR. SYS. 1869 B-3.

[131] Davison, *Ottoman Diplomacy and Reforms*, pp. 333-334.

[132] Ali Fuat Türkgeldi, *Mesail-i Mühimme-i Siyasiye* (Ankara: Türk Tarih Kurumu, 1957), vol. 1, pp. 60-61; G. F. de Martens (ed.), *Nouveau Recueil général des Traités* (Göttingen: Dieterich, 1843-1875), vol. 15, pp. 670-671, protocol of session 11, April 19, 1855. Cited in Davison, *Ottoman Diplomacy and Reforms*, pp. 336-337.

[133] Davison, *Ottoman Diplomacy and Reforms*, p. 337.

[134] Text in J. C. Hurewitz, *The Middle East and North Africa in World Politics: a Documentary Record* (New Haven: Yale University Press, 1975), vol. 1, p. 320. Cited in Davison, *Ottoman Diplomacy and Reforms*, p. 338.

[135] Davison, *Ottoman Diplomacy and Reforms*, p. 338.

The Rothschilds and the Fourth Point

The multinational partnership that the Rothschilds founded was the biggest bank in the world between 1815 and 1914.[136] Their firm mainly operated in Britain, France and Germany.[137] The Rothschilds were at the same time major industrial investors. They financed the development of railways in the 1830s and 40s in France, Austria and Germany. "Indeed, by the 1860s James de Rothschild had built up something like a Pan-European railway network extending northwards from France to Belgium, southwards to Spain and eastwards to Germany, Switzerland, Austria and Italy".[138] They also invested in mines producing gold, copper, diamonds, rubies and oil.[139] For the Rothschilds, as for many other Jewish families who migrated in the nineteenth century, social assimilation or integration into the countries where they settled raised a challenge to their faith, although the weakening of discriminatory legislation allowed them to acquire wealth and social prestige.[140] The promulgation of the Republic did not change, for instance, the attacks of French anti-Rothschild litera-ture in the 1870s.[141] Although they encountered anti-Jewish sentiment, and other Jewish families preferred to convert to Christianity as a solu-tion to such pressures, they opted to preserve their attachment to Judaism and to play an important role in the preservation of the interests of vari-ous Jewish communities. "They did this not only in their home town of Frankfurt, but consistently in almost every state where they did business thereafter as well as in some countries (for example, Rumania and Syria) where they had no economic interests".[142] The Rothschilds saw their finan-cial power as a way of defending the interests of their co-religionists.[143] Other Jews considered them their leaders in the quest for equal civil and political rights.[144] They secured, for instance, the admission of Jews to the House of Commons in the 1840s and 50s.[145] "It was a strategy which suited the Rothschilds well, allowing them to pursue their own

---

[136] Niall Ferguson, *The World's Banker: The History of the House of Rothschild* (Weidenfeld & Nicolson: London, 1998), p. 3.

[137] Ferguson, pp. 31-32.

[138] Ferguson, p. 7.

[139] Ferguson, p. 7.

[140] Ferguson, p. 9.

[141] Ferguson, p. 19.

[142] Ferguson, p. 9.

[143] Ferguson, p. 22.

[144] Ferguson, p. 23.

[145] Ferguson, p. 23.

familial strategy of penetrating the social and political elites where they lived without converting from Judaism; and allowing them to do good works on behalf of their 'co-religionists' while at the same time acquiring quasi-royal status in the eyes of other Jews".[146]

The common point between the Camondos and the Rothschilds was the fact that they institutionalised new practices of philanthropy in France and the Middle East throughout the nineteenth century. The Rothschilds became the avant-garde of these new practices through the institutionalisation of new norms of behaviour among Jewish economic elites. The new form of philanthropy aimed to go beyond national frontiers and ameliorate the conditions of Jewish communities in decline, particularly in the Middle East.[147] On the political side, the Rothschilds understood the importance of proximity to politicians who determined financial, domestic and foreign policies. In the same way, politicians understood the importance of proximity to the Rothschilds for the sake of solvency of the states they governed.[148] Their influence extended to British royalty as well as to Victorian politicians.[149]

The Crimean War strengthened the primacy of the family in the field of public finance. The Rothschilds financed the war expenses of France and Britain.[150] The other combatant country searching for funding in 1855 was the Ottoman Empire itself, and the Rothschilds were ready to lend to it.[151] When, France and Britain were involved in the Crimean War because of the situation of Ottoman Christian subjects, in March 1854 Jewish leaders drew the attention of both governments to the status of Jews in the Ottoman Empire and the Danubian principalities. Their objective was to ensure that Jews be included in any future arrangement affecting the status of non-Muslims in Ottoman Turkey. The initiative was taken by the Rothschilds in England and France by appealing to Foreign Secretary Lord Clarendon and the Ottoman ambassadors in Paris and London. They requested that the advantages and privileges granted to Ottoman Christians be similarly extended to the Jewish population.[152]

---

[146] Ferguson, p. 23.

[147] Cf. Nora Şeni & Sophie Le Tarnec, *Les Camondo ou l'Eclipse d'une Fortune* (Actes du Sud, 1997), pp. 42-58.

[148] Ferguson, p. 9.

[149] Ferguson, p. 10.

[150] Ferguson, pp. 582-584.

[151] Ferguson, p. 584.

[152] *Minute Books of the Board of Deputies of British Jews* (hereafter JBD), VII, pp. 252-257. *Allgemeine Zeitung des Judenthums* (hereafter AZJ), 3 April 1854,

A committee was instituted in order to secure the position of Ottoman Jews in terms of enjoying equal rights with Christian subjects.[153]

In reply to the Rothschilds' appeal, Clarendon responded that the privileges granted to Ottoman Christians would be extended to Ottoman Jews as well.[154] Unfortunately, the efforts of Jewish leaders remained fruitless; the Jewish question was not raised at the Paris Peace Conference[155] and the fourth point remained limited to Christians only.[156] The status of Jews in the Ottoman Empire was, however, discussed for the first time during the negotiations between the ambassadors of Britain, France and Austria before the Paris Congress. Although the fourth point referred to Christians only, Jews were included in all the arrangements provided for other non-Muslim subjects of the empire.[157]

The inclusion of Jews in the fourth point in one way or another was Stratford's work,[158] since his policy was to obtain equality between Muslim and non-Muslim subjects of the Ottoman Empire in order to secure its survival.[159] The Jewish question was also considered at home. Lord Palmerston, the British prime minister, always maintained that the territorial integrity of the Ottoman Empire could only be assured by internal reforms,[160] of which equal treatment of all inhabitants independently of their beliefs was the central point. Thus, he paid special attention to the situation of Jews in the Ottoman Empire, and particularly in Palestine, from 1839 to 1841.[161] "Let me recommend the Jews to your

---

pp. 173-174. See also the *Jewish Chronicle* (hereafter JC), 28 April 1854, pp. 254-255. Cited in Eliyahu Feldman, "The Question of Jewish Emancipation in the Ottoman Empire and the Danubian Principalities after the Crimean War," *Jewish Social Studies*, vol. 41, no. 1 (Winter 1979), p. 41.

[153] Şeni & Le Tarnec, pp. 49-52.

[154] PRO, FO 78/1052. From Foreign Office to Montefiore, 15 May 1854. See also *JC*, 7 April 1854, p. 232. Cited in Feldman, p. 42.

[155] Cf. *JC*, 25 January 1856, pp. 460-461. Cited in Feldman, p. 43.

[156] *JC*, 25 January 1856, p. 65. Cited in Feldman, p. 43.

[157] PRO, FO 78/1171. From Stratford to Clarendon, 16 January 1856; 17 January 1856; 19 January 1856. Cited in Feldman, pp. 43-44.

[158] FO 78/1173. From Stratford to Clarendon, 13 February 1856. Cited in Feldman, p. 44.

[159] Cf. Temperley, "The Last Phase of Stratford de Redcliffe", pp. 216-259. Cited in Feldman, p. 44.

[160] PRO, FO 78/1236. From Lord Malmesbury to Cowley, 25 May 1858. Cited in Feldman, p. 44.

[161] PRO, FO 78/391, from Palmerston to Ponsonby, 24 November 1840; FO 78/427, 17 December 1841; FO 78/428, 21 April 1841; FO 78/430, from Ponsonby to Palmerston, 21 January 1841; FO 78/432, 27 March 1841. Cited in Feldman, p. 44.

special care", he wrote privately to Lord Ponsonby, the British ambassador to the Porte on February 26, 1841.[162] Similarly, when the British, French and Austrian ambassadors to the Porte conducted their negotiations on the fourth point in Istanbul in 1856, Palmerston instructed Stratford that he should keep in mind the inclusion of Jews.[163] His telegram dated January 26, 1856 was received after the text of the arrangements had been already decided. Montefiore, another British banker and the president of the London committee, intervened a second time on January 25, 1856. Finally, the provisions regarding the fourth point were extended to non-Muslims instead of being limited only to Christians. In other words, the provisions of the fourth point referred to non-Muslims in order to not exclude Ottoman Jews.[164]

After the promulgation of the 1856 Reform Edict, Redcliffe received the official French translation from Fuad Pasha.[165] Before its promulgation, Redcliffe ascertained that the articles regarding privileges and reforms remained loyal to the French original.[166] Since Redcliffe was told that there were some doubts as to the precision of the sultan's edict with respect to the articles in French, originally agreed upon during the negotiations on the fourth point, and that the printed translations in Greek and French were also thought to be imperfect, he consulted Percy Smythe and Frederick Pisani, members of his staff.[167] "The one is a project, the other a decree, and the measures and resolutions which appear as simple statements in the former are enforced with authority in the latter, by the Sultan taking occasion to speak in the first person", Percy Smythe responded after having compared, with the assistance of Frederick and

---

[162] Charles K. Webster, *The Foreign Policy of Palmerston* (2nd ptg., London, 1969), p. 763, n. 2. Cited in Feldman, p. 44.

[163] PRO, FO 78/1159, 24 January 1856, telegram no. 97. Cited in Feldman, p. 44.

[164] PRO, FO 78/1232, from Montefiore to Clarendon, 25 January 1856. FO 78/1159, from Clarendon to Stratford, 28 January 1856; FO 27/1109 to Cowley, 28 January 1856. Cited in Feldman, pp. 44-45.

[165] MAEF, Mémoires et Documents, vol. 51. Turquie, 1854-56. Part XVIII, Eastern Papers, Correspondence respecting Christian privileges in Turkey, presented to both Houses of Parliament by Command of Her Majesty (London: Harrison and Sons, 1856). From Stratford de Redcliffe to the Earl of Clarendon, February 21, 1856.

[166] MAEF, Mémoires et Documents, vol. 51. Turquie, 1854-56. Part XVIII, Eastern Papers, Correspondence respecting Christian privileges in Turkey, presented to both Houses of Parliament by Command of Her Majesty (London: Harrison and Sons, 1856). From Stratford de Redcliffe to the Earl of Clarendon, February 13, 1856.

[167] MAEF, Mémoires et Documents, vol. 51. Turquie, 1854-56. Part XVIII, Eastern Papers, Correspondence respecting Christian privileges in Turkey, presented to both Houses of Parliament by Command of Her Majesty (London: Harrison and Sons, 1856). From Stratford de Redcliffe to the Earl of Clarendon, March 6, 1856.

Etienne Pisani, the Ottoman text of the firman with the original French memorandum drawn up by the three representatives of the British, French and Austrian governments.[168] They also added that they could not detect any difference amounting to a discrepancy or material variation between the two documents. If there were small differences, this was due to the respective peculiarities of Ottoman Turkish and French idioms and did not affect the sense.[169] The following textual analysis of the 1856 Reform Decree focuses on these terminological differences between the Ottoman text and the translations into French and Armenian.

The Reform Edict of 1856: Textual Analysis

The Reform Edict was proclaimed on February 18, 1856.[170] The conceptual analysis of the French version of the Reform Edict is based on the translation sent by Fuad Pasha stating that this was the official text.[171] The text of the edict began with a concern for happiness (*saadet/ bonheur*): since his accession to the throne, all the efforts of the sovereign had been oriented towards the happiness of all classes of imperial subjects (*kaffe-i sunuf-ı tebea-i şahane/toutes les classes des sujets*) entrusted to his rule by God. Like the Ottoman and French texts, the Armenian text also used the concept of happiness (*erch'ango'wt'iwn*). *Sunuf*, the Ottoman equivalent of "classes", meant rank, way of life, or status. The Armenian text refers to the expression of "subjects of all ranks" (*amen asdijani hbadagner*).

---

[168] MAEF, Mémoires et Documents, vol. 51. Turquie, 1854-56. Part XVIII, Eastern Papers, Correspondence respecting Christian privileges in Turkey, presented to both Houses of Parliament by Command of Her Majesty (London: Harrison and Sons, 1856). From P. Smythe to Stratford de Redcliffe, March 1, 1856.

[169] MAEF, Mémoires et Documents, vol. 51. Turquie, 1854-56. Part XVIII, Eastern Papers, Correspondence respecting Christian privileges in Turkey, presented to both Houses of Parliament by Command of Her Majesty (London: Harrison and Sons, 1856). From P. Smythe to Stratford de Redcliffe, March 1, 1856. Inclosure in no. 57.

[170] For the Ottoman text, see BOA, I.MMS. 6/245. For the French text, see MAEF, CP, January-February 1856. Annex to the political despatch dated 21 February 1856; from the Sublime Porte (Fuad Pasha). See also MAEF, Mémoires et Documents, vol. 51. Turquie, 1854-56. Part XVIII, Eastern Papers, Correspondence respecting Christian privileges in Turkey, presented to both Houses of Parliament by Command of Her Majesty (London: Harrison and Sons, 1856); from Redcliffe to Clarendon, February 21, 1856. For the Armenian text, see *Awedaper*, February 27, 1856 & March 12, 1856. The newspaper refers to a text translated into Armenian from the official translation without mentioning whether the translation was from French or Ottoman.

[171] See MAEF, CP, January-February 1856. Annex to the political despatch dated 21 February 1856, from the Sublime Porte (Fuad Pasha).

Unlike the Imperial Rescript, the Reform Edict does not express any idea of Ottoman decline. On the contrary, the point of departure is that these efforts of the sovereign concerning the happiness of his subjects had been productive. Consequently, the level of development (*mamuriyet*) and wealth (*servet*) of the state and the nation (*mülk ü millet*) were increasing. The ideas of development and prosperity and the simultaneous use of the state and the nation provide a certain continuity between the 1839 Imperial Rescript and the 1856 Reform Edict. Again, the Ottoman equivalent of the term "nation" (*millet*) should be read with a certain national connotation and as the conceptualisation of an Ottoman nation rather than as a religious entity. The Armenian text translated this passage as the increase in happiness of the nation and of the wealth of Ottoman countries. We may keep in mind that the Armenian equivalent of the term "nation" (*azk*) has a religious connotation like the term "*millet*". However, the debates in the newspapers of the time lead us to think that the content of the Armenian term was also slowly evolving towards a more national and secular connotation.[172]

The objective of the Reform Edict is defined as the renewal and enlargement of new regulations (*nizamat-ı cedide/les règlements nouveaux*) instituted in order to attain a state of affairs be fitting Ottoman dignity (*şan/dignité*) and the high and important position (*mevki-i âli ve mühimme/la position*) that the Ottoman Empire occupied among civilised nations (*milel-i mütemeddine/nations civilisées*). The Armenian text also refers to state dignity (*de'ro'wt'ean arzhanabado'wo'wt'iwn*) and to the empire's position (*tirq*) among civilised nations (*qaghaqaganacadz azker*) as well as to the renewal and enlargement of regulated arrangements (*sahmano'wadz garkatro'wt'iwn*). The decree announces a new era in which all classes of imperial subjects (*kaffe-i sunuf-ı tebea-i şahanem/tous mes sujets*), united to each other by cordial ties of subjecthood (*revabıt-ı kalbiyye-i vatandaşi/rapports cordiaux de patriotisme*), are equal in the eyes of the sovereign. The surprising word here is *vatandaşi*, which the French text translates as *patriotisme* (*rapports cordiaux de patriotisme*). *Vatandaş* is the equivalent of citizen in the modern sense of the term. To translate *vatandaşi* as "citizenship" is anachronistic, as it refers to a much later meaning of the word. If we consider that the 1856

---

[172] See the discussions in *Masis*, 12 November 1859; 25 February 1860; 8 July 1860; 14 July 1860; 24 January 1857; 6 October 1860; 27 October 1860; 3 November 1860; 17 November 1860; 10 March 1862; 17 March 1862.

Reform Decree was first drafted in French,[173] the use of *vatandaşi* may be considered an attempt by the Ottomans to find a word that might correspond to the French term "*patriotisme*", which derives from "*patrie*" (fatherland). Similarly, *vatandaşi* derives from *vatan* (fatherland). This may be the first-ever use of *vatandaş*.[174] The Armenian text also refers to the equality of all subjects and defines their attachment to each other in terms of the close relationship of citizenship (*hah'renagco'wt'ean serd h'arapero'wt'iwnnero'v*). Compared to the Imperial Rescript, the instrument of justification of the Reform Edict changes from conformity with the shari'a into improvement of the conditions of Ottoman subjects according to the dignity and the position the Ottoman Empire occupies among the civilised nations.[175]

The edict, in both the Ottoman and French versions, confirms once more that the Gülhane Rescript provided all the subjects of the Ottoman Empire, without exception, security of life, property and honour regardless of religion or sect (*her din ve mezhepte bila-istisna/sans distinction de classes ni de culte*). The French text differs only slightly in that it replaces "sect" with "class". The Armenian text states that these guarantees (*erashxawo'ro'wt'iwn*) are to be enjoyed without any distinction of rank (*asdijan*) and religion (*gronq*). These guarantees granted by the sultan are once again confirmed and consolidated by the text of the Reform Edict. The text states that all privileges and spiritual exemptions (*bil-cümle imtiyazat ve muafiyet-i ruhaniye/tous les privilèges et immunités spirituels*) granted by the ancestors of the sultan to the Christian and other non-Muslim communities (*Hıristiyan ve sair tebea-i gayr-i Müslime cemaatlere/les communautés chrétiennes ou d'autres*

---

[173] However, the individual or collective memoranda drafted in French on the fourth point do not contain any passage regarding the "cordial ties of patriotism". The use of a similar expression appears in a draft of the firman annexed to Redcliffe's despatch to Clarendon, in which Redcliffe talks about his efforts to ascertain that "the Turkish version, as prepared for the sultan's firman, of the concerted articles relating to privileges and reforms, agrees completely with the original in French". This draft of the firman talks about "subjects united to one another by the bonds of cordiality and the same patriotism" ("classes de sujets attachées les unes aux autres par les liens d'une entente cordiale et par le même patriotisme" in French). MAEF, Mémoires et Documents, Turquie, vol. 51. Turquie, 1854-56. Part XVIII, Eastern Papers, Correspondence respecting Christian privileges in Turkey, presented to both Houses of Parliament by Command of Her Majesty (London: Harrison and Sons, 1856); from Stratford de Redcliffe to the Earl of Clarendon, February 13, 1856.

[174] I thank Prof. Eldem for drawing my attention to these comments about *vatandaşi*.

[175] Ardıç, p. 94.

rites non-musulmans), which are subjects of the Ottoman Empire, will be confirmed once again in writing and maintained. The Armenian text talks about Christian and non-Muslim communities (*Qrisdo'neah' gam Mahme'dagan chegho'gh o'wrish gronqe' eghadz hasarago'wt'iwnner*) without referring to their Ottoman subjecthood; however, it mentions their establishment under sultanic protection, like the French text, and discusses spiritual privileges (*ho'kewo'r arantznashno'rho'wt'iwnner*) and authorisations (*ardono'wt'iwnner*).

The text stipulates that each Christian and non-Muslim community (*Hıristiyan ve tebea-i gayr-i Müslime-i sairenin her bir cemaati/chaque communauté chrétienne ou d'autre rite non-Musulman*), within a fixed period of time, is obliged to examine current privileges and exemptions. They should cooperate with a commission that would be temporarily formed in the patriarchates under the supervision of the Sublime Porte and with the approval of the sultan in order to proceed to the reforms required by the norms of civilisation and current thought (*asar-ı medeniyet ve malumat-ı müktesebe/les progrès des lumières et du temps*) and submit the results to the Porte. Like the French text, the Armenian version refers to Christian and non-Muslim communities in general (*Qrisdo'neah' gam Mahmedagan chegho'gh o'wrish gronqe' eghadz ame'n me'g hasarago'wt'iwny*) without mentioning Ottoman subjecthood, while the Ottoman text refers to Christian and non-Muslim communities which are subjects of the Ottoman Empire. Thus, the omission of the issue of subjecthood in the French and Armenian texts calls into question whether the reforms were extended to other non-Muslims (for instance, the colony of foreigners, who were numerous enough to be considered as "communities" and who also built their own churches). In the French text, the principles of the reforms are based on the Enlightenment and progress. The Armenian text refers to the Enlightenment (*lo'wsawo'ro'wt'iwn*) and the progress of the times (*zhamanagi h'ar'ach'timo'wt'iwn*). The authorisations and powers (*ruhsat ve iktidar/ pouvoirs*) conceded to patriarchs and Christian bishops by Sultan Mehmed II and his successors should be adapted to the position which these communities were provided, and the elections of the patriarchs should be reformed. After the revision of the current regulations regarding election, the principle of nominating patriarchs for life would be applied precisely in accordance with their firman of investiture. Patriarchs, metropolitans, archbishops, bishops and rabbis would swear loyalty upon entry to office according to a formulation agreed upon between the Sublime Porte and the spiritual chiefs of diverse communities.

The Reform Edict placed the movable property and real estate of the Christian clergy under guarantee. The edict entrusted the administration of the affairs of each Christian and other non-Muslim community, subject of the empire (*Hıristiyan vesair tebea-i gayr-i Müslime cemaatlerine milletçe olan maslahatlarının idaresi*), to an assembly composed of the clergy and the people (*ruhban ve avamı beyninde müntehib azadan mürekkep bir meclis*) of each *millet*. While the Ottoman text talks about the *millet* administration of each community, the French text refers to a temporal administration (*l'administration temporelle des communautés chrétiennes ou d'autres rites non-musulmans*). Similarly the French text refers to a communal assembly composed of clerics and laymen (*une assemblée choisie dans le sein de chacune des dites communautés parmi les membres du clergé et des laïcs*). The conceptualisation of the Armenian text is similar to that of the French. It refers to the temporal administration (*zhamanagawo'r gar'avaro'wt'iwn*) of Christian and other non-Muslim communities by an assembly of clerics (*egeghecagan*) and laymen (*ashxaragan*).

The selection and nomination of Ottoman civil officialdom would depend, the edict stated, on the sovereign will of the sultan, but all Ottoman subjects, independently of their *millet* affiliation, would be admissible to public offices according to their capacities and skills. The Ottoman text refers to the term "*millet*" as if the empire was an amalgamation of various *millets*, while the French text uses the term "nationality" as if the empire was an amalgamation of nationalities. Similarly, the Armenian text refers to the non-discrimination of nationalities (*ar'anc azkah'no'wt'ean me'ch' xdro'wt'iwn ynelo'w*). In any case, in his memorandum addressed to the Earl of Clarendon on May 1855 on the religious privileges of Ottoman Christians, Ali Pasha himself made use of the term "*nationalité*" when pointing out that sultanic toleration was so expansive that the diverse populations of the empire had preserved their nationality, religion and laws at the moment of their defeat and conquest by the Ottomans. Surprisingly, Ali Pasha also uses the term "*minorité*" (minority) when mentioning these defeated populations in his memorandum.[176] Ottoman subjects were equally admissible to schools of the military or public administration. Similarly, each community was

---

[176] MAEF, Mémoires et Documents, vol. 51. Turquie, 1854-56. Part XVIII, Eastern Papers, Correspondence respecting Christian privileges in Turkey, presented to both Houses of Parliament by Command of Her Majesty (London: Harrison and Sons, 1856); from Musurus to the Earl of Clarendon, May 13, 1855. Inclosure in no. 2, Memorandum.

permitted to open scientific, professional or industrial schools provided that the modes of education and the nomination of teachers would be under the supervision of a mixed council of public instruction whose members would be nominated by the sultan.

According to the edict, commercial or penal cases between Muslim (*ehl-i İslam*) and Christian or other non-Muslim (*Hıristiyan vesair tebea-i gayr-i Müslime*) subjects, or between Christian subjects (*tebea-i Iseviyye*) and other non-Muslim subjects (*tebea-i Iseviyye vesair tebea-i gayr-i Müslimden mezahib-i muhtelife*), would be heard publicly in mixed assemblies (*muhtelit divan*). The French text refers to mixed tribunals (*tribunal mixte*) instead of mixed assemblies. The Reform Edict does not abolish patriarchal courts. Special cases such as inheritance between Christians or other non-Muslim subjects (*Hıristiyan vesair tebea-i gayr-i Müslimeden*) could be transferred to the councils of patriarchs or communities. The French text uses the term "special civil cases such as inheritance" (*les procès civils spéciaux comme ceux de succession*) while the Ottoman text omits the term "civil" (*hukuk-ı irsiye gibi deavi-i mahsusa*) and the Armenian keeps it (*masnawo'r qaghaqagan tader, zo'r orinag zhar'anko'wt'ean*). The Armenian text also used terms such as "*hamagron*" (entity of people belonging to the same religion) and "*hamazk*" (entity of people belonging to the same nation) when defining the parties in these civil cases. The Reform Edict was also an incomplete text in the sense that penal and commercial laws as well as the codification of procedures to be applied in mixed tribunals were not ready: they would be prepared in the near future and translated into the various languages used in the Ottoman Empire.

The Reform Edict refers to the harmonisation of human rights (*hukuk-ı insaniye/droits de l'humanité*) with those of justice (*hukuk-ı adalet/droits de la justice*) when stipulating the conditions for reforming Ottoman prisons and the prohibition of persecutions. The Armenian text also uses the equivalents of these terms (*martasiragan irawo'wnq & artaro'wt'ean irawanc*). The organisation of the police would be regulated in the Ottoman capital as well as in the provinces in order to guarantee the security of life and property to all subjects (*kaffe-i tebea/tous les sujets*). The text stipulated that equality of taxes (*verginin müsavatı/égalité des impôts*) implies equality of burdens (*tekalif-i sairenin müsavatı/égalité des charges*), just as equality of rights (*hukukça olan müsavat/égalité des droits*) implies equality of duties (*vezaifçe olan müsavat/égalité des devoirs*). In that respect, Christian and other non-Muslim subjects should, like Muslims, fulfil their military service. The legislation regarding the conditions of the admission of Christians to the Ottoman army, as well as the conditions of their military service, would be completed in the near future.

The mode of election of members among Muslim, Christian and other subjects composing the provincial assemblies, as well as the regulations regarding their organisation, would be reformed so as to guarantee the expression of votes. Laws regulating the purchase, sale and acquisition of property would be equally applied to Ottoman subjects, and land ownership would be allowed to foreigners in the Ottoman Empire. The Reform Edict also recognises the equality of taxation independent of the class and religious denomination (*sınıf ve mezheplerine bakılmayarak/ sans distinction de classe ni de culte*) of subjects, while also promising to remedy abuses in the collection of taxes, especially the tithe, and to replace the system of tax farming with direct taxation. The Armenian text again refers to non-discrimination according to rank (*asdijan*) and religion (*gronq*) in the equalisation of taxation. Local taxes would be established in such a way that they would not harm production or movement in domestic trade. The special taxes collected in the provinces would contribute to public works and the construction of communication routes by sea or land. A special law had already been promulgated for the regulation of the state budget; accordingly, the state budget would be fixed every year and published.

The chiefs and one official of each community, designated by the Sublime Porte (*her bir cemaatin rüesasıyla taraf-ı eşref-i şahanemden tayin olunacak birer memurları*), would take part in the resolutions of the Supreme Council of Justice regarding the circumstances that interested the generality of the subjects (*tebea-i saltanat-ı seniyemin umuruna ait*). The Armenian text refers to circumstances related to the public interest of Ottoman subjects (*hbadagnero'wn hasaragac oko'wdy*) and uses the term "deputy" (*eresp'o'xan*) instead of "official". The mandate of these functionaries would be annual and they would not be hindered when voting or expressing their ideas in either the ordinary or extraordinary sessions of the Council. Laws against corruption would be applied to all the subjects of the empire without considering their class and the nature of their functions. The creation of banks and other similar institutions to reform the monetary and financial system and to increase the material resources of the empire was put on the state's agenda. Roads and canals would be constructed in order to facilitate communication and increase the country's sources of wealth. All obstacles against the development of commerce or agriculture would be abolished. The sciences, arts and European capital would be implemented for the sake of this development.

3. New Trends: the 1860s

Millet *Constitutions: the Beginning of Constitutional Debate in the* *Ottoman Empire*

The Ottoman Empire was established as an empire of difference. The adoption of the *millet* system probably emerged from the need of the Ottoman state to take into account the organisational and cultural differences of the various religious-ethnic groups under its rule.[177] Firstly, the term designated a community of people belonging to the same religious creed and was used in the framework of different expressions: hence the *millet-i İslamiye* in the sense of the people of Islam; the *millel-i mahkume* in the sense of the non-Muslim *millet*s; and the *millel-i erbaa* designating the four religious communities, Muslims, Greeks, Armenians and Jews, etc. Secondly, it also referred to the "body of doctrine" or "common practice" peculiar to one of these confessions in expressions such as *millet* worship, *millet* ritual or *millet* law. In the third place, the term also meant the institutional framework or structure of the religious communities together with their ecclesiastical hierarchy and their administrative organs and regulations.[178] The *millet* system was first based on religion and second on ethnicity. Religion provided a universal framework of beliefs despite covering ethnic and linguistic differences of the communal structure. For instance, the Greek Patriarchate of Constantinople housed all the Orthodox dyophysites (Greeks, Bulgarians, Serbians, Albanians, Wallachians, Moldavians, etc.) while the Armenian Patriarchate of Constantinople comprised Armenians, Syrians, Chaldeans, Copts, Georgians, etc.[179] The idea of a separate religious identity evolved towards national consciousness and nationalism in the 1860s through the reform of the *millet* structures.[180] Consequently, the *millet* system acquired a national connotation towards the end of the nineteenth century, thus altering the equilibrium between the universalism of faith and ethno-cultural particularisms.[181]

According to traditional narratives, Mehmed the Conqueror gave definitive form to the *millet* system by establishing "separate", "parallel"

---

[177] Cf. Karpat, "*Millet*s and Nationality", p. 141.
[178] Davison, "The *Millet*s as Agents of Change", p. 320.
[179] Karpat, "*Millet*s and Nationality", p. 146.
[180] Cf. Davison, "The *Millet*s as Agents of Change", p. 333.
[181] Cf. Karpat, "*Millet*s and Nationality", p. 147.

and "autonomous organisations" for his Orthodox, Armenian and Jewish communties and by nominating the Greek and Armenian patriarchs and the chief rabbis.[182] However, Benjamin Braude questions these foundation myths and observes that they are almost entirely similar: this similarity should be a source of suspicion in the sense that they contradicted the practices and norms of the given community.[183]

Before the Ottoman conquest of Istanbul, for instance, there was no Armenian patriarch in Istanbul and other established spiritual centres were beyond the borders of the Ottoman Empire. The catholicosates of Etchmiadzin and Aghtamar and most of historical Armenia were under the control of two other Turkmen factions, the Akkoyunlular and Karakoyunlular. Consequently, the accounts according to which families from Bursa and other regions were resettled in Istanbul after the conquest[184] were grounded in the fact that Mehmed II probably preferred to move Armenians from sensitive areas to a relatively secure place.[185] In order to challenge the influence of these religious centres on Ottoman Armenians, Mehmed II created an alternative patriarchal institution in Istanbul.[186] Similarly, Kevork Bardakjian also questions the veracity of these traditional narratives. Mehmed II's *berat* to Yovakim, if there was one, did not survive.[187] The authority of the Patriarchate grew with the conquest of new territories.[188] Based on some colophons, Bardakjian also identifies the existence of some independent bishops heading independent Armenian communities in diverse cities before the fall of Constantinople.[189] "The existence, then, of at least four bishops with uncertain territorial jurisdiction, strongly suggests that the Ottomans recognised the Armenian communities separately, an arrangement which was probably based on financial expediency and which remained in effect, it appears, long after Mehmed II's death".[190]

---

[182] "Introduction," in Avigdor Levy (ed.), *The Jews of the Ottoman Empire* (Princeton, New Jersey: Darwin Press, 1994), pp. 42-43.

[183] Benjamin Braude, "Foundation Myths of the *Millet* System," in Braude and Lewis (eds.), *Christians and Jews in the Ottoman Empire*, vol. 1, pp. 74-83.

[184] Michael Chamich, *History of Armenia*, tr. Johannes Avdall (Calcutta, 1827), vol. 2, pp. 329-330. Cited in Braude, "Foundation Myths of the *Millet* System", p. 81.

[185] Braude, "Foundation Myths of the *Millet* System", p. 82.

[186] Levy, "Introduction", p. 44.

[187] Kevork B. Bardakjian, "The Rise of the Armenian Patriarchate of Constantinople," in Braude and Lewis (eds.), *Christians and Jews in the Ottoman Empire*, vol. 1, p. 89.

[188] Bardakjian, p. 90.

[189] Bardakjian, p. 91.

[190] Bardakjian, p. 91.

An Armenian Patriarchate did not exist for the whole empire and Armenian communities were recognised as independent groups according to their geography and administrative division.[191] Moreover, a *berat* issued in 1764 shows the way in which the Armenian community was defined: "*altı cemaat tâbir olunur Ermeni reâyası*" (the Armenian subjects known as the six congregations). In the same *berat*, the Patriarchate was referred to as "*İstanbul ve tevabi-i Ermeni Patrikliği*" (the Armenian Patriarchate of Istanbul and its dependent districts), "*İstanbul ve perakende-i Rumeli ve Anadolu ve tevabi-i Ermeniyan Patrikliği*" (the Armenian Patriarchate of the scattered communities of Rumeli and Anatolia and Istanbul and its dependent districts).[192] Bardakjian states that the *altı cemaat* probably refers to the six families that Mehmed II brought with Yovakim.[193] As late as 1844, when the election of a new patriarch was on the agenda, the Porte decreed that the *altı cemaat* would elect their head.[194] "If Yovakim was proclaimed as the 'patriarch' of those transferred from Bursa and Ankara and of the local Armenian population, his 'patriarchal' realm could not have gone beyond Stambul, Galata, and, possibly, Scutari".[195]

Towards the end of the eighteenth century, one may talk about the rise of a universal Patriarchate due to various factors: the investiture of the catholicos of Etchmiadzin in Istanbul in 1725, the growing importance of the changing structure of power relations within the Armenian community and the centralisation efforts of the Porte.[196] The Ottoman capital had an impact on the intellectual and moral life of the provinces, and the Patriarchate benefited from the privileged position of the imperial city. The patriarchal elections took place in Istanbul without any objection from the provinces.[197] The Armenian *amira* class, the influential and quasi-aristocratic laity who played an intermediary role between the Porte and the community in patriarchal elections, was located in Istanbul. By the nineteenth century, the rivalry of the catholicosates, the rise of

[191] Bardakjian, p. 92.
[192] Avedis Berberyan, *Badmo 'wt 'iwn Hah 'o 'c* (History of the Armenians), (Constantinople, 1871), pp. 227-228. Cited in Bardakjian, p. 92.
[193] Mikayel Çamçyants, *Badmo 'wt 'iwn Hah 'o 'c* (Venedik, 1786), vol. 3, p. 500. Cited in Bardakjian, p. 92.
[194] Alboyacıyan, p. 201. Cited in Bardakjian, p. 92.
[195] Bardakjian, p. 92.
[196] Cf. Levy, "Introduction", p. 44; Bardakjian, pp. 94-97.
[197] Alboyacıyan, pp. 102-104. Also cited in Koçunyan, "Long Live Sultan Abdülaziz, Long Live the Nation, Long Live the Constitution!", p. 194.

the Armenian financial elites known as the *amira*s and the fall of Etchmiadzin into Russian hands gave *de facto* authority to the Armenian
patriarch of Istanbul over all the Apostolic Armenians of the Ottoman
Empire.[198]

A process of institutionalisation also followed the universalisation of
the Armenian Patriarchate. Patriarch Hovannes Golod gave equal rights
to the clergy and the laity in the administration of patriarchal affairs.
Thus the assembly he convened in 1725 in the Mother Church after the
death of the catholicos could be considered the first of the national general assemblies called to elect clergy to that office. Bishops, *vartabed*s
(celibate priests), *kahana*s (married parish priests) and the civil notables
of Istanbul participated in this assembly. Starting from that day, the election of the patriarchs was executed by this assembly. If the 1764 *berat*
recognised the existence of such an assembly, the 1831 *berat* given to
Patriarch Stepannos Ağavni more clearly certified its position by recognising its right to elect the patriarch. What remained vague in this affair
was the rule of the composition of the National General Assembly. In
any case, however, the assembly was composed of the ecclesiastical
class and the Armenian notables of Istanbul.[199] Soon, other bodies started
to emerge within the Armenian Patriarchate. In 1847, an imperial order
established spiritual and civil bodies within the Armenian Patriarchate
of Istanbul. Subsequently, the patriarch was asked to consult these bodies in the administration of communal-religious affairs.[200] In addition to
traditional professional categories such as goldsmiths, *sarraf*s and directors of mints, the inclusion of those trading with Europe into the Civil
Assembly of the Armenian Patriarchate was, in my opinion, a new
development that facilitated the infiltration of western ideas into patriarchal circles.[201] These two bodies gathered under the presidency of the
patriarch: one deliberated on religious matters and the other on temporal
issues. Elected by the General Assembly operating within the Armenian
Patriarchate of Istanbul, they administered community affairs from 1847
until May 24, 1860.[202] In parallel with the official institutionalisation of

---

[198] George A. Bournoutian, *A Concise History of the Armenian People (From Ancient Times to the Present)*, (Costa Mesa, Calif: Mazda Publishers, 2003), pp. 186-188.

[199] Alboyacıyan, pp. 125-137.

[200] Alboyacıyan, pp. 301-313.

[201] See the details regarding the imperial order and the composition of the Civil Assembly in BOA, I.MSM 33/937, 10 Cemazeyilevvel 1263/26 April 1847.

[202] Alboyaciyan, p. 314.

a temporal assembly within the Armenian Patriarchate of Istanbul in 1847, the Sublime Porte introduced lay members into the Synod of the Greek Patriarchate despite the objections of the patriarch and the clergy, who were against the secularisation of communal institutions.[203]

Braude also draws attention to the fact that the foundation myths contradicted the norms of the Jewish community, which had never been hierarchical.[204] Although rabbis Moses Capsali (1420-95) and Elijah Mizrahi (1496-1526) served as chief rabbis and were recognised by the sultan, some other authors see no evidence from the fifteenth and sixteenth centuries of a Chief Rabbinate with jurisdiction covering all the Ottoman lands, arguing that the authority of Capsali and Mizrahi was limited to the Ottoman capital. In that respect, such an office may have existed but its authority was probably limited to Istanbul, and the roles of Capsali and Mizrahi were more to represent the Jewish community before the sultan rather than to exercise religious power over all Ottoman Jewry.[205]

With regards to the Jews, there were no accepted conceptions and traditions of central authority and hierarchical organisation.[206] In fact, the most basic unit of Jewish self-government was the congregation, a voluntary association of families and individuals around their synagogue. Leadership was shared by religious and lay heads in each congregation. These congregations shared a "cultural-religious legacy of language, dialect, and particular customs connected with their ritual".[207] Ottoman Jewish society was very heterogeneous, since it contained Italian, Sephardim, Ashkenazi and Romaniote Jews: it was thus in the interest of the Ottoman state to impose a central authority over these separate and distinct

---

[203] George Young, *Corps de Droit ottoman* (Oxford: Clarendon Press, 1905), v. 2, p. 13. See also Athanasia Anagnostopulu, "Tanzimat ve Rum Milletinin Kurumsal Çerçevesi: Patrikhane, Cemaat Kurumları, Eğitim," (The Theoretical Framework of Tanzimat and the Greek *Millet*: Patriarchate, Communal Institutions, Education) in Pinelopi Sthathis (ed.), *19. Yüzyıl İstanbul'unda Gayrimüslimler* (İstanbul: Tarih Vakfı, 1999), pp. 1-35.

[204] Braude, "Foundation Myths of the *Millet* System", p. 75. See also İsmail Aydıngün and Esra Dardağan, "Rethinking the Jewish Communal Apartment in the Ottoman Communal Building," *Middle Eastern Studies*, vol. 42, no. 2 (Mar., 2006), pp. 319-334, here p. 320.

[205] Stanford Shaw, *The Jews of the Ottoman Empire and the Turkish Republic* (Basingstoke: Macmillan, 1991). Avigdor Levy, *The Sephardim in the Ottoman Empire* (Princeton, NJ: The Darwin Press, 1992). Cited in Aydıngün and Dardağan, p. 321.

[206] Levy, "Introduction", p. 45.

[207] Levy, "Introduction", p. 46.

groups.[208] Jewish sources refer to Rabbi Capsali, the chief rabbi officially appointed following the conquest of Istanbul, as the head of all the congregations of Istanbul.[209] "Did the Ottomans aim to support a statewide Jewish authority, as in the case of the Orthodox Church, or did they intend to establish a strong centre in the capital only, as in the Armenian model, and allow the internal dynamics within the community to determine its future development?"[210] After Rabbi Capsali, the Ottoman government avoided giving official sanction to the appointment of succeeding rabbis.[211] The influx of European Jews and the individual tendencies of congregations which enjoyed a certain level of autonomy curtailed the centralising approach of the Ottoman state, since Jewish structures of self-government were characterised by a high degree of decentralisation and a structure different from the Orthodox and Armenian models.[212] After the destabilisation of the Balkans following the Greek and Serbian uprisings, the Ottomans aimed to promote the principle of a pluralistic Ottoman society. The first step was the formal recognition of Ottoman Jewry as one of the official communities of the empire; thus, the office of the chief rabbi came into existence in 1835. The state introduced the official position of *haham başı*, which was equal in principle to that of Orthodox and Armenian ecclesiastical leaders. Like them, he was a civil and religious leader and the official representative before the Ottoman authorities.[213] However, it was only in 1909 that the Ottoman government conferred the title "Chief Rabbi of All the Jews of the Capital and its Dependencies and of All the Jews resident in the Ottoman Empire".[214]

The official recognition of the office of the chief rabbi can also be interpreted within the framework of the Porte's centralisation policy.[215] European governments in the modern period generally considered Ottoman rule over Christian subjects an internal affair of the Ottoman state.

---

[208] Levy, "Introduction", pp. 47, 53-54.

[209] Joseph R. Hacker, "Ottoman Policy toward the Jews and Jewish Attitudes toward the Ottomans during the Fifteenth Century," in Braude and Lewis, *Christians and Jews in the Ottoman Empire*, vol. 1, pp. 122 and 126, note 31. Levy, "Introduction", p. 54.

[210] Levy, "Introduction", p. 56.

[211] Levy, "Introduction", p. 58.

[212] Levy, "Introduction", p. 58.

[213] Levy, "Introduction", pp. 105-106.

[214] Esther Benbassa, *Un Grand Rabbin sépharade en politique 1892-1923* (Paris: Presses du CNRS, 1990), pp. 26-32. Cited in Levy, "Introduction", p. 107.

[215] Aydıngün and Dardağan, p. 321.

However, the foundation of an independent Greece, celebrated by some Europeans, and Russian demands for the protection of the rights of the Orthodox subjects of the Ottoman Empire during the Crimean War offered precedents for the "internationalisation of local grievances".[216] The "politicisation" of "religious difference" made the administration of non-Muslims more difficult in comparison to the past. The Powers competed among themselves "to champion the interests of different religious communities".[217] Moreover, Ottoman centralisation aimed at strengthening the Orthodox structures of various non-Muslim *millet* administrations, which were challenged by the proselytism of the Great Powers.

The proclamation of the French Revolution in 1789 strengthened Catholic expansion in the Near East. The 1790 Constitution dissolved all missionary orders. However, the destruction of French orders channeled them towards Ottoman lands. France did not plan to destroy the missions in the Orient, because they represented the French state and constituted an element of influence in Ottoman lands.[218] Of all Ottoman Christians, Armenians were the most attracted by western missionary activities. Even some members of the *amira* class converted to Catholicism when their children attended missionary schools. "A report made after an apostolic visitation there in August 1700 recorded eight thousand Armenian Catholics in Istanbul, so far exceeding the French and Italian in number that the word 'Catholic' was reserved for them, while Westerners were known as Franks or Latins."[219]

Religiously, the Ottoman Armenians were a unified community until 1830. Despite all efforts at reconciliation, the unity of the Armenian Church could not be achieved. The Armenian papal clergy was divided into two antagonistic groups: the Collegians, named after the College of Propaganda, opted for the "complete conformity of the Armenians to the Roman Catholic Church in doctrine and worship" while the Mekhitarists remained faithful to the Armenian tradition and the conservation of the Armenian language in the liturgy. At the end of the Russo-Turkish War of 1828-29, France and Britain required from the sultan the return of papal exiles and the establishment of a civil institution for the Catholics of the empire independent of the Armenian Patriarchate. The Catholics

---

[216] Hanioğlu, pp. 67-69.

[217] Findley, "The Tanzimat", p. 16.

[218] Charles Frazee, *Catholics and Sultans: The Church and the Ottoman Empire* (London: Cambridge University Press, 1983), p. 164.

[219] Frazee, p. 178.

obtained freedom of worship under Ottoman rule so long as they built their own churches and did not attend those of the foreigners. On May 24, 1831, the Catholic Armenians of the Ottoman Empire were recognised as a *millet* by an imperial edict of Mahmud II.[220] The head of the Catholic Armenian community, mentioned as a bishop in the *berat* dated 1831 and as a patriarch in the *berat* dated 1834, was elected by an assembly of bishops and laymen. He was also entrusted with the representation of four other sects: Maronites, Melchites, Syrians and Chaldeans united with Rome. The Ottoman state aimed to counteract foreign influence over the Christian communities of the empire by establishing a unified Catholic family.[221] The imperial *berat* dated January 5, 1831, recognised the priest elected by the Catholic community as the bishop of All Catholics within the Ottoman Empire on the condition that he collected the annual taxation determined by the state.[222] These provisions of the *berat* framed the Catholic *millet* as an economic unity as well as religious-legal one subjected to the jurisdiction of the Catholic bishop: his responsibilities extended from tax collection to the ordination of priests, from matrimonial issues to inheritance matters.[223]

Under the pressure of Sir Stratford Canning, in 1847 the Ottoman government recognised freedom of conscience for Protestant converts. The head of the new community occupied the same position as the patriarch among the Armenians or Greeks.[224] In 1850, the Protestant community was assigned the legal status of a *millet*.[225] "In November, 1850, a charter was granted to the Protestants by His Imperial Majesty, Sultan Abdul Medjid, completing and confirming their distinct organisation as a civil community, and securing to them equal religious rights with the older Christian organizations".[226] The charter of 1847 was a ministerial act and could be cancelled after a change of ministry. However, the decree of 1850 emanated from the authority of the sultan. "It secured

---

[220] Vartan Artinian, *The Armenian Constitutional System in the Ottoman Empire, 1839-1863: a Study of Its Historical Development* (Istanbul: [s. n.], 1988), pp. 33-38.

[221] Young, v. 2, pp. 98-99.

[222] Patriarcat arménien catholique, bérat, 5 janvier 1831. Cited in Baron I. de Testa, vol. 5, p. 138.

[223] Hovannes Tcholakian, *L'Eglise Arménienne Catholique en Turquie* (İstanbul: Ohan Matbaacılık, 1998), pp. 30-31.

[224] William Goodell, *Forty Years in the Turkish Empire* (New York: Robert Carter and Brothers, 1876), p. 330.

[225] A. J. Arberry, *Religion in the Middle East* (London: Cambridge University Press, 1969), v. 1, pp. 499-500.

[226] Goodell, p. 352.

perpetually to the Protestants the right of choosing their own head, of transacting business, of worship, of burial, free from all molestation, and promised to them protection by the imperial government against persecution."[227] The Ottoman Empire was beginning to regulate the governance of various religious entities by inviting them to elaborate their community regulations.[228] Accordingly, the Greek Orthodox and Armenian communities successively declared their organic laws in 1862 and 1863. The Jewish community promulgated their regulation in 1865. Some of the new community regulations were already called "constitutions" and institutionalised representative bodies for the management of communal affairs.

The Armenian Constitutional Experience

In the late eighteenth century, a group of Armenian merchants from India played an important role in the emergence of the first Armenian constitutional movement. Settled in Agra, Delhi, Bombay, Surat, Calcutta, Madras and several other towns, they accumulated wealth and acted as philanthropists for Armenian educational, cultural, intellectual and political movements in India. The fate of Indian Armenians took a new turn with the conquest of Bengal by the British East India Company. The communities of Madras and Calcutta emerged as centres of political revival in response to British hegemony. If the domination of the East India Company, which operated almost like a colonial power, weakened the Armenian merchants of Madras and Calcutta and subjugated them to discrimination and various restrictions, the merchants acquired experience of how to adapt themselves to the rules and regulations of the British and to adopt their economic, social and cultural concepts. The new process led them to preserve their ethnic identity through communal solidarity and education and to cultivate the ideal of an independent Armenia free from foreign domination.[229] The Madras movement also

---

[227] Goodell, pp. 352-353.

[228] Sultan Abdülmecid's Hatti Hümayun reaffirming the privileges and immunities of the non-Muslim communities, 18 February 1856. [U. S., 46th Cong., Spec. Sess. (March 1881), Senate, Exec. Documents, vol. 3, No. 3, *The Capitulations*, by E. A. Van Dyck, part 1, pp. 108-111]. Cited in J. C. Hurewitz, *Diplomacy in the Near and Middle East: A Documentary Record, 1535-1914* (New Jersey: D. Van Nostrand, 1956), v. 1, pp. 149-153.

[229] Vazken Ghougassian, "The Quest for Enlightenment and Liberation: The Case of the Armenian Community of India in the Late Eighteenth Century," in Richard G.

had a "Pan-Armenian" nationalistic orientation aiming at the liberation of Armenia from Persian and Ottoman rule and the re-establishment of historical Armenia, concretised in the draft constitution *O'ro'kah't' P'ar'ac* (the Snare of Glory).[230]

The Madras movement was centered on Joseph Emin and the Armenian merchant and philanthropist Shahamir Shahamirian, who established the first Armenian printing press in India. Emin was born in Hamadan (Iran) in 1726. After the Afghan occupation of Isfahan, he joined his merchant father in Calcutta and was inspired by the British Enlightenment. He went to London in 1751, where he also met Edmund Burke, the future British statesman and political writer. Burke's support provided Emin with access to British intellectual circles.[231] Although the official author of *O'ro'kah't' P'ar'ac* is mentioned as Shahamirian's son, Hagop, modern Armenian scholarship has attributed the authorship of the draft constitution to Shahamir himself. One may also think that the work was perhaps a collective product to which Emin might have contributed.[232] This is because a draft of a constitution is mentioned in his adventures, although it may not be the one formulated by the Madras Armenians. Emin exchanged ideas with Sir William Jones about the nature of the government to be established in Armenia, and Jones recommended the adoption of a "mixed government". Jones (1746-94) was a famous orientalist and was appointed judge of the Supreme Court of Calcutta in 1783.[233] "A mixed government, therefore, like that of England, is the only form approaching to a state of natural society and likely to be permanent; if your design was to transplant our constitution to Armenia, I heartily lament your disappointment, though I cannot wonder at it. [...] Let me also advise you to discard forever the Asiatick style of panegyrick, to which you are too much addicted; weak minds only are tickled with praise, while they, who deserve it receive it with disdain".[234] Such were

---

Hovannisian and David N. Myers, *Enlightenment and Diaspora: the Armenian and Jewish Cases* (Atlanta, Georgia: Scholars Press, 1999), pp. 241-242, 250-253.

[230] Ghougassian, pp. 242, 244, 253-254. *Kirq ano'waneal O'ro'kah't' P'ar'ac* [Book called the Snare of Glory] (Madras: Shahamirian Press, 1773).

[231] Ghougassian, pp. 242, 243, 250-253.

[232] Ghougassian, p. 254.

[233] Joseph Emin, *Life and Adventures of Emin Joseph Emin, 1726-1809, an Armenian*, written in English by himself (London, 1792; second edition, by Amy Apcar (ed.), Calcutta: Baptist Mission Press, 1918). Cited in Apcar, p. xix.

[234] Gardens, August 10, 1788. Sir William Jones to the author. Cited in Amy Apcar, pp. xix-xx.

Sir William's words to Emin. In his book, the latter noted that he visited England "to see the admirable European system of wise laws and useful regulations".[235] All these details draw attention to how colonial or foreign Powers and their individual agents sought to expand their legal conceptions at a crossroads of commerce.

One may also question the impact of *O'ro'kah't' P'ar'ac* on the constitutional course taken by the Ottoman Armenian community in the early nineteenth century. The writings of Armenian intellectuals who drafted a constitution for their communal administration within the Ottoman Empire do not refer to the Madras movement but rather mention their European sources of inspiration. Joseph Emin visited the Ottoman Empire in 1759 on his way to Etchmiadzin,[236] but his visit preceded the printing of *O'ro'kah't' P'ar'ac*. He passed through Aleppo, Erzurum, İskenderun and several Armenian villages, and met the Muslim population as well as Armenian notables in Anatolia. Mention is made of an Armenian notable who was at the same time the banker of the grand vizier.[237] However, nothing in his adventures clarifies the fraternisation of Indian Armenians with those of the Ottoman Empire around a constitutional idea. Interestingly enough, Krikor Margosyan, who was supposed to draft the 1857 Armenian regulation, had been trading with India for a long time. He had also participated in the peace negotiations during the Crimean War as a translator for the Ottoman Foreign Ministry.[238]

Although the target of the two movements was different, both of the constitutions developed common points. The title of *O'ro'kah't' P'ar'ac*, which literally means "the snare of glory", did not directly make allusion to a constitution, but the Ottoman Armenian counterpart was entitled *Azkah'in Sahmanatro'wt'iwn Hah'o'c* (Armenian National Constitution). The text of *O'ro'kah't' P'ar'ac* instead considers the initiative as a "*garkatro'wt'iwn*" (arrangement).[239] The reader encounters, however,

---

[235] Emin, *Life and Adventures*, p. 2.

[236] Emin, *Life and Adventures*, pp. 129-161.

[237] Emin, *Life and Adventures*, pp. 129-161.

[238] Vahan Zartaryan, *H'ishadagaran: Hah' Erewelinero'w Gensakragannery, Lo'wsangarnery, Tzer'akirnery, Kro'wt'iwnnery, 1512-1912* (Memorial Book on the Biographies, Photographs, Manuscripts, and Writings of Armenian Notables), (Istanbul: Zartaryan, 1912), pp. 213-217. See also Cololyan, vol. 3, p. 37.

[239] *O'ro'kah't' P'ar'ac, T'arkmano'wt'iwny Kraparic & Dzano't'akro'wt'o'wnnery Panasiragan Kido'wt'o'wnneri Do'gdo'r, Pro'feso'r Bo'gho's Xach'adrh'ani* (*O'ro'kah't' P'ar'ac,* Its Translation from Classical Armenian and Its Presentation by Professor Boghos Khaçadıryan, Doctor of Philology), (Yerevan: Hayasdan, 2002), p. 16.

the words "*sahmanel*" (to limit or to stipulate) and "*sahman*" (limit but also law in an eighteenth-century context), from which the word "*sahmanatro'wt'iwn*" (constitution) was derived.[240] Like its Ottoman Armenian counterpart, the text drafted in India promoted the importance of law, legality and order in the governance of communal life,[241] and also made use of the expression "*sahmano'wadz ore'nq*" (limited law) to give the idea that law is a set of limitations[242] which even the will of the sovereign cannot surmount.[243] Thus, the sovereign is also limited by law.[244] It is also interesting to note that the Armenian version of the 1856 Reform Edict referred to a similar concept of regulated/limited arrangements (*sahmano'wadz garkatro'wt'iwn*).[245] Again, like its Ottoman Armenian counterpart, *O'ro'kah't' P'ar'ac* promoted the idea of popular sovereignty[246] and named the people as the supreme authority of the state and the Armenian National Assembly or the House of Armenians as the highest governing body:[247] it was responsible for electing the president of the country in *O'ro'kah't' P'ar'ac*[248] and the Armenian patriarch of Istanbul in the National Constitution. Other similarities are the separation of the religious and temporal spheres and the autonomy of the respective authorities from one another despite the loyalty expressed to the Armenian Apostolic Church.[249] Equally, both documents note the importance of education for both sexes[250] and communal assistance for the poor and the needy.[251]

Western influences on Indian Armenians were mainly British, although the networks of Shahamirian's circle were wider thanks to his various commercial ties. Joseph Emin himself spent his life in a larger zone extending from India to Britain, including Persia, the Ottoman Empire,

---

[240] *O'ro'kah't' P'ar'ac, T'arkmano'wt'iwny Kraparic*, pp. 20, 34, 36, 37, 39.

[241] *O'ro'kah't' P'ar'ac, T'arkmano'wt'iwny Kraparic*, pp. 16, 20, 34, 36, 37, 39.

[242] *O'ro'kah't' P'ar'ac, T'arkmano'wt'iwny Kraparic*, p. 21.

[243] *O'ro'kah't' P'ar'ac, T'arkmano'wt'iwny Kraparic*, p. 80; Article 18. See also Ghougassian, pp. 254-255.

[244] *O'ro'kah't' P'ar'ac, T'arkmano'wt'iwny Kraparic*, p. 14.

[245] See p. 94 in this book.

[246] *O'ro'kah't' P'ar'ac, T'arkmano'wt'iwny Kraparic*, p. 14.

[247] *O'ro'kah't' P'ar'ac, T'arkmano'wt'iwny Kraparic*, p. 80; Article 18. See also Ghougassian, pp. 254-255.

[248] *O'ro'kah't' P'ar'ac, T'arkmano'wt'iwny Kraparic*, p. 80; Article 20.

[249] *O'ro'kah't' P'ar'ac, T'arkmano'wt'iwny Kraparic*, pp. 139, 192; Articles 155, 156, 397.

[250] *O'ro'kah't' P'ar'ac, T'arkmano'wt'iwny Kraparic*, p. 139; Article 158.

[251] *O'ro'kah't' P'ar'ac, T'arkmano'wt'iwny Kraparic*, p. 140; Article 162.

the Caucasus, Russia and Germany.[252] It is possible to situate the
O'ro'kah't' P'ar'ac within the framework of a modern constitutional
project, since it distances itself from divine law and ancestral traditions
and is instead founded on the human will.[253] Moreover, a Judicial Plan
was formulated in India in 1772 by Warren Hastings, governor-general
of the East India Company. The Judicial Plan was the first Anglo-Indian
code and dealt with civil and penal laws. In 1773, the British Parliament
also voted through the Regulating Act: this applied to the practices of the
East India Company under Hastings' authority and aimed, among other
things, to fight corruption in commercial matters.[254] It is also interesting
that the term *"garkatro'wt'iwn"* (arrangement) was often used in the
O'ro'kah't' P'ar'ac to mean "constitution". The arrangement evokes a
commercial setting and also perhaps helps us to imagine the regulatory
context of the East India Company, which operated like a state. The aim
of the Madras movement was before all liberation and territorial reunifi-
cation under a secular authority and on the basis of law. In that respect,
the Madras circle differed from other Armenian centres like Istanbul and
Etchmiadzin, which were organised around religious authorities.[255]
Although the Catholicosate of Echmiadzin tried to resolve the question
of unity by creating a spiritual union between Armenians around a
national church, the Madras group opted for a political and territorial
solution.[256]

Those influences which penetrated the Armenian *millet* structure in the
Ottoman Empire and the ways in which the latter adapted new ideas to
its structures were quite complex.[257] After 1830, Ottoman Armenians
divided into three distinct communities: Gregorians, Catholics and Protestants. Prior to the official recognition of their final draft in 1863, the
Apostolic Armenians drafted two statute laws in 1857 and 1860. The
1860 draft received tacit agreement from the Ottoman government. When
the first anniversary of the 1860 National Constitution was celebrated on
May 28, 1861 in Hünkar İskelesi, the organisational committee rented

---

[252] Saténig Batwagan-Toufanian, "Le Piège de l'Orgueil, la Constitution d'un Etat de
droit en Arménie" (Unpublished PhD dissertation, Paris: Ecole des Hautes Etudes en
Sciences sociales, 2013), p. 166.

[253] Batwagan-Toufanian, pp. 38-39.

[254] http://www.legalservicesindia.com/article/article/development-of-adalat-system-
during-the-time-of-warren-hastings-252-1.html). Cited in Batwagan-Toufanian, p. 39.

[255] Batwagan-Toufanian, p. 85.

[256] Batwagan-Toufanian, p. 110.

[257] Cf. Davison, *Ottoman Diplomacy and Reforms,* p. 422.

two boats from the imperial shipyard. Four imperial soldiers escorted the procession when the participants went ashore. Selim Pasha donated 100 piasters during the celebrations.[258] The informal presence of Ottoman state employees during the anniversary was a sign of the tacit and unofficial transition to the new statute law. The content of the celebrations are also worthy of analysis to understand the linkages Ottoman Armenians saw between their community law and wider European constitutional movements. An arch was erected at the ceremony site and decorated with flowers: a photograph of the sultan was placed facing the sea. On the interior side of the cloth was written in Armenian script: "Long live the nation, long live the constitution, May 24, 1860". At table, glasses were raised to the Ottoman government, to the proclamation of the National Constitution, to the sultan, to the catholicos, to the Armenian patriarch of Istanbul, to the contributors of the community and to its administration. After the banquet, European dances were performed and speeches were delivered in Ottoman and Armenian.[259] The slogans of the celebrations show the multiple loyalties of Ottoman Armenians to both the sultan and the religious authorities of the Armenian Church while the acclamations of "long live the constitution and long live the nation" recall those of European constitutional revolutions and reveal how Armenians identified their community statute law with western constitutions. They also demonstrate how they could reconcile the idea of communal sovereignty with a broader allegiance to sultanic sovereignty. In that respect, the National Constitution was a compromise between these multiple allegiances.

The celebrations that marked the official recognition of the 1863 National Constitution allow us to discover other linkages. On this occasion, Hünkar İskelesi hosted two national ceremonies at the same time: the proclamation of the 1863 Armenian National Constitution and the third anniversary of the Constitution of the Italian monarchy. About 15,000 people convened in Hünkar Iskelesi. A vault was decorated in white and red flags, in the middle of which the *tuğra* of the sultan was placed. In addition to the wishes addressed to the Ottoman sultan, the flags bore the slogans "love", "union", "law" and "loyalty". The newspaper *Masis* recounted that the Italian community also decorated the site with flags, laurels and flowers in which were located the photographs

---

[258] *Masis*, 7 June 1861.
[259] *Masis*, 7 June 1861.

of King Victor Emmanuel and Garibaldi. The Italian consul also con-
gratulated Bishop Nerses and the participants on the promulgation of
the Armenian National Constitution. All the participants unanimously
exclaimed: "Long live the Armenian nation, long live Italy, long live the
brotherhood of nations, long live Sultan Abdülaziz".[260] The overlapping
of the two ceremonies may seem surprising at first sight but the common
feature that united Italians and Armenians around the same table was
certainly the limitations they imposed on their religious authorities, one
on the temporal powers of the Papacy and the other on those of the Patriarchate, thus finally leaving room for the expression of the popular will.

The Road to the Armenian National Constitution[261]

The story of the proclamation of the National Constitution reflects
the interplay of internal dynamics, such as the rise of the intelligentsia,
the concomitant decline of the influence of the clergy and *amira* class
and the partial mobilisation of the masses for a representative, legal and
legitimate communal administration. The emergence of two opposing
wings accompanied the preparatory phase of the National Constitution:
the "Enlightened", who were in favour of the National Constitution, and
the "Retrogrades", who opposed the administration of the community
by such a regulation. The Armenian National Constitution was the work
of Armenian intellectuals, most of whom pursued their careers in
France. It was the first attempt to organise the life of the Armenian
community according to the ideals of nineteenth-century French constitutionalism. Some of the names who gathered around the idea of the
constitution were inseparable from each other: Nigoğos Balyan, Hagop
Balyan, Krikor Odyan and Nahabed Rusinyan.[262] Architect of the palace
and adviser of the sultan in fine arts, Nigoğos Balyan (1826-58) was
the founder of the idea of a constitution as expressed during a session
of the National Assembly in 1870.[263] Nigoğos had been involved in the
process secretly so as not to oppose his father, who aligned himself with

---

[260] *Masis*, 1 June 1863.

[261] For an earlier and detailed analysis of the genesis of the Armenian National
Constitution and other community regulations, see also Koçunyan, "Long Live Sultan
Abdülaziz, Long Live the Nation, Long Live the Constitution!", pp. 189-210.

[262] *Kegho'wni*, 1 June 1902, pp. 42-44.

[263] Kevork Pamukciyan, *Biyografileriyle Ermeniler* (Biographies of Armenians),
(İstanbul: Aras Yayıncılık, 2003), pp. 95-97.

the opponents of the movement.[264] Thanks to the presence of Hagop Balyan, Ortaköy became the centre of Armenian intellectual life. Armenian writers and artists encountered each other at Balyan's house in Ortaköy to study the promotion of the Armenian language and theatre. Nahabed Rusinyan was the soul of these encounters.[265] Except for Krikor Odyan, who studied law in Paris, none of the other draftsmen (Serviçen Effendi, Nahabed Rusinyan, Nigoğos Balyan or Garabed Ütüciyan) were trained as lawyers. Serviçen and Rusinyan were physicians, while Ütüciyan was a journalist.[266] In terms of contacts with the Ottoman bureaucracy, Serviçen was probably the strongest member of this constitutionalist group. This also explains how he became a senator after the proclamation of the 1876 Ottoman Constitution.[267] He held a range of professional positions, from an honorary professorship at the Imperial School of Medicine to the position of chief physician of the *Seraskerat* (Ottoman Ministry of War),[268] something which enhanced his relations with the state. As for Krikor Odyan, he was involved in French political life; he participated in sessions of the French Parliament, was in touch with French statesmen such as Thiers, Gambetta, Jules Simon and Jules Ferry and admired French writers like Lamartine, Musset and Hugo.[269] This explains why Odyan was sent to Paris and London after the proclamation of the Ottoman Constitution to publicise the new regime.

In fact, the French way of democratising society had a great impact on these Armenian intellectuals. The French Revolution had weakened the powers of the Roman Catholic Church. The law of the Civil Constitution of the Clergy, proclaimed in 1790, subordinated the church to state authority.[270] The decree of secularisation, adopted in November 1789, put

---

[264] Alboyacıyan, pp. 329-332.

[265] *Kegho'wni*, 1 June 1902, pp. 43-44.

[266] Hrant Asadur, *Timasdo'werner* (Profiles), (İstanbul, 1921), p. 32. Cited in Artinian, p. 62.

[267] Elke Hartmann, "The 'Loyal Nation' and Its Deputies: the Armenians in the First Ottoman Parliament," in Christoph Herzog & Malek Sharif (eds.), *The First Ottoman Experiment in Democracy* (Istanbul: Orient Institut, 2010), p. 191.

[268] *Notice biographique sur le Dr. Servicen Effendi lue devant la S. I. de Médecine dans sa Séance du 3 décembre 1897 par le Dr. V. Torkomian* (Extrait de la Gazette médicale d'Orient), (Constantinople: Imprimerie A. Christidis, 1898), pp. 1-7.

[269] M. Gazmararyan, *Kriko'r Odeani Ko'harnery* (Krikor Odyan's Gems), (İstanbul: Der Sahakyan, 1931), v. 2, p. 9.

[270] Constitution civile du Clergé decreed on July 12 and August 21, 1790. See for the text, Pierre Larousse, *Grand Dictionnaire universel du 19ème Siècle* (Paris: Administration du Grand Dictionnaire universel, [1866]), v. 4, pp. 1046-1047.

church properties at the disposal of the French nation.[271] The debate on whether church properties belonged to the Armenian community and on communal rights over their management, put on the agenda of Armenian constitutionalists, was the extension of the same anti-clerical and secular policies. The French state supervised all religious orders after 1768, systematically limiting the activities of Jesuits and Franciscans: the 1790 Constitution dissolved all missionary orders.[272] Moreover, the French state reorganised Catholic and Protestant religious institutions in 1802. Accordingly, a consistorial system was established for the Protestants.[273] French Jewry believed that an official organisation of their faith along the same lines would bring equality, the maintenance of the liberal principles of 1789 and their emancipation.[274] A consistorial structure following the Protestant model was conceived in 1806 and created in 1808-09 for French Jewry.[275] The French consistorial system had an impact on the restructuring of Ottoman Jewry in the new regulation promulgated in 1865. One may also question whether Armenian draftsmen took into consideration the reshaping of the French "*régime des cultes*" after the French Revolution and how the 1848 Revolution affected confessional structures by bringing universal suffrage into their election processes. In general, Armenian intellectuals preferred to mention the impact of the French Revolution and constitutionalism as a model. However, the networks Krikor Odyan discussed opens up new avenues of research on the relations Ottoman Armenians might have had with other confessional communities in the West.

Odyan narrated how Rusinyan experienced the 1848 Revolution and how he got almost involved in: he also discussed how the movement established the principle of universal suffrage, gave voice to a national spirit and spread the idea of a constitution. He noted that Nigoğos Balyan was another child of the 1848 Revolution, although he returned from Paris (where he studied architecture) to Istanbul much earlier. Odyan remarked that Nigoğos had been influenced by the 1830 literary

---

[271] Pierre Albers & René Hedde, *Manuel d'Histoire ecclésiastique* (Paris: Librairie Lecoffre, 1939), v. 2, p. 364.

[272] Frazee, p. 164.

[273] Phyllis Cohen Albert, *The Modernization of French Jewry: Consistory and Community in the Nineteenth Century* (Hanover, New Hampshire: Brandeis University Press, 1977), p. 56.

[274] Albert, p. 56.

[275] Albert, pp. 45-46.

movement during which Thiers and Guizot published their works. In addition to Guizot, Odyan also evoked the impact of Victor Cousin's philosophical thoughts and of Michelet and Quinet's struggle against "fake religiosities". Odyan noted that Balyan had been Quinet's student.[276] Among these networks, Guizot was of Protestant origin and was a devoted member of the consistory of the Reformed Church in Paris until his death.[277] If the consistorial model inspired Armenian draftsmen, then Guizot might have been one of the potential nodes of these networks. His identity as a member of a religious minority in France might have been already attractive to Armenian draftsmen.[278] One may also recognise the traces of his views on censitary suffrage and the importance of education between the lines of the National Constitution.[279] Edgar Quinet's lectures at the Collège de France attacked Roman Catholicism: Quinet praised the Reform as a capital moment on the way to freedom and proposed the Constitution of the United States to France, where the persistence of clerical and monarchical traditions would be major obstacles against the progress of democracy.[280] For Quinet, inclination towards Protestantism was the dividing line between successful and failed revolutions. The ones which could not break their ties with Catholicism, including the French Revolution, were among the unsuccessful models. He concludes that the fate of revolutions depends on harmony between political society and its spiritual counterpart.[281]

A comparative study on the evolution of the National Constitution from the first text in 1857 to the final text ratified in 1863 allows us to examine the initial expectations of community members and draftsmen in favour of a new regulation and the ways in which these expectations were reshaped by the state authorities. As early as 1857, the Armenian community submitted a *millet* constitution. However, the draft was

---

[276] Gazmararyan, v. 2, pp. 29-46.

[277] Laurent Theis, *Guizot: La Traversée d'un Siècle* (Paris: CNRS, 2014), pp. 105, 2251.

[278] Theis, p. 225.

[279] Theis, pp. 129, 1220-1233.

[280] Marcel du Pasquier, "Edgar Quinet et la Pensée protestante en Suisse romande: Ernest Naville, Charles Secrétan, Amiel, Merle d'Aubigné, Ferdinand Buisson," *Revue de théologie et de philosophie*, vol. 8, no. 1 (1958), pp. 2-3.

[281] Simone Bernard-Griffiths, "Autour de la Révolution d'Edgar Quinet. Les Enjeux du Débat Religion-Révolution dans l'Historiographie d'un Républicain désenchanté," *Archives de Sciences Sociales des Religions*, vol. 66, no. 1 (1988), pp. 53-54.

rejected by the Sublime Porte. In the report of the Tanzimat Council,[282] the hierarchy among non-Muslim communities was cited as one of the reasons for the rejection of the draft. Accordingly, it was to the Greek Orthodox Patriarchate that was first to promulgate its *millet* regulation. When its turn came, the Armenian Patriarchate proclaimed its statute law.[283] In his entry on the Ecumenical Patriarchate, George Young states that a certain spiritual pre-eminence was given by the Ottoman government to that Patriarchate among the other Christian communities. We may perhaps interpret the hierarchy within this framework.[284] The same report also stated that some of the provisions of the 1857 text went beyond the expectations of the Ottoman government without mentioning the real content of divergent views.[285] The emphasis put on Etchmiadzin as the higher religious authority for the entire Armenian world and the explicitly lower position of the Armenian patriarch of Istanbul as the religious leader of Armenians inhabiting the Ottoman Empire probably provoked discontent within the Ottoman state. Similarly, the fact that the Armenian patriarch of Istanbul was an Ottoman subject but would receive his title of bishopric from the catholicos of Etchmiadzin, who would remain the principal reference point for spiritual issues the patriarch could not resolve, was certainly another reason for the rejection. The patriarch of Istanbul was an Ottoman subject in subsequent constitutions. While the 1860 text stipulates that the patriarch is a bishop ordained by the catholicos of Etchmiadzin, the 1863 text only requires that the person elected as patriarch should be worthy of the confidence and respect not only of the community but also of the government.[286] In parallel, the provisions on the protectoral committee, concerned with Armenian schools in Europe, might have again disturbed the Ottoman authorities because of its territorial scope. The fact that these stipulations were omitted or formulated in other ways in the 1860 and 1863 texts gives us the impression that the latter were probably provisions which did not meet governmental expectations. Moreover, the mention that this regulation concerned Gregorian Armenians was suppressed in the subsequent two

---

[282] BOA, I.MVL 16736, lef 3. Cited in Ueno Masayuki, "The First Draft of the Armenian *Millet* Constitution," *AJAMES* (Annals of Japan Association for Middle East Studies), no. 23-1 (2007), pp. 213-251. Here, p. 222.

[283] Masayuki, pp. 215-222.

[284] Young, vol. 2, p. 13.

[285] Masayuki, p. 223.

[286] Masayuki, p. 226.

texts. The 1860 and 1863 National Constitutions do not mention the "Gregorian" Armenian Church but refer to the *"Hah'asdaneah'c* Church" meaning the Church of Armenians. The term *"Hah'asdaneah'c"* derives from *"Hah'asdan"* (Armenia). However, the use of this derivative form has a symbolic value, since it designates the attachment of the two constitutions to the Mother See and the traditions of the Armenian Church as institutionalised in Etchmiadzin. The fact that the two texts avoided using the word "Gregorian" shows the secular character of the two National Constitutions.

In the minds of Ottoman Armenian intellectuals, the 1860 Constitution created a kind of extra-territorial[287] autonomy that would enable the community to operate independently through national institutions, which were themselves based on secular fundamentals. From 1860 to 1863, it is clear that the constitution lost this notion of autonomy: the document itself was transformed into a piece of machinery whose functioning continually depended on the interference of the Ottoman government. The fact that "whenever the national administration is mentioned in the 1860 text, it is replaced by the term 'nation' in the 1863 Constitution" leads us to the conclusion that the Armenian community was considered by the state as a social entity without any specific authority that the term national administration generates. This is not to say that this term is not mentioned in any part of the 1863 Constitution: however, the provision that the "patriarch of Istanbul is the medium for the execution of the orders of the Ottoman government in particular circumstances" in the 1863 Constitution makes allusion to the supreme authority of the imperial government, which could turn the "constitutional cog" as it required. The article strengthens the position of the Ottoman state in relation to the autonomous sphere of the community while the patriarch is considered an intermediary who determined the limits of that autonomy. The relations clause of the 1860 Constitution turns the national administration into an authorised negotiator before the Sublime Porte for the protection of the religious and political rights of the Armenian community. However, the 1863 Constitution makes it an executive body positioned between the Armenian patriarch of Istanbul and the Sublime Porte. Accordingly the National General Assembly, which represents the will

---

[287] The term was used by Anahide Ter Minassian, *Ermeni Kültürü ve Modernleşme* (Armenian Culture and Modernisation), trans. Sosi Dolanoğlu (İstanbul: Aras Yayıncılık, 2006), p. 127.

of the nation, is the first authority of the national administration in the 1860 text, while the Armenian patriarch of Istanbul is elevated to the highest pinnacle of the national administration in the 1863 text. Through these differences, we could conclude that the 1860 Constitution anticipates a secular authority, the national administration, as the negotiator with the Sublime Porte while the 1863 text foresees the mediation of a religious authority, the patriarch of Istanbul.

As for the institutions of the National Constitution, the regulation shared executive power within the community between the Armenian patriarch on the one hand, and provincial prelates, community assemblies and councils on the other.[288] In order to respect a balanced share of power, the Constitution distributed administration and supervision to different authorities. Accordingly, the General Assembly was responsible for the election of community leaders (the patriarchs of Istanbul and Jerusalem), the nomination and supervision of the religious and civil assemblies for the settlement of questions beyond their competences, and the preservation of the principles of the National Constitution while empowering the Religious Assembly for religious matters and the Civil Assembly for secular issues. The General Assembly was composed of 20 ecclesiastical deputies elected by the clergy of Istanbul, 40 provincial deputies and 80 deputies elected by the quarters of Istanbul. A total number of 120 lay deputies from the provinces and the capital thus dominated the composition of the Assembly as a principle of secularisation. The Constitution authorised four councils of supervision, such as the Educational Council, the Economic Council, the Financial Council and the Judicial Council, as well as executive bodies including the Council for Monasteries, the Committee on Wills, and the Trustees of the Hospital. The Provincial Assemblies, as well as the Provincial Religious and Civil Assemblies, were the decentralised organs of this central administrative structure. The Constitution thus defined a chain of competences and duties according to which each sub-body was accountable to a higher organ.

The Armenian National Assembly: a Legitimate Intermediary

The Armenian National Assembly, instituted by the 1863 Armenian National Constitution, operated as an authority claiming recognition of

---

[288] Télémaque Tutundjian, *Pacte politique entre l'Etat ottoman et les Nations non-musulmanes de la Turquie* (Lausanne: Imprimerie G. Vaney-Burnier, 1904), p. 84.

rights both from the Ottoman government and the Great Powers. With the possession of a Constitution as an internationally recognised legal instrument and as a device of modernity and civilisation, the Assembly legitimised its claims on the grounds of popular will and popular representation. As the National Constitution was recognised by the government as part of Ottoman legislation, Armenian leaders, from the patriarch to the lower ranks of the communal hierarchy, considered themselves, through the document, the legal and legitimate interlocutors with the Ottoman government as well as the Great Powers.

The minutes of the Armenian Patriarchate of Istanbul from 1860 to 1876 also exemplify the functioning of the Armenian National Assembly as an intermediary body between the Porte and the Armenian population for the emancipation of their civil, economic and political status in the Ottoman Empire. The Assembly presented two reports to the Sublime Porte. The first, dated April 11, 1872, was entitled "Provincial Reports of Oppressions" and compiled the most important *takrir*s (notes) presented by the Armenian Patriarchate about oppressions.[289] The basis of the first report was the generalisation of complaints addressed by prelates in the last eight years in Anatolia. Consequently, the National Assembly, in its session of November 27, 1870, constituted a special commission in order to examine the nature of these oppressions. The commission sent circulars to prelacies and informed them about the provincial situation. The report was thus the result of complaint records kept at the Patriarchate for the last 20 years and of those sent by the prelates.[290] The complaints were generally sent from provinces far from the Ottoman capital, which had communication difficulties because of the distance.[291] A second report regarding the provinces of Anatolia was presented by the *ad hoc* commission nominated by the Armenian National Assembly on September 10, 1876.[292] The second report basically discussed the same issues on the

---

[289] *Deghegakirq Kawar'agan Harsdaharo'wt'eanc* (Reports on Provincial Oppressions), (Istanbul: Dbakrutyun Aramyan, 1876). The report was submitted by the commission to the National Assembly on October 8, 1871. This principal headline of the report was read in the session dated 18 February 1872 of the National Assembly.

[290] The report was presented to the Grand Vizier Mahmud Nedim Pasha and bore the seal of the Armenian Patriarch Mıgırdiç Khrimyan. *Kawar'agan Harsdaharo'wt'eanc*, p. 1.

[291] *Deghegakirq Kawar'agan*, p. 2.

[292] *Les Arméniens de Turquie: Rapport du Patriarche arménien de Constantinople à la Sublime Porte*, traduit de l'arménien par K. S. Achguerd (Paris: Ernest Leroux, 1877), p. I.

grounds that the registers of the Patriarchate showed the extent to which the first report remained without any fruitful result. The report was also published in French in 1877.[293]

If we combine the results of both reports, we see that the National Assembly suggested the collaboration of community bodies with the local government in order to contribute to the supervision and reinforcement of governmental measures. The reports touched upon the issue of community representation in local government. Local administrative assemblies included, among others, the heads of non-Muslim populations. However, these members, the reports continued, were not the real representatives of their respective communities. Their selection was arbitrary and membership in any local assembly was the privilege of a limited number of men. The Armenian Patriarchate suggested, through the reports, that the list of elected members in these assemblies should be widened and its composition should have a more representative nature. It was compulsory to consult the approbation of the respective provincial prelate when preparing the list of non-Muslim candidates. In the same way, communal provincial assemblies should be consulted during the election of candidates representing non-Muslim communities in local government.[294] The selection of Armenian members should be executed by the provincial bodies of the community administration. This was a legitimate demand, as the communal provincial administration was constitutionally organised thanks to the *irade* of the sultan: the administration was elected by popular vote and enjoyed the trust of the community.[295]

In addition to obtaining better representation within Ottoman public administration, the reports of the Armenian National Assembly concentrated on the issue of unfair taxation,[296] forced conversion to Islam and forced labour. It was reported between the lines that people from the Armenian population were forced to perform labour (*angarya*) during the construction of buildings belonging to the imperial palace. Financial con-

---

[293] *Rapport du Patriarche arménien*, p. II.

[294] *Deghegakirq Kawar'agan*, pp. 3-4.

[295] *Deghegakirq Kawar'agan*, p. 43.

[296] *Deghegakirq Kawar'agan*, pp. 1-3. The military tax of those who had died or migrated was collected from the people who stayed. Taxes on real estate and profit taxes were unjustly collected from non-Muslims compared to Muslims. The poor were exploited by tax farmers and some of the Ottoman functionaries were secretly collaborating with unjust tax farmers.

tributions were unjustly demanded from the Armenian population for the construction of palace buildings.[297] Efforts were made to convert women and children to Islam. More interestingly, the reports stated that when female converts wanted to return to their initial religion, not only they but the whole Armenian population in the proximity were subjugated to acts of violence and pillage. Because of the non-admission of the testimony of non-Muslims, many instances of kidnapping, looting and assassination remained unpunished.[298] Ottoman penal and civil codes were not duly applied and priority was given to shariʿa courts.[299]

The reports mentioned the transgression of the rights of ownership of the Armenian population as a result of either population resettlement[300] or the non-registration of church or schools property as communal property.[301] Successive *takrir*s on the problems of private property were sent by the Patriarchate. Although commissions were nominated by the government for the investigation and dismissal of guilty provincial officials, late-comers were neither removed from the land of which they unjustly took possession nor were the decisions for the dismissal of state functionaries put into practice. In some cases, no response followed the *takrir*s sent to the government by the Patriarchate. In some provinces, Muslims prevented Christians from acquiring new property or from constructing churches.[302] In others, the complaints were considered to be without grounds and the result of the provocations of Armenian prelates.[303] We can gather from the reports that the Armenian patriarch collaborated with his Greek Orthodox counterpart in order to appeal to the Ottoman Foreign Ministry in issues regarding land ownership.

[297] *Deghegakirq Kawar'agan*, pp. 40-42.

[298] Cf. *Deghegakirq Kawar'agan*, pp. 5-6, 41; *Rapport du Patriarche arménien*, pp. 13-15.

[299] Cf. *Rapport du Patriarche arménien*, pp. 13-16.

[300] *Deghegakirq Kawar'agan*, Account of the *takrir* dated 1289 Şaban 6 / September 27, 1872, pp. 14-15. In some cases, Circassians were settled by provincial state functionaries in the farms cultivated by Armenians without considering that, according to Ottoman legislation, the land belonged to those who cultivated it.

[301] *Deghegakirq Kawar'agan*, pp. 26-33, 35. When any member of the Armenian clergy died, the Porte permitted the local government to sell, for instance, the farm on which the clergyman was living, even though the latter was national property. During the official recording of real estate by state officials, many properties of the Armenian Church and schools were not recorded as communal property.

[302] *Deghegakirq Kawar'agan*, p. 15.

[303] *Deghegakirq Kawar'agan*, pp. 15-16.

The reports put emphasis on the consideration of local languages. The orders of the Sublime Porte should be published in the official newspapers of each governorship, and Ottoman law codes (*düsturs*) should be translated in the language of each community of the empire. Their translation and disclosure were essential. The reports also addressed the agrarian question and the systematic oppression to which the Armenian agricultural population was subjected.[304] In order to promote the progress of agriculture in Anatolia and provide the cultivator with relative well-being and security, it was necessary to defend the rights of ownership and encourage cultivators to acquire lands in order to reach a certain degree of development.[305] The Armenian patriarch particularly emphasised the importance of recognising the farmers as the owners of the land they cultivated.[306]

Both of the patriarchal reports reveal the parallel between communal/local demands and the proposals addressed by the Great Powers for the emancipation of non-Muslims. There is no doubt that communal agents were communicating their complaints to foreign actors as well. What the Armenian patriarch suggested about agrarian reforms was no different from what Count Andrassy suggested on the same issue. In that respect, Ottoman Armenians, as well as other non-Muslims, were instrumental in the transmission of the deficiencies of Ottoman public administration and were, in one way or another, the indirect and informal authors of reform suggestions emanating from foreign state actors.

In December 1876, the Armenian National Assembly discussed whether the community should take part in the debates concerning constitutional reforms in the Ottoman Empire. A report was prepared by the commission which had previously dealt with oppression in the Ottoman provinces. The latter legitimised the expression of the National Assembly's voice in the matter of reform on the grounds that the Armenian community was governed by a constitution previously ratified by the Sublime Porte and that its application was sufficient sign of the communal character of order and legislation. On behalf of the Armenian community of Turkey, the deputies of the Armenian National Assembly expressed their expectation that the Ottoman state and the friendly Powers would take the situation of various

---

[304] *Deghegakirq Kawar'agan*, pp. 40-42.

[305] *Rapport du Patriarche arménien,* pp. 39-43. Nerses, Patriarch, 24 Recep 1291 (August 24, 1874).

[306] *Rapport du Patriarche arménien,* pp. 40-42.

Ottoman populations into equal consideration. The granting of equal rights without discrimination, their communiqué stated, was the precondition of offering equal opportunities of development and civilisation into Ottoman populations.[307] The Assembly strongly criticised the grant of special privileges to some provinces instead of general reforms for the whole country. The communiqué of the Armenian National Assembly shows the self-perception of Armenians as a previously organised "constitutional community" and how they used this self-perception as an argument to express their opinion on the shaping of the Ottoman Constitution. In addition to his report, also published in French,[308] the Armenian Patriarch of Istanbul Nerses visited Bourgoing and Chaudordy as well as the other delegates of the Conference of Constantinople in order to attract their attention to the situation of his co-religionists in the eastern Ottoman provinces.[309] His visit, as well as the mention of his report in *The Times*[310] and its publication in French, was also a way of using external assets in order to provoke internal change.[311]

The special interest of the Great Powers in the rebellions of Bulgaria, Bosnia and Herzegovina caused some agitation among other non-Muslim populations of the Ottoman Empire. Ottoman Greeks, considering themselves as "the most advanced" and "the most civilised" Christian population of the empire, were alarmed not only in Istanbul but also in the provinces and sent petitions to the Porte to protest against the special rights and privileges granted to the Christian populations of Slavic descent and to demand general and equal reforms. One of the petitions, which came from Epirus and Thessaly and was presented by the Greek patriarch, argued that if some special privileges were to be granted, they should be given first to the Greek population, not only because of their importance in the empire but also because "the Porte, in its present dominion over a large portion of the Empire is the successor of the Sovereignty of the Greek nation".[312] Ottoman Greeks legitimised their

---

[307] *Adenakro'wt'iwnq Eresp'o'xanagan Ynthano'wr Zho'gho'vo'h'*. Bashdonagan Hradarago'wt'iwn. Azkah'in Badriarqaran, G. Bo'lis (Minutes of the National General Assembly. Official Publication. The Armenian Patriarchate of Istanbul). December 3, 1876 & December 10, 1876. See also *Masis*, January 2, 1877.

[308] *Rapport du Patriarche arménien, 1877*.

[309] MAEF, CP, Turkey 1876, December 1876, vol. 407. Here December 9, 1876. From Bourgoing to Decazes.

[310] *The Times*, October 5, 1876.

[311] *The Times*, October 5, 1876.

[312] *The Times*, December 2, 1876.

discourse on the grounds of continuity between Byzantium and the Greek *millet*, since doing so demonstrated a legacy of statehood, administrative experience and a certain level of civilisation. The discourse of civilisation would be a strong argument for having a say in the constitutional debate. Catholic Armenians and Jews also joined these initiatives. The chief rabbi addressed himself to the grand vizier in order to discuss the future position of Ottoman Jews.[313]

The Regulation of the Ecumenical Patriarchate

The regulation of the Ecumenical Patriarchate was entitled *Genikoi/ Ethnikoi Kanonismoi* (General/National Ordinances). The Greek term "*kanonismos*" was used as an equivalent of law or regulation.[314] In fact, the Ottoman term "*kanun*" (law) probably derived from this Greek equivalent. Following the imperial instruction of April 1857 regarding the codification of historical privileges after the promulgation of the 1856 Reform Edict, a national assembly composed of seven metropolitans and 21 lay representatives, of whom ten were from the capital and eleven from the provinces, gathered in Istanbul. As one might expect from this lay majority, the new institutions this national assembly drafted had a more democratic character than had previously been the case. In fact, the Synod responsible for patriarchal election had included three lay members from 1770 but the restructuring undertaken in the 1820s excluded any lay representation. The five ecclesiastical members of the National Assembly, supported by the Greek patriarch, opposed the laicisation of national institutions.[315] The main reason for preventing secularism within the Greek Orthodox Patriarchate was perhaps the Bulgarian issue. Unlike the Armenian Patriarchate of Istanbul, the Greek Orthodox Patriarchate ruled over ethnically and linguistically diverse peoples: its jurisdiction also covered the Bulgarian population, which required a separate ecclesiastical structure in this period.[316] The secularisation of the Greek Patriarchate could have sharpened the nationalisation of different ethnic identities under the eaves of Orthodoxy.

---

[313] *The Times*, December 2, 1876.

[314] Johann Strauss, "A Constitution for a Multilingual Empire", pp. 37-38.

[315] Young, vol. 2, p. 13.

[316] MAEF, Private Papers of Thouvenel, PA-233, vol. 2. From Joseph de Barozzi to Thouvenel, March 21, 1860; April 25, 1860.

The reform of the Greek Orthodox Patriarchate was similar to that of the Armenian Patriarchate of Istanbul. In 1860, when the Greek patriarch resigned, the *Journal de Constantinople* announced that the election of his successor would be held according to the new regulation elaborated by the national reform commission. The new regulation was not ratified by the Porte, as in the Armenian case, when the election took place in accordance with the new principles. The former regulation still had some supporters and was not legally abolished.[317] The Grand Vizier Ali Pasha asked the Greek logothete to convene some metropolitans and notables in order to put an end to the strife within the Greek Orthodox Church and to decide on the mode of the election of the patriarch. Thus they gathered *ad hoc* in the residence of Fuad Pasha, the Ottoman foreign minister.[318]

The enactment of the Greek regulation allowed for the involvement of Neo-Phanariot circles (families who replaced the old Phanariots, whose position was shaken after the independence of Greece) and the rising economic elites (merchants and bankers) in the management of the temporal affairs of the Patriarchate.[319] The National Mixed Council, instituted by the regulation, eradicated the old "Gerontismos" system, which operated until the mid-nineteenth century and allowed the Synod's bishops to dominate the affairs of the community in collaboration with the patriarch.[320] If the most important reform was the participation of the laity in electing the patriarch, the choice of the individual who would become patriarch remained under the control of the Holy Synod.[321] Although the Armenian National Constitution was a more secular text compared to its Greek counterpart, it put emphasis on the supremacy of the list prepared by the Religious Assembly by stressing that an individual whose name was not on the list could not be elected patriarch.

Unlike its Armenian counterpart, the Greek regulation limited the role of guilds both in the patriarchal election process and in the administration of patriarchal affairs, much to the benefit of Neo-Phanariots and the

[317] MAEF, CP, May 1860, vol. 344. From Lavalette to Thouvenel, May 29, 1860.

[318] MAEF, Private Papers of Thouvenel, PA-233, vol. 2. From Joseph de Barozzi to Thouvenel, June 19, 1860.

[319] Dimitrios Stamatopoulos, "From *Millet*s to Minorities in the 19th-Century Ottoman Empire: an Ambiguous Modernization," in S. G. Ellis, G. Halfadanarson & A. K. Isaacs (eds.), *Citizenship in Historical Perspective* (Pisa: Edizioni Plus, 2006), pp. 256, 260.

[320] "For the establishment of the Gerontismos regime", see Th. H. Papadopoullos, *The History of the Greek Church and People under Turkish Domination* (Brussels: Bibliotheca Graeca Aevi Posterioris, 1952). Cited in Stamatopoulos, pp. 260, 270.

[321] Stamatopoulos, p. 260.

bourgeois merchants and bankers.[322] In the Armenian case, the National Constitution also resulted from the class struggle between the *amira* and the *esnaf*, which included guild members. The list of members reflects the decreasing number of *amira*s in the community assemblies and the involvement and diversification of professional backgrounds (from middle-class traders to big merchants) after 1847. The decrease of the social power and economic influence of the *amira*s was also tied to the suppression of tax farming by the Tanzimat reforms.[323] In contrast with the Armenian *millet*, a group of bankers promoted their supremacy in the Greek Orthodox and Jewish cases through their reformist efforts.[324] The reform that would be brought to the community through the Greek regulation also targeted the ascendency of Neo-Phanariots with regard to patriarchal affairs and the eradication of Russian influences from the administration of the Patriarchate. Neo-Phanariots were pro-western and supported the reform process.[325]

Unlike its Armenian and Jewish counterparts, the statute law of the Greek community does not transfer the management of temporal and religious matters to two separate authorities. These affairs were instead governed by a Mixed Council headed by an archbishop and consisting of four archbishops and eight laymen. The four archbishops should be members of the Holy Synod and elected by the patriarch and the Holy Synod. As for lay members, the patriarch would invite the inhabitants of the imperial capital, the neighborhood and the shores of the Bosporus to elect representatives according to the distribution assigned to each quarter. These representatives, the Holy Synod and the members of the Mixed Council would form an electoral college. The Holy Synod thus had weight in the election of the lay members of the Mixed Council. The Mixed Council would supervise the schools, hospitals and charitable establishments of the nation, manage the financial administration of these institutions and the churches of Istanbul and settle disputes, which arose among nationals.[326]

The Holy Synod, which consisted of twelve metropolitans and was headed by the patriarch, represented the spiritual authority for all Christians who came under the authority of the Greek Patriarchate. The mission

---

[322] Stamatopoulos, p. 260.
[323] Artinian, p. 53. Cited in Stamatopoulos, pp. 263, 270.
[324] Stamatopoulos, p. 265.
[325] Stamatopoulos, p. 260.
[326] Young, vol. 2, pp. 21-25.

of the Holy Synod was to administer the spiritual affairs of the nation in conformity with canonical laws, manage the monasteries and seminaries of the capital, nominate archbishops, see to it that Orthodox Christians were protected against all acts which could corrupt their religious opinions and provide books regarding the education of the clergy and Christians. For the latter purpose, a printing house was to be established within the Patriarchate and the patriarch was to arrive at a consensus with the minister of public education regarding the publication of all books except those directly concerning theological matters. Moreover, the Holy Synod was to supervise the education of all the national schools. It would function in collaboration with the metropolitans in the provinces. The patriarch should accept and execute the decisions taken by the majority of the Holy Synod. However, the Holy Synod could not execute any decision without the knowledge of the patriarch and vice versa. If the patriarch did not act in conformity with his spiritual duties and insisted upon his attitude, the Holy Synod and the Mixed Council could refer to the Sublime Porte for his deposition.[327] The statute stipulates that when the patriarchal throne was vacant, the Holy Synod should elect a *locum tenens* in collaboration with the Mixed Council from the metropolitans of Istanbul and communicate his name to the Sublime Porte for ratification. Then the metropolitans of the provinces would be invited to notify their candidate in 41 days. The members of the Holy Synod and the metropolitans of Istanbul would add their votes to those of the provinces. Lay delegates from 28 provinces would also come to Istanbul in order to express their choices. In that respect, patriarchal elections mobilised participation beyond Istanbul and included the provinces as well.[328]

The Regulation of the Jewish Millet

Archival evidence allows us to trace the impact of the French consistorial model on the restructuring of the Ottoman Jewish community, which also drafted a new regulation after the 1856 Reform Edict. It was Napoleon I who had the idea of organising the Jewish confession on a legal basis like other creeds by instituting corporate bodies and hierarchical religious and lay functionaries and by legally determining their

---

[327] Young, v. 2, pp. 25-27.
[328] Young, v. 2, pp. 28-29.

modalities of appointment and defining their rights and duties.[329] He convened an assembly of all the most distinguished Jews of the empire on July 15, 1806. As a further step (February 9, 1807), he assembled the Grand Sanhédrin, whose mission was to sanction the outcome of the debates emanating from the assembly of Jewish notables. Finally Napoleon published a decree (March 17, 1808) regulating the various institutions of Judaism for the Jewish community of the whole empire.[330]

The members of the first central consistory were elected by the emperor from the Sanhédrin.[331] The history of the Grand Sanhédrin went back to the time of the Prophet Moses. The term meant "assembly" and housed experts of Jewish law. The word was borrowed by Napoleon I to gather a Sanhédrin before the organisation of the French consistory. Napoleon's aim was to gather a general assembly of Spanish, Portuguese, Italian, German and French Jews that represented more than three quarters of European Jewry. Its acts would be placed next to those of the Talmud as articles of belief and principles of religious legislation. For that purpose, Napoleon I sent an invitation and notification to all the synagogues of Europe, including those of France, in order to enable them to send deputies who would contribute to the acts of the Grand Sanhédrin. The solutions proposed to various questions would be regulated as theological decisions or principles, which would have the force of religious and ecclesiastical law. It would form a second legislation of Jews, conserving the essential character of the law of Moses while adapting it to the present situation of Judaism. Instead of a rabbinical assembly, which would only consider the doctrine, Napoleon's aim was to gather a more populous assembly which would supersede rabbinical authority and consider the interests of the Jewish people.[332] The Grand Sanhédrin, which was supposed to be composed of the most enlightened Jews of Europe, would suppress from the legislation of Moses the laws belonging to the historical situation of the Jews in Palestine.[333] The rabbis would not preach anything contrary to the doctrines of the Sanhédrin. Another question was to distinguish the lines between the

---

[329] S. Debré, "The Jews of France," *The Jewish Quarterly Review*, vol. 3, no. 3 (April 1891), p. 368.

[330] Debré, p. 369.

[331] Debré, p. 372.

[332] M. Schwabe, "La Correspondance de Napoléon 1er et le Grand Sanhédrin," *Archives israélites: recueil religieux, moral et littéraire*, vol. 24 (1863), pp. 933-939.

[333] Schwabe, *Archives israélites*, vol. 24 (1863), p. 939.

Grand Sanhédrin and the French state in the regulation of a new form of Jewish organisation in France. For the French state, there was also a need to demand secular/legal stipulations for political ends, especially from the perspective of the integration of Jews into the French nation.[334]

An imperial edict gave the force of law to the regulation, according to which a synagogue and a consistory should be established in each department with a Jewish population of at least 2,000. Departments with fewer than 2,000 Jews would merge with other contiguous departments in order to reach the required population and constitute one consistory. A central consistory, which would be at the top of the consistorial hierarchy, was established in Paris.[335] The consistorial system put the Jewish religion under the control of the laity and centralised power in the hands of the central consistory.[336] The latter was an intermediary body between the ministry of cults and the departmental consistories.[337] For instance, the central consistory retained the right to suspend or dismiss rabbis or request the ministry to dismiss them. Similarly, the departmental consistories had the right to propose the dismissal or suspension of the district's communal rabbis.[338] The consistorial model was subject to several modifications. After the 1848 Revolution, the 1844 ordonnance was revised in light of universal suffrage.[339] The 1850 election resulted in the significant increase in orthodox and conservative opinions. A decree of July 9, 1853 recaptured the elections from the hands of the people and returned them to consistorial control. Departmental grand rabbis would be elected by the local consistory, voting with 25 notables chosen by universal suffrage. Universal suffrage applied to the election of lay members to the consistory for another ten years.[340] A new decree was promulgated on August 29, 1862 in order to increase the authority of the central consistory and restrict the voice of the people in the choice of rabbis and lay consistory members. The 1862 decree thus eliminated people who did not financially contribute to Jewish institutions recognised by the consistories. It thereby protected the financial interests of the consistories and prevented the very

---

[334] Schwabe, *Archives israélites*, vol. 24 (1863), pp. 937-938.
[335] Albert, pp. 57-59.
[336] Albert, p. 61.
[337] Albert, pp. 368-378.
[338] Albert, p. 71.
[339] Albert, pp. 79, 112-116.
[340] Albert, pp. 85, 116.

orthodox masses from influencing the fate of Jewish communities.[341]
The consistorial system resulted from the modern secular state recognising multiple religious traditions under the supervision of a centralised
state that was fostering integration. The consistory aimed to support a
progressive, moderately liberal identity in terms of religious opinions and
stood in favour of social and economic integration.[342] The organisation of
the French Jewry along consistorial lines was not without social tensions.
Jewish society was fragmented into various segments: some opted for
reforms, lay control of communal life and increasing centralisation of
consistorial power while others insisted on orthodoxy, tradition and
rabbinical power.[343]

There was also a Jewish question in Europe, and the gradual construction of the consistorial system reflected the shaping of a new Jewish
identity in France. In the first half of the nineteenth century, according
to the *Archives israélites*, Russia housed the most numerous Jewish
population (around 1,400,000 people). Austria followed with a population of around one million.[344] The Jewish population numbered about
150,000 in the Ottoman Empire by the early nineteenth century.[345]
Around 88,000 Jews inhabited France while Britain was home to around
45,000. The rest of a population of one million and half was spread
across various countries.[346] Once the *Archives israélites* noted in 1853
that although a bill for the political equality of British Jews was rejected
in the House of Lords by a majority, Lord Aberdeen voted for the bill
despite being among those who rejected it two years previously.[347]
In Prussia, the University of Breslau conferred the grade of doctor to a
Jew, Sigmund Freud, for the first time. This promotion took place in the
faculty of philosophy.[348] In France as well, Jewish citizens were forcing

---

[341] Albert, pp. 92-93, 116-117.
[342] Albert, pp. 45-55, 303-314.
[343] Albert, pp. 51-55.
[344] *Archives israélites*, vol. 29 (1868), pp. 892-93.
[345] Moshe Ma'oz, "Changing Relations between Jews, Muslims, and Christians during
the Nineteenth Century, with Special Reference to Ottoman Syria and Palestine," in Avigdor Levy (ed.), *Jews, Turks, Ottomans: a Shared History, Fifteenth through the Twentieth
Century* (Syracuse, New York: Syracuse University Press, 2002), p. 108.
[346] *Archives israélites*, vol. 29 (1868), pp. 892-893.
[347] *Archives israélites*, vol. 14 (1853), p. 295.
[348] *Archives israélites*, vol. 14 (1853), p. 706.

open the doors of well-known public educational institutions (the Ecole normale supérieure, the Lycée Charlemagne, etc.).[349]

The Crimean War was instrumental for a rapprochement between the leaders of the central consistory and Ottoman Jewish reformers. The war attracted the attention of French Jews to the living conditions of their Ottoman counterparts, especially those in Palestine. They found that the empire's Jews were in a state of fanaticism, inertia, ignorance and inactivity, totally rejecting any idea of reform.[350] Mr Philippson, the rabbi of Magdebourg, addressed a memorandum to the central consistory for the creation of an institution in Europe that would supervise the training of young Jews from Turkey. He also targeted the training of Ottoman Jews in the big European cities in order to enable them to spread civilisation among the Jews of the Orient and provide moral emancipation. Philippson asked that the central consistory intervene to support this philanthropic action.[351]

A common meeting was organised between the Paris consistory and the central consistory in order to discuss measures for the moral and civil emancipation of oriental Jews. Philippson's project was rejected. Mr Cohn, a member of the central consistory of Paris and head of the *Comité de Bienfaisance*, a consistorial institution for providing public welfare,[352] proposed that he should examine the situation in Jerusalem by visiting the city. He also advanced the idea that the Jews of Palestine would never send their children to Europe for educational purposes. The only means to spread public instruction and the taste for work would be the foundation of good schools in local places. These were the means used by Protestant missionaries in Palestine for the purpose of proselytism. Cohn suggested the foundation of a hospital, school and a monthly newspaper in Hebrew and the establishment of permanent relations between the Jews of Palestine and those of Europe. Mr Frank, vice-president of the central consistory, insisted on the necessity to work for the emancipation of the Jews of Turkey in general and pointed out that the question of Jerusalem was secondary. If they only dealt with Palestine, he said, this would give rise to old prejudices against European Jews and the impression that they

---

[349] *Archives israélites*, vol. 14 (1853), p. 656.

[350] *Archives israélites*, vol. 15 (1854), p. 401.

[351] Archives of the Israelite Central Consistory of France (hereafter Consistoire central), Procès verbaux des Délibérations, no. 5., January 23, 1848-July 1st, 1871. Session of May 31, 1854.

[352] Debré, pp. 426-427.

were looking for their real country elsewhere. De Rothschild did not share the fears of Frank since he could not see any inconvenience in dealing with Jerusalem, a place of veneration for all confessions. In his view, there was also a religious question which was important beyond the question of civilisation.[353] Cohn also proposed to the consistory that they start a public subscription for all the Jewish communities of France in order to help provide financial assistance to oriental Jews.[354] They decided to address a circular to all departmental consistories for this subscription.[355]

French Jews appropriated the civilisational discourse of the West: *"Le Consistoire central ayant pris la resolution de se metre en rapport avec tous les centres de populations israélites de l'Europe, à l'effet de secourir, instruire et civiliser les Juifs d'Orient et particulièrement ceux de Jérusalem, décide qu'il sollicitera, par une souscription publique, les moyens d'action qui se révèleraient après une enquête préalable faite sur les lieux, et dès aujourd'hui arrête que l'introduction de jeunes orientaux en Occident sera une des premières mesures à mettre en pratique"*.[356] To help them thus became a matter of philanthropy and civilisation, a *mission civilisatrice*. The central consistory also decided to get in touch with other urban centres inhabited by European Jewry and to open a public subscription with their collaboration in order to bring their financial assistance to the Jews of the Orient and to acquaint oriental Jews with the civilisation of Europe by offering educational opportunities. A preliminary survey was also on the agenda to inquire in detail about the living conditions of oriental Jews and set up the means of action. This inquiry was entrusted to Albert Cohn, who would visit the Orient to collect information.[357]

---

[353] Consistoire central, Procès verbaux des Délibérations, no. 5., January 23, 1848-July 1st, 1871. Session of June 6, 1854.

[354] Consistoire central, Procès verbaux des Délibérations, no. 5., January 23, 1848-July 1st, 1871. Session of October 18, 1854.

[355] Consistoire central, Procès verbaux des Délibérations, no. 5., January 23, 1848-July 1st, 1871. Session of November 13, 1854.

[356] *Archives israélites*, vol. 15 (1854), pp. 445-446. See also Consistoire central, Procès verbaux des Délibérations, no. 5., January 23, 1848-July 1st, 1871. Session of March 23, 1854.

[357] *Archives israélites*, vol. 15 (1854), pp. 445-446. See also Consistoire central, Correspondance, 1850-1859. Here, June 12, 1854. M. Philippson, Rabbi of Magdebourg, no. 7307.

In 1854, Albert Cohn visited Jerusalem and Istanbul: he suggested to the sultan that Jewish subjects could benefit from being placed on an equal footing with Christian communities.[358] Within the framework of this *mission civilisatrice*, many philanthropic activities were undertaken in the Ottoman Empire by European Jewry. A Jewish hospital was opened with the financial assistance of the Rothschild family and other European Jewish notables in Jerusalem in 1854.[359] There were around 8,000 Jews in Palestine in the 1850s according to the *Archives israélites*; Rothschild's hospital seems to have come into existence as a Jewish alternative in a geographical context where Protestant missions were very powerful and had efficient philanthropic institutions that might attract Ottoman Jews.[360] The idea to develop agriculture in order to ameliorate the material conditions of Palestinian Jews and to reduce the number of famines was also put on the table.[361] Furthermore, European Jews initiated a network of schools in Istanbul, Izmir and Alexandria in order to spread "public instruction": professors of French were also sent to these Ottoman cities. The school was seen as a means to reach civilisation, prosperity and moral and intellectual development. These outcomes would allow philanthropy to tackle more than just customs of idleness and pious mendicity.[362]

Cohn conducted a second trip to Jerusalem in the summer of 1856. He mastered Hebrew, Arabic, German and Italian and had an impact on Jews from different geographical backgrounds. He passed from Jerusalem to Istanbul, where he stayed from August 14 to August 26. Cohn visited the school of Hasköy, which had been founded two years ago, in order to inspect the current state and progress of the institution. He also paid visits to the bureaucrats of the Sublime Porte, the ambassadors of France and Austria, the chief rabbi, the famous banker Camondo and the members of the Jewish committee of public instruction in Istanbul.[363] J. de Castro was the vice-president of this committee, which counted

---

[358] Isodore Loeb, *Biographie d'Albert Cohn*, chapitre IX. Cited in Abraham Galante, *Documents officiels turcs concernant les Juifs de Turquie: recueil de 114 lois, règlements, firmans, bérats, ordres et décisions de tribunaux* (Istanbul: Haim, Rozio, 1931), pp. 1-2. *Takvim-i Vekayi*, no. 96, 1250 (1836). Cited in Galante, *Documents officiels*, p. 2.

[359] *Archives israélites*, vol. 15 (1854), p. 491.

[360] *Archives israélites*, vol. 14 (1853), p. 681. *Archives israélites*, vol. 15 (1854), p. 368.

[361] *Archives israélites*, vol. 15 (1854), p. 371.

[362] Isidore Cahen, "Chronique du mois," *Archives israélites*, vol. 16 (1855), pp. 40-41.

[363] *Archives israélites*, vol. 17 (1856), pp. 578-585.

A. Camondo, H. Hatem, H. Palaci and A. B. Bezonana among its members.[364] He participated in a dinner organised at the Austrian embassy on the occasion of their national day, during which he encountered Prokesch. He commemorated the memory of Jewish soldiers who died during the Crimean War in the defence of the Ottoman Empire. During his discourse at the synagogue of Galata, he put emphasis on the importance of France as a country of tolerance, civilisation and justice. He said a prayer both in Hebrew and French for the memory of the dead as well as for the sultan, the French emperor and the Allied Powers.[365] The *Archives israélites* refer to the August 25 issue of the *Presse d'Orient*, accoding to which Albert Cohn, after having visited Grand Vizier Ali Pasha, Mehmed Rüşdü Pasha, the minister of war, and Fuad Pasha, the foreign minister, was also welcomed by the sultan. Cohn expressed his satisfaction with the state of schools in Istanbul, Cairo, Alexandria and Jerusalem. He expressed his deep gratitude for the equality proclaimed in the Reform Edict and the hope that a greater number of Ottoman Jews would be able to attend the imperial school of medicine and be sent to Europe in order to complete their studies.[366]

The Road to the Jewish Regulation

In the key communities of Istanbul, Salonica and Izmir, an important element of lay leadership was composed of Jews of Italian origin: the names Camondo, Fernandez, Modano and Morpurgo were associated with the process of westernisation.[367] By the middle of the nineteenth century, the Francos came into contact with European Jews who were spreading western culture and education in the Orient.[368] Jewish newspapers such as the *Jewish Chronicle* and the *Archives israélites* in the 1840s and 50s reported their economic misery and ignorance: they also commented on, in Ludwig Philipson's (the editor of the *Allgemeine Zeitung des Judenthums*) words, the Jewish Eastern Question.[369] This western Jewish discourse echoed positively among the Francos in the

---

[364] *Archives israélites*, vol. 20 (1859), pp. 536-537.
[365] *Archives israélites*, vol. 17 (1856), pp. 578-585.
[366] *Archives israélites*, vol. 17 (1856), pp. 585-586.
[367] Aron Rodrigue, "The Beginnings of Westernisation and Community Reform among Istanbul's Jewry, 1854-1865," in Levy (ed.), *The Jews of the Ottoman Empire*, p. 439.
[368] Rodrigue, p. 440.
[369] Rodrigue, p. 440.

Ottoman Empire. One of them, Jacques de Castro, had trained in the Imperial School of Medicine (opened in 1827) and was a senior medical officer at the military hospital of Haydarpaşa: in 1848, he communicated with the editor of the *Archives israélites* to voice the necessity of liberating the Jews of the Levant from their state of ignorance and the fanatics of their community.[370] In a letter published in the *Archives israélites* in 1853 signed by L. Allatini, J. Modiano and S. Allatini, all the Franco bankers in Salonica thanked the French Rothschilds for their funds to the city and hoped that their relationship would bring the benefits of civilisation to their poor and ignorant co-religionists.[371] Another Franco was Abraham Camondo. He was from a family that had migrated from Venice to Istanbul in the seventeenth century. The family acquired Austrian citizenship in the eighteenth century.[372] In the 1840s, Abraham Camondo emerged as one of the leaders of the Jewish community. His bank grew in importance and played a major role in the financing of the Ottoman war effort during the Crimean War. Camondo was in close contact with leading Ottoman officials, especially with Fuad Pasha.[373]

Alphonse de Rothschild, a member of the French central consistory, was in Istanbul at the moment when the Reform Decree was promulgated in February 1856: he convened the Jewish notables of the city.[374] The *Univers israélite* mentioned that the chief rabbi addressed a circular to his co-religionists in order to communicate the decisions taken during this meeting. The content of this circular seems to signal the first institutions which would take shape for the administration of Ottoman Jewish communities: a committee of notables composed of foreigners who had inhabited the city for long time; and a second committee of public instruction composed of foreign and local Jews. Foreign Jews would contribute to the committee of public instruction with their knowledge while local members would raise money for the maintenance of schools. The circular already established the chief rabbi and the committee of notables as administrative authorities which could utilise force in order to ensure the observation of the regulations. The circular also foresaw a provincial organisation for the community together with the gathering of

---

[370] Rodrigue, p. 441.
[371] Rodrigue, p. 441.
[372] Rodrigue, p. 442.
[373] Rodrigue, p. 443.
[374] Rodrigue, p. 445.

committees of notables in relevant cities under the supervision of their chief rabbis.[375]

"As in the Orthodox *millet*, the 'reformers' were led by a powerful banker, in this case Abraham Camondo. Camondo led within the Jewish *millet*, supporting the election of two 'reformist' Chief Rabbis in the 1860s: Ya'akov Avigdor (1860-63) and Yakir Gueron (1863-71)".[376] Like the Greek and Armenian *millet*s, the Jewish community was also divided between tradition and modernity. The Jewish primary school, founded in 1854 in Piri Pasha and placed under the auspices of Abraham Camondo, became the target of the reactionary wing, which considered instruction in French a sin: they intended to excommunicate the count. The same attacks were repeated when the *Alliance israélite* founded a school in Istanbul in 1875.[377] The reactionary rabbis blacklisted the *Journal israélite* of Gabbai for having published an article on free masonry.[378] Ubicini describes the situation of the Jewish community and explains how, starting from 1859, the dissentions produced by the antagonism between clerical and lay elements troubled the community and shook the former institutions without giving the new ones any chance of being established.[379] Two antagonistic wings arose within the Jewish community under the names of *lo'wsawo'real* (the "enlightened") and *xawareal* (the "retrogrades"), qualifiers borrowed from the two rival segments of the Armenian community in that period.[380] Starting from 1859, antagonism between the secular elements of Jewish society and the clergy disrupted the old institutions.[381] The *lo'wsawo'real*s conceived of the reorganisation of the Jewish community on the model of the Armenian community. They informed the Ottoman government of their project, which complied, after all, with the spirit of the 1856 Reform Edict in the sense that every non-Muslim community was asked to revise its former privileges and immunities. An *irade* dated 2 Sefer 1280 (July 19, 1863)

---

[375] *Univers israélite*, April 1856, no. 8, pp. 337-344.

[376] C. G. A. Clay, *Gold for the Sultan: Western Bankers and Ottoman Finance, 1856-1881: a Contribution to Ottoman and to International Financial History* (London, New York: Tauris, 2000), pp. 24-25. Cited in Stamatopoulos, pp. 264-265.

[377] Galante, *Juifs de Turquie*, v. 5, pp. 8-10.

[378] Galante, *Documents officiels*, pp. 8-9.

[379] Ubicini, *Etat présent de l'Empire ottoman* (Paris: Librairie militaire de J. Dumaine, 1876), pp. 205-206. Cited in Galante, *Documents officiels*, pp. 8-9.

[380] Galante, *Juifs de Turquie*, v. 5, p. 12.

[381] Ubicini, *Etat présent de l'Empire ottoman*, pp. 205-206. Cited in Galante, *Juifs de Turquie*, v. 5, p. 12.

authorised the chief rabbi of Edirne to go to Istanbul to function as a *locum tenens* of the city (the chief rabbi of Istanbul had been dismissed) and to preside over the elaboration of the statute of the Jewish community following the example of the patriarchs.[382] According to M. Franco, the regulation of the Jewish *millet* was first drafted in Judaeo-Spanish and then translated into Ottoman Turkish by Yehezkel Gabay (1825-96),[383] who founded the *Jurnal Yisraelit* in Istanbul in 1860. Gabay was considered the father of Jewish journalism in the Ottoman Empire and was an experienced translator from Ottoman Turkish. His translation of the Ottoman penal code into Judaeo-Spanish was published in 1860 and he was the first Jewish employee of the Ottoman Ministry of Education.[384] The Judaeo-Spanish draft of the Jewish regulation also made use of the term "constitution", as it was entitled *Konstitusyon para la nasyon yisraelita de la Turkia*.[385]

Although Ottoman Greeks and Armenians were granted their statute laws in 1862 and 1863 respectively, Ottoman Jews only obtained the recognition of their regulation in 1865. This delay might have resulted from the lack of clear definitions regarding their position in the 1856 Reform Edict. Although the latter stipulated that every Christian and other non-Muslim community would, under the inspection of the Sublime Porte, revise their actual immunities and privileges, the edict only referred to the revision of the powers conceded to Christian patriarchs and bishops by Sultan Mehmed II and his successors, without touching upon the position of the chief rabbi.[386] Moreover, the 1856 Reform Edict was the result of pressures emanating from the European Great Powers, who were

---

[382] See the *Journal israélite* of 2 August 1863. Cited in Galante, *Juifs de Turquie*, v. 5, p. 12.

[383] See M. Franco, *Essai sur l'Histoire des Israélites de l'Empire ottoman depuis les Origines jusqu'à nos Jours* (Paris: Durlacher, 1897), p. 169. Cited in Strauss, "A Constitution for a Multilingual Empire", p. 24.

[384] Strauss, "A Constitution for a Multilingual Empire", p. 24.

[385] Elena Romero, *La Creación Literaria en Lengua Sefardí* (Madrid: Ed. MAPFRE, 1992), p. 202. See also regarding "constitution", Rodrigue, pp. 439-456. The text was reprinted in 1913. See *Hahamkhane Nizamnamesi, Estatuto organiko dela komunidad israelita promulgado en data del 23 de agosto de 1287* (Konstantinopla, Imprimeria Izak Gabay, Galata, 1913). Cited in Strauss, "A Constitution for a Multilingual Empire", p. 37, fn. 87.

[386] Sultan Abdülmecid's Hatti Hümayun reaffirming the privileges and immunities of the non-Muslim communities, 18 February 1856. [U. S., 46th Cong., Spec. Sess. (March 1881), Senate, Exec. Documents, vol. 3, No. 3, *The Capitulations*, by E. A. Van Dyck, part 1, pp. 108-111]. Cited in Hurewitz, *Diplomacy in the Near and Middle East*, v. 1, p. 150.

more concerned about the two major Orthodox communities (Greek and Armenian) than the Ottoman Jewish community due to their own vested interests.[387]

The Jewish statute law mainly targeted the restriction of the powers of the rabbis. However, the statute law only covered the Jewish community of Istanbul. The statutes of the other Jewish communities of the Ottoman Empire applied more or less the same principles adopted by the community of the capital with small modifications.[388] The assumption was that such a reform would emanate from the Jewish community of Istanbul and the rest would be subordinate to the Jewish leadership in the Ottoman capital. The *hahambaşı* would be the temporal head of the community throughout the empire and the spiritual head of the Istanbul region. At the same time, individual Jewish communities would be governed by committees of notables including rabbis and lay members, a provincial version of the capital's model. Some eight rabbinical districts were created in addition to Istanbul, each of them having a *hahambaşı*: this number increased during the 19th century.[389] Accordingly, the chief rabbi became, like the patriarchs, the head of the Jewish community and was supposed to execute the orders of the Ottoman imperial government. The statute law of the Ottoman Jewish community was similar to its Armenian counterpart in the sense that it established separate bodies, the Religious and Civil Councils, for the management of temporal and religious affairs. The chief rabbi was bound by the application of the regulation and could be indicted in case of transgression. This quest for conformity to the regulation somewhat reflects the respect of legality as a secular principle.[390] The Chief Rabbinate also housed a General Assembly, which was responsible for the election of the chief rabbi. His election should also be submitted to the approbation of the Sublime Porte, as with his Armenian and Greek counterparts. The General Assembly was composed of 60 lay and 20 ecclesiastical members. The lay majority was an important step towards secularisation. According to the regulation, 60 lay members were elected by the Jewish people in Istanbul and its suburbs. When the question regarded the election of the chief

[387] Cf. Galante, *Juifs de Turquie*, v. 6, p. 309.

[388] Galante, *Juifs de Turquie*, v. 5, p. 12.

[389] Daniel J. Schroeter, "The Changing Relationship between the Jews of the Arab Middle East and the Ottoman State in the Nineteenth Century," in Levy (ed.), *A Shared History*, p. 95.

[390] Young, v. 2, pp. 148-155.

rabbi, 40 temporary members, invited by the chief rabbinates of Edirne, Bursa, Izmir, Thessaloniki, Bagdad, Cairo, Alexandria and Jerusalem, would also be a part of the General Assembly. The statute law conceived the collection of a communal tax called *kisba*. Although the statute law stipulated that the chief rabbi had to refer to councils or to competent commissions to handle all questions submitted to his authority by the Sublime Porte or by other means, the regulation did not mention any organisational scheme in which specific councils or commissions were instituted according to their areas of responsibilities.[391]

Daniel J. Schroeter states that such an arrangement with the Jews of the empire bore a certain resemblance to the French consistorial system.[392] M. Franco, when describing the road to the Jewish regulation, mentioned that the investiture of Jacob Avigdor as chief rabbi in 1860 was followed by the establishment of an assembly of notables (*Meclis-i Cismani* or Civil Assembly). These representatives of the nation were elected by the people in every quarter of Istanbul among the rich, notable and educated families. In that period, the presidency of this assembly was confided to Abraham Camondo. This assembly used to gather once a week in a place located in Galata with the participation of the chief rabbi. When mentioning this assembly of notables, Franco used the word "*consistoire*", indicating that this term had entered the vocabulary of Ottoman Jews as a result of the impact of the French model.[393]

As for the provinces, the notion of single rabbinical authority had little meaning because of the absence of a clerical hierarchy in Judaism.[394] The relationship between the chief rabbi in Istanbul and the local rabbis was not clearly defined in the 1865 regulation.[395] When electing a chief rabbi, delegates from other communities would join the General Assembly and would elect him from a choice of five candidates. The statute did not indicate who had the right to elect the representatives of each quarter in charge of electing members of the General Assembly. Like the Armenian Constitution, it favoured the lay element: the *Meclis-i Umumi* had full executive powers and reduced the power of the rabbinate. The paralysis in community affairs continued after 1865 with the resignation of different committees. The fact that each Jewish quarter had an autonomous

---

[391] Galante, v. 5, pp. 13-26. See also Young, v. 2, pp. 154-155.
[392] Schroeter, pp. 93-94.
[393] Franco, pp. 161-162.
[394] Schroeter, p. 95.
[395] Schroeter, pp. 95-97.

position with "weak links to the chief rabbinate", combined with the
conflictual divisions between reformists and traditionalists, prevented
the statute law from enabling an efficient community administration.[396]

In 1896, the community of Izmir convoked a General Assembly representing all the synagogues of the city and chose a Community Council
as its central administration. In 1908, on the eve of Jewish emigration
to Latin America, the Community Council of Izmir proclaimed its general statute.[397] The regulation of the Jewish community of Izmir seems
to have served as a reference for the constitutional documents of the
Unión Israelita Chevet Ahim of Havana (Cuba) and the *Sociedad Comunidad Israelita Sefaradi de Buenos Aires* (Argentina), both founded in
1914 by Jews coming from the Ottoman Empire and thus providing a
unified framework of communal organisation to the entire Judaeo-Spanish-
speaking sector.[398] The general statute of the *Unión Israelita Chevet
Ahim* of Havana was certified by the governor of Havana in 1918, while
the Argentinian body obtained legal recognition with the granting of
personería jurídica in 1919 by the general inspector of justice.[399] The
draftsmen of the general statutes of both Havana and Buenos Aires were
originally from Izmir, and their emigration to Latin America started in
the aftermath of the Young Turk Revolution because of the strengthening
of Turkish nationalism.[400] The mapping of models up to the migration to
Latin America helps us to observe that although the texts reflect similar
aspirations of community organisation, each time they encountered the
challange of adaptating to different patterns of historical development
and societal/communal dynamics.[401] For instance, the administration of

[396] Rodrigue, pp. 452-453.

[397] Abraham Galante, *Histoire des Juifs d'Anatolie, Les Juifs d'Izmir (Smyrne)*
(Istanbul: Babok, 1937), v. 1, pp. 18, 274-289. Cited in Margalit Bejarano, "Constitutional
Documents of two Sephardic Communities in Latin America (Argentina and Cuba),"
Jewish Political Studies Review, vol. 8, no. 3-4 (Fall 1996), p. 129.

[398] Bejarano, pp. 127-148.

[399] Unión Israelita "Chevet Ahim," *Estatutos Generales* (Habana, 1918), Sender
Kaplan Archives, Miami Beach; Kahal Kadosh y Talmud Tora La Hermandad Sefaradi,
Minutes, February 9, 1919, from the *Minutes Book of the Asociación Comunidad Israelite
Sefaradi de Buenos Aires*, Central Archives for the History of the Jewish People,
HM2/1422b (hence: ACIS, Minutes). Cited in Bejarano, p. 128.

[400] George Weinberger, "The Jews in Cuba," *The American Hebrew and Jewish
Messenger*, vol. 102, no. 14 (February 1918); Harry Sandberg, "The Jews of Latin
America," *American Jewish Yearbook*, vol. 19, 1917, pp. 84-86; Interview with Moise
Bensignor, Miami 1984, Oral History Division, Institute of Contemporary Jewry. Cited in
Bejarano, p. 128.

[401] Cf. Bejarano, p. 127.

Chevet Ahim served the immigration policy of the Cuban government and prevented Jewish immigrants from becoming a public burden by dealing with their integration process, a vital role since they lacked consular representation to protect them.[402]

New Institutions: *the* Alliance israélite universelle

The *Alliance israélite universelle* was a "transnational ethnic-religious network", which suggested legal and social change "otherwise than by the formation of an independent territorial state".[403] It was at the same time a network of Jewish elites which perhaps lacked the "formal political capabilities" of states[404] but nevertheless had the power to change the "legal discourse"[405] through a cultural association involved in humanitarian efforts.[406] One of the conditions which prepared the success of the *Alliance israélite* was that it worked within a context of "open-ended" and "unstable relations of power".[407] "A second trait that allowed the Alliance to survive for almost a century as a public political ethnic entity was the particular dual face the network assumed: on the one hand, the Alliance was working under the shield of the strong French state while on the other hand, the Alliance was represented in international gatherings by powerful individuals whose authority derived from their role in their states".[408] The Alliance began its mission in 1860, its main objective being the acquaintance of the Jews of the Orient with the methods of liberal French education and the amelioration of their moral and material living standards.[409] The statutes of the Alliance evolved over time but the three main goals of the institution remained the same: to work everywhere for the emancipation and moral progress of the Jewish people,

---

[402] Bejarano, p. 131.

[403] Moria Paz, "A Non-Territorial Ethnic Network and the Making of Human Rights Law: the Case of the Alliance Israélite Universelle," *Interdisciplinary Journal of Human Rights Law*, vol. 4:1 (2010), pp. 1-24. Here, p. 1.

[404] Cf. Paz, p. 1.

[405] Cf. Paz, p. 4.

[406] Cf. Paz, p. 17.

[407] Paz, p. 22.

[408] Paz, pp. 22-23.

[409] André Chouraqui, *Cent Ans d'Histoire: L'Alliance Israélite Universelle et la Renaissance juive contemporaine* (Paris: Presses universitaires de France, 1965), p. 161. Cited in Derek Angus Frenette, "L'Alliance Israélite Universelle and the Politics of Modern Jewish Education in Bagdad, 1864-1914" (Unpublished MA Thesis, Simon Fraser University, 2005), p. 1.

to provide effective support to those who suffered because they were Jewish and to encourage all publications pursuing this goal.[410] The *Alliance israélite* was a powerful association that was not limited to the territory of France, but spread over several points of the globe: it had gathered 5,000 adherents from America, Asia, Africa and Europe paying subscriptions. Nonetheless France was privileged as the first country which had emancipated the Jews and made them equal to citizens of religions.[411]

The Alliance played an important role in strenghtening the relations of the Jewish communities throughout the Ottoman Empire and the worldwide Jewish diaspora.[412] With the establishment of the Alliance in Turkey in 1863, Camondo became the president of the Istanbul Regional Committee and a member of the Central Committee in Paris, a position he held until his death in 1873.[413] The inauguration of the Committee took place in Istanbul in the famous Hôtel d'Angleterre with the participation of Crémieux, the former French minister of justice, as the president of the *Alliance israélite* on November 21, 1864.[414] It was probably not a coincidence that the regulation of the Jewish community was promulgated just after. One may also add a third trait which, among others, ensured the success of the *Alliance*. In exchange for the backing that the French government offered, French was the educational language in all the institutions of the Alliance. It thus had the ambition of propagating French ideas and civilisation in the Middle East and Africa, particularly in the Muslim states of the Mediterranean basin.[415] The *Alliance* served as a model for the foundation of a similar organisation, the Armenian General Benevolent Union, in 1906 by Boghos Noubar Pasha.[416]

---

[410] Chouraqui, p. 412. Cited in Frenette, p. 3.

[411] "Discours de M. Crémieux," *Archives israélites*, vol. 27 (1866), p. 1071.

[412] Levy, "Introduction", pp. 114-115.

[413] Rodrigue, p. 443.

[414] Şeni & Le Tarnec, pp. 58-61.

[415] MAEF, ADP (Affaires diverses politiques), Turquie, 1814-96. March 4, 1879. From the *Alliance Israélite Universelle* to the French foreign minister; Ministère des Affaires étrangères, ADP (Affaires diverses politiques), Turquie, 1814-1896. Alliance Israélite Universelle, August 27, 1879.

[416] Claire Mouradian, "Une Emule de l'Alliance: l'Union générale arménienne de Bienfaisance," in André Kaspi, *Histoire de l'Alliance israélite universelle, de 1860 à nos Jours* (Paris: Armand Colin, 2010), pp. 64-67.

Young Ottomans

In the 1860s, other currents such as the Young Ottoman movement were also working in a constitutional direction. The intellectual foundations of this new movement were built by the poet Şinasi Effendi. Namık Kemal himself recognised the intellectual leadership of the latter for the Young Ottomans.[417] Şinasi's publications acquainted the Ottoman audience with nineteenth-century literary, social and political movements in Europe. He started his career as a clerk in the bureau of the Imperial Ottoman Artillery. Encouraged by Reşid Pasha, he went to Europe and stayed in Paris until 1853, where he studied public finance and literature. He was in touch with Samuel de Sacy, Alphonse de Lamartine and liberal circles in the French capital. After his return to Istanbul, he devoted himself to the literary sphere and published his own newspaper, *Tasvir-i Efkar* (Description of Opinions), which became a medium for the expression of new literary and political ideas.[418] Şinasi also became the founder of the modern school of Ottoman literature.[419] An article of his which defended the principle of "no taxation without representation" was published in his *Tasvir*.[420] The newspaper also spread natural law theories by serialising the translation of Vattel's *Droit des Gens*.[421] Among others, Şinasi also published a single series entitled "The Financial System of France" and thus presented the principles of parliamentary government to his readers.[422] He greatly contributed to the development of the Ottoman political mind by defending the rights of the people as a result of their obligations and thus introduced elements of western political rationality.[423] Şinasi's writings reflected a certain appreciation of the "civilising mission" of Reşid Pasha and saw the well-being of the empire in the process of Europeanisation.[424] He had a rationalistic approach to law that differed from the Ottoman-Islamic tradition.[425] "In Şinasi's

---

[417] Kuntay, vol. 1, p. 377. Cited in Mardin, p. 252.

[418] Mardin, pp. 252-256.

[419] E. J. W. Gibb, *A History of Ottoman Poetry* (London: Luzac, [1900-1909]), vol. 5, p. 28. Cited in Mardin, p. 265.

[420] Mardin, p. 254.

[421] "Hukuk-ı Milel," *Tasvir-i Efkar*, 4 Sefer 1279-17 Muharrem 1282/August 1, 1862-June 12, 1865. Cited in Mardin, p. 261.

[422] "Fransa Umur-u Maliyesi Hakkında," 16 Muharrem 1280-5 Rebiülevvel 1280/July 3, 1863-August 20, 1863. Cited in Mardin, p. 262.

[423] Mardin, p. 266.

[424] Mardin, pp. 266-267.

[425] Mardin, p. 269.

scheme what was being praised was neither divine law nor the less orthodox *Kanunname*, the product of the sultan's will. It was the vizier's law which was praised".[426] His idea of a human lawgiver other than the ruler separates him from the Ottoman classical thought, for which law is either the law of God or that of the ruler.[427] His reflections on the papal problem in the columns of the *Tasvir-i Efkar* and his defence of the Italian government show his appreciation for the separation of church from state.[428] What perhaps separated Şinasi from Namık Kemal was the fact that the former was inspired by the West and that he believed in the superiority of European intellectual novelties and political thought; thus, he did not try to reconciliate them with Islam.[429]

For the Young Ottomans, the most important event was the letter addressed by the Turco-Egyptian Pasha Mustafa Fazıl, brother of the Khedive of Egypt İsmail Pasha, to the Ottoman sultan to ask for the establishment of a constitutional regime in the Ottoman Empire. The letter, written in 1866, popularised the idea that Ottoman decline might be prevented with changes to the political structure.[430] In his letter to the sultan, he expressed his admiration for the France of 1789 and emphasised that French emancipation was made possible only when despotism had been defeated and the principle of freedom had triumphed. Similarly, Ottoman regeneration, in his view, resided in the establishment of a constitution that would guarantee perfect equality of rights and duties between Muslims and Christians, limit the power of the sovereign as well as abuses of power, respect freedom and individual dignity and guarantee private property. Mustafa Fazıl insisted on the French model of political governance because France had realised social, political and institutional transformation in order to emerge from financial crises and arbitrary power. He gave the examples of the king of Piedmont, who liberalised his country through a constitution, and of Austria, which had established constitutional freedom. Mustafa Fazıl did not consider the shariʿa an appropriate basis for governmental frameworks. There were, he stated, no Christian or Muslim politics, only justice, and politics were the

---

[426] Mardin, p. 272.
[427] Mardin, pp. 271-272.
[428] "Roma Meselesi," *Tasvir-i Efkar*, Selh-i Zilhicce 1278/June 28 1862. Cited in Mardin, p. 269.
[429] Cf. Mardin, p. 275.
[430] Mardin, pp. 24-40, 276-282.

achievement of this justice.[431] The constitutional statute of the monarchy of Sardinia-Piedmont, granted by King Charles Albert in 1848, became the political charter of the whole of Italy in 1860. The Italian Constitution to which Mustafa Fazıl referred recognised the Catholic religion as the only religion of the state while tolerating other religions. Legislative power was collectively exercised by the king and two chambers, the Senate and the Chamber of Deputies. Interestingly enough, the Senate welcomed among its members some of the clergy (archbishops and bishops): this was similar to its Ottoman counterpart, which housed the spiritual heads of various *millet*s.[432]

The translation of Mustafa Fazıl's letter to Abdulaziz in 1867 by the Young Ottomans was a major contribution to Ottoman constitutionalism. The letter analysed the causes of the decadence of the Ottoman Empire and introduced another approach to state affairs. The letter stressed, as in the Gülhane Rescript, that the decline could be arrested via structural changes. According to Fazıl, the efficiency of the state machinery could not be provided by the increase of control and measures of centralisation but by liberating the citizen from the grasp of the state. Tyranny in the Ottoman Empire was attributed by Mustafa Fazıl to the fact that governmental elite was not responsible to public opinion. He argued that the excesses of statesmen could be counterbalanced by the establishment of a responsible government. Mardin comments that Fazıl's constitutional model, reflected in his letter, recalled the works of Italians such as Mazzini and d'Azeglio, and his approach to the ethical aspects of government was inspired by the moralistic views of Gioberti's work, *Prolegomeni del Primato Morale e Civile degli Italiani*.[433] Mustafa Fazıl Pasha later broke his ties with the Young Ottomans some time in 1873-74 and died at the beginning of December 1875.[434]

One may also question whether Mustafa Fazıl's letter was intentionally translated in 1867, since this was the year in which Sultan Abdülaziz I visited Europe (France, Britain, Prussia, Austria and Belgium).[435] Fuad Pasha, Ottoman foreign minister, and the future Sultan Abdülhamid II,

---

[431] *Lettre adressée au Feu Sultan Abdul Aziz par le Feu Prince Moustafa Fazil*, 1866 (Caire: A. Costagliola, 1897), pp. 11-17. See also Mardin, pp. 24-40, 276-282.

[432] Larousse, v. 4, p. 1049.

[433] Mardin, pp. 276-282.

[434] Mardin, p. 77.

[435] See for details, Ali Kemali Aksüt, *Sultan Aziz'in Mısır ve Avrupa Seyahati* (Sultan Aziz's Visit to Egypt and Europe), (Ahmed Sait Oğlu Kitabevi, 1944), pp. 114-198.

who was 25 years old at that time, accompanied the sultan during his trip. Although sources do not indicate any concrete relation between Abdülaziz I's visit to Europe and the compilation of constitutional input from any country he visited, they refer to the sultan's objective to bring ideas of regeneration from Europe to the empire and to personally observe the institutions that ensured the superiority of Christian nations.[436] Ali Pasha's political testament also refers to the study of European constitutions and social customs by Abdülaziz I.[437] Midhad Pasha himself confirmed in his memoirs that Ali and Fuad Pashas encouraged Sultan Abdülaziz I to visit Europe in order to personally observe the development and administrative forms of European states and to dissipate his suspicion that freedom and equality among Ottoman peoples could endanger the independence of the state.[438]

As for Namık Kemal, he was born in the town of Tekirdağ and studied at the rüştiye's of Beyazit and Valide, the eight-year schools founded during the Tanzimat period on the western model. When he came to Istanbul in around 1857-58, he worked for the Translation Bureau of the Customs and then of the Porte. He reached a wide audience thanks to the simplicity of his Turkish and his patriotic style: his poetry looked to the salvation of the fatherland. In that respect, he went further than his predecessor Şinasi Effendi in the use of a modern vernacular. His second contribution was the popularisation of the notion of hürriyet (freedom).[439] Namık Kemal spoke of the fatherland not only as a geographic unit but also as a strong emotional tie and a "sacred idea resulting from the conglomeration of various noble feelings such as the people, liberty, brotherhood, interest, sovereignty, respect for one's ancestors, love of the family, and childhood memories".[440] Key words in Namık Kemal's statements include the expressions "Osmanlı" (Ottoman), "ümmet" (community), "millet" (in its traditional meaning of a religious group or with the connotation of nation) and "mezheb" (denomination): these terms point to his national allegiance.[441] It is quite interesting to note that the various constitutional drafts analysed in Chapter III reflect

---

[436] Aksüt, pp. 88, 92.

[437] Ali Pasha, Testament politique, p. 16.

[438] Midhad Paşa, Mirat-ı Hayret (Mirror of Surprise), vol. 2 of Midhad Paşa'nın Hatıraları, ed. Osman Selim Kocahanoğlu (İstanbul: Temel Yayınları, 1997), p. 33.

[439] Mardin, pp. 283-285.

[440] Namık Kemal, "Vatan", pp. 264-265. Cited in Mardin, p. 327.

[441] Mardin, p. 327.

a long discussion over the concepts "everyone" (*herkes*), "all Ottomans" (*Osmanlıların kaffesi*), "Ottoman individuals" (*Osmanlı efradı*) and "every Ottoman" (*Her Osmanlı*), as well as the expression "each of the subjects of the Ottoman state" (*Tebea-i Devlet-i Osmaniye'den herkes*): expressions like "Ottoman" and "all Ottomans" were finally preferred in the text of the Ottoman Constitution.

Kemal's channels of inspiration were not only western: he was also influenced by the classical poet Leskofçalı Galip and Islamic standards of justice. His thought and political philosophy may be captured through the articles he wrote for the newspapers *Hürriyet* and *İbret*. Most of his articles focused on fundamental theoretical issues: divine justice, religious law and the observance of Islamic principles. He compared the ideas of the Enlightenment regarding governmental issues with the political thought of Islam. In his view, natural law overlaps with the divine justice established by the Qur'an.[442] The conclusion that might be extracted from Kemal's articles was the necessity of establishing the system of *meşveret*, the Islamic equivalent of representative government. In his view, the shari'a was the equivalent of common law in Islam, and he believed that the former included the structure of government and the fundamental rights of subjects. He was opposed to the movement of secularisation which started in the Tanzimat period.[443] "Thus, starting from the premise that freedom was a divine grant, he would go on to state that a community ("*ümmet*") could be free only when it had been assured of its personal rights ("*hukuk-u şahsiye*") and of its political rights (*hukuk-u siyasiye*")".[444] The security of personal rights depended on the functioning of impartial and competent courts while political rights would be secured by the separation of powers (*kuvvetlerin taksimi*) and the establishment of representative government.[445] Kemal did not vehemently insist on the drafting of a constitution or on the wresting of a constitutional charter from the state. In his view, the shari'a already provided fundamental political rules and principles to guide rulers. He insisted however on the need to make all the laws of the land other than the shari'a accessible to all. He stated that laws and regulations should be written in a language understandable

---

[442] Mardin, pp. 283-293.
[443] Mardin, pp. 308-315.
[444] Mardin, pp. 308-309.
[445] Mardin, pp. 308-309.

to all. Moreover, he suggested the codification of various laws and charters (such as the Imperial Rescript or the Reform Edict) proclaimed at different dates by the Ottoman state. The revision and consolidation processes of these charters should be inspired, in his view, by "existing foreign constitutions". If the provisions of these charters were to be included in a new constitution of the Ottoman Empire, the text should be in harmony with the principles of Islamic law. Moreover, the proclamation of a constitutional regime in the Ottoman Empire would not be something new. A mechanism of governmental control was in use in the Ottoman Empire before the centralising tendencies of Mahmud and the rise of a new bureaucracy.[446] According to Kemal, the Ottoman system of government was in fact a "legitimate government" in which the ulema maintained the legislative power while the sultan and his viziers controlled the executive power and the Janissaries checked the actions of the executive.[447] He concluded that this primitive arrangement resulted in continuous struggles between the government and the Janissaries in bloody revolutions. "Thus, concluded Kemal, historical evidence 'unfortunately' pointed to the necessity of confining government to the hands of 'a well-qualified group' of limited size which would take care of the matters of state. There was no other way to invest this group with legitimate authority and to control their actions than by having 'recourse to delegation'".[448]

Namık Kemal also insisted that a suitable model for the Turks was the constitution of France's Second Empire. He rejected the constitution of the United States because it was a republic and those of Prussia and England because both were based on the representation of an aristocracy, which did not exist in the Ottoman Empire.[449] "To Namık Kemal, the French Constitution appeared to include the most suitable combination of checks and balances for Turkey, for it had been able to create 'an era of happiness' in France, a country generally given to violent revolution".[450]

---

[446] Namık Kemal, "Usul-u Meşveret," *Hürriyet*, September 14, 1868, pp. 1, 6. Cited in Mardin, p. 310.

[447] Namık Kemal, "Hasta Adam," Hürriyet, December 7, 1868, p. 1. Cited in Mardin, p. 310.

[448] Namık Kemal, "Usul-u Meşveret," *Hürriyet*, September 14, 1868, pp. 1, 6. Cited in Mardin, pp. 310-311.

[449] Namık Kemal, "Usul-u Meşveret," *Hürriyet*, September 14, 1868, p. 7. Cited in Mardin, p. 311.

[450] Namık Kemal, "Usul-u Meşveret," *Hürriyet*, September 14, 1868, p. 7. Cited in Mardin, p. 311.

Kemal also speaks of the Belgian Constitution as the most suitable constitutional system.[451] Based on the French model, Kemal proposed the creation of a governmental system composed of three bodies: a Council of State, a Senate and a lower Chamber, all under the supervision of the sultan. The legislative body (composed of elected members while members of the Council of State were to be nominated by the sovereign) and the Senate would approve or reject legal projects prepared by the Council of State: the lower Chamber would control only the budget.[452] Kemal later expressed his new admiration for Prussia in a memorandum he sent to Ali Pasha, wherein he suggested looking to Germany in the future rather than to France and England.[453] This change was probably the result of the Franco-Prussian War, which, in Kemal's mind, replaced France with Germany as "the most successful embodiment of Western civilisation".[454] Namık Kemal also discussed the position of the sultan in this scheme. He maintained that the Ottoman Empire could not adopt the French system, which took some part of the responsibility from the shoulders of the government to place it on the emperor, who became responsible to the people. Neither could the Ottomans take all responsibility from the shoulders of the sultan to make the government responsible, as in England. Kemal suggested the compromise of making the sultan responsible for his actions and his will.[455] In addition to the concept of responsibility, Kemal's writings also conceptualised a certain idea of equality, which meant "equality before the law": equality results from the dignity of the person and the creation of man by God.[456] Kemal was influenced by European ideological currents and was a cultural translator at the same time. He translated Montesquieu, discussed Voltaire and Condorcet, and followed Garibaldi and Mazzini as nationalist models. He spent periods of exile in Paris, London and Geneva, where he published newspapers that were prohibited in Istanbul. However, he was attached to the revival of Islam and to the shariʿa as the basis of society

---

[451] Namık Kemal, "Memur," *İbret*, October 7, 1872. Cited in Mardin, p. 311.

[452] Namık Kemal, "Usul-u Meşveret," *Hürriyet*, September 21, 1868, pp. 2, 6. Cited in Mardin, p. 311.

[453] The text may be found in [Namık Kemal], "Kemal Bey'in Bir Mütalaa-i Siyasi-yesi," *Mecmua-i Ebüzziya*, 1 Muharrem 1298/December 4, 1880, pp. 225-231. Cited in Mardin, pp. 61-62.

[454] Mardin, pp. 61-62.

[455] Namık Kemal, "Usul-u Meşveret," *Hürriyet*, September 14, 1868, p. 8. Cited in Mardin, p. 312.

[456] Namık Kemal, "Müsavat", *M. S. E.*, p. 377. Cited in Mardin, p. 319.

and government. He tried to find Islamic linguistic equivalents for the concepts of the Enlightenment. He was critical of some of the functionaries of the Porte imitating Europe,[457] and gathered around him a small group of dismissed functionaries such as Ziya Pasha.[458] As an eminent figure of Young Turkey, he founded two main newspapers in Istanbul, *İbret* (The *Example*) and *Sıraç* (The *Lantern*): as chief editor, Kemal wrote pieces for these papers criticising the current political system. He was thus considered an adversary in palace circles.[459]

As for Ziya Pasha, he differed from Namık Kemal in terms of personality and career. The former was experienced as an administrator and expressed his concerns for the amelioration of administrative practices in the Ottoman Empire, while Kemal acted as a theorist who dealt with general principles of politics. Ziya Pasha entered the Translation Bureau and was influenced by the classical poet Fatin Effendi, who enabled him to acquire Ottoman-Islamic culture. Like Şinasi Effendi, Ziya Pasha was Reşid Pasha's protégé and was appointed secretary to the imperial palace in 1855. He learnt French and made translations from this language. After the death of Reşid Pasha, Ziya Pasha was targeted by Ali Pasha, against whom he attempted to organise an intrigue: as a consequence, he was pushed away from key state positions. He became the closest collaborator of Namık Kemal during their exile years and contributed to the newspaper *Hürriyet* with his articles.[460] In one of its issues, Ziya's stand on the idea of freedom shows us how he and perhaps other Young Ottomans understood the term along with its western political connotations and the extent to which they contextualised their opposition to governmental practices within the framework of global struggles for freedom:[461]

> As in Britain, the United States and France many thousand patriots were destroyed by imprisonment, exile or at the hands of the executioner, so one example of this has also been seen in our land. Those supporters of freedom, who wished to change the way of government were either dismissed, imprisoned or executed.

---

[457] Sami Zubaida, "Cosmopolitanism and the Middle East," in Roel Meijer (ed.), *Cosmopolitanism, Identity and Authenticity in the Middle East* (Surrey: Curzon, 1999), p. 22.

[458] MAEF, Papier Adolphe Thiers, PA-AP 170, vol. 5, Copies of Correspondence, May 11, 1871-May 13, 1873. Here April 16, 1873. From Voguë to Count Rémusat.

[459] MAEF, Papier Adolphe Thiers, PA-AP 170, vol. 5, Copies of Correspondence, May 11, 1871-May 13, 1873. Here April 16, 1873. From Voguë to Count Rémusat.

[460] Mardin, pp. 337-340.

[461] *Hürriyet*, 16 Rebiülevvel 1285/6 July 1868, p. 2f. Cited in Czygan, p. 943.

"The efforts of the Young Turkey Party are primarily directed", he stated, "to the substitution of the *will of the nation*, that is to say of the population of the Empire without distinction of race or religion, for the arbitrary power of a few individuals".[462] Like Namık Kemal, he saw the salvation of the Ottoman Empire in the creation of a national assembly, but he was quite timid in taking one step further and making the sultan responsible. His governmental scheme clearly indicated his respect for the monarchical principle. While proposing the creation of a National Assembly, he emphasised that the "legitimate independence" of the sultan should not be curtailed.[463] Ziya Pasha argued that the subjects of the Ottoman Empire were not mature enough to be aware of their own interests, but good government and the institution of representation would achieve these goals. He believed that the decline of the Ottoman Empire was caused by the degradation of the imperial function and included in his proposals the idea that bureaucrats should be held responsible to a National Assembly. The idea that the sovereign would cause no harm and that he should not be held responsible conformed quite strongly with the Islamic conception of government. His conceptualisation of freedom was similar to that of Namık Kemal in the sense that it was a divine grant to men. However, he also developed his conceptualisation by putting freedom into relation with law: "Elaborate laws were made according to the particular composition of every nation and according to its characteristics and mores. There has never existed at any time a tribe which lived in society without being tied to a more or less regular system of laws [...]. Thus liberty is found with attachment to laws".[464] In that respect, he also maintained that the shariʻa should not be disregarded. Such indifference would risk degeneration and the loss of cultural identity in the Ottoman context.[465] Ziya Pasha criticised Reşid Pasha and his successors for not having defended the legitimate position the shariʻa should occupy in the Ottoman Empire vis-à-vis the European norms of justice and accused them of not having adopted any efficient policy to challenge the European belief that "the shariʻa prevents justice, humanity and progress".[466]

---

[462] Ziya Pasha, letter to the French newspaper *Liberté*; French original and English translation in the *Levant Herald* (Istanbul), October 20, 1868. (Italics in quotation are those of Mardin). Cited in Mardin, pp. 346-347.

[463] Mardin, pp. 347-348.

[464] Mardin, pp. 349-352; The quotation from Ziya Paşa, "Yeni Osmanlıların Ecille-i Azasından... Ziya Beyefendi," *Hürriyet*, July 6, 1868, p. 2. Cited in Mardin, p. 352.

[465] Mardin, pp. 352-353.

[466] *Hürriyet*, 5 April 1869, p. 7. Cited in Czygan, p. 947.

He also argued that the bad image of the shariʿa in Europe was due to its harsh application and that existing Islamic law should be improved instead of the promulgation of new laws.[467] Ziya Pasha attributed the decline of the Ottoman Empire to the weakening of the sultanate and to the rise of ministers who instrumentalised the sultans in order to achieve their policies. This was why imperial power lost strength day by day.[468] Ziya also criticised high-ranking Ottoman bureaucrats for their external policy, which had triggered European interference. These criticisms were also reflected in some of his articles in *Hürriyet*:

> He [Reshid Pasha] believed he would please European governments by putting their diplomats' requests for favours to the fore. This deference with its ill-timed manœuvring opened the doors to interference, which [later] he was not able to close again.[469]

The agency and importance of the Young Ottomans lay in the fact that, for the first time, an organised group made extensive use of the mass media to express their criticisms vis-à-vis their government either in the Ottoman context or in Europe after exile.[470] The variety of ideas expressed by their principal members reflects the heterogeneous character of the movement. Some were firmly committed to the European style of emancipation and constitutionalism while others were in search of identity and cultural authenticity and tried to reconcile the European ideas of the Enlightenment and constitutionalism with the principles of Islam.[471] Cyzgan's article argues that the Patriotic Alliance targeted political change by introducing consultative principles and that their action was described as a "plot against Ali Pasha and some other ministers".[472] It seems that they principally opposed the political orientation taken by the Tanzimat bureaucracy, which, in their view, reduced the freedom of action of the the sultanate in Ottoman political governance. This element becomes clearer in Namık Kemal's way of contextualising the sultan as a supervising authority in his constitutional scheme and Ziya Pasha's attribution of the Ottoman decline to the

---

[467] Czygan, p. 947.
[468] Ziya Pasha, "Hatıra," *Hürriyet*, January 4, 1869, p. 5. Cited in Mardin, p. 356.
[469] *Hürriyet*, 12 April 1869, p. 8. Cited in Czygan, p. 947.
[470] Mardin, p. 4.
[471] Cf. Mardin, p. 4.
[472] Czygan, p. 944.

strength of ministers. Moreover, they targeted the population as an audience and the rights of the people also became an object of discussion in the political sphere. "With the articulation of the people's rights in the press, they began the process of establishing the voice of the general public as a political factor".[473] As the draft constitutions the book analyses in Chapter III are not authored, we may argue cautiously that Ziya Pasha and Namık Kemal, who occupied seats in the Drafting Commission implicitly as Young Ottomans, might have played a determining role in shaping the content of discussions over sultanic and ministerial responsibility, the prerogatives and the counterweight of the sultan vis-à-vis other legislative, executive and judiciary bodies, the importance of Turkish and the relationship between the law and its limits. The final text of the Ottoman Constitution reflects, as we will see in Chapter III, their conservative stand over these questions. Moreover, as the Young Ottomans suffered from exile and imprisonment because of their political ideas and opposition, one may also consider their role in shaping the relevant provision regarding these issues. While the Ottoman Constitution does not talk about the "people", this category does appear in the final text in a more national form: "*Osmanlılar*" (Ottomans) or "*Osmanlıların kaffesi*" (all Ottomans).

The rest of my investigation shows that Ottoman non-Muslims were fascinated by the idea of constitutions throughout the nineteenth century. The constitution had symbolic value and was the embodiment of equal recognition and the equal enjoyment of civil and political rights. This promising legal framework would also allow them to identify themselves with international society. Non-Muslim communities played an important role in the constitutionalisation of the Ottoman Empire and pursued different strategies to that purpose. They first constitutionalised the administration of their communal sphere. This modification pushed the state to harmonise new communal structures with Ottoman legislation; in turn this harmonisation forced legislators to conceptualise a new egalitarian legal system for the whole empire. Although the main purpose of this chapter has been to search for the answer to whether non-Muslims were one of the driving forces behind the establishment of a constitutional mode of governance in the Ottoman Empire, it has only offered some examples of non-Muslim agency. The chapter is a modest attempt at providing some of the narratives of agency within the wider context of

---

[473] Czygan, p. 952.

Ottoman history. *Takrir*s,[474] memorials, reports and similar internal instruments of pressure were mobilised by non-Muslims upon the violation of their rights. However, these instruments of intimidation produced a limited effect on the Ottoman state, which was the real wielder of coercion. The fact that many elements of the reform decrees that concerned non-Muslims remained a dead letter is proof of this limited effect. Although the Reform Edict of 1856 became an international stipulation together with community constitutions to promise equality of rights both in the treatment of non-Muslims by the Ottoman government as well as in the administration of the communal spheres, the Great Powers did not themselves respect this equality of rights and preferred one community over the others according to the interplay of international politics. This explains why Bulgarians were favoured in 1876 at the expense of other non-Muslims and why the importance of the Ottoman Constitution was overshadowed by the agenda of the Conference of Constantinople. As regards the institutional agency of non-Muslims, one should keep in mind that the chapter analysed how the textual framework of community regulations or constitutions may be interpreted as the emergence of constitutional thought in the Ottoman context without dealing with their application. As far as the Armenian National Constitution was concerned, the application process showed that the communal entity, not being a state, lacked the instruments of sanction or, in other words, did not possess the coercive power to impose the stipulations of the Constitution on community members. Grand Vizier Ali Pasha was perhaps right in describing the Armenian National Constitution as a "square wheel".[475] One would not expect different narratives from the application process of other community regulations. Moreover, the treatment of the agency of non-Muslims together with that of the Young Ottomans leads us to the idea that all social segments of the Ottoman society, either Muslim or non-Muslim, were in search of new tools of legitimacy and that they questioned conformity to global models in order to resolve this crisis in governance, either communal or more general. They tried to make a synthesis between tradition and solutions coming from the West.

---

[474] Cf. Tutundjian, pp. 105-113.
[475] Saro'wxan, p. 59.

CHAPTER II

ACTORS, INTERACTIONS AND NEGOTIATIONS IN 1875-76

The territorial loss prevented in 1856 happened in the 1870s. The rebellions that broke out in 1874 in Herzegovina spread to Bosnia, Montenegro and Bulgaria in 1876. The political destabilisation led to the deposition of two sultans (Abdülaziz I and Murad V) and Abdülhamid II came to the throne in 1876.[1] During the Balkan crisis in 1875, the European Powers claimed autonomy for Bosnia and Herzegovina. The Ottoman state strongly opposed the grant of administrative autonomy to the European provinces on the grounds that it would harm the authority and prestige of the Porte in all parts of the empire. Both the diplomatic discussion of internal questions and the interference of the Powers in the relations between Bosnia and Herzegovina and the Ottoman authorities would be transgressions of the rights of the Porte's sovereignty and independence. Moreover, an exceptional form of government for the insurgent provinces would provoke disorders in other parts of European Turkey.[2] In December 1875, Musurus Pasha, the Ottoman ambassador to London, immediately confirmed the engagement of his government in completing recently decreed reforms and making them public as soon as arrangements could be made for bringing them into effect. He observed that the question of reforms and the administration of the empire were exclusively within the competence of the Ottoman state and that the sultan could not accept proposals for reforms from any other power, since such was incompatible with the independence of the Ottoman Empire and with the provisions of the Treaty of Paris. In return, the British government refused any assistance to the Porte until they had more complete information about the reform project.[3] This stage was the beginning of a

---

[1] Findley, "The Tanzimat", p. 16.

[2] PRO, FO 78/2674, Lord Derby to the Marquis of Salisbury, November 21, 1876.

[3] PRO, FO 78/2436. Instructions addressed to Her Majesty's Embassy at Constantinople respecting Administrative and Financial Reforms in Turkey: 1856-1875. Derby to Henry Elliot, December 8, 1875.

process in which the Porte communicated the content of new reforms to the Powers until the proclamation of the Ottoman Constitution.

The Porte's answer to the Austrian proposals (the Andrassy Note) was conveyed to the representatives of the Six Powers in an official note.[4] The Porte accepted the first four points (full religious freedom, abolition of tax farming, amelioration of the agricultural situation of farmers, and institution of a local commission composed of an equal number of Muslims and non-Muslims in order to supervise the general execution of all the reforms). The fifth point regarding the use of direct taxes for the needs of the province itself did not conform to the general system of imperial financial administration. On February 11, 1876, the imperial government decreed that four points out of five formulated in the Andrassy Note should be executed in Bosnia and Herzegovina.[5] The British government considered the conditions of peace proposed by the Porte inadmissible, and the other Great Powers adhered to this point.[6]

1. The Great Powers and their Representatives

Britain's Position

British consuls regularly reported the administrative and financial deficiencies of the Ottoman Empire to their government and advised structural improvements. The reports that covered the Tanzimat era also formulated consular views on the application of the reform decrees. The existence of the reports in the archives of the Ottoman Foreign Ministry shows that they were not just for informing the British government. There is no doubt that the reports provided Her Majesty's Government with concrete grounds when formulating its ultimatums to the Ottomans. However, factual evidence reveals that consular reports were also used to pressure the Ottoman government and were sent to high-ranking Ottoman bureaucrats to urge the state to make institutional changes.[7]

---

[4] PRO, FO 78/2469 From Henry Elliot, February 13, 1876.

[5] MAEF, Mémoires et Documents, vol. 101. Turquie. Conférence de Constantinople, 1876-1877. Documents divers, Réunions préparatoires, Protocoles. Here Response of the Porte to the Andrassy Note by Rashid Pasha, Ottoman Foreign Minister, February 13, 1876.

[6] MAEF, CP, September-November 1876, vol. 406. September 24, 1876.

[7] See for example BOA, HR.SYS. 1869 D-2. Henri Bulwer sent to Ali Pasha, Ottoman foreign minister, on November 19, 1860, a copy of the printed reports of British consuls relating to the conditions of Christians in Turkey.

The reports varied from one another in terms of their content but some general traits can be extracted from independent accounts.

The fact that the 1839 Gülhane Decree remained a dead letter in some provinces is a *leitmotif* of the consular reports.[8] Abuses by state officials still existed in one province or another, and some rapacious men still dominated the provincial councils in order to promote their own interests. The local assemblies were less favourable to progress and good government than the officials of the Porte. Insecurity of life and property reigned in rural districts. Ottoman Christian authorities, namely the spiritual leaders and the primates (*kocabaşı*), were more rapacious and tyrannical than the Ottoman authorities. Bishops and metropolitans committed acts of oppression and cupidity against their flocks.[9] Consular reports also underlined the fact that Greek and Armenian bishops and the chief rabbi attended the assemblies but were subjected to humiliation when they gave an independent opinion.[10]

Consular reports mentioned the negative impact of tax farming. They put emphasis on the neglected interests of two classes of population, the peasantry and the merchants. The peasantry still complained about tax farmers because of the extra levy. Taxes were not high in the Ottoman Empire but the mode of collection and exaction from farmers was oppressive. British consuls advised that taxes needed to be levied by the government instead of tax farmers, who cheated both sides and enriched themselves. Most importantly, agriculture and trade needed a certain impetus. There was a lack of confidence in the government. The chief aim of the government should be to restore that confidence. A large amount of money, hoarded by Christians as well as Muslims, would circulate freely if confidence in the stability of the state was restored, thus creating an atmosphere of prosperity. Provincial banks for loans, savings and deposits could be a solution.[11]

According to the consuls, the commercial court system did not function well. Reports underlined the necessity of separate courts for civil, criminal and commercial suits in every province and the independence of the judiciary system. They advised that Ottoman courts should be headed by a president without any local connections and interests. Tribunals

---

[8] BOA, HR. SYS. 1869 B-2. British Consular Reports dated February 1849.
[9] BOA, HR.SYS. 1869 D-2.
[10] BOA, HR. SYS. 1869 B-2. British Consular Reports dated February 1849.
[11] BOA, HR. SYS. 1869 D-2. Papers relating to the Condition of Christians in Turkey, Foreign Office, 1860.

should be independent of provincial governors and depend on the minister of justice. Magistrates should not have any executive power. The executive power should be vested exclusively in the governor of the province and in sub-governors acting under his authority. The judicial functions of the local assemblies should be curtailed and their interference in executive power prevented.[12]

Even after the promulgation of the 1856 Reform Edict, the reports referred to inequalities depending on religion: the evidence of a Muslim had more weight than that of a Christian or a Jew, and Christians and Jews were not allowed to hold the public offices assigned to Turks. Thus the presidents of tribunals were invariably Muslims. Christian members were not able to protect their co-religionists from acts of injustice. Christian evidence was not admitted in the courts. No offices were confided to Christians in local government, military service or the police. British consuls reported that Christians preferred to enter the army instead of paying the exemption tax provided that they were recruited in separate regiments.[13]

Consular reports also reflect the extent to which Britain intended to penetrate the Ottoman Empire through judicial, financial and military structures. My personal conviction is that Egypt was the principal model for Britain when shaping its mode of penetration. It expected to develop a second Egypt in the Ottoman Empire. The British Foreign Secretary John Russell once proposed the establishment of a mixed tribunal in which the Ottoman minister of justice would sit together with the judge of the consular court for the settlement of all matters necessitating a special jurisdiction.[14] British intentions to penetrate the Ottoman judiciary are clearer in later periods. The British suggested that a higher court of appeal should be established in Istanbul in which the Porte should also accept the employment of foreign judges.[15] The element on which the British placed special importance was the establishment, in the Ottoman

---

[12] BOA, HR. SYS. 1869 D-2. Papers relating to the Condition of Christians in Turkey, Foreign Office, 1860. See for instance, Sir H. Bulwer to Lord J. Russell, July 31, 1860 transmitting the replies of Consul Blunt. Inclosure in no. 8, p. 42. Pristina, July 14, 1860.

[13] BOA, HR. SYS. 1869 D-2. Papers relating to the Condition of Christians in Turkey, Foreign Office, 1860. See for instance, Consul-General Longworth to Sir H. Bulwer, Belgrade, July 14, 1860, p. 20.

[14] PRO, FO 78/2436. Instructions addressed to Her Majesty's Embassy at Constantinople respecting Administrative and Financial Reforms in Turkey: 1856-1872. Lord J. Russell to Sir H. Bulwer, May 31, 1860 # No. 238.

[15] PRO, FO 78/2674, Lord Derby to the Marquis of Salisbury, November 20, 1876.

Empire, of a local and central international tribunal after the Egyptian model.[16] This model was undergoing a five-year trial in Egypt: if the results were successful, the old courts in which the qadi applied the law of the Qur'an would probably be absorbed into the new international court system.[17] Britain's ambition was thus to introduce the same court system into the Ottoman Empire.

It seems that the Ottoman financial sphere was not exempted from penetration. The British government exercised pressure during different financial crises on the Ottoman government to send British experts for the improvement of finances. It was even Russell's idea that the Ottoman financial administration should be partly composed of foreigners for a while.[18] One of his preoccupations was whether a British expert from the Treasury in London was desirable in Istanbul and whether such a person could receive an appointment and an adequate salary from the Porte.[19] The Foreign Office even targeted the Ottoman military sphere. The British ambassador to Madrid once sent an explanatory despatch about the organisation of the *guardia civil* in Spain and instructed Redcliffe to communicate these papers to the Sublime Porte in order to suggest that a similar force might be practicable in the Ottoman Empire.[20]

After the signing of the Paris Treaty, the main concern of the British Foreign Office was the inadequacy of its consulate-general in Istanbul

---

[16] PRO, FO 78/2680, From Salisbury to Derby, November 21, 1876 # no. 1. (Paris).

[17] MAEF, CP, Turkey 1876, December 1876, vol. 407. From Bourgoing to Decazes.

[18] PRO, FO 78/2436. Instructions addressed to Her Majesty's Embassy at Constantinople respecting administrative and financial reforms in Turkey: 1856-1872. From Russell to Sir Henry Bulwer, March 31, 1862. PRO, FO 78/2436. Instructions addressed to Her Majesty's Embassy at Constantinople respecting administrative and financial reforms in Turkey: 1856-1872. From the Foreign Office to Henry Bulwer, June 27, 1859; PRO, FO 78/2436. Instructions addressed to Her Majesty's Embassy at Constantinople respecting administrative and financial reforms in Turkey: 1856-1872. Lord J. Russell to Sir H. Bulwer. October 18, 1860 # no. 561. Note to be presented by Sir H. Bulwer to Aali Pasha. Inclosure in no. 73; PRO, FO 78/2436. Instructions addressed to Her Majesty's Embassy at Constantinople respecting administrative and financial reforms in Turkey: 1856-1872. Note to be presented by Sir H. Bulwer to Aali Pasha [n.d.]; PRO, FO 78/2436. Instructions addressed to Her Majesty's Embassy at Constantinople respecting administrative and financial reforms in Turkey: 1856-1872. From the Foreign Office to Sir Henry Bulwer, December 31, 1861.

[19] PRO, FO 78/2436. Instructions addressed to Her Majesty's Embassy at Constantinople respecting administrative and financial reforms in Turkey: 1856-1872. From Russell to Sir Henry Bulwer, May 19, 1863.

[20] PRO, 78/2436. Instructions addressed to Her Majesty's Embassy at Constantinople respecting administrative and financial reforms in Turkey: 1856-1872. Foreign Office to Stratford de Redcliffe, July 21, 1857.

when it came to dealing with judicial and commercial business, the amount of which increased after the peace between Turkey and the Powers.[21] Many British subjects were attracted by the opening of banks and the construction of roads, railways and other commercial enterprises in the Ottoman Empire as a result of the provisions of the 1856 Reform Edict. The law which allowed foreigners to hold landed property, when executed, would afford further encouragement to British settlers. Consequently, the business of the consulate, instead of diminishing, would be greatly increased in the future.[22] Therefore, Her Majesty's Government envisaged appointing a Commission of Inquiry, which also incorporated a legal expert, Mr Hornby, to investigate the efficiency of the current judicial systems in force in the Ottoman capital.[23]

Hornby was appointed to fill the office of judge of the supreme consular court. He was instructed by the Foreign Office to keep in mind the prevailing nature of British law and rules of practice in the settlement of legal cases in Istanbul. He was also warned to take into consideration local customs and practices among the mercantile community in the Levant.[24] Hornby was asked to communicate to his government his observations about the changes and reforms he might judge necessary for the adaptation of British law to the peculiarities of the mercantile community in Istanbul. The main concern of the Foreign Office in the establishment of a judicial unit of inquiry within the consulate-general was thus the exclusive benefit of British subjects or people under British protection who had been contributing to the increase of revenue in Britain. Their benefits were after all the British government's benefits.[25]

Hornby was also supposed to develop close relations with the judicial and executive officers of the Ottoman state apparatus. In Clarendon's view, the best mode of obtaining influence was by good example. He suggested to Hornby that he should push the Turkish government to more closely imitate the legal as well as the commercial systems of Europe and that he should demonstrate by evidence and daily experience that these systems functioned better than those of Turkey. The law officers of the

[21] PRO, FO 781/9. The Earl of Clarendon to Stratford de Redcliffe, May 30, 1856 # No. 2.

[22] PRO, FO 781/9. Report of Consul-General Cumberbatch to the Commission.

[23] PRO, FO 781/9. The Earl of Clarendon to Stratford de Redcliffe, May 30, 1856 # No. 2.

[24] PRO, FO 781/9. Foreign Office, September 18, 1857. From Clarendon to Hornby.

[25] PRO, FO 781/9. Foreign Office, September 18, 1857. From Clarendon to Hornby.

Crown expected that Hornby's experience would help them to create some general principles of commercial and criminal law as a guide to consuls in the outports and to constitute a Levant code. Hornby was entrusted with the mission of devoting some portion of his time to placing the British criminal and commercial jurisdiction on secure and satisfactory foundations in the East.[26] I interpret the effort of the British government in constituting a code of the Levant as a strategy for competing with France in terms of influence over the Ottoman legal system. Since the French judicial system was conceived as an ideal type, legal reforms were extensively borrowed from the Napoleonic codes in the nineteenth century: the Ottoman Empire was no exception.[27] Some documents in the archives of the Ottoman Foreign Ministry confirm the impact of the French civil code on the Ottoman legal system and especially on the Ottoman commercial code.[28]

Nevertheless, neither the despatches of the Foreign Office nor consular reports refer to British support for the Ottoman constitutional process. Palmerston was, however, an advocate of constitutionalism in Europe. He promoted constitutionalism everywhere and interfered in the internal affairs of states for this cause. "He sent volunteers, arms and money to help the constitutionalists in Spain and Portugal. He helped them by loans in Greece, he defended constitutionalist states like Belgium and Piedmont both in word and deed".[29] However, for Turkey, Palmerston was anti-constitutional. The question of why Palmerston supported reforms and not a constitution in the Ottoman Empire is a crucial one. Every British foreign minister from Palmerston to Lansdowne, whether liberal or conservative, was indifferent to the constitutionalisation of the Ottoman Empire. In their view, the remedy in the Ottoman case was enlightened absolutism and not a constitution.[30] Between 1834 and 1839, Palmerston sent British military and naval instructors to help Mahmud II improve his finances, army and navy, but all of them found it difficult to influence the Ottomans.[31]

---

[26] PRO, FO 781/9. Foreign Office, September 18, 1857. From Clarendon to Hornby.
[27] Rubin, "Legal Borrowing", pp. 281-282.
[28] BOA, HR.SYS. 1869 D-1.
[29] Temperley, "British Policy", p. 157.
[30] Temperley, "British Policy", p. 158.
[31] Vide F. S. Rodkey, "Lord Palmerston and the Rejuvenation of Turkey, 1830-41," in *Journal of Modern History*, vol. 1 (December 1929), pp. 570-593. Cited in Temperley, "British Policy", p. 158.

In 1839, Reşid Pasha favoured parliamentary reform, but was cautious about expressing his constitutionalist ideas under Mahmud II. After the death of Mahmud, he established the representative principle in local assemblies, but he stopped there. He received no help in this from either Ponsonby, who remained ambassador until 1841, or from Stratford Canning, who returned as ambassador in 1842 and remained until 1858. Canning's idea of reform also had a purely administrative and humanitarian character. "But why did he not go further? Why did he not desire a parliamentary system as an organ for first obtaining, and then protecting, the new order?"[32] In his memorandum on reform, he said that "[t]here is no question of transferring any portion of power from the [Turkish] sovereign to his subjects".[33] A month later, Palmerston was giving the same direction to another diplomat: "Her Majesty's Government have not advised the Sultan to follow the example of Pope Pius IX and to grant constitutional institutions to the Ottoman Empire".[34]

One of the reasons why parliamentary reform was not envisaged by Stratford might be the nature of the sultan's power and the disbelief of British statesmen in the limitation of his authority:[35] the decree of the sultan had to be confirmed by the fatwa of the sheikh ül-Islam. "The Shadow of God" could not be criticised or made responsible, and the responsibility of his ministers was limited since they were the servants of the sultan. The Ottoman political system did not have political parties behind it.[36] Bulwer, who succeeded Stratford Canning as British ambassador to the Porte, continued to back financial and administrative reforms and proposed the reorganisation of the provincial assemblies and the improvement of the elective system, making it more representative: however, he did not follow any policy of parliamentarism.[37] Bulwer's objection to a parliamentary system or even an imitation of it in the provincial councils was formulated in 1862 in one of his despatches. As an alternative to the perspective of Thouvenel, who suggested establishing local councils in the provinces, he advanced the argument that "[a] Council

---

[32] Temperley, "British Policy", p. 159.

[33] [Public Record Office], F[oreign] O[ffice], 78/773. From Stratford, No. 84 of 12 March 1849, ends Memo. Cited in Temperley, "British Policy", pp. 159-160.

[34] F. O. 65/360. To Mr. Buchanan (St Petersburg), no. 102 of 20 April 1849. Cited in Temperley, "British Policy", p. 160.

[35] Temperley, "British Policy", p. 167.

[36] Temperley, "British Policy", p. 160.

[37] Engelhardt, *La Turquie et le Tanzimat*, v. 1, p. 172. Bulwer's own account is in FO 195/630, no. 224 of 26 May 1860 and FO 78/1506, no. 274 of 23 May. Cited in Temperley, "British Policy", p. 162.

here, acting as a Representative Body from the Provinces and containing naturally men of the different creeds and races that are found there would either be a mute assembly in the hands of the Government or a turbulent and contentious one tending to promote confusion and to render more deadly existing feuds".[38]

The promulgation of the Ottoman Constitution coincided in 1876 with the Balkan crisis and the Conference of Constantinople that aimed to find a solution to the Eastern Question. Like the rest of the Great Powers, Britain avoided supporting the Ottoman Constitution during the Conference. The arguments of the British government were based on the economic and political aspects of the reform question. Compared to their policy in 1856, the change in the line of British conduct was remarkable in 1876. Feelings in Britain had changed very much since the Crimean War.[39] Russell threw himself into the movement for the support of the insurgents in the European provinces of Ottoman Turkey during the Balkan crisis. He was the first statesman to break with the past and to give his hearty approval to revolt.[40]

Her Majesty's Government would not offer any assistance to the Ottoman state, as it did during the Crimean War, by elaborating a counter-argument with France against Russian claims.[41] Musurus was warned in the strongest terms that the Ottoman government could not count upon assistance from Lord Derby and Benjamin Disraeli.[42] Russophobia was an important element of pressure on Britain to change its foreign policy towards the Ottoman Empire.[43] Britain could no longer advance any convincing argument against Russian claims, according to which all former Ottoman reforms became dead letters: in their view, the Ottoman Constitution would not be an exception.[44]

The Marquis of Salisbury was appointed, conjointly with Sir Henry Elliot, British ambassador to the Porte, to represent Britain at the Conference of Constantinople in 1876.[45] The fact that Lord Salisbury did not act on behalf of the Ottoman Empire during the Conference of Constantinople

---

[38] FO 78/1649. From Bulwer, No. 132 of 19 March 1862. Cited in Temperley, "British Policy", pp. 162-163.

[39] PRO, FO 78/2450, From the Foreign Office to Elliot, May 28, 1876.

[40] PRO / 30 / 22 / 17, From Arthur Gordon to Lord Russell, January 30, 1875.

[41] PRO, FO 78/2674, Lord Derby to the Marquis of Salisbury, January 9, 1877.

[42] PRO, FO 78/2674, Lord Derby to the Marquis of Salisbury, January 9, 1877.

[43] PRO, Cf. FO 78/2476, From Elliot, November 4, 1876.

[44] See for details, MAEF, Mémoires et Documents, vol. 116. Turquie, Documents divers, 1859-67. Russian observations on the *hatt-ı humayun*.

[45] PRO, FO 78/2674, Lord Derby to the Marquis of Salisbury, November 21, 1876.

was aimed at making Russo-Turkish military confrontation inevitable. This confrontation would then allow Britain to acquire greater political and economic influence in the Near East.[46] In other words, the British government was trying to obtain some concessions from the Ottoman Empire, especially in relation to the island of Cyprus, after a Russo-Turkish war. British diplomacy did not, however, sever relations with the Ottoman state, which could engender rapprochement with Russia.[47]

Another aspect of the problem was probably the financial cost of constitutional support. It might be supposed that the new liberal ministry which came to power in 1868 would have defended the cause of parliamentary reform in the Ottoman Empire as they had done while in opposition. However, the only way to achieve this would have been to use financial influence to provoke political changes in the Ottoman Empire. Gladstone, the British prime minister, found Turkey in a financial crisis and wished to avoid wasting British money on a crumbling financial fabric.[48] In his brochure *The Bulgarian Horrors and the Question of the East*, Gladstone tried to influence public opinion to reverse British policy on the Ottoman Empire and to work in concert with other European nations for the abolition of Ottoman rule in Bulgaria.[49] The Bulgarian affair transformed European public opinion and led them to the idea that the fusion of Muslims with Christians in the Ottoman Empire was impossible.[50] In the despatches from August to September, Lord Derby asked his ambassador Sir Henry Elliot to tell the Porte that the Bulgarian catastrophe negatively influenced British sympathies towards the Ottoman Empire and that British public opinion had reached such a point that the government could not defend the Ottoman Empire in case of a military conflict with Russia.[51]

The real motive of the anti-Turk campaign was also the suspension of the payment of foreign loans in 1876.[52] "Inasmuch as the majority of

---

[46] Cf. Kirakossian, pp. 51-52.

[47] R. W. Seton-Watson, *Disraeli, Gladstone and the Eastern Question* (London: Frank Cass, 1962), p. 139. Eastern Papers. Part LXVIII, 1876-1877 (London, 1884), pp. 1094-1096. Cited in Kirakossian, p. 53.

[48] Temperley, "British Policy", p. 166.

[49] W. E. Gladstone, *Bulgarian Horrors and the Question of the East* (London: J. Murray, 1876), pp. 31-32. Cited in Kirakossian, p. 49.

[50] Mahmud Celaleddin Paşa, v. 1, p. 200.

[51] Turkey no. 1 (1876-1877). Correspondence respecting the Conference in Constantinople and the affairs in Turkey (London, 1877), p. 159. Cited in Kirakossian, p. 50.

[52] Berkes, p. 219.

the bondholders of the Ottoman loans were located in France and England, it was in these two countries that the greatest outcry was heard against the action."[53] While western diplomacy supported the Ottoman Empire against Russia before and after the Crimean War, an anti-Turkish campaign spread after the empire's financial moratorium in 1875 and the suspension of the payment of foreign loans drawn from Paris and London.[54] On October 6, 1875, Elliot received an enclosed note from Safved Pasha, the Ottoman foreign minister, transmitting an imperial order for the reduction of the interest on the foreign debt. A modification was introduced into the first project that entirely repudiated half of the interest. According to the *irade*, half of the interest could be paid in cash and the other half in bonds bearing interest at five years.[55] A similar note was also communicated to the French ambassador.[56] This declaration, which alluded to the reduction of interest on Turkey's public debt and to a financial moratorium, was considered shocking both in the empire and abroad, and shook the credibility of the Ottoman state. Even the partial payment of coupons ceased after a single payment in January 1876.[57] The British view of the matter was that the announcement of reforms by the Porte could not be accepted as sufficient for pacification. Similar kinds of general assurances had previously been offered but were executed imperfectly. The British government also did not consider the Ottoman Constitution a serious initiative. Salisbury stated that the checks upon abuses by the instruments of the new constitution were too hypothetical.[58]

Individual Agencies

The Case of Sir Henry Elliot

As a British ambassador to the Porte, Elliot followed a different line than his government towards the Ottoman Empire. The extent to which

---

[53] Donald C. Blaisdell, *European Financial Control in the Ottoman Empire* (New York, 1929), p. 81. Cited in Berkes, p. 219.

[54] Berkes, p. 224.

[55] PRO, FO 78/2388. From Elliot to Derby, October 7, 1875 # 641.

[56] PRO, FO 78/2388. From Elliot to Derby, October 7, 1875 # 643.

[57] Edhem Eldem, *A History of the Ottoman Bank* (Istanbul: Ottoman Bank Historical Research Center, 1999), pp. 128-132.

[58] PRO, FO 881/3045. From the Marquis of Salisbury to the Earl of Derby, January 4, 1877.

Elliot represented official British policy is quite vague. His correspondence with the Foreign Office shows that he disagreed with many aspects
of British policy, especially in the shaping of the provincial structure in
the Balkans. According to him, the European Powers had only an imperfect acquaintance with the real state of affairs in Herzegovina. Most
people felt sympathy for the Christian populations rising against Muslim
domination and misrule. However, in his view, "it would be a complete
mistake to attribute the present movement to the grievances of which the
populations of the Herzegovina may have a legitimate right to complain".
According to him, these grievances were much more the pretext than
the cause of the insurrection, which was in fact the result of the great
national Slavic movement fostered by Russia and, in recent years, encouraged by Austria. Superficial observers attributed these agitations to resistance against tithe extractions or acts of fiscal extortion. He stated that
the remedies proposed in Herzegovina were chimerical.[59]

Elliot considered two alternatives, which could offer the prospect of the
maintenance of order and tranquillity in the province. If the Turks were
to be expelled from the region, there were two options: one was Bosnia's
annexation to Serbia, which would no doubt encounter the resistance of
Austria. The other was its incorporation into Austria, which would be
opposed by the inhabitants of the province. Bosnia might be of no great
financial benefit to the empire, he said, but it could provide the largest
number of troops for the imperial service. Nothing would induce the sultan or his government to sacrifice an important Muslim population by
leaving them at the mercy of a hostile Christian majority. He argued that
the abuses and maladministration that occurred under Ottoman rule should
not be underestimated but that any attempt towards withdrawing of the
northern province from the direct administration of the Ottoman capital
would lead to further dismemberment.[60] According to Elliot, the concern
of the Ottoman Empire should be to place the Slavic populations in as
good a position as those of Austria from the standpoint of land tenure.[61]

Although the British government officially adhered to the Andrassy
Note, Elliot criticised it on the grounds that the reforms suggested by
Andrassy had been already adopted by the Porte through the firman of

---

[59] PRO, FO 78/2386, From Elliot to Derby, September 3, 1875 # no. 512.
[60] PRO, FO 78/2386, From Elliot to Derby, September 3, 1875 # no. 512.
[61] PRO, FO 78/2390, Sir Henry Elliot to the Earl of Derby, November 21, 1875 #
no. 770.

December 12, 1875, which was communicated to the embassies a day before it was promulgated. They could not ask the Porte to communicate the same principles a second time through the Andrassy Note.[62] Contrary to the Russian policy of providing Bosnia, Herzegovina and Bulgaria with a large measure of local autonomy without political separation, Elliot maintained that any mention of the word "autonomy" as applied to Bulgaria should be avoided.[63] The British ambassador was anxious about the Russian project, especially since Russia interpreted the term "administrative autonomy" in different ways. This divergence over terminology was the heart of the problem. Elliot left to the Porte, which he judged the most competent body, the care of applying the reforms and regulating local affairs as well as the guarantees against arbitrary power.[64] According to him, the Ottoman government should rely on its own resources to suppress the insurrection and should deal with it as a "local outbreak" instead of giving it international importance by asking for the support of the other Powers. If vigorous measures had been taken at the outbreak of the insurrection for the restoration of order, it would not have attained such proportions and there would not have been any grounds for proposing a consular mission to the disturbed districts. A consular mission was incompatible with the independent authority of the Porte and would lead to foreign sympathy vis-à-vis the insurrection as well as to further diplomatic interference in the internal affairs of the Ottoman Empire.[65]

By the end of 1875, Midhad gradually announced the content of his constitutional project to Elliot.[66] Elliot communicated his positive ideas on Midhad Pasha to his government. In his view, Midhad was the most energetic and liberal of Turkish statesmen and a man of action and active thought: he always advocated equality between Christians and Muslims and wished to exert control over the power wielded by the grand vizier as well as the sultan. He was opposed to centralisation and in favour of giving the provincial populations much autonomy in their own affairs. He spoke strongly to Elliot against the grant of special institutions to Slavic provinces. He was hated, Elliot argued, by General Ignatieff, who

---

[62] PRO, FO 78/2469, From Henry Elliot, January 4, 1876.
[63] PRO, FO 78/2474, From Henry Elliot, September 22, 1876.
[64] MAEF, CP, September-November, 1876, vol. 406. From Charles de Moüy to Decazes, November 8, 1876.
[65] PRO, FO 78/2448, From Derby to Elliot, January 25, 1876 # no. 52.
[66] PRO, FO 78/2391, Elliot to Derby, December 14, 1875 # no. 831.

spoke of him as a brigand and madman. The dislike was reciprocal. He was the hope of reformist Muslims and Christians, but was disliked by conservative Muslims.[67] Ignatieff also spread the rumour that Midhad Pasha would revolt against the Ottoman state by mobilising the power of public opinion and change the political regime of the Ottoman Empire within palace circles.[68] Elliot spoke of Midhad as if he were the head of a movement of regeneration for the Ottoman Empire, which seemed to him quite ready for the inauguration of a constitutional regime: he also expressed his admiration for the softas.[69]

In his despatches to the Foreign Office, Elliot clearly defended the Ottoman constitutional project. He observed that the extension and real application of the law of the *vilayet*s would offer a better perspective than any other scheme proposed for better provincial administration and for the improvement of the conditions of the people.[70] Elliot recognised that the weakness of the government and the inability of its agents to break the influence of people of local importance constituted the greatest part of provincial maladministration and were the subject of most of the complaints addressed by the different classes of the empire. However, the establishment of foreign control would create an *imperium in imperio* and would render provincial government nearly impossible. Although the Powers were only interested in Christians, he said, the whole administration required reform, and harmony between the two races would not be attained by placing one of them under foreign guardianship while the other part had to rely upon Turkish officials.[71]

There was, for him, reason to believe that the new Ottoman sovereign wanted to inaugurate a new order and his sincerity should be tested without putting the administration of the empire under foreign control.[72] The creation of a Senate and a representative assembly in the capital might

[67] PRO, FO 78/2476, From Elliot, December 19, 1876.

[68] Midhad Paşa, *Tabsıra-i İbret*, v. 1, p. 264.

[69] MAEF, Papier Decazes Fonds nominatifs PA-AP 54 vol. 7, 1875-1877. Here May 24, 1876. From M. de Bourgoing, French ambassador to Duc Decazes, French foreign minister.

[70] PRO, FO 78/2674, Lord Derby to the Marquis of Salisbury, November 20, 1876.

[71] PRO, FO 198/42. Turkey no. 1 (1877). Correspondence respecting the affairs of Turkey, presented to both Houses of Parliament by Command of Her Majesty, 1877. From Sir Henry Elliot to the Earl of Derby, October 20, 1876.

[72] PRO, FO 198/42. Turkey no. 1 (1877). Correspondence respecting the affairs of Turkey, presented to both Houses of Parliament by Command of Her Majesty, 1877. From Sir Henry Elliot to the Earl of Derby, October 20, 1876.

seem surprising and the manner in which these institutions would work doubtful, but in any case they would institute useful control over the actions of the different departments of the state. The scheme of provincial administration was the one on which the prosperity and the future condition of the population would be built. He maintained that, instead of granting exceptional privileges to the insurgent provinces, he was convinced that the Porte should adopt the only line of conduct that could be followed with safety and "without the certainty of giving rise to fresh movements in the less privileged Provinces, and of increasing the strong animosity already existing between the rival Christian races".[73] Elliot expressed the idea that the Italian government was mistaken in supporting the notion that Russian influence be increased by including the Greek provinces in a general measure of reform. Once privileges were given to the Slavs, the Greeks would begin agitating anew for similar benefits.[74]

In November 1876, *The Times* published a letter arguing that the grand vizier, upon the suggestion and encouragement of Sir Henry Elliot, was putting forward restrictions which the representatives of the guaranteeing Powers would not have any difficulty overruling. The British government denied these allegations.[75] However, it seems that rumours were circulating in the opposite direction: "Sir Henry Elliot would not fail to advise the Porte to do everything in its power by administrative reforms to facilitate the restoration of peace".[76] These rumours even reached Count Schouvaloff, Russian ambassador to London, and General Ignatieff. Upon the statements of Elliot that Britain would abandon the project of reform it had suggested and that the project advanced by Midhad Pasha was preferable to the system of local autonomy, the Russian representatives asked Lord Derby the extent to which Elliot was representing the British government.[77]

---

[73] PRO, FO 198/42. Turkey no. 1 (1877). Correspondence respecting the affairs of Turkey, presented to both Houses of Parliament by Command of Her Majesty, 1877. From Henry Elliot to the Earl of Derby, October 12, 1876.

[74] PRO, FO 78/2475, From Elliot, October 29, 1876.

[75] PRO, FO 78/2682. From the Earl of Derby to Sir Henry Elliot, November 23, 1876.

[76] PRO, FO 198/42. Turkey no. 1 (1877). Correspondence respecting the affairs of Turkey, presented to both Houses of Parliament by Command of Her Majesty, 1877. From Sir A. Buchanan to the Earl of Derby, June 28, 1876.

[77] PRO, FO 198/42. Turkey no. 1 (1877). Correspondence respecting the affairs of Turkey, presented to both Houses of Parliament by Command of Her Majesty, 1877. From the Earl of Derby to Lord A. Loftus, October 26, 1876.

Elliot's presence was the principal obstacle to the Russian provincial project. General Ignatieff was probably making every effort to eliminate Elliot from the Conference of Constantinople. If Elliot was removed, the Conference would remain in the hands of the Russian ambassador: the other ambassadors would not be in a position to stand up to him.[78] Salisbury was, for Ignatieff, a less unfriendly adversary compared to Elliot. Ignatieff feared the charming aspect of liberal reforms conceded by the Sublime Porte; this would render his struggle more difficult. He tried to negotiate with Ottoman ministers to convince them that the shortest road was to arrange matters directly with Russia and not to submit to the humiliation of a conference.[79] He succeeded in convincing the conservative strata of Ottoman ministers that the promulgation of the constitution would harm the results of the Conference. He also succeeded in discrediting Midhad Pasha. Zichy, the Austro-Hungarian ambassador, denied the virtues of the Ottoman Constitution, an attitude which gave more power to General Ignatieff and the conservative Ottoman ministers.[80] Unlike Baron Prokesch Osten, who acted in complete harmony with the British embassy and frustrated the plans of Russian diplomats, Zichy was a *persona gratissima* to the Russians.[81] Elliot did not hide his hostility towards Ignatieff. Unlike Ignatieff, who was opposed to the promulgation of reforms, Elliot was recommending their immediate publication. He even had a private audience with the sultan and insisted on this conclusion.[82]

"To the accusation of being a blind partisan of the Turks", Elliot responded that his conduct was never guided by "any sentimental affection for them", but by the principles of a former foreign policy which considered the dismantlement of the Ottoman Empire a principal threat to Britain's interests.[83] Elliot stated in private correspondence that the

---

[78] MAEF, Papier Decazes Fonds nominatifs PA-AP 54 vol. 7, 1875-1877. Here October 26, 1876. From M. de Bourgoing, French ambassador to Duc Decazes, French foreign minister.

[79] MAEF, Papiers d'agents, Duc Decazes (Louis-Charles), agents spéciaux, Vienne, Rome, Berlin, Constantinople, 1873-77, vol. 5. Here Constantinople, November 14, 1876.

[80] MAEF, Papiers d'agents, Duc Decazes (Louis-Charles), agents spéciaux, Vienne, Rome, Berlin, Constantinople, 1873-77, vol. 5. Here Constantinople, November 27, 1876.

[81] Sir Henry G. Elliot, *Some Revolutions and Other Diplomatic Experiences*, edited by his daughter (Gertrude Elliot), (London: John Murray, 1922), pp. 204-205.

[82] MAEF, PA-AP 122, Correspondance politique du Comte de Moüy, 1876-78, no. 37, vol. 1. November 28?, 1876.

[83] PRO, FO 198/42. Turkey no. 1 (1877). Correspondence respecting the affairs of Turkey, presented to both Houses of Parliament by Command of Her Majesty, 1877. From Sir Henry Elliot to the Earl of Derby, September 4, 1876.

maintenance of Turkish authority was a political necessity. The proposal to turn Bosnia and Herzegovina into an autonomous tributary state was an absurd remedy that would lead Muslim and Christian populations to civil war.[84]

Elliot reacted strongly to General Ignatieff's suggestion that implied the exclusion of a Turkish representative from the Conference of Constantinople: "If a Conference is to end by decisions which are to be imposed upon the Porte, sufficient violence will be done to the feelings of the Turks as an independent nation without the additional humiliation of their being concerted by foreign Representatives in their own capital".[85] He reminded them of Article 9 of the Treaty of Paris, according to which the Powers promised not to interfere individually or collectively in relations between the sultan and his subjects or in the internal administration of the country. The Powers had, according to him, the formal right to intimate to the Porte that they would not abstain from interference until the reforms promised by the Reform Edict were fully carried out. But if the Powers directly proposed the measures by which the reforms were brought into practice or directly superintended their application, this could cause disappointment to those who wished for real progress in the empire. Elliot suggested that the Porte be given time for the realisation of reforms that would secure equality to all races.

Unlike Gortchakoff, Elliot considered the upheavals provoked by the Young Ottomans the beginning of a liberal tendency which would limit the power of the sultan and start a new constitutional era. In Gortchakoff's view, these upheavals would destabilise the Ottoman government and end in chaos.[86] For the French, the continuation of these revolutionary movements meant the gradual loss of the sultan's throne.[87] French diplomatic archives describe Elliot as somebody who encouraged the Turks in their resistance. All the arguments that they heard from the mouths of the Turks in order to justify their attitude,

[84] PRO / 30 / 22 / 17, From Elliot to Russell, September 11, 1876.

[85] PRO, FO 198/42. Turkey no. 1 (1877). Correspondence respecting the affairs of Turkey, presented to both Houses of Parliament by Command of Her Majesty, 1877. From Sir Henry Elliot to the Earl of Derby, October 20, 1876.

[86] MAEF, Papier Decazes Fonds nominatifs PA-AP 54, vol. 7, 1875-1877. From Gortchakoff to Count Schouvaloff, May 14/26, 1876.

[87] MAEF, Papier Decazes Fonds nominatifs PA-AP 54 vol. 7, 1875-1877. Here May 24, 1876. From M. de Bourgoing, French ambassador to Duc Decazes, French foreign minister.

stated Bourgoing, the French ambassador to the Porte, were also expressed by Elliot himself.[88]

When the Conference of Constantinople ended on January 20, 1877, Sir Henry Elliot was called to England in order to report upon the state of affairs in Turkey in accordance with the instructions of Her Majesty's Government, which appreciated his desire to continue at his post given its effect on his health.[89] The subsequent removal of Elliot was interpreted in different ways. One interpretation was that, after the emergence of the Eastern Question in 1876, Disraeli intended to change the British ambassador to the Porte and informed the queen that he would replace him with Sir Henry Layard:[90] "What we want is a man of the necessary experience and commanding mind at this moment in Constantinople–and one not too scrupulous. But such men are rare everywhere".[91] Gladstone and the Liberals considered Layard pro-Turkish; when they returned to power in 1880, they sent George Goschen as a special ambassador.[92] Sir Henry Elliot's removal in 1877 by Disraeli was interpreted as a means for the British government to attempt to act in concert with the other Great Powers to exercise pressure; equally, "a new representative ... would have more weight with the Porte than one whom they have looked upon as Turkish as themselves".[93] Sir George Campbell, for instance, expressed his ideas on Elliot in the following terms:[94] "The British Embassy and its surroundings have been the very focus of philo-Turk and anti-Russian feeling". He did not see any peaceful settlement of the Eastern Question unless Elliot was recalled from Istanbul: in this way, the British hoped to show that they had abandoned the pro-Turkish policy. If Elliot remained British ambassador, the Turks would have difficulties

---

[88] MAEF, Papier Decazes Fonds nominatifs PA-AP 54 vol. 7, 1875-1877. Here May 24, 1876. From M. de Bourgoing, French ambassador to Duc Decazes, French foreign minister.

[89] PRO, FO 198/42. Turkey no. 2 (1877). Correspondence respecting the Conference at Constantinople and the affairs of Turkey, 1876-77, presented to both Houses of Parliament by Command of Her Majesty, 1877. The Earl of Derby to Sir Henry Elliot, February 5, 1877.

[90] Royal Archives H11/272, Disraeli to Queen Victoria, 22 December 1876. Cited in Jones, p. 178.

[91] G. Waterfield, *Layard of Nineveh* (London: J. Murray, 1963), pp. 355-356. Cited in Jones, p. 178.

[92] Jones, pp. 178-179.

[93] Originals in Royal Archives C35/43, 44. Cited in Jones, p. 179.

[94] George Campbell, *A Handy Book on the Eastern Question. Being a very recent view of Turkey* (London: John Murray, 1876). Cited in the *The Times*, December 11, 1876.

becoming aware of the change in policy. "He is an old diplomatist of the old school, bred in that policy of supporting the Turk which has hitherto been followed by Whig and Tory alike".[95] Elliot expressed his antagonism toward General Ignatieff and his support of the Turks so openly that he was accused of "a want of discretion and prudence".[96]

A Russian Scheme: an American-Authored Autonomy of Bulgaria

Nineteenth-century Russian policy aimed at attracting the different ethnic layers of Ottoman society through protectionist discourse. The Russian government even gained influence over a number of Ottoman functionaries.[97] After the defeat of France by Prussia in 1870, French influence at the Porte and the palace weakened while the Russian impact gained ascendency.[98] Russian ideas even made some progress in Istanbul and in the councils of the Ottoman government. Russian action also influenced some ministers of the sultan.[99] The Grand Vizier Mahmud Nedim Pasha was even nicknamed Nedimoff because of his pro-Russian tendencies.[100]

The scheme regarding administrative autonomy for the province of Bulgaria authored by Schuyler, American secretary of legation to the Porte, and Prince Tsereteleff, second secretary of the Russian embassy, was confidentially communicated by Ignatieff to Salisbury. This scheme differed very little from the proposals attributed to the Russian government by the *Cologne Gazette*.[101] General Ignatieff was the indirect author of the scheme requiring an autonomous Bulgaria. The French considered the Russian scheme a serious threat to the Treaty of Paris, as Russia would again play the role of protector of oppressed Ottoman Christians.[102] Regardless of whether because Ignatieff could convince the British or not,

---

[95] *The Times*, December 11, 1876.

[96] *The Times*, December 11, 1876.

[97] MAEF, Papiers d'agents, Duc Decazes (Louis-Charles), agents spéciaux, Vienne, Rome, Berlin, Constantinople, 1873-77, vol. 5. Here Constantinople, October 30, 1875.

[98] Davison, *Nineteenth-Century Ottoman Diplomacy and Reforms*, p. 111.

[99] MAEF, Papiers d'agents, Duc Decazes (Louis-Charles), agents spéciaux, Vienne, Rome, Berlin, Constantinople, 1873-77, vol. 5. Here Constantinople, October 30, 1875.

[100] See also Mahmud Celaleddin Paşa, v. 1, p. 60.

[101] PRO, FO 78/2680, From Salisbury to Derby, December 8, 1876.

[102] MAEF, Papier Decazes Fonds nominatifs PA-AP 54 vol. 7, 1875-1877. Here October 26, 1876. From M. de Bourgoing, French ambassador to Duc Decazes, French foreign minister.

Britain's stance also evolved towards concepts of autonomy and self-government in the administration of Ottoman provinces.[103] "Her Majesty's Government believed that if some such system of local self-government could be established, it would form the best guarantee for the well-being of these provinces, and open the way to the general adoption of reformed and constitutional Government throughout the Turkish Empire".[104]

Eugene Schuyler (1840-90) was America's "best-qualified diplomat, one of its first PhDs, and a friend of Tolstoy, translator of Turgenev, and biographer of Peter the Great".[105] After graduating from Yale College in 1859, he entered law school at Columbia College in New York City. He studied Russian[106] and completed his doctorate at Yale in classical philology in 1861.[107] The American reception of Russian writers (Turgenev, Tolstoy, etc.) started with his translations.[108] His interest in Russian literature and his closeness to famous Russian writers gained him access to famous literary salons and political circles.[109]

Schuyler became one of America's first Russian experts after having served the United States in Russia for a decade.[110] He was appointed American consul in Moscow in 1866.[111] During his two years there, he made a long trip to Orenburg, a military centre from whence Russian armies were adding large areas of Muslim Central Asia to the empire: this was a region in which Schuyler was interested.[112] In 1873, he was officially invited there by General Konstantin Kaufman, Russia's military governor in Central Asia.[113] American diplomatic posts were lower-level legations directed by ministers rather than by ambassadors. Most were made up of one subordinate officer, the secretary of the legation.[114] Based on his experience in Turkic-speaking Central Asia, Schuyler

---

[103] PRO, FO 78/2674, Lord Derby to the Marquis of Salisbury, November 20, 1876.

[104] PRO, FO 78/2674, Lord Derby to the Marquis of Salisbury, November 20, 1876.

[105] Peter Bridges, "Eugene Schuyler, the Only Diplomatist," *Diplomacy and Statecraft*, 16 (2005), pp. 13-22. Here p. 13.

[106] Bridges, p. 14.

[107] Ralph P. Rosenberg, "Eugene Schuyler's Doctor of Philosophy Degree: A Theory Concerning the Dissertation," *The Journal of Higher Education*, vol. 33, no. 7 (October 1962), pp. 381-386. Here, p. 386.

[108] Rosenberg, p. 385.

[109] Bridges, p. 14.

[110] Bridges, p. 13.

[111] Bridges, p. 14.

[112] R. J. Jensen, "Eugene Schuyler and the Balkan Crisis," *Diplomatic History*, vol. 5, no. 1 (Winter 1981), pp. 23-39; here 25. Cited in Bridges, p. 15.

[113] Bridges, p. 16.

[114] Bridges, p. 15.

considered himself qualified to become minister in Istanbul. He failed
to get the position, but he was appointed in 1876 to a dual commission
as secretary of the legation and consul-general under the new minister
Horace Maynard.[115]

Soon after his arrival to Istanbul in 1876, Maynard was confronted
with the Bulgarian crisis. Schuyler was sent to the Bulgarian province
to investigate. He was also joined by Prince Tsereteleff.[116] Schuyler's
job was to report to his minister in Istanbul, who would then report to
Washington. But this was not enough for Schuyler, who was interested
in publishing a book on Russia and Central Asia when he was in
St Petersburg and wrote a number of articles about Russia for *Scribner's
Magazine*. On August 29, 1876, his friend MacGahan, a journalist who
accompanied him to the Bulgarian province, published the text of
Schuyler's preliminary report to Maynard in his London paper.[117]
"It was taken as authoritative, coming from an American official".[118]
The report inspired William Gladstone to write his pamphlet about the
"atrocities in Bulgaria". Gladstone's pamphlet had an influential impact
on public opinion in Europe, particularly in the Balkans, Russia and
Britain.[119] Schuyler continued to meet Prince Tsereteleff when he
returned to the American legation in Istanbul and helped the Russians
to draft a constitution for an autonomous Bulgaria without authorisation
from Washington.[120]

The United States was thus unknowingly involved in the constitutional
arrangement of Bulgaria through the activities of Eugene Schuyler.
Schuyler acted as an instrument of Russian policy and was involved in
the drafting of the Bulgarian Constitution by Ignatieff.[121] "Ignatieff
involved Schuyler in the writing of the Constitution of Bulgaria not only
because of his knowledge of law and his sympathy for Bulgarians, but
also because he was credible."[122] Ignatieff's main plan was to engage
Schuyler in such a way that the constitutional draft would be in harmony
with the Russian political agenda and so that Russia could convince

[115] Bridges, p. 16.
[116] Bridges, p. 17.
[117] Bridges, p. 18.
[118] Bridges, p. 18.
[119] Patricia Herlihy, "Eugene Schuyler and the Bulgarian Constitution of 1876," in
Ferdinand Feldbrugge (ed.), *Russia, Europe, and the Rule of Law* (Leiden & Boston:
Martinus Nijhoff Publishers, 2007), pp. 165-167.
[120] Bridges, p. 18.
[121] Herlihy, pp. 169-171.
[122] Herlihy, p. 171.

the European diplomats who assembled in Istanbul to discuss the Eastern Question within the framework of the Conference of Constantinople through a neutral and competent personality.[123] Schuyler also authored a book entitled *Turkistan; Notes of a Journey in Russian Turkistan, Khokand, Bukhara, and Kuldja*[124] in 1876 when the Ottoman Constitution was drafted. It would be interesting to investigate further how his impressions of these provinces were received by the Ottomans at a moment when provincial reform was being undertaken.

The Russian scheme was also a local reform in that it developed a set of measures applicable to Bosnia, Herzegovina and Bulgaria. However, in contrast to the Andrassy Note, the reform process would be carried out not only through the use of local populations but also by two international commissions of control appointed by the guaranteeing Powers so that they could monitor the execution of regulations and assist local authorities in different measures affecting order and public safety. For instance, in Bosnia, Herzegovina and Bulgaria, Christian governors-general (*vali*s) would be appointed, as in Lebanon, by the Porte for five years, but only with the consent of the guaranteeing Powers. The *vali* could also be a foreigner if there were no suitable Ottoman subjects available. The international commission of supervision would also penetrate the Ottoman judicial system: half of the judges in civil and criminal tribunals would be nominated by the *vali*s with the assent of the Administrative Council and the other half by the international commission. The members of the Court of Appeal would be appointed by the Porte on the recommendation of the *vali*s and with the assent of the Powers.

In addition to religious freedom and the improvement of rural conditions, the Russian project further developed principles of decentralisation, self-government, popular representation and election in the provincial administration. Compared to former British reform proposals, this plan went still further by defending the principle of autonomy.

Bulgaria would thus constitute an autonomous province of the Ottoman Empire. The administrative unit would be the canton (*nahiye*), with an average of 5,000 to 10,000 inhabitants. Muslims and Christians would be grouped into distinct cantons. The cantons would possess a large

---

[123] Marin V. Pundeff, *Bulgaria in American Perspective: Political and Cultural Issues* (Boulder, CO: Columbia University Press, 1994), note 28, 231, n. 84. Cited in Herlihy, p. 172.

[124] Eugene Schuyler, *Turkistan; Notes of a Journey in Russian Turkistan, Khokand, Bukhara, and Kuldja* (New York: Scribner, Armstrong & Co, 1876).

degree of self-government through the cantonal council. They would administer themselves and would deal, without any interference from superior authorities, with the distribution of taxes, the construction and maintenance of roads, the organisation of police, etc. The inhabitants, without any distinction of creed, would elect a cantonal council composed of the delegates of each commune. The mayor would be placed at the head of this council and the canton: he would be selected by the governors-general from three candidates elected by the cantonal council.

Tax farming and the tithe would be completely abolished. Provincial assemblies would deliberate publicly and control finances. Provincial assemblies and cantonal councils would have the power to collect taxes. They would draw up the provincial budget. The assembly of the province would establish general regulations related to taxation. The provincial assembly and the cantonal councils would have the right to vote additional taxes for the needs of the province or of the cantons. Thus, the Russian scheme aimed to confer the control of revenue and local expenditure onto provincial assemblies and cantonal councils. A sum would be fixed by the commission, not exceeding one third of the average revenue of the province, to be paid to the Porte for public debt and general expenses annually for five years. The rest of the revenue would be assigned to the requirements of the central government and to the province. Prefects of departments would be appointed by governors among Christians or Muslims according to the dominant creed.

The scheme strengthened Christian religious institutions by recognising the exclusive jurisdiction of ecclesiastical authorities and courts for special cases concerning religious matters: local languages in the tribunals and public administration were put on the same footing as Turkish. The Russian scheme also prohibited the employment of irregular troops and stipulated the formation of a local militia. A militia and a gendarmerie would be formed with the participation of Christians according to their proportion of the general population. Subaltern officers would be named by the governor-general. The police would be formed by the governors (*mutasarrif*s) among Christians and Muslims according to their proportion of the general population. Ignatieff also proposed the employment of neutral forces, which would consist of 6,000 Belgians or Italians.[125]

---

[125] PRO, FO 78/2680, From Salisbury to Derby, December 9, 1876 # no. 14. FO 78/2680, From Salisbury to Derby, December 17, 1876. FO 78/2686, 6ème Protocole, Séance du 27 décembre 1876 & 8 janvier 1877.

The Austrian Scheme: the Andrassy Note

The process of the elaboration and promulgation of the Ottoman Constitution of 1876 was overshadowed by the Eastern Question. Following the crisis in the Balkans, a possible solution for Bosnia-Herzegovina was proposed on December 30, 1875 by the Andrassy Note (named after the Austro-Hungarian foreign minister) and approved by the five Great Powers.[126] The proposal contained in Count Andrassy's despatch of December 30 obtained the support of the British Cabinet and constituted the basis of general consent.[127]

The process in which the Andrassy Note took shape before the Conference of Constantinople offers a perfect example of how each of the Great Powers invariably formed their policy in correspondence with those of the others. In the aftermath of rebellions in Bosnia and Herzegovina, the Ottoman effort to promulgate new reforms in order to satisfy the insurgents becomes an instrument of rivalry and negotiations between Russia, Austria and Britain. However, the rivalry was not only intergovernmental. Opinion was also divided within the different political circles of each government.

It was proposed to Lord Clarendon that the Powers should give no choice to Turkey with regard to the acceptance of the Austrian note and warn it that if it refused to accept the note both in word and substance, they could no longer aid it in its contest with Russia. When the note arrived in Istanbul, Ottoman ministers interpreted it as a threat to the independence of Turkey and as the establishment of a Russian protectorate over the Christian subjects of the empire. On August 26, Lord Aberdeen, a member of the House of Lords, informed his fellow peers that the Porte desired to alter the note and expressed his doubt as to whether Russia would accept the modifications. The attempt to revise it

---

[126] PRO, FO 198/42. Turkey no. 1 (1877). Correspondence respecting the affairs of Turkey. Presented to both Houses of Parliament by Command of Her Majesty, 1877. From Prince Gortchakoff to Count Schouvaloff (communicated to the Earl of Derby by Count Schouvaloff), November 27, 1876.

[127] PRO, FO 198/42. Turkey no. 1 (1877). Correspondence respecting the affairs of Turkey. Presented to both Houses of Parliament by Command of Her Majesty, 1877. From Prince Gortchakoff to Count Schouvaloff (communicated to the Earl of Derby by Count Schouvaloff), November 27, 1876. MAEF, Mémoires et Documents, vol. 101. Turquie. Conférence de Constantinople, 1876-1877. Documents divers, Réunions préparatoires, Protocoles. Here Response of the Porte to the Andrassy Note by Rashid Pasha, Ottoman Foreign Minister, February 13, 1876.

failed because of irreconcilable differences within the British Cabinet.[128] For the French, the Andrassy Note was a repetition of the principles of the 1856 Reform Edict.[129] Consequently, the Powers themselves (and the different wings within each of the Powers) could not come to an agreement on how the Andrassy Note was to be modified.

Unlike Prince Gortchakoff, Count Andrassy strongly objected to the idea of granting autonomy to Bosnia and Herzegovina. Andrassy agreed with Lord Derby that the insurgents should be content with reforms already proposed provided that there were proper guarantees for their execution. If the proposals went beyond reforms, this could strengthen the fanatical party in Istanbul. For the British, it was problematic for a foreign government to frame a scheme of administration for a Turkish province. There were local peculiarities, tendencies and customs which should be taken into account and which only local knowledge could judge.[130] However, as far as discussions advanced, Britain and the rest of the Powers evolved towards the idea of granting administrative autonomy to the disturbed provinces.[131]

The process before the promulgation of the Andrassy Note depicts even better the sharpness of the European rivalry and the extent to which notes, decrees and schemes, which differed from one another not so much in terms of their content but in their forms of coercion and priorities, were proclaimed one after the other just to dominate the discourse of reform. Hence, in September 1875, some months before the proclamation of the note, Sir Henry Elliot told the grand vizier that the Porte should give evidence of its determination to remedy the grievances expressed in the northern provinces. If this was not done, the governments interested in the maintenance of tranquillity in the region would propose some special measures to satisfy the people.[132]

In a confidential despatch to Derby, Elliot reported that Andrassy was trying to persuade the German and Russian governments and that these three Powers would agree upon a project for the administration of Bosnia.[133] Ignatieff told him in strict confidence that Adrassy's proposal,

---

[128] PRO / 30 / 22 / 17, From Arthur Gordon to Lord Russell, January 30, 1875.

[129] MAEF, CP, January-April, 1876, vol. 403. From Decazes to Bourgoing. January 9, 1876.

[130] PRO, FO 881/3066.

[131] PRO, FO 881/3066.

[132] PRO, FO 78/2387, From Elliot to Derby, September 21,1875 # no. 577.

[133] PRO, FO 78/2388, Elliot to the Earl of Derby, October 3, 1875.

though not liked by the Russian government, had been accepted in St Petersburg.[134] Elliot was alarmed by Ignatieff and the idea that the Austrian project was seen with favour by the Russian government. Following Ignatieff's message, Elliot immediately alarmed the grand vizier and the Ottoman foreign minister in order to urge the Porte to make satisfactory administrative reforms for the Christian population in Bosnia and Herzegovina. His intention was to "defeat the object of the Austro-Hungarian Government".[135]

Although the Andrassy Note was the outcome of views exchanged between the three courts of Austria-Hungary, Russia and Germany, Ignatieff's intention was to provoke the Porte into dismissing the Andrassy Note.[136] For that reason, Ignatieff presented the Andrassy Note as a project harmful to Ottoman dignity.[137] His ambition was to prevent Austria from becoming a protector of Slavic populations in the eyes of the Christians of Turkey.[138] He successively continued to provoke Elliot and pretended to express his preference for negotiating Ottoman reforms with the guaranteeing Powers.[139] In fact, his attitude was duplicitous. The Russian side was trying to give the impression that they were maintaining the Ottoman Empire's right to independence whilst also shoving all the blame for Herzegovina upon the Austro-Hungarian government.[140]

From the correspondence of Elliot with the Earl of Derby on December 1, 1875, it is clear that the Ottoman Council of Ministers approved most of the new reforms and that they would be promulgated in a few days.[141] However, it seems that the Austrian ambassador to the Porte, by order of Count Andrassy, urged the grand vizier not to promulgate any new project of reform. The Austrians, Elliot wrote, insisted on the determination of reforms by the concert of the Powers who had signed the

---

[134] PRO, FO 78/2388, Elliot to the Earl of Derby, October 8, 1875 # no. 648.

[135] PRO, FO 78/2388, Elliot to the Earl of Derby, October 15, 1875.

[136] MAEF, CP, January-April, 1876, vol. 403. From Bourgoing to Decazes, January 3, 1876, no. 1.

[137] MAEF, CP, January-April, 1876, vol. 403. From Bourgoing to Decazes, January 12, 1876, no. 7.

[138] MAEF, CP, January-April, 1876, vol. 403. From Bourgoing to Decazes, January 19, 1876, no. 11.

[139] PRO, FO 78/2390, Elliot to the Earl of Derby, November 6, 1875.

[140] PRO, FO 78/2390, Elliot to the Earl of Derby, November 11, 1875 # no. 739.

[141] PRO, FO 78/2391, Sir Henry Elliot to the Earl of Derby, December 1st, 1875 # no. 803.

Treaty of Paris. The British recommended, however, that the required reforms should be promptly brought into practice unless the Austrian government presented satisfactory reasons for their delay. "Rashid Pasha believes", Elliot wrote, "that Count Andrassy's object is to cause it to appear that the initiative of the concessions proceeds from him".[142] All this interference clearly demonstrates that the main struggle of the Powers was not for reform itself but about which government would play a dominant role in the reform processes.

After the Austrian and Russian interventions, the British government was not slow to dominate the process. Elliot's suggestion was to send an official note to the foreign representatives in which it would be communicated that a new reform decree was issued by the sultan "for the purpose of putting all his subjects upon the footing of equality which they had not hitherto fully enjoyed".[143] Hence, the decree ordering the reforms was communicated to the embassies with provisions agreeing to Elliot's suggestions.[144] The Porte's policy was thus to adhere to the propositions of Count Andrassy by sanctioning them with its own imperial order, which then became a part of Ottoman legislation.[145] The imperial firman of December 12, 1875, relayed general provisions on the reorganisation of the Ottoman court system, taxation, property, the rights and privileges of different communities, and religious freedom, but added almost nothing new to former decrees. More importantly, the firman recognised that non-Muslims had been deprived of the right of land ownership in some parts of the Ottoman Empire and affirmed that the relevant law would be applied equally to all subjects in the future. In fact, the right of land ownership was also something on which the Andrassy Note would elaborate.[146] Elliot's support for the promulgation of the firman regarding new reforms in the insurgent provinces prior to the release of the Andrassy Note may be interpreted as an effort to prevent any reform project from being authored by the rival Powers.

Elliot was authorised to give general support to the proposals contained in the Andrassy Note in late January 1876.[147] Despite the official

---

[142] PRO, FO 78/2391, Sir Henry Elliot to the Earl of Derby, December 8, 1875 # no. 814.
[143] PRO, FO 78/2391, Sir Henry Elliot to the Earl of Derby, December 10, 1875.
[144] PRO, FO 78/2391, Sir Henry Elliot to the Earl of Derby, December 14, 1875.
[145] Cited in MAEF, CP, January-April, 1876, vol. 403.
[146] PRO, FO 78/2391, Sir Henry Elliot to the Earl of Derby, December 14, 1875.
[147] PRO, FO 78/2448, From Derby to Elliot, January 25,1876 # no. 52.

authorisation of his government, he did not hide the fact that Britain was constrained by the behaviour of the other Great Powers.[148] His governmental constraints indicate how much the Powers based their actions on each other's behaviour and how they lacked a stable policy of westernisation for the Ottoman Empire. Their policy changed from one day to the next as they tried to guess how the others would act.

The Content of the Andrassy Note

Unlike the British reform schemes, the Andrassy Note concentrated on the reform of a certain locality, Bosnia-Herzegovina. As Austria's main concern was the pacification of its border with the Ottoman Empire rather than general principles of reform, the note resulting from confidential exchanges between Petersburg, Berlin and Vienna focused on the measures of appeasement of troubles in the region. The Andrassy Note consisted of the contextualisation of some of the general problems of Bosnia and Herzegovina. It was not only through the Andrassy Note that the deprivation of full religious freedom and equality before the law for Christian populations, the necessity of fiscal reforms and the misery of the peasantry due to illegal maintenance of the tax farming system were reported to the Ottoman government.[149] Suggestions regarding the exclusive use of direct taxes by the provinces in order to increase financial resources and well-being also emerged from British consular reports in earlier periods.[150] Andrassy legitimised, however, the distinctiveness of his note on the grounds that former reform decrees were not applied in Bosnia and Herzegovina and that the *irade* of October 2, 1875 and the firman of December 12, 1875 were only interested in general principles for improving imperial public administration rather than the pacification of the provinces. The note insisted on the idea that the principles proclaimed by the Porte were not applicable if pacification was not fully assured in the insurgent provinces.

---

[148] MAEF, Papier Decazes Fonds nominatifs PA-AP 54 vol. 7, 1875-1877. Here September 1, 1875. From M. de Bourgoing, French ambassador, to Duc Decazes, French foreign minister.

[149] PRO, FO 78/2675, Salisbury to Derby, Vienna, November 29, 1876.

[150] PRO, FO 78/2674, Lord Derby to the Marquis of Salisbury, November 20, 1876. See for examples, BOA, HR. SYS. 1869 B-2; BOA, HR. SYS. 1869 D-2; PRO, FO 78/2436. Instructions addressed to Her Majesty's Embassy at Constantinople respecting Administrative and Financial Reforms in Turkey: 1856-1872.

The improvement of the conditions of rural populations was crucial in the Andrassy Note.[151] The unhappy condition of Bosnian and Herzegovinian Christians was connected in the note to the nature of relations between the rural population and landowners. Agrarian difficulties were due to the fact that the landlord class differed either in religion or nationality from the labourers. In the provinces, nearly all of those properties not belonging to the state or to the mosques were in the hands of Muslims, while the agricultural class was composed of Christians of both creeds. The note envisaged the possibility of finding some combination which would permit peasants to acquire portions of the waste land which the state put up for sale on easy terms. These rural issues had already been cited in British consular reports in the 1860s.[152] However, the fact that the execution of the proclaimed reforms would not be submitted to the control of provincial governments, but to the supervision of a commission of notables of the country (equally composed of Muslims and Christians and elected by the inhabitants of the province according to a mode of election determined by the Porte) was a novelty of the Andrassy Note.[153] In other words, Andrassy trusted the internal forces of the Ottoman Empire for supervision. In contrast, the British envisaged the strengthening of the *vilayet* administration by the appointment of a *vali* (governor-general) whose nomination should be subject to the approval of the ambassadors of the guaranteeing Powers.[154]

On the initiative of Lord Derby on November 5, 1876, the contracting Powers recognised the necessity of organising a conference in order to find a solution to the Eastern Question, avoid the renewal of hostilities between Montenegro, Serbia and the Porte and ameliorate the situation of Christians in Bulgaria, Bosnia and Herzegovina.[155] European representatives gathered for the Conference of Constantinople on December 23, 1876.[156]

---

[151] PRO, FO 78/2674, Lord Derby to the Marquis of Salisbury, November 20, 1876.

[152] See for examples, BOA, HR. SYS. 1869 D-2. Papers relating to the Condition of Christians in Turkey, Foreign Office, 1860. Consul Skene to Sir H. Bulwer, Aleppo, August 4, 1860, pp. 57-58.

[153] PRO, FO 881/3084. Count Andrassy to Count Beust, Budapest, December 30, 1875. Communicated to the Earl of Derby by Count Beust, January 3.

[154] PRO, FO 78/2674, Lord Derby to the Marquis of Salisbury, November 20, 1876.

[155] PRO, FO 78/2675, Salisbury to Derby. MAEF, CP, September-November 1876, vol. 406. From Derby to Lyons (British ambassador to Paris), November 4, 1876.

[156] PRO, FO 78/2675, Salisbury to Derby.

During the Conference, the term "autonomy" was the principal point of conflict between Lord Derby and Count Andrassy, who rejected the expression. According to Derby, the term did not designate any measure that could harm the integrity of the Ottoman Empire or create a situation analogous to that of the vassal principalities. Andrassy, however, thought that it should be eliminated from the text of the propositions made to the Porte. According to him, "autonomy" would signify administrative independence, the elimination of the Turkish element from public offices, the creation of a national militia and a rupture between the provinces and central authority.[157] Andrassy's position was also fragile vis-à-vis his government. Archduke Albert's party was gaining ground over the German constitutional party which Andrassy joined. Andrassy wrote a series of incendiary articles on the Eastern Question by accusing Russia of having favoured insurrection in the Balkans.[158] The Conference of Constantinople turned to the profit of Russia, and Austria entered the orbit of Russian policy. Gortchakoff admitted that the union of Bosnia with Serbia and of Herzegovina with Montenegro would be contrary to the vital interests of Austria. In return, Austria admitted the principle of a partial territorial exchange to the profit of Serbia and Montenegro in the eventuality of their victory. The only concession that Andrassy obtained was that the eventual territorial exchange could only take place with the consent of the guaranteeing Powers.[159]

2. A MULTI-LAYERED LIBERAL EFFORT AMONG OTTOMANS

Abdülaziz's rule and Mahmud Nedim's government proved inefficient in solving the problems of insurrection, finance, European diplomatic intervention, Pan-Slavic pressure and famine.[160] The anxiety of the financial moratorium and Abdülaziz I's inefficient rule led Ottoman liberals to proclaim a "Manifesto of Muslim patriots", which they forwarded to the

---

[157] MAEF, Mémoires et Documents, vol. 101. Turquie. Conférence de Constantinople, 1876-1877. Documents divers, Réunions préparatoires, Protocoles. September 21, 1876. From the ambassador of France, Voguë in Vienna, to the French Foreign Minister. Confidential.

[158] MAEF, Papiers d'agents, Duc Decazes (Louis-Charles), agents spéciaux, Vienne, Rome, Berlin, Constantinople, 1873-77, vol. 5. Here from Paris, April 18, 1876.

[159] MAEF, Papiers d'agents, Duc Decazes (Louis-Charles), agents spéciaux, Vienne, Rome, Berlin, Constantinople, 1873-77, vol. 5. Here Cracovia, July 12, 1876.

[160] Davison, *Reform, 1856-1876*, p. 311.

leading statesmen of Europe on March 9, 1876.[161] The anonymous text criticised the regime and proposed the liberal opposition, namely the energetic and moderate party of Midhad Pasha, as a solution to Abdülaziz I's despotic rule and extravagance. They also demanded the establishment of an Ottoman Parliament, composed of the representatives of different religions of Turkey, for better government and the amelioration of finances.

In May 1876, a softa (theological student) demonstration followed the manifesto urging the sultan to dismiss the Sheikh ül-Islam Hasan Fehmi Effendi and the Grand Vizier Mahmud Nedim Pasha and to replace them with Hasan Hayrullah Effendi and Mehmed Rüşdü Pasha respectively.[162] Mahmud Nedim Pasha's known sympathy for General Ignatieff, who was considered an intriguer in the eyes of the general public, provoked the Muslim and Bulgarian populations of the empire to react against one another. Hasan Fehmi Effendi's subservience to the Russian ambassador turned these two men into traitors as far as the theological students were concerned.[163] The softas, whose number was estimated to range from 5,000 to 60,000 by various sources,[164] represented the largest organisable group in the capital since most Ottoman soldiers were on campaign in the Balkans.[165]

"By the spring of 1876 this general discontent, focussed on the Ottoman government, found leadership in strategically placed groups of civil officials, military leaders, and theological students whose temporary coalescence made possible the *coup d'état* of May 30".[166] Although Abdülaziz I hoped that ministerial changes would appease the general discontent, they did not protect him from being deposed by a military

[161] Devereux, p. 31. *The Times* of June 17, 1876 reported the manifesto as addressed to Lord Derby and as it appeared in a French newspaper of Istanbul, *Stamboul*, on June 2, 1876. The manifesto seems to have been sent to Disraeli, Lord Derby, Lord Granville (a former state secretary), Marshall MacMahon (the president of the French Republic), Mr Thiers (the French ex-president), Mr Gambetta (a French statesman), Prince Bismarck (the German chancellor) and Mr Visconti Venosta (the Italian foreign minister).

[162] Devreux, pp. 32-33.

[163] Ahmed Midhad Effendi, *Üss-i İnkılab: Kırım Muharebesinden II. Abdülhamid Han'ın Cülusuna kadar*, yayına haz. Tahir Galip Seratlı (The Basis of Revolution: from the Crimean War to Abdülhamid's Accession to the throne: Transliterated and Simplified by Tahir Galip Seratlı) (İstanbul: Selis Kitaplar, 2004), v. 1, pp. 165-169.

[164] Both the lower and the higher figures are Elliot's. PRO, FO 78/2457, Elliot to Derby, May 9, 1876. Cited in Davison, *Reform, 1856-1876*, p. 325.

[165] Davison, *Reform, 1856-1876*, p. 325.

[166] Davison, *Reform, 1856-1876*, p. 311.

coup d'état planned by the new Grand Vizier Mehmed Rüşdü Pasha, the Minister of War Hüseyin Avni Pasha and Midhad Pasha, the minister without portfolio.[167] Süleyman Pasha, then director of military schools, commended the troops which took Abdülaziz I into custody after his deposition. The new Sheikh ül-Islam Hasan Hayrullah Effendi proclaimed a fatwa (canonical decree) legitimising the deposition of the sultan.[168]

Abdülaziz I's deposition was preceded by a palace revolution or *coup d'état*, which may have resulted from the failure of negotiation with the sultan. After the softa demonstration, the new Grand Vizier Mehmed Rüşdü Pasha urged the sultan to undertake some new reforms in the Ottoman administration mainly based on Midhad Pasha's programme, which included the curtailment of the civil list, the limitation of the sultan's arbitrary power and a change in foreign policy to emancipate the Ottoman state from Russian ascendency. However, these suggestions were not welcomed by the sultan.[169] Texts from the Qur'an circulated to demonstrate that the form of government it praised was democratic, that the absolute power of the current sultan was a violation of the rights of the people unsanctioned by sacred law and that a sovereign who violated the interests of the state should not be obeyed.[170] Consequently, the triumvirate of Mehmed Rüşdü Pasha, Hüseyin Avni Pasha and Midhad Pasha, who met at the last Council of Ministers, decided on the deposition of the sultan and to raise to the throne Mehmed Murad, nephew of Sultan Abdülaziz I and eldest son of the late Sultan Abdülmecid, the oldest surviving male of the imperial dynasty.[171]

The liberals were also encouraged by the idea that the future sovereign, Murad V, was a supporter of constitutionalism.[172] As Murad had promised to promulgate a constitution, his first act was to invite expatriated

---

[167] *Journal des Débats*, June 2, 1876; *The Times*, June 1 & June 16, 1876.

[168] See for the details regarding Abdülaziz I's deposition, Süleyman Hüsnü Paşa, *Hiss-i İnkılab* (The Feeling of the Revolution), (Istanbul: Tanin Matbaası, 1326); Mahmud Celaleddin, *Mirat-ı Hakikat: Tarih-i Mahmud Celaleddin Paşa* (The Mirror of Truth: The History of Mahmud Celaleddin Pasha), (Istanbul: Matbaa-i Osmaniye, 1326-1327). Cited in Devereux, p. 33, fn. 27. For the text of the fatwa, see also Ahmed Midhad Effendi, *Üss-i İnkılab*, v. 1, p. 287. See also *The Times*, June 8, 1876. The grounds for the fatwa was that Sultan Abdülaziz I had lost the use of his intellectual faculties, did not possess any knowledge of political affairs, administered the money of the state according to his caprices and ruined the state and the people without settling religious and civil affairs.

[169] *The Times*, June 8, 1876.

[170] Elliot, pp. 231-232.

[171] *The Times*, June 8, 1876.

[172] See for details, Devereux, pp. 32-33.

Young Ottomans (such as Namık Kemal) to return home.[173] However, Murad shifted his position on the grounds that the knowledge and training of the people were not suitable to the constitution of a National Assembly and that the state should be reformed by strengthening its security and financial situation.[174] On June 15, 1876, when Hüseyin Avni Pasha was killed by a Circassian army captain, Midhad's power was strengthened.[175] Hüseyin Avni Pasha was said not to approve of the reforms that would limit the power of the crown.[176]

Before constitutional discussions could evolve, Ottoman political life was again shaken up by the suicide of Abdülaziz I. His enthronement by a military *coup d'etat*, combined with his uncle's death, negatively influenced the mental health of Murad V.[177] Various sources interpreted the reasons behind the deaths of both Abdülaziz I and Hüseyin Avni differently, without proving one or the other. "In the phrase of a witty journalist, Abdülaziz was suicided".[178] Similarly, suspicions also appeared about Hüseyin Avni's murder connecting it to the competition between reformist and conservative wings.[179] In the meanwhile, Sultan Murad V's mental health deteriorated rapidly.[180] On September 1, after a convincing interview with Hamid, Murad V's half-brother, on his inclination towards a constitutional regime and the certification of a number of physicians, foreign as well as Turkish, of the incurability of Murad V, the Cabinet obtained a fatwa authorising the latter's dethronement: Abdülhamid II was proclaimed the new sultan.[181] Abdülhamid's enthronement was not without military pressure. When the issue was under discussion at the Grand Vizierate, the *Serasker* (minister of war) Redif Pasha threatened military intervention if the investiture of Abdülhamid II was delayed by the Grand Vizier Mehmed Rüşdü Pasha.[182] The investiture of the former

---

[173] Devereux, p. 34.

[174] Mahmud Celaleddin Paşa, v. 1, p. 117. Cited in Devereux, pp. 34-35.

[175] Devereux, p. 37.

[176] *Journal des Débats*, June 17, 1876.

[177] Davison, *Reform, 1856-1876*, pp. 341-343.

[178] Charikles [Aristarchi Bey?], "Türkische Skizzen in Briefe an eine Freundin," *Deutsche Zeit-und Streit-fragen*, VI: 83/84 (1877), p. 16. Cited in Davison, *Reform, 1856-1876*, p. 342. See also pp. 341-342 in general for comments.

[179] Davison, *Reform, 1856-1876*, p. 346.

[180] Devereux, p. 39.

[181] Devereux, p. 43.

[182] Mahmud Celaleddin Paşa, *Mirat-ı Hakikat*, prep. by. İ. Miroğlu et al. (İstanbul: Tercüman, 1980), v. 2, pp. 12-13.

sultan, Murad V, in the *Seraskerat* and not in the Ottoman palace[183] was probably a symbolic indicator of the power of the military classes in the settlement of politics. The fatwa of his dethronement was given by Kara Halil Effendi and the Sheikh ül-Islam Hasan Hayrullah Effendi,[184] both of whom occupied seats in the Drafting Commission of the Ottoman Constitution.

3. DIASPORAS AND ETHNIC LOBBIES

The Ottoman constitutional process mobilised networks and actors beyond its territorial borders, including diasporas. The case studies of the Armenian diaspora of Manchester and of the Jewish diaspora of France exemplify the power of ethno-religious ties in constructing transnational networks of solidarity and their function as ethnic lobbies in order to influence the foreign policy of their host lands in favour of their co-religionists in the homeland.[185]

The Armenian Diaspora of Manchester

Manchester was considered the industrial centre of the cotton trade.[186] Armenians, particularly those from Istanbul and Izmir, settled in the commercial centres of London, Manchester and Liverpool from 1830-35.[187] The signing of the commercial treaty between Britain and Turkey in 1838 accelerated relations between Britain and the Ottoman capital.[188] Armenians were already the owners of successful textile businesses in

---

[183] Midhad Paşa, *Tabsıra-i İbret*, vol. 1, pp. 188-189.

[184] Mahmud Celaleddin Paşa, v. 2, pp. 15-17.

[185] Gabriel Sheffer, "The Politics of Ethno-National Diasporas," in Lisa Anteby-Yemini, William Berthomière & Gabriel Sheffer, *Les Diasporas: 200 Ans d'Histoire* (Rennes: PUR, 2005), p. 134. See also Tony Smith, *Foreign Attachments: The Power of Ethnic Groups in the Making of the American Foreign Policy* (Cambridge: Harvard University Press, 2000); M. S. Saideman, *The Ties that Divide: Ethnic Politics, Foreign Policy, and International Politics* (New York: Columbia University Press, 2001). Cited in Yossi Shain, *Kinship & Diasporas in International Affairs* (Ann Arbor: University of Michigan, 2007), pp. 6, 128, 141.

[186] Joan George, *Merchants in Exile: The Armenians in Manchester, England, 1835-1935* (Princeton and London: Gomidas Institute, 2002), p. 1.

[187] Moushegh Yebisgobos (Bishop), *Manche'stri Hah' Kagho'wt'y* (The Armenian Community of Manchester), (Azk: Boston, 1911), pp. 13, 29.

[188] Evelyn Waugh, *When the Going was Good* (London: Duckworth, 1945), p. 144. Cited in George, p. 4.

Istanbul or Izmir and opened branches in Manchester to directly buy from manufacturers and ship the goods throughout the Ottoman Empire. In that respect, they became the pioneers of an Armenian "trade diaspora" in Britain.[189] By the 1850s, they had already acquired a certain level of wealth.[190] Many of the Manchester merchants received their education and knowledge of English in missionary schools. The chief establishments were Robert College (Istanbul), the American College for Girls (Istanbul), Euphrates College (Kharput) and the Anatolian College (Marsovan).[191] The Armenian newspaper *Orakir* recorded that the Armenian population of Manchester reached about 80-90 people in 1873 and consisted of traders and students who had migrated from the Ottoman Empire and Russia.[192] The period extending from 1873 to 1878 was the most active period for the Armenian community of Britain. In 1874, they dealt with the chronic famine which plagued the eastern provinces (Van and Muş) of the Ottoman Empire. They sent financial aid to these provinces in order to protect the Armenian population. As a result of this famine, many Ottoman Armenians died, some converted to other religions and others migrated. The integrity of the Armenian population was thus threatened, and the Armenian Patriarchate of Istanbul asked for more financial help from the Armenian community of Manchester.[193] The issue of famine inspired a more permanent collaboration between the two communities.[194] The famine committee, founded in November 1874 in Manchester, sent a call not only to the Armenian residents of the city but also to British philanthropists, opening a branch in London.[195]

The Armenians of Manchester were also alerted to the emergence of the Armenian question in the Ottoman Empire.[196] In October 1876, the community discussed whether they could publish articles in British newspapers (especially in the *Daily News*) to heighten public awareness of the problem. Since negotiation initiatives with the Ottoman government had already exhausted, the solution appeared to be increasing the awareness of the conditions of provincial Armenians in the Christian

---

[189] George, p. 5.
[190] George, p. 9.
[191] V. M. Kurkjian, *A History of Armenia* (New York: AGBU, 1958), pp. 455-456. Cited in George, p. 18.
[192] *Orakir G. Bolso'h'* (Daily of Istanbul), 28 July 1875.
[193] Moushegh Yebisgobos (Bishop), pp. 55-60.
[194] Moushegh Yebisgobos (Bishop), pp. 55-60.
[195] Moushegh Yebisgobos (Bishop), p. 64.
[196] Moushegh Yebisgobos (Bishop), p. 66.

European governments. In London, Seth Apcar headed the publication movement that intended to draw attention to the reality of Ottoman Armenians.[197] Apcar descended from an influential family that had migrated from Julfa, Persia, to Bengal in the early nineteenth century. Its fortune was made by trade with China in opium. The family firm, Apcar & Co., had for many years its own line of steamships between Calcutta and the treaty ports.[198] *The Times* thus mentioned a long memorial on the grievances of the Armenians, written by Seth A. Apcar and presented to the chancelleries of the Great Powers, which complained of mistreatments, restrictions of liberties, the seizure of their property and forced conversions.[199] During the Conference of Constantinople, a British clergyman presented an English booklet to Lord Salisbury in the name of Ottoman Armenians. This booklet was entitled *The Armenians and the Eastern Question* and had been published in London. Its objective was to draw the attention of the Conference to the situation of Armenians in the Ottoman Empire through the intermediary of British delegates.[200]

The Camondos: Another Banking Family

The Camondos were among those Jewish banking families of nineteenth-century Istanbul whose wealth was comparable to that of the Rothschilds. The Camondos first emerged through their bank I. Camondo et Cie in the first half of the nineteenth century. They were known to be the private bankers of Reşid, Ali and Fuad Pashas (the three key bureaucrats of the reform period) as well as their counsellors. They also maintained a partnership with the bankers of Galata, a group mostly made up of Orthodox Greeks in Istanbul (Zografos, Zarifis, Baltazzis, etc.), who were involved in foreign finance and associated with European capital. In 1869, the family moved the main branch of the Camondo Bank to Paris in conjunction with their gradual settlement in the French capital, while the family's banking and real-estate business continued to flourish through their *chargés d'affaires* in Istanbul. As the Ottoman government was appealing to foreign financial groups for credit, especially after the

---

[197] Moushegh Yebisgobos (Bishop), p. JP.

[198] Sir A. A. Apcar, Obituary. *The Times*, April 19, 1913. See also Jacob Seth Mesrovb, *History of the Armenians in India from the Earliest Times to the Present Day* (Calcutta: Published by the author, 1895), p. 127; Seth Mesrovb, pp. 126-128.

[199] *The Times*, November 13, 1876.

[200] Saro'wxan, p. 154.

1856 Reform Edict, it was more profitable for the Camondos to conduct business from a financial centre like Paris. They progressively became, in Istanbul as well Paris, one of the most important patrons of the arts in the late nineteenth and early twentieth centuries. The Camondos also worked for the transformation of the urban fabric in Istanbul. In the aftermath of the Crimean War, they contributed to the municipality reform in Istanbul by granting credit for the renovation of some districts (Galata, Pera and Tophane). In 1870, together with their partners and the Ottoman Imperial Bank, they established the *Société des Tramways de Constantinople*, which installed the first urban rail transportation in Istanbul.[201]

From Paris, Count Camondo wrote to the Ottoman Minister of Foreign Affairs Safved Pasha on December 1, 1876, before the Conference of Constantinople and the promulgation of the Ottoman Constitution, to defend the rights of his co-religionists in the Ottoman Empire.[202] He expressed his expectation that the Ottoman government would clarify either in the treaty or the convention to be signed at the end of the Conference that the non-Muslim populations of the empire included not only Christian Serbs and Bulgarians but also Jewish subjects of the Porte. He underlined that the Jewish population of the Ottoman Empire should not once again be victims of intolerance as they had been in Rumania, despite the stipulations of the Treaty of Paris.[203]

Ethnic Solidarity beyond Diasporas

In 1876, when a constitutional model for the Ottoman Empire was discussed and the Conference of Constantinople debated the grant of special privileges to some populations of the Ottoman Empire, the *Alliance israélite universelle* was the driving force behind the protection of the rights of the Jewish population. In 1876, Charles Netter, special envoy of the Central Committee of the *Alliance israélite*, left

---

[201] Şeni & Le Tarnec, pp. 11-41. Nora Şeni, "The Camondos and Their Imprint on 19th-Century Istanbul," *International Journal of Middle East Studies* 26 (1994), pp. 663-675.

[202] BOA, HR. SFR. 4 299/93.

[203] The 1866 Rumanian Constitution stipulated that all Christian rites would enjoy equal political rights. The enjoyment of these rights could be extended to other religious communities by legislative arrangements. See also Baron I. de Testa, *Recueil des Traités de la Porte ottomane avec les Puissances étrangères* (Paris: Amyot, 1882), vol. 5, p. 300.

Paris for Istanbul in order to submit to the members of the Conference of Constantinople a memorial in favour of his co-religionists in the Ottoman Empire.[204] The memorial was submitted by the delegates of the Jewish populations of France, Britain, Germany, Austria, Italy, Belgium, Holland and Switzerland, who had convened in Paris on December 11, 1876 to discuss religious freedom and to urge French representatives not to make any distinction between different religions. In addition to complete civil, political and religious equality in the Ottoman provinces, Jewish delegates required the revision of the Convention of Paris of 1858 regarding the Jews of Rumania in order to provide them with the full enjoyment of civil and political rights.[205] In 1876, during the Conference of Constantinople, Lord Derby also received a deputation from the Council of the Anglo-Jewish Association at the Foreign Office which presented the same memorial.[206]

Since autonomy had been granted to the Danubian principalities, the memorial stated, the conditions of Jews had worsened. The Danubian principalities were reorganised by a convention concluded in Paris in August 1858 and renamed the United Principalities of Wallachia and Moldavia. Article 46 of the convention stipulated that Moldavians and Wallachians of all Christian rites enjoyed equal political rights. The enjoyment of these rights could be extended to other religious communities by legislative arrangements.[207] The association asked that the present opportunity be taken for a revision of the European treaties of 1856 and 1858 between all the Great Powers. Montefiore, president of the London Committee of Deputies of British Jews, transmitted to Lord Derby the request that the Jews, together with their social, civil and political rights, be placed on an equal footing with Muslim and non-Muslim subjects, and that the position of Jews resident or travelling in these provinces be secured in the most effectual manner possible when measures were proposed for the better government of the provinces of the Ottoman Empire.[208]

---

[204] MAEF, CP, Turkey 1876, December 1876, vol. 407. December 27, 1876. From Decazes? to Bourgoing.

[205] MAEF, ADP (Affaires diverses politiques), Turquie, 1814-1896. From the *Alliance Israélite Universelle* to Duc Decazes, Comité central. December 22, 1876.

[206] MAEF, CP, Turkey 1876, December 1876, vol. 407.

[207] PRO, FO 78/2682. From Lord Derby to the Marquis of Salisbury, December 20, 1876.

[208] PRO, FO 78/2682. November 29, 1876. From Montefiore to Lord Derby.

The Committee of Rome of the *Alliance israélite universelle* addressed a letter on December 31, 1876 to the Italian Foreign Minister Melegari in order to request that he submit the memorial elaborated by the Jewish Congress gathered in Paris to the Italian representatives participating in the Conference of Constantinople. The Alliance also asked Melegari to welcome their French co-religionist Charles Netter, who had been entrusted with the mission of defending the Jewish cause before the members of the Conference. The letter put emphasis on the necessity of reorganising the Ottoman provinces around the principle of equality without any religious discrimination. As for the discrimination experienced by the Jewish population in Serbia and Rumania, the letter argued that the Jewish question was not an internal issue. If the sufferings of Christians, the letter continued, necessitated the interference of the Powers in the internal affairs of the Ottoman Empire, European intervention in the emancipation of Jews would not be an attack on the autonomy of the principalities.[209]

4. THE OTTOMAN GOVERNMENT'S POSITION

In September 1876, Henry Elliot told Derby that the decisions of the Porte were unofficially in favour of the creation of a general elective assembly, the complete and strict application of the *vilayet* system, the extension of the powers of provincial councils and control over the acts of the government and local authorities. Elliot commented that this was the general application of the measures contained in the Andrassy's Note across the whole empire. The organisation of municipalities and the reorganisation of police in the provinces, he said, would apply to Bosnia, Herzegovina and Bulgaria as well as to the rest of the empire.[210] The terms of the protocol and administrative autonomy were entirely rejected by the Council.[211] The Porte still hoped for disunity among the Powers and expected that it would be defended by Britain in the end.[212] In his private papers regarding the Conference of Constantinople, the French representative Chaudordy himself commented that the Ottoman

---

[209] Italian Foreign Ministry, Archives in Rome hereafter MAE, Moscati 6/1456.
[210] PRO, FO 198/42. Turkey no. 1 (1877). Correspondence respecting the affairs of Turkey, presented to both Houses of Parliament by Command of Her Majesty, 1877. From Sir Henry Elliot to the Earl of Derby, September 27, 1876.
[211] PRO, FO 78/2475, From Henry Elliot, October 3, 1876.
[212] PRO, FO 78/2475, From Lord Lyons, October 3, 1876.

Constitution was promulgated in accordance with the principles in the Andrassy Note. Andrassy was expecting to obtain an official guarantee of the decree of 20 October and the firman of 12 December from the government of the sultan. Thus the official communication of the constitutional act was the first step in meeting Andrassy's expectations. However, the promulgation of the Ottoman Constitution was not satisfactory for the other participants of the Conference, whose objective was to examine the new administrative institutions in the two provinces of Bosnia and Bulgaria.[213]

Musurus Pasha informed the British Foreign Office that a scheme of reforms would be communicated to the Powers in the near future to avoid the use of the expression "administrative autonomy".[214] A telegraph sent by Safved Pasha, the minister of foreign affairs, to Ottoman ambassadors in London, Paris, Rome, Vienna, Berlin and St Petersburg on October 12, 1876, more or less alludes to the formulation of the Ottoman Constitution. He announced that a commission, established under the presidency of Midhad Pasha and composed of Muslim and Christian high officials, was elaborating new laws. Instead of announcing the future establishment of the Ottoman Constitution, his telegraph alluded to "new institutions", including a Senate nominated by the state and a General Assembly elected by the inhabitants of the provinces and of the capital which would vote on, among other things, laws about taxation and the empire's budget.[215]

After this telegraph, Safved Pasha sent an official circular to the ambassadors of the Six Great Powers in order to acquaint them with the new institutions on October 17, 1876. We understand from the points which Safved Pasha emphasised in this circular that the state was trying to convince the Great Powers of the virtues of an alternative programme of reforms in order to refute their requirement for the autonomy of some Ottoman provinces. Safved Pasha emphasised provincial law, which was a weak point of Ottoman central administration. He recognised that the previous provincial reforms could not meet the expectations of the population. He stated that older provincial laws would be complemented by additional reforms that could control the use of administrative authority. The aim was to generalise the reforms required by the Great Powers for Bosnia and

---

[213] MAEF, Papier Chaudordy PA 46. Affaires turques. 1876-77. vol. 9. December 23, 1876.

[214] PRO, FO 78/2452, From the Foreign Office to Elliot, October 2, 1876.

[215] BOA, HR. SYS 1864-1, Savfet Pasha's telegraph to Ottoman ambassadors, 12 October 1876. See also *La Turquie*, October 27, 1876.

Herzegovina to all the provinces of the empire. Safved Pasha was trying to convince his European audience that the provincial reform which would soon be launched would be preferable to the special privileges asked by the European Powers for some provinces at the expense of others. In this official note, Safved emphasised once again that the commission headed by Midhad Pasha was formulating the constitutive laws of two assemblies that would be established in the Ottoman Empire. The use of the term "constitutive laws" alluded more directly to the term "constitution".[216] When communicating the Porte's official note about the content of the new reforms to Derby, Elliot stated: "No mention is made of administrative autonomy, and the above must be taken as a counter-proposal".[217]

After the official communiqué to the European Powers, the Ottoman ambassadorial circle worked to reproduce the echo that this communication made in major European capitals. The real intention of this communiqué was, in my opinion, to measure the European reactions to the Ottoman constitutional reform in progress before its official promulgation and whether it could supersede the requirements of the Powers.[218]

The Ottoman ambassadors in the European capitals did not hesitate to publicise the importance of these new institutions. Edhem Pasha, Ottoman ambassador to Berlin, wrote to Safved Pasha in November that he was trying to explain the extent to which the establishment of these new institutions was preferable to the grant of privileges to some provinces.[219] The Ottoman ambassador to Vienna, Aleko Vogorides, communicated his personal opinion to Safved Pasha, writing in his despatch of November 4, 1876 that the generalisation of reforms to all Ottoman provinces was the only way to consolidate well-being in the monarchy and that the grant of special privileges to some provinces would destroy the administrative unity of the empire by generating conflict among the different populations.[220] In another despatch, Vogorides communicated that according to Count Robillant, the Italian ambassador, the new Ottoman reforms had no value in the eyes of Europe since no Christian participated in the

---

[216] We came cross this official note, which was also sent to Ottoman diplomats on 17 October 1876. BOA, HR. SYS 1864-1, 17 October 1876.

[217] PRO, FO 198/42. Turkey no. 1 (1877). Correspondence respecting the affairs of Turkey, presented to both Houses of Parliament by Command of Her Majesty, 1877. From Henry Elliot to the Earl of Derby, October 12, 1876.

[218] BOA, HR. SYS 1864-1, Musurus to Safved Pasha, 30 October 1876; 2 November 1876.

[219] BOA, HR. SYS 1864-1, Edhem Pasha to Safved Pasha, 4 November 1876.

[220] BOA, HR. SYS 1864-1, Aleko Vogorides to Safved Pasha, 4 November 1876.

deliberations. Vogorides tried to convince the Italian ambassador that Christian bureaucrats were also involved in the preparatory phase of the reform process.[221] It is also striking that the Ottoman state nominated bureaucrats of Greek origin to ambassadorial posts: Musurus Pasha in London, Aleko Vogorides in Vienna, Aristarki Bey in Washington, Aleksandr Karateodori in Brussels and Fotiyades Bey in Athens. The intention was probably to make the reform process more convincing in the eyes of European public opinion by using the relatively easier time that Christian subjects had interacting with western bureaucracy.

On November 8, 1876, Safved Pasha transmitted to Ottoman embassies the first results of the work of the commission dealing with the creation of the new National Assembly and pointed out that this would serve as the basis of the new Ottoman Constitution. Thus the term "constitution" was already used in November before its official promulgation on December 23, 1876: the Ottoman constitutional project was a counter-proposal against European demands for autonomy in the Balkans. These results consisted only of instructions regarding the transitional mode of election of the National Assembly. Safved also announced that a definitive electoral law and the internal organisation of deliberative assemblies were in progress. Ottoman ambassadors were asked to send some exemplars of Safved's new communiqué to the respective foreign offices. Consequently, this communiqué did not fail to emphasise that the imperial government was showing, through the first results of the commission, its firm intention to bring into practice the prescriptions of the imperial firman in the very near future.[222] Moreover, the list of Ottoman embassies to which this communication was sent was extended. In addition to the embassies of Paris, London, Rome, Vienna, Berlin, and St Petersburg, those of Tehran, Athens, Washington and Brussels were also included.

The financial preoccupations of Europe were in the meantime appeased by a letter, sent on December 27, 1876 from Midhad Pasha to the Ottoman Bank, stating that the law of October 6, 1875 which deferred the payment of the interest had caused problems in the empire's financial system and could be considered abolished with the proclamation of the constitutional regime.[223] The grand vizier expressed the view that a new

---

[221] BOA, HR. SYS 1864-1, Aleko Vogorides to Safved Pasha, 7 November 1876.

[222] BOA, HR. SYS 1864-1, Safved Pasha to Ottoman ambassadors, 8 November 1876.

[223] BOA, HR. SFR. 4 299/97, 27 December 1876. FO 78 / 2683, From Elliot to Derby, January 5, 1877. (Received January 12). Inclosure in no. 111. Extract from the Levant Herald of January 3, 1877.

bill that would satisfy the holders of foreign public debt could be voted on as soon as the Ottoman Parliament convened. Midhad's statement could be interpreted as a way of appeasing the discontent arising in Europe over Ottoman foreign debt.

Needless to say, Ottoman ambassadors were trying to publicise the results of the commission's work in their respective countries.[224] Similarly, the Ottoman ambassadorial circle transmitted the reactions of Europe vis-à-vis the proclamation of the Ottoman Constitution on December 23, 1876. In some cases, Ottoman ambassadors tried to change prejudices or negative opinions in favour of the Ottoman Constitution.[225] Thus, the Ottoman diplomacy functioned as a mechanism of conviction that tried to shape European public opinion in favour of the Ottoman Constitution. Some representative extracts from the reaction that the proclamation of the Ottoman Constitution provoked in European capitals show that the Ottoman ambassadors did not always receive positive feedback, but nevertheless endeavoured to legitimise its promulgation.

Before and after the promulgation of the Ottoman Constitution in 1876, Musurus worked to publicise the importance of the new institutional reforms to the British and took Derby's pulse frequently in order to gage any negative feeling on his part regarding the reform process.[226] When *The Times* and the *Daily News* presented criticisms of the viability of the Ottoman Constitution and the suitability of the empire for this regime, Musurus Pasha sought to refute these arguments through the *Morning Post*, the *Daily Telegraph* and the *Standard*.[227] Needless to say other Ottoman diplomats accomplished the same tasks in other European capitals: Aleko Vogorides in Vienna, Aristarki Bey in Washington, Aleksandr Karateodori in Brussels and Fotiyades Bey in Athens.[228]

---

[224] BOA, HR. SYS 1864-1, Edhem Pasha to Safved Pasha, 18 November 1876; Aleko Vogorides to Safved Pasha, 18 November 1876; A. Tevfik to Safved Pasha, 23 November 1876; Esad Bey to Safved Pasha, 24 November 1876; Aleksandr Karateodori to Safved Pasha, 28 November 1876.

[225] BOA, HR. SYS 1864-1, Turkhan Bey to the Ottoman Ministry of Foreign Affairs, 26 December 1876; Tefvik Bey to the Ottoman Ministry of Foreign Affairs, 26 December 1876; Aleksandr Karateodori to Safved Pasha, 29 December 1876. Fotiyades Bey to Safved Pasha, 2 January 1877.

[226] BOA, HR. SYS 1864-1, Musurus to Safved Pasha, 30 October 1876; 2 November 1876.

[227] BOA, HR. SYS 1864-1, Musurus Pasha to Safved Pasha, 28 December 1876.

[228] See for examples BOA, HR. SYS 1864-1, Edhem Pasha to Safved Pasha, 18 November 1876; Aleko Vogorides to Safved Pasha, 18 November 1876; A. Tevfik to Safved Pasha, 23 November 1876; Esad Bey to Safved Pasha, 24 November 1876; Aleksandr Karateodori to Safved Pasha, 28 November 1876.

The Special Mission of Odyan Effendi

In the 1860s, Odyan was the head of the Foreign Correspondence Office, into which he had been recruited in 1857 as simple redactor.[229] In the coming 15 years, Odyan occupied the position of president of the Armenian National Assembly.[230] When the Ottoman provincial law was promulgated in 1864, Midhad was appointed governor of the *vilayet* of the Danube,[231] while Odyan became political director and was charged with maintaining relations with foreign diplomatic agents and subjects of the province.[232] Odyan worked successively as secretary within the Ministry of Foreign Affairs (1870) and Justice (1871), and as undersecretary of state within the Ministry of Commerce (1871) and Publics Works (since 1875).[233] Odyan was promoted to the rank of *bala* (the rank below vizier) in 1876 and was nominated to membership of the Council of State as well as the Drafting Commission of the Ottoman Constitution. His nomination to the Council of State would have given him, like it did Ohannes Çamiç, a certain weight in the Drafting Commission, which worked in close cooperation with the Council of State.[234] Odyan Effendi was described as the "right hand of Midhad Pasha" in the sources of the period.[235] It was even argued that his influence over the constitutional process was so considerable that Midhad's conceptualisation of the constitution was attributed to him.[236]

In mid-1876, some newspapers announced mysterious trips for Odyan Effendi. For instance, the *Journal des Débats* wrote that he was expected to go to Ems for health reasons but that the real reason behind this departure was to visit the Russian Emperor Alexander in order to complain about General Ignatieff and ask for his recall from Istanbul in the name of the government.[237] Other visits to Britain and France for health reasons were also announced, but were viewed as diplomatic missions.[238]

---

[229] Arthur Beylérian, "Krikor Odian (1834-1887): Un Haut Fonctionnaire ottoman," *Revue du Monde arménien moderne et contemporain*, vol. 1 (1994), p. 47.

[230] Beylérian, p. 47.

[231] Davison, *Ottoman Diplomacy and Reforms*, p. 100; Beylérian, pp. 47-48.

[232] FO 195/831, letter of Ali Pasha to W. Stuart, British chargé d'affaires to Constantinople, 28 March 1865, no. 13 288/9. Cited in Beylerian, pp. 48-49.

[233] Beylérian, pp. 52-53.

[234] Gazmararyan, v. 2, p. 8.

[235] See for instance *The Times*, January 14, 1876.

[236] Frédéric Macler, *Autour de l'Arménie* (Paris: Librairie E. Nourry, 1917), p. 268.

[237] *Journal des Débats*, July 4, 1876.

[238] *Journal des Débats*, June 23, 1876; June 30, 1876.

Midhad's plan was to promulgate the Constitution before the Conference of Constantinople in order to avoid the impositions of the Powers.[239]
However, when the Conference started, the Powers insisted on the
admission of the proposals they formulated.[240] In his mind, there was
one concession that the Porte could make: to communicate the Constitution formally and officially to the Conference. This would enable the
European Powers to insist on the application of its principles but it
would be less binding than a formal treaty. Before presenting this offer
to the European Powers, however, Midhad preferred to verify whether
Britain and France would agree on the issue. He sent Odyan Effendi to
Paris and London with the approval of the Cabinet in order to gather the
reactions of the British and French governments to this proposal.[241]

On January 4, 1877, Lord Derby had been presented by the Ottoman
ambassador Musurus to Odyan Effendi, who arrived in England with a
special mission assigned by the Porte: he delivered a letter from Midhad
Pasha. Odyan Effendi recapitulated the history of recent events and
the reasons for which the Ottoman state refused the proposals made by
the plenipotentiaries during the Conference of Constantinople.[242] Odyan
seems to have negotiated about the provincial issue: the organisation of
the provincial administration, which would be drawn up by Turkish
ministers after receiving the approval of the Powers, would be a part of
the general plan and subsumed under the same agreement. The whole
system of reforms granted by the sultan to his subjects would thus be
placed under the guarantee of the Powers, who would have the right to
watch over the manner in which it was carried out.[243]

Odyan Effendi also visited Lord Beaconsfield on January 8, 1877 with
Musurus. With regard to the reforms, both of the Ottoman ministers
expressed their objection to the creation of Bulgaria and to its borders,
which would include a large portion of land inhabited by a Greek population. Odyan also explained that the stipulation that the governors of
the new province or provinces of Bulgaria must be Christian presented

---

[239] Cf. Ali Haydar Midhad, *The Life of Midhad Pasha. A Record of his Services, Political Reforms, Banishment, and Judicial Murder* (London: John Murray, 1903), pp. 114-147.
Mahmud Celaleddin Paşa, v. 1, p. 193. Cited in Devereux, p. 55.

[240] See also Devereux, pp. 92-94.

[241] See Mahmud Celaleddin Paşa, v. 1, pp. 234ff., for a discussion of Odyan's mission.
Cited in Devereux, pp. 93-94.

[242] PRO, FO 78/2674, Lord Derby to the Marquis of Salisbury, January 4, 1877.

[243] PRO, FO 78/2674, Lord Derby to the Marquis of Salisbury, January 10, 1877.
FO 78/2683, From Derby to Elliot, January 11, 1877 # No. 743.

difficulties to the Porte because of the small number of Christians available for such high appointments. As for the guarantees, the proposals that Ottoman troops should be withdrawn to the principal towns, leaving the policing of the country to foreign gendarmerie, and that a commission of foreigners would have power to exercise all the functions of government were humiliating: they were concessions that no independent power with any self-respect could make. Odyan Effendi continued that he was himself a Christian and an Armenian and knew well the feeling dominant in various parts of the empire. The grant of exceptional advantages to the Slavic provinces would create jealousy and dissatisfaction elsewhere. Odyan repeated that they could embody the Constitution in a protocol and place it under a European guarantee that would give the Powers the right to intervene on behalf of any portion of the sultan's subjects who were suffering from misgovernment. He mentioned that the special constitution granted to the districts of Lebanon was also secured by a protocol and it had never been argued that the Porte had failed to fulfil its responsibilities.[244]

However, the Foreign Office was surprised by Odyan Effendi's guarantees and questioned how the Ottoman government could advance such a suggestion. He seemed to be simultaneously refusing to grant special privileges to only three provinces on the basis of national sovereignty while proposing guarantees that would put the whole empire under the supervision of the European Powers. The Foreign Office did not know whether Midhad had obtained the sultan's approval when suggesting such a guarantee or whether Midhad had forced the sultan to refuse the proposals of the Conference of Constantinople by threatening the continuity of the sultanate. The Foreign Office seemed to consider the second a probability.[245]

After his conversation with Lord Derby, Odyan Effendi telegraphed the Porte that it was difficult to convince Russia as long as the Bulgarians

---

[244] PRO, FO 198/42. Turkey no. 2 (1877). Correspondence respecting the Conference at Constantinople and the Affairs of Turkey, 1876-77, presented to both Houses of Parliament by Command of Her Majesty, 1877. Memorandum no. 186. Foreign Office, January 13, 1877.

[245] BOA, YEE 16/13, 6 Rebiülevvel 1327/28 March 1909. Mithat Paşa'ya ve Mavi Kitaba dair makaleler (Articles related to Midhad Pasha and the Blue Book). It seems that somebody interpreted the statements of British statesmen included in the Blue Book in order to comment on internal Ottoman politics, but the author of this file is unknown. Some of the comments on Midhad Pasha, including the individual opinions and judgments of the unknown author, seem to have been extracted from the statements of the Foreign Office, translated into Ottoman Turkish and dated 13 Kanun-ı sani (January) 1877.

were not satisfied. Consequently, it was necessary to realise some of the points mentioned during the Conference of Constantinople together with the application of the Ottoman Constitution. If peace was concluded with Serbia and Montenegro, Russia would have less to protest. On these recommendations of Odyan Effendi, Midhad tried to constitute a mixed police organisation composed of Muslims and Bulgarians in Sofia, Edirne and the Danube; to assure the selection of governors and vice-governors from Bulgarians; to proclaim a general amnesty for those involved in uprisings; to reopen the provincial general assemblies which had been suspended by Mahmud Nedim Pasha; and to suppress the tithe. Midhad Pasha also sent instructions to the provinces to begin the election of members to the Chamber of Deputies.[246] We also understand from Odyan Effendi's message that Midhad organised the gendarmerie in Rumelia with French officers and that he undertook the reorganisation of finances with British experts.[247] However, at the moment when Midhad Pasha was preparing some of these concessions, Abdülhamid II sabotaged the process by sending an imperial order according to which non-Muslim students would not be accepted to Ottoman military schools; thus an important provision of the Ottoman Constitution was changed.[248]

As public opinion had an influential role in politics in democratic countries, Odyan suggested to Midhad Pasha that they should publish the proposals of the Conference in order to publicly explain their illogical and unjust character and to justify the Ottoman attitude. Thus, another dimension of Odyan Effendi's mission was to shift public opinion, both in Paris and London, in favour of the Ottoman government.[249] From the angle of the Ottoman archives, which contain the telegraphs of Odyan Effendi to the Grand Vizierate in early 1877, the main objective of his mission was to have a positive impact on public opinion in Paris and London, where the Ottoman government was under attack for not having accepted the proposals of the Conference of Constantinople.[250] His telegraph to the Grand Vizierate regarding his meeting with Disraeli reported how Odyan reacted to the appointment of Christian

---

[246] Midhad Paşa, *Tabsıra-i İbret*, vol. 1, pp. 214-215.

[247] BOA, HR. SYS 1863-3, From Odyan, Paris to the Grand Vizier, January 24, 1877.

[248] From Midhad Pasha to *Mabeyn-i Hümayun* (the private secretariat of the palace), 9 Muharrem 1294/24 January 1877. Cited in Midhad Paşa, *Tabsıra-i İbret*, vol. 1, p. 309.

[249] Bekir Sıtkı Baykal, "Midhad Paşa'nın Gizli Bir Siyasi Teşebbüsü," (The Secret Political Initiative of Midhad Pasha) in *III. Türk Tarih Kongresi, Ankara, 15-20 Kasım 1943* (Ankara: Türk Tarih Kurumu, 1948), pp. 472-473.

[250] BOA, HR.TO 554/41; 3 January 1877.

governors in Bulgaria and the supervision of the region by an international commission. He emphasised that even though the Sublime Porte
accepted the measures proposed by the delegates of the Conference, the
character of these measures was incompatible with the stipulations of
the Ottoman Constitution. As his meeting with Disraeli was organised
when the sessions of the Conference of Constantinople were in progress,
Odyan tried to informally negotiate amendments to the initial proposals
presented by the European delegates. He notified the Grand Vizierate
that even if he did not know their exact content, the Ottoman government could expect the submission of new proposals by the delegates of
the Conference.[251] In their telegraphs to the Grand Vizierate, Odyan
Effendi and Sadık Pasha, the Ottoman ambassador to Paris, described
their meeting with Thiers. They reported that the promulgation of the
Ottoman Constitution did not produce the impact they had expected in
the French newspapers *Débat* and *République*, which still had doubts
about its application.[252] In one of his telegraphs to the Grand Vizierate,
Odyan reported the course of his visit to Lord Derby and how he tried
to convince him that the application of the constitution would be less
difficult in the Ottoman Empire than in the Catholic countries of Europe.
The suppression of the Bulgarian uprising in 1876 by the Ottoman government led to an angry public reaction in Europe and the United States.
During his meeting with Derby, Odyan tried to legitimise the Ottoman
attitude to the Bulgarian issue.[253] When discussing the application of the
Ottoman Constitution during his encounter with Jules Simon, Odyan
again expressed his view that the process would be less difficult since
the empire did not have a clergy and practise a religion like Catholicism.[254] Odyan also met Sir Northcote, the Chancellor of the Exchequer,
in order to assure him that he would publicise the Ottoman Constitution
as an "Ottoman investment for the real needs of the country and not
for those of politics" in the British Parliament. Odyan Effendi also
dissipated the chancellor's doubts about the liberal character of the new
constitutional development.[255]

---

[251] BOA, HR.TO 554/44; 8 January 1877.

[252] BOA, HR.TO 554/45; 22 January 1877.

[253] BOA, HR.TO 554/28; 30 January 1877.

[254] BOA, HR. SYS 1863-3, From Odyan, Paris to the Grand Vizier, January 24, 1877.

[255] BOA, HR. SYS 1863-3, From Odyan, London to the Grand Vizier, February 4,
1877.

It is possible to conclude that Odyan acted as a mediator between the Ottoman state and the European Powers. The promotion of the Ottoman Constitution and opposition to the proposals of the Conference of Constantinople from a Christian subject would be more efficient and credible in the eyes of European diplomacy. The selection of an Armenian delegate was probably the best way to show the European Powers how much the granting of special privileges to Slavic provinces led to jealousy and dissatisfaction among the other Christian populations of the Ottoman Empire.

The Provincial Law and the Ottoman Counter-Project

The constant dilemma of the Tanzimat period lay in the two contradictory tendencies of centralisation and decentralisation.[256] Centralisation was desirable in order to bring into effect state-originated reforms, to put an end to the exploitation of rural populations by local landowners and to increase control over governmental revenues. Decentralisation was desirable in order to appease nationalist/separatist movements.[257] This dilemma was reflected in Ottoman provincial law. The provincial reform started with the granting of different degrees of authority through local councils. The *vilayet* law first applied to the Danubian province in 1864 and then to the whole empire in 1867.[258] The law provided the division of the empire into provinces called *vilayet*s, which were placed under the governors-general (*vali*s) named by the sultan. Each *vilayet* was divided into sanjaks (districts) under the administration of a governor (*mutessarıf*). The sanjak was divided into cazas (cantons) under the jurisdiction of a *kaymakam*. The caza was divided into communes. Groups of small

---

[256] Davison, *Reform, 1856-1876*, p. 136. Cited in Walter F. Weiker, "The Ottoman Bureaucracy: Modernisation and Reform," *Administrative Science Quarterly*, vol. 13, no. 3, Special issue on Organisations and Social Development (Dec. 1968), p. 464.

[257] Weiker, pp. 464-465.

[258] See the *Vilayet Nizamnamesi* (Provincial Law), *Düstur*, 1. Tertip (Istanbul, 1289), pp. 608-624 and the *Tuna Vilayet Nizamnamesi* (Provincial Law of the Danube), BOA, I.MMS no. 1245. Also see M. Hüdai Şentürk, *Osmanlı Devleti'nde Bulgar Meselesi*, 1850-1875 (The Bulgarian Question in the Ottoman State), (Ankara: Türk Tarih Kurumu, 1992), pp. 253-271 "for the differences between these two copies of the *nizamname* and their transliteration into the Latin alphabet". Cited in Mehmet Çelik, "Tanzimat in the Balkans: Midhad Pasha's Governorship in the Danube Province (Tuna Vilayeti), 1864-1868" (Unpublished MA Thesis, Bilkent University, 2007), p. 2, fn. 1. For the French translation of the provincial law of the Danube, see *Loi constitutive du Département formé sous le nom de Vilayet du Danube* (Constantinople: Imprimerie centrale, 1865).

villages not sufficiently important to form independent cazas were incorporated into the nearest cazas as *nahiye*s. The governor's office was divided into departments of civil, financial, police, political and legal affairs. The governor was granted authority over all officials in the province, but his authority was counterbalanced by the sultan's power to appoint sanjak and caza officials and by the responsibility of the various heads of departments to their respective ministries in addition to their responsibilities to the governor-general.[259]

In order to make the government more approachable and to soften religious divisions, the executive structure of the provincial administration was complemented by a system of mixed courts, general assemblies and administrative councils at the province, sanjak and caza levels.[260] The governor-general was assisted by an administrative council, composed of the chief magistrate, who was the head of the Sheri (Muslim religious tribunals), the director of finance, the director of external affairs and four other members (two elected by the Muslim population and two by the non-Muslim population). There was also a general council for each *vilayet*, composed of four members for each sanjak (two Muslims and two non-Muslims). It was the general council's duty to deal with local matters and transmit its resolutions through the governor-general to the imperial government. The governor was also assisted by an administrative council, composed of the qadi of the caza, the mufti of the chief town and the spiritual heads of the non-Muslim population, the sub-director of finance, the director of correspondence of the sanjak, and two Muslim and two non-Muslim permanent members. The lieutenant-governor of each caza also had an administrative council of three Muslims and three non-Muslims. In each commune, there was a council called the "*Conseil des Anciens*", composed of Muslim and non-Muslim members. The spiritual chiefs of the Muslim and non-Muslim populations were *ex officio* members of the council, which regulated the distribution of taxes and questions of public health and agriculture.[261] It should be noted, however, that representation, as perceived by the bureaucrats of the Tanzimat, was not entirely associated with the idea of democracy. It was rather a policy for obtaining the cooperation of different ethno-religious groups and the advice of their respected leaders

---

[259] Davison, *Reform, 1856-1876*, pp. 146-147. Weiker, p. 465.
[260] Davison, *Reform, 1856-1876*, pp. 146-147. Weiker, pp. 465-466.
[261] PRO, FO 78/2674. From Derby to Salisbury, November 20, 1876.

for better administration without allowing them to participate in political decision-making. The perspective was similar when, in 1845, two non-Muslim headmen from each province were invited to the capital to give information on local problems and suggest new reforms.[262] Far from achieving the principle of representation, the councils became instruments of domination by the governors or unrepresentative local elites.[263]

Safved Pasha's note of October 12, 1876 to foreign representatives intended to add a general assembly to this scheme of provincial administration, which would be elected by the inhabitants of the *vilayet*s and the capital to vote on the budgets and laws of the empire.[264] Safved Pasha himself indicated that the note of October 12, which presented a new programme of reforms, was a response to the programme of the British government, which also included the application of the Andrassy Note. The Porte's main argument was that the proposals of the Powers regarding the autonomy of the provinces went beyond the British programme during the Conference of Constantinople. The Ottoman plenipotentiaries presented the Ottoman Constitution as an oath of guarantee against the proposals of the European Powers and argued that these proposals contradicted constitutional principles.[265]

During the Conference of Constantinople, the Ottoman plenipotentiaries refused to give their agreement to the proposals of the Powers, which adhered to the Russian scheme. From the fourth protocol of the Conference, we can see that the Ottoman counter-project was communicated to the six Powers either at the end of December 1876 or in early January 1877.[266] During the seventh session of the Conference, the Ottoman plenipotentiaries accepted the terms of the Andrassy Note but refused their assent to other proposals.[267] The grand vizier offered to extend the Andrassy Note to Bulgaria.[268] This puts into question whether the Ottoman government received the support of the Austrian government, since the Austrians were against the formation of a large Bulgarian state.[269] The Ottoman counter-project did not make any mention of certain points

---

[262] Ahmed Lütfi Effendi, *Tarih*, vol. 8, pp. 15-17. Cited in Hanioglu, p. 76.

[263] Weiker, p. 466.

[264] PRO, FO 78/2674, From Derby to Salisbury, November 20, 1876.

[265] PRO, FO 78/2686, 6ème Protocole, Séance du 27 décembre 1876 & 8 Janvier 1877.

[266] PRO, FO 78/2686, 4ème Protocole, Séance du 20 décembre 1876, 1er Janvier 1877.

[267] PRO, FO 78/2676, From Salisbury to Derby, January 11, 1877.

[268] PRO, FO 78/2678, From Salisbury to Derby, January 12, 1877.

[269] PRO, FO 78/2677, From Salisbury, December 13, 1876.

imposed by the Powers, such as the employment of foreign soldiers in the gendarmerie and the international commission of supervision. The counter-project submitted for the consent of a future legislative assembly, not yet created, contained the abolition of the tithe and tax farming, the establishment of tribunals, the mode of the nomination of judges and the duration of their mandate, the election process and the attributes of different administrative councils. The counter-project categorically rejected the creation of a local militia in the three provinces consisting of Muslims and Christians in proportion to the population (the Porte accepted that the gendarmerie would recruit non-Muslim members but refused the fact that the number of non-Muslims should be proportionate to their share of the population); the use of the languages of the country on the same footing as Turkish; the nomination of the governor-general by the Porte for a period of five years with the consent of foreign ambassadors and his dismissal by the verdict of an independent tribunal; the selection of the governor by the governor-general; the settlement of the proportion of direct taxes payable to the central government by an independent authority and local control of taxation; and the prohibition of the future colonisation of the Circassians. The counter-project stipulated that the governors-general, governors, directors of finances and treasurers could only be removed at the discretion of the Porte. The verdicts of different councils would not have any force without the consent of the Porte.[270]

The European plenipotentiaries considered the Ottoman counter-project. Derby received a confidential report according to which the plenipotentiaries of the six Powers agreed upon certain modifications in the proposals made to the Porte: these were drawn up by Count Chaudordy in a manner which would likely raise the least objection from the Ottoman government. The introduction of a foreign police force should be abandoned and substituted with an Ottoman gendarmerie with European officers. There should be one commission composed of resident consuls in order to supervise the execution of the intended reforms.[271]

The 1876 Ottoman Constitution provided an imprecise framework for provincial administration, stipulating that further details would be fixed by another law.[272] The archives of the Ottoman Foreign Ministry contain

---

[270] PRO, FO 78/2470, From Elliot to Lord Derby, January 20, 1877. FO 78/2676, from Salisbury to Derby, January 1, 1877. FO 78/2677, from Salisbury to Derby, 31 December 1876.

[271] PRO, FO 78/2683, From the FO to Salisbury, January 4, 1876.

[272] "The Ottoman Constitution, Promulgated the 7th Zilbridje, 1293 (11/23 December, 1876)," Articles 108-112, pp. 384-385.

pages of drafts in French regarding provincial administration.[273] The author of these drafts was not indicated in the relevant file. If we can rely on the accounts of Abdülhamid II's brother-in-law, Mahmud Celaleddin, an Ottoman executive assembly started to prepare drafts for the application of the reform after the admission of the Andrassy Note. In the meantime, Ignatieff elaborated a draft entitled "administration of *nahiyes*" and sent it to the Ottoman Foreign Ministry. The translation of this draft was approved by the executive assembly as if it had been written by the Ottoman Foreign Ministry and was sent to the Cabinet.[274] These draft documents might be the ones authored by Ignatieff. These were followed in the same file by another document, again in French, entitled "constitutive law project instituting the bases of administrative, judiciary, financial and military organisation of the empire".[275] I maintain that the last draft was formulated by the anti-Russian wing of the Ottoman Foreign Ministry as a counter-response to Ignatieff's initiative. Midhad Pasha himself stated that some of the proposals of the Conference of Constantinople had been revised in official and informal meetings by Ottoman delegates in accordance with the spirit of the Ottoman Constitution.[276] This shows that Ottoman delegates were trying to find a compromise between European proposals and the spirit of the constitutional reform even after the promulgation of the Ottoman Constitution, which was still being developed because of its incomplete provisions.

The Ottoman counter-project of provincial reform, which seems to have been formulated by the Ottoman Foreign Ministry, targeted not only the three provinces of the Balkans but all Ottoman territory. It made some concessions and found a certain compromise between Ottoman views of the issue and the conceptualisation of provincial reform by Britain, Russia, France (whose influence was rather on legal codes) and Austria after the rebellions in the Balkans.

The project established the administrative divisions of a province. The province would be administered by a governor nominated by the sultan.

---

[273] BOA, HR. SYS 1864-1.

[274] Mahmud Celaleddin Paşa, v. 1, pp. 113-114.

[275] BOA, HR. SYS 1864-1. Projet de loi constitutive instituant les bases de l'organisation administrative, judiciaire, financière et militaire de l'Empire ottoman.

[276] Extracted from Midhad Pasha's statement at the Grand Divan convened by Midhad Pasha in order to discuss the proposals of the Conference of Constantinople. See for details, Ali Fuat Türkgeldi, *Mesail-i Mühimme-i Siyasiye* (Important Political Affairs), Bekir Sıdkı Baykal (ed.), (Ankara: Türk Tarih Kurumu, 1957), v. 2, pp. 8-15. Cited in Midhad Paşa, *Tabsıra-i İbret*, v. 1, pp. 288-293.

In the projects advanced by the European representatives, the governor would be nominated by the Porte but with the consent of the European Powers. The compromise offered by the Ottoman government was that the governor should belong to the faith of the majority of the provincial population. In the provinces in which the governor was Muslim, his undersecretary would be Christian and vice-versa. This concession corresponded to the requirements of the European Powers for the appointment of a Christian governor to the provinces of Bosnia, Herzegovina and Bulgaria and for the integration of more Christian functionaries into Ottoman public administration. The undersecretary would be also appointed by the sultan but the other functionaries of the provincial administration would be nominated by the governor on the proposal of the general council of the province. This was also an element proposed by the projects of the European representatives. Other elements were imported from the projects of the European Powers previously cited: thus a municipal council would be entrusted with the task of collecting taxes through collectors which it would nominate on its own, independently of the Porte. Legal and administrative acts would be promulgated both in Turkish and in the language of the majority of the population (although this was limited to the European provinces of the Ottoman Empire and to the islands).

Nizamiye (civil, criminal) laws would be completed on the basis of their European counterparts. As regards the civil code, the French model would be adopted with some modifications in accordance with the customs of the country. Gaps would be filled in the code of commercial and civil procedures in use. The commercial and penal codes in use would be confirmed. The code of criminal instruction would be formulated on the basis of French and British legislation. Thus the Porte probably intended to end the complaints of the European Powers about the lack of European references in terms of the legal codification in the Ottoman Empire. The lack of reference points difficulties in the preservation of the rights of European nationals in the courts.

The counter-project also developed a financial dimension. The total amount of taxes for each *vilayet* would be determined according to the general needs of the state and the province. A financial legislation commission would be established in the Ottoman capital in order to develop the new regime of taxation. The commission would also establish a project of payment of the internal and external public debt. With the last article, the Ottoman government probably expected to prevent the transfer of the surplus of the three provinces to the Ottoman foreign debt, as suggested by the Great Powers, by increasingly centralising the administration of debts.

Four commissions of administrative, judicial, financial and military legislation were entrusted with the task of elaborating laws and regulations for the development of the general principles proclaimed in the project; each of the commissions would be composed of five members nominated by the sultan from notabilities in each speciality. In case of need, the sultan could also refer to foreign specialists. The Ottoman state probably intended to satisfy the desire of the Powers and especially that of Britain by employing foreign functionaries in Ottoman public administration. Moreover, the *Journal des Débats* announced that the idea to extend the measures prepared for Bosnia, Herzegovina and Bulgaria to the whole empire made some progress in Britain. Instead of local autonomy and distinct reforms for privileged provinces, Lord Stratford de Redcliffe, former ambassador to the Porte, seemed to be behind a general plan of reorganisation that would apply to the whole Ottoman Empire in order to preserve territorial integrity. Redcliffe suggested constituting a half Muslim, half Christian commission. This would also house European commissioners. In that respect, one may also question the extent to which the counter-project instituting the bases of administrative, judicial, financial and military organisation in the Ottoman Empire was partially inspired by the perspectives of Britain's liberal wing, represented by Redcliffe, since the idea of a mixed commission seems to be similar in both projects.[277]

The draft of provincial administration laid down plans for the organisation of the Ottoman gendarmerie, local police and army. Safved Pasha, having refused all the proposals of the Conference (some because they were contrary to the principles of an independent government, others because they contradicted the Ottoman Constitution), announced that "to show its desire of an understanding and its deference towards Europe", the Porte accepted the project of forming a corps of volunteers incorporating foreign cadres recruited on neutral territory.[278] Safved Pasha sent the Ottoman representatives in London, Paris and Brussels a confidential despatch on May 19, 1878 in order to inquire whether these governments could send officers up to the rank of captain for the

[277] *Journal des Débats*, October 12, 1876.
[278] *The Times*, January 6, 1877.

reorganisation of the Ottoman army and whether they could help in the selection of the candidates.[279] In May 1878, Musurus confidentially discussed the issue with Lord Salisbury. The latter asked him if it was possible to recruit captains, as well as officers above or below that grade, from Britain. Musurus recommended the recruitment of one or two colonels and two or three majors.[280] Karateodori Effendi communicated from Brussels on May 20, 1878, that the Belgian Ministry of Foreign Affairs was not able to decide on the issue on its own because of Belgium's neutrality.[281] The idea of the recruitment of Belgian troops was advanced by one of the French plenipotentiaries as a neutral force for assisting in the maintenance of peace in Bulgaria during the Conference of Constantinople. The project of employing a Belgian police force was a compromise between Russian occupation and the employment of a purely Ottoman force.[282] The Ottoman government thus found an intermediate solution by employing foreign soldiers in the Ottoman army.

The Drafting Commission: a Platform of Tensions

The Drafting Commission of the Ottoman Constitution was established by an imperial decree in October 1876 under the chairmanship of Midhad Pasha. The list of the participants is still controversial given disputes in the sources, although the imperial decrees that officialised the members of the Commission dissipate the controversies to some extent. The Drafting Commission welcomed members of different backgrounds, mostly civil officials but also participants from the ulema and military: non-Muslim bureaucrats were not neglected. Hence, the Commission was a heterogeneous group in terms of its professional, ideological, legal and ethno-religious background. The intention of this section is to inquire how the Commission might have debated the Ottoman constitutional issue and come to an agreement on the selection of European constitutional models by focusing on selection parameters and the principal elements of tensions between the different members. The Commission reveals the extent to which the Ottoman state was composed of antagonistic wings and how this antagonism shaped the Ottoman constitutional

---

[279] BOA, HR. SYS 1864-1, Safved Pasha to the Ottoman representatives, 19 May 1878.
[280] BOA, HR. SYS 1864-1, Musurus to Safved Pasha, 20 May 1878.
[281] BOA, HR. SYS 1864-1, Karateodori Effendi to Safved Pasha, 20 May 1878.
[282] PRO, FO 78/2684, From the Earl of Derby, December 15, 1876.

process. The prevalence of the sultan and his circle over the process will show that the central government in its narrow and Ottoman sense was identified with the personality of the sultan and his few favourites. The Drafting Commission was also the embodiment of a quest for identity and cultural authenticity in opposition to Europe, although European constitutional models were under examination.[283]

The "Constitutional Calendar"

In December 1875, the British ambassador Elliot noted in his despatches that the discontent with the government had reached such a point that some leading men were seriously thinking of addressing a petition to the sultan regarding the state of the empire and urging him to establish control over the administration. Elliot remarked that something of a "constitutional nature" was on the agenda.[284] Midhad Pasha, then minister of justice, resigned on the grounds that the reform project prepared by the Grand Vizier Mahmud Nedim Pasha and reflected in the 1875 imperial firman of December 12 was incomplete: the reforms "did not touch the root of the vice of the administration which was that of excessive centralisation".[285]

Midhad Pasha seemed to conceptualise a draft constitution in his mind much earlier than 1876, first mentioning his plan to Sir Henry Elliot in 1875. He formulated his project around the same major institutional concepts, namely the establishment of a national assembly and the principles of centralisation and ministerial responsibility. The assembly would assure the responsibility of ministers before the nation. In order to make the assembly totally national, the latter would house deputies regardless of racial and religious affiliation. Centralisation would control the governors-general in the provinces. The fact that Midhad Pasha planned the proclamation of the Ottoman Constitution long before shows that his main intention was not to use the constitution as a weapon in the Conference of Constantinople.[286] In order to see whether his constitutional project would be supported by Britain, Midhad also made inquiries with

---

[283] Meijer, "Introduction," in Meijer, pp. 1-3.
[284] PRO, FO 78/2391, Elliot to Derby, December 10, 1875 # no. 821.
[285] PRO, FO 78/2391, Elliot to Derby, December 14, 1875 # no. 831.
[286] This summary of Midhad's project is based on an article Sir Henry Elliot wrote in the *Nineteenth Century* of February 1888. Cited in Midhad Paşa, *Tabsıra-i İbret*, v. 1, pp. 304-305.

regards to its reception by British public opinion through Henry Elliot. The British ambassador gave him signs of support, responding to him that the British disliked absolutist regimes and would welcome constitutional monarchy in the Ottoman Empire.[287] Elliot even had an audience with Abdülaziz I in order to convince him to bring the new reforms into practice. He gave him "mortal offence" by adding that "a spirit had risen of which every European country had had experience, that the institutions of the past were no longer suited to the present age, and that everywhere the people were beginning to expect to have a certain control over those who conducted their administration".[288] Midhad's interaction with Elliot in the matter of a more radical reform was perhaps the beginning of the constitutional calendar.

After Aziz's deposition, Midhad drafted a decree of accession that referred to the transition of the Ottoman Empire to constitutional government and ministerial responsibility. He encountered the opposition of both Hüseyin Avni and Mehmed Rüşdü, who joined Sadullah Bey,[289] the newly-appointed palace secretary, in stating that the sultan does not wish to constitute a national assembly on the grounds that Ottoman society was not suited to such an innovation. Consequently, Midhad's draft of the decree of accession was changed so as to avoid any reference to a constitution.[290]

Despite Midhad's failure to shape the content of the decree regarding Murad V's accession to the throne, his popularity was made manifest on the evening of June 2, 1876, when a crowd of softas walked towards his home crying "Long live the Sultan", "Long live Midhad" and "Long live the Constitution".[291] Midhad also gained popularity before international public opinion. *The Times* wrote in its issue of June 8, just after Abdülaziz I's deposition, that Midhad was designated by public acclamation

---

[287] Based on an article Sir Henry Elliot wrote in the *Nineteenth Century* of February 1888. Cited in Midhad Paşa, *Tabsıra-i İbret*, v. 1, pp. 304-305.

[288] Elliot, pp. 229-230.

[289] Sadullah Pasha was a friend of Namık Kemal who contributed to the translation of Mustafa Fazıl's letter to Abdülaziz I proposing a constitutional regime. Cited in Davison, *Reform, 1856-1876*, p. 340.

[290] Süleyman Paşa, pp. 60-61; Mahmud Celaleddin, v. 1, pp. 117-118, 126. Cited in Davison, *Reform, 1856-1876*, p. 340.

[291] Y. Haluk Şehsuvaroğlu, *Sultan Aziz, Hususi, Siyasi Hayatı, Devri* (Sultan Aziz, His Private and Political Life, His Era and His Death), (İstanbul: Hilmi Kitabevi, 1949), p. 110. See also Comte E. de Kératry, *Mourad V: Prince-Sultan-Prisonnier d'Etat, 1840-1878*, 2nd edition (Paris, 1878), pp. 142-143. Cited in Devereux, p. 36. The event was also reported in the *Journal des Débats*, June 12, 1876.

as the successor to Mehmed Rüşdü Pasha.[292] "Midhad Pasha especially, is credited with character and energy commensurate with his first-rate talents, and he is supposed that he will not in office disavow those notions as to the practicability of the establishment of something like Constitutional rule in Turkey, for which he made himself conspicuous at the head of the Opposition".[293] These statements by *The Times* show that he was already considered the leader of a constitutional movement long before the establishment of the Drafting Commission. His international recognition also engendered internal promotion: he was promoted from minister without a portfolio to president of the Council of State.[294]

Constitutional debates first began at the meetings of grand councils. Two council meetings were held to discuss constitutional reform before the institution of the Commission. Süleyman Pasha (director of military schools), Kara Halil Effendi (commissioner of fatwa), Seyfeddin Effendi (*kazasker* of Anatolia and a member of the Council of State), Mahmud Celaleddin Pasha (Abdülhamid II's brother-in-law), Namık Pasha (minister without a portfolio) and Mehmed Rüşdü Pasha (grand vizier) were the most well-known figures in these discussions.[295] The professional background of the participants indicates that initially the debate took place between religious, military and civil elites. Midhad Pasha seems to have developed his draft constitution after the Grand Council of 8 June, 1876,[296] which was a meeting of theologians and jurisconsults of Islamic law organised by the sheikh ül-Islam in his office to discuss with Midhad Pasha whether and the extent to which a representative constitution could be reconciled with the fundamental principles and doctrines of Islam. Midhad Pasha was welcomed favourably.[297] The discussions were lively, but the Council decided unanimously on the creation of a representative chamber: the task of elaborating this project was entrusted to Midhad Pasha.[298] The Sheikh ül-Islam Hayrullah Effendi was said, however, to soften the radical character of his reforms.[299] Namık Pasha, then minister

---

[292] *The Times*, June 8, 1876.
[293] *The Times*, June 8, 1876.
[294] *The Times*, June 16, 1876.
[295] Mention is made of the meetings of July 8 & 15, 1876. See for details Devereux, pp. 36-38.
[296] *Journal des Débats*, July 29, 1876.
[297] *Journal des Débats*, July 6, 1876.
[298] *The Times*, June 21, 1876. Mahmud Celaleddin Paşa, v. 2, p. 81. *Revue de Constantinople*, June 11, 1876.
[299] *Journal des Débats*, June 21, 1876.

without a portfolio, accepted the establishment of a chamber provided that membership was restricted to Muslims. During this discussion, the Grand Vizier Mehmed Rüşdü Pasha advanced the argument that the people were not ready for such an innovation.[300] During a session of the Grand Council of July 15, 1876, Midhad presented the bases of his project.[301] His preliminary programme was based on equality between Muslims and non-Muslims; the admission of Christians to state offices, including the Grand Vizierate; the creation of a Chamber of Deputies (four deputies from each province and sixteen deputies from the capital), proportionate to the number of communities; the responsibility of the ministers before this Chamber of Deputies; the abolition of the article of the shariʿa repudiating the testimony of Christians to the benefit of Muslims; and the irremovability of judges and state officials in the absence of misconduct. It was also noted that the application of this project would engender the suppression of the Grand Vizierate and that the grand vizier would become a simple president of ministers. The functions of the National Assembly were already defined as the supervision of finances, the voting of the budget, the revision of civil and internal laws and the promulgation of new legislation if necessary, and the creation of industries and the protection of commerce and agriculture.[302] Midhad Pasha once stated that, in addition to religious temples, the new assembly would be the temple of the fatherland in which Muslims and Christians would discuss, in an atmosphere of brotherhood and freedom, the new laws and the application of the reform.[303]

The copies of his draft constitution started to circulate after the meeting of July 15, 1876 among the participants of the council.[304] The session of the Council of Ministers on July 15 was a turning point in the sense that several ulemas and high-ranking functionaries participated in the meeting and discussed the bases of the projected constitution.[305] In July, upon Midhad's complaint that nothing was done to carry out the organic reforms for which the Grand Council expressed its opinion and he himself

---

[300] İsmail Hami Danişmend, *İzahlı Osmanlı Tarihi Kronolojisi* (An Annotated Chronology of Ottoman History) (Istanbul, 1955), vol. 4, p. 280. Cited in Devereux, p. 37.

[301] *Journal des Débats*, July 29 & 31, 1876; *Levant Herald*, July 17, 1876; *The Times* (London), July 17 & August 5, 1876. Cited in Devereux, pp. 37-38.

[302] *Revue de Constantinople*, June 11, 1876.

[303] *Revue de Constantinople*, July 23, 1876.

[304] *Journal des Débats*, July 29, 1876.

[305] *The Times*, July 17, 1876.

intended to realise, Henry Elliot warned the grand vizier that the delay would strengthen the position of opponents. Mehmed Rüşdü Pasha's pretext was that the sultan was unable to attend to business. Although he was himself in favour, the promulgation of a reform seemed impossible under these conditions. If the object was to abolish or limit the sultan's prerogatives, he questioned how it could be possible to promulgate such a concession when the sultan himself was not in a state to understand the nature of the concessions he was making. The validity of the new law could be contested by the opposition and the next sultan.[306] Grand Vizier Mehmed Rüşdü Pasha profited from Murad V's mental disorder and attempted to dominate the administration of state affairs. However, discontent with the sultan assuming the Islamic functions of his position given his mental disorder and blame against Rüşdü Pasha for his ambition to dominate state affairs by eliminating the sultan's presence were spreading among the members of the ulema.[307]

Athough Hüseyin Avni did not share the idea of instituting a constitution, he believed it was necessary to depose the sultan in order to save the empire.[308] Hüseyin Avni was not a constitutionalist: his real motive in joining the *coup d'état* was rather his patriotic ambition to curb the Balkan rebellion and reduce Russian influence. He was "a Tanzimat man only in so far as army reform went".[309] Once Süleyman Pasha had clearly expressed his support for Midhad Pasha and his constitutional programme, Hüseyin Avni silenced Süleyman Pasha by stating that soldiers should not intervene in politics.[310] On June 15, 1876, Hüseyin Avni Pasha was killed. "With Avni gone, Midhad, although officially only the President of the Council of State, became the *de facto* head of the government".[311]

---

[306] PRO, FO 198/42. Correspondence respecting the affairs of Turkey. Turkey no. 1 (1877). From Sir Henry Elliot to the Earl of Derby, July 25, 1876, no. 15.

[307] Mahmud Celaleddin Paşa, v. 2, pp. 11-12. Elliot, pp. 246-247.

[308] See for details, Devereux, pp. 32-33.

[309] Süleyman Paşa, pp. 9-10, 17; Ahmed Saib, *Vaka-i Sultan Abdülaziz* (The Episode of Sultan Abdülaziz), (Kahire: Hindiye Matbaası, 1320), pp. 167-168; *Levand Herald*, 5 July 1876; Emile de Kératry, *Mourad V. Prince, Sultan, Prisonnier d'Etat (1840-1878) d'après des Témoins de sa Vie* (Paris: Dentu, 1878), pp. 103-105. Cited in Davison, *Reform, 1856-1876*, p. 318.

[310] Danişmend, *Osmanlı Tarihi Kronolojisi*, v. 4, p. 280. Cited in Devereux, p. 37. The discussion between Hüseyin Avni and Süleyman Pasha occurred at the meeting held by the sheikh ül-Islam of June 8, 1876.

[311] Devereux, p. 37.

Other councils followed that of June 15, 1876. Contradictory news circulated about the presidency of the council that would deal with the elaboration of the reform programme. First, Server Pasha was appointed as the president of the reform council,[312] and the project elaborated by Midhad Pasha was set aside.[313] The Porte turned its attention to the Ottoman Constitution, although they avoided using the word.[314] In August, the scheme for an Ottoman Constitution elaborated by Midhad Pasha was ready for consideration by Grand Vizier Mehmed Rüşdü Pasha, who would then bring it before the Council of Ministers for deliberation. Midhad's project provoked, however, strong opposition from the ulema and especially from the sheikh ül-Islam, who had been appointed the previous May for his liberal ideas.[315] The grand vizier, aware that opinion was divided among the members of the Cabinet, left the matter in abeyance. The Cabinet was divided by two conflicting parties, the liberals and the conservatives. The conservatives, headed by the sheikh ül-Islam, stated that the discussion of political matters at a moment when Ottoman soldiers were confronting the enemies of the country would provoke the masses. The liberals, on the contrary, expressed the view that the accomplishment of the sultan's promises would gather patriots around the Ottoman throne and obtain the sympathy of Europe.[316]

"While the domestic political situation thus made the liberal cause appear hopeless, the liberals had a valuable asset in the foreign situation".[317] The diplomatic pressure from the European Powers for the settlement of the Balkan crisis constituted a new turning point: on September 26, a Grand Council composed of ministers, ulema, military leaders and high functionaries (about 70 people) convened at the Porte to discuss whether the Porte should concede to the proposals of the Powers for peace in the Balkans (status quo in Montenegro and Serbia, administrative autonomy for Bosnia and Herzegovina, and reforms in Bulgaria). The participants rejected the proposals and Midhad took the opportunity to advance the necessity of a constitutional system that would generalise the reforms not only for the Balkan provinces but for

---

[312] *The Times*, August 18, 1876.
[313] *The Times*, August 24, 1876.
[314] *The Times*, August 24, 1876.
[315] *The Times*, August 5, 1876.
[316] *The Times*, August 8, 1876.
[317] Devereux, p. 45.

the whole empire as an alternative solution to the Powers' suggestions.[318] "It was variously reported that there would be an assembly of seven hundred and twenty members, which resembled a proposal by Küçük Said Bey, or of one hundred and twenty members of whom three fourths would be elected, which sounded like Midhad's project".[319] One might think that two draft constitutions, one by Küçük Said and the other by Midhad Pasha, were discussed during the session of the Grand Council on September 26.[320]

After Abdülhamid's accession, the Drafting Commission of the Ottoman Constitution was instituted on October 8, 1876. What made it different from the other grand councils which had convened after June 1876 to debate the constitutional issue was the official announcement of its institution to the European Powers through Safved Pasha's circular of October 12, 1876. It is true that various rumours regarding the former grand councils and their deliberations on constitutional reform also circulated, but none of them emanated from an official source. Thus, the functioning of the Commission became an international commitment for the Porte and an irreversible step towards drafting the Ottoman Constitution. Midhad Pasha was named as the head of the Commission.[321]

The Composition of the Drafting Commission

The list of the members making up the Drafting Commission differs from one source to the other. Mithat Cemal Kuntay's list,[322] included in his book within the framework of Namık Kemal's ideas regarding the Commission's members, nearly overlaps with an archival list contained in the imperial decree of October 8, 1876, which officially institutionalised the Drafting Commission with a core list of members.[323] According

---

[318] Mahmud Celaleddin Paşa, v. 1, pp. 188-189. Cited in Devereux, p. 45.

[319] *Levand Herald*, September 28 and 30, 1876. Cited in Davison, *Reform, 1856-1876*, p. 368.

[320] Davison, *Reform, 1856-1876*, p. 368.

[321] *Journal des Débats*, October 13, 1876.

[322] Mithat Cemal Kuntay (1885-1956) was a Turkish writer and jurist. He gave a list of the members of the Drafting Commission in his biography of Namık Kemal. See Mithat Cemal Kuntay, *Namık Kemal: Devrinin İnsanları ve Olayları Arasında* (Namık Kemal: Among The Men and Events of his Time), v. 2, part 2 (İstanbul: Maarif Basımevi, 1956), pp. 75-85. See also Kılıç, *Osmanlı Devleti'nde Meşrutiyet'e Geçiş*, pp. 43-50 & Devereux, pp. 259-260.

[323] See Appendix II for the list of members of the Drafting Commission in a comparative table which includes Kuntay's list together with those of the imperial decrees.

to the document, the core list of names was decided by the Cabinet which gathered that day at the Sublime Porte: it was then submitted to the approbation of the sultan.[324] The functions of the Drafting Commission were described as the formulation of the Ottoman Constitution and the internal regulations of the General Assembly and the responsibilities of ministers and civil officialdom.[325] Two other decrees show that additional names were added to the core list in October and November 1876.[326] Selda Kılıç observed that the number of participants in the Commission then reached 37.[327] The subsequent inclusion of names indicates that the participation of additional members was constantly negotiated behind the scenes. There were also some ambiguities over the chairmanship of the Drafting Commission; for instance, Ubicini mentions Server Pasha as the president.[328] However, the imperial decree instituted the Commission under the chairmanship of Midhad Pasha.

If civil functionaries dominated the Drafting Commission, the ulema occupied an undeniably better position than military officers.[329] Kara Halil Effendi, the commissioner of fatwa, was the one who religiously legitimised the dethronement of Abdülaziz I on the grounds of his incapacity to deal with political affairs.[330] The participation of the *kazasker*s of Rumelia and Anatolia, the two chief religious judges and the most high-ranking officials of the ulema after the sheikh ül-Islam, was a guarantee that the Drafting Commission's decisions would conform to the principles of the shari'a and the interests of the ulema class.[331]

A secret report written by Nusret Pasha to Abdülhamid II, the principal opponent of Midhad Pasha during the establishment of the Danubian *vilayet*,[332] contains a list of Midhad's supporters. Interestingly, the names on the list overlap with those of some members of the Drafting

---

[324] BOA, I. DUIT 91/10, 19 Ramazan 1293/8 October 1876.

[325] BOA, I. DUIT 91/10, 19 Ramazan 1293/8 October 1876.

[326] BOA, İ. DUIT 91/3. 14 Şevval 1293/2 November 1876: Namık Kemal Bey, Mehmed Sahib Molla Bey, Asım Effendi and Yanko Effendi were added to the core list on November 2, 1876; BOA, DUIT 91/2. From Said Pasha, 19 Ramazan 1293/8 October 1876: the inclusion of Abidin Bey, commissioner of the Stock Exchange, was thus decreed by the sultan on October 8, 1876.

[327] Kılıç, "1876 Anayasası'nın Bilinmeyen İki Tasarısı", pp. 565-569.

[328] A. Ubicini, *La Constitution ottomane du 7 Zilhidje 1293 (23 Décembre 1876) expliquée et annotée* (Paris: Cotillon, 1877), p. 9. See also for details, Devereux, p. 47, fn. 27.

[329] See Appendix II for the professional backgrounds of the members.

[330] Mahmud Celaleddin Paşa, v. 1, p. 165.

[331] Yılmaz, p. 16.

[332] Çelik, pp. 35-36.

Commission.[333] If we consider the people described as Midhad's supporters in Nusret's report as the supporters of progressive ideas and constitutional reform within the Drafting Commission, we may assume that at least half of the civil functionaries in the Commission were in favour of the proclamation of the Ottoman Constitution.[334]

Nusret's report also reveals that Ramiz Effendi was from the Mevlevi order and not a Sunni.[335] More interestingly, it was argued that the Mevlevi lodge of Yenikapı was a meeting point for Young Ottomans to discuss constitutional matters.[336] It seems that Midhad Pasha even bought a farm house near the lodge and that he was the close friend of the Mevlevi Sheikh Osman Selahaddin Dede. It also seems that the latter introduced Midhad Pasha to Prince Abdülhamid and was the only eyewitness of his promise to promulgate the Ottoman Constitution when he came to the throne.[337] This calls into question the extent to which non-Sunni Islamic orders were involved in the constitutional affair and if they expected the equalisation of their orders with Sunni Islam.

Almost one third of the Commission was composed of members of the Council of State. In fact, the Drafting Commission was attached to the Council of State to help with technical cooperation.[338] Some evidence of the time being considered, one might also think that the Drafting Commission was instituted within the Council of State.[339] If the Ottoman Foreign Ministry was the negotiator of reforms with the Great Powers, the Council of State accomplished the technical dimension of the reforms. In August 1876, before the establishment of the Drafting Commission, Midhad Pasha proposed an efficient reorganisation of the Council of State's staff as well as the distribution of salaries for the sake of economy.[340] In fact, one aspect of Midhad's reforms was efficient use of the state's financial resources for the sake of economic improvements.

Among the civil functionaries, three were of Armenian origin (Odyan Effendi, Vahan Bey and Ohannes Çamiç Effendi), while three others (Yanko Effendi, Aleksandr Karateodori Effendi, and Sava Pasha) were of

[333] BOA, YEE 79/60. From Nusret, 10 Ağustos 1294/22 August 1878.
[334] BOA, YEE 79/60. From Nusret, 10 Ağustos 1294/22 August 1878.
[335] BOA, YEE 79/60. From Nusret, 10 Ağustos 1294/22 August 1878.
[336] Ekrem Işın, İstanbul'da Gündelik Hayat (Everyday Life in Istanbul), (İstanbul: İletişim Yayınları, 1995), p. 290. Cited in Midhad Paşa, Tabsıra-i İbret, v. 1, p. 175.
[337] See Işın, p. 290. Cited in Midhad Paşa, Tabsıra-i İbret, v. 1, pp. 174-175, fn. 74.
[338] BOA, I. DUIT 91/3. 14 Şevval 1293/2 November 1876.
[339] Kuntay, v. 2, part 2, p. 56.
[340] BOA, I. DUIT 58/37, 9 Ağustos 1292/21 August 1876.

Greek descent. Vahan Effendi wrote a treatise on Ottoman commercial law which was published by imperial order in 1861.[341] Sava Pasha was a specialist in Islamic law and would publish a book on its theoretical framework much later.[342]

Sava Pasha was also the director of the Imperial Galatasaray Lycée in 1876. He was described by the French as someone familiar with the principles and methods of French secondary education. In 1876, the sultan decided to restore the Ottoman Imperial Lycée in Galatasaray to its former historical location by moving the institution from Gülhane, where it had been transferred some years after the death of Ali Pasha.[343] In fact, one may follow from Sava Pasha's correspondence with the grand vizier that the former requested the moving of the institution to its traditional location. Sava Pasha complained of the insufficiency of space in Gülhane in light of the increasing number of students attending the school.[344] "The Lycée was placed in the midst of the Christian quarter and at the centre of European ideas" noted the French embassy after the move. The French government also appreciated the perseverance of the director and made him an officer of the *Légion d'Honneur*.[345] The Galatasaray Lycée was a source of tensions between France and the Ottoman Empire in 1876, as it was the Porte's intention to reduce the intellectual and moral influence of the University of France to a minimum in this institution. Although the French government awarded Sava Pasha with the *Légion d'Honneur* for having defended French interests, it accused him some months later of pursuing only his personal benefit and decided to campaign for his dismissal.[346] The presence of Sava Pasha in the Drafting Commission probably had symbolic value. He was, after all, the director of an institution founded to train Ottoman students as future bureaucrats.

---

[341] BOA, I. MVL 452/20206, 23 Safer 1278/30 August 1861.

[342] Savvas Pacha, *Etude sur la Théorie du Droit musulman*, 2 vol. (Paris: Marchal & Billard, 1892-98).

[343] French Ministry of Foreign Affairs, Diplomatic Archives, ADP (Affaires diverses politiques), Turquie, 1814-1896. Galata-Serai (Lycée de). From Bourgoing to Decazes, April 21, 1876.

[344] BOA, I DUIT 115/55. From Sava Pasha to the Grand Vizier, 15 Zilkade 1292/13 December 1875.

[345] French Ministry of Foreign Affairs, Diplomatic Archives, ADP (Affaires diverses politiques), Turquie, 1814-1896. Galata-Serai (Lycée de). From Bourgoing to Decazes, April 21, 1876.

[346] MAEF, CP, July-August 1876, vol. 405. From Bourgoing to Decazes. July 10, 1876, no. 100 & From Bourgoing. July 28, 1876.

The Agenda of the Drafting Commission

An official communication[347] dated 11.N.1293/September 30, 1876 from the chief scribe of the Ottoman palace (*Mabeyn Başkatipliği*) to the Grand Vizierate and the imperial order[348] dated 7.Z.1293/December 24, 1876 to Midhad Pasha on the occasion of the promulgation of the Ottoman Constitution reflect the spirit and the administrative process in which said constitution was drafted. Since the drafting of the Ottoman Constitution, together with the internal regulation of a General Assembly and the rules regarding the responsibilities of ministers and state officials, should conform to the principles of the shari'a, a special commission (*cemiyet-i mahsusa*) composed of ministers, the ulema and other state functionaries was instituted for the study of the administrative regimes of civilised states and the selection of legislation which could prove exemplary for the Ottoman Empire. The second step of the drafting process was the submission of this special commission's work to the Council of Ministers for examination. The final step was the approval of the draft constitution by the sultan. The tone of both documents reveals that changes in the internal affairs of the state and the expansion of external relations were provoked by the administrative insufficiency of the current governmental form of the empire. This insufficiency was behind the idea of drafting a constitution. More importantly, however, the institution of a General Assembly seems to have been a counter-response to the requirement of administrative autonomy for Bosnia, Herzegovina and Bulgaria.

The Drafting Commission met formally four times a week in the quarters of the Council of State and organised night sessions at the houses of Midhad, Damad Mahmud and Server.[349] A special council which included some of the members (Kemal, Ziya, Abidin Bey and Süleyman Pasha who headed it) of the Drafting Commission was also instituted with the purpose of examination.[350] The constitutional draft was developed by various appointed sub-committees. One of the committees was headed by Ahmed Cevded Pasha and was charged with the preparation

---

[347] BOA, YEE 71/43.

[348] BOA, YEE 71/38. See also Ahmed Midhad Effendi, *Üss-i İnkılab* (The Essentials of Reform), 2 vol., edited by Tahir Galip Seratlı (İstanbul: Selis Kitapları, 2004), here vol. 2, pp. 173-174.

[349] *İttihad*, January 6, 1877, cited in Kuntay, v. 2, part 2, p. 57. Cf. *Levant Herald*, November 23, 1876. Cited in Devereux, p. 48.

[350] Kuntay, v. 2, part 2, pp. 82, 91.

of a law on provincial administration.[351] Some of the members of the
Drafting Commission from the ulema (Kara Halil Effendi and İsmail
Seyfeddin Effendi)[352] were also members of this Council of *Mecelle*, an
initiative for the drafting of the Ottoman civil code. Ahmed Cevded
Pasha did not seem to be a strong supporter of the Ottoman Constitution.
Midhad's son, Ali Haydar, noted that when the proclamation of the Otto-
man Constitution was discussed at the General Council (*Meclis-i
Umumi*), Ahmed Cevded argued that since a clever sultan (meaning
Abdülhamid II) had come to the throne, the proclamation of a constitution was unnecessary.[353] He was such a royalist as to appreciate Napoleon III's accession from the presidency of the French Republic to the
position of emperor of France.[354] The second committee worked under
Server Pasha to draft a press law. The most important committee was
the one headed by Ziya Bey: it included Namık Kemal, Ohannes Çamiç,
Ramiz Effendi, Sava Pasha, Abidin Bey and Hayrullah Effendi. The
function of this committee was to draft the constitution itself with an
internal regulation for legislative bodies and an electoral law.[355] Namık
Kemal even argued that Ziya Pasha, Sava Pasha, Ohannes Çamiç and
Abidin Bey elaborated the draft constitution submitted to the sultan.[356]
The committee met every day. The proposals of the committee were first
submitted to Midhad and then distributed to all commission members to
be discussed at a general meeting of the full Commission. The articles,
rejected by a majority of votes, were returned to the Commission for
modification.[357] The Drafting Commission also tried to recruit a steno-
grapher to record the minutes of the Chamber of Deputies. However, the
Commission noticed that nobody in the Ottoman Empire was familiar
with this European way of keeping records. Consequently, the solution
was to recruit an expert from Europe to teach stenography. The Spanish
embassy at the Porte recommended Mr Bondini, who taught stenography

[351] *İttihad*, January 6, 1877, cited in Kuntay, v. 2, part 2, p. 57. Cf. *Levant Herald*,
November 23, 1876. Cited in Devereux, p. 48.
[352] Kuntay, v. 2, part 2, pp. 77-78.
[353] Midhad Paşa, *Tabsıra-i İbret*, v. 1, p. 210, fn. 95, Ali Haydar Midhad's note.
[354] Ahmed Cevded Paşa, *Tarih-i Cevded* (İstanbul: Darü't-Tıbaat'ül Amire, 1288), v. 1,
pp. 19-20. Cited in Kuntay, v. 2, part 2, pp. 82-83.
[355] *İttihad*, January 6, 1877, cited in Kuntay, v. 2, part 2, p. 57. Cf. *Levant Herald*,
November 23, 1876. Cited in Devereux, p. 48.
[356] From a letter of Namık Kemal to Ahmed Midhad Effendi, Cited in Kuntay, v. 2,
part 2, p. 58, fn. 10.
[357] *Levant Herald*, November 23, 1876. Cited in Devereux, pp. 48-49.

to the Italian Parliament. An imperial order sanctioned his recruitment for that purpose in December 1876.[358]

Midhad's plan for the early meeting of Parliament was accepted by the Cabinet and sanctioned by the sultan, but the first electoral law was rejected. On October 10, in a meeting attended by the ulema, ministers and other dignitaries, it was decided to form a special committee composed of Server Pasha, Kara Halil Effendi, Kadri Bey and Ahmed Hulusi Effendi.[359] The work of the special committee appeared on October 28 with an officially promulgated regulation. The seven-article regulation included important changes. The number of the deputies for the Chamber was increased from 120 to at least 130 members. No mention was made of the length of term or the size of the Senate. Although the opening day of the Ottoman Parliament was fixed at December 1, this date was delayed to March 1 for the first year.[360] On October 28, 1876, the instructions regarding the transitory mode of elections of the Chamber of Deputies were also published in the *Official Gazette* (*Takvim-i Vekayı*): the main question of national representation was thus resolved.[361] In early November, the provisions of the temporary election process of the members of the National Assembly were publicised in the press.[362] *La Turquie* announced that a council had gathered in Midhad's residence on November 17 to discuss a project of law regarding the Ottoman Parliament.[363]

Sources indicate different dates for the completion of the Drafting Commission's work, but the draft constitution followed an approval process by various state departments as described in the official communication cited above. According to some, the Commission completed its work by November 20 and Midhad unofficially submitted a draft (of 140 articles) to Abdülhamid II.[364] Other sources state that the Commission finished its work on December 1. Midhad Pasha, who did not take an ostensible part in the Commission but provided all the materials and became the spirit of the sessions, gathered the grand vizier and the

---

[358] BOA, I. DUIT 11/106. 17 Zilkade 1293/4 Aralık 1876.

[359] *Stamboul*, October 11, 1876. The fourth name was probably meant to be Ahmed Hilmi Effendi of the Drafting Commission. Cited in Devereux, p. 50.

[360] Aristarchi Bey, *Législation ottomane* (1878), pp. 306-309. Cited in Devereux, p. 51.

[361] Ubicini, *La Constitution ottomane*, p. 11.

[362] *La Turquie*, November 3, 1876.

[363] *La Turquie*, November 18, 1876.

[364] Mahmud Celaleddin Paşa, v. 1, p. 221. Cited in Devereux, p. 53.

ministers in his mansion to read the draft constitution and decide on the definitive text.[365] Finally, some documents suggest that the Commission finished the task of elaborating the constitution on December 4, 1876 and submitted the results to the grand vizier on December 5.[366] One day after the approval of the draft by the Council of Ministers on December 6, the draft was officially submitted to Abdülhamid II.[367] Midhad was appointed grand vizier on December 19, 1876.[368]

Midhad's Banishment and the Suspension of the Ottoman Constitution

The intrigues surrounding the dethronement of two sultans pushed Abdülhamid II to strengthen the position of the sultanate by breaking the power of the Sublime Porte and by concentrating the administration of state affairs in his hands. Consequently, he attempted to eliminate Mehmed Rüşdü Pasha, the Sheikh ül-Islam Hasan Hayrullah Effendi and Midhad Pasha from the Ottoman bureaucracy, as they were involved in the dethronement of Abdülaziz I, and to reconstitute a Cabinet from people he trusted. However, as these bureaucrats had supporters in the military and the Ottoman population, he did not dare to risk their sudden dismissal. He chose rather to wear them down gradually. He constituted a consultative commission within the inner palace for the administration of state affairs under his supervision: it contained his brother-in-law Mahmud Pasha, Mahmud Pasha's brother-in-law British Said and others.[369] In fact, it was Mahmud Celaleddin Pasha himself who recommended British Said and Little Said to the sultan for their incorporation into the palace circle.[370] As British Said received his training in Britain and had been positively received by Midhad Pasha, it was in the interest of the sultan to nominate him as a guarantee both to the constitutionalists and to Britain, the support of which was needed against Russia.[371]

---

[365] Ubicini, La Constitution ottomane, pp. 11-12. See also Devereux, pp. 46-59.

[366] See Journal des Débats, December 5, 1876.

[367] Süleyman Paşazade Sami, Süleyman Paşa Muhakemesi: 1293 Osmanlı-Rus Muharebesi (The Trial of Süleyman Pasha: The Ruso-Turkish War of 1293), (Konstantiniye: Matbaa-i Ebüzziya, 1328 [1912], pp. 57-58. Levant Herald, December 7, 1876. Cited in Davison, Reform, 1856-1876, p. 378.

[368] Ubicini, La Constitution ottomane, p. 12.

[369] Cf. Mahmud Celaleddin Paşa, v. 2, pp. 18-21.

[370] İ. Hakkı Uzunçarşılı, Midhad Paşa ve Taif Mahkumları (Midhad Pasha and Taif's Captives), (Ankara: Türk Tarih Kurumu, 1970), p. 130. Cited in Burhan Çağlar, İngiliz Said Paşa ve Günlüğü (Jurnal), (British Said Pasha and His Diary), (İstanbul: Arı Sanat Yayınevi, 2010), p. 20.

[371] Danişmend, Osmanlı Tarihi Kronolojisi, v. 4, p. 290. Cited in Çağlar, pp. 20-21.

Ubicini noted that the majority of the Drafting Commission was composed of enlightened men voting for liberal measures. Only some ulemas were hesitant, not because of any bad will but due to scruples of conscience; nothing had prepared them for the task that suddenly fell on their shoulders. The scruples and anxiety of the ulema were increased by the violent polemics of Ottoman newspapers contesting the participation of Christians in governance, considering this to be against the shariʿa. The limitation of the authority of the sultan by an assembly seemed considerably less contestable since the Qur'an itself legitimised the consultation of an assembly. The main question of contestation between the constitutionalists and their opponents was whether this assembly should house Christians or not. Although the ulema were troubled by the echoes of these controversies, they were convinced by the sheikh ül-Islam, who aligned with the majority of the Commission and the constitutionalists.[372]

Midhad Pasha was able to convince the influential members of the ulema. The latter even preached on the legitimacy of the constitutional regime: according to a verse of the Qur'an and hadiths, consultation on state affairs within the General Assembly was religiously legitimate. Even Seyfeddin Effendi, the *kazasker* of Anatolia and a member of the Council of State, defended more than others the legitimacy of the *meşveret* (consultative regime). The involvement of the ulema members and *kazasker*s in the discussion of constitutional reform legitimised the project on Islamic grounds and facilitated negotiations with opponents.[373]

Opinion seems to be divided among the softas. They addressed a letter to Midhad Pasha in the first week of August 1876 and threatened his assassination if he persisted in the constitutional initiative. The softas reacted particularly strongly to governmental affairs with Christian subjects. Their argument was that other governments such as Russia, France and Britain had prevented their Tatar, Arab, Indian and Muslim subjects from participating in government.[374]

The softas were supposed to be the most strongly opposed to the new institutional framework that would be established through the Constitution. Their support was provided thanks to the man at the head of the organisation, the Sheikh ül-Islam Hayrullah Effendi. The latter was one of Midhad's few real personal friends. He used both his "official position"

---

[372] Ubicini, *La Constitution ottomane*, pp. 10-11.
[373] Mahmud Celaleddin Paşa, v. 2, p. 41.
[374] MAEF, CP, Juillet-Août 1876, Tome 405. From Bourgoing to Decazes. August 16, 1876.

and his "personal character" to ensure the success of the constitutional process.[375] The house and person of Hayrullah Effendi became a sort of "parliamentary centre" which would exercise no less influence in the Parliament itself.[376] Ali Haydar, Midhad's son, noted that erudite softas made every effort to seeing a constitution proclaimed and would form a counterweight by mobilising the ordinary people, Muslim or non-Muslim, if Abdülaziz I objected to the establishment of a constitutional regime. They even distributed Qur'anic verses according to which the constitutional regime perfectly conformed to the shari'a: these also declared that it was religiously unacceptable to obey a sultan (Abdülaziz I) who violated the rights of the people and did not consider the interests of the country. They thus prepared for the dethronement of Sultan Abdülaziz I.[377]

The softas identified the constitutional project with Midhad Pasha. When the latter was banished by Abdülhamid II, there were "legions of softa volunteers" who considered the "cause of Midhad" and that of the constitution "identical". They prepared for the fall of Mahmud Nedim Pasha and supported the constitutional movement by introducing popular control.[378] The deposition of Abdülaziz I and the enthronement of his nephew Murad V, together with the resignation of Mehmed Rüşdü Pasha and the transition of the Grand Vizierate to Midhad Pasha, were described as a success of softas.[379] They propagated the idea that the Qur'an was the book of law and freedom and that deviating from it meant the enslavement of the people. They had the support of the army and "a certainty that either there would be no struggle or only a short one, and of no doubtful issue".[380]

There was continuous tension between Midhad Pasha and the staff of the palace secretariat, which argued that Midhad intended to concentrate power in his hands through a prime ministry. The real objective of the palace staff was not to protect the sultan or to guarantee his independence. They thought that, upon the admission of the principle of ministerial responsibility, their intervention in state affairs would cease: this would harm their power and personal interests.[381]

---

[375] *The Times*, March 27, 1877.
[376] *The Times*, March 27, 1877.
[377] Midhad Paşa, *Tabsıra-i İbret*, p. 192, Ali Haydar Midhad's note.
[378] *The Times*, March 27, 1877.
[379] *The Times*, May 26, 1876.
[380] *The Times*, May 26, 1876.
[381] Mahmud Celaleddin Paşa, v. 2, p. 83. See also Elliot, p. 250.

More importantly, Abdülhamid II gave signals of his preference for an entente with the Powers rather than for the promulgation of the Constitution. The Marquis of Salisbury, a delegate at the Conference of Constantinople, had a long audience with the sultan. The latter told him that his life was in danger but his remarks did not indicate very clearly any opinion on the proposals of the Conference.[382] The British were aware of the fact that during the meeting of ministers held at the palace in order to decide on the proposals of the Conference of Constantinople, the sultan expressed his desire for an arrangement with the Powers. It was Midhad Pasha who influenced the Council to come to a collective decision of resistance against the proposals of the Powers.[383] The sultan was rather anxious to accept the terms of the Powers until the end of the meeting. Midhad Pasha resisted and arranged the Council accordingly.[384]

From the political correspondence of the French diplomat Count Charles de Moüy, it is clear that the promulgation of the Constitution by Midhad was considered a threat to the sovereign rights of the sultan. The rumour that Midhad was thinking of founding a republican regime was another motive behind his banishment.[385] Some archival documents from the Yıldız Palace collection also allude to the struggle of power between Midhad Pasha and the sultan. Midhad was accused of establishing a hegemony over the internal politics and foreign policy of the empire and acting like the president of a republic. "If the promulgation of the Constitution is delayed", Midhad threatened Abdülhamid II, "I would burden you with the bad consequences of this delay". For those opposed to a constitution, it represented an instrument at Midhad's disposal for making his power equal to that of the sultan (or even greater than it). Midhad Pasha also seized the presidency of the Ottoman Cabinet and thus dominated the functioning of the empire as well as that of the sultanate.[386]

---

[382] PRO, FO 198/42. Turkey no. 2 (1877). Correspondence respecting the Conference at Constantinople and the affairs of Turkey, 1876-77, presented to both Houses of Parliament by Command of Her Majesty, 1877. The Marquis of Salisbury to the Earl of Derby. December 26, 1877.

[383] PRO, FO 881/3052. From the Marquis of Salisbury to the Earl of Derby. January 16, 1877.

[384] PRO, FO 881/3054. From the Marquis of Salisbury to the Earl of Derby. January 19, 1877.

[385] MAEF, PA-AP 122, Correspondance politique du Comte de Moüy, 1876-78, no. 37. Second interim, from January 27, 1877 to February 19 1878. First part, January 27-July 30 1877. Here February 7, 1877.

[386] BOA, YEE 16/13, 6 Rebiülevvel 1327/28 March 1909. Mithat Paşa'ya ve Mavi Kitaba dair makaleler (Articles related to Midhad Pasha and the Blue Book). It seems that

Article 113 of the Ottoman Constitution allowed the sultan to banish those who threatened the security of the state on the grounds of credible police information. Accordingly, Midhad Pasha was forced to resign on February 7, 1877 and was exiled to Europe. Midhad's position was not a secure one. "It was an incessant struggle for life against the numerous adverse influences and personal enemies, both domestic and foreign. Every step which he took or prepared to take in carrying out his policy could only be gained by a new and successful struggle".[387] His fall was considered to be the result of a palace intrigue.[388] The list of his enemies was quite long. However, there was behind this the Old Turkey Party and a number of old functionaries who were against the extension of Midhad's administrative ideas to the whole empire. There was also the foreign influence, which was collaborating with the palace to remove Midhad "as the chief obstacle to an understanding".[389] In order to face these enemies, he gained influence over the Young Turkey Party, which was mostly composed of men who had not been in power and who were less capable of defending him. Midhad Pasha's fall was also connected to his refusal to conclude peace with Serbia until Prince Milan expressed and guaranteed his peaceable intent. The sultan was convinced by the Old Court Party to replace him in return for a settlement. Midhad's fall was interpreted by Europe as an indication that the Porte would agree on the proposals of the recent Conference.[390]

Chapter II has endeavoured to reconstruct the backdrop of the reform programmes and tried to depict how the Great Powers positioned their policies according to each other's strategies. The chapter clearly demonstrates that the European Great Powers did not adopt separately or collectively any consistent programme of constitutional reform for the Ottoman Empire. Their proposals merely emerged from local crises, rebellions, the changing circumstances of international politics and their desire for survival and better political and economic penetration into the Ottoman Empire rather than from preoccupation with constitutional

---

somebody interpreted the statements of British statesmen included in the Blue Book as comments on internal Ottoman politics, but the author of this file is unknown. The ideas of this section are extracted from the statements of the author entitled *Midhad Paşa ile Kanun-ı Esasi* (Midhad Pasha and the Ottoman Constitution).

[387] *The Times*, February 7, 1877.
[388] *The Times*, February 7, 1877.
[389] *The Times*, February 7, 1877.
[390] *The Times*, February 7, 1877.

reforms. Memorandums, notes and reform proposals followed one another in 1876 in rapid succession, without differing in terms of content: they were tools of domination that distinguished one Power from the others. When questioning the agency of foreign Powers in the making of Ottoman constitutional reforms, the chapter shows the inconsistency of their foreign policy from 1856 to 1876, the change in their strategic priorities and the terms of their rivalry. Combined together, the results of Chapters I and II on trans-imperial religious minorities also draw attention to various types of transnational spaces, ranging from ethno-religious communities' various administrative bodies and networks to diasporas, which engendered social ties, exchange and solidarity that question the modes of political governance of sovereign states. The particular and symbolic nature of these social ties, embedded by "emotional depth" and "moral obligation",[391] engendered efficient strategies for penetrating and transforming the policies of sovereign states in order to obtain the equal treatment of different ethno-religious groups. They may have indirectly democratised the social fabric of their country of origin as well as their host land.

The study of some European diplomatic archives shows that the issue of reforms was negotiated not only between the Ottoman Foreign Ministry and the representatives of European Powers, but also between European central governments and their representatives, who did not always act in accordance with the agenda of the government they represented. They sometimes opposed the constraints of their state structure on the grounds that personal experience of the environment, geographical proximity to Ottoman territory and familiarity with its political culture allowed them to make decisions different from those of their respective governments. The use of this margin for individual initiative caused their recall from their diplomatic missions. The individuality of agencies shows how individual agents had different ambitions from than the states they represented and how their personal ambitions were reflected in the issue of reform. It also unveils how the issue of interaction between foreign actors and their local associates has been neglected so far in the interpretation of diplomatic history and how the study of individual exchanges may shed light on the linkages that transform global movements into local developments. Although archival documents are insufficient in clarifying the nature of and motivations for the solidarity

---

[391] Faist, p. 9.

between Henry Elliot and Midhad Pasha, it is worth asking what informal dynamics define the relationship of individuals who acted beyond
their state policy. The consideration of the diplomatic body together
with ideological clashes, tensions, agreements and disagreements
between individual agents and the governmental centre makes the state
a more palpable and human institution and less of than an abstract entity
manifesting itself as a homogeneous apparatus. The differentiation of
state agencies from the individual agency of diplomats in the book
intends only to show the ideological fragmentation of the state in Europe
as well as in the Ottoman Empire and to reflect the complex world of
diplomatic relations.

CHAPTER III

DRAFTS AND THE FINAL VERSION OF THE OTTOMAN CONSTITUTION: TEXTUAL AND POLITICAL ANALYSIS

"The history of the attempt to establish constitutional government in Turkey in 1875 and 1876 is not known as it deserves to be".[1] When Robert Devereux, the author of the *First Ottoman Constitutional Period*, quoted these words by Henry Elliot, he underlined that this statement dating from 1880 was valid 80 years later. Because of the lack of documents, the statement may be still true to some extent. Devereux wrote that when the Drafting Commission started work, there were nearly 20 projects, including Midhad's draft and others prepared by Namık Kemal, Süleyman Pasha, Küçük ("Little") Said Pasha and other, anonymous, authors.[2] In his book *Üss-i İnkılab* (The Bases of the Revolution), Ahmed Midhad Effendi states that Midhad's draft served as the basis for the discussions of the Ottoman Constitution. Given that his draft instituted a Chamber of Deputies while omitting a section on the Council of Notables (or Senate in European terms) and neglecting to sufficiently develop the sections related to the general rights of Ottomans and the sultan, the courts, the Ottoman provincial administration and finances, Ahmed Midhad Effendi writes that Said Pasha, the chief scribe of the palace, drafted a more complete text based on the French Constitution: the sultan took this into consideration together with Midhad's draft.[3] Namık Kemal reacted to these statements by stating that the Drafting Commission took into consideration neither Midhad's draft nor Said Pasha's translation of the French Constitution. He even added that the Commission reviewed all monarchical constitutions available and almost 1,000 books. Consequently, the Ottoman Constitution was not, Namık

---

[1] Sir Henry Elliot, "The Death of Abdul Aziz and of Turkish Reform," *The Nineteenth Century* XIII (February, 1880), p. 276. Cited in Devereux, p. 15.

[2] Devereux, p. 49.

[3] Ahmed Midhad Effendi, pt. 2, pp. 199, 321. Cited in Kuntay, v. 2, part 2, pp. 89-90.

Kemal argued, a degraded version of either Midhad's draft or the Constitution of the French Republic.[4]

The confusing dimension is that the sources do not refer to only one Midhad's draft or only one Said's draft. In addition to Midhad's draft constitution *Kanun-ı Cedid* (the New Law), published in Ahmed Midhad Effendi's book,[5] the Ottoman constitutional historian Tarık Zafer Tunaya also refers to a handwritten draft he found in the archives of the Yıldız Palace collection.[6] However, Tunaya does not give any bibliographical reference for this archival document. Filiz Karaca, who studied the Ottoman Constitution of 1876 together with all the amendments made prior to 1918 claims that she found the archival document to which Tunaya referred and also gave the relevant bibliographical reference.[7] In fact, the first part of the document[8] to which Karaca refers contains a draft constitution that resembles Midhad's draft published in Ahmed Midhad Effendi's book. However, the draft is neither entitled *Kanun-ı Cedid* nor signed by Midhad Pasha. The latter begins directly with the provisions without bearing a title. However, some of the internal provisions of the draft constitution use the term "*Kanun-ı Cedid*" (articles 10, and 56 & 57 regarding the revision of the constitutional text). The archival document seems to be a preliminary version of the published draft constitution. For instance, the provisions regarding the Council of State and public instruction of Ottomans were developed later in the published version. However, a crucial difference is quite thought-provoking: the initial version does not talk about the sacred character of the sultan's person and his legal immunity. It stipulated rather that the orders of the executive power, conforming to law, were sacred and those who opposed them would be punished.[9] This statement was perhaps a way of recognising the superiority of law and was well-grounded in the relationship between legality and

---

[4] Kuntay, v. 2, part 2, pp. 90-92.

[5] For the printed version see Ahmed Midhad Effendi, *Üss-i İnkılab*, v. 2, pp. 321-333 and Appendix III.

[6] Tunaya, *Siyasal Gelişmeler*, v. 1, pp. 7-8; Tunaya, "Midhad Paşa'nın Anayasa Tasarısı: Kanun-ı Cedid," (The Draft Constitution of Midhad Pasha: *Kanun-ı Cedid*) in Murat Belge (under the direction of), *Tanzimat'tan Cumhuriyet'e Türkiye Ansiklopedisi* (Encyclopaedia of Turkey from Tanzimat to Republic) (İstanbul: İletişim Yayınları, 1985), v. 1, p. 30.

[7] Filiz Karaca, *Osmanlı Anayasası: Kanun-ı Esasi* (The Ottoman Constitution: Kanun-ı Esasi) (İstanbul: Doğu Kütüphanesi, 2009), p. 13, fn. 46. The archival document to which she refers is coded as BOA, YEE 71/21.

[8] BOA, YEE 71/21. See the original document in Appendix IV.

[9] BOA, YEE 71/21, Article 55.

the sacredness of the person of the sultan. At least two issues of *The Times* also publicised the general content of Midhad's draft constitution.[10]

One does not notice any radical contradiction or difference between these various versions of Midhad's draft constitution except in the idea of the sultan's sacredness, later incorporated in Ahmed Midhad's work, and the surprising absence of a Senate. These different texts show the progress of his project and ideas over time. More interestingly, in a confidential conversation with Elliot, Midhad Pasha confessed that his objective was to take a first step towards a more liberal system. During this conversation, Elliot objected to the establishment of a Senate in the Ottoman Empire, as proposed by Midhad, on the grounds that a Senate named by the government could not control either the palace or the grand vizier. Midhad Pasha responded that this body would be nominated by the government at first but he was aiming to gradually make it elective and thus by degrees obtain constitutional control over the sovereign.[11] One may wonder why the idea of a Senate only appears in his confidential conversation with Elliot and then disappeared from his later drafts. However, the telegraph of Safved Pasha, minister of foreign affairs, sent to Ottoman ambassadors in London, Paris, Rome, Vienna, Berlin and St Petersburg on October 12, 1876, announced that a commission under the presidency of Midhad Pasha was elaborating "new institutions". These new institutions, which followed the general plan outlined in Midhad's draft, also included a Senate nominated by the state.[12] Among multiple possibilities, one can argue that this note was another advanced version of Midhad's draft constitution. It is true that the new institutions announced in the note were also the results of the collective work of the Drafting Commission which had just been appointed by imperial decree some days before on October 8, but one can hardly believe that the Commission could come across such a developed outline of institutions in such a short period of time without an initial draft. Also, the official note of October 12 could have hardly announced a Senate among the future institutions of the Ottoman Empire if Midhad, the president of the Drafting Commission, had disagreed with such a plan.

[10] *The Times*, June 21 & August 8, 1876.
[11] PRO, FO 78/2391, Elliot to Derby, December 14, 1875 # No. 832.
[12] BOA, HR. SYS 1864-1, Savfet Pasha's telegraph to Ottoman ambassadors, 12 October 1876.

The second part of the archival document to which Karaca refers as Midhad Pasha's draft contains another draft that resembles Said Pasha's draft constitution.[13] Nothing other than the similarity of the provisions proves that this draft was authored by Said Pasha. The archival document was merely entitled *Kanun-ı Esasi* (Ottoman Constitution) without bearing the name of its author. When one compares each article, one notices that the version published by Ahmed Midhad Effendi as Said Pasha's draft was a developed version of the archival document. The most striking difference between the two texts is the use of certain French institutional words such as "Senate" and "senators" instead of their Ottoman equivalents and the use of the French "territory" instead of the Ottoman "country" (*memleket*) in the draft constitution published by Ahmed Midhad Effendi. The French inspiration for the archival text was limited to the calculation of the senators' salaries in francs.[14] These terminological differences probably indicate the progress of ideas over time, but one may also wonder whether Ahmed Midhad Effendi, who wrote his book about the basis of the Ottoman reform as an apology for Abdülhamid II, distorted the original texts.

The other confusing dimension regarding both Midhad's and Said Pasha's archival constitution drafts is that they both bore the seal of the Commission for the Examination of Documents (*Evrak-ı Tetkik Komisyonu*). More interestingly, the seal is dated 1327 (1909) and not 1876, although they were documents of the first constitutional era. A brief contextualisation of the aforementioned Commission and a chronology of events will, however, clarify the issue. The 1908 Young Turk Revolution followed 32 years of Hamidian absolutism and opened the second constitutional era in the Ottoman Empire. The revolution, which started in the Balkans, quickly spread throughout the empire, pushing Abdülhamid II to re-establish the Ottoman Constitution of 1876 and reopen Parliament on July 3, 1908. Nine months after the opening of the Ottoman Parliament, the *contrecoup* of April 13, 1909, the intention of which was the restoration of absolutist monarchy, broke out. The monarchist attempt failed due to the determination of the Unionists to preserve the constitutional regime and the intervention of a section of the military, the Third Army Corps, which departed from Thessaloniki and remained

---

[13] BOA, YEE 71/21. See the original document in Appendix V.
[14] Kılıç, "1876 Anayasası'nın Bilinmeyen İki Tasarısı", pp. 560-562.

loyal to the revolution.[15] The Chamber of Deputies met shortly thereafter and decided on the deposition of Abdülhamid II and his replacement with Mehmed Reşad V.[16]

The Commission for the Examination of the Documents of the Yıldız Palace was founded after the incident of March 31 (corresponding to April 13 in the Hegirian calendar) in which the army besieged the palace[17] where Abdülhamid II had moved in April 1877. The Yıldız Palace became the key space in Abdülhamid II's reign.[18] The main target of the Commission was to collect political documents, especially those tracing Abdülhamid's 33-year rule, and to confiscate and examine the secret *jurnal*s (reports) submitted to him by a network of palace spies and informers. The investigation progressed from early May until August 1909 with the collaboration of a few members from the Chamber of Deputies and the Senate.[19] Some of the documents that could have shed light on the Hamidian period were destroyed.[20] The Ottoman Constitution of 1876 was re-promulgated without revision on July 23, 1908. A commission (*Meclis-i Encümen*) was established to discuss amendments to the former constitution. Although the discussions regarding constitutional revision started on April 7, 1909, the revisions were accomplished after the March 31 incident and promulgated on August 21, 1909.[21] The seal on both Midhad's and Said's drafts indicates that they were examined by the members of the Commission. If the motivation behind the military intervention of April 1909 was the self-representation of the army as the protector of the constitutional regime in the Ottoman Empire,[22] the

[15] Aykut Kansu, *Politics in Post-Revolutionary Turkey, 1908-1913* (Leiden: Brill, 2000), p. 77.

[16] Kansu, p. 116.

[17] *Osmanlı*, no. 36, April 21, 1909. Cited in Zekeriya Türkmen, "31 Mart Olayı'ndan sonra Yıldız Evrakı Tedkik Komisyonu'nun Kuruluşu, Faaliyetleri ve Yıldız Sarayı'nın Araştırılması," (The Foundation of the Commission for the Examination of Documents of the Yıldız Palace after the Incident of 31 March, its Activities and the Investigation of the Yıldız Palace) in *XIII. Türk Tarih Kongresi, Ankara, 4-8 Ekim 1999. Kongreye Sunulan Bildiriler* (13th Turkish Historical Congress, Ankara, 4-8 October 1999. Proceedings submitted to the Congress) (Ankara: Türk Tarih Kurumu, 2002), v. 3, pt. 1, p. 561.

[18] Türkmen, p. 559.

[19] Türkmen, pp. 565-569.

[20] Türkmen, p. 574.

[21] Burhan Gürdoğan, "İkinci Meşrutiyet Devrinde Anayasa Değişiklikleri," (Constitutional Amendments in the Second Constitutional Era) *Ankara Üniversitesi Hukuk Fakültesi Dergisi*, XVI/1-4 (1959), p. 91. Cited in Karaca, pp. 25-26.

[22] *İkdam*, no. 5354, April 21, 1909. Yunus Nadi, İhtilal ve İnkılab-ı Osmani (İstanbul, 1325), pp. 149-151. Cited in Türkmen, p. 560.

examination of the documents related to the first constitutional era by
the military just before constitutional revision is not surprising.

Namık Kemal's argument that the Commission's draft was based on
the examination of 1,000 books is probably an exaggeration if we
consider that the Ottoman Constitution was drafted in quite a short period
of time, from October to December. We must also keep in mind that
Midhad's and Said's drafts were discussed in the Grand Council of
September 26 and that some of the participants then occupied a seat in
the Drafting Commission of the Ottoman Constitution. If one examines
the evolution of articles into the final text of the Ottoman Constitution,
as indicated in the comparative table of Appendix VII, one notices that
the draft constitution of 130 articles prepared by the Drafting Commission was the product of a fusion of some aspects of both drafts.

Midhad's draft is relatively short and composed of sections on the
Ottoman state, the person of the sultan and the Ottoman dynasty,
the Council of Ministers and public functionaries, the Council of State,
the Chamber of Deputies, the rights and duties of Ottoman subjects,
executive power and the revision of the Constitution.

The draft of Said Pasha, chief scribe of the Imperial Office, is a more
developed text which includes sections on subjecthood, the rights of subjects, governmental, legislative, executive, judiciary and military powers,
the Council of Notables, the Council of State, internal administration,
special provisions, transitory dispositions and the revision of the Constitution. His draft is mentioned by Ahmed Midhad Effendi as being based
on the French Constitution.[23]

In Midhad's view, in terms of industrial and technical innovations and
development, European civilisation was built on the idea of security and
the principles of freedom and equality within whose framework citizens
could develop their human capacities. In his opinion, religious differences
between Ottoman subjects should not be an obstacle for the practice of
freedom and equality. In fact, discord between various Ottoman subjects
was not a matter of religious difference but rather the result of bad governance and different levels of development. Midhad stated that the equalisation of Ottoman subjects in terms of civil and individual rights would
create a unity of interests and undermine divergences, rivalries and enmity

---

[23] For the printed version, see Ahmed Midhad Effendi, *Üss-i İnkılab*, v. 2, pp. 333-355
and Appendix VI.

between the various segments of the population.[24] One notices from the comparative table of Appendix VII that the item on equality did not change much from his draft constitution to the Constitution of 1876. The case is similar for the idea of individual liberty. Midhad was practically the creator of the provisions on equality and individual liberty while Said's draft is silent on these matters, although both conceptualised quite a liberal framework for the freedom of expression and the press. Similarly, both Midhad and Said developed the most liberal provision on religious freedom among the other draft constitutions, stipulating equal protection for all religions without privileging one over the others. Said also mentioned the right to found associations, something that other draft constitutions and the Ottoman Constitution itself never took into consideration. He was also the creator of the people's right to petition state authorities, something that would be developed in the coming draft constitutions.

Midhad Pasha also put emphasis on the importance of the Chamber of Deputies as the protector of civil and individual rights. He stated that there were legislation, tribunals and assemblies in the Ottoman Empire but what the empire lacked was an overall authority that could protect the continuity of these institutions. He touched upon the deficiency of private initiative and economic liberalism on the one side, and of technical and industrial know-how on the other. In his view, the high rates of capital interest were an obstacle for the development of economic liberalism. Moreover, the preparation of legislation to codify the opening and functioning of banks and transactions would encourage industrial investment in the Ottoman Empire.[25] He also considered the necessity of agricultural credit for financial assistance to farmers.[26] In Midhad's view, the state treasury consisted of the capital that was collected from the population in order to protect the greatness of the state as well as the security of the population. Consequently, the latter was the real owner of the state treasury. If the state budget was in deficit, the debts also belonged to the population. In civilised countries, the collection of state income and expenditure was under the control of the Chamber of Deputies, which was elected by the population. Thus, the latter should also have a say in public borrowing.[27] His provisions on the financial supervision of the

---

[24] Midhad Paşa, *Mirat-ı Hayret*, v. 2, pp. 32-33.
[25] Midhad Paşa, *Mirat-ı Hayret*, v. 2, pp. 36-37.
[26] Midhad Paşa, *Tabsıra-i İbret*, v. 1, p. 49.
[27] Midhad Paşa, *Mirat-ı Hayret*, v. 2, p. 55.

Chamber of Deputies had a considerable effect on the Ottoman Constitution except for the clauses stipulating the regulation of state debt, internal or external, by the Chamber. Said's draft does not assign such a strong role to the Chamber of Deputies and vaguely mentions it under the section regarding legislative power.

Midhad aimed to put ministers under the control of the Chamber of Deputies in order to avoid state extravagance.[28] His draft constitution stipulates the collective responsibility of the Council of Ministers as well as the individual and penal responsibilities of its members: it indirectly recognises the responsibility of the Council before the Chamber of Deputies. Albeit in a less detailed fashion, Said's draft also recognised ministerial responsibility. This principle was adopted in later drafts and in the Ottoman Constitution itself as a result of Midhad and Said's influence. However, the Ottoman Constitution of 1876 raised all possible barriers to weaken ministerial responsibility.[29]

Midhad's draft constitution, with the different versions which this book maps in various sources (archives, newspapers and books), drew the profile of a sovereign state with territorial integrity whose administration was based on the shari'a: however, there was not a complete separation of the legislative, executive and judicial branches. In that respect, he clearly defined the boundaries of the Ottoman state, the sultanate, the Ottoman dynasty, the Council of Ministers, Ottoman subjecthood and the rights of Ottomans. Midhad's draft affected the Ottoman Constitution in terms of reference to the shari'a, sultanic prerogatives and the public law of Ottoman subjects. However, the different localisation of the provisions transformed their logic. For instance, Midhad perceived the shari'a as the administrative principle of the state. Consequently, he localised the attachment of the empire to the shari'a in the provisions regarding the Ottoman state. The Ottoman Constitution refers to Islam as a state religion instead of considering the shari'a to be an administrative principle in the clauses regarding the rights of Ottoman subjects. Accordingly, the Ottoman Constitution, while maintaining Islam as state religion, protected the free exercise of religions recognised in the empire and the religious privileges granted to the different communities on condition that public order and good morals were not offended.

---

[28] Midhad Paşa, *Tabsıra-i İbret*, v. 1, p. 275.
[29] Tunaya, "Kanun-ı Cedid", pp. 30-32.

More interestingly, Midhad's draft counterbalances the weight of the sultan in the administration of the Ottoman state. The presence of the sultan together with his dynasty and special prerogatives (dismissal and nomination of ministers, signing of treaties with foreign states, proclamation of war and peace, decision regarding military operations, convocation and dissolution of the Chamber of Deputies, command of the army, etc.) within the 1876 Ottoman Constitution's clauses regarding the state identified, at first sight, the sultan with the state in relation to other organs separately enumerated under their respective titles. In contrast, Midhad inverted the formal presence of the sultan by limiting his clauses regarding the state to territorial integrity and reference to the shariʿa. He reserved a separate chapter for the sultan and his dynasty and distinguished them from the state as an institution. Midhad's objective was to break the power of the palace in order to strengthen the power of the government.[30]

Although the Ottoman Constitution assigned the sultanate to the oldest member of the Ottoman dynasty, Midhad granted the sultanate to the oldest member of the Ottoman dynasty who was at the same time of sound mind. This is particularly significant if one considers that Abdülhamid II's brother, Murad V, was deposed on grounds of insanity. More importantly, Midhad challenged the power of the sultan by introducing two offices, the Prime Ministry and the Council of Ministers, into the exclusive space assigned to the sultanate. The office of Grand Vizierate was abolished by Midhad and the presidency of the Council of Ministers was transferred from the sultan to one of the ministers, who was named prime minister: he was to nominate the Cabinet under imperial approval. All important internal and external affairs and politics should be discussed within the Council of Ministers, although their decisions were to be executed upon imperial approval. As the person of the sultan was sacred, Midhad's draft recognised his immunity but transferred more responsibility to the ministers. Thus, Midhad's draft strengthened the position of the prime minister and the Cabinet as an alternative source of authority.[31]

In addition to the prime minister and the Cabinet, the Council of State was the third authority to share the sultan's executive power. Unlike the Ottoman Constitution, which does not even mention the Council of State

---

[30] Mahmud Celaleddin Paşa, v. 1, p. 187.
[31] Tunaya, "Kanun-ı Cedid", pp. 30-31.

under a separate title, Midhad's draft designed a Council of State able to intervene before the Council of Ministers and even the sultan when laws and regulations were not duly executed. In Midhad's text, the Council of State is not solely limited to the executive field but also interferes in the legislative process: each law and regulation was to be discussed within the Council of State before being submitted to the approval of the Chamber of Deputies and the sultan. More importantly, executive power could not by itself make laws and regulations but only order the Council of State to elaborate the laws and regulations that it considered necessary.

Like Midhad Pasha, Said Pasha also strengthened the position of the Council of State. The dismissal of diplomatic representatives, commanders of the navy and army, governors and other high-ranking civil officials should be negotiated with the Council of Ministers. Similarly, the dismissal of civil officials elected by popular vote should be negotiated with the Council of State. Provincial and municipal assemblies could be dissolved by the sultan but only with the consent of the Council of State. Although the sultan was the head of the Council and his members were nominated with his approval, their dismissal could be assured with the decision of the *Millet* Assembly (National Assembly). Both the sultan and the *Millet* Assembly had priority in the establishment and revision of laws, but both parties had to negotiate laws with the Council of State. The latter also had the function of inspection and supervision over the general administration.

Midhad's categorisations of the state, the sultan, the premiership, the Council of Ministers, the Council of State, the legal status of public functionaries and equal access to public offices did not make it entirely into the 1876 Ottoman Constitution. However, to a large extent, these principles shaped the Commission's 130-article draft except for the explicit mention of the premiership and the Council of State. Even if the subsequent draft constitutions and the Ottoman Constitution itself did not develop a separate section on the Council of State, the technocratic aspect of the institution was kept and the bills of laws continued to be prepared by the Council in the constitutional framework of 1876 as a result of both Midhad's and Said's provisions on the issue.

Midhad's draft does not explicitly mention legislative power and the National Assembly but does have a long section on the Chamber of Deputies. In contrast, Said's draft has a long section on legislative power, describing a National Assembly and a Chamber of Deputies, although it is less detailed compared to Midhad's text. In this section, Said's text restricts the sultan's prerogatives. For instance, the sultan did not have the power to dissolve the *Millet* Assembly or to suspend the constitution or the provisions of similar legislation. Even if the sultan supervised the protection of the state, he cannot decide on his own to declare war without the consent of the *Millet* Assembly. If a legal project was not published in due time, the head of the *Millet* Assembly could order its publication. However, these liberal positions did not seem to affect the drafting process.

Although at first sight Said Pasha's draft seems to counterbalance the position of the sultan through the *Millet* Assembly or the Council of State, other points strengthened sultanic power. First of all, his text contains a strong clause about subjection (*metbuiyyet*). The text stipulates that subjection is to the person of the sultan; this means that the sultan is again identified with the Ottoman state as an institution, like in the Ottoman Constitution. However, if one follows the evolution of the idea of subjecthood, one notices that it is Midhad's conceptualisation which affects the Drafting Commission.

In Said's draft, the Senate seems to have been established for the enhancement of sultanic power. Composed of members considered by the sovereign to be appropriate to this post, the Senate is the guardian of the Constitution and general freedoms. No law can be published without being submitted to the approval of the Senate. The interpretation of the constitution also belongs to the Senate. The latter could submit a legal project concerning the greater interests of the Ottoman *millet* by writing a statement to the sultan. The Senate could ask for the revision of the constitution; if its proposal was accepted by the sultan, the revision was established by a decree of the Senate. If the *Millet* Assembly was dissolved by the sultan, the Senate was to undertake the administration of the government until a new assembly was convened. Thus, an organ whose members and head were nominated by the sultan possessed many legislative and executive powers. Although all of these provisions regarding the Senate did not shape the legislative process, the Senate possessed greater power to control the bills of laws submitted by the Chamber of Deputies. Said Pasha's draft may have also opened the way to the decree-laws of the Cabinet, developed by the subsequent draft constitutions and then adopted by the text of 1876. His draft stipulates that the sultan has the competency to submit legal projects to the Chamber of Deputies through ministers.

If Said Pasha's draft lacked the concept of a sovereign state with territorial boundaries and a national language, it established a clearer separation of powers between the legislative (*kuvve-i kanuniye*), executive (*kuvve-i hükümet*) and judicial (*kuvve-i adliye*) branches. It even suggested a fourth power, that of the military (*kuvve-i askeriye*), which affected the drafting of the Ottoman Constitution. His draft constitution also initiated a provision about martial law without detailing the circumstances in which such law should come into force. His archival draft constitution literally designated martial law as the state of siege (*muhasara hali*, the literal translation of the French term "*état de siège*").[32] If we consider that Said Pasha composed his draft constitution on the basis of various French constitutions and that he translates "*Assemblée nationale*" into Ottoman Turkish as "*Millet* Assembly", we may then think that he saw the *millet* as the equivalent of the nation. Such means that the term "*millet*" may have begun to possess a national connotation in the midst of these constitutional debates. The version incorporated into Ahmed Midhad Effendi's book talked about customary administration (*idare-i örfiye*) in designating martial law. One may question the extent to which martial law, which is a military administration, is connected with customs, but perhaps one way to legitimise martial law as a new concept was to find such a link.

The merger of Midhad's and Said's drafts probably served as a point of departure for the initial development of provisions regarding legislative power that were finally mentioned under the titles of "General Assembly", "Council of Notables" and "Chamber of Deputies", so as to avoid the word "power". Executive power, mentioned literally in both drafts, was never used in the following drafts or in the Ottoman Constitution. Said Pasha's judicial power, something lacking in Midhad's text, was quite different from the provisions of the sections on "Courts" and the "High Court", the latter of which would judge high-ranking state officials and all others accused of high treason or an attempt against the safety of the state, in the later drafts. Midhad Pasha also brings a framework of national awareness to the Constitution. He was the creator of provisions regarding the Turkish language, knowledge of which was compulsory for access to public offices and the uniformisation of Ottoman public instruction and schools under common laws. Midhad had reservations regarding the unification of public instruction: his concern

---

[32] BOA, YEE 71/21.

was to not hinder the distinctiveness of religious instruction in the various *millet*s. If further steps in the drafting process consolidated his provision on public instruction by adding state supervision over schools, the relevant article was incorporated into the Ottoman Constitution with Midhad's initial principles. Midhad's conceptualisations of both the issue of language and the question of public instruction reveal to some extent that a Turkish national awakening was at work. The Turkish language was mentioned instead of the Ottoman language. Moreover, the consolidation of a common language and common principles of public instruction was probably expected to create a social fabric that would undermine the communal compartmentalisation of Ottoman society.

1. Draft Constitutions: the Commission's Work

One of the records of the Yıldız Palace collection refers to the correction of a constitutional draft of 130 articles by Safved Pasha, the minister of foreign affairs in 1876.[33] There is no evidence in the draft itself that these handwritten corrections were Safved Pasha's work. Similarly, the document does not provide any details about the author or authors of the draft before Safved's revisions. Zafer Tunaya himself referred to these corrections as Safved Pasha's work without explaining the basis for this assumption.[34] Selda Kaya Kılıç, who studied the draft, presents her doubts about the corrections belonging to Safved Pasha.[35]

Moreover, what is misleading is the fact that the document is dated 27 April 1909 in the catalogue of the Ottoman archives. Safved Pasha died in 1883. Consequently, he could not have corrected the draft in 1909. This date corresponds to the period in which the Commission for the Examination of the Documents of the Yıldız Palace was founded and in which the revisions of the second constitutional era started. Although the document does not bear the seal of the Commission like Midhad's and Said's archival texts do, a draft dated April 1909 makes one wonder whether the document was a draft constitution belonging to the first constitutional era that was examined either by the Commission for the Examination of the Documents of the Yıldız Palace and/or by the Drafting

---

[33] BOA, YEE 41/7, 6/R/1327/27 April 1909. Kanuni Esasi müsveddesinin Safved Paşa kalemi ile düzeltilmiş nüshası (Draught of the Constitution corrected by Safved Pasha). See the original document in Appendix VIII and the comparative table in Appendix VII.

[34] Kılıç, "1876 Anayasası'nın Bilinmeyen İki Tasarısı", p. 573, fn. 32.

[35] Kılıç, "1876 Anayasası'nın Bilinmeyen İki Tasarısı", p. 573, fn. 32.

Commission of the second constitutional era. There is, however, one concrete sign proving that the document was a draft constitution from 1876: Article 130 of the draft refers to a provisional instruction of October 28, 1876 regarding the elections of the General Assembly. The relevant article then passed into the Ottoman Constitution of 1876, in which it was registered as Article 119. The provision was removed during the constitutional amendments of 1909.[36] The second question is why the draft constitution may have been corrected by Safved Pasha, who was not a member of the 1876 Drafting Commission. We need to remember that once the draft was prepared by the Commission, it was supposed to be submitted to the Ottoman Cabinet. Although he was not a member of the Drafting Commission, Safved Pasha was a member of the Cabinet and was probably asked to review the text. One may also assume that Safved's ideas carried a certain weight for Abdülhamid II, since the former, as an Ottoman foreign minister, was familiar with European ideas, reactions and political attitudes.

Selda Kaya Kılıç refers to this document as a second draft constitution which followed the first draft of 113 articles.[37] This book offers a different reading of the draft constitution supposedly corrected by Safved Pasha. Ubicini wrote that when the Drafting Commission's text of 140 articles was submitted to the Council of Ministers on December 1, important changes were made to the initial text and many provisions were eliminated. Thus, a text of 140 articles was reduced to 119 articles. Midhad Pasha endeavoured to conserve the liberal character of the initial text, but his efforts encountered the opposition of Mehmed Rüşdü Pasha.[38] Considering the liberal character of the draft constitution submitted for Safved's correction, one might conclude that the latter was the draft presented to the Council of Ministers on December 1. Either Ubicini confused the 140- and 130-article drafts (as he did Midhad and Server Pashas when announcing the president of the Drafting Commission) or the draft of 130 articles that this book studies was preceded by a text of 140 articles. The latter was said to contain (like the 113-article draft) an article according to which the various populations of the Ottoman Empire were authorised to learn and teach the languages native to them.[39] Our draft of

---

[36] See Karaca, p. 56.

[37] Kılıç, *Osmanlı Devleti'nde Meşrutiyet'e Geçiş*, pp. 54-86.

[38] Ubicini, *La Constitution ottomane*, pp. 11-12.

[39] Cf. Mehmed Zeki Pakalın, *Son Sadrazamlar ve Başvekiller* (The Last Grand Viziers and the Premiers) (Istanbul, 1942), vol. 1, p. 339. Cited in Devereux, pp. 55-56.

130 articles contained a provision with the same stipulation on the language issue. The conservative ministers, and especially İngiliz Said Pasha, argued that this provision would put all local languages on an equal footing with Turkish. Thus, the Cabinet deleted the relevant article and replaced it with a provision in which Turkish was declared the sole official language.[40] This draft of 130 articles was probably accomplished by the Drafting Commission, which took Midhad's and Said's texts as the points of departure.

The liberal character of the draft does not only derive from the language issue. This was also the draft in which the sultanate was described in a different section to the Ottoman state, as in Midhad's draft; thus, the person of the sultan was not identified as an institution. Moreover, the prerogatives of the sultan were enumerated, probably with the intention of defining their boundaries. Within the framework of individual liberties, penalties, imprisonments and, more importantly, exiles without legal grounds were prohibited. The provision regarding the right of Ottoman subjects to petition a competent authority as well as the General Assembly in order to address their complaints about the misconduct of public functionaries or the infractions of laws was developed in Midhad's draft. Similarly, the article on equality progressed in the sense that Ottomans were equal not only before the law but also in terms of rights and duties. If the draft does not directly mention that the Grand Vizierate was to be replaced by a premiership, a softer provision denoting the change of the title into the chairmanship of ministers was an allusion to it. The term "grand vizier" was used only once in the relevant provisions in order to clarify that the grand vizier was the president of ministers who had a say in the election of other ministers. The draft recognises the penal, individual and collective responsibility of ministers for their ministries but, compared to the 1909 constitutional amendment, which literally recognises their individual and collective responsibility before the Chamber of Deputies,[41] the article of recognition in the 130-article draft constitution is vague. One can infer by the subsequent article mentioning the complaint of the Chamber of Deputies in the case of deficiency in their responsibilities that the competent authority for controlling ministerial responsibility was the Chamber of Deputies. Nevertheless, compared to following draft constitutions and the Constitution of 1876

---

[40] Cf. Pakalın, vol. 1, p. 339. Cited in Devereux, pp. 55-56.
[41] Karaca, p. 39.

itself, it at least outlines the framework in which ministerial responsibility can be questioned: high treason to the state, attempts to abolish the Constitution, corruption and abuse of power, and waste of assets belonging to the state treasury. Moreover, once the responsibility of a minister or ministers was questioned, the whole process from the accusation to the transfer to the High Court for trial was pursued by the Chamber of Deputies. In a further draft which Namık Kemal corrected himself, he reacted to the removal of criteria enumerating the cases in which ministerial responsibilities could be questioned as being from the "Commission's draft", thus alluding to the Drafting Commission. This statement by Namık Kemal proves once more that the 130-article draft was the Commission's work, as it is the only draft containing such an enumeration.

Another liberal aspect of the 130-article draft constitution was the part that non-Muslim communities and their regulations occupied in the Ottoman provincial administration: in each caza, there would be a council belonging to each of the different religious communities to be charged with the control of the administration of real property revenues, the funds of pious foundations (vakıf), in accordance with the usage or the principles fixed by their founders or by testamentary dispositions, and the administration of orphan funds. These councils would be governed by the elected body of each community in accordance with special regulations. These councils would depend on the local authorities and general councils of each province. The relevant provision also specified that the head of the council of the Muslim community would be the mufti of the caza or a member of the ulema while the head of each council of non-Muslim communities would be the spiritual chief or the representative of each community "as stipulated in their regulations" (Article 122), a statement that foresaw the cooperation of community regulatory texts with the wider social pact of the constitution.

Nevertheless, the last part of the provision designating the heads of the councils of the different religious communities and their communal regulations was removed from the Ottoman Constitution. This removal left vague the ways in which the communal heads would be elected by avoiding any reference to their community regulations and instead bound their councils by a special regulation that would be established in the future (Article 111). Moreover, the following provision of the initial draft, which specified how the general council of each province would be composed of the representatives of various communities, was removed from the Ottoman Constitution (Article 123).

One of the interesting changes that Safved or another draftsman made was on the issue of religion. The Commission's draft recognised Islam as the state religion. While maintaining this principle, the state guaranteed the free practice of the other religions recognised in the Ottoman Empire on the condition of respect for public security and good morals. Safved Pasha scored out the sentences regarding Islam as the state religion and the maintenance of this principle and kept only the state guarantee of the free practice of religions on the condition of respect for public security and good morals. Safved also removed the limits of the shari'a on individual liberty. Moreover, he rendered Ottomans equal before the law and in terms of rights and duties independently of religious affairs.

Safved Pasha's changes within the provisions of the Cabinet attempted to strengthen both the position of the head of the Cabinet (the grand vizier) and ministerial responsibility. In the Commission's draft, the ministers are supposed to refer to the sultan with regard to affairs beyond the limits of their powers (Article 30). Safved's corrections transformed the article in such a way that the ministers must refer to the head of the Cabinet for questions beyond the limits of their powers. This change was reflected in the Ottoman Constitution (Article 29). Safved Pasha's corrections placed the decision process over the decree-laws of the Cabinet in the hands of the Chamber of Deputies, and thus eliminated the Senate from the process (Article 39). The Commission's draft instituted a General Assembly composed of the Senate and the Chamber of Deputies, and the initiative which stated that the capacity to propose or to modify a law belonged only to the Cabinet, the Senate or the Chamber of Deputies. In the case of such a request, the draft of the law would be prepared within the Council of State and then submitted to the Chamber of Deputies and the Senate for examination. Safved added that this entire process would function with the knowledge of the sultan. This change by Safved, which strengthened the power of the sultan within the legislative process, was the most authoritarian intervention he made in the initial text. It was reflected in the Ottoman Constitution. In the case of the proposition of a new law or the modification of an existing one, the request should be submitted first to the sultan; should there be any reason for it, the Council of State would then be charged by imperial order to prepare the draft. The drafts of laws from the Council of State could be then submitted to the Chamber of Deputies and the Senate before final approval by the sultan (articles 53-54).

More interestingly, Safved preferred to use the term "Ottoman sub-jects" over "everyone" or "everybody" in order to impose boundaries. The Commission's draft, prior to his corrections, stated that instruction is free and that everyone is authorised to give public or private instruction on condition of respect for the laws (Article 15). Safved scored out the word "everyone" and replaced it with the expression "everyone from the subjects of the Ottoman state" (*tebea-i Devlet-i Aliye'den herkes*). It might have been thought that the term "everybody" extended the right to give public or private instruction to foreign nationals and thus put into question whether this "everybody" also applied to foreign or missionary schools operating in the Ottoman Empire. Safved thus limited educa-tional activities to Ottoman subjects through his corrections, which were reflected in their entirety in Article 15 of the Ottoman Constitution.

We can also see from Safved Pasha's corrections that he carefully distinguished the concepts "everyone" (*herkes*), "all Ottomans" (*Osmanlıların kaffesi*), "Ottoman individuals" (*Osmanlı efradı*) and "every Ottoman" (*Her Osmanlı*) from his expression "each of the sub-jects of the Ottoman state" (*tebea-i Devlet-i Osmaniye'den herkes*), with which he replaced them. However, in some parts of his draft, he replaced the term "Ottoman individuals" with that of "subject of the Ottoman state": these replacements were reflected in the final text of the 1876 Ottoman Constitution. Within his framework, there was probably a strict overlapping between the state and Ottoman subjecthood, and individuals did not exist independently from subjection to the state.[42] In fact, this overlapping was also the framework of the Ottoman *millet* system. How-ever, the differentiation he made between these concepts was not always strictly observed in all the provisions of the Ottoman Constitution.

Interestingly, we can see by his corrections that, if not to individuality as a modern concept, he did pay attention to the principle of representa-tion. Article 65 of the 1876 Ottoman Constitution stipulates that the num-ber of members which would make up the Chamber of Deputies was fixed at one deputy for every 50,000 male inhabitants under Ottoman subjection. This provision corresponded to Article 72 of the initial draft, to which Safved added a geographical and administrative limit for this number of deputies; accordingly, the number of deputies was fixed at one deputy for every 50,000 male inhabitants in each Ottoman province. This means that the provinces would be represented in the Chamber of Depu-

---

[42] See, for instance, the corrections he made for this purpose in Articles 8, 14, 15, 17, 22, etc. of the initial draft.

ties according to the proportion of their male population. However, this administrative limit was not reflected in the text of the Ottoman Constitution.

2. From the Commission's Work
to the Council of Ministers' Amendments

The Commission's draft constitution seems to have become the subject of a struggle between the palace, the Commission and the Council of Ministers.[43] "Abdülhamid followed a process of asking various ministers and officials for their views on the draft, probably to play one against another".[44] The Foreign Minister Safved Pasha may have been one of them. In fact, the latter did not really believe in the Ottoman Constitution. He thought that the people should create a constitution, not be granted one by a sovereign.[45] Abdülhamid II also intended to benefit from the popularity of some of the draftsmen among the people and have it appear as if he was a liberal sultan. This was his intention in nominating Namık Kemal to the membership of the Drafting Commission.[46] When the constitutional draft was submitted to the sultan, he showed it to antagonists such as Namık Pasha and Mehmed Rüşdü Pasha, the grand vizier. The latter was not in favour of a constitutional regime; if there had been no foreign danger, he would never have given his consent for such a change.[47] When he was asked for comments, he adopted a shaky position and reacted against the articles regarding the enumeration of the sultan's duties at the beginning of the Constitution on the grounds that such would decrease the glory of the sultan before public opinion and limit sultanic prerogatives. He proposed the elimination of these provisions, arguing that the power of the sultan could not be bound by limitations. He also suggested the suppression of the articles regarding the creation of a premiership instead of the Grand Vizierate and the appointment of ministers by the premier. He insisted on the continuation of the Grand Vizierate and on the nomination of ministers by the sultan.[48]

---

[43] Davison, *Reform, 1856-1876*, p. 376.
[44] Davison, *Reform, 1856-1876*, p. 376.
[45] *Said Paşa'nın Hatıratı* (Memoirs of Said Pasha), (İstanbul: Sabah Matbaası, 1328 [1912]), v. 2, p. 32. Cited in Kuntay, v. 2, part 2, p. 61.
[46] Cf. Kuntay, v. 2, part 2, pp. 24, 57.
[47] Mahmud Celaleddin Paşa, v. 2, pp. 82-87.
[48] Mahmud Celaleddin Paşa, v. 2, pp. 82-87.

This perhaps explains why, on November 26, Abdülhamid II sent a letter to Midhad Pasha stating that the constitution contained some provisions that did not conform to the rules and tendencies of the country. He underlined that the needs of Ottoman subjects should be reconciled with the rights of the Ottoman state in the new arrangements. Consequently, the draft constitution would be discussed by the Cabinet according to these fundamental principles.[49] What he understood by rights of the state were probably those of the sultan. In order to accelerate the process, Midhad Pasha wrote to the chief scribe of the palace on November 28 that the draft constitution might contain some imperfections, but that if the constitution was not proclaimed before the Conference of Constantinople, the Ottoman state would be obliged to accept the proposals of the European Powers.[50]

Some newspapers reflected the conflict between Midhad Pasha and the grand vizier, who opposed the former's efforts to promulgate the constitution before the Conference of Constantinople.[51] Like his predecessor Mahmud Nedim Pasha, Grand Vizier Mehmed Rüşdü Pasha was said to be influenced by General Ignatieff. It was even argued that Midhad Pasha's constitution was corrected, amended and shortened by Mehmed Rüşdü Pasha; according to some newspapers, it became almost unrecognisable.[52] The Ottoman government denied these rumours, announcing that the development of the reforms was about to come to its end.[53] In addition to the sultan's prerogatives and the continuation of the Grand Vizierate, ministerial responsibility was among the most contested provisions between liberals and conservatives.[54] It was said that the Council of Ministers probably accepted Mehmed Rüşdü's argument that the enumeration of the sultan's powers would be a limitation on his authority. This explains why a preamble of general principles like those of the 1839 Rescript was added to the draft constitution.[55]

[49] Letter from Abdülhamid II to Midhad Pasha, 9 Zilkade 1293/26 November 1876. Cited in Midhad Paşa, *Tabsıra-i İbret*, v. 1, p. 306.

[50] From Midhad Pasha to the chief scribe of the *Mabeyn* (private secretariat of the Ottoman palace), 11 Zilkade 1293/28 November 1876. Cited in Midhad Paşa, *Tabsıra-i İbret*, v. 1, pp. 307-308.

[51] *Journal des Débats*, December 8, 1876. *La Turquie*, December 14, 1876.

[52] *Journal des Débats*, December 16, 1876. *La Turquie*, December 29, 1876.

[53] *La Turquie*, December 14, 1876.

[54] *Journal des Débats*, December 18, 1876.

[55] İbnülemin Mahmud Kemal İnal, *Osmanlı Devri'nde Son Sadrazamlar* (The Last Grand Viziers in the Ottoman Period), (İstanbul, 1940-1953), pp. 343-344, n. 3; Kuntay, v. 2, part 2, pp. 88, 90-91, 98. Cited in Davison, *Reform, 1856-1876*, p. 378.

All these rumours emerging from the pages of memoirs and newspapers seem to have a textual reflection in the Ottoman archives. Another record of the Yıldız Palace collection also contains a pile of draft constitutions bearing the seal of the Commission for the Examination of the Documents of the Yıldız Palace and dated 1909.[56] Among three draft constitutions, the record also contained a draft and a corrected version of a bylaw regarding the Council of Ministers and its duties, said by the archival catalogue to have been corrected by Said Pasha, Namık Kemal, Mahmud Pasha (Abdülhamid II's brother-in-law) and other statesmen. Again, nothing proves that the views on the bylaw of the Council of Ministers belong to the bureaucrats mentioned by the catalogue. Similarly, the authors or the correctors of the draft constitutions included in the record are not indicated.

Selda Kaya Kılıç comes to the conclusion that one of these documents was an unknown draft of the Ottoman Constitution corrected by Namık Kemal. She considers it to be one of the first texts that the Commission prepared. In her view, the draft constitution that Safved or another corrector amended followed this draft, which was supposed to have been corrected by Namık Kemal.[57] However, if one looks at the drafts carefully, one notices that Safved's draft constitution, which this book considers to be the Commission's work, preceded these two draft constitutions, since some of the amendments suggested by Safved Pasha were adopted by these two other drafts. Interestingly, the articles regarding the definition of the state, the sultanate and the prerogatives of the sultan are absent in these two texts, which are almost the same before the corrections. More importantly, in these two drafts the grand vizier loses his voice in the selection of ministers. Similarly, the provisions regarding ministerial responsibility are weakened. The ministers are responsible for the acts of their ministry but the mention of individual or collective responsibility is removed. These drafts also include the preliminary form of the famous Article 113, which gave the sultan the exclusive right to expel those considered injurious to the safety of the Ottoman state. More strangely, both of the draft constitutions start with a preamble. The preamble is an

---

[56] BOA, YEE 71/33. Kanun-ı Esasi Layıhasıyla Meclis-i Vükelanın Vazifelerine Müteallik Kararname üzerinde, Namık Kemal Bey, Eski Sadrazam Said Paşa ve Mahmud Paşa ve diğer bazı devlet ricalinin mütalaalarını havi taslak çalışmaları (Draft of the Constitution together with Drafts of a Bylaw Related to the Duties of the Council of Ministers Containing the Views of Namık Kemal, Said Pasha, Mahmud Pasha and Other Statesmen).

[57] Kılıç, *Osmanlı Devleti'nde Meşrutiyet'e Geçiş*, pp. 54-55.

introductory paragraph resembling that of former imperial decrees: it
explains the reasons for which the text of the Ottoman Constitution was
drafted (strengthening of the administrative foundations of the Ottoman
Empire, happiness and legal equality of Ottoman subjects, access to civilisation, etc.) and connects the text to Abdülhamid II's decree of enthronement from September 11, 1876 (21 Şaban 1876) and the good intentions
of the sultan for granting such a favour. Moreover, the Tanzimat guarantees
recognising the security of life, property and honour, granted to all Ottoman subjects without religious discrimination since the Imperial Rescript
of 1839, are again put under the special protection and defence of the
sultan. Nevertheless, this is not to say that these drafts referring to the
Tanzimat trilogy disregard other legal guarantees over life and property.
Reference to the Tanzimat seems to be purely ideological. The amendments of the first draft also added a clause putting the property rights and
allowance of the Ottoman imperial family under public guarantee.

Considering the less liberal character of the drafts, and the similarity to
the discussions provoked by Grand Vizier Mehmed Rüşdü Pasha, the
change of articles and the inclusion of a preamble, one may assume that
these two drafts are those which the Council of Ministers amended. In
other words, this is the transformation of the Drafting Commission's work
into the amended version by the Council of Ministers. Thus, the texts of
the draft constitutions take on the traditional style of former Tanzimat
decrees, which were favours granted by the sultan to his population.

One of these two draft constitutions mentioned above is a text of 114
articles,[58] while the other contains 113 articles.[59] As previously mentioned, both of the texts might have been the Drafting Commission's
work which was amended by the Council of Ministers upon the conservative reaction of the Grand Vizier Mehmed Rüşdü Pasha. The texts
still contain new amendments for which it is difficult to find an author
or authors. It is not very clear from the bibliographical note of the archival catalogue whether one should attribute the authorship of Said Pasha,
Namık Kemal, Mahmud Pasha and others only to the bylaw regarding
the Council of Ministers or also to these draft constitutions contained in
the same file. One may remember from the comparative table that the

[58] BOA, YEE 71/33. See the original document in Appendix IX and the comparative
table in Appendix VII.
[59] BOA, YEE 71/33. See the original document in Appendix X and the comparative
table in Appendix VII.

draft of 114 articles is the text where the initial form of Article 113 emerges in someone's handwriting merely as a marginal note without a number.

Mahmud Pasha, Abdülhamid II's brother-in-law, was said to be influenced by the Muhiddin plot, wherein Muhiddin Effendi and his supporters organised agitation and counter-propaganda against the Constitution: after a police investigation, Midhad Pasha was successful in assuring their banishment with Abdülhamid II's approval. Consequently, he suggested to the sultan that he should add a provision that would permit him to expel anyone who could endanger his safety. Küçük Said Pasha, chief scribe of the palace, protested against the article on the grounds that such a provision could destroy the meaning of the Constitution. Abdülhamid II threatened not to promulgate the Constitution if the Cabinet opposed the inclusion of the article.[60] Mahmud Celaleddin Pasha, who was appointed *amedi*[61] (a kind of private secretary in the Ottoman Ministry of Foreign Affairs) during the dethronement of Abdülaziz and the enthronements of Murad V and Abdülhamid II, related that the article was the idea of Said Pasha, chief scribe of the palace, and Damad Mahmud Pasha, and that it encountered opposition because it was found to be contrary to the spirit of a document that made mention of personal freedoms and ministerial responsibility. Although Midhad Pasha worked for the exclusion of Article 113 from the constitutional draft, he failed and had to agree on its inclusion instead of endangering the promulgation of the Constitution.[62] Said Pasha himself denied drafting the article in his memoirs.[63] It was also argued that Midhad did not really find the article to be against his principles. He was, after all, behind the banishment of people involved in the Muhiddin plot.[64] He may have expected to exile the opponents of the Ottoman Constitution. To Ziya's and Namık Kemal's

[60] Cf. Şehsuvaroğlu, p. 183. Pakalın, v. 1, p. 34. Cited in Devereux, pp. 57-58. Kuntay, v. 2, part 2, pp. 63-64 (where a passage from İngiliz Said Pasha's memoir, *Jurnal* [Journal], is also reproduced to show the views of Mahmud and Said Pashas on Article 113, fn. 1).

[61] For more information, see M. Mehdi İlhan, "An Overview of the Ottoman Archival Documents and Chronicles," *Ankara Üniversitesi Dil ve Tarih Coğrafya Fakültesi Tarih Bölümü Tarih Araştırmaları Dergisi*, vol 27, no. 44 (2008), pp. 24-25, 27-28.

[62] Cf. Mahmud Celaleddin Paşa, v. 2, pp. 84-87; v. 1, p. 12. See also Elliot, p. 250.

[63] Said Paşa, *Said Paşa'nın Hatıratı*, v. 2, part 2, pp. 243-244, n. 1. Cited in Davison, *Reform, 1856-1876*, p. 379, fn. 88.

[64] İsmail Hami Danişmend, "İlk Meşrutiyetin İç Yüzü," (The True Story of the First Constitutional Regime), *Milliyet*, May 18, 1952. Cited in Devereux, p. 58, fn. 53.

demands that the clause be removed, Midhad Pasha responded that such a reaction could endanger the promulgation of the Ottoman Constitution. Ziya even suspected Midhad Pasha of having somehow planned the inclusion of Article 113 in the Constitution.[65] The emergence of Said Pasha and Mahmud Pasha in the debates regarding Article 113 in the sources of the time partially justifies the mention of their names in the archival catalogue with regards to the last pile of drafts. However, if Said Pasha reacted against the provision, as he argued in his memoirs, this is not visible among the amendments to the draft of 114 articles.

Selda Kaya Kılıç attributes the authorship of the marginal notes appearing on the second draft of 113 articles to Namık Kemal for the reasons she rightly explains.[66] It seems that Namık Kemal addressed some petitions to Abdülhamid II in order to criticise the amendments of the Council of Ministers to the draft constitution. One of his criticisms was related to the removal of the provisions regarding the rights and prerogatives of the sultan from the beginning of the text on the grounds that these would be an infraction of the rights of both the caliphate and sultanate. Another related to the replacement of these provisions by a preamble recalling the spirit of the Tanzimat Rescript. Namık Kemal stated that the mention of the rights and prerogatives of the sultan in the constitution was a provision generally respected by constitutional monarchies and that their removal would endanger said rights and prerogatives.[67] Similarly, in the last marginal note of the draft constitution of 113 articles, a handwritten statement reacts against the removal of said provisions because the rights and prerogatives of the sultan had lost their legal ground.[68] Namık Kemal's second criticism was regarding the inclusion of a preamble to the beginning of the draft constitution: such transformed the constitution into a favour granted by the sultan and thus reduced its value in the eyes of Europe.[69] The similarity of content between Namık Kemal's petitions and the handwritten views expressed in the marginal notes of the 113-article draft constitution leads us to think

---

[65] Sami, p. 58. n. 3; Fevziye Abdullah Tansel, *Hususi Mektuplarına Göre Namık Kemal ve Abdülhak Hamid* (Namık Kemal and Abdülhak Hamid as Seen in Their Private Correspondence), (Ankara: [s. n.], 1949), p. 29. İnal, *Son Sadrazamlar*, pp. 345-346. Cited in Davison, *Reform, 1856-1876*, p. 379.

[66] Kaya Kılıç, *Osmanlı Devleti'nde Meşrutiyet'e Geçiş*, pp. 54-57.

[67] Kuntay, v. 2, part 2, p. 97.

[68] *Mecmua-ı Ebüziyya*, vol. 154, pp. 40-43. Cited in Kuntay, p. 87.

[69] Kuntay, v. 2, part 2, p. 98. See also İnal, *Son Sadrazamlar*, pp. 343-344, n. 3; Kuntay, v. 2, part 2, pp. 88, 90-91, 98. Cited in Davison, *Reform, 1856-1876*, p. 378.

that the amendments to the text were Namık Kemal's work, as Selda Kaya Kılıç argued.[70]

When, on December 6, the Cabinet approved the constitution of 119 articles and then presented the document to the sultan, the latter requested Küçük ("Little") Said, his aide-de-camp İngiliz ("British") Said[71] and Süleyman Pasha to submit their comments. The three stated that the modifications were convenient and that the text was much better than before.[72] They are said to have approved the constitution in the form it had before the changes by the Council of Ministers.[73] In fact, the third draft constitution contained in the file also including the bylaw of the Council of Ministers is a text of 119 articles[74] that removes the preamble recalling the spirit of the Tanzimat and scores out the Tanzimat guarantees: it also reinstitutes the articles regarding the definition of the Ottoman state and the prerogatives of the sultan.

If one has a look at the drafting process of the Ottoman Constitution from the debates begun with Midhad to the final text of the Constitution itself, the evolution of the most contested articles leads us to interesting conclusions, as shown in the comparative table of Appendix VII.

Considering the fact that Midhad, Said and the Drafting Commission imagined a constitution without any preamble recalling the Tanzimat decrees, especially the Imperial Rescript of 1839 and the Reform Decree of 1856, one might think that reformist draftsmen intended to break the traditional mode of law-making in order to evolve towards a much more modern constitutional text and away from charters granted by the sultan. Unlike the reactions of the Council of Ministers, the liberal wing of the Commission might have imposed such a break if we consider that no preamble was added to the final text of the Ottoman Constitution. The ideological trajectory of the Tanzimat guarantees putting life, honour and property under state protection is the same. The text of the Ottoman

[70] See all the marginal notes, Kaya Kılıç, pp. 161-165.

[71] The nickname of Said Pasha originated in the fact that he was one of the students of the Ottoman Engineering School sent to Britain for training. It was not a coincidence that British Said was nominated Abdülhamid II's aide-de-camp at a moment when the Ottoman Empire had to play the British card against Russian interventions. See Çağlar, p. 12.

[72] Şehsuvaroğlu, p. 182. Cited in Devereux, p. 57.

[73] Sami, pp. 12-14, n. 2 and 58-62; Şehsuvaroğlu, p. 182. Cited in Davison, *Reform, 1856-1876*, p. 380.

[74] BOA, YEE 71/33. See the original document in Appendix XI and the comparative table in Appendix VII.

Constitution laid legal foundations for their protection instead of instituting a vague concept of state protection. However, the amendments of the Council of Ministers attempted to put the property rights and allowances of the Ottoman imperial family under public guarantee: this attempt was successful, as the relevant amendment was incorporated into the Ottoman Constitution. The definition of the state evolved so as to overlap in the final text with that of the sultanate. Midhad's point of departure was to define the Ottoman state in terms of territorial integrity and its political regime based on the shari'a. The sultanate was separately defined from the state in a different section together with the prerogatives of the sultan, who was at the same time the caliph and protector of Islam. These definitions progressed with the work of the Drafting Commission mentioning Istanbul as the capital of the Ottoman state and enlarging the prerogatives of the sultan. The amendments of the Council of Ministers removed these definitions on the grounds that the relevant provisions attempted to limit sultanic power. It seems that the Drafting Commission and the Council of Ministers came to a compromise in the final text of the Ottoman Constitution. The definition of the Ottoman state as drafted by the Commission was kept but its basis in the shari'a was removed; instead the Ottoman state adopted a state religion, which was Islam. The 119-article draft constitution shows that there was an attempt to put the sultanate and the prerogatives of the sultan into a separate section entitled "the person of the sultan", but the scoring out of the title shows that the parties could not come to an agreement on the issue until the last moment. Hence the title separating the definition of the Ottoman state from that of the sultanate is removed from the final text of the Ottoman Constitution, thus demonstrating an overlapping between the sultanate and the state.

As for the rights and duties of Ottoman subjects, the evolution of the article on the equality of Ottoman subjects independently of their religious affiliation shows that this was one of the least contested issues. The Drafting Commission also added another dimension: equality in terms of rights and duties, something that the Ottoman Constitution itself recognised. Similarly, the article on Ottoman subjecthood followed an easy trajectory, reaching the Ottoman Constitution without any substantial change. It is, however, interesting to note that the Drafting Commission felt the need to emphasise each time that the concepts of equality and the status of being Ottoman were exempted from any religious discrimination. Midhad conceptualised individual liberty as being beyond religious discrimination and communal affiliation and prohibited exile or imprisonment without any legal grounds. The Drafting Commission added more solid legal and moral dimensions to the concept: Ottomans enjoyed individual liberty on condition of not violating the liberty of others and were exempted from punishment, exile or imprisonment except when determined by law. Strangely, however, the Drafting Commission also added the framework of the shari'a to the legal and moral limits of individual freedom. The article reached the Ottoman Constitution without the limits imposed by the shari'a, including only a moral and legal perspective. More importantly, however, the mention of exile and imprisonment was removed from the Ottoman Constitution. The final text only referred to a general concept of punishment (*mücazat*), determined by law alone, to limit individual freedom. The Drafting Commission conceptualised the most developed article on taxation by recognising the equality of Ottoman subjects in terms of taxation, the proportionality of taxes to the economic power of ratepayers, their conformity with special regulations and the control of the Chamber of Deputies over the policy of the government in the matter of taxation. The evolution of the article shows that draftsmen could not come to an agreement on the control of the Chamber of Deputies over governmental policies in the matter of taxation. Finally, the Ottoman Constitution does not literally mention equality in terms of taxation but only recognised the proportionality of taxes to the economic power of ratepayers and their conformity with special regulations. In the initial phase, religious freedom was defined by Midhad as the free exercise of various religions of the empire on the condition of not violating good morals and public safety, and their equal protection by the state. Within the Drafting Commission, which also housed the high-ranking members of the ulema, the relevant provision evolved into recognition of a state religion, Islam, while guaranteeing the free practice of other religions. The article's ups and downs further on reveal that the principal element of controversy was the recognition or non-recognition of Islam as state religion. Finally, the Ottoman Constitution accepted Islam as such, but added another detail: the Ottoman Constitution also guaranteed the exercise of privileges previously granted to various communities. Nevertheless, the provision does not clarify whether these privileges signify the community constitutions promulgated in the aftermath of the Crimean War or the former communal fabrics that preceded these constitutions. The expression "as previously" (*kemakan*) gives a certain ambiguity to the provision in the sense that one does not know how far one can go back in the time frame. It seems that the annexation of the privileges in Article 11 of the Ottoman Constitution was Midhad's work; he wrote to the sultan on December 22, 1876, one day before the promulgation of the Ottoman Constitution, that changes had been made to Article 11 so that the clause "the enjoyment of religious privileges granted to different communities will occur as in ancient times", which had been previously skipped, was now included. He put particular emphasis on the use of "as in ancient times" in the article.[75] If freedom of the press was recognised by the Ottoman Constitution, freedom of expression, developed by Midhad and Said, the freedom to found associations and the abolition of the death penalty in the matter of political crimes, which only Said thought of, were never taken into consideration in the later stages of drafting as well as in the Constitution itself.

The evolution of the article on the access of Ottoman subjects to public offices, which eliminated all the subjective barriers or obstacles (i.e. nobility and all manner of affiliations) and regularised the issue on the basis of concrete laws allowing all Ottoman subjects to take such offices according to their aptitude, again brings a vague and subjective framework to the question. No concrete/objective tools were provided including laws to testify the capacity and aptitude of Ottoman subjects in order to regulate their access to offices in the Ottoman Constitution. The article on public functionaries follows a similar itinerary. From a framework in which their nomination to the civil service would be permitted according to their diplomas and training, the article again evolves towards the nomination of public functionaries according to their merit and capacity. The only solid ground in this nomination process is law, but one might doubt whether legislation can impose objective tools for measuring the suitability of public functionaries in terms of their educational background. Midhad's draft also brings the idea of progress to public functionaries, but further drafts, including the Ottoman Constitution, do not even mention it. The non-progress of the public functionary is not cited among the reasons of dismissal. However, as arbitrary dismissals were the common concern of all Ottoman bureaucrats, all the drafts agreed at least on the principle that officials could not be dismissed or changed unless legal grounds justified these dismissals.

If one has a look at the situation of the Council of Ministers, one notices that it regressed from an alternative source of authority into an authority at the service of the sultan. The creation of the premiership within the Council of Ministers, as Midhad expected, encountered the

---

[75] BOA, I. MMS. 55/2510, 5 Zilhicce 1293/22 December 1876.

opposition of Grand Vizier Mehmed Rüşdü Pasha and probably the Council of Ministers. The individual and collective responsibility of ministers was also weakened in the Ottoman Constitution, regressing towards a vague concept of responsibility for the acts of the ministry without any differentiation between individual and collective responsibility. Throughout the drafting process, when the idea of creating a premiership was present, the term "president of the Council of Ministers" was more often used instead of "grand vizier". As this idea was undermined towards the end of the drafting process, the vocabulary changed: the preferred term was now the Grand Vizierate.

One also notices through changes from the initial drafts to the final text of the Ottoman Constitution that the draftsmen struggled against one another for a stronger Chamber of Deputies or General Assembly and a weaker Council of Ministers, or a stronger Council of Ministers and a weaker Chamber of Deputies or General Assembly. For instance, when one or more members of the Chamber of Deputies lodged a complaint against a minister, the whole process from deliberation until a decision by vote on the course to be taken against the accused minister, including an address demanding his trial at the Higher Court (*Divan-ı Ali*), was conducted by the different bodies of the Chamber of Deputies. The Ottoman Constitution puts the grand vizier at the final phase which submits the process to imperial sanction, thus weakening the control the Chamber of Deputies had over the ministers. When investigating any deficiency in ministerial acts, one might doubt whether a grand vizier nominated by the sultan could be as objective as the Chamber of Deputies, elected by the population.

Similarly, in case of urgent necessity, if the General Assembly could not convene, the Council of Ministers could make dispositions without waiting for the General Assembly; after imperial sanction, these dispositions would have the force of law until the final decision of the General Assembly when it did convene, provided that they respected the principles of the Ottoman Constitution. The text of the Drafting Commission strengthened the position of the General Assembly, stating that these dispositions will cease to become law if rejected by the Assembly once it convenes. It also underlines that the entire responsibility for these dispositions belongs to the Council of Ministers. However, until the article took its final form in the Ottoman Constitution, the disposition regarding the possibility of rejection by the General Assembly was scored out, thus rendering the negotiations between the Council of

Ministers and the former vague in the case of conflict over the acceptance of the decrees undertaken by the ministers. The article was adopted
by the Ottoman Constitution, removing the provision putting responsibility for the decrees on the shoulders of the Council of Ministers.

The Council of State was conceptualised by Midhad as an organ that
could challenge the power of the Council of Ministers and even that of
the sultan. Its functions extended from the executive field to the legislative process. Nevertheless, its status in the Ottoman Constitution regressed
into a simple technocratic office where bills of laws would be prepared
at the request of the legislative branch. The Council of State was not even
assigned a separate section.

Although the Drafting Commission shared legislative power between
the Council of Ministers and the two organs of the General Assembly
(the Chamber of Deputies and the Council of Notables) before the compulsory imperial sanction, the amendments of the Council of Ministers
put the legislative process under the control of the sultan, who even
decided whether the legal projects submitted by the legislative bodies
were worthy of being submitted to the Council of State for elaboration.
The Council of Notables or the Senate, the members of which were nominated by the sultan, was conceived as another sultan-oriented body to
check the conformability of the legislative process with the principles of
the Constitution, religion, the rights of the sultan, freedom, the integrity
and security of the Ottoman state, etc. Although the Chamber of Deputies
was supposed to represent popular will as an elective legislative body, it
reached the Ottoman Constitution with a gradual weakening of its com-
petencies before the Council of Ministers and the Senate. The Chamber
already lost some of its major responsibilities as conceptualised by Midhad (regulation of state debt, negotiation of financial policies including
internal or external borrowing, taxation, adjustment of the state budget
and public expenses, discussion of legal projects, and supervision of state
departments in terms of the application of regulations) after the revision
of the draft by the Commission. The amendments of the Council of Ministers restricted its legislative initiative to bills of laws related to the
Constitution and financial issues. Moreover, as the comparative table of
Appendix VII shows, the number of deputies and their increase for better
representation were contested issues. Although the number was fixed at
one deputy for every 50,000 Ottoman male inhabitants, this number was
chagned to one per every 80,000: the question of better representation
was disregarded by the final text of the Ottoman Constitution.

Article 118 of the Ottoman Constitution stipulated that all dispositions of laws, regulations, usages and customs in force would continue to be applied "until they were modified or abrogated by laws and regulations". The use of "until" in the sentence offered the prospect of change in the near future. However, an imperial order sanctioned the transformation of the expression "until they were abrogated" into "as far as they were not abolished", although only on official copies.[76] This undermined the expectation of changes in existing laws and customs which might have contradicted the application of the Ottoman Constitution.

3. WHICH EUROPEAN CONSTITUTIONS?[77]

Some articles of the 1867 Austrian Constitution regarding the emperor's prerogatives, his immunity and sacred character, the responsibility of ministers and state functionaries for their acts within the limits of their powers and the application of the Constitution and the judgment of the accused ministers were translated into Ottoman Turkish in August 1907. This translation was probably preparation before the promulgation of the Ottoman Constitution of 1908 and the completion of the constitutional amendments that strengthened ministerial responsibility in 1909. This translation makes one wonder whether the Austrian Constitution acted as a reference for the 1876 Ottoman Constitution. Archival sources do not indicate any concrete sign of this. However, a comparison of the two constitutions in terms of the translated provisions on the government, the functioning of civil officialdom and executive power reveals similarities. The prerogatives of the Austrian and Ottoman sovereigns were more or less similar in the 1867 and 1876 texts. However, the international sphere of action of the Austrian emperor was counterbalanced by the approval of the bicameral Imperial Council for the conclusion of commercial treaties or those concerning his subjects. There were similar nuances in other provisions as well. For instance, if a complaint was addressed against a minister on account of his lack of responsibility, the order for his trial would be submitted for the sanction of the sovereign: the accused minister would be judged in a high court in both the Ottoman and Austrian

[76] BOA, DUIT 91/4, 8 Zilkade 1293 / 25 November 1876. From Said Pasha.
[77] For an earlier analysis of the impact of European constitutions on the 1876 *Kanun-ı Esasi*, see also Koçunyan, "The Transcultural Dimension of the Ottoman Constitution", pp. 235-258.

cases, with the only difference being that, in the Austrian example, the minister would be judged by ordinary courts for penal crimes he might have committed.[78] The limits on the emperor's prerogatives and ministerial responsibility are better defined in the Austrian Constitution.

These similarities lead us to believe that the 1867 Austrian Constitution might have been taken into consideration in the drafting of the 1876 Ottoman Constitution. In fact, the Austro-Hungarian Constitution was used as a model by Midhad since Austria-Hungary housed a diversity of races and religions.[79] The immunity, sacredness and inviolability of the emperor (principles that appear in other European constitutions as well, such as the Italian Constitution,[80] the 1831 Belgian Constitution[81] and the French Constitutions of 1791,[82] 1814, 1815, 1830, etc.) left aside, the general rights of citizens mentioned in the Austrian Constitution of 1867 seem to have influenced those of Ottoman subjects in the initial draft constitutions. Particularly the language issue, stipulated in the draft constitution of 130 articles, seems to have been inspired by its Austrian counterpart: the Austrian Empire recognised equal rights for all languages of the empire in public instruction and public affairs. Moreover, public schools were organised in such a way that each race would have the necessary means for instruction in its own language: equally, there was to be no coercion in terms of instruction in another language. While the 130-article draft does not talk about the equality of the languages spoken in the Ottoman Empire, the various peoples are authorised to teach and learn the languages native to them. However, the Austrian Constitution recognises more explicitly the cultural diversity of the population; thus all the races of the Austrian Empire have equal and inviolable rights to preserve and cultivate their nationality and language. Neither the draft constitutions nor the Ottoman Constitution itself develop such a framework for the Ottoman Empire. The Ottoman state recognised rather the historical privileges of various *millet*s, which also included a certain freedom of public instruction and religious education in community schools through which national cultures, including language, could be cultivated. Like their Austrian counterparts, Ottoman subjects were authorised to

---

[78] BOA, YEE 112/13. From the Ottoman Embassy of Vienna, Veli (translator), 30 Temmuz 1323/12 August 1907.

[79] *Journal des Débats*, October 20, 1876.

[80] Larousse, v. 4, p. 1049.

[81] *Inventaire raisonné*, v. 12, p. 694.

[82] Larousse, v. 4, p. 1037.

found establishments of public instruction or education. In the Austrian Constitution, religious instruction in the schools depended on the Church or on the religious society in charge of the school. In both empires, the state had the right of supervision over public instruction and education.[83]

As documents directly issued by the state and the sultan himself, the decrees enthroning Abdülaziz I, Murad V and Abdülhamid II are worthy of being studied in terms of their constitutional value. As a result of the promulgation of the 1856 Reform Edict, Abdülaziz I's act of enthronement[84] talks about the happiness, prosperity and well-being of all Ottoman subjects; the guarantee of life, honour and property for everyone; loyalty to the shariʿa for the state's consolidation; respect for laws, rights and duties; the ordering of the administrative and financial affairs of the state; the economic use of public income to avoid extravagance; and the equality of all subjects of various creeds and *millet*s before justice, without neglecting God's assistance for the realisation of all this. Thus, the decree of accession refers to principles peculiar to constitutional frameworks. As the transition of the Ottoman Empire to a constitutional regime was the requirement of a reformist bureaucratic party after his accession to the throne, it is quite normal that Abdülaziz I's text does not refer to a new text on which these principles will be based.

What is perhaps more interesting is the act of enthronement of Murad V, who came to the throne by way of his promise to promulgate a constitution. After having mentioned the deterioration of state affairs, both internal and external, and the lack of confidence expressed by public opinion, Murad V's text[85] talks about the determination of state affairs by an essential text and strong laws, on which public administration will be based and which will conform to the capabilities of the Ottoman populations and to the dispositions of the shariʿa. Murad V adds that the nature of these laws will be discussed among ministers. He refers to the reorganisation of the Council of State and Judicial Ordinances, the ministries of public instruction and finances, as well as to the reorganisation of other state departments. He puts particular emphasis on the control of finances and avoiding public expenses beyond the state budget.

---

[83] *Inventaire raisonné*, v. 12, pp. 702-703. See also The Austrian Constitution of 1867 available at http://mjp.univ-perp.fr/constit/at1867-1.htm (accessed 24.01.2013).

[84] See the text, Ahmed Midhad Effendi, *Üss-i İnkılab*, v. 1, pp. 294-296 and Appendix XII.

[85] See the text, Ahmed Midhad Effendi, *Üss-i İnkılab*, v. 1, pp. 401-403 and Appendix XIII.

The historical value of this act of enthronement undoubtedly lies in its reference to a new text on which state affairs will be based.

Abdülhamid II's act of enthronement[86] is the text of a late-comer; it refers to almost the same principles, attributing the troubles and difficulties encountered by the state to the non-respect of the shari'a, the non-application of laws and regulations and to arbitrary rule. Unlike Murad V, who mentions a new administrative text without directly pronouncing the magic word "constitution", Abdülhamid II makes reference to the institution of a General Assembly which will supervise the arrangement and application of laws and regulations in accordance with the dispositions of the shari'a and the needs of the country, as well as the equilibrium between public income and expenditure. Like Murad V, Abdülhamid II also envisages the reorganisation of state affairs regarding public administration, finances and security. Although the last two texts refer to the elaboration of a new administrative text and the institution of a General Assembly (*Meclis-i Umumi*), they do not promise the adoption of a constitutional regime in the Ottoman Empire. After all, any regime may promise a new administrative text and an assembly without being bound by a constitutional framework.

A letter sent from the Ottoman embassy in Brussels to the Ottoman Ministry of Foreign Affairs on September 5, 1892 described the procedures according to which the sessions of the Belgian Parliament had been suspended for constitutional revision and informed how long it took for the king to proclaim the new Belgian Constitution.[87] This letter regarding the suspension of Belgian Parliament perhaps reflects many intentions. Midhad Pasha was forced to resign on the grounds of Article 113 of the Ottoman Constitution on February 7, 1877 and was exiled to Europe. This article gave the sultan the exclusive right to expel from Ottoman territory those who, after police investigation, were considered dangerous to the safety of the state. After the opening of the Ottoman Parliament on March 19, 1877, Abdülhamid II, on the recommendation of the Grand Vizier Ahmed Vefik Pasha, suspended the General Assembly.[88] One possible motive for examining this suspension procedure is that the Belgian Constitution had previously served as a reference to the 1876 Ottoman

---

[86] See the text, Ahmed Midhad Effendi, *Üss-i İnkılab*, v. 2, pp. 281-285 and Appendix XIV.

[87] BOA, Y. A. HUS. 280/92, 15 Rebiülahır 1311/26 October 1893.

[88] Tunaya, *Siyasal Gelişmeler*, pp. 15-16.

Constitution and the sultan wanted to know more about the policy of Belgian parliamentary suspension in order to legitimise the interruption of the Ottoman Parliament by way of a European model. The letter might also have been sent for informative purposes only. The archival records of the Ottoman Foreign Ministry display the efforts of Ottoman embassies to carefully follow all kinds of constitutional revisions, parliamentary suspensions and similar developments in Europe. However, other sources confirm the use of the Belgian Constitution as a reference by the Ottomans. Newspapers also made allusion to the use of Belgian institutions as a model.[89] Moreover, Bancroft Davis, American minister to Berlin, once commented that the sultan "collected the Ottoman Constitution from Belgium and proclaimed it in the Ottoman Empire".[90] Davis does not clarify to which sultan he was referring. The French ambassador to the Porte also reported that the adoption of the Belgian Constitution, which prevailed in all of Europe, was on the agenda of Ottoman reformers.[91]

When carefully examined, one notices that both the Belgian and Ottoman constitutions begin with a territorial concern. Both of them define their territories and their provincial divisions. The Belgian Constitution also authorised the use of all local languages but the inspiration of Ottoman draftsmen seems more Austrian than Belgian with regards to this question.[92] When it is the text of a hereditary monarchy, the Belgian Constitution belongs to a more liberal tradition than its Ottoman counterpart in the sense that all powers emanate from the nation. Neither the draft constitutions nor the Ottoman Constitution itself developed the idea of national sovereignty. Legislative power was exercised collectively by the sovereign, the Chamber of Representatives and the Senate, and the initiative of law belonged to each of these three branches in the two constitutions.[93] The Chamber of Representatives was composed of deputies directly elected by the citizens, who paid a certain amount of tax determined by electoral law in the Belgian Constitution, something more

---

[89] See for instance, *La Turquie*, June 23, 1876.

[90] BOA, HR. SYS. 1869-18. From Aristarki (Ottoman Legation of Washington) to the Ottoman Foreign Minister Server Pasha, February 19, 1878 & Extract from the despatch of Davis to M. Fish, Legation of the States, Berlin, January 4, 1877.

[91] MAE, Archives diplomatiques (Paris), Correspondance politique, Mai-Juin 1876, Tome 404. From Bourgoing to Decazes, June 7, 1876.

[92] The Belgian Constitution of 1831 is available at http://mjp.univ-perp.fr/constit/be1831.htm (accessed 24.01.2013).

[93] *Inventaire raisonné*, v. 12, pp. 693-694.

or less similar to the Ottoman case. Unlike in the Ottoman Constitution, however, the Senate was also elected. One may remember that Midhad, when discussing the institution of a Senate within the Ottoman Constitution, was also thinking of an elected house in the long term:[94] one may question whether the Belgian Constitution was something projected rather than directly materialised in the Ottoman Constitution.

The disappointments of Ottoman liberals due to the growing possibility of European intervention led them to publish the "Manifesto of Muslim Patriots", which was forwarded to European statesmen in March 1876.[95] The manifesto put emphasis on the necessity of a Parliament on the "English model" and requested European "understanding" and "patience" for the achievement of this goal.[96] Among the records consulted so far, the manifesto is the only document to refer to an English model. However, newspapers referred to the adoption of British institutions when the idea of reform was publicly discussed in the period preceding the proclamation of the Ottoman Constitution.[97] In his diary, Elliot himself stated that Midhad "could rely upon the hearty sympathy of the British nation for an attempt to obtain something like an imitation of its own institutions".[98] In general, the European press reflected European hostility towards the Ottoman Constitution.[99] Among others, the recognition of Islam as a state religion was one of the reasons why the constitution was unacceptable in the eyes of Europe. However, in England, the monarch was also the head of the Church of England, which had the privileges of an official state church.[100]

Midhad's text assigns the legislative power to the Chamber of Deputies. *The Times* of June 21, 1876 mentions that this national assembly was called *Meclis-i Memalik* (Assembly of the Country) in Midhad's vocabulary. The number of provinces would be approximately 24 (some of them, like Bosnia, being divided into more than one) and each would send four deputies: the total number of deputies would not exceed 110 except for the members of the Ottoman capital at a number of six or eight. Istanbul and its immediate neighbourhood would not belong to any province and

---

[94] *Inventaire raisonné*, v. 12, pp. 693-694.
[95] Devereux, p. 31.
[96] Devereux, p. 32.
[97] See for instance *La Turquie*, June 23, 1876.
[98] Elliot, p. 229.
[99] Devereux, pp. 87-91.
[100] Devereux, p. 90.

would be administered by the Ministry of the Police.[101] The issue of *The Times* dated August 8, 1876, together with the draft published by Ahmed Midhad Effendi in his *Üss-i İnkılab* and the draft of the Yıldız Palace collection, provided a more advanced version of the Chamber of Deputies, according to which the latter would consist of 120 members, 40 of whom would be appointed by government and 80 of whom elected by popular vote. For the first year, the 80 elective deputies would be nominated by the general councils of the provinces already existing and elected by the people upon the principle of direct universal suffrage. After the first year, the election of the deputies would proceed in accordance with a new electoral law that the Chamber itself would discuss and vote on during its first session.[102] The election of deputies by the general councils (*conseils généraux* in French; *Meclis-i Umumi* in Ottoman) whose seats were located in the country towns (*chef-lieu*) of the provinces was the application of suffrage at two degrees, an electoral system that France possessed in 1789, on condition that the general councils would be elected by the delegates of the nation.[103]

The temporary electoral law recalls the provincial elections stipulated in the Armenian National Constitution, according to which the deputies of the provinces should be elected by the general assemblies of each province. For Istanbul, the electoral law stipulated the formation by all "property owners" of an electoral college for popular vote.[104] This overlaps with the same principle as that of the "dues-paid electors" of the Armenian National Constitution, which was based on the goal of economic power for Istanbul.[105] Moreover, the fact that the capital would provide more deputies than the provinces was another similarity with the electoral principles of the Armenian National Constitution. Namık Kemal also referred to the *millet* assemblies of non-Muslims as a model for the future Ottoman Chamber of Deputies.[106]

The similarities are more consistent with the French constitutional movement. The Ottoman Constitution was also said to be based on

---

[101] *The Times*, June 21, 1876.

[102] *The Times*, August 8, 1876.

[103] *Revue de Constantinople*, June 11, 1876.

[104] Davison, *Reform, 1856-1876*, pp. 374-375. See also *La Turquie*, November 3, 1876.

[105] Artinian, p. 94.

[106] Kuntay, v. 1, p. 185, quoting his "Answer to the Gazette du Levant" of 1867. Cited in Roderic Davison, *Essays in Ottoman and Turkish History, 1774-1923: The Impact of the West* (Austin: Texas University Press, 1990), p. 103.

"a legislature consisting of two chambers [...], not differing widely in its constitution from that which existed in France during the Second Empire".[107] This statement of Salisbury concerns the French Constitution of 1852, which instituted the Second Empire and made Louis-Napoleon Bonaparte the emperor of the French under the name of Napoleon III.[108] The 1852 Constitution attributed almost dictatorial powers to the latter;[109] accordingly, the legislative power was collectively exercised by the president of the republic, the Senate and the legislative body, but only the president had the right to initiative of law. He could convoke, delay, prorogue or dissolve the legislative body. In the case of dissolution, he must convoke the new legislative body within six months, which is quite a long period. During this interval, the Senate, on the proposition of the president, provided what was necessary for the functioning of the government including emergency measures. By way of a report to the president of the republic, the Senate could lay the foundations for a legal project presenting national interests.[110] These stipulations show that the president, through the Senate, could dominate the whole legislative process once the legislative body became paralysed. Similarly, the sultan could dominate the legislative process through the Council of Ministers and the Senate on the grounds of urgency or national interests, two governing bodies the members of which he nominated on his own.

If one goes back to the draft constitutions of the Ottoman Commission, one notices that almost the entire French constitutional course was examined by Ottoman reformers, even if some of principles did not materialise in the final Constitution of 1876. For instance, Said Pasha's draft constitution resembled the French Constitution of 1848 with its National Assembly of 750 deputies; in its abolition of the death penalty in the matter of political crimes; in the sultan submitting an account of the general state of affairs to the General Assembly every year, as in the French Republic; and in the mention of martial law (*état de siège*, also formulated in the Constitution of 1852).[111] His provision on freedom of the press indicates that he had read the French Constitution of 1815. His mention of the non-formation of extraordinary commissions or tribunals in any circumstance and the prohibition of the re-establishment of the

---

[107] PRO, FO 78/2676, From Salisbury to Derby, January 13, 1877.
[108] Larousse, v. 4, pp. 1045-1046. *Inventaire raisonné*, v. 12, p. 658.
[109] *Inventaire raisonné*, v. 12, p. 658.
[110] Larousse, v. 4, p. 1046.
[111] Larousse, v. 4, pp. 1044-1045.

penalty of sequestration (the latter also mentioned in the French Constitution of 1814) in his draft are a proof of his consideration of the French Constitution of 1830. Like the French Constitution of 1814, which was a granted charter (*charte octroyée*), the Ottoman Constitution of 1876 was a grant by the sultan to his subjects. Article 113 of the Ottoman Constitution bears some elements of the Law of General Security (*Loi de sûreté générale* in French) promulgated by Napoleon III in 1858, which allowed for the deportation from French territory, without trial, of anyone convicted of political crimes deemed a threat to public security.[112]

4. THE FINAL TEXT OF THE OTTOMAN CONSTITUTION

The Ottoman Constitution was proclaimed on December 23, 1876.[113] The term *"Kanun-i Esasi"* (Basic Law) was chosen as the Ottoman equivalent of "constitution". However, the French term *"konstitüsyon"* appears in Ottoman texts at earlier stages.[114] Moreover, the first *millet* regulation of the Armenian community, drafted in 1857 before the 1863 National Constitution and rejected by the Sublime Porte, was named *"Himnagan Gano'nq"* (Basic Laws) in Armenian and *"Nizamat-ı Esasiye"* (Basic Regulation) in Ottoman Turkish.[115]

Kostaki Effendi Antopulo and Yanko Effendi Ökiyades, members of the Council of State, were appointed for the official translation of the

[112] See for details, Vincent Wright, "La Loi de Sûreté générale de 1858," in *Revue d'Histoire moderne et contemporaine*, vol. 16, no. 3 (July-September 1969), pp. 414-430.

[113] For the official translation in French see PRO, FO 198/42, From Elliot to Derby, December 23, 1876, Inclosure in no. 118. The official French translation was followed in the same file by an English translation, which was probably that of the British embassy to the Porte. See also Demétrius Nicolaïdes (publié par), *Doustour-i Hamidié. Appendice à la Législation ottomane contenant les lois et règlements promulgués à partir de l'année 1874-1878* (Constantinople: Journal Thraki, 1878), pp. 7-25. When presenting the general outline of the constitutional text, my work is based on the English translation without neglecting to compare the terminological differences between the Ottoman, French, English and Armenian texts. For the Ottoman text, see *Düstur*, 1. Tertip (First Series), vol. 4, pp. 4-20 and Appendix XV; also cited in Suna Kili, *Osmanlı ve Türk Anayasaları* (Ottoman and Turkish Constitutions), (İstanbul: Boğaziçi Üniversitesi Yayınları, 1980), pp. 1-14. For the official Armenian translation, see *Masis*, December 26, 28, 30, 1876. For another Armenian translation, see also *Sahmanatro't'iwn Osmanean* (Ottoman Constitution), translated from French by Mihran H. Sıvacıyan ([s.l.]: [s.n.], 1876). Some concepts are different in Sıvacıyan's translation.

[114] Strauss, "A Constitution for a Multilingual Empire", p. 36.

[115] For the Ottoman text, see BOA, I.MVL 16736/lef 1. Cited in Masayuki, pp. 215, 247.

Ottoman Constitution into Greek. Elias Effendi, director of the archives of foreign affairs, and Boğos Effendi Parnasyan, vice-chief of the press office, were appointed for the official translation of the Ottoman Constitution into Armenian.[116] When the translations were accomplished, the text of the Constitution would be officially transmitted to the patriarchates, which, in turn, would send the translations to the provinces.[117]

The nineteenth century was characterised by rebellions in the Balkan provinces to establish new independent states which would not be subjugated to Ottoman sovereignty.[118] As a response to these separatist tendencies and debates regarding the autonomy of some European provinces, the constitution started with a concern for territorial integrity: Article 1 stipulated that the Ottoman Empire comprised the current territory together with the privileged provinces and constituted an "indivisible whole, from which no portion can be detached under any pretext whatever".

The question of territorial integrity was inseparable from the issue of Ottoman sovereignty. The 1876 Ottoman Constitution does not introduce the notion of popular sovereignty like some of its European counterparts. Sovereignty was associated with sultanic authority: the Ottoman sovereignty, which includes in the person of the sovereign the supreme caliphate of Islam, belongs to the eldest prince of the House of Osman, in accordance with the rules established *ab antiquo* (Article 3). This means that Ottoman sovereignty was in fact the property of the Ottoman dynasty. Furthermore, Abdülhamid II assigned a political function to Islam through the institution of the caliphate. The objective of this new policy, which was called Pan-Islamism, was not to gather Islamic countries under Ottoman rule; rather it was used as a political tool against the imperialist policies of the Great Powers.[119] Pan-Islamism was an Ottoman response to the Pan-Slavic policies of Russia and the protectionist claims of the Great Powers vis-à-vis non-Muslim communities. The rule of seniority was also stipulated in this article. The codification of seniority could be conceived as the result of the spread of the nineteenth-century idea that

---

[116] *La Turquie*, December 30, 1876.

[117] *La Turquie*, December 29, 1876.

[118] Quataert, pp. 54-55.

[119] Ahmed Yaşar Ocak, "Islam in the Ottoman Empire: A Sociological Framework for a New Interpretation," in Kemal H. Karpat & Robert W. Zens (eds), *Ottoman Borderlands: Issues, Personalities and Political Changes* (Madison: The University of Wisconsin Press, 2003), p. 195.

a ruler who was not from the Ottoman dynasty could also accede to the throne.[120] We should also keep in mind that Khedive İsmail Pasha, "Istanbul's close rival" in the process of modernisation, succeeded in changing the rule of succession after his two predecessors.[121] The Ottoman dynasty probably felt its position was endangered and tried to guarantee its continuity through this article.

Sultanic sovereignty was also consolidated by Article 113; accordingly the sultan held the exclusive right to expel those who were considered dangerous to the safety of the state from Ottoman territory. Furthermore, in the case of disturbance in any corner of Ottoman territory, the imperial government had the right to proclaim a state of siege which "consists in the temporary suspension of civil rights" (in the English translation of the Ottoman Constitution). The French and Armenian translations mention the suspension of civil (*civil*/*qaghaqah'in*) laws instead of rights. However, *mülkiye*, which was translated from Ottoman into other languages as the equivalent of "civil", means "what is non-religious and non-military". Although the sultan's authority covered a large spectrum of prerogatives (Article 7: appointment of the ministers, minting money, conclusion of treaties with the Powers, declaration of peace and war, execution of the provisions of the shari'a, gathering of the General Assembly, dissolution of the Chamber of Deputies, and command of land and sea forces), his person was immune and sacred (Article 5). The 1876 Ottoman Constitution shows that the legal frameworks of 1839 and 1856 evolved from the statement of individual liberties (religious freedom, happiness, prosperity, guarantee of life, honour, property, etc.), institutional emancipation (amelioration of the provinces, reform in the Ottoman tax system, regularisation of the military service, etc.) and the particularisms of non-Muslim communal spheres towards uniform legislation. The apparent principle of representation in the different state departments was overshadowed by the consolidation of the central power around the sultan.

The Ottoman sultan, under the title of "supreme caliph", declared himself as the protector of the Muslim religion while continuing to be the sovereign of all Ottomans (Article 4). Thus the Ottoman Constitution of 1876 brought the idea of separation of the sultan-caliph's religious

---

[120] Hakan T. Karateke, "Who is the Next Ottoman Sultan? Attempts to Change the Rule of Succession during the Nineteenth Century," in Itzchak Weismann & Fruma Zachs (eds.), *Ottoman Reform and Muslim Regeneration: Studies in Honour of Butrus Abu-Manneh* (London: Tauris, 2005), p. 44.

[121] Karateke, p. 49.

authority from his political sovereignty; this meant that the sultan held political power over all Ottomans while at the same time he held the position of caliph for Muslim subjects.[122] "This may have been due to Ottoman concern about arousing French and British anxieties, given their large Muslim colonies and the delicate state of international relations".[123] Thus, the Constitution responded to the religious protectionism of the Great Powers over Ottoman non-Muslims by creating an Islamic equivalent over the transnational Islamic community.

After the enumeration of general provisions regarding the Ottoman Empire (articles 1-7), the Constitution passed to the definition of the public law of the Ottomans (articles 8-26). This section establishes the equal conditions of being an Ottoman subject without distinction of faith (Article 8); the inviolability of personal liberties (Article 10); the freedom of press (Article 12); the power of forming commercial, industrial or agricultural companies for Ottoman subjects (Article 13); the freedom of education (Article 15) under state supervision (Article 16); the equality of all Ottomans before the law "with the same rights and duties towards their country" and "without prejudice to religion" (Article 17); the evaluation and distribution of taxes in proportion to the fortune of each taxpayer (Article 20); the guarantee of property, real or personal (Article 21); the inviolability of the domicile (Article 22); the prohibition of the confiscation of property and forced labour (Article 24); of the exaction of any sum of money for various reasons except by virtue of law (Article 25), and of torture (Article 26).

According to Article 11, Islam was the state religion. While maintaining this principle, the state would protect the free exercise of other religions professed in the Ottoman Empire and the religious privileges granted to various communities, however provisionally. State protection was offered "on condition of public order and morality not being interfered with". According to French diplomatic records, Midhad's objective was the unification of internal legislation. As a partisan of the famous formula "free church within a free state", Midhad would suppress national communities as civil organisations entrusted with a certain political autonomy. In Midhad's view, this result could only be obtained by the establishment of a uniform civil legislation and the creation of municipalities organised

---

[122] Ş. Tufan Buzpınar, "The Question of Caliphate under the Last Ottoman Sultans", in Weismann & Zachs, p. 19.
[123] Buzpınar, p. 25.

without prejudice to religion or race. If this ideal was reached, inequalities between Ottoman subjects would be suppressed together with the pretexts of interference by the European Powers.[124] In that respect, we may assume that the Ottoman Constitution was aiming at the gradual weakening of communal regulations in the long term. Another question was which Islam was the state religion. The Ottoman Empire was composed of many Muslim orders, and Sufi sects were alternatives to Sunni orthodoxy.[125] Although the tendency of the Ottoman dynasty towards Sunni orthodoxy was implicit, the Ottoman Constitution does not mention any sectarian Islamic preference, probably for the sake of covering other Islamic populations.

In addition to freedom of education, the Ottoman version of the Constitution aims at harmonising and regulating the public instruction given to Ottomans without harming the religious affairs of diverse communities. The French version is closer to the Ottoman one in that it inserts the condition of not harming the religious education of diverse communities. The English translation does not talk about diverse communities but rather diverse districts. The Armenian translation expresses more clearly that there would be no interference in the religious education of diverse communities (Article 16). There is, however, a conceptual difference between non-interference and not harming the sphere of religious education.

Articles 27 to 38 define the functioning of the Cabinet. The sultan appoints the grand vizier, the sheikh ül-Islam and other ministers (articles 27-28). The Cabinet meets under the presidency of the grand vizier. State affairs, domestic or foreign, are under the competency of the Council of Ministers. Their measures should, however, be submitted to the approval of the sultan (Article 28). The grand vizier takes initiatives on the issues presented to him by the ministers but refers to imperial sanction for the final decision (Article 29). Unlike the sultan, the ministers are responsible for their acts (Article 30). Nevertheless, some other provisions of the Constitution instituted a process that would prevent ministerial responsibility from being questioned; for instance, any complaint addressed by the Chamber of Deputies against a minister should be approved by the sultan before the accused minister is brought to trial

---

[124] MAEF, Papier Adolphe Thiers, PA-AP 170, vol. 5, Copies of Correspondence, May 11, 1871-May 13, 1873. Here October 16, 1872. It is not very clear from the formulation of the sentences whether the objective to establish a uniform legislation was Midhad's or Halil Pasha's (then minister of foreign affairs) idea.

[125] Barkey, *Empire of Difference*, p. 26.

before the High Court (Article 31).[126] If the Chamber of Deputies throws out a bill together with their motivations and the minister insists on the adoption of the bill, the sultan has the competence to order either a change of ministers or the dissolution of the Chamber of Deputies on condition of their re-election (Article 35). "Here again the power of Parliament was tempered by a sin of omission".[127] What would happen for instance if the sultan did not either dismiss the minister or dissolve the Parliament? He could just order the minister to withdraw the bill in question and then promulgate it himself through his power to issue decrees.[128] One may also talk about the same "sin of omission" with regard to ministerial decrees; when the Ottoman Parliament was not in session, ministers were authorised to issue decrees which, once approved by the sultan, would have the force of law so long as they were not contrary to the Ottoman Constitution (Article 36). Although the article stipulated that these decrees would be presented to the approval of the Ottoman Parliament when it was in session, it did not clarify what would happen if the Parliament did not give consent to these decrees. It is not clear from the article whether the submission of the decrees to the Parliament has an informative purpose.[129] Article 38 brings another set of omissions regarding ministerial responsibility: when the Chamber of Deputies, by a majority of votes, demanded a minister to appear before it to give explanations regarding his ministry, said minister could choose to send a subordinate in his place or to postpone his appearance. However, the article failed to clarify how long the minister could postpone this appearance and the consequences of his delay and his explanations thereof that are deemed unsatisfactory by the Chamber of Deputies.[130] Articles 39 to 41 define the framework in which public office is exercised.

Articles 42 to 53 define the functioning of the General Assembly, which was composed of two Chambers, the Senate and the Chamber of Deputies (Article 42). All the resolutions were to be voted on by an absolute majority of members in both chambers (Article 51). The initiative to propose a bill or change an existing law belonged to the Cabinet. The Senate and the Chamber of Deputies might also use such an initiative but only in matters regarding their duties. In the event of such a proposal,

[126] Devereux, pp. 67-68.
[127] Devereux, p. 68.
[128] Devereux, p. 68.
[129] Devereux, pp. 68-69.
[130] Devereux, p. 69.

the demand would be submitted by the grand vizier to the sultan; the Council of State was thus empowered by an imperial decree to prepare the legal project (Article 53).

Drafts of bills prepared by the Council of State were first submitted to the Chamber of Deputies and then to the Senate. Even if it passed both chambers, no bill could become law without imperial order. If a bill was thrown out by either of the chambers, it could not be proposed a second time during the same session (Article 54). Each bill must pass in both chambers by a majority of votes; each article and the whole bill must be voted by the majority of each of the two chambers (Article 55).

Articles 60 to 64 cover the Senate, whose members were nominated by the sultan for life (articles 60 & 62). The Senate examined bills and the budget communicated by the Chamber of Deputies (Article 64). Articles 65 to 80 are related to the functioning of the Chamber of Deputies. The number of deputies was fixed at one deputy for every 50,000 males of Ottoman nationality. The election was to be held by secret ballot. The Constitution stipulated that the electoral law would be determined by a special law in the future (articles 65 & 66). In that respect, the Constitution is an incomplete text. The general elections of deputies were to be held every four years (Article 69). The Chamber of Deputies discussed the bills, and adopted, amended or rejected the provisions regarding Ottoman finances or the Constitution. It examind the general expenditure of the state and created the budget (Article 80).

What is also worthy of attention is the ways in which the Ottoman Senate was named in the different texts. The Ottoman text refers to the Chamber of Notables (*Meclis-i Ayan*). In fact, while the term "*ayan*" literally means "notables", it also corresponded in the Ottoman context to a powerful class of territorial magnates. The *ayan*s were practically identified with tax farmers and had established hereditary self-rule in the provinces.[131] In addition to the use of the word "Senate" in the French and English translations, the latter also named this body "*la Chambre des Seigneurs*" and "the House of Lords". The Armenian translation of the word is quite different. It refers to the Armenian equivalent of the word "Senate" (*dzerago'h'd*), which literally means a "Council of Senior People". The word "*dzerago'h'd*" is more loyal to the spirit of the Constitution, since the Ottoman Senate would be composed of members who had exercised the functions of minister, governor-general, commandant

---

[131] Cf. Abu-Manneh, pp. 75-78.

of the army, ambassador, patriarch, grand rabbi, etc. Thus, the Armenian
text puts emphasis on the seniority of the Senate members both in terms
of their previous functions and their age (*dzerago'h'd* derives from the
word "dzer", which means "old"). The choice "Chamber of Notables" in
the Ottoman version was probably an attempt to evoke the terminology
of the British model, namely the House of Lords.

Articles 81 to 95 define the position of law courts. Unlike the English
and Ottoman texts, which successively announce this section under the title
of "Law Courts" and "Judges" (*Mehakim*), the French and Armenian texts
entitle it "Judicial Power" (*Pouvoir judiciaire*/*Tadagan ishxano'wt'iwn*).
Accordingly, judges were irremovable but could resign. In case of judicial
condemnation, their promotion, displacement or dismissal were subject to
legislation (Article 81). The sittings of all tribunals were to be public and
the publication of judgements was authorised (Article 82). Both the French
and English texts (Article 83) stipulate that any person, in the interest of
his defence, can make use of the means permitted by the law (*des moyens
permis par la loi*) before the tribunal. The Ottoman text mentions the use
of legitimate means (*vesait-i meşrua*) instead of laws. The concept of legitimate means is quite vague in comparison with the framework of concrete
laws, and the limits of legitimacy are not well-defined in the Constitution.

Affairs concerning the shari'a are heard in the tribunals of the Sheri
while civil affairs are heard in civil tribunals (Article 87). Unlike the
French and English texts, the Ottoman text makes a distinction between
Sheri and regular affairs (*deavi-i şeriye* & *deavi-i nizamiye*) as well as
between Sheri and regular courts (*mehakim-i şeriye* & *mehakim-i
nizamiye*). *Nizam* and *nizami* were often used to differentiate "civil" law
from "religious" (*şeri*) law. In fact, the term "*nizamiye*" derives from
nizam (order) and literally identifies the new-style courts as the "products
of the reforms".[132] The Armenian translation makes the distinction
between "Sheri" and "civil" (*qaghaqah'in*) affairs and "Sheri" and "civil"
tribunals. A High Court was formed by 30 members, of whom ten were
senators, ten counsellors of state and ten chosen among the presidents
and members of the Court of Cassation and Court of Appeal. All the
members were nominated by lot. The High Court gathered when necessary by imperial order. According to its English translation, its function
was the trial of ministers, the president and the members of the Court of
Cassation and all other people accused of treason or crimes against the

---

[132] Findley, "The Tanzimat", p. 20.

safety of the state (Article 92). The French version, in addition to crimes against the safety of the state (*attentat contre la sûreté de l'Etat*), mentions that of lese-majesty (*lèse-majesté*), which was an offense against the dignity of a reigning sovereign. The Ottoman version is closer to the French translation through its use of terms such as "*hukuk-ı şahane aleyhinde hareket etme*" (acts against the rights of the sovereign) and "*devleti bir hal-i muhatara-ı ilkaya tasaddi eyleme*" (act which endangers the state). The Armenian translation talks about acts against the safety of the state (*bedo'wt'ean abaho'vo'wt'ean te'm*) and "high treason" (*dzanr tawajano'wt'iwn*). Moreover, the Ottoman text does not literally refer to a "High Court" but to a "Supreme Council" (*Divan-ı Ali*). In fact, the term "*Divan*" designates an advisory assembly headed by the sultan or the sovereign in Islamic states. *Divan* was probably chosen instead of the more legal term "court" in the Ottoman translation, as the High Court was in principle a gathering by imperial order. The Armenian translation also uses the term "High Court" (*Partzrako'h'n Adean*). The decisions of the High Court were to be taken by a two-thirds majority of its members (Article 94). It was possible to quash its decisions by recourse to the Court of Cassation (Article 95). According to the French and English translations, the Court of Cassation would interpret civil and penal laws; the Council of State administrative laws; and the Senate the articles of the Constitution (Article 117). The Ottoman translation does not refer to civil and penal laws, but rather mentions a more general term such as "affairs of justice" (*umur-ı adliye*) for laws to be interpreted by the Court of Cassation.

Articles 96 to 107 are related to Ottoman finances. Taxes were to be fixed and collected in accordance with laws (Article 96). A budget law evaluated the receipts and expenses of the state, and taxes for the profit of the state were regulated by this law from their assessment to their collection (Article 97). The budget bill was voted upon by the General Assembly for one year (articles 98 & 102). No expenses could be incurred beyond the budget except by virtue of law (Article 100). A Court of Accounts was to be created for the examination of the operations of financial functionaries as well as of the yearly accounts presented by various ministries: every year it would address a special report to the Chamber of Deputies as well (Article 105). The Court of Accounts would be composed of twelve irremovable members nominated by imperial order, who could only be removed by decision of the majority of the Chamber of Deputies (Article 106). The budget was perhaps the only legislative task that the Parliament and the Chamber of Deputies could dominate if one considers how they were overshadowed by other state departments in the processes of legislation.[133]

Articles 108 to 112 are dedicated to the administration of the provinces, based on the principle of decentralisation. The section of provincial administration is incomplete in the sense that the organisational details were to be fixed in the future (Article 108). Unlike the French and English translations, which made use of the term "decentralisation" itself, the Ottoman text, instead of using the principle of decentralisation, refers rather to the enlargement of powers (*tevsi-i mezuniyet*) and to the separation of responsibilities (*tefrik-i vezayif*). The Armenian translation literally adopts the principle of decentralisation (*daragetro'nacman sgyzpo'wnq*). Another incomplete section regards municipal business, which would be administered in Istanbul and the provinces by elected municipal councils. However, their organisational scheme as well as their function and the election of their members had not yet been fixed by special laws (Article 112). The functions of the Provincial Council-General are defined in the French and English translations as the right to deliberate on matters of "public utility" such as the establishment of means of communication, the organisation of institutions of agricultural credit, the development of manufactures, commerce and agriculture and the diffusion of education (Article 110). The Ottoman translation refers rather to public works (*umur-ı nafıa*) instead of using the term "public utility". The Armenian text uses the term "public utility" (*hasaragac oko'wd*). In addition to public instruction, the Ottoman text refers to the moral dimension of education, though the principles according to which this dimension would be accomplished again remain vague. The Armenian translation mentions education in general terms without considering the moral dimension.

According to the Ottoman provincial administration, in every canton there would be a council related to each of the different communities. The council would be charged with the administrative control of the real property revenues of pious foundations, the employment of funds or properties assigned to charity by testamentary acts and the administration of funds for orphans. Each council would be composed of members elected by the community it represents; these councils would function under the rule of local authorities and the councils-general of the provinces (Article 111).

---

[133] Cf. Devereux, p. 71.

The election of provincial counsellors by the community they represented was in fact a suggestion expressed by the Armenian Patriarchate through its provincial report of oppressions in 1872, mentioned in detail in Chapter II. All four translations stipulate that all laws, regulations and customs in force at that time would continue to be applied if not modified by other laws and regulations (Article 118).

The general frame of the discussions within the Drafting Commission as well as within bureaucratic circles before and after the proclamation of the Constitution shows that the selection of models went beyond the French, Belgian and Prussian constitutions as argued in many previous studies which deal with Ottoman constitutional history.[134] In that respect, 1,000 books mentioned by Namık Kemal are symbolic and metaphorical, representing the fact that the Drafting Commission consulted a rich variety of constitutions. The narrowing of the draft text from a more liberal perspective to a more conservative framework shows that the very centre of the government was interested in European constitutional models not in order to offer a more democratic regime to Ottoman subjects, but so as to provide a European armature to the old tools of state authoritarianism and the legitimation of sultanic power. The centre considered the drafting process to be a set of political calculations measuring the concessions that any constitutional choice would impose on the exercise of sultanic sovereignty, administrative centralisation and the application of the shariʿa. The common text resulting from the Drafting Commission's work gives the impression that the horizon of the Commission was broader than that of the central government. For the Commission, the members of which ranged from moderates to radicals, the whole issue was to find a more global solution to old questions such as the inclusion of non-Muslims in state governance, the limitation of sultanic power by representative bodies and principles for facing the increasing intervention of Europe. Some members of the Drafting Commission were probably interested in constitution drafting in the real sense of the term and in the content of constitutional models as frameworks of freedom, mutual rights and duties between the state and the subjects.

---

[134] See for examples, Davison, *Reform, 1856-1876*, p. 388; Lewis, "Turkey", pp. 11-12.

CONCLUSION

This book shows the transcultural and transnational dimension of the genesis of the first Ottoman Constitution. The chapters show the evolution of a continuous set of negotiations: the negotiation of internal forces with external dynamics and the negotiation of domestic actors over constitutional concepts and state power, the negotiation of various cultural milieus on the idea of reform in the Ottoman Empire. The resonances with which European constitutional concepts and issues such as legitimacy, the restriction of political power, lawful government, liberty, equality, the rule of people and the treatment of minorities reached the Ottoman context and the ways in which these concepts were altered and acquired new meanings or equivalents during their adaptation to the imperial political culture shed light on the cultural aspects of the idea of justice and on the social construction of constitutional law.[1] In a more general sense, the investigation of Ottoman constitutional history goes beyond the study of a national narrative and constitutional history itself. It reconstructs at the same time the terms of power relations between the Great Powers and the Ottoman Empire and the cultural divides which differentiated their understanding of law and politics. It also unveils the teleological use of "legal standards" by the Powers.

The study of such a multi-layered negotiation helps us to question to a certain extent the dominant narrative of externalist conventional historiography, according to which the nineteenth-century Ottoman Empire underwent a linear process of westernisation between 1839 and 1876, the zenith of which was the promulgation of the Ottoman Constitution. It is true that we may talk about the domination of western diplomatic, political and ideological forces in the shaping of Ottoman reforms. It is also true that "1839 was made *for* Europe" and that "1856 was made *by* Europe",[2] but not *exactly as* Europe wanted. Although the book accepts European domination over Ottoman internal politics as a point of departure, it also unveils how the Ottoman Empire endeavoured to curb

---

[1] Fernanda Pirie and Judith Scheele, *Legalism: Community and Justice* (Oxford: Oxford University Press, 2014), pp. 1-24.

[2] I am quoting from Prof. Edhem Eldem's preliminary report on the dissertation.

this domination. If the archival materials demonstrate the agency of France, Britain and Austria in the shaping of the 1856 Reform Edict, they also bring into view the limits of their agency. The negotiations on the fourth point illustrate that there was a threshold beyond which the Powers encountered Ottoman resistance. What were the elements that defined this threshold? This is perhaps an important issue that this book is unable to entirely clarify. However, this threshold obliged the Powers to make some compromises. Contrary to common understandings of the paradigms of westernisation and decline, the Ottoman state responded to European political domination with resistance, rigidity or whatever it might be called. This resistance shows the existence of a strong state tradition and that the state was politically strong even in a period of decline. Moreover, the archival research demonstrates once again that the externalist conventional historiography loses its footing in 1876. If 1839 was made *for* Europe and 1856 was made *by* Europe, 1876 was made by the Ottomans and for the Ottomans against the will of Europe. Although the Ottoman Constitution incorporated certain administrative, institutional and financial principles already evoked in the proposed reforms emanating from European foreign offices and integrated institutions from the European constitutional experience, the Great Powers never realised such a constitutional end for the Ottoman Empire. Considered from these angles, westernisation is perhaps better defined as integration rather than homogenisation. In this integration process, non-western cultures endeavoured to keep some of their authenticity. This concept also allows us to go beyond the narrow framework of an "expansionist Europe unilaterally superimposing itself on a passive world" and to "find a representation of the world as the field of human contestation in which [...] societies and peoples are not thereby transformed into one, or even made more alike".[3]

The draft constitutions studied throughout the last chapter show, as the textual embodiment of internal controversies, that the process initiated a broader, richer and more liberal debate around the issue before resulting in an authoritarian text. Equally, the quality of these debates points to a certain political maturation that a limited circle of bureaucrats seems to have attained. If this liberalisation was generalised to the entire Ottoman bureaucracy, it would probably have been difficult for Abdülhamid II to curb their power. In that respect, the final text hides and overshadows the

---

[3] Michael Geyer and Charles Bright, "World History in a Global Age," *The American Historical Review* 100 (1995), pp. 1046, 1059.

richness of the preceding debates and textualises the expectations and monopolies of powerful segments of Ottoman society over the reform issue. The book remains mechanistic in the sense that it only studies bureaucratic behaviour around the constitutional reform. The chapters focus on administrative and diplomatic processes and their textual outcomes (rescripts, decrees, etc.) and bureaucratic effects, which reflect the relations of power within Ottoman society. The book neglects the epistemological process and the production of constitutional thought beyond the narrow context of administrative reforms. This epistemological process undoubtedly comprised richer dimensions: the intellectual trajectories and exchange of internal and external actors, their cultural and ideological parameters, the places of production and diffusion of constitutional knowledge (universities, newspapers, erudite journals, etc.) and the emergence of principles, concepts, theories and doctrines. The Ottoman constitutional process was also framed by an internal intellectual movement that the book only unveiled within the framework of two Young Ottomans, Kemal and Ziya Pashas, both members of the Drafting Commission. The leaders of this movement studied the philosophers of the eighteenth century; European public law and the revolutionary movements of 1789, 1830 and 1848; reinterpreted the principles of Islam in the light of their knowledge of European institutions; and found analogies between the first institutions of Islam and those of modern Europe. This intellectual movement intended to introduce European institutions into the Ottoman Empire by demonstrating that these institutions did not contradict the principles of the shari'a: they tried to convince the wider public that the dislocation of the Ottoman Empire resulted from the absolutism of the sultan.[4] Considered from this angle, the constitutional process is richer and more mature than what the final text of the Ottoman Constitution and the book itself reflect. If a new constitutional history were to be rewritten, it should focus not only on final products but also on a rich variety of earlier textual productions and debates in order to map the real elements of political maturation and democratisation instead of lingering on artificial reconstructions from 1808 to 1876.

The inclusion of community discourses and those of the Young Ottomans enables us to hear the resonances of the reform issue in various religious contexts. In that respect, one may notice the extent to which

---

[4] Y. A., *Midhad Pacha, La Constitution ottomane et l'Europe* (Paris: Imprimerie Topographique Jean Gainche, 1903), pp. 5-7.

Muslims and non-Muslims experienced common trajectories when questioning the content of legal reform, either within the communities or
wider Ottoman society. The main issue was perhaps how to find equilibrium between tradition, religion and modernity and how to fix the boundaries between administrative principles and religious dogma in communal
governance or the limits between politics, state administration and Islam
for social governance. The discursive interventions of various actors of
different religious affiliations show the extent to which religion affected
the social construction of constitutional law in the Ottoman context. The
use of primary sources in different languages (especially Ottoman Turkish, French and Armenian) helps us to capture how key constitutional
concepts varied from one linguistic context to the other and how terminological differences shape differently the construction and understanding of law in various linguistic landscapes. The variety of languages and
texts and the multiple political and legal meanings that may be extracted
from various versions enabled the state to project alternative visions of
politics, legitimacy and legal order and to speak to wider audiences.[5]
"The polyphony, dissonance, and divergence of these texts call into question the myth of a unitary and sacrosanct constitution, even at the moment
of founding".[6] Although this variety of legal documents was a strategic
move to integrate the various cultural domains of the empire, it could
have also been source of misunderstandings and conflicts between the
Ottoman state and the different audiences it targeted.

Communal translations (in my case the Armenian translations) give the
impression that major Ottoman communities, instead of using Ottoman
political terminology, created equivalents in their respective languages
through borrowings from French and thus demonstrated their "cultural
independence".[7] "One may interpret this as an attempt of the language
users to distance themselves from the languages of the rulers".[8] The second point is that French was the model and the source for this terminology. The different versions of legal texts reflect religious and ideological
divisions between the different Ottoman communities and call into question the extent to which Ottoman Turkish had a "unifying effect" in the
Ottoman Empire.[9] The most striking example of this ideological division

---

[5] Cf. Hussin, pp. 149, 152.
[6] Hussin, p. 152.
[7] Cf. Strauss, "A Constitution for a Multilingual Empire", p. 51.
[8] Strauss, "A Constitution for a Multilingual Empire", p. 51.
[9] Strauss, "A Constitution for a Multilingual Empire", p. 51.

was the omission of the words alluding to the secular such as "civil", "temporal", and "laymen" in Ottoman texts, although the Armenian and French texts used their equivalents. It is true that the words *nizam* and *nizami* were used to make a distinction between civil and religious realms, but their use was limited to the courts in the decree texts and were avoided as much as possible. Avi Rubin claims that the equivalent of the term "secular" was absent in Ottoman judicial jargon and that the "distinction between secular and religious legal spheres" was an invention of the post-Ottoman period.[10] However, dictionaries and some legal texts referred to the terms "dünyevi" (temporal) and "cismani" (material but also temporal) and reciprocated, if not exactly, a certain idea of secularity in the Ottoman legal vocabulary.[11] These terminological differentiations were probably a part of Ottoman state policy according to which non-Ottoman texts were instruments of image-making. The use of a secular vocabulary could offer a liberal and modern image of the Ottoman Empire to the West. The Ottoman text remained, however, the legal reference. Only the Ottoman version of regulations was recognised in Ottoman courts as it was considered more reliable.[12] However, the 1839 Imperial Rescript, the 1856 Reform Edict and the 1876 Ottoman Constitution had official translations into French. One may also raise the question whether these terminological differences sharpened the clashes between the state and the communities or the Ottomans and Europeans and their respective representation of each other. The Ottoman state conceived of the social, public and legal sphere within the framework of religiosity while the communities evolved towards secular perspectives.

A treatise entitled *Devlet-i Aliye'deki Islahat-ı Kanuniye* (Reform of Law in the Ottoman Empire), written by a Dutch author in Ottoman Turkish, also sheds light on the issue of terminological differences which engendered a divergence of spirit between the original text of the decrees

---

[10] Rubin, *Ottoman Nizamiye Courts*, p. 57.

[11] See for instance, A. Calpha, *Dictionnaire de Poche Français-Turc* (Paris: Garnier Frères, 1865), pp. 230, 403. The dictionary translates the terms "*laïque*" and "*temporel*" as "*dünyevi*". In a similar way, the Ottoman version of the Armenian National Constitution refers to "*Cismani Meclis*" (Temporal Council) when designating the Civil Council of the Armenian Patriarchate. See *Düstur*, birinci tertib, cüz-i sani (v. 2), (İstanbul: Matbaa-i Amire, 1289 [1872]), *Nizamat-i İdare-i Müteferrikat* ("Regulations of Different [*Millet*] Administrations"): *Ermeni Patrikliği Nizamatı* ("Regulation of the Armenian Patriarchate"), p. 946.

[12] BOA, YA. RES. 10/89, 28 Cemaziyelevvel 1298/28 April 1881.

and their translations into European languages.[13] In light of the author's comments, one may raise the question whether the Ottoman state intended to distance itself from European political culture by keeping the Islamic tone and terminology in the Ottoman texts of the reform decrees. For instance, the author argued that the 1839 Imperial Rescript did not institute equality of law (*müsavat-ı hukukiye*) between Muslims and non-Muslims as Europeans understood it: "Equality within the framework of the shari'a was staggered as equality among Christians, as equality among Jews and as equality among Muslims and these levels of equality were differentiated from one another. The shari'a did not recognise equality among Muslims and Christians or Muslims and Jews. But the European diplomats of the time could not interpret the Imperial Rescript in the light of these differences of meaning. Similarly, the penal law was translated into the French text of the Rescript as penal code. But the penal law to which the Ottoman text of the Rescript referred had an Islamic connotation, which was quite different from the set of attributes or associations implied by the French penal code". "In fact", he maintained "the most important inaccuracy was to reciprocate the Ottoman word Tanzimat, which alluded to good administration (*hüsn-i idare*), with its French equivalent of reform". The issue of religious freedom was also interpreted differently: "the Ottoman state allowed religious freedom as the freedom to practise the religion with which people were born while Europeans understood it as the easy conversion of people from one to the other".

Focusing on the historical aspect of the relations of non-Muslim communities with an Islamic state, the book also sheds light on current questions regarding minority issues, religious pluralism, secularisation and the separation of religion and state or the separation of state and politics in Turkey. It also opens new avenues for investigating the place of religion in legislative and legal processes in Islamic countries. The Arab Spring reopened these debates in countries such as Yemen, Egypt and Tunisia. We are in a century where we are experiencing the return of religion as a "post-modern phenomenon". The line between the public and the private is again blurred and societies face the challenge of finding an efficient

---

[13] BOA, YEE 10/58. The name of the author is not indicated but we understand from the third page of the document that he was Dutch. The author also underlines that he was acquainted with the shari'a. The document is undated but if we consider that the author talks about reforms that succeeded the 1876 Ottoman Constitution and the Young Turks, the treatise was probably drafted in the 1900s or just before.

way to redefine state neutrality against the re-politicisation of religion.[14] Some of the constitutionalist discourses in my study pushed back religion to the private sphere and contributed to the privatisation of religion in the Ottoman context. The book thus offers an empirical laboratory in which various issues regarding the place religion occupies in social life are investigated with its historical dimensions.

The idea of reform in community governance dominated the public agenda of non-Muslims and accelerated exchanges with their co-religionists in Europe. These exchanges brought emancipation to community structures, as Ottoman non-Muslims were inspired by the democratic rights their co-religionists enjoyed in Europe. For the sake of focus, the book mainly reflected on the debates of Armenian and Jewish leaders in order to investigate how they conceptualised a new community structure in the light of emancipation ideas they imported from the confessional/ organisational patterns of western contexts and how these communal debates contributed to the constitutional thought of Ottoman society. After all, the treatment of minorities was one of the most important constitutional issues, and non-Muslims brought important insights into the question by fostering a new community identity in the nineteenth-century Ottoman Empire.

The agency of traders was undoubtedly considerable in this exchange, since they were non-state actors operating across borders not only in terms of the exchange of products but also of ideas. Trading agents created transnational spaces that "may range from highly formalised structures and processes at one end of the scale to relatively informal ones at the other end".[15] The 1838 Anglo-Ottoman Commercial Treaty and the 1839 Imperial Rescript that followed were also the result of encounters between foreign industrialists and Ottoman traders that pushed their state for the codification of new commercial "formalised structures". It was not a coincidence that new commercial codes followed this process. The Imperial Rescript received support among Ottoman traders residing in England. The Rescript also produced a great sensation in Alexandria. The governor of Egypt, Mehmed Ali Pasha, promulgated

---

[14] Karl-Heinz Ladeur, "The Myth of the Neutral State and the Individualisation of Religion: the Relationship between State and Religion in the Face of Fundamentalism," in Susanna Mancini & Michel Rosenfeld, *Constitutional Secularism in an Age of Religious Revival* (Oxford: Oxford University Press, 2014), pp. 35-37.

[15] Faist, p. 1.

freedom on exports in order to gain popularity.[16] Among non-state agents, traders were probably the most powerful in engendering chain reactions between distant localities and in homogenising these localities ideologically and legally thanks to the control they exerted over different territories through the circulation of their goods as symbolic bearers of new ideas. Traders operating through trans-imperial networks also had a better experience of encountering and dealing with diversity. The movements of capital and commodities overlapped with the trajectories of rules and business know-how. In the case of non-Muslim traders and agency, their commercial paths, operating on a large scale from Ottoman Turkey to Western Europe and South Asia, crossed with their diasporic ties. On the one hand, the democratisation of the Ottoman Empire would serve their commercial interests. On the other, the emancipation of the Ottoman social fabric would offer better political and civil rights to Ottoman non-Muslims, who were connected to their European counterparts in terms of familial bonds and co-religionist ties. This interaction between trans-imperial communal networks also worked in the reverse direction. Western religious minorities, or diasporas in some cases, were preoccupied with the fate of their co-religionists in the Ottoman Empire, perceived their emancipation as a "*mission civilisatrice*" and internalised the civilisational discourse of their empires. All this overlaps with the policies of the Central Jewish Consistory of France and of the *Alliance israélite universelle*, those of the Anglo-Jewish Association and the actions lauched by the Camondos and British Armenians. Relations between states and these trans-imperial non-state actors were asymmetrical in terms of power and authority. Even states differed from each other in terms of economic and political influence. In that respect, the efficiency of these actors was limited to a certain extent. Nevertheless, they gave a voice to their co-religionists that would otherwise never have been considered and attracted the attention of international society to their living conditions.

In addition to trade, the second tool of encounter is diplomacy in its narrow and wider sense. The consideration of diplomatic history from the standpoint of human encounters by including network analysis paves the way to the broadening of diplomatic history beyond the simple sum of encounters between states and international relations. Thus, the new diplomatic history becomes a novel tool for understanding international

---

[16] BOA, HR. SYS. 1869 A-2.

society as something other than a composite of different states: it is instead conceived of as an entity of individuals caught between personal aspirations, perceptions, calculations and initiatives on the one hand, and state constraints, policies and interests, on the other. The book shows that while ambassadors and consuls possessed a certain margin of initiative, real political power was monopolised by the actors of central governments both in the Ottoman Empire and Europe. Despite all efforts of the Ottoman ambassadorial ring to publicise the Ottoman Constitution abroad, the sultan and Lord Salisbury, the British delegate at the Conference of Constantinople, seemed to negotiate the proposals of the Conference rather than the application of the Constitution. Ambassadors and consuls were data collectors, and policymakers to a certain extent, but they had limited access to the final decision process. However, the consideration of ideological clashes, tensions, agreements and disagreements between individual agents and their respective governments gives a more tangible and human character to diplomatic history. In that respect, diplomatic history no longer focuses only on the relations between states, but examines diplomats in terms of both their individual traits and their place in collective state identity.

If the book cannot entirely respond to the issue, it at least raises the question of what constitutes individual weight in this collective identity. As opposed to Henry Elliot, Redcliffe, for instance, created a more successful individual profile as a British ambassador to the Porte. He struggled against any foreign rival influence over the Ottoman Empire. Although Russia and France sometimes provoked his envy and indignation, Redcliffe exerted a quasi-despotic influence on the Ottoman Empire without sharing his power. Redcliffe even threatened the position of some Ottoman ministers if they sympathised more with his French counterparts.[17]

This diversity of interests existed not only among each of the Great Powers and the Ottoman Empire but also among the various segments of the same state. Ideological differences between Whigs and Tories engendered, for instance, ambassadorial change at the Foreign Office.[18] The dismissal of Sir Henry Elliot should be interpreted as the outcome of this

---

[17] MAEF, Mémoires et Documents, Turquie, vol. 114, Documents divers, 1855-1856. Résumé de la Correspondance politique de l'ambassade de l'Empereur à Constantinople, août 1855-décembre 1856.

[18] Jones, p. 216.

ideological fragmentation of the British state in 1876. "The failure of the Conference and the subsequent war brought about the defeat of the Reforming party in Turkey; it was crushed, and its heads placed at the mercy of the Sultan Abdul Hamid. Sir Henry deplored this to the end of his life, and it was especially bitter to him as having resulted from the action of the Liberal party in England, who might have been expected to support any movement for Reform".[19]

Not only states but also foreign individuals or non-political institutions emerge from the archival sources as the authors of memorials, memorandums or treatises suggesting a different line of Ottoman reforms. Case studies also show that the border between individual or institutional involvement and state backing was blurred. In a different manner, one has difficulties in classifying the initiative of Benoît Musolino, a colonel and deputy of the Italian Parliament who submitted a memorandum of administrative, financial and military reforms to the Sublime Porte in late 1875 through the intermediary of Karateodori Effendi. Musolino was depicted in the Ottoman documents as somebody who criticised the Great Powers' politics vis-à-vis the Sublime Porte and as a friend of the Ottoman Empire. The Grand Vizier Midhad Pasha found his memorandum interesting and had it sent to the Council of State for examination.[20] The Ottoman Empire received word of the negative impressions of the Italian Foreign Minister Melegari and the Italian press regarding the Ottoman Constitution, with Melegari stating that the constitutional reform would be a dead letter and would not offer sufficient guarantees to the Christian populations, who would remain in the minority in the Ottoman Parliament.[21] However, Musolino talked about giving support to the Ottoman government for the compilation of laws and regulations that would complete the Ottoman Constitution and thus differentiated himself from the official policy of his government. One may encounter similar case studies justifying the extent to which the involvement of individual agents and networks went beyond the control of their respective government in the matter of Ottoman reforms, and the extent to which the adjectives of nationality, such as Italian, British, French, etc., had a variety of connotations that ranged from the national

[19] Elliot, p. ix.

[20] BOA, HR. SYS 1863-3. From Benoît Musolino to Midhad Pasha, January 10, 1877. From Esad Bey, Ottoman ambassador to Rome, to Midhad Pasha, January 12, 1877. From the Grand Vizier [Midhad Pasha] to Esad Bey, February 15, 1876.

[21] BOA, HR. SYS 1864-1, Esad Bey to Safved Pasha, 12 January 1877.

to the individual, and that these contradicted one another under the umbrella of the same nationality.

Reform, emancipation and similar concepts, promoted as part of a humanitarian stance with respect to the governance of populations in the Ottoman Empire, amounted largely to a conformist rhetoric, a form of political correctness already devoid of any hope of application or viability. The question of reforms was more the object of diplomatic negotiation, concessions and calculations rather than a policy geared towards social, political and economic improvements in the Ottoman Empire. The opposition of Russia was also a major reason for the mobilisation of the bureaucratic circle of the palace known for its Russian tendencies. If we are to believe A. Tevfik Bey, the Ottoman ambassador to St Petersburg, the Russian government even prevented the press and the intelligentsia from adopting a favourable stance with respect to the proclamation of the Ottoman Constitution. Tevfik Bey drew attention to the Russian fear that the promulgation of the Ottoman Constitution would encourage opponent groups to rebel against autocracy in Russia.[22] Halil Şerif Pasha (1872-73), a former foreign minister, himself confessed that the defeat of France was the principal cause of internal troubles in the Ottoman Empire. It was with the support of the French embassy, he said, that Reşid, Fuad and Ali Pashas found the necessary force to resist the caprices of the palace and maintain the policy of reform. In the 1870s, Europe could not make its voice heard in the palace. The French embassy, he continued, preferred to avoid the risk of taking steps with the other Great Powers against Russia as in 1856.[23]

We may read Halil Şerif Pasha's statements as the consolidation of Russian ascendancy. Although its empirical research focuses on French and British ascendancy in the Porte, this book fails to illustrate in detail the Russian impact except in some cases, as reported from other archives. The same concern applies to the study of other Great Powers, such as Austria and Germany, and even beyond. For instance, although the 1855 Ottoman commercial law, together with its subsequent revisions in the 1860s and the annexation of the law of maritime commerce in 1864, was said to be mainly inspired by French legislation, it also contained many elements from Prussian, Dutch, Portuguese, Spanish, Sardinian and

---

[22] BOA, HR. SYS 1864-1, A. Tefvik Bey to Safved Pasha, 15 January 1877.

[23] Cf. MAEF, Papier Adolphe Thiers, PA-AP 170, vol. 5, Copies of Correspondence, May 11, 1871-May 13, 1873. Here November 27, 1872.

Sicilian legislation. The Ottomans borrowed various legal principles from different countries,[24] and this was not limited to the traditions of the Great Powers of Europe. As the comparative table of Appendix VII shows, Namık Kemal refers to the Greek Parliament in terms of the small number of its deputies, which shows that the Greek example did not escape Ottoman attention. While the Tunisian Constitution of 1861 was suspended three years later, Egypt, Serbia and Rumania still had their national assemblies: one may wonder about the extent to which these precedents affected Ottoman political thought. In 1867, both Mustafa Fazıl and Namık Kemal referred to these parliamentary examples for the Ottoman Parliament.[25] This book cannot depict the unlimited plurality of this borrowing process.

Having followed the complex trajectories of the constitutional process, the reader likely faces frustration when they come to ask whether there was a decisive moment that ended these continuous stages of negotiations. It was full of multiple contradictions and dynamics, none of which can be privileged over the others as a pattern of efficient agency for finally framing our discussion on the Ottoman reform. There are, however, some issues that this endless chain of negotiations with external dynamics clarifies despite all the ambiguities it creates for the reader.

Although it is erroneous to argue that the constitutional experience of the Ottoman Empire was merely the result of nineteenth-century westernisation, at the same time it would be difficult to deny the influence of external factors. Even if we exclude the importance of European impact on the constitutional process in order not to overshadow the internal impetus, the Ottoman reform experience cannot be understood merely in terms of local/national history.

Hüseyin Yılmaz argues that the nineteenth-century Ottoman constitutional movement was the result of previously existing local traditions, that military, financial and religious institutions which progressively developed in order to challenge sultanic power provided traditional grounds for the legitimisation of a parliamentary system in the Ottoman Empire and that these "autonomous structures" presented some similarities with the constitutional developments of Western Europe.[26] In a similar manner,

---

[24] Cf. BOA, YEE 10/58, pp. 64-65.

[25] Moustafa-Fazil Pacha, *Lettre adressée*, p. 17; Kuntay, v. 1, p. 212, n. 25; *Hürriyet*, September 29, 1868. Cited in Davison, *Reform, 1856-1876*, pp. 365-366.

[26] Yılmaz, pp. 1-30.

Baki Tezcan draws attention to the importance of internal dynamics in the creation of the Second Ottoman Empire, characterised by the development of an early modern polity comparable to its European counterparts. However, he also underlines that this polity was empowered by the monetisation of the Ottoman economy, which did not happen independently of the spreading of a wide network of markets over Asia, Europe and Africa.[27] He also gives the example of "England [which] had inherited a medieval institution called parliament, whereas the Ottomans had a military corporation, the Janissary corps, which transformed itself into a political organisation"[28] when comparing the transformation of internal dynamics between Europe and the Ottoman Empire in order to create an early modern polity for challenging royal power. The military rebellions of the late sixteenth and early seventeenth centuries had an economic rationale, such as the debasement of the currency, the distribution of tax farms and the consolidation of the power of the palace's officers, who assigned tax farms to their clients.[29] This leads us to the idea that the empowerment of certain social groups resulted in the limitation of sultanic authority for the interests of those groups rather than in a constitutionalist argument covering the interests of a wider public.

Returning to the constitutional process, even if we could talk about the maturation of Ottoman political thought before 1876, the reformist bureaucratic segment of Ottoman society needed European support in order to realise a Constitutional Revolution in the Ottoman Empire. The Ottoman Foreign Ministry shared the content of the Ottoman Constitution with European foreign offices in order to verify whether or not the provisions were appreciated by the Great Powers and if the reformists could count on European support. Two sultans were dethroned for not promulgating the Ottoman Constitution, but the Grand Councils that gathered to discuss the issue still did not result in a drafting process. It was only after the announcement of a Drafting Commission by Safved Pasha to the representatives of the Great Powers that an irreversible process began. Odyan Effendi was sent to Europe to publicise the Ottoman Constitution and to call for external support. The "autonomous structures" which were said to provide the traditional grounds of parliamentary rule, namely the Grand Vizier Mehmed Rüşdü Paşa and the Minister

---

[27] Tezcan, pp. 13, 17.
[28] Tezcan, p. 242.
[29] Tezcan, p. 190.

of War Hüseyin Avni Pasha, were nearly present in 1876 but, along with the reformist bureaucracy, they contributed to the dethronement of Sultan Abdülaziz I not for a constitutionalist cause but rather for personal aspirations and the consolidation of their power. Only the Sheikh ül-Islam Hayrullah Effendi seemed to be partial to aligning with the constitutionalists after being convinced by Midhad.

The Ottoman Constitution, announced pompously by cannon fire, had a short life of about a year, like that of former Tanzimat decrees, which became dead letters in the long run. One might ask, inevitably, what the Constitution finally meant. Was it a new diplomatic game to gain time in the face of external pressure? Was it a real political process or just a pretentious way of hiding a new state strategy? Was it the culminating point of the Tanzimat period? Might we finally talk about a generalised process of political maturation and democratisation from 1808 to 1876?

As Yaycıoğlu emphasises, the Deed of Agreement established a clear distinction between the state and the sultan. Although the supervision of the agreement would be provided by the sultan, the state was not an instrument in the hands of the former but rather an objective mechanism in which the sultan was an essential element. In other terms, the state and the sultanate were defined as the common umbrella of both the central and provincial elites. The concepts "contractor" (*müteahhit*) and "guarantor" (*zamin*), together with "guarantee" (*kefalet*), defined the main framework of relations between the signatories of the agreement establishing a set of rules to limit the sphere of action of one another.[30] When coming across the final text of the Ottoman Constitution, we notice that the distinction between the state, the sultanate and the sultan disappear and the sultan identifies himself with the state apparatus. In that respect, it would be difficult to find a linear continuity from 1808 to 1876. However, we may also note that the main contractors of the agreement, the grand vizier, the ulema, the military, the sheikh ül-Islam and local notables, were the main actors in the Tanzimat developments. Although the 1839 Imperial Rescript and the 1856 Reform Edict promised to curb the power of local notables, this promise remained a dead letter: the electoral system of the 1876 Ottoman Constitution privileged the position of local elites in the Parliament.

It is clear from the debates that Ottoman draftsmen did not refer to the Deed of Agreement as their point of departure, using instead both the

---

[30] Yaycıoğlu, pp. 701-705.

Tanzimat and Reform decrees as their references. The discussion on the preamble that the Council of Ministers intended to incorporate into the Ottoman Constitution responds more clearly to the question of whether Ottomans themselves saw linear progress and maturation from the Tanzimat Decree to the 1876 Constitution. Namık Kemal's reaction to the incorporation of the preamble referring to the decree of accession of Abdülhamid II and to his good intentions is a clear indication that some draftsmen intended to break with former Tanzimat decrees, which did not fit the spirit of a constitution since they were charters granted by the sultan; however, other draftsmen saw the continuity of a legacy from 1839 to 1876. Namık Kemal reacted to the mention of the 1839 Imperial Rescript and its guarantees among the articles of the draft constitution elaborated by the Council of Ministers on the grounds that the mention of other decrees was omitted. His reaction to such an omission indicates that draftsmen found complementarity in the succession of decrees promulgated throughout the Tanzimat period. Namık Kemal's approach to the preamble of the draft constitution illustrates how some of his contemporaries refused to see a linear continuity between the Tanzimat period and the 1876 process without entirely denying the whole legacy of decrees. We may rather find continuity in the fact that legal reforms were often mediated and negotiated among bureaucratic, religious, and military elites. As an Ottoman specificity, the bureaucratic elites also included the intellectual layers of society. In moments when the liberal elites, either bureaucratic or intellectual, were weakened by existing power relations, they knew how to use foreign pressure as an asset in order to impose their reform policy on the state and democratise the fabric of political governance. Midhad's defeat and the suspension of the Ottoman Constitution were indicators that this liberal wing was weak when it came to mediating democratisation with conservative forces in the country and needed foreign support to curb their power. This partially explains the fraternisation of domestic bureaucrats with foreign diplomats and, in more concrete terms, the friendly relations between Midhad and Henry Elliot.

Linear maturation does not seem to have existed in the minds of Tanzimat intellectual-bureaucrats, who were expected to represent the highest level of democratisation. The comparative table of Appendix VII reflects the ups and downs of Namık Kemal himself. While reproaching the shortening of articles regarding ministerial responsibility in the draft constitution, Namık Kemal reacted at the same time to the fact that the

Council of Ministers was headed by the grand vizier, noting that the latter was recognised as an authority other than the sultan and not all the deliberations of the Council met with the approval of the sultan. Despite an approach which almost favoured the sultan, he defended better representation in the Ottoman Parliament, arguing that the latter was the greatest school of political science; he thus opposed narrowing the sphere of influence of the Chamber of Deputies in the process of law-making. This shows the extent to which the issue of reforms was something ambiguous in the minds of the draftsmen; one might question how such a process, full of contradictions and ambiguities even at the personal level, could be incorporated into a linear/macro development.

It would be an oversimplification to reduce the Ottoman constitutional process to mere tactics. In more general terms, the process from 1839 to 1876 was full of ups and downs; the search for a linear maturation and a grand narrative of gradual democratisation is an artificial reconstruction of the period. After the promulgation of the Gülhane Rescript, Reşid Pasha tried to change the general principles of the Rescript into a "program of action" through a series of laws and regulations for the reorganisation of the different branches of the Ottoman government.[31] The new legal and administrative reorganisation provided the ruling class with new experiences.[32] The reform movement was successful within certain spheres: legislation, elite formation, expansion of government, inter-communal relations, etc.[33] The acts of 1839, 1856 and 1876 engendered a wave of legislation, namely new penal and commercial codes, land laws and a new network of *nizami* (regular) courts.[34] Although the new codes might be considered a step towards secularisation, the tension between the shari'a and secular legislation continued in later periods. "In 1876, Abdülhamid's decree of promulgation still echoed the Gülhane decree's reference to 'laws conformable to the shari'a' by affirming the constitution's conformity to the provisions of the *şeriat* (*ahkam-ı şer-i şerif*)".[35] Although the Tanzimat was a period of socio-economic change, the government's revenues proved insufficient for meeting the costs of the reform policies.[36]

---

[31] Devereux, p. 22.
[32] Cf. Devereux, p. 30.
[33] Cf. Findley, "The Tanzimat", p. 17.
[34] Findley, "The Tanzimat", p. 20.
[35] Kili and Gözübüyük, *Türk Anayasa*, pp. 29-30. Cited in Findley, "The Tanzimat", p. 21.
[36] Findley, "The Tanzimat", p. 33.

The reconciliation of equality with individual, communal and imperial levels was a difficult task.[37] "Yet the struggle to reconcile the rights of the individual, the community and the totality has proven central to the development of modern polities around the world. The Tanzimat reformers faced their version of this problem at a time when identity and difference were becoming politicised in new ways".[38] A comprehensive concept of Ottomanism offered the guidelines for this reconciliation.[39] The main target of Ottoman constitutionalism was to refute the grounds of European pressures for "pro-Christian reform". "A constitutional regime, it was argued, would turn all Ottoman subjects into equal citizens, thereby ending all community-specific privileges within the empire and removing the logical basis for European criticism".[40] The Ottoman Constitution is an interesting example for tracing how the state passed from the particularistic definition of communal interests to the determination of the public good for Ottoman society at the intersection of communality, diverse religions, Ottomanism and the recognition of Islam as a state religion.

On the other hand, the ideological struggles that centred on the constitutional process and the gradual narrowing of the initial liberal project until it became the final text of the Ottoman Constitution being considered, one cannot deny that the Ottoman Constitution of 1876, like the rest of other Tanzimat charters, had a strategic dimension for the state. As Chapter I shows, Britain and France clearly stated that they would not back the Ottoman Empire before the Russian threat if the Reform Decree was not proclaimed. In its turn, the Ottoman state also knew how to take advantage of this diplomatic manoeuvre. At a moment when Europe was preoccupied with the fate of religious minorities, the Reform Decree, which was almost a sub-document of an international commitment like the Paris Treaty, appeared to be a tactic of Ottoman centralisation: the Ottoman state took the initiative, through the Reform Decree, to institutionalise the blurred administrative structures of non-Muslims, which engendered European intervention, regularise the rather spontaneous arrangements between community agents and the state and incorporate their legal components into Ottoman legislation. The decree was a pragmatic device of stabilisation at a moment when waves of proto-nationalism were trying to define the

---

[37] Findley, "The Tanzimat", p. 28.
[38] Findley, "The Tanzimat", p. 28.
[39] Cf. Findley, "The Tanzimat", p. 28.
[40] Hanioğlu, p. 114.

borders of communal identities. Ali Pasha, one of the key figures of this process, wrote in his testament that the whole struggle was about the definition of Ottoman frontiers, the rights of the people and the establishment of these rights in order to avoid contestation from Europe. Each concession made was to avoid bigger sacrifices in the face of European requirements. He himself added that the limits of these concessions were defined by the interests of the state, the rights of the sovereign and the preservation of his absolute power, which, because of its sacred character, could not accept any compromise. He also confessed that the bureaucrats had difficulties in finding a compromise between the consolidation of sultanic power and the measures necessitated by the circumstances. He did not hide that they sometimes paid a cost for these compromises and that their success was endangered by the immediate circles around the throne.[41]

> *Her zamandan ziyade şimdi devletimize lazım olan şey haddim olmayarak vükelanın ittifakıdır Maazallah beyninize tefrika düşer ise yeniden vükelayı kim intihab ü nasb edecekdir Yine haddim olmayarak arz ederim ki bu mesele dahi pek ağırdır Bazı rivayete nazaran beyninizde ittifak-ı tamme yokmuş Bazı zevat-ı celadet-simata söz anlatılmalı Hele takliden bir konstitüsyon yapılmadığına şu zamanda teşekkür olunur Avrupa'da cümlenin efkârı dahi bu merkezdedir Bize konstitüsyon değil enstitüsyon lazımdır Bunları teh'iye eylemeli Şimdiki halde muharebeleri muvaffakkiyetle bitirelim cümlesi olur Fakat hemen şimdi olamaz Bora ve fırtınada harab evin çatısını tamire kalkışmağa benzer.*

Dare I say that what our state needs most at this moment is unity among ministers? God forbid if dissension were to enter among you, who would be able to choose and appoint ministers again? Again, dare I say that this matter too is of much gravity? According to some rumours, there is not a perfect consensus among you. Some great men should be made to understand this. Most of all, one should be thankful at this point that no constitution is established in imitation [of Europe]. Everyone is of the same opinion in Europe, too. It is not a constitution, but rather institutions that we need. These should be prepared. At present, let us end the conflict with success, the rest will follow. But it cannot be done right now. It would be like repairing the ruined roof of a house during a tempest and strong wind.[42]

---

[41] Ali Pasha, *Testament politique*, pp. 5-8.
[42] BOA, Y.EE. 44/13. Edhem Pasha to Safved Pasha, Berlin, 23 August, 1876. I thank Prof. Edhem Eldem very much for communicating this document to me as well as for providing the transcription into Turkish, the English translation and his comments on the issue.

This correspondence between Edhem and Safved Pashas is important in the sense that both would become Ottoman delegates to the Conference of Constantinople and defend the Constitution against the proposals of the Great Powers of Europe in December 1876. Interestingly enough, the unity of the Council of Ministers as a pragmatic settlement and the defence of a status quo mattered much more than the Constitution itself for Edhem Pasha. His statements also show that the conservatism of bureaucrats arguing that the country was not ready enough for a constitutional turn had not changed much since Reşid Pasha, who advanced the same argument. Moreover, Edhem Pasha's confession that the country needed institutions more than a constitution sounds like he possessed a certain awareness that a change of regime would not bring much to the existing institutions if substantial reforms were not accomplished.

A striking point of the constitutional process was the rise of Ottoman Muslim or non-Muslim physicians as bureaucrats. For instance, Fuad Pasha, the most important figure of the Tanzimat period, and Serviçen Effendi and Nahabed Rusinyan, who reformed the legal structure of the Armenian community, first studied medicine before becoming involved in Ottoman politics. The main reason for this was probably the fact that "[t]he School of Medicine became not only a secular scientific institution, but also the most effective channel through which liberal and national ideas fomented and disseminated".[43] When Mahmud II modernised the traditional medical institutions and founded a State Medical School, *Tıbhane-i Amire*, in 1827, some European physicians were also appointed as teachers. Some of the graduates were also sent to Europe for further studies.[44] We might assume, then, that the Ottoman Medical School became an institution in which European political concepts circulated and its students became politicised. It was also one of the first institutions where students of various creeds could socialise. The last chapter also points to the bureaucratisation of the Ottoman military ranks. The military class was always strong and heavily involved in politics in the Ottoman Empire before the constitutional process. However, the novelty lies perhaps in the fact that the military segment expressed its opinion and brought its contribution to the process not by using rebellions but by taking their seats in the Drafting Commission.

---

[43] Berkes, p. 194.
[44] Berkes, pp. 112-113.

Moreover, Süleyman Pasha, then director of military schools, occupied his place among the bureaucrats, whose advice was sought by the sultan just before the promulgation of the Ottoman Constitution. Again, nothing is surprising in this evolution. The military institutions were the ones where reforms were undertaken first. This allowed for the circulation of modern ideas and the politicisation of the Ottoman military class.

The individual contributions of various members of the Drafting Commission to the making of the Ottoman Constitution are the most important missing pieces of the constitutional puzzle. Few individual contributions, like those of Midhad, Said and Safved Pashas, and Namık Kemal, emerge from draft constitutions. My emphasis on individuals is not to say that some are more important than others; rather, I suggest that the mapping of personal ways of thinking can better highlight the large spectrum of convergences and divergences between draftsmen, the hostilities of modernists, moderates and conservatives, and allow an empirical study of modernism, moderation and conservatism from the way in which they are expressed by their proponents. Given the lack of appropriate documentation, we often study these ideological currents without penetrating the psychology of individuals who adhered to them. Furthermore, Musurus, like Odyan Effendi, also promoted the interests of his community when defending the Ottoman constitutional project before British diplomats. The Ottoman Constitution fit the expectations of Ottoman Greeks and Armenians more than the grant of special privileges to the Slavic populations of European Turkey. The promotion of the Ottoman Constitution and the opposition of the empire to the proposals of the Conference of Constantinople made by Christian subjects would have been more efficient and credible in the eyes of European diplomacy. Thus the Ottoman Foreign Ministry could mobilise the support of two important community blocs, the Armenians and Greeks, as an alternative to granting special privileges to Slavic populations, through the diplomatic posts it offered to their co-religionists.

It would also be very interesting to document how non-Muslim draftsmen cooperated with their Muslim counterparts within the Drafting Commission. If relevant documents existed in the archives, this could have allowed us to trace how Ottoman diversity took shape at personal levels through the fusion of the ideas of people belonging to different cultural, religious and legal traditions. The lack of such documents prevents us from going beyond the abstract dimension of concepts and from embodying them through human encounters. Moreover, if the importance of the different units, especially of the Translation Office, is emphasised in the making of the Ottoman constitutional movement, the role of the Council of State is underestimated in Ottoman historiography. It was reported that the Council housed 21 non-Muslim people, Catholic and Gregorian Armenians, Greeks, Jews and Bulgarians in 1868.[45] While the study of the Council's interference was beyond the scope of this book, it would be interesting to note how different ethnic identities inter-acted in the technical dimension of the Ottoman Constitution.

---

[45] *Mémorial diplomatique*, 14 May 1868. Cited in BOA, HR.SYS. 1869 D-6.

APPENDICES

NEGOTIATIONS ON THE FOURTH POINT AND THE FINAL TEXT OF THE 1856 REFORM EDICT

Collective Text

1) Des mesures efficaces seront prises pour que les garanties promises à tous les sujets de Sa Majesté le Sultan par le hatti-schérif de Gulhané et les lois ~~de~~ du Tanzimat, sans distinction de classe ni de culte, reçoivent leur plein et entier effet. Ces principes seront rappelés et consacrés de nouveau par un ~~a~~Acte solennel, émané du Souverain.

2) La Sublime Porte ~~ne fera aucune difficulté de proclamer~~ proclame la reconnaissance et le maintien de tous les privilèges spirituels accordés *ab antiquo*, et à des dates postérieures, à toutes les communautés non-Musulmanes établies dans l'Empire, sous l'égide de Sa Majesté le Sultan.

3) Chaque communauté non-Musulmane sera tenue, dans un délai fixé, et avec le concours d'une Commission formée *ad hoc* dans son sein, de procéder, avec la haute approbation de sa Majesté le Sultan, dont un délégué assistera aux délibérations, à l'examen de ses immunités et privilèges ~~actuelles~~ actuels, et ~~d'y introduire~~ d'y discuter et soumettre à la Sublime Porte les réformes exigés[1] par le progrès des lumières et du temps. Les pouvoirs concédés aux Patriarches et aux Evêques des rits Chrétiens par le Sultan Mahomet II et ses successeurs, seront mis en harmonie avec la position nouvelle

Reform Edict

Les garanties promises de notre part à tous les sujets de mon Empire par le Hatti-i-Humaïoun de Gulhané et en conformité de Tanzimat, sans distinction de classes ni de culte, pour la sécurité de leurs personnes et de leurs biens et pour la conservation de leur honneur, sont aujourd'hui confirmées et consolidées; et pour qu'elles reçoivent leur plein et entier effet, des mesures efficaces seront prises.

Tous les privilèges et immunités spirituels accordés *ab antiquo* de la part de mes ancêtres, et à des dates postérieures, à toutes les communautés chrétiennes ou d'autres rites non-Musulmans établies dans mon Empire, sous mon égide protectrice, seront confirmés et maintenus.

Chaque communauté Chrétienne ou d'autre rite non-Musulman, sera tenue, dans un délai fixé et avec le concours d'une Commission formée *ad hoc* dans son sein, de procéder, avec ma haute approbation et sous la surveillance de ma Sublime Porte, à l'examen de ses immunités et privilèges actuels, et d'y discuter et soumettre à ma Sublime Porte les réformes exigées par les progrès des lumières et du temps. Les pouvoirs concédés aux Patriarches et aux Evêques des rites Chrétiens par le Sultan Mahomet II et ses successeurs, seront mis en harmonie avec la position nouvelle que mes

---

[1] This should be "exigées".

que les intentions généreuses de sa Majesté le Sultan assurent à ces communautés. Le principe de la nomination à vie des Patriarches, après la révision des règlements d'élection aujourd'hui en vigueur, sera exactement appliqué. conformément à la teneur de leurs firmans d'investiture.
Les Patriarches, les Métropolitains, Archévêques et Evêques seront assermentés à leur entrée en fonctions d'après une formule concertée en commun entre la Sublime Porte et les chefs spirituels des différentes communautés.

Les redevances ecclésiastiques, de quelque forme et nature qu'elles soient, seront supprimées, et remplacées par la fixation des revenus des Patriarches et Chefs des communautés, et par la location[2] l'allocation de traitements et de salaires équitablement proportionnés à l'importance, au rang et à la dignité des prêtres divers membres du clergé.
Il ne sera porté aucune atteinte aux propriétés mobilières et immobilières des divers clergés Chrétiens. Toutefois l'administration temporelle des communautés non-Musulmanes sera placée sous la sauvegarde d'une assemblée, choisie dans le sein de chacune des dites communautés parmi les membres du clergé et des laïques.

4) Dans les villes, bourgades, et villages, où la population appartiendra en totalité au même culte, il ne sera apporté aucune entrave à la réparation, d'après leur plan primitif, des édifices destinés au culte, aux écoles, aux hôpitaux, et aux cimetières. Les plans de ces divers édifices, en cas d'érection nouvelle approuvés par les Patriarches ou Cchefs de communautés, seront simplement soumis à la Sublime Porte, qui devra les approuver ou faire ses observations dans un délai déterminé.

intentions généreuses et bienveillantes assurent à ces communautés. Le principe de nomination à vie des Patriarches, après la révision des règlements d'élection aujourd'hui en vigueur, sera exactement appliqué, conformément à la teneur de leurs firmans d'investiture.

Les Patriarches, les Métropolitains, Archévêques, Evêques, et Rabbins seront assermentés à leur entrée en fonctions, d'après une formule concertée en commun entre ma Sublime Porte et les chefs spirituels des diverses communautés.

Les redevances ecclésiastiques, de quelque forme et nature qu'elles soient, seront supprimées et remplacées par la fixation des revenus des Patriarches et chefs des communautés et par l'allocation de traitements et de salaires équitablement proportionnés à l'importance du rang et à la dignité des divers membres du clergé.
Il ne sera porté aucune atteinte aux propriétés mobilières et immobilières des divers clergés Chrétiens; toutefois, l'administration temporelle des communautés Chrétiennes ou d'autres rites non-Musulmans, sera placée sous la sauvegarde d'une aAssemblée, choisie dans le sein de chacune des dites communautés, parmi les membres du clergé et et les laïcs.

Dans les villes, bourgades, et villages où la population appartiendra en totalité au même culte, il ne sera apporté aucune entrave à la réparation, d'après leur plan primitif, des édifices destinés au culte, aux écoles, aux hôpitaux, et aux cimetières. Les plans de ces divers édifices, en cas d'érection nouvelle, approuvés par les Patriarches ou Chefs de communautés, devront être soumis à ma Sublime Porte, qui les approuvera par mon ordre impérial, ou fera ses observations dans un délai déterminé.

[2] This is probably "l'allocation".

Chaque culte, dans les localités où ne se trouveront point d'autres confessions religieuses, ne sera soumis, dans ses manifestations extérieures, à aucune espèce de restriction. Dans les villes, bourgades, et villages où les cultes sont mélangés, chaque communauté, habitant un quartier distinct, pourra également, en se conformant aux prescriptions ci-dessus indiquées,[3] réparer et consolider ses églises, ses hôpitaux, ses écoles, et ses cimetières. Lorsqu'il s'agira de la construction d'édifices nouveaux, l'autorisation nécessaire sera demandée à la Sublime Porte, par l'organe du Patriarche ou chef de communauté à la Sublime Porte, et la Sublime Porte qui prendra une décision souveraine en accordant cette autorisation à moins d'obstacle administratif. L'intervention de l'autorité administrative dans tous les actes de cette nature, sera entièrement gratuite. Le Gouvernement prendra des mesures pour assurer à chaque culte, quel que soit le nombre de ses adhérents, la pleine liberté de son exercice.

5) Aucun sujet de Sa Majesté le Sultan, à quelque culte qu'il appartienne, ne sera ni insulté ni molesté, encore moins persécuté ou puni à raison de ses opinions religieuses.[4]
Vu que tous les cultes sont et seront librement pratiqués dans les Etats ottomans, aucun sujet de Sa Majesté le Sultan ne sera gêné dans l'exercice de la religion qu'il professe, et ne sera en aucune manière inquiété à cet égard. Personne ne pourra être contrainte à changer de religion.

Chaque culte, dans les localités où ne se trouveront pas d'autres confessions religieuses, ne sera soumis à aucune espèce de restriction dans la manifestation publique de sa religion. Dans les villes, bourgades et villages où les cultes sont mélangés, chaque communauté, habitant un quartier distinct, pourra également, en se conformant aux prescriptions ci-dessus indiquées, réparer et consolider ses églises, ses hôpitaux, ses écoles et ses cimetières. Lorsqu'il s'agira de la construction d'édifices nouveaux, l'autorisation nécessaire sera demandée par l'organe des Patriarches ou chefs des communautés à ma Sublime Porte, qui prendra une décision souveraine, en accordant cette autorisation, à moins d'obstacles administratifs. L'intervention de l'autorité administrative dans tous les actes de cette nature sera entièrement gratuite. Ma Sublime Porte prendra des mesures énergiques pour assurer à chaque culte, quel que soit le nombre de ses adhérents, la pleine liberté de son exercice.

Toute distinction ou appellation tendant à rendre une classe quelconque des sujets de mon Empire inférieure à une autre classe, à raison du culte, de la langue ou de la race, sera à jamais effacée du Protocole Administratif. Les lois séviront contre l'usage, entre particuliers ou de la part des autorités, de toute qualification injurieuse ou blessante.
Vu que tous les cultes sont et seront librement pratiqués dans mes Etats, aucun sujet de mon Empire ne sera gêné dans l'exercice de la religion qu'il professe et ne sera d'aucune manière inquiété à cet égard. Personne ne pourra être contrainte à changer de religion.

---

[3] The correct form should be the former one ("indiquées").

[4] The order of the fifth and sixth articles was reversed. The sixth article on religious freedom, which became the fifth article, was almost redrafted. The order will be again reversed in the final text of the Reform Edict, but the content will be almost the same.

6) Toute distinction ou appellation tendant à rendre une classe quelconque des sujets de Sa Majesté le Sultan inférieure à une autre classe à raison du culte, de la langue, ou de la race, sera à jamais effacée du Protocole Administratif. Les lois séviront contre l'usage entre particuliers, ou de la part des autorités, de toute qualification injurieuse ou blessante.

7) Tous les sujets de Sa Majesté le Sultan, sans distinction de nationalité, seront admissibles aux emplois publics et aptes à les occuper, selon leur capacité et leur mérite, et conformément à des règles d'une application générale.

8) Tous les sujets de Sa Majesté le Sultan seront indistinctement reçus dans les Ecoles Civiles et Militaires du Gouvernement, aujourd'hui existantes, ou qui seraient créées à l'avenir, s'ils remplissent d'ailleurs les conditions d'âge et d'examen spécifiées dans les Règlements Organiques des dites Ecoles. De plus chaque communauté est autorisée à établir des Ecoles Publiques de Science, d'Art, et d'Industrie; seulement le mode d'enseignement et le choix des professeurs dans les écoles de cette catégorie seront sous le contrôle d'un Conseil Mixte d'Instruction Publique dont les membres seront nommés par Sa Majesté Impériale.

9) Toutes les affaires civiles ou criminelles dans lesquelles seraient mêlés des Mussulmans avec des non-Mussulmans, ou des non-Mussulmans de rits différents, seront déférées à des Tribunaux Mixtes. Comme il est décidé que des Tribunaux Mixtes et Spéciaux seront institués pour juger les procès criminels entre des Musulmans et des non-Musulmans, ou des non-Musulmans de rites différents,

La nomination et le choix de tous les fonctionnaires et autres employés de mon Empire étant entièrement dépendante de ma volonté souveraine, tous les sujets de mon Empire, sans distinction de nationalité, seront admissibles aux emplois publics et aptes à les occuper, selon leurs capacités et leurs mérites, et conformément à des règles d'une application générale.

Tous les sujets de mon Empire seront indistinctement reçus dans les Ecoles Civiles et Militaires du Gouvernement, s'ils remplissent d'ailleurs les conditions d'âge et d'examen spécifiées dans les Règlements Organiques des dites Ecoles. De plus, chaque communauté est autorisée à établir des Ecoles Publiques de Sciences, d'Arts et d'Industrie. Seulement le mode d'enseignement et le choix des professeurs dans les écoles de cette catégorie, seront sous le contrôle d'un Conseil Mixte d'Instruction Publique, dont les membres seront nommés par un ordre souverain de ma part.

Toutes les affaires commerciales, correctionnelles et criminelles entre des Musulmans et des sujets Chrétiens ou autres non-Musulmans, ou bien des Chrétiens ou autres de rites différents non-Musulmans, seront déférées à des Tribunaux Mixtes.

et que des Tribunaux de Commerce Mixtes existent déjà pour les affaires commerciales, un code pénal, un code commercial, et des codes de procédure relatifs à ces tribunaux sont sur le point d'être complétés et le seront au plus tôt. Les procès ayant trait aux affaires civiles continueront à être jugées[5], d'après les lois et les règlements par devant les Conseils Mixtes des Provinces en présence du Gouverneur et du Juge du lieu. Les procès civils spéciaux, comme ceux de succession ou d'autre de ce genre, entre les sujets de même rit, pourront à leur demande être renvoyés par les Conseils des Patriarches ou des communautés.

L'audience de ces Tribunaux sera publique. Les parties y seront mises en présence et produiront leurs témoins, dont les dépositions seront reçues indistinctement sous un serment prêté selon la loi religieuse de chaque culte.

~~10) Les lois pénales, civiles et commerciales, et les règles de procédure à appliquer dans les Tribunaux Mixtes, seront complétées le plus tôt possible et codifiées. Il en sera publié, sous les auspices de la Porte, des traductions dans toutes les langues en usage dans l'Empire.~~
Les lois pénales, correctionnelles, commerciales et les règles de procédure à appliquer dans les Tribunaux Mixtes, seront complétées le plus tôt possible et codifiées. Il en sera publié, sous les auspices de la Porte, des traductions dans toutes les langues en usage dans l'Empire.[6]

~~11~~10) Il sera procédé, dans le plus bref délai possible, à la réforme du système pénitentiaire dans son application aux

L'audience de ces Ttribunaux sera publique; les parties seront mises en présence et produiront leurs témoins, dont les dépositions seront reçues indistinctement, sous un serment prêté selon la loi religieuse de chaque culte.

Les procès ayant trait aux affaires civiles continueront d'être publiquement jugés, d'après les lois et les règlements, par devant les Conseils Mixtes des Provinces en présence du Gouverneur et du Juge du lieu. Les procès civils spéciaux, comme ceux de succession ou autres de ce genre, entre les sujets d'un même rite Chrétien ou autre non-Musulman, pourront, à leur demande, être envoyés par devant les Conseils des Patriarches ou des communautés.

Les lois pénales, correctionnelles, commerciales et les règles de procédure à appliquer dans les Tribunaux Mixtes, seront complétées le plus tôt possible et codifiées. Il en sera publié des traductions dans toutes les langues en usage dans l'Empire.

Il sera procédé, dans le plus bref délai possible, à la réforme du système pénitentiaire, dans son application aux maisons

---

[5] The correct form should be "jugés".

[6] Article 10 is incorporated into the end of Article 9. The incorporated part is slightly amended.

maisons de détention, punition, ou de correction, et d'autres établissements de même nature, à afin de concilier les droits de l'humanité avec ceux de la justice. Aucune peine corporelle, même dans les prisons, ne pourra être appliquée que conformément à des règlements disciplinaires émanés de la Porte, et tout ce qui ressemblerait à la torture sera radicalement aboli.

Les infractions à ce sujet seront sévèrement réprimées et entraîneront en outre de plein droit la destitution des autorités qui les auraient ordonnées et des agents qui les auraient commises.

12 11) L'organisation de la police, dans la capitale, dans les villes de province et dans les campagnes, sera révisée de façon à donner à tous les sujets paisibles de Sa Majesté le Sultan les garanties désirables de sécurité quant à leurs personnes et à leurs biens.

13 12) L'égalité des impôts entraînant l'égalité des charges, comme celle des devoirs entraîne aussi celle des droits, les non-Musulmans, comme les Mussulmans, satisfaire aux obligations de la Loi de Recrutement. Le principe du remplacement ou du rachat sera admis. Il sera publié, dans le plus bref délai possible, une loi complète sur l'organisation et sur le mode d'admission et de service des sujets non-Mussulmans dans l'armée, réglant l'avancement dans la hiérarchie et le traitement affecté à chaque grade. La position d'activité et celle de réforme des officiers seront également garanties. Il sera publié, dans le plus bref délai possible, une loi complète sur le mode d'admission et de service des sujets non-Musulmans dans l'armée, de manière à leur assurer la position la plus convenable.

14 13) Il sera procédé à une réforme dans la composition des Conseils Provinciaux et Communaux, pour garantir la sincérité des choix des délégués des communautés

de détention, de punition et de correction, et autres établissements de même nature, afin de concilier les droits de l'humanité avec ceux de la justice. Aucune peine corporelle, même dans les prisons, ne pourra être appliquée que conformément à des règlements disciplinaires émanés de ma Sublime Porte, et tout ce qui ressemblerait à la torture sera radicalement aboli.

Les infractions à ce sujet seront sévèrement réprimées, et entraîneront en outre, de plein droit, la punition, en conformité du Code Criminel, des autorités qui les auraient ordonnées et des agents qui les auraient commises.

L'organisation de la police dans la capitale, dans les villes de province et dans les campagnes, sera révisée de façon à donner à tous les sujets paisibles de mon Empire, les garanties les plus fortes de sécurité quant à leurs personnes et à leurs biens.

L'égalité des impôts entraînant l'égalité des charges, comme celle des devoirs entraîne celle des droits, les sujets Chrétiens et des autres rites non-Musulmans devront, ainsi qu'il a été antérieurement résolu, aussi bien que les Musulmans, satisfaire aux obligations de la Loi de Recrutement. Le principe de remplacement ou du rachat sera admis. Il sera publié dans le plus bref délai possible, une loi complète sur le mode d'admission et de service des sujets Chrétiens et d'autres rites non-Musulmans dans l'armée.

Il sera procédé à une réforme dans la composition des Conseils Provinciaux et Communaux pour garantir la sincérité des choix des délégués des communautés

Musulmanes et non-Musulmanes, et la liberté des votes dans les Conseils. La Porte avisera à l'emploi des moyens les plus efficaces ~~pour~~ de connaître exactement et de contrôler le résultat des délibérations et des décisions prises.

Musulmanes, Chrétiennes et autres, et la liberté des votes dans les Conseils. Ma Sublime Porte avisera à l'emploi des moyens les plus efficaces de connaître exactement et de contrôler le résultat des délibérations et des décisions prises.

~~15~~14) ~~Les lois qui régissent l'achat, la vente, et la disposition des propriétés immobilières seront communes à tous les sujets de Sa Majesté le Sultan. Le droit de propriété foncière sera concédé aux étrangers, sous l'observation des lois qui régissent la matière, et l'obligation d'acquitter les mêmes charges que les indigènes.~~

Comme les lois qui régissent l'achat, la vente et la disposition des propriétés immobilières sont communes à tous les sujets du Sultan, Sa Majesté est aussi disposée à permettre aux étrangers de posséder des propriétés foncières dans ses Etats, en se conformant aux lois et en acquittant les mêmes charges que les indigènes, et après les arrangements qui auront lieu avec les puissances étrangères.

Comme les lois qui régissent l'achat, la vente et la disposition des propriétés immobilières sont communes à tous les sujets de mon Empire, il pourra être permis aux étrangers de posséder des propriétés foncières dans mes Etats, en se conformant aux lois et aux règlements de police, en acquittant les mêmes charges que les indigènes, et après que des arrangements auront lieu avec les Puissances étrangères.

~~16~~15) Les impôts sont exigibles au même titre de tous les sujets de Sa Majesté le Sultan, sans distinction de classe ou de ~~culte.;~~ on avisera aux moyens les plus promptes[7] et les plus énergiques de corriger les abus dans la perception des impôts, et notamment des dîmes. Le système de la perception directe sera successivement, et aussitôt que faire se pourra, substitué au régime des fermes dans toutes les branches des revenus de l'Etat.
Tant que ce système demeurera en vigueur, il sera interdit, sous les peines les plus ~~sévères;~~ à tous les agents de l'autorité et à tous les membres des Medjlis de se rendre ~~adjudicataires~~ adjudicatoires des fermes qui seront annoncées avec

Les impôts sont exigibles au même titre de tous les sujets de mon Empire, sans distinction de classe ni de culte. On avisera aux moyens les plus prompts et les plus énergiques de corriger les abus dans la perception des impôts, et notamment des dîmes. Le système de la perception directe sera, successivement et aussitôt que faire se pourra, substitué au régime des fermes dans toutes les branches des revenus de l'Etat.
Tant que ce système demeurera en vigueur, il sera interdit, sous les peines les plus sévères, à tous les agents de l'autorité et à tous les membres des Medjlis de se rendre adjudicataires des fermes qui seront annoncées avec publicité et

---

[7] The correct form should be "prompts".

publicité et concurrence, ou d'avoir une part quelconque d'intérêt dans leur exploitation.

Les impositions locales seront autant que possible calculées de façon à ne pas affecter les sources de la production ou à entraver le mouvement du commerce intérieur.

~~17~~16) Les travaux d'utilité publique recevront une dotation convenable, à laquelle concourront les impositions particulières et spéciales des provinces appelées à jouir de l'établissement des voies de communication par terre et par eau.

~~18~~17) Le budget des recettes et dépenses de l'Etat sera communiquée,[8] à une époque périodique, et autant que possible par prévision d'une année, au Grand Conseil de Justice. Le budget sera annuellement publié, et l'on procédera à la révision des traitements affectés à chaque emploi.

~~19~~18) Les ~~e~~Chefs et un ~~d~~Délégué de chaque communauté désignés par la Sublime Porte, seront appelés à prendre part aux délibérations du ~~Grand~~ Conseil Suprême de Justice dans toutes les circonstances qui intéresseraient la généralité des sujets de Sa Majesté le Sultan. Ils seront spécialement convoqués à cet effet par le Grand Vizir. Le mandat des ~~d~~Délégués sera annuel. Ils prêteront serment en entrant en charge.

Tous les membres du Conseil, dans les réunions ordinaires et extra-ordinaires, émettront librement leurs avis et leurs votes sans qu'on puisse jamais les inquiéter à ce sujet.

~~20~~19) Les lois contre la corruption, la concussion, ou la malversation seront appliquées, d'après les formes légales, à tous les sujets de Sa Majesté le Sultan, quelle que soit leur classe et la nature de leurs fonctions.

---

concurrence, ou d'avoir une part quelconque d'intérêt dans leur exploitation.

Les impositions locales seront, autant que possible, calculées de façon à ne pas affecter les sources de la production, ni à entraver le mouvement du commerce intérieur.

Les travaux d'utilité publique recevront une dotation convenable, à laquelle concourront les impositions particulières et spéciales des Provinces appelées à jouir de l'établissement des voies de communication par terre et par mer.

Une loi spéciale ayant déjà été rendue, qui ordonne que le budget des recettes et des dépenses de l'Etat sera fixé et communiqué chaque année, cette loi sera observée de la manière la plus scrupuleuse. On procédera à la révision des traitements affectés à chaque emploi.

Les chefs et un délégué de chaque communauté, désigné par ma Sublime Porte, seront appelés à prendre part aux délibérations du Conseil Suprême de Justice dans toutes les circonstances qui intéresseraient la généralité des sujets de mon Empire. Ils seront spécialement convoqués à cet effet par mon Grand Vizir. Le mandat des délégués sera annuel; ils prêteront serment en entrant en charge.

Tous les membres du Conseil, dans les réunions ordinaires et extra-ordinaires, émettront librement leurs avis et leurs votes sans qu'on puisse jamais les inquiéter à ce sujet.

Les lois contre la corruption, la concussion, ou la malversation seront appliquées, d'après les formes légales, à tous les sujets de mon Empire, quelle que soit leur classe et la nature de leurs fonctions.

---

[8] The correct form should be "communiqué".

2120) Il est à désirer que la Sublime Porte annonce l'intention de s'occuper au plus tôt de la réforme de son système monétaire, et de la création d'institutions du crédit public.

On s'occupera de la création de banques et d'autres institutions semblables pour arriver à la réforme du système monétaire et financier, ainsi que de la création de fonds destinés à augmenter les sources de la richesse matérielle de mon Empire.

On s'occupera également de la création de routes et de canaux qui rendront les communications plus faciles et augmenteront les sources de la richesse du pays. On abolira tout ce que peut entraver le commerce et l'agriculture. Pour arriver à ces buts, on recherchera les moyens de mettre à profit les sciences, les arts et les capitaux de l'Europe et de les mettre ainsi successivement en exécution.

THE DRAFTING COMMISSION
OF THE OTTOMAN CONSTITUTION

Affiliation of the Member	Name	Profession
Civil	Midhad Pasha	President of the Council of State
Civil / Former Ulema	Ahmed Cevded Pasha	Minister of Justice
Civil	Server Pasha	Minister of Public Works
Civil	Kani Pasha	Minister of Indirect Taxes
Civil	Namık Pasha	Minister without portfolio
Civil	Kadri Bey	Prefect of Istanbul
Civil	Ziya Bey	Undersecretary of Education
Civil	Odyan Effendi	Undersecretary of Public Works
Civil	Aleksandr Karateodori Effendi	Undersecretary of Foreign Affairs
Civil	Vahan Bey	Undersecretary of Justice
Civil	Namık Kemal Bey*	Member of the Council of State
Civil	Sava Pasha	Director of the Imperial Lycée
Civil	Abidin Bey**	Commissioner of the Stock Market
Civil	Ohannes Çamiç Effendi	Member of the Council of State
Civil	Yanko Effendi*	Member of the Council of State
Civil	Samih Pasha***	Minister without portfolio
Civil	Mehmed İzzed Pasha***	Minister of Police
Civil	Kostaki Bey****	Head of the Sixth Municipal Circle
Civil	Sami Pasha****	Not mentioned
Civil	Ömer Effendi****	Member of an assembly of investigation
Military	Mahmud Mesud Pasha*****	Chief of Staff
Military	Aziz Pasha*****	Member of the Central War Council
Ulema	Kara Halil Effendi	Commissioner of Fatwas
Ulema	İsmail Seyfeddin Effendi	Member of the Council of State
Ulema	Asım Yakub Effendi*	*Kazasker* of Anatolia
Ulema	Ahmed Esad Effendi	*Kazasker* of Roumelia
Ulema	Mehmed Sahib Molla Bey*	Member of the Council of State

Affiliation of the Member	Name	Profession
Ulema	Ahmed Hilmi Effendi	President of the Court of Cassation, Civil Section
Ulema	Mustafa Hayrullah Effendi	President of the Üsküdar Civil Court
Ulema	Ömer Hilmi Effendi	Undersecretary of Wakfs
Ulema	Emin Effendi***	Member of the Council of State
Ulema	Ramiz Effendi	Member, Council of State & Court of Cassation

* Included in the archival list on November 2, 1876.
** Included in the archival list on October 8, 1876.
*** Not included in the archival list.
**** Not included in Kuntay's list.
***** Included in the archival list not by their names but by their profession.

MIDHAD PASHA'S CONSTITUTIONAL MODEL
AS PUBLISHED IN *ÜSS-İ İNKILAB*

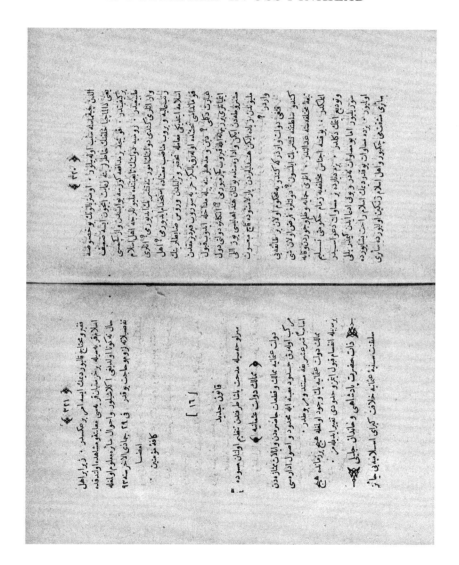

اوله‌رق سلالهٔ آل عثماندن اکبر وارشد اولاده عائددر .

ذات حضرت پادشاهی حسب الخلافه دین اسلامك حامی ونکهبانی وقوهٔ بریه و بحریه‌نك برنجی قوماندانیدر .

وکلانك عزل ونصبی ودول اجنبیه ایله معاهدات عقدی وحرب وصلح اعلانی وحرکات عسکریه وکافهٔ تدابیر ملکیه‌نك اتخاذ و اجراسی و مجرمینك عفوی و مجلس مبعوثانك عقد و فسخی ذات حضرت پادشاهینك امتیاز مخصوص ومقدسیدر .

ذات حضرت خلافتپناهینك نفس همایونی مقدس وهر درلو مسؤلیتدن مصون و محفوظدر .

محافظهٔ شان سلطنت ایچون مخصص اولان تخصیصات سنیه‌نك تدارکی عمومه‌نك وظایفندندر حسب الاقتضا ضم وتعدیل ایدیله‌جك اولور ایسه مجلس مبعوثان قراری اوزره تعیین اولنور .

صدارت مطلقه مسندی ملغادر هیئت وکلا ریاستی طرف حضرت پادشاهیدن باش وکیل نامیله وکلادن برینه احاله ووکلا هیئتی انك رأیی ایله انتخاب و ارادهٔ سنیه ایله نصب اولنور .

مجلس وکلا باش وکیلك ریاستی تحتنده عقد اولنوب داخلی وخارجی کافهٔ امور مهمه و پولتیقه‌نك مرجعیدر . مذاکراتك قرارلری ارادهٔ سنیه ایله اجرا اولنور .

دوائر مهمهٔ دولتك ریاست ونظارتلرنده بولنان ذوات وکلالق مسندینی وامتیازینی حائز اولوب وکلادن هر بری تعیین اولنان مأذونیت دائره‌سنده وظیفه‌لرینی اجرایه مرخص ومأذوندر .

ادارهٔ دولتجه مخل امنیت اولان وقانون جدیدا احکامنه مخالف بولنان اجراآت عمومیده هیئتجه وهر دائره‌نك وظایف معینه‌سنه دائر اولان احوالده دخی منفرداً وکلا مسؤلدر .

مسؤلیتدن تبریهٔ ذمت ایده‌میان وکلا ایچون مجلس مبعوثانده اکثریت ایله سلب امنیته قرار ویرلدکده مضبطه‌سی رئیس واسطه‌سیله طرف شاهانه‌یه طوغریدن طوغری‌یه تقدیم اولنور بو حالده وکلا هیئتجه و یا منفرداً استعفایه مجبور اولورلر .

وکلا استعفا ایتدکده قبول و عدم قبولی رأی شاهانه‌یه منوطدر .

وکلانك هیئتجه استعفالری قبول بیورلدقده یا انلردن ویا خارجدن برذاته طرف شاهانه‌دن ریاست وکلا مأموریتی تفویض بیوریلوب هیئت وکلانك تشکیلی اکا احاله قلنور وهیئت وکلادن شخصا متهم بولنمیانلر هیئت جدیده‌یه التحاق ایده‌بیلورلر اکر هیئتدن بری استعفا ایدر ایسه انك یرینه رئیس وکلا بولنان ذات دیکرینی انتخاب ایدوب ارادهٔ سنیه اوزرینه نصب اولنور .

٣٢٤

کرك بالفعل مأمور بتده اولان وکرك معزول بولنان وکلانك اجرای محاکمه‌لری مجلس مبعوثان استدعاسی اوزرینه تعلق ایده‌جك ارادهٔ سنیه‌یه موقوفدر ·

ذات حضرت پادشاهی هرنوقت تنسیب بیورر ایسه مجلس وکلایه ریاست ایدر ·

مأمورین

هرمأمور طریق ومسلك مخصوصندن یتشمك لازمدر · مأموریتلرك مسلك وطریقی تنظیم اولنه‌جق مکاتب دروسلریله تعیین اولنه‌جغندن اشبو مکاتبك یوم تنظیمندن بش‌سنه مدت مرورنده شهادتنامه‌سی اولمیان هیچ برکیمسه‌نك مأموریت استدعاسنه صلاحیتی اولمیه‌جقدر ·

بش سنه مدتده بولندیغی مأموریتلرده حسن خدمت وترقی کوسترن هربرمأمورك طلب مکافاته صلاحیتی واوتوز سنه لکه‌سز خدمات دولتده بولنمش و یاخود اثنای خدمتده برعلته دوچار اولمش اولان مأمورك دخی تقاعد معاشنه اهلیتی اولور مأموریتلرك مسلکلری و مکافاتك انواعی وتقاعد معاشنك صورت تخصیصی نظامات مخصوصه ایله تعیین اولنه‌جقدر ·

نظاماً جنحه‌سی ثابت اولمدقجه و ترقی ایتدکچه و یاخود دولتجه برسبب مشروع ومقبوله مستند لزوم اولمدقجه هیچ

٣٢٥

برمأمور مأموریتندن چیقاریله‌مز · بیوك وکوچك نظر قانونده مساوی اولمغله برمأمورك آمرینه اطاعتی قانونك تعیین ایتدیکی دائره‌یه مخصوصدر · هرمأموریتك دائرهٔ وظیفه‌سی معین اولمغله هرکس وظیفه‌سی دائره‌سندن مسؤل ومعاتب اولور ·

شورای دولت

شورای دولت وضع اصلیمی اوزره تجدید و تنظیم اولنه‌جقدر ·

شورای دولتك رئیس واعضاسی طرف شاهانه‌دن عزل ونصب اولنور ·

شورای دولت اولا کافهٔ قوانین و نظامات لایحه‌لرینی بعدالتدقیق تصدیقه ثانیاً طرف حکومتدن کندینه حواله اولنه‌جق امور ومصالح ملکیه حقنده رأینی اعطایه ثالثا ملکیه مأمورلری ایله عدلیه مأمورلری بیننده تعیین وظیفه‌دن طولایی ظهوره کلان اختلافاتی فصله رابعاً متن نظامات و قوانینده عارض اوله‌جق شبهاتی حل و تفسیره خامساً مأمورین دولتك مأموریتلرندن طولایی اقتضا ایدن محاکماتك اجراسنه مأموردر ·

شورای دولت قوهٔ اجرائیه‌نك وظایفنه اصلا مداخله ایده‌مز · فقط قوانین ونظاماتك نقصان و بولنسز برصورتده

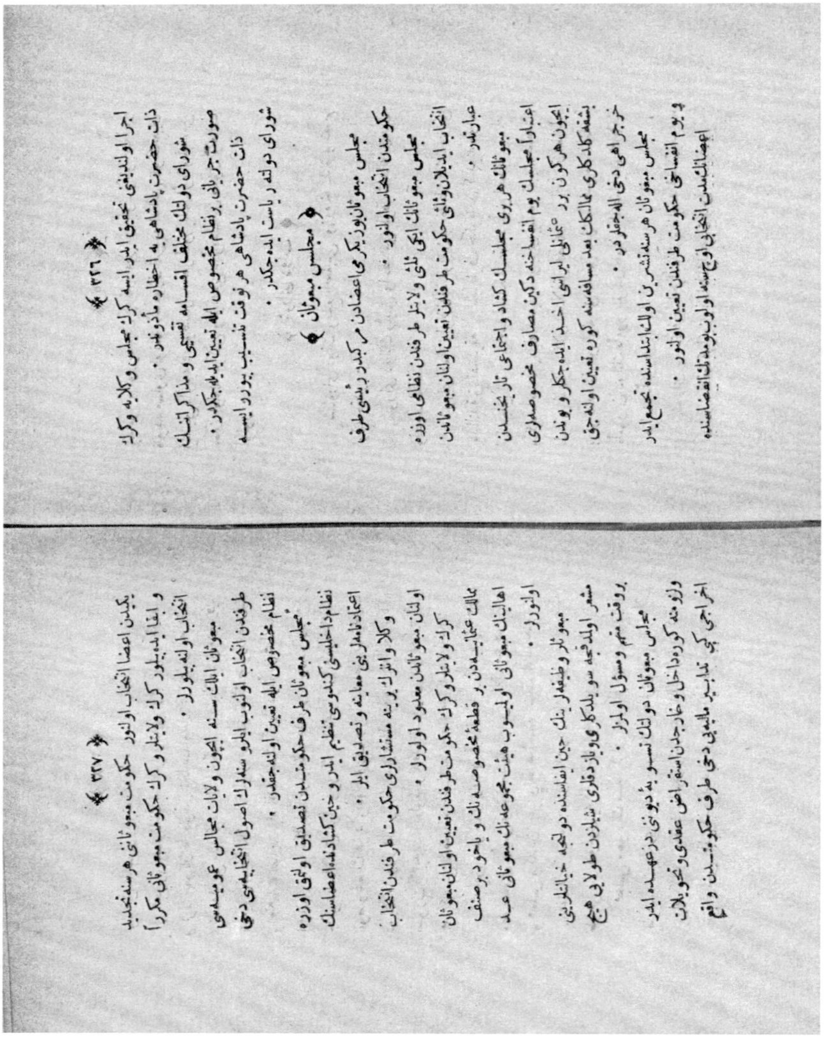

﴾ ۳۲۸ ﴿

اولەجق طلب اوزرینە مذاکرە ایلر .

مجلس مبعوثانك اساس وظایفی اولا کرك حکومت وکرك مبعوثان طرفلرندن تکلیف اولنان قوانین و نظامات لایحەلرینی مذاکرە ثانیا حکومت ایلە بالاتفاق مصارف عمومیەیی تعیین ایتمك ثالثا واردات عمومیەنك صورت صرف واستعمالنە نظارت ایلە اقتضاسنە کورە دوائردن محاسبات استمك رابعا تکالیف عمومیەنك مقدار و صورت توزیعنە حکومتلە بالاتفاق قرار ویرمك خامسا قوانین ونظامات موضوعەنك هر دائرەدە صورت جریاننە نظارت ایدوب دولت مأمورلرندن برینك مغایر نظام وقانون افعال وحرکاتی صورت صحیحەدە معلوم اولدقدە شورای دولتدە اجرای محاکمەسنی بامضبطە طلب ایتمك خصوصلرندن عبارتدر .

مجلس مبعوثان ویرەجکی قرارلرە دائر تنظیم ایدەجکی مضبطەلری رئیس واسطەسیلە مجلس وکلایە عرض ایدر و مجلس وکلادن اجرای مقتضاسنە تشبث اولندیغنە دائر بر هفتە ظرفندە جوابی آلەمز ایسە کیفیتی بامضبطە طوغریدن طوغری یە ذات شاهانەیە عرض و بیان ایلر .

مجلس مبعوثانك مذاکراتی علنی اولەجق و رئیس طرفندن نشری تنسیب اولنان ضبطلری طبع ایلە اعلان ایدیلەجکدر فقط حاضر بولنان مبعوثانك ثلثی مذاکرەنك خفی اولمسنی طلب ایدر ایسە اولوجهلە مذاکرە اولنەجقدر .

﴾ ۳۲۹ ﴿

مجلس مبعوثانك تجمعی اثنادە مبعوثاندن بری بر جنحە وجنایتدن طولایی اتهام اولنور ایسە مجلس مذکور طرفندن اتهامنە سبب کافی بولندیغنە قرار ویرلدکجە محاکمەسنە مبادرت اولنمیەجقدر .

مجلس مبعوثان لااقل اعضالك نصفی حاضر اولمدقجە مذاکرەیە مبادرت ایدەمز . وکافۀ قرار حاضر اولان مبعوثانك اکثریت آراسیلە قبول اولنور .

مجلس مبعوثانك قرارلرینە دائر ذات حضرت پادشاهی طرفندن قبول وتصدیق بیورلمیان خصوصات موجود بولنان مبعوثانك مدتی بالانقضا یکیلری انتخاب اولنمدقجە تکرار موقع مذاکرەیە قونیلەمز . انجق حکومت سنیە اومدت ایچندە رضا وموافقت کوسترر ایسە اولجهلە دخی تکرار مذاکرەیە قونیلور .

ذات حضرت پادشاهی هر نوقت منافع دولت ضمننده لزوم کورور ایسە مجلس مبعوثانی فسخ ووقت معیننده غیری وقتدە دخی جمع ایدەبیلور . انجق اولوجهلە مجلسك فسخندە التی ماه ظرفندە دیکر مجلسك عقد واجتماعی دخی امر ایدر .

﴾ تابعیت عثمانیە وعثمانلولرك حقوق ووظایفی ﴿

تابعیت دولت عثمانیەدە بولنان افرادك جملەسنە بلااستثنا عثمانلی تعبیر اولنور .

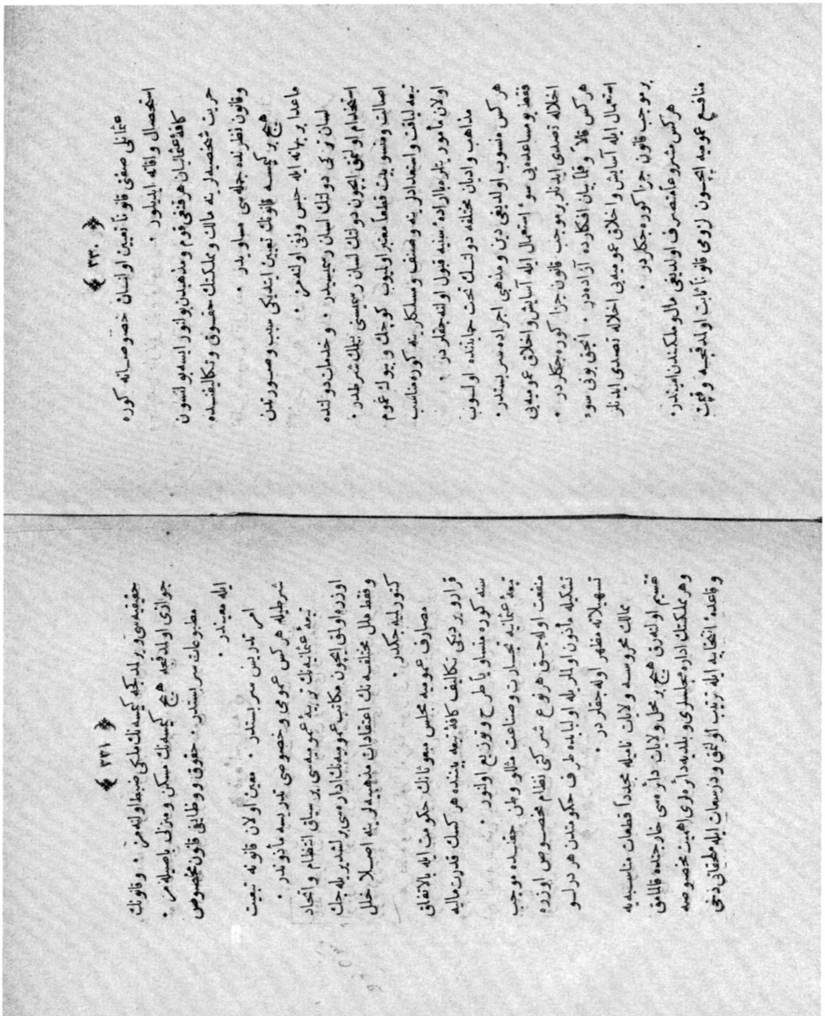

MIDHAD PASHA'S CONSTITUTIONAL MODEL
FROM THE OTTOMAN ARCHIVES

Y.EE.00071

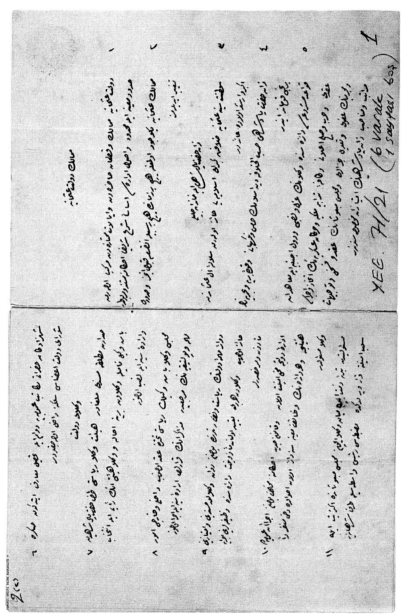

Y.EE.00071

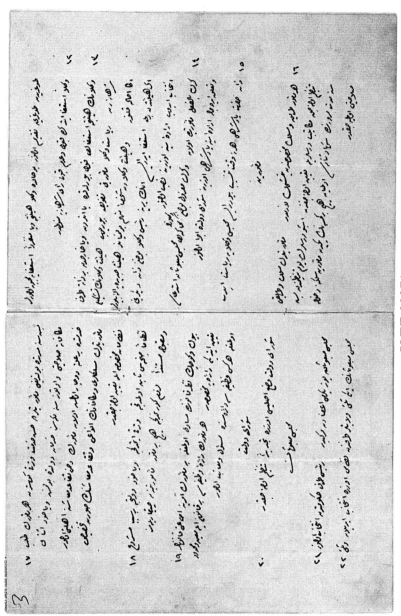

Y.EE.00071

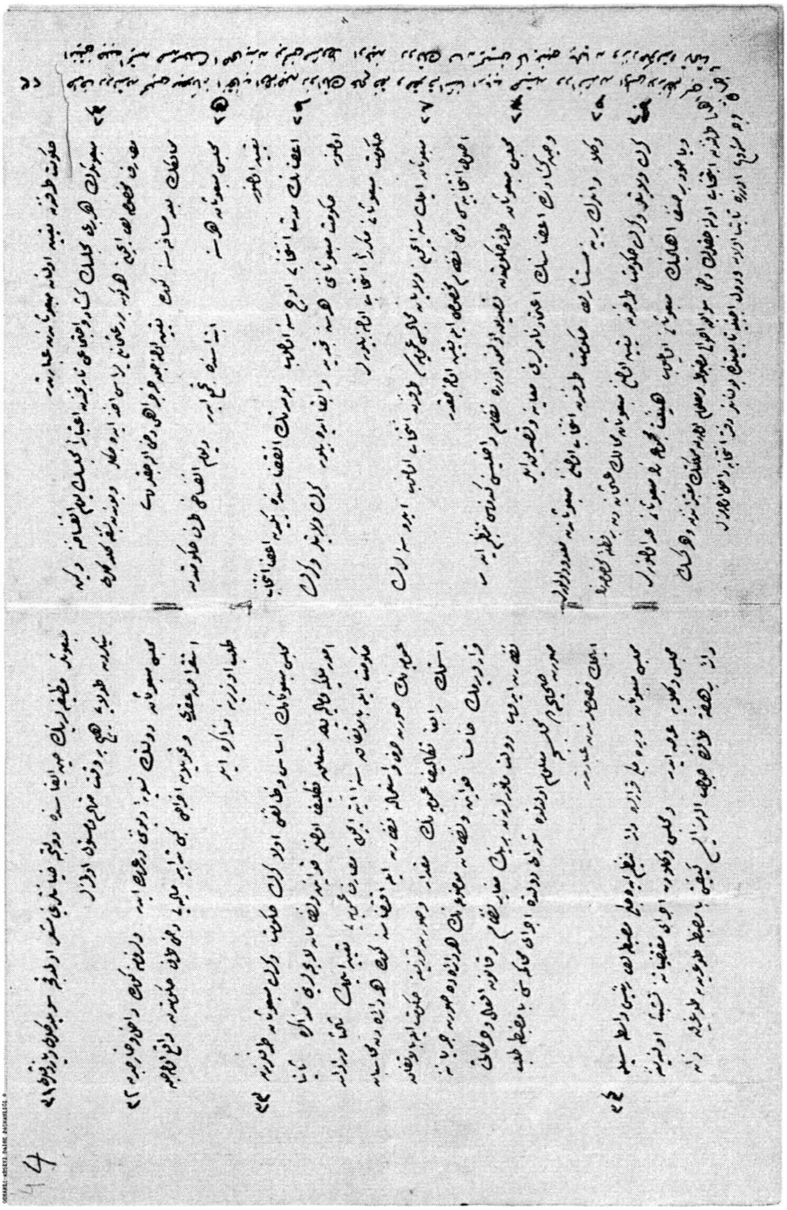

Y.EE.00071

Y.EE.00071

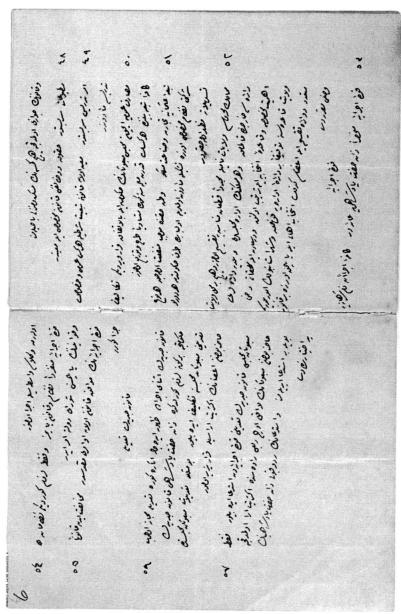

APPENDIX V

SAID PASHA'S CONSTITUTIONAL MODEL
FROM THE OTTOMAN ARCHIVES

Y.EE.00071

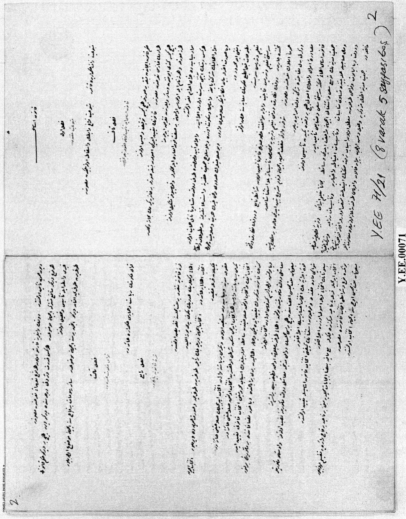

Y.EE 74/21 (8 varak 5 sayfası 69)

Y.EE.00071

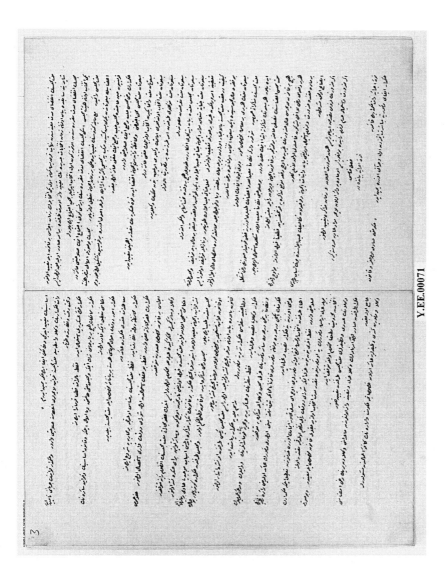

Y.EE.00071

Y.EE.00071

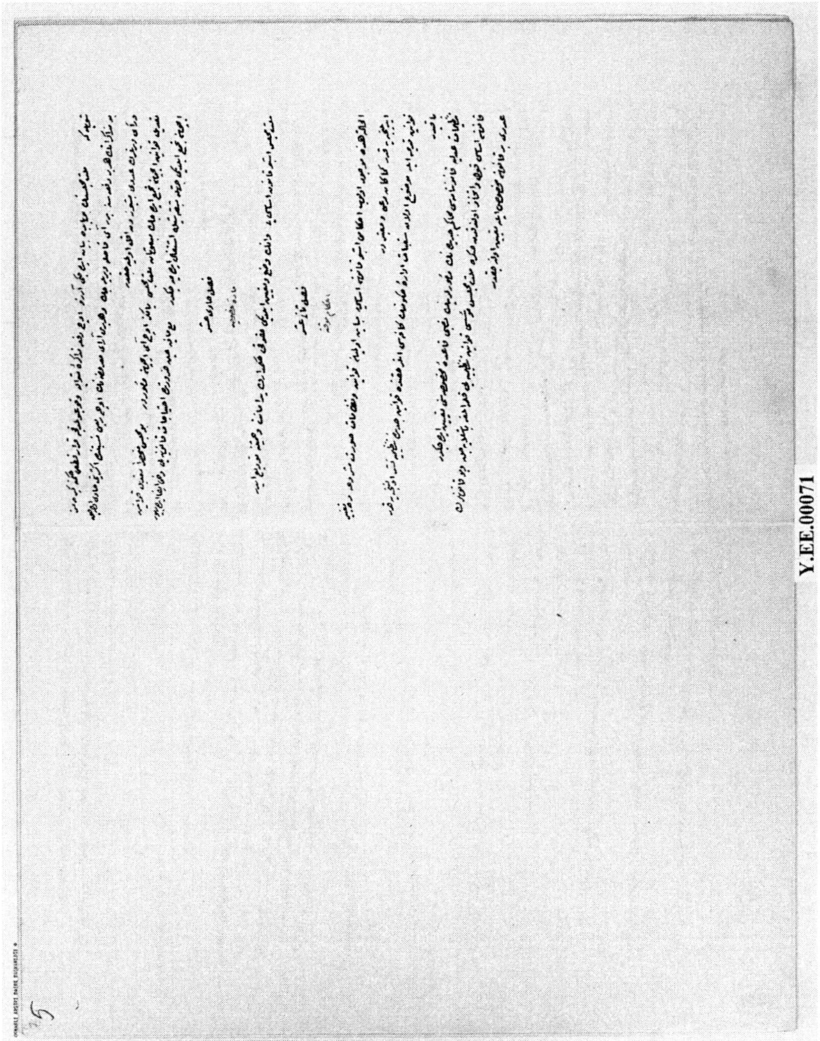
Y.EE.00071

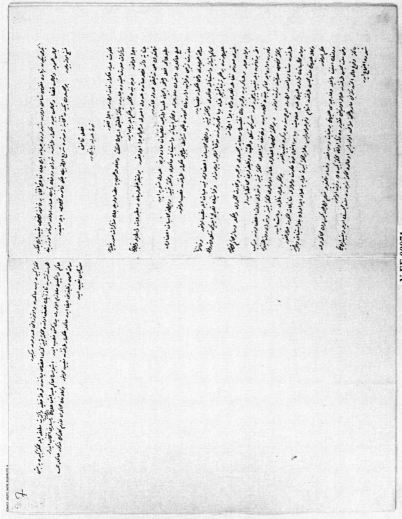

Y.EE.00071

APPENDIX VI

SAID PASHA'S CONSTITUTIONAL MODEL
AS PUBLISHED IN *ÜSS-İ İNKILAB*

﴾ ٣٣٤ ﴿

هر آدمك خانه‌سی تعرضدن مصوندر . قانونك تعيين ايلديكی اصولدن بشقه صورتله بر خانه‌يه كيرمك مجاز دكلدر .

هيچ كيمسه كندی او يندن وسائر ويلرندن تفريق ايديله‌مز .

هر نه صورتله ونه نام ايله اولورسه اولسون برصفت فوق‌العاده ايله محكمه‌لر وقوميسيونلر تشكيل اولنه‌مز .

مواد سياسيه‌ده جزای اعدام لغو اولنمشدر .

هركس دينك آيينی سربست اوله‌رق اجرا ايدر واجرای آيين خصوصنده طرف دولتدن متساويا نائل حمايت اولور .

افراد اهالينك شركت بامعه وآسايش وسكونت اوزره وبلا سلاح جمعيت عقدينه واستدعا تقديمنه ومطبوعات واسطه‌سيله وباصورت اخرله بيان افكار اتمكه صلاحيتلری واردر وبو صلاحيتلرك حدودی دخی غيرك حريت وصلاحيت وعمومك امنيتی ايله محدوددر .

مطبوعات قبل الطبع حكومتك معاينه‌سنه عرض اولنمز .

تعليم وتدريس سربستدر .

سربستیٔ تعليم وتدريس قابليت وآدابه موافقت خصوصلرنده قانوناً معين اولان شرائطه تابع ودولتك نظارت ودقتی تحتنده جاريدر . دولتك نظارت ودقتی

﴾ ٣٣٥ ﴿

تعليم وتربيه مخصوص وبلا استثنا شاملدر .

عموماً املاك تعرضدن مصوندر . شو قدر واركه منفعت عموميه ايچون لزوم مشروع تبين ايلديكی حالده بر ملكك پشين ودكرلی بدل مقابلنده تركنی دولت امر ايده بيلور .

مصادرهٔ اموال واملاك اصولی هيچ بروقتده يكيدن تأسيس اولنه‌مز .

قانون اساسی اهالیٔ مملكته سربستیٔ سعی وصنايعی تأمين ايدر .

جمعيت مدنيه‌نك توسع واشتغالی ايچون مراجعت ايلديكی وسائط مجاناً تعليم ابتدائی وتربيهٔ خصوصيهٔ صناعيه‌لر ومال صاحبيله عمله بيننده تساویٔ مناسبات وتأسيسات احتياطيه واعتباردن وتأسيسات زراعيه وشركت اختياريه ودولت ويا ايالات ونواحی طرفلرندن معطل اولان اسباب ثروت مملكتك ايشلدلمسنه منحصر اوله‌رق اتخاذ قلنه‌جق تأسيسات نافعه‌در .

جمعيت مدنيه اطفال متروكه‌يه وعليل ومسن اولوب بيوايه قالان واقرباسی طرفندن اعانه اولنه ميانلره معاونت ايلر .

ديون عموميه تأمين اولنمشدر . دولتك داينلرينه قارشو اولان هرنوع تعهداتی تعرضدن مصوندر .

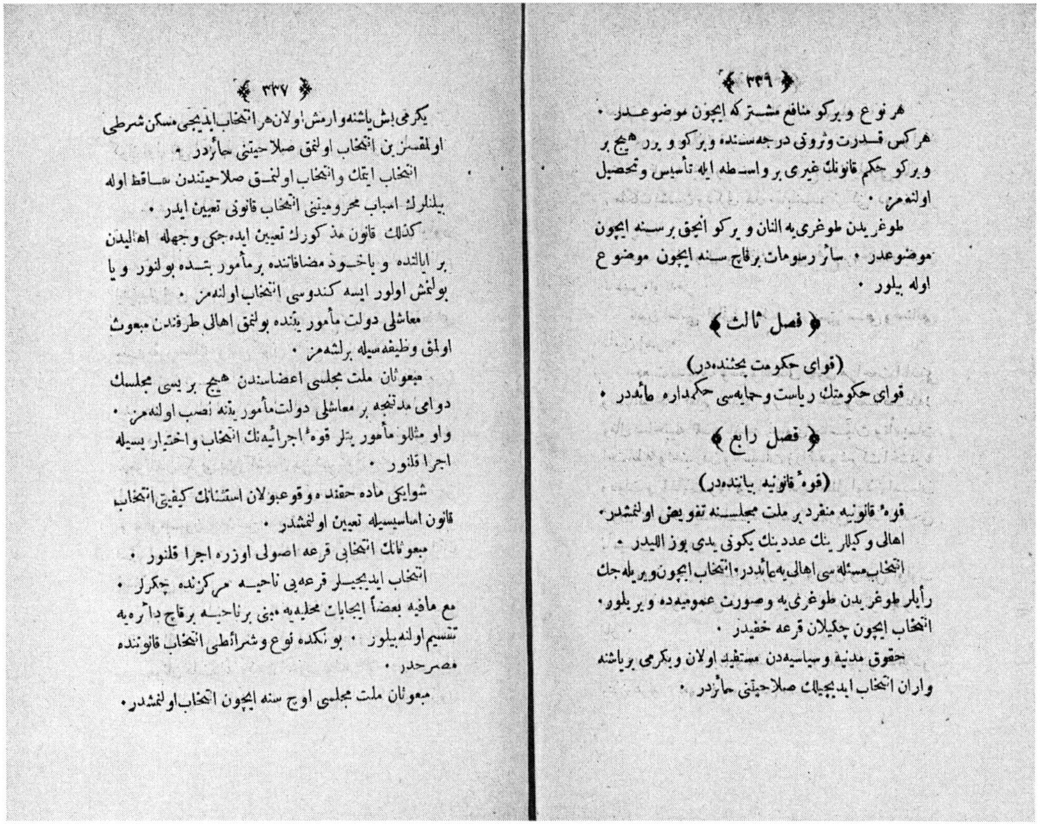

﴿ ٣٣٦ ﴾

هر نوع و برکو منافع مشترکه ایچون موضوعدر .

هر کس قدرت وثروتی درجه‌سنده ویرکو ویرر هیچ بر ویرکو حکم قانونك غیری بر واسطه ایله تأسیس وتحصیل اولنه‌مز .

طوغریدن طوغری‌یه النان ویرکو انجق بر سنه ایچون موضوعدر . سائر رسومات برقاچ سنه ایچون موضوع اوله بیلور .

﴿ فصل ثالث ﴾

(قوای حکومت بخنده‌در)

قوای حکومتك ریاست وحمایه‌سی حکمداره عائددر .

﴿ فصل رابع ﴾

(قوۀ قانونیه بیانده‌در)

قوۀ قانونیه منفرد بر ملت مجلسنه تفویض اولنمشدر .

اهالی وکیللرینك عددینك یکونی یدی یوز الیدر .

انتخاب مسئله‌سی اهالی‌یه عائددر . انتخاب ایچون ویریله‌جك رأیلر طوغریدن طوغری‌یه وصورت عمومیه‌ده ویریلور . انتخاب ایچون چکیلان قرعه خفیدر .

حقوق مدنیه وسیاسیه‌دن مستفید اولان ویکرمی بریاشنه واران انتخاب ایدیجیلك صلاحیتنی حائزدر .

﴿ ٣٣٧ ﴾

یکرمی بش یاشنه وارمش اولان هر انتخاب ایدیجی مسکن شرطی اولمقسزین انتخاب اولنمق صلاحیتنی حائزدر .

انتخاب ایتمك وانتخاب اولنمق صلاحیتندن ساقط اوله بیلنلرك اسباب محرومیتنی انتخاب قانونی تعیین ایدر .

کذلك قانون مذکورك تعیین ایده‌جکی وجهله اهالیدن بر ایالتده ویاخود مضافاتنده بر مأمور بتده بولنور ویا بولنمش اولور ایسه کندوسی انتخاب اولنه‌مز .

معاشلی دولت مأمور یتنده بولنمق اهالی طرفندن مبعوث اولمق وظیفه‌سیله برلشه‌مز .

مبعوثان ملت مجلسی اعضاسندن هیچ بریسی مجلسك دوامی مدتنجه بر معاشلی دولت مأموریتنه نصب اولنه‌مز . واو مثللو مأموریتلر قوۀ اجرائیه‌نك انتخاب واختیاریله اجرا قلنور .

شوایکی ماده حقنده وقوعبولان استثنانك کیفیتی انتخاب قانون اساسیسیله تعیین اولنمشدر .

مبعوثانك انتخابی قرعه اصولی اوزره اجرا قلنور .

انتخاب ایدیجیلر قرعه‌یی ناحیه مرکزنده چکرلر . مع مافیه بعضاً ایجابات محلیه‌یه مبنی بر ناحیه برقاچ دائره‌یه تقسیم اولنه‌بیلور . بونکده نوع وشرائطی انتخاب قانوننده مصرحدر .

مبعوثان ملت مجلسی اوچ سنه ایچون انتخاب اولنمشدر .

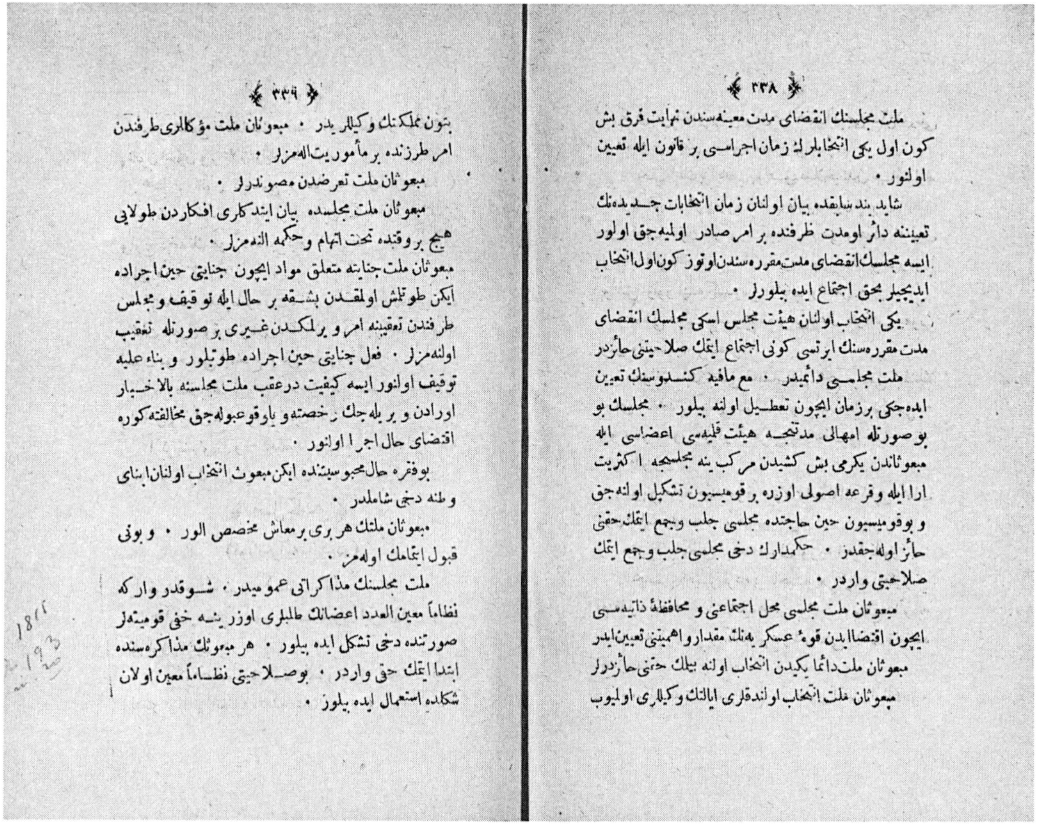

﴿ ٣٣٨ ﴾

ملت مجلسنك انقضای مدت معینه‌سندن نهایت فرق بش
کون اول یکی انتخابلرك زمان اجراسی بر قانون ایله تعیین
اولنور ٠

شاید بند سابقده بیان اولنان زمان انتخابات جدیده‌نك
تعیننه دائر اومدت ظرفنده بر امر صادر اولمیه‌جق اولور
ایسه مجلسك انقضای مدت مقرره‌سندن اوتوز کون اول انتخاب
ایدیجیلر بحق اجتماع ایده بیلورلر ٠

یکی انتخاب اولنان هیئت مجلس اسکی مجلسك انقضای
مدت مقرره‌سنك ایرتسی کونی اجتماع ایتمك صلاحیتنی حائزدر
ملت مجلسی دائمیدر ٠ مع مافیه کندوسنك تعیین
ایده‌جکی برزمان ایچون تعطیل اولنه بیلور ٠ مجلسك بو
بوصورتله امهالی مدتنجه هیئت قلمیه‌سی اعضاسی ایله
مبعوثاندن یکرمی بش کشیدن مرکب ینه مجلسجه اکثریت
ارا ایله وقرعه اصولی اوزره بر قومیسیون تشکیل اولنه‌جق
و بوقومیسیون حین حاجتده مجلسی جلب وجمع ایتمك حقنی
حائز اوله‌جقدر ٠ حکمدارك دخی مجلسی جلب وجمع ایتمك
صلاحیتی واردر ٠

مبعوثان ملت مجلسی محل اجتماعنی و محافظهٔ ذاتیه‌سی
ایچون اقتضا ایدن قوهٔ عسکریه‌نك مقدار و اهمیتنی تعیین ایدر
مبعوثان ملت دائما یکیدن انتخاب اولنه بیلمك حقنی حائزدرلر
مبعوثان ملت انتخاب اولندقلری ایالتك وکیلاری اولمیوب

﴿ ٣٣٩ ﴾

بتون مملکتك وکیللریدر ٠ مبعوثان ملت موکللری طرفندن
امر طرزنده بر مأموریت الەمزلر ٠

مبعوثان ملت تعرضدن مصوندرلر ٠

مبعوثان ملت مجلسده بیان ایتدکلری افکاردن طولایی
هیچ بر وقتده تحت اتهام و محکمه الەمزلر ٠

مبعوثان ملت جنایته متعلق مواد ایچون جنایتی حین اجراده
ایکن طوتلمش اولمقدن بشقه بر حال ایله توقیف و مجلس
طرفندن تعقیبنه امر و یرلمکدن غیری بر صورتله تعقیب
اولنەمزلر ٠ فعل جنایتی حین اجراده طوتیلور و بناء علیه
توقیف اولنور ایسه کیفیت درعقب ملت مجلسنه بالاخبار
اورادن ویریله‌جك رخصته و یاوقوعبوله‌جق مخالفته کوره
اقتضای حال اجرا اولنور ٠

بوفقره حالمحبوسیتده ایکن مبعوث انتخاب اولنان ابنای
وطنه دخی شاملدر ٠

مبعوثان ملتك هر بری برمعاش مخصص الور ٠ و بونی
قبول ایتمامك اولەمز ٠

ملت مجلسنك مذاکراتی عمومیدر ٠ شو قدر وارکه
نظاما معین العدد اعضانك طلبلری اوزرینه خفی قومیته‌لر
صورتنده دخی تشکل ایده بیلور ٠ هر مبعوثك مذاکره‌سنده
ابتدا ایتمك حقی واردر ٠ بوصلاحیتی نظاما معین اولان
شکلده استعمال ایده بیلور ٠

٣٤٠

ملت مجلسی اعضاسنك برفضله نصفی حاضر بولنمدقجه برقانون ایچون ویریلان رأیلر معتبر اوله‌مز .

هیچ بر قانون لایحه‌سی (حال ضرورتك غیریده) اوچ دفعه موقع مذاکره‌یه قونلمقسزین قطعیاً قبول اولنه‌مز بواوچ دفعه‌نك هر بردفعه‌سی دخی لااقل بشر کون فاصله‌لی اولمق لازم کلور .

برماده حقنده ضرورت ولزوم استعجال اولدیغنی بیان واثبات ایچون وقوعبولان تکالیفك حین اجراسنده بونك اسباب موجبه‌سی ایضاح اولنمق مشروطدر .

اکر ضرورتك لزومنی تصدیق ایدرایسه همان ضرورتی واعلان وزمان مذاکره‌یی تعیین ایدر .

اکر ضرورت و استعجاله عدم لزوم رأینده بولنور ایسه اوماده‌یه دائر اولان لایحه مواد عادیه صره‌سنه کیرر .

فصل خامس

(قوهٔ اجرائیه بیانده‌در)

قوهٔ اجرائیه ذات حکمداریده قائمدر

حکمدار ایفای مأموریته مباشرت ایتزدن اول وجه آتی اوزره یمین ایدر .

(حکومتجه صادق اوله‌جغمه وقانون اساسینك تعیین ایلدیکی وظائفی ایفا ایده‌جکمه یمین ایدرم)

٣٤١

ذات حکمدارینك وکلا واسطه‌سیله ملت مجلسنه قوانین لایحه‌لری تقدیم ایتمکه صلاحیتی واردر و حکمدار قواننك جریاننی تأمین ایدر وتحت دقت ونظارتنده طوتار .

حکمدار قوهٔ عسکریه‌یی استعمال ایدر فقط بالذات قطعاً قوماندا ایده‌مز .

حکمدار وکلانك غیری مأمورین ایله طوغریدن طوغری‌یه مکاتبه ایده‌مز .

حکمدار ممالکك هیچ بر پارچه‌سنی ترك ایتمکه طوغریدن طوغری‌یه ومجلس ملتی طاغتمغه و یاقانون اساسینك وقوانین سائره‌نك احکامنی تعطیل ایتمکه قادر اوله‌مز .

حکمدار امور دولتك احوال عمومیه‌سنی هرسنه بر بیاننامهٔ مخصوص ایله ملت مجلسنه عرض ایدر .

معاهدات عقدی حکمداره عائددر .

حکمدار محافظهٔ دولته نظارت ایدر فقط ملت مجلسنك رضاسی اولمدقجه بر محاربه‌یه شروع ایده‌مز .

حکمدارك عفو مجازاته حق واردر . فقط بو حقك استعمالندن اول شورای دولتك قراری استحصال اولنور .

عفو عمومی اجراسی برقانون مخصوص صدورینه متوقفدر .

وکلا وسائر کیمسه‌لر محکمهٔ کبیرهٔ عدلیه‌جه محکوم اولور ایسه انلرك عفو مجازاتی ملت مجلسنك انضمام رأینه متوقفدر .

٣٤٢

احكامى مستعجل اولان قوانين ملت مجلسنده قبول اولنديغى تاريخدن اوچ كون وسائر قوانين برآى صكره نشر اولنور .

نشر قوانين ايچون معين اولان اشبو مدتلر ايچنده حكمدار برقانونك تكرار مذاكره ايدلمسنى اسباب موجبه‌يى حاوى بر بيانامه ايله مجلس ملتدن طلب ايده‌بيلور . مجلس دخى مذاكره ايدر . اوقانون قطعى الحكم اولور و مجلس طرفندن حكمداره كوندريلور بو حالده اوقانون قوانين مستعجله‌يه مخصوص اولان مهلت ايچنده نشر ايديلور .

قانون بالاده بيان اولنان مدتلر ايچنده نشر اولنميه‌جق اولور ايسه ملت مجلسى رئيسى طرفندن امر نشره ابتدار اولنور .

دول اجنبيه سفراسى حكمدار نزدينه مأموردرلر .

مراسم مليه‌يه حكمدار رياست ايدر .

حكمدار وكلايى نصب و عزل ايدر . فقط سفرانك و عساكر بريه و بحريه و باش قوماندانلرينك و واليلرك و پاى تخت عساكر ملكيه‌سى باش قوماندانك و مدعى عموميلرك ونظاماً برنجى درجه‌ده و سائر بيوجك صنفده بولنان مأمورينك عزلى مجلس وكلا ايله مذاكره‌يه متوقفدر .

حكومتك ايكنجى درجه‌ده بولنان مأمورلرى شرائط نظاميه‌سى دائره‌سنده اوله‌رق عائد اولديغى دائره ناظرينك

٣٤٣

عرضى اوزرينه حكمدار طرفندن نصب وعزل اولنور .

اهالى طرفندن انتخاب اولنمش قوه اجرائيه مأمورلرينى اوچ آى مدتى تجاوز ايتامك اوزره خدمتلرندن تعطيل ايلمكه حكمدارك صلاحيتى واردر . فقط انلرى بتون بتون عزل ايتمكه شوراى دولتك رأيى منضم اولمدقجه مقتدر اولمز .

بويله عزل ايدلمش مأمورلرك يرينه اوماًمور يتلره نقدر مدت انتخاب اولنه‌ميه‌جقلرى قانون مخصوص ايله معيندر و بو صورتله انتخابدن محروميت مطلقا محكوم اولمغه توقف ايدر .

وكلانك عددى و وظيفه‌لرى ملت مجلسى طرفندن تعيين قلنور .

حكمدار طرفندن صادر اولان امرنامه‌لرك وكلا نصب وعزلنه دائر اولنلرندن ماعداسى وكلادن برينك دخى امضاسنى جامع اوله‌جقدر .

وكلا و مأمورين كندى وظيفه‌لرينه عائد اولان خصوصاتجه حكومت واداره‌نك كافه اعمالندن مسؤلدرلر .

ملت مجلسنك فسخنه ويا تعطيل مذاكراتنه ويا خود دوام مأموريتنجه ممانعته دائر تشبثات وقوعبولور ايسه قانون اساسى اخلال اولنمش عد اولنور و بو اخلال عمومه حق ادعايى موجب اولور .

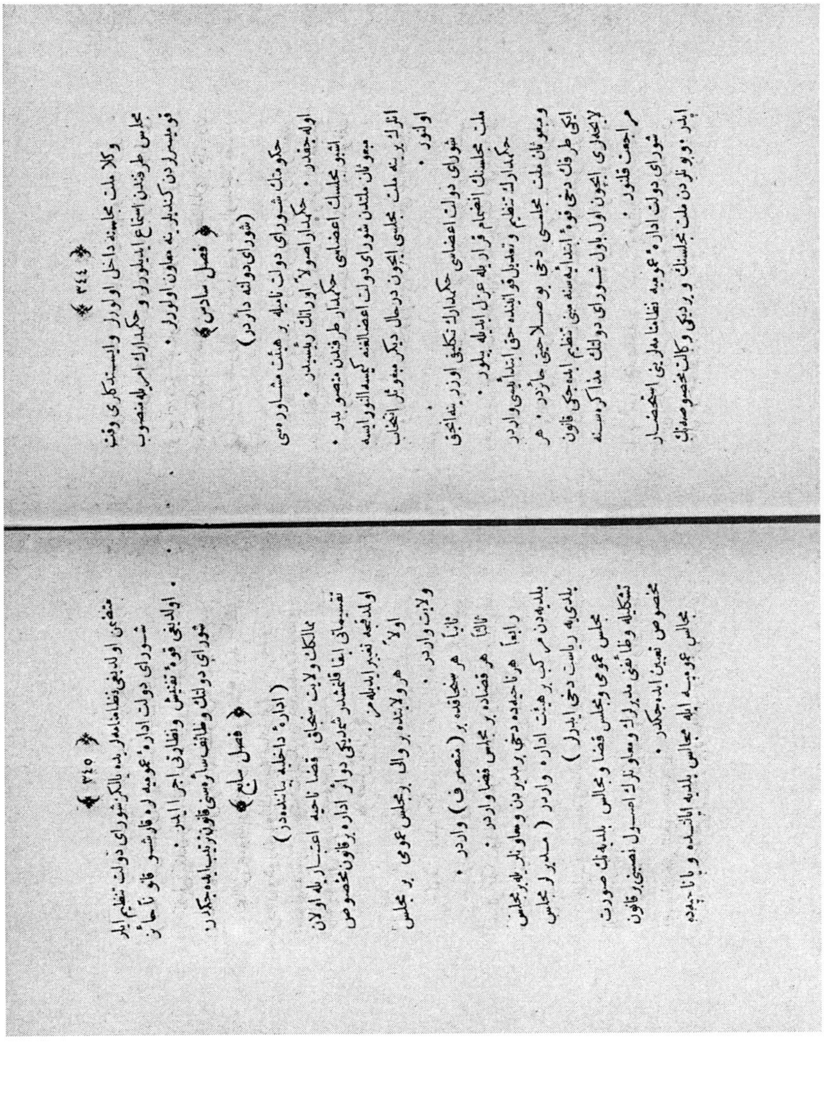

٣٤٤

وكلا ملت مجلسنه داخل اولورلر وايستدكلري وقت
مجلس طرفندن استماع ايديلورلر وحكمدارك امريله منصوب
قوميسرلردن كنديلرينه معاون اولورلر .

فصل سادس

(شوراى دولته دائردر)

حكومتك شوراى دولت ناميله بر هيئت مشاورەسى
اولەجقدر . حكمدار اصولاً اورانك رئيسيدر .
اشبو مجلسك اعضاسى حكمدار طرفندن منصوبدر .
مبعوثان ملتدن شوراى دولت اعضالغنه كيمسه النورايسه
انلرك يرينه ملت مجلسى ايچون درحال ديگر مبعوثلر انتخاب
اولنور .
شوراى دولت اعضاسى حكمدارك تكليفى اوزرينه انجق
ملت مجلسنك انضمام قراريله عزل ايديله بيلور .
حكمدارك تنظيم وتعديل قوانينده حق ابتدائيسى واردر
ومبعوثان ملت مجلسى دخى بو صلاحيتى حائزدر . هر
ايكى طرفك دخى قوۀ ابتدائيەسنه مبنى تنظيم ايدەجكى قانون
لايحەلرى ايچون اول باول شوراى دولتك مذاكرەسنه
مراجعت قلنور .
شوراى دولت ادارۀ عموميه نظامنامەلرينى استحضار
ايدر وبونلردن ملت مجلسنك ويرديكى وكالت مخصوصەنك

٣٤٥

متضمن اولديغى نظامنامەلر بده يالكز شوراى دولت تنظيم ايلر
شوراى دولت ادارۀ عموميه لره قارشو قانوناً حائز
اولديغى قوۀ تفتيش ونظارتى اجرا ايدر .
شوراى دولتك وظائف سائرەسنى قانون ترتيب ايدەجكدر .

فصل سابع

(ادارۀ داخليه بيانندەدر)

ممالكك ولايت سنجاق قضا ناحيه اعتباريله اولان
تقسيماتى ابقا قلنمشدر شمديكى دوائر اداره برقانون مخصوص
اولمدقجه تغيير ايديلەمز .
اولاً هر ولايتده بر والى بر مجلس عمومى بر مجلس
ولايت واردر .
ثانياً هر سنجاقده بر (متصرف) واردر .
ثالثاً هر قضاده بر مجلس قضا واردر .
رابعاً هر ناحيەده دخى بر مديردن ومعاونلريله بر مجلس
بلديەدن مركب بر هيئت اداره واردر (مديرلر مجلس
بلديەيه رياست دخى ايدرلر)
مجلس عمومى ومجلس قضا ومجالس بلديەنك صورت
تشكيله وظائفى مديرلرك ومعاونلرك اصول نصبينى برقانون
مخصوص تعيين ايدەجكدر .
مجالس عموميه ايله مجالس بلديه ايالتنده و [illegible]

متمكن اهالينك طوغريدن طوغري‌يه رأيلريله انتخاب اولنور هر قضا مجلس عمومي‌يه بر اعضا انتخاب ايدر .

يكرمي بيكدن زياده نفوسي شامل اولان شهرلرده جريان ايده‌جك قاعدهٔ انتخابي برقانون مخصوص تعيين ايده‌جكدر .

مجالس عموميه و مجالس قضا ومجالس بلديه حكمدار طرفندن وشوراي دولتك رأيله صادر اولان امرنامه‌اوزرينه فسخ اولنه‌بيلور . بو مجلسلرك يكيدن انتخابنه‌مدتده شروع اولنه‌بيله‌جكي قانون مخصوص ايله معيندر .

فصل ثامن

(قوهٔ عدليه بيانده‌در)

حكومت عدليه حكمدار نامنه اوله‌رق اجرا قلنور .

مذاكرات صورت علنيه‌ده جاريدر . يالكز علنيتي آسايش مملكت واخلاق عموميه‌يه مضر اوله‌بيله‌جك مذاكرات صورت خفيه‌ده اجرا اولنور و بونيده محكمه بر حكم ايله بيان ايدر .

جنايته دائر خصوصاتده عدول اصولي مرعي الاجرا اوله‌جقدر .

پولتيقه جنحه‌لرينك ومطبوعات واسطه‌سيله وقوعبولان تهمتلرك حق تدقيقي عدوله عائدر .

مطبوعاتجه فعلي وجنحه ايچون طلب اولنه‌جق تضمينات

ماده‌لريني تسويه ايدر .

صلح حاكملري وانلرك ملازملري ومحاكم ابتدائيهٔ استينافيه حاكملري ومحكمهٔ تميز وديوان محاسبات اعضالري ملازمت ترتيبي وقوانين اداره‌نك كوستره‌جكي شرائط موجبنجه حكمدار طرفندن نصب اولنور .

مدعئ عموميلري دخي حكمدار نصب ايدر .

محاكم ابتدائيه واستينافيه حاكملري ومحكمهٔ تميز وديوان محاسبات اعضالري قيد حيات ايله نصب اولنورلر وقانوناً عليهلرنده برحكم ترتب ايتمينجه عزل و ياخود بيلرندن موقتاً مهجور ايديله‌مزلر وقوانينك تصريح ايلديكي شكل وشروطك غيري صورتله تقاعدلكلري دخي اجرا اولنه‌مز .

ديوان حربلر وعساكر بريه و بحريه‌نك تفتيش ومعاينه مجلسلري بحريه وتجارت محكمه‌لري و حكمسلري وسائر محاكم مخصوصه اخر برقانون ايله تغيير ايديلنجه‌يه قدر شمديكي شكل وهيئت وظيفه‌لريني محافظه ايدرلر .

مأمورين اداره ايله محاكم بيننده ظهور ايدن وظائف نزاعلري محكمهٔ تميز وشوراي دولت اعضالرندن مركب بر محكمهٔ مخصوصه معرفتيله رؤيت اولنور وبو محكمهٔ مخصوصه عائد اولدقلري محكمهٔ تميز وشوراي دولت هيئتلري طرفندن متساوي العدد اوله‌رق اوچ سنه‌ده بركره تعيين قلنور .

بو محكمه‌يه عدليه ناظري رياست ايدر .

﴾ ٣٤٨ ﴿

دیوان محاسباتك قرارلری علیهنده عدم صلاحیت
و یاسوء استعمالات قوهٔ حکومت دعوالری منازعات محکمه‌سنه
حواله قلنور .

وکلا علیهنده ملت مجلسی طرفندن اتهام وقوعبولور
ایسه دعوا بر محکمهٔ کبیرهٔ عدلیه‌یه حواله ایله اوراده بلا
استیناف و بلا تمییز حکم اولنور .

دولتك امنیت داخلیه وخارجیه‌سی علیهنده بر جنایت
وسوء قصد وفساد تهمتاریله متهم اوله‌جق کیمسه‌لرك محاکه‌لری
دخی ملت مجلسی طرفندن حواله اولنه‌دیغی تقدیرده ذکر
اولنان محکمهٔ کبیره‌ده رؤیت اولنور .

یالکز وقوع حال التمش سکزنجی ماده حکمنه موافق
اولور ایسه اوحالده محکمهٔ مزبوره ملت مجلسنك امریله
وتعیین ایده‌جکی شهرده اجتماع ایدر .

محکمهٔ کبیره بش حاکمدن واوتوز التی عدولدن مرکبدر .
هر سنه تشرین ثانی آینك نصف اولنده محکمهٔ تمییز
کندی اعضاسی میانندن قرعهٔ خفیه واکثریت مطلقه ایله
محکمه‌یه بش حاکم وایکیسی ملازم اوله‌رق یدی کشی نصب
ایدر . اشبو بش حاکم حین اجتماعلرنده رئیسلرینی ایچلرندن
انتخاب ایدرلر .

مدعی عمومی وظیفه‌سنی ایدن حاکلر حکمدار طرفندن
تعیین اولنور .

﴾ ٣٤٩ ﴿

وکلانك محاکمه‌سی لازم کلدکده مذکور حاکملری ملت
مجلسی تعیین ایدر .

اوتوز التیسی عدول ودردی ملازم اولمق اوزره قرق
کشیدن مرکب ارکان عدولیه ایالات مجالس عمومیه‌سی
اعضاسی میانندن آلنور . مبعوثان ملت عدول هیئتنه
داخل اوله‌مز .

محاکه ایچون تصحیح اولنان کونده حاضر بولنه‌جق عدولر
التمشدن نقصان ایسه محکمهٔ کبیره رئیسی لاجل الاتمام محکمه‌نك
بولندیغی ایالتك مجالس عمومیه اعضاسندن دخی قرعه ایله
عدولر الوب عدد مذکوری اکمال اولنور .

عذر معتبر حاصل ایده‌میان عدولدن بیك فرانقدن اون
بیك فرانقه قدر جزای نقدی اخذیله و بش سنه مدتدن
زیاده اولمق اوزره حقوق سیاسیه دن محرومیتله مجازات
اولنورلر .

متهم ومدعی عمومی مواد عادیه‌ده اولدیغی وجهله رد
صلاحیت حقنی اجرا ایدرلر . متهمك قباحتلی اولدیغنه
دائر عدول طرفندن آرانك ایکی ثلثی درجه‌سنده اکثریتی
حاوی اولدیغی حالده صحیح عد اولنه‌مز .

وکلانك مسؤل اولدیغی کافهٔ احوالده ملت مجلسی متهم
اولان ناظری ایجابنه کوره کرك محکمهٔ کبیرهٔ عدلیه‌یه وکرك
محاکم عادیه‌دن برینه حواله ایده بیلور .

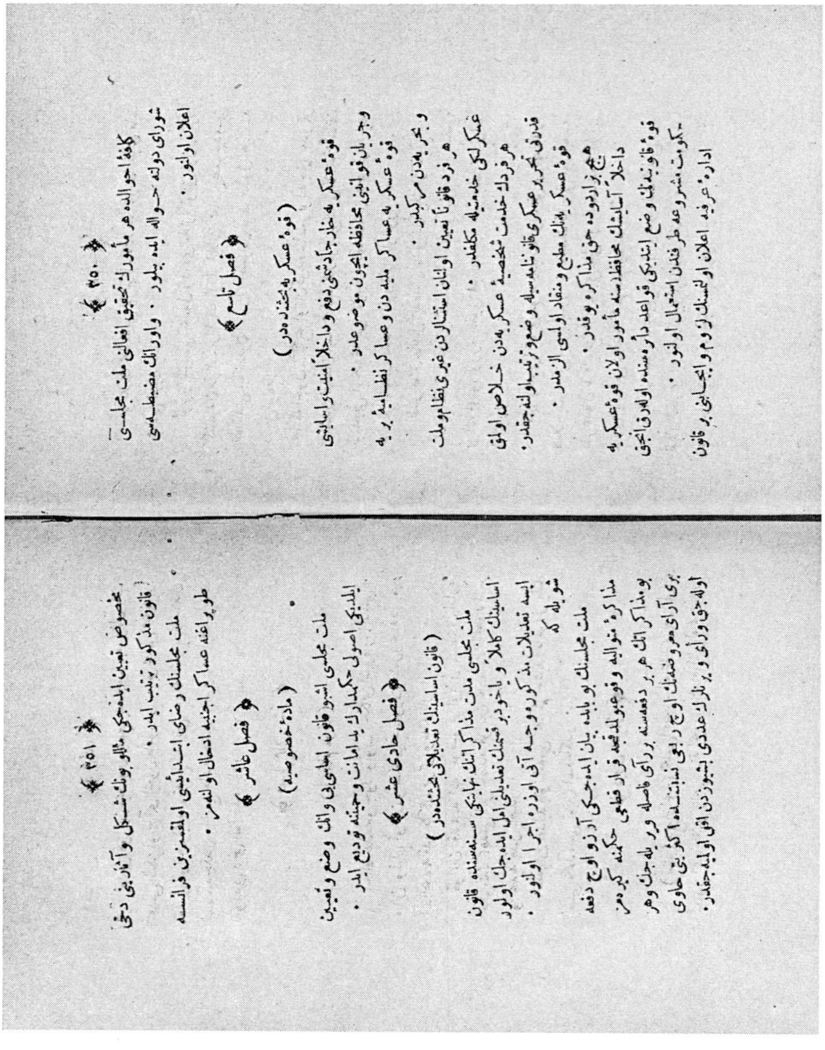

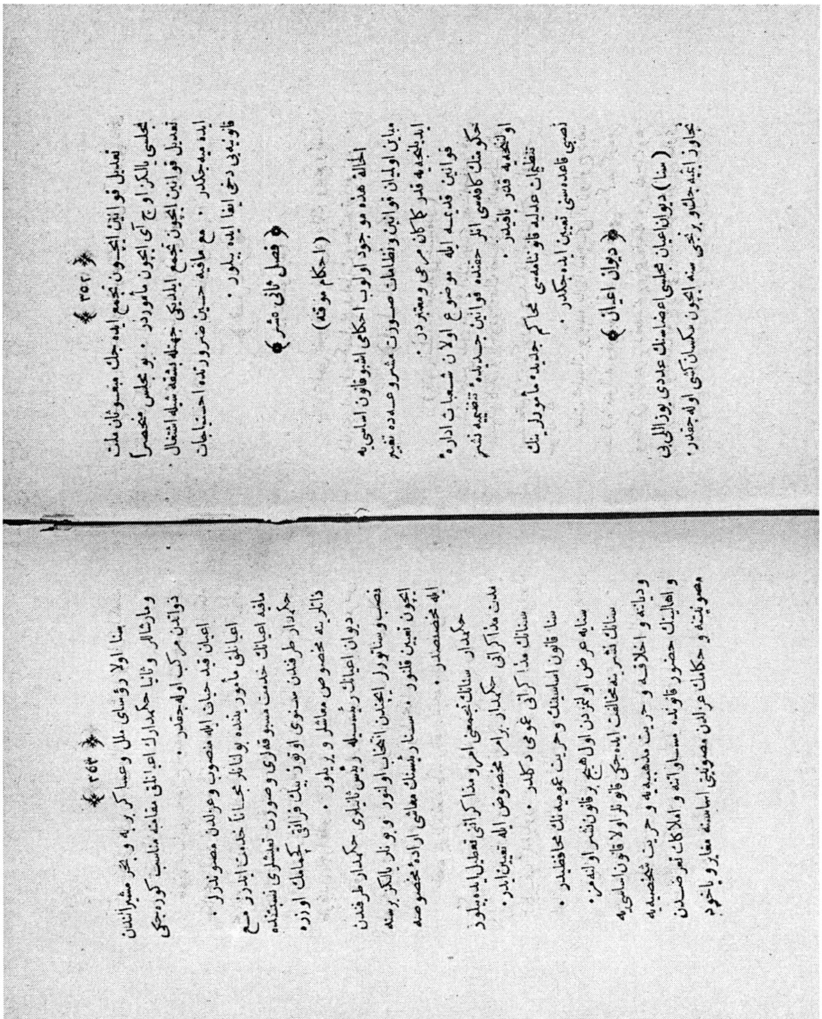

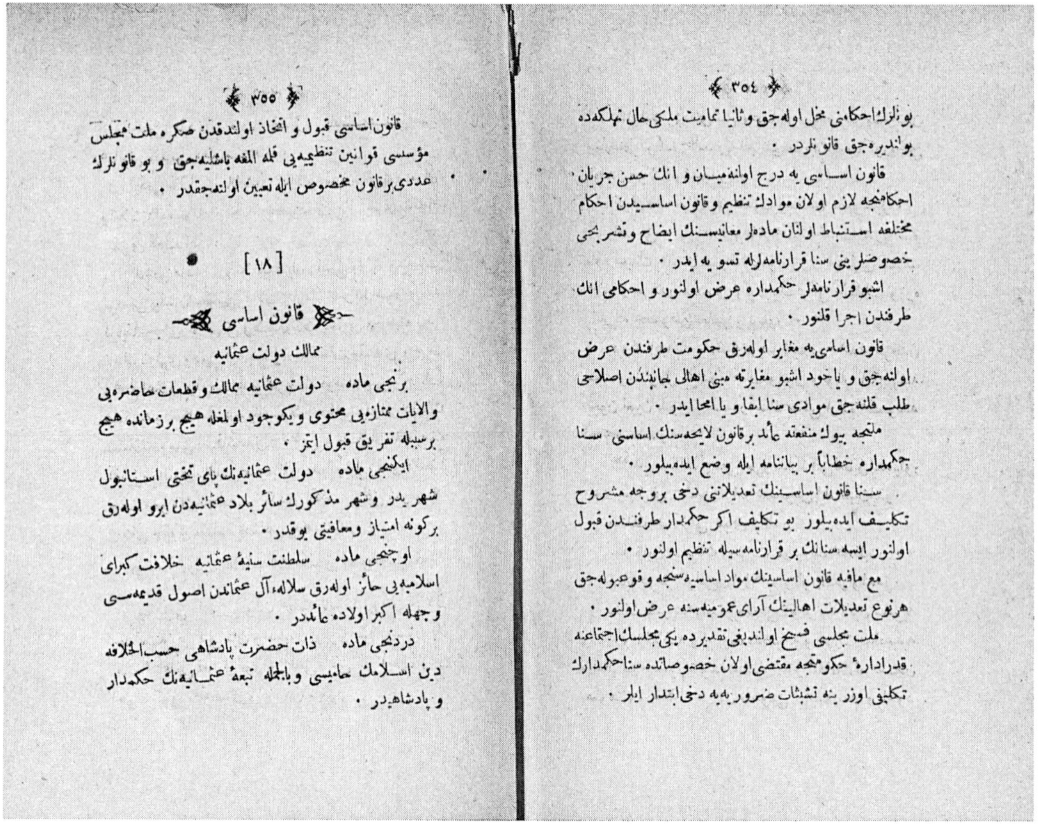

٣٥٤

بونلرك احكامنی مخل اوله جق و ثانیا تمامیت ملکی حال تهلکه ده بولندیره جق قانونلردر .

قانون اساسی یه درج اولنه میان و انك حسن جریان احكامنجه لازم اولان موادك تنظیم و قانون اساسیدن احكام مختلفه استنباط اولنان ماده لر معانیسنك ایضاح و تشریحی خصوصلرینی سنا قرارنامه لرله تسویه ایدر .

اشبو قرارنامه لر حكمداره عرض اولنور و احكامی انك طرفندن اجرا قلنور .

قانون اساسی یه مغایر اوله رق حكومت طرفندن عرض اولنه جق و یاخود اشبو مغایرته مبنی اهالی جانبندن اصلاحی طلب قلنه جق موادی سنا ابقا و یا امحا ایدر .

ملتجه بیوك منفعته عائد بر قانون لایحه سنك اساسنی سنا حكمداره خطاباً بر بیاننامه ایله وضع ایده بیلور .

سنا قانون اساسینك تعدیلاتنی دخی بروجه مشروح تكلیف ایده بیلور بو تكلیف اگر حكمدار طرفندن قبول اولنور ایسه سنانك بر قرارنامه سیله تنظیم اولنور .

مع مافیه قانون اساسینك مواد اساسیه سنجه وقوعبوله جق هرنوع تعدیلات اهالینك آرای عمومیه سنه عرض اولنور .

ملت مجلسی فسخ اولندیغی تقدیرده یكی مجلسك اجتماعنه قدر اداره حكومتجه مقتضی اولان خصوصاتده سنا حكمدارك تكلیفی اوزرینه تشبثات ضروریه یه دخی ابتدار ایلر .

٣٥٥

قانون اساسی قبول و اتخاذ اولندقدن صكره ملت مجلس مؤسسی قوانین تنظیمیه یی قلمه المغه باشلیه جق و بو قانونلرك عددی بر قانون مخصوص ایله تعیین اولنه جقدر .

[١٨]

قانون اساسی

ممالك دولت عثمانیه

برنجی ماده دولت عثمانیه ممالك و قطعات حاضره یی والایات ممتازه یی محتوی و یكوجود اولمغله هیچ بر زمانده هیچ بر سببله تفریق قبول ایتمز .

ایكنجی ماده دولت عثمانیه نك پای تختی استانبول شهریدر و شهر مذكورك سائر بلاد عثمانیه دن ایرو اوله رق بر گونه امتیاز و معافیتی یوقدر .

اوچنجی ماده سلطنت سنیه عثمانیه خلافت كبرای اسلامیه یی حائز اوله رق سلاله آل عثماندن اصول قدیمه سی وجهله اكبر اولاده عائددر .

دردنجی ماده ذات حضرت پادشاهی حسب الخلافه دین اسلامك حامیسی و بالجمله تبعه عثمانیه نك حكمدار و پادشاهیدر .

COMPARATIVE TABLE OF THE DRAFT CONSTITUTIONS AND THE OTTOMAN CONSTITUTION OF 1876 FROM THE STANDPOINT OF THE FORMULATION OR INSERTION OF CERTAIN PROVISIONS

Insertion of a Preamble in the Draft Constitution

Midhad Pasha's draft.	No preamble.
Said Pasha's draft.	No preamble.
Draft submitted to [Safved Pasha]*; [very probably the Drafting Commission's work]; draft of 130 articles.	No preamble.
The preceding draft corrected by [Safved Pasha].	No preamble.
A draft constitution of 114 articles (probably the Council of Ministers' work); noted by the archival catalogue as the draft constitution; put together with a bylaw related to the duties of the Council of Ministers and supposed to contain the views of [Namık Kemal, Said and Mahmud Pashas and others] on the bylaw.	Preamble resembling the decree model.
Additions/corrections on the draft constitution of 114 articles.	The preamble remains as it is.
Draft with Namık Kemal's marginal notes and reactions to some provisions; a very similar draft to the previous one of 113 articles; probably the work of the Council of Ministers.	Namık Kemal reacts to the preamble on the grounds that the latter transforms the Ottoman Constitution into a favour granted by the Porte and reduces its value before Europe.
The 119-article draft preceding the 1876 Constitution.	No preamble.
The Ottoman Constitution of 1876.	No preamble.

* The names in brackets indicate that their authorship regarding the constitutional drafts is in question.

Reference to Tanzimat and/or to its Legal Guarantees

Midhad Pasha's draft.	No reference to Tanzimat guarantees – provisions protecting real and personal property from lawless expropriation except for public utility determined by law and in exchange of its value, and protecting everyone's domicile against raids except by law. Provisions considering as public duty the procuration of the imperial allowance for the preservation of the glory of the sultanate, but necessitating the decision of the Chamber of Deputies in case of revision or increase of this allowance.
Said Pasha's draft.	No mention of Tanzimat guarantees but protecting real property, allowing expropriation for legitimate need and public interest by the state in exchange for its value, prohibiting the re-establishment of the sequestration law, defending the domicile from aggression and prohibiting entry into somebody's domicile except for a legal reason.
Draft submitted to [Safved Pasha]; [very probably the Drafting Commission's work]; draft of 130 articles.	No reference to Tanzimat but placing the honour and dignity of Ottoman subjects under the protection of the government and of common guarantee; prohibiting expropriation of real and personal property except for public utility and in exchange for its material value, and the authorities' entry by force into anybody's domicile except in cases determined by law; considering sequestration a crime and prohibiting confiscation of property in all cases.
The preceding draft corrected by [Safved Pasha].	Almost the same articles with additional corrections emphasising the exchange of value by law and protecting the domicile from aggression and prohibiting confiscation of property except by law.
A draft constitution of 114 articles (probably the Council of Ministers' work); noted by the archival catalogue as the draft constitution; put together with a bylaw related to the duties of the Council of Ministers and supposed to contain the views of [Namık Kemal, Said and Mahmud Pashas and others] on the bylaw.	Inclusion of Tanzimat guarantees on life, property and honour. Provisions on property adopted with [Safved Pasha's] corrections but divided into two succeeding articles and changing few words, not affecting the content.

Additions/corrections on the draft constitution of 114 articles.	No correction of Tanzimat guarantees but the addition of a clause putting the property rights and allowance of the Ottoman imperial family under public guarantee. No correction of other property rights.
Draft with Namık Kemal's marginal notes and reactions to some provisions; a very similar draft to the previous one of 113 articles; probably the work of the Council of Ministers.	Namık Kemal reacts to the mention of the Tanzimat in the draft on the grounds that the only reference to the Imperial Rescript annihilates the decrees promulgated thereafter. No correction on property rights.
The 119-article draft preceding the 1876 Constitution.	Reference to Tanzimat and to its guarantees as part of the general rights of Ottoman subjects but then scored out; placing in a separate article the honour and dignity of Ottoman subjects under the protection of the Ottoman government and of common cooperation. The word "dignity" was scored out (or the entire article was eliminated since the clause finally disappeared). The article putting the property and allowance of the Ottoman imperial family under public guarantee reappears. Provisions on property, adopting the same principles as mentioned in the 114-article draft and previously drafted by [Safved Pasha].
The Ottoman Constitution of 1876.	No mention of Tanzimat guarantees on honour and dignity. Adoption of the article on property rights, as previously drafted. Adoption of the article guaranteeing the property rights of the Ottoman imperial family.

Definition of the Ottoman State

Midhad Pasha's draft.	The Ottoman state defined in terms of territorial integrity and its regime essentially based on the shari'a.
Said Pasha's draft.	No definition of the state.
Draft submitted to [Safved Pasha]; [very probably the Drafting Commission's work]; draft of 130 articles.	Almost the same definition of the state with less emphasis on the invariability of its territorial borders and additionally mentioning Istanbul as the capital of the state; but without granting any privileged position to it in comparison with other provinces.

The preceding draft corrected by [Safved Pasha].	No correction by [Safved Pasha] on the article.
A draft constitution of 114 articles (probably the Council of Ministers' work); noted by the archival catalogue as the draft constitution; put together with a bylaw related to the duties of the Council of Ministers and supposed to contain the views of [Namık Kemal, Said and Mahmud Pashas and others] on the bylaw.	Removal of the definition of the state.
Additions/corrections on the draft constitution of 114 art.	
Draft with Namık Kemal's marginal notes and reactions to some provisions; a very similar draft to the previous one of 113 articles; probably the work of the Council of Ministers.	At the end of the draft, Namık Kemal reacts to the removal of the articles defining the Ottoman state.
The 119-article draft preceding the 1876 Constitution.	Definition of the Ottoman state as drafted in the text submitted to [Safved Pasha], but including the provision that Ottoman legislation is based on the shari'a in its first article, and then scoring out the provision.
The Ottoman Constitution of 1876.	Definition of the Ottoman state as drafted in the text submitted to [Safved], but no mention of the shari'a in the articles regarding the Ottoman state.

Subjecthood

Midhad Pasha's draft.	All the subjects of the empire are called Ottomans without exception; the quality of being Ottoman is determined by law.
Said Pasha's draft.	Subjection is to the person of the sultan; it cannot be transferred to someone else or cancelled.
Draft submitted to [Safved Pasha]; [very probably the Drafting Commission's work]; draft of 130 articles.	All the subjects of the empire are called Ottomans without exception; the quality of being Ottoman is determined by law; adds that all subjects are called Ottomans without exception, no matter what religion they practise; united in one article.
The preceding draft corrected by [Safved Pasha].	No correction by [Safved] but the article strangely scored out.

A draft constitution of 114 articles (probably the Council of Ministers' work); noted by the archival catalogue as the draft constitution put together with a bylaw…	Adoption of the article as formulated in [Safved's] draft.
Additions/corrections on the draft constitution of 114 art.	
Draft with Namık Kemal's marginal notes and reactions to some provisions; a very similar draft to the previous one…	No correction by Namık Kemal.
The 119-article draft preceding the 1876 Constitution.	Adoption of the article as formulated in [Safved's] draft.
The Ottoman Constitution of 1876.	Adoption of the article as formulated in [Safved's] draft.

The Sultanate

Midhad Pasha's draft.	The sultanate mentioned in a different title with the Ottoman dynasty than the section regarding the Ottoman state; associated with the caliphate of Islam and united in the person of the sultan, the caliph and protector of Islam; belonging to the oldest sound-minded prince of the Ottoman dynasty; prerogatives of the sultan defined as the first commander of the army and navy, appointment/dismissal of ministers, signing of treaties with foreign powers, declaration of war and peace, practice of military operations and administrative measures, amnesty, convocation/dissolution of the Chamber of Deputies; his person immune and sacred.
Said Pasha's draft.	No direct mention of the sultanate. Said Pasha mentions the sultan as the sovereign. The sovereign supervises the preservation of the state but he cannot start war without the consent of the *Millet* Assembly; he has the right to remit penalties but after the decision of the Council of State; general amnesty is subject to a special law; he nominates and revokes the ministers; he signs treaties.
Draft submitted to [Safved Pasha]; [very probably the Drafting Commission's work]; draft of 130 articles.	The sultanate mentioned in a different title than the Ottoman state, associated with the caliphate of Islam and united in the person of the sultan, the caliph and

	protector of Islam and also the sultan and sovereign of all Ottoman subjects; the sultanate belonging in accordance with rules established *ab antiquo* to the eldest prince of the Ottoman dynasty. Prerogatives of the sultan additionally to those defined in Midhad's draft: he confers grades and functions; gives the insignia of his orders; invests the chiefs of the privileged provinces; mints money; his name is pronounced in the mosques during public prayers; he follows the execution of the dispositions of the shariʿa and the laws; remits or commutes the penal laws; convokes or prorogues the General Assembly; and if necessary, dissolves the Chamber of Deputies on condition of proceeding to re-elections.
The preceding draft corrected by [Safved Pasha].	No correction by [Safved] on the article.
A draft constitution of 114 articles (probably the Council of Ministers' work); noted by the archival catalogue as the draft constitution; put together with a bylaw related to the duties of the Council of Ministers and supposed to contain the views of [Namık Kemal, Said and Mahmud Pashas and others] on the bylaw.	Removal of articles regarding the sultanate.
Additions/corrections on the draft constitution of 114 art.	
Draft with Namık Kemal's marginal notes and reactions to some provisions; a very similar draft to the previous one of 113 articles; probably the work of the Council of Ministers.	At the end of the draft, Namık Kemal reacts to the removal of articles regarding the sultanate on the grounds that the prerogatives of the sultan would not have any legal basis and would endanger the sultanate.
The 119-article draft preceding the 1876 Constitution.	Re-adoption of the article on the sultanate, almost as drafted in the text submitted to [Safved's] attention but adding that the sultan is immune and his person sacred. A separate title on the person of the sultan was drafted after the first two articles but then scored out.
The Ottoman Constitution of 1876.	Re-adoption of the article on the sultanate, almost as drafted in the text submitted to [Safved's] attention without neglecting the provision regarding the immunity of the sultan and the sacred character of his person. Separate title introducing his person and the sultanate removed.

Individual Liberty

Midhad Pasha's draft.	All Ottomans enjoy individual liberty no matter what religion they practise and what community they belong to. Nobody can under any pretence suffer imprisonment or exile except in cases determined by law.
Said Pasha's draft.	No mention of individual liberty.
Draft submitted to [Safved Pasha]; [very probably the Drafting Commission's work]; draft of 130 articles.	All Ottomans enjoy individual liberty on condition of not attacking the liberty of others and not violating the limits determined by the shari'a and the laws. Moreover, individual liberty is inviolable. Nobody can under any pretence suffer any penalty, imprisonment or exile except in the cases determined by law (provisions expressed in two subsequent articles).
The preceding draft corrected by [Safved Pasha].	"Limits of law and of the shari'a" removed; Ottomans enjoy liberty on condition of not attacking the liberty of others. Mention of "exile and imprisonment" removed; individual liberty is inviolable and nobody can be punished except for reasons determined by law.
A draft constitution of 114 articles (probably the Council of Ministers' work); noted by the archival catalogue as the draft constitution; put together with a bylaw related to the duties of the Council of Ministers and supposed to contain the views of [Namık Kemal, Said and Mahmud Pashas and others] on the bylaw.	Adoption of the article as formulated in [Safved's] draft after his corrections.
Additions/corrections on the draft constitution of 114 art.	
Draft with Namık Kemal's marginal notes and reactions to some provisions; a very similar draft to the previous one of 113 articles; probably the work of the Council of Ministers.	Adoption of the previous article. No correction by Namık Kemal.
The 119-article draft preceding the 1876 Constitution.	Adoption of the article as formulated in [Safved's] draft after his corrections. A few corrections reflect a desire to return to the initial form of the article before [Safved's] corrections but they are scored out in the final instance.
The Ottoman Constitution of 1876.	Adoption of the article as formulated in [Safved's] draft after his corrections.

Taxation

Midhad Pasha's draft.	All Ottomans are equal in terms of taxation. The Chamber of Deputies, in cooperation with the government, decides on taxation for public expenses and taxes are collected equally from people in accordance with their capabilities.
Said Pasha's draft.	Taxation is necessary for public interests and taxes are collected from people in accordance with their capabilities and fortune and only by law.
Draft submitted to [Safved Pasha]; [very probably the Drafting Commission's work]; draft of 130 articles.	Taxes are collected from people according to their capabilities and in equal proportions in accordance with new regulations. The General Assembly, in cooperation with the government, deliberates on taxation for public expenses.
The preceding draft corrected by [Safved Pasha].	Principle of equality, cooperation between the General Assembly and the government removed. Ottoman subjects pay the tax in accordance with special regulations, proportionally, according to everyone's capabilities.
A draft constitution of 114 articles (probably the Council of Ministers' work); noted by the archival catalogue as the draft constitution; put together with a bylaw related to the duties of the Council of Ministers and supposed to contain the views of [Namık Kemal, Said and Mahmud Pashas and others] on the bylaw.	Ottoman subjects pay the tax in accordance with special regulations but with the mention that taxes would be proportional to people's capabilities.
Additions/corrections on the draft constitution of 114 art.	
Draft with Namık Kemal's marginal notes and reactions to some provisions; a very similar draft to the previous one of 113 articles; probably the work of the Council of Ministers.	Adoption of the previous article. No correction by Namık Kemal.
The 119-article draft preceding the 1876 Constitution.	Adoption of the previous article. However, there was an initiative to again insert the mention that "the General Assembly in cooperation with the government deliberates on tax regulations" but the mention was scored out.
The Ottoman Constitution of 1876.	Taxes are collected from everyone in accordance with his financial capabilities and with special regulations.

Religious Freedom

Midhad Pasha's draft.	Different religions enjoy the protection of the state. Everyone is free to practise his religion on condition of not abusing this freedom or violating security and good morals.
Said Pasha's draft.	Everyone is free in the exercise of his own form of worship and the state grants equal protection for the free practice of religious services.
Draft submitted to [Safved Pasha]; [very probably the Drafting Commission's work]; draft of 130 articles.	The religion of the state is Islam. While maintaining this principle, the state guarantees the free practice of other religions recognised in the empire on condition of respecting public security and good morals.
The preceding draft corrected by [Safved Pasha].	[Safved] scored out the sentences regarding the consideration of Islam as the state religion and the maintenance of this principle, and kept only the state guarantee on the free practice of religions recognised in the Ottoman Empire on condition of respecting public security and good morals.
A draft constitution of 114 articles (probably the Council of Ministers' work); noted by the archival catalogue as the draft constitution; put together with a bylaw related to the duties of the Council of Ministers and supposed to contain the views of [Namık Kemal, Said and Mahmud Pashas and others] on the bylaw.	First the article was formulated in [Safved's] way.
Additions/corrections on the draft constitution of 114 art.	[Safved's] considerations were set aside and the article was returned to its previous form in which a state religion was accepted.
Draft with Namık Kemal's marginal notes and reactions to some provisions; a very similar draft to the previous one of 113 articles; probably the work of the Council of Ministers.	Namık Kemal reacted to the article on the grounds that the word "protection" was dangerous and was inconvenient from both the standpoint of the shari'a and rationality.
The 119-article draft preceding the 1876 Constitution.	The provision that the legislation of the Ottoman state is based on the dispositions of the shari'a was added as the first article of the Constitution but then scored out; a similar provision exists in Midhad's draft,

	which stipulates that the regime of the Ottoman state is based on the dispositions of the shariʻa. Namık Kemal's comments were disregarded and the article was accepted in its previous form, naming a state religion. A marginal note also adds that the Ottoman Constitution guarantees the exercise of privileges granted to various communities as formerly.
The Ottoman Constitution of 1876.	The previous article entirely accepted with the addition that the Ottoman Constitution guaranteed the exercise of privileges granted to various communities as formerly.

Freedom of Press

Midhad Pasha's draft.	The press is free. Its rights and duties are determined by a special law.
Said Pasha's draft.	People may express opinion through the press. The latter cannot be subject to the control of the government before going to print.
Draft submitted to [Safved Pasha]; [very probably the Drafting Commission's work]; draft of 130 articles.	The article is again brought to its previous form as drafted by Midhad.
The preceding draft corrected by [Safved Pasha].	[Safved] puts forth the idea of limiting the press by law.
A draft constitution of 114 articles (probably the Council of Ministers' work); noted by the archival catalogue as the draft constitution; put together with a bylaw related to the duties of the Council of Ministers and supposed to contain the views of [Namık Kemal, Said and Mahmud Pashas and others] on the bylaw.	The freedom of the press is first stipulated using [Safved's] approximate formulation.
Additions/corrections on the draft constitution of 114 art.	The press becomes free within limits determined by law.
Draft with Namık Kemal's marginal notes and reactions to some provisions; a very similar draft to the previous one of 113 articles; probably the work of the Council of Ministers.	No correction by Namık Kemal.
The 119-article draft preceding the 1876 Constitution.	The article is again brought to the form drafted by Midhad but then scored out, stating that the press is free within limits determined by law.
The Ottoman Constitution of 1876.	Preceding version adopted.

Freedom of Expression

Midhad Pasha's draft.	Everyone is free to express opinion in oral and written forms on condition of not violating security and good morals.
Said Pasha's draft.	Freedom of expression through the press on condition of not violating the freedom of others and public security.
Draft submitted to [Safved Pasha]; [very probably the Drafting Commission's work]; draft of 130 articles.	Not mentioned.
The preceding draft corrected by [Safved Pasha].	Not mentioned.
A draft constitution of 114 articles (probably the Council of Ministers' work); noted by the archival catalogue as the draft constitution; put together with a bylaw related to the duties of the Council of Ministers and supposed to contain the views of [Namık Kemal, Said and Mahmud Pashas and others] on the bylaw.	Not mentioned.
Additions/corrections on the draft constitution of 114 art.	Not mentioned.
Draft with Namık Kemal's marginal notes and reactions to some provisions; a very similar draft to the previous one of 113 articles; probably the work of the Council of Ministers.	Not mentioned.
The 119-article draft preceding the 1876 Constitution.	Not mentioned.
The Ottoman Constitution of 1876.	Not mentioned.

Authorisation to Found Commercial/Agricultural Companies

Midhad Pasha's draft.	Ottoman subjects have the right to found commercial, industrial or similar companies for the interest of the fatherland in accordance with special regulations, and would benefit from facilities offered by the government.
Said Pasha's draft.	Ottoman subjects have the right to found companies on condition of respecting the freedom of others and public security.
Draft submitted to [Safved Pasha]; [very probably the Drafting Commission's work]; draft of 130 articles.	Ottoman subjects have the right to found all kinds of companies for commerce, crafts (*sınaat*) and agriculture within the limits determined by law.

The preceding draft corrected by [Safved Pasha].	No correction by [Safved].
A draft constitution of 114 articles (probably the Council of Ministers' work); noted by the archival catalogue as the draft constitution; put together with a bylaw related to the duties of the Council of Ministers and supposed to contain the views of [Namık Kemal, Said and Mahmud Pashas and others] on the bylaw.	Adoption of the previous article but the word "*ziraat*" (agriculture) is replaced by "*felahat*" (also agriculture).
Additions/corrections on the draft constitution of 114 art.	
Draft with Namık Kemal's marginal notes and reactions to some provisions; a very similar draft to the previous one of 113 articles; probably the work of the Council of Ministers.	No correction by Namık Kemal.
The 119-article draft preceding the 1876 Constitution.	Adoption of the preceding article.
The Ottoman Constitution of 1876.	Adoption of the preceding article.

Authorisation to Found Associations

Midhad Pasha's draft.	Not mentioned.
Said Pasha's draft.	Ottomans have the authorisation to found associations on condition of not being armed or violating the liberty of others and public security.
Draft submitted to [Safved Pasha]; [very probably the Drafting Commission's work]; draft of 130 articles.	Not mentioned.
The preceding draft corrected by [Safved Pasha].	Not mentioned.
A draft constitution of 114 articles (probably the Council of Ministers' work); noted by the archival catalogue as the draft constitution; put together with a bylaw related to the duties of the Council of Ministers and supposed to contain the views of [Namık Kemal, Said and Mahmud Pashas and others] on the bylaw.	Not mentioned.
Additions/corrections on the draft constitution of 114 art.	Not mentioned.
Draft with Namık Kemal's marginal notes and reactions to some provisions; a very similar draft to the previous one of 113 articles; probably the work of the Council of Ministers.	Not mentioned.
The 119-article draft preceding the 1876 Constitution.	Not mentioned.
The Ottoman Constitution of 1876.	Not mentioned.

Authorisation to Petition

Midhad Pasha's draft.	Not mentioned.
Said Pasha's draft.	Said briefly discusses the authorisation to petition.
Draft submitted to [Safved Pasha]; [very probably the Drafting Commission's work]; draft of 130 articles.	One or several Ottoman subjects will have the authorisation to address petitions to a competent authority, as well as to the General Assembly, to complain of the conduct of functionaries or infractions of laws.
The preceding draft corrected by [Safved Pasha].	[Safved] reinforces the article by adding that Ottoman subjects may address their petitions as litigants, and changed the future tense of the article into the present tense in order to indicate that the authorisation to petition was not something new.
A draft constitution of 114 articles (probably the Council of Ministers' work); noted by the archival catalogue as the draft constitution; put together with a bylaw related to the duties of the Council of Ministers and supposed to contain the views of [Namık Kemal, Said and Mahmud Pashas and others] on the bylaw.	Preceding article adopted including [Safved's] corrections.
Additions/corrections on the draft constitution of 114 art.	
Draft with Namık Kemal's marginal notes and reactions to some provisions; a very similar draft to the previous one of 113 articles; probably the work of the Council of Ministers.	Namık Kemal reacts to the status of litigant.
The 119-article draft preceding the 1876 Constitution.	Namık Kemal's objections first considered. The article was first drafted without including the "status of litigant" but was then restored to the form it took after Safved's corrections.
The Ottoman Constitution of 1876.	Adoption of the preceding form of the article.

Equality

Midhad Pasha's draft.	All Ottomans are equal before the law and in the eyes of legislation no matter what religion they practise or community they belong to.
Said Pasha's draft.	Not mentioned.
Draft submitted to [Safved Pasha]; [very probably the Drafting Commission's work]; draft of 130 articles.	All Ottomans are equal before the law and in terms of rights and duties.
The preceding draft corrected by [Safved Pasha].	With [Safved's] additions, all Ottomans are equal before the law and in terms of rights and duties "outside sectarian affairs".

A draft constitution of 114 articles (probably the Council of Ministers' work); noted by the archival catalogue as the draft constitution; put together with a bylaw related to the duties of the Council of Ministers and supposed to contain the views of [Namık Kemal, Said and Mahmud Pashas and others] on the bylaw.	The article is almost the same with only a few changes in wording not affecting the general meaning; "sectarian affairs" become "condition of religion and sects". (Religion is more comprehensive).
Additions/corrections on the draft constitution of 114 art.	
Draft with Namık Kemal's marginal notes and reactions to some provisions; a very similar draft to the previous one of 113 articles; probably the work of the Council of Ministers.	No correction by Kemal.
The 119-article draft preceding the 1876 Constitution.	Ottomans are equal before the law and in terms of rights and duties outside conditions of religion and sects as previously accepted. The word "practice" was proposed instead of "condition".
The Ottoman Constitution of 1876.	Ottomans are equal before the law and in terms of rights and duties outside conditions of religion and sects as previously accepted. The word "practice" was not accepted.

Turkish as an Official Language and Other Languages

Midhad Pasha's draft.	Turkish as an official language. It is compulsory to know the official language to be recruited for public services.
Said Pasha's draft.	Not mentioned.
Draft submitted to [Safved Pasha]; [very probably the Drafting Commission's work]; draft of 130 articles.	Each of the various populations of the Ottoman Empire is authorised to learn and to teach the language native to them. The official language of the state being Turkish, it is compulsory to know this language in order to be recruited for public office.
The preceding draft corrected by [Safved Pasha].	[Safved] scored out the term "various" (various populations) and the phrase "the official language of the country is Turkish".
A draft constitution of 114 articles (probably the Council of Ministers' work); noted by the archival catalogue as the draft constitution; put together with a by law...	[Safved's] changes are accepted and the article changes into: Everyone of the Ottoman Empire is authorised to learn and to teach the language native to him but in order to be recruited for public service, it is compulsory to know Turkish, the official language of the state.

Additions/corrections on the draft constitution of 114 art.	
Draft with Namık Kemal's marginal notes and reactions to some provisions; a very similar draft to the previous one...	No correction by Namık Kemal.
The 119-article draft preceding the 1876 Constitution.	The new article scores out the provision: "everyone of the Ottoman Empire is authorised to learn and to teach the language native to him". Thus it remains: in order to be recruited for public service, it is compulsory to know Turkish, the official language of the country.
The Ottoman Constitution of 1876.	The preceding article is accepted, thus excluding the learning and teaching of languages native to the various populations.

Public Instruction

Midhad Pasha's draft.	Instruction is free. Everyone is free to give public or private courses of instruction on condition of conforming to the law. For the sake of regularisation and unification of the general education of Ottoman subjects, the administration of all schools is united, but this would not adversely affect the religious beliefs of various *millet*s.
Said Pasha's draft.	The freedom to instruct must conform to legislation in terms of good morals and is under the supervision of the state. This supervision comprises the matter of instruction and moral education.
Draft submitted to [Safved Pasha]; [very probably the Drafting Commission's work]; draft of 130 articles.	Instruction is free. Everyone is free to give public or private courses of instruction on condition of conforming to the law. The schools will be under state supervision for the regularisation and uniformisation of the education of Ottoman subjects, but this state supervision would not affect the content of the religious education of various *millet*s.
The preceding draft corrected by [Safved Pasha].	[Safved] added that special measures would be undertaken for the purposes of regularisation and unification.
A draft constitution of 114 articles (probably the Council of Ministers' work)...	Adoption of the preceding article including [Safved's] additions.
Additions/corrections on the draft constitution of 114 art.	

Draft with Namık Kemal's marginal notes and reactions to some provisions; a very similar draft to the previous one…	Adoption of the preceding article. No correction by Kemal.
The 119-article draft preceding the 1876 Constitution.	Adoption of the preceding article.
The Ottoman Constitution of 1876.	Adoption of the preceding article.

Access to Public Offices

Midhad Pasha's draft.	Nobility and affiliation not being credible, all Ottoman subjects are admitted to public offices by imperial order in accordance with their loyalty and capabilities, their class and professions.
Said Pasha's draft.	Not mentioned.
Draft submitted to [Safved Pasha]; [very probably the Drafting Commission's work]; draft of 130 articles.	Midhad's article is developed: nobility, affiliation and other similar elements being subjective, all subjects will be admitted to public offices in accordance with their aptitude and loyalty, and their professions which will be regulated by law.
The preceding draft corrected by [Safved Pasha].	[Safved] scored out many parts of the article and added some new provisions: Ottoman subjects will be admitted to public offices that suit their aptitude.
A draft constitution of 114 articles (probably the Council of Ministers' work); noted by the archival catalogue as the draft constitution; put together with a bylaw related to the duties of the Council of Ministers and supposed to contain the views of [Namık Kemal, Said and Mahmud Pashas and others] on the bylaw.	A nearly identical article is adopted.
Additions/corrections on the draft constitution of 114 art.	
Draft with Namık Kemal's marginal notes and reactions to some provisions; a very similar draft to the previous one of 113 articles; probably the work of the Council of Ministers.	No correction by Namık Kemal.
The 119-article draft preceding the 1876 Constitution.	The article is first brought back to the version before [Safved's] corrections but then all the provisions alluding to the exclusion of factors of nobility, affiliation and other subjective elements are scored out, and the article remains nearly the same as the preceding one.
The Ottoman Constitution of 1876.	All subjects will be admitted to public offices according to their aptitude and capacity.

Death penalty

Midhad Pasha's draft.	Not mentioned.
Said Pasha's draft.	Abolished in political matters.
Draft submitted to [Safved Pasha]; [very probably the Drafting Commission's work]; draft of 130 articles.	Not mentioned.
The preceding draft corrected by [Safved Pasha].	Not mentioned.
A draft constitution of 114 articles (probably the Council of Ministers' work); noted by the archival catalogue as the draft constitution; put together with a bylaw related to the duties of the Council of Ministers and supposed to contain the views of [Namık Kemal, Said and Mahmud Pashas and others] on the bylaw.	Not mentioned.
Additions/corrections on the draft constitution of 114 art.	Not mentioned.
Draft with Namık Kemal's marginal notes and reactions to some provisions; a very similar draft to the previous one of 113 articles; probably the work of the Council of Ministers.	Not mentioned.
The 119-article draft preceding the 1876 Constitution.	Not mentioned.
The Ottoman Constitution of 1876.	Not mentioned.

The Council of Ministers

Midhad Pasha's draft.	The Grand Vizierate is abolished. The presidency of the Council of Ministers is assigned by the sultan to a minister named "premier", who will elect the ministers of the Council to be appointed by imperial order. The Council of Ministers is the locus of internal and external political affairs and its deliberations are executed by imperial order. Ministers have personal and collective responsibility for their acts before the Chamber of Deputies, and resign individually or collectively in the case of deficiency in their responsibility following the decision of the Chamber of Deputies and the submission of the relevant official report to the sultan by the president of the Chamber. But Midhad's draft does not clarify how the accused minister(s) will be judged. Moreover, their resignation is subject to the sultan's approval.

Said Pasha's draft.	Not mentioned under a separate title as in Midhad's draft but the provisions regarding the Council of Ministers are disseminated under the title of "executive power", which belongs to the sultan. The number and the responsibility of ministers are determined by the *Millet* Assembly. Ministers and functionaries are responsible for the acts of the government, and the public administration for the matters concerning their responsibilities.
Draft submitted to [Safved Pasha]; [very probably the Drafting Commission's work]; draft of 130 articles.	The title of absolute delegate, (namely that of the grand vizier), is transformed into the presidency of ministers. The draft assigned the nomination of the president of ministers and of the sheikh ül-Islam to the sultan but gave initiative to the president of ministers for the selection of the rest of the ministers. The draft stipulated the composition of the Council of Ministers (by hierarchical order: the grand vizier (president of the Council); the sheikh ül-Islam; the president of the Council of State; and ministers of internal affairs, defence, navy, foreign affairs, justice, finances, public instruction, public works, commerce and agriculture). The president of the Council is one of these ministers. The Council is the locus of internal and external affairs and its deliberations are executed by imperial order. Ministers refer to the sultan for affairs beyond the limits of their powers. Ministers have personal, collective and penal responsibilities for their acts. The Chamber of Deputies addresses a complaint in the case of deficiency in their individual and collective responsibility, something that indirectly alludes to their responsibility before the Chamber. In the case of penal responsibility, the accused minister is judged by the High Court. His transfer to the High Court, albeit decided in the Chamber of Deputies by vote, is subject to the approval of the sultan. The ministers can make dispositions in case of necessity without waiting for the convention of the General Assembly in order to defend the state against danger and to

	preserve public security, and these dispositions will have the provisional force of law until the convention of the General Assembly, in which they can be rejected. Ministers bear the responsibility for the dispositions which they make and which should conform to the principles of the Constitution. In case of a conflict between the Council of Ministers and the Chamber of Deputies due to the rejection of a legal project submitted by the Council to the Chamber and on which the ministers insisted despite the Chamber's rejection, the ministers resign. The sultan decides on either a change of ministry or the dissolution of the Chamber on condition of the re-election of the deputies.
The preceding draft corrected by [Safved Pasha].	The office of Grand Vizierate is designated the presidency of ministers. (A different formulation of the preceding article, removing the word "transformation"). The position of president of the Cabinet preserved its role in the election process of the rest of the ministers. The article regarding the composition of the Council of Ministers is scored out as if disapproved of. The ministers refer to the president of the Cabinet (and not to the sultan as previously stated) for questions beyond the limits of their powers. The president refers to the Cabinet if necessary for these questions and then submits them to the approval of the sultan. [Safved] scored out the article regarding submitting the resignation of ministers to the sultan's approval. Ministerial responsibility reinforced: ministers are also responsible for the decisions made by the Council and bearing their signature. With [Safved's] changes, these decree-laws of the Cabinet will have the force of law until the convention of the Chamber of Deputies (he thus eliminated the Senate from the process). No change to the article relevant to the conflict between ministers and the Chamber of Deputies.

A draft constitution of 114 articles (probably the Council of Ministers' work); noted by the archival catalogue as the draft constitution; put together with a bylaw related to the duties of the Council of Ministers and supposed to contain the views of [Namık Kemal, Said and Mahmud Pashas and others] on the bylaw.	[Safved's] formulation on the status of the grand vizier as the head of ministers and his voice in the selection of the rest of the ministers is adopted. No stipulation on the composition of the Council of Ministers. The Council of Ministers is responsible for the acts and practices related to their service but the direct mention of individual and collective responsibilities is removed. More importantly, as they are responsible before the Chamber of Deputies, in case of complaint by the Chamber of a deficiency in ministerial responsibility, the whole process of accusation against the minister or ministers until the request for his trial at the Higher Court is conducted by the different organs of the Chamber of Deputies. In this draft, it is the head of the Council of Ministers who intervenes in the final phase of this process to submit the request for trial of the accused minister to imperial sanction. The condition of re-election of the Chamber of Deputies within the term fixed by law is added to the draft so as to guarantee the re-election of the deputies in case of a conflict between the Chamber and the ministers in the matter of a legal project. [Safved's] attempt at reinforcing the control of the Chamber of Deputies over the decree-laws is adopted in the draft.
Additions/corrections on the draft constitution of 114 art.	The most important change is that the grand vizier, who is the president of the Council of Ministers, has no voice in the selection of ministers, directly nominated by the sultan.
Draft with Namık Kemal's marginal notes and reactions to some provisions; a very similar draft to the previous one of 113 articles; probably the work of the Council of Ministers.	Namık Kemal reacts to the fact that the grand vizier is the head of the Council of Ministers. Since all ministers are responsible, he states, if they refer to an authority other than the sultan, then the principle of responsibility cannot function. In the preceding draft, the Council of Ministers refers to the sultan, if necessary submitting their deliberations for his approval. Namık Kemal reacts to this article stating that in a normal state, the

	deliberations of the Council of Ministers always need the sultan's approval. He reacts to the shortening of the article on ministerial responsibility and to the intervention of the head of the Council when submitting the request for trial of the minister accused by the Chamber of Deputies to the sultan's approval. He also objects to the removal of the condition of ministerial responsibility on the decree-laws as stated in the draft submitted to [Safved].
The 119-article draft preceding the 1876 Constitution.	The provision that the grand vizier is the head of the Council of Ministers is removed. The relevant article directly talks about the nomination of the grand vizier and the sheikh ül-Islam by the sultan. The former article regarding the composition of the Council of Ministers was redrafted but then scored out. Throughout the entire section regarding the Council of Ministers, the term "president of the Council of Ministers" was avoided when referring to the grand vizier. In previous drafts, these two terms were used alternatively, but the draft in question only uses the term "grand vizier". However, it mentions only once that the Council convenes under the presidency of the grand vizier. The draft reflects an attempt at submitting all the deliberations of the Council to the sultan's approval as stated by Kemal. However, it then stipulates that certain deliberations needing imperial sanction will be submitted for the sultan's approval. Consequently, the provision that ministers first refer to the grand vizier for questions beyond the limits of their powers is retained. Ministerial responsibility was again redrafted in detail but then scored out and shortened as in the preceding draft. Despite Kemal's objections, it is the grand vizier and not the head of the Chamber of Deputies who submits the request for trial of the accused minister for imperial sanction. The condition of re-election of the deputies within the limits fixed by law is retained. Ministerial responsibility was again redrafted for

	decree-laws but then scored out and the relevant article restored to its preceding form.
The Ottoman Constitution of 1876.	The provisions regarding the Council of Ministers are included in the Ottoman Constitution as in the preceding draft.

Public Functionaries

Midhad Pasha's draft.	The draft stipulated the institution of special school courses for the training of public functionaries; within a period of five years after the institution of these courses, nobody will be admitted to public offices without diploma. No public functionary can be dismissed unless he does not make progress, a legal reason justifies this dismissal, this dismissal is judged necessary by the government for a legitimate reason or he resigns. Each official must obey his superior's orders only if they conform to the limits determined by law. The powers of each office are determined and each official is responsible within the limits of his powers.
Said Pasha's draft.	No special section on public functionaries. The sultan can appoint and dismiss ministers. However, the dismissal of diplomats, the commanders of army and navy, governors or other public functionaries of the first order is subject to negotiation with the Council of Ministers. The public functionaries of the second order of the government can be appointed or dismissed by the sovereign upon the request of the minister to which they belong within the limits of regulations. The sovereign cannot dismiss the entire body of functionaries of the executive branch, elected by the people, without the approval of the Council of State.
Draft submitted to [Safved Pasha]; [very probably the Drafting Commission's work]; draft of 130 articles.	Nominations to public office will take place in conformity with regulations and the merit and capacity of functionaries. No public functionary can be dismissed

	or changed unless a legal reason justifies this dismissal, he resigns or the dismissal is judged necessary by the state. The powers of each office are determined by special regulations and each official is responsible within the limits of his power. Each official must obey his superior's orders only if they conform to the limits determined by law. For acts contrary to the law, obedience to a superior cannot relieve the official who executed them from responsibility.
The preceding draft corrected by [Safved Pasha].	Before [Safved's] corrections, public offices are determined by law. His corrections make the article vaguer by putting the emphasis not on the determination of public offices by law but on the determination of the conditions of nominations to public offices by law. [Safved's] additions seem to change the determination by law of the conditions regarding the obedience of the official to his superior: although the respect and obedience of the official to his superior is a praised virtue, obedience does not relieve the official from responsibility (a thin scoring out seems to remove the perspective of law in the issue of obedience). No change on the rest of provisions.
A draft constitution of 114 articles (probably the Council of Ministers' work); noted by the archival catalogue as the draft constitution; put together with a bylaw related to the duties of the Council of Ministers and supposed to contain the views of [Namık Kemal, Said and Mahmud Pashas and others] on the bylaw.	[Safved's] corrections on the determination of public offices are adopted: the conditions of nomination of officials to different public offices will take place in conformity with regulations and their merit and capacity. The officials appointed under these conditions cannot be dismissed or changed unless a legal reason justifies the dismissal, the official himself resigns or the reason is judged necessary by the state. [Safved's] corrections on the powers of each office are not accepted. The powers of each office are determined by law and each official is responsible within the limits of his power. The conditions of obedience of officials to their superiors are again determined by law.

Additions/corrections on the draft constitution of 114 art.	Each official must obey his superior's orders only if they conform to the limits determined by law.
Draft with Namık Kemal's marginal notes and reactions to some provisions; a very similar draft to the previous one of 113 articles; probably the work of the Council of Ministers.	No correction by Kemal. The preceding form of the article is accepted.
The 119-article draft preceding the 1876 Constitution.	The preceding form is accepted.
The Ottoman Constitution of 1876.	The preceding form is accepted.

The Council of State

Midhad Pasha's draft.	The president and the members of the Council are nominated and dismissed by the sultan. The Council of State is able to intervene before the Council of Ministers and even the sultan when laws and regulations are not duly executed. Its function is not solely limited to the executive field but also influences the legislative process: each law and regulation is discussed within the Council of State before being submitted to the approval of the Chamber of Deputies and to that of the sultan. More importantly, the executive power, which belongs to the sultan, but is executed in his name by the ministers, cannot individually make dispositions and can only order the Council of State to elaborate laws and regulations that it judged necessary.
Said Pasha's draft.	The sovereign is the head of the Council of State, the members of which are nominated by the sultan. However, the members of the Council can only be dismissed upon the request of the sultan and by the decision of the *Millet* Assembly. The sovereign has the right to elaborate or amend legislation, like the *Millet* Assembly. Both of the institutions first refer to the Council of State for the elaboration of legislation. The Council of State has the power of inspection and supervision over public administrations.

Draft submitted to [Safved Pasha]; [very probably the Drafting Commission's work]; draft of 130 articles.	No separate section on the Council of State but the bills of laws are first elaborated in the Council of State.
The preceding draft corrected by [Safved Pasha].	No correction by [Safved].
A draft constitution of 114 articles (probably the Council of Ministers' work); noted by the archival catalogue as the draft constitution; put together with a bylaw related to the duties of the Council of Ministers and supposed to contain the views of [Namık Kemal, Said and Mahmud Pashas and others] on the bylaw.	No separate section on the Council of State but the bills of laws are first elaborated in the Council of State.
Additions/corrections on the draft constitution of 114 art.	
Draft with Namık Kemal's marginal notes and reactions to some provisions; a very similar draft to the previous one of 113 articles; probably the work of the Council of Ministers.	No correction by Namık Kemal.
The 119-article draft preceding the 1876 Constitution.	No separate section on the Council of State but the bills of laws are first elaborated in the Council of State.
The Ottoman Constitution of 1876.	No separate section on the Council of State but the bills of laws are first elaborated in the Council of State.

The General Assembly

Midhad Pasha's draft.	No mention of the General Assembly.
Said Pasha's draft.	The *Millet* Assembly is mentioned under the section of "legislative power". Said Pasha envisages an assembly of 750 deputies. Among others, the most important criteria for election is the enjoyment of political and civil rights. The election of deputies takes place by the drawing of lots. Interestingly enough, Said's draft does not mention how laws are elaborated by the Assembly under the section of "legislative power". Legislative power is described rather under the section of the Council of State. The sovereign has the right to submit bills of laws to the *Millet* Assembly through the Council of Ministers. Similarly, the *Millet* Assembly has

	the right to elaborate or amend legislation. Both first refer to the Council of State for the elaboration of bills. The sovereign can insist on the adoption of a legal project, which becomes law after reexamination in the *Millet* Assembly. Said does not clarify whether this renegotiation in the *Millet* Assembly can result in a veto.
Draft submitted to [Safved Pasha]; [very probably the Drafting Commission's work]; draft of 130 articles.	The draft has a separate section on the General Assembly, which is composed of the Chamber of Deputies and the Council of Notables. The initiative to propose a law or modify an existing law only belongs to the Council of Ministers, the Council of Notables or the Chamber of Deputies. In the case of such a request from any of these bodies, the draft of the law will be first elaborated in the Council of State and will be submitted for examination first to the Chamber of Deputies and then to the Council of Notables. When the draft is separately approved by both of the bodies, it will be submitted for imperial sanction so as to have the force of law.
The preceding draft corrected by [Safved Pasha].	[Safved's] handwriting added only that this entire process will function with the knowledge of the sultan.
A draft constitution of 114 articles (probably the Council of Ministers' work); noted by the archival catalogue as the draft constitution; put together with a bylaw related to the duties of the Council of Ministers and supposed to contain the views of [Namık Kemal, Said and Mahmud Pashas and others] on the bylaw.	The draft brought restrictions to the proposition of a law or to the modification of an existing law emanating from the Chamber of Deputies and the Senate, which will address such a demand on matters comprised within their duties. In such a case, the demand will be submitted by the grand vizier to the sultan and if there is any reason for it, the Council of State will be charged by imperial order to elaborate the draft upon information provided by the relevant Department. The draft, elaborated at the Council of State, will be first submitted to the Chamber of Deputies and then to the Council of Notables for examination. When the draft is separately approved by both of these bodies, it will be submitted for imperial sanction so as to have the force of law.

Additions/corrections on the draft constitution of 114 art.	
Draft with Namık Kemal's marginal notes and reactions to some provisions; a very similar draft to the previous one of 113 articles; probably the work of the Council of Ministers.	No correction by Namık Kemal but he reacts to the fact that the propositions of laws emanating from the Council of Ministers do not need imperial sanction before discussion while those of the Council of Notables and of the Chamber of Deputies do. He accused the draftsmen of ignorance for having transformed the relevant provision of the Drafting Commission into this and for initiating such a process of imperial sanction, as all legal projects are submitted for final imperial approval.
The 119-article draft preceding the 1876 Constitution.	The preceding form is accepted.
The Ottoman Constitution of 1876.	The preceding form is accepted.

The Council of Notables/The Senate

Midhad Pasha's draft.	Although Midhad had in mind the institution of a Senate, the archival evidence does not provide enough detail for a comparison.
Said Pasha's draft.	The Senate is composed of the heads of the *millet*s, the marshals of the army and navy, and those who are considered by the sovereign to be appropriate to this post. The head of the Senate as well as the other senators are nominated for life by the sultan and are protected from dismissals. The Senate is the guardian of the Ottoman Constitution and of general liberties. No law can be published before being submitted to the Senate. The latter opposes the publication of laws against the Ottoman Constitution, religion, good morals, religious freedom, individual liberty, equality of the people before the law, the inviolability of rights on private property, the protection of judges against dismissals or other dispositions endangering the integrity of the state. The Senate can address a statement to the sultan with regards to the proposition of a law regarding the greater interests of the *millet*. The Senate can also propose the revision of

	the Ottoman Constitution through a special proposition and if the proposition is admitted by the sultan, a decree of the Senate follows the process. However, the revisions regarding the fundamental points of the Ottoman Constitution are subject to the general vote of the population. In case of the dissolution of the *Millet* Assembly, the Senate accomplishes the necessary initiatives for the administration of the government upon the proposition of the sovereign until the convention of the new Assembly.
Draft submitted to [Safved Pasha]; [very probably the Drafting Commission's work]; draft of 130 articles.	No change on the conditions of nomination of senators but no special public functionary enumerated to be nominated senator. The functions of the Senate are more limited compared to Said's draft: the Senate examines the legal projects and budget, submitted by the Chamber of Deputies and sends them back to the Chamber of Deputies with its opinion if it finds something contrary to religion, the rights of the sultan, freedom, the principles of the Constitution, the integrity of the state, the internal security of the country, the defence and the preservation of the fatherland and customs. It transmits the legal projects that it approves to the president of the Council of Ministers. If it judges it necessary, it communicates to the relevant ministry the petitions it receives with a complementary opinion.
The preceding draft corrected by [Safved Pasha].	[Safved's] handwriting added another option: in case the Senate finds the legal projects and budget contrary to the dispositions enumerated in the preceding draft, the Senate's other option is to absolutely refuse the projects instead of sending them back to the Chamber of Deputies.
A draft constitution of 114 articles (probably the Council of Ministers' work); noted by the archival catalogue as the draft constitution; put together with a bylaw related to the duties of the Council of Ministers and supposed to contain the views of [Namık Kemal, Said and Mahmud Pashas and others] on the bylaw.	Those who can be nominated senators are again enumerated and the list is enlarged: accordingly, those who retired from the offices of minister, governor-general, marshal, *kazasker* (added later), diplomat, patriarch, chief rabbi (added later) together with the generals of the army and navy. The functions of the Senate are as in the previous draft including [Safved's] additions. The only change is the transmission of petitions received by the Senate to the relevant ministries, if judged necessary.

Additions/corrections on the draft constitution of 114 art.	The functions of *kazasker* and chief rabbi are added later. The second change is in the transmission of petitions received by the Senate: they go to the Grand Vizierate instead of to the relevant ministries.
Draft with Namık Kemal's marginal notes and reactions to some provisions; a very similar draft to the previous one of 113 articles; probably the work of the Council of Ministers.	Namık Kemal reacted to the enumeration of public functionaries who can be nominated as senators.
The 119-article draft preceding the 1876 Constitution.	The previous article is adopted but the words "the president of the Council of Ministers" is scored out, to be replaced by the Grand Vizierate in the provision stating that the Senate transmits the legal projects it accepts to the president of the Council of Ministers. There was an attempt in the draft at communicating the petitions to the relevant ministry as formulated in the draft submitted to [Safved's] attention. However, the ministry is scored out and replaced with the Grand Vizierate. There was also an attempt at eliminating the list enumerating the public functionaries appropriate to the office of senator but then the list was again added.
The Ottoman Constitution of 1876.	The final form of the preceding article is accepted.

The Chamber of Deputies

Midhad Pasha's draft.	The Chamber of Deputies is composed of 120 members, two thirds of which are elected by the provinces according to a regulation, while one third is nominated by the government. For the first year, the deputies will be elected by the general councils of the provinces, and a special electoral regulation will be elaborated for subsequent years. The Chamber of Deputies regulates the debts of the state, negotiates financial measures such as the signing of internal and external loans upon the request of the government. The essential functions of the Chamber of Deputies are to discuss the legal projects submitted by the government and the deputies; to supervise the ways in which state income is spent and to ask for reports from state departments; to fix general expenses in

	cooperation with the government; to determine the amount and method of distribution of the general tax in cooperation with the government; to supervise the application of regulations in the state departments; to warn the Council of State of their infractions and of impending trials. The sultan can convene or dissolve the Chamber of Deputies before the ordinary time for the interests of the state. But in the case of its dissolution, the new Chamber shall convene within six months.
Said Pasha's draft.	No special section on the Chamber of Deputies but brief mention under the section regarding the legislative power, without clarification of its essential functions.
Draft submitted to [Safved Pasha]; [very probably the Drafting Commission's work]; draft of 130 articles.	The number of deputies is fixed at one deputy per every 50,000 male Ottoman subjects. The Chamber of Deputies discusses the legal projects elaborated in the Council of State, and accepts, rejects or revises them. It examines the general expenses of the state comprised in the budget, the amount of which it fixes in cooperation with the ministers. It also determines, in cooperation with the ministers, the nature, amount and method of assessment and realisation of the receipts in order to cover expenses.
The preceding draft corrected by [Safved Pasha].	[Safved] added an administrative as well as a geographical unit to the number of deputies; accordingly, the number of deputies is fixed at 50,000 male Ottoman subjects per province. No correction by [Safved] on the functions of the Chamber of Deputies.
A draft constitution of 114 articles (probably the Council of Ministers' work); noted by the archival catalogue as the draft constitution; put together with a bylaw related to the duties of the Council of Ministers and supposed to contain the views of [Namık Kemal, Said and Mahmud Pashas and others] on the bylaw.	[Safved's] addition of a geographical unit is not adopted but the number of 50,000 is retained. The Chamber of Deputies will discuss the drafts of law that are submitted to it. It will adopt, amend or reject the dispositions concerning the Constitution or finances. It examines the general expenses of the state comprised in the budget, the amount of which it fixes in

	cooperation with the ministers. It also determines, in cooperation with the ministers, the nature, amount and method of assessment and realisation of the receipts in order to cover expenses.
Additions/corrections on the draft constitution of 114 art.	The number of deputies is fixed at one deputy per 80,000 male Ottoman subjects.
Draft with Namık Kemal's marginal notes and reactions to some provisions; a very similar draft to the previous one of 113 articles; probably the work of the Council of Ministers.	The number of deputies is fixed at one deputy per 80,000 male Ottoman subjects. Namık Kemal reacts to the number of 80,000 on the grounds that the council of election, including males and females, does not exceed 50,000 in any state. The enlargement of the council of election means that the electors will elect the people they do not know. To have one deputy for every 80,000 male inhabitants means that the Ottoman Assembly will be smaller than the Greek one. However, the Assembly is the greatest school for politics. The greater the number of the deputies in an assembly, the more people who are trained for better service to the state. Namık Kemal also reacts to the restriction of the sphere of influence of the Chamber of Deputies which is limited to the dispositions related to the Constitution and finances because all laws in one way or another touch these two domains.
The 119-article draft preceding the 1876 Constitution.	The number of 80,000 is adopted. There was an attempt at redrafting the article in its initial form, allowing the Chamber of Deputies to discuss the projects of laws elaborated in the Council of State and eliminating the restrictions brought to its sphere of intervention (only over dispositions regarding the Constitution and finances), but the article retained its shape of the preceding draft.
The Ottoman Constitution of 1876.	The number of deputies is again fixed at one deputy for every 50,000 male Ottoman subjects. The restrictions regarding the sphere of intervention of the Chamber of Deputies are not removed and the article remains as in the preceding draft.

Measures against Revolution/Martial Law

Midhad Pasha's draft.	Not mentioned
Said Pasha's draft.	Difference of terminology between his archival draft talking about the state of siege (*muhasara hali*, the literal translation of the French *état de siège*) and the printed version of his draft talking about customary administration (*idare-i örfiye*), an equivalent of military rule for a temporary period and urgent conditions. In both drafts, the proclamation of military rule is determined by a special law.
Draft submitted to [Safved Pasha]; [very probably the Drafting Commission's work; draft of 130 articles.	In the case of a revolution in any part of the territory, the Ottoman government has the right to proclaim a customary administration in the locality in question for a temporary period. The word "customary administration" is mentioned in parentheses and defined: it consists of the temporary suspension of civil laws (*nizamat-ı mülkiye*). The mode of administration of the locality under "customary administration" will be determined by a special law.
The preceding draft corrected by [Safved Pasha].	No correction by Safved on martial law but at the end of the draft, [Safved] wrote a preliminary article that he could not finish and which seems to be an initial phase of Article 113; however, it only talked about the infraction of internal security and an action of treason against the state. But this initial provision does not talk about the expulsion of individuals from the Ottoman territory.
A draft constitution of 114 articles (probably the Council of Ministers' work); noted by the archival catalogue as the draft constitution; put together with a bylaw related to the duties of the Council of Ministers and supposed to contain the views of [Namık Kemal, Said and Mahmud Pashas and others]...	The article is almost the same but the beginning changes in the sense that customary administration will be proclaimed once the signs of a revolution are confirmed.
Additions/corrections on the draft constitution of 114 art.	An initial form of Article 113 is added in handwriting: the sultan has the exclusive right to expel from the Ottoman Empire those who threaten the security of the Ottoman state.

	Then a second statement, again added in handwriting, indicates that the expulsion of individuals is on the basis of reliable information collected by the police administration.
Draft with Namık Kemal's marginal notes and reactions to some provisions; a very similar draft to the previous one of 113 articles; probably the work of the Council of Ministers.	Namık Kemal suggests the use of the term "military administration", stating that the use of the term "customary administration" is not correct.
The 119-article draft preceding the 1876 Constitution.	Article 113 takes its final form; some of the corrections added in handwriting to the preceding text are accepted while some are rejected. The term "customary administration" is preferred over "military administration". Accordingly: in case of proof or signs of a revolution in any part of the Ottoman territory, the Ottoman state has the right to proclaim customary administration, which consists of the temporary suspension of civil laws. The mode of administration of the locality under customary rule will be determined by law. The sultan has the exclusive right to expel from the Ottoman territory those who, on the basis of reliable information collected by the police administration, are found injurious to the safety of the state.
The Ottoman Constitution of 1876.	Entire adoption of the article.

DRAFT CONSTITUTION CORRECTED
BY [SAFVED PASHA]

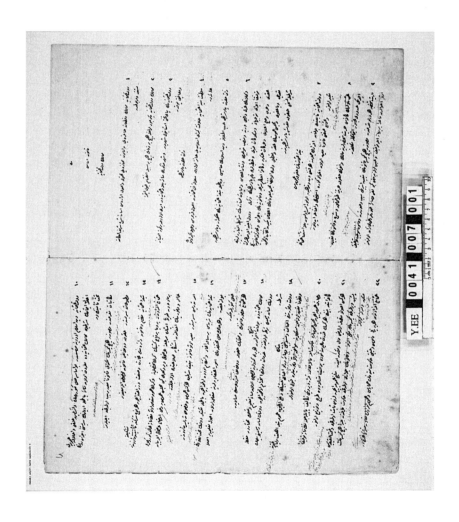

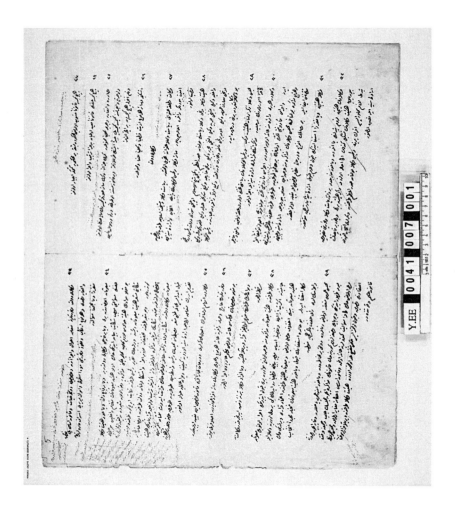

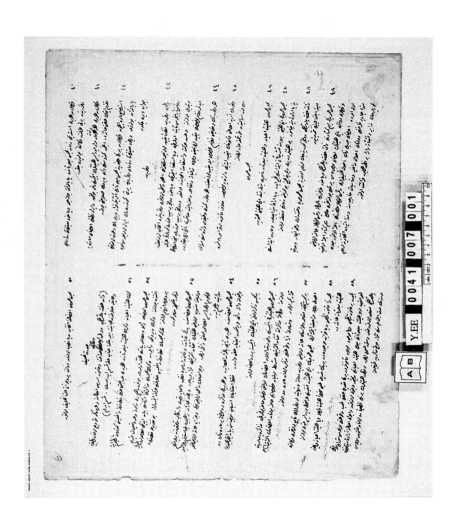

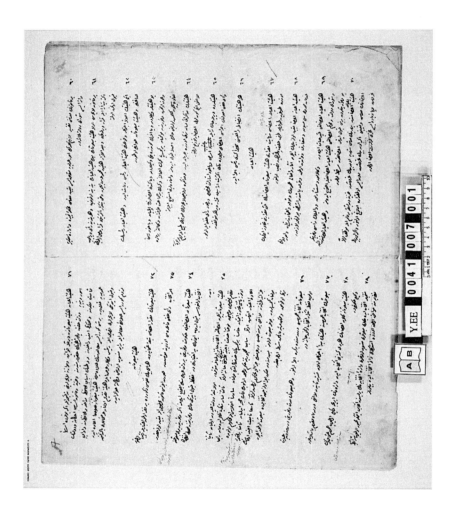

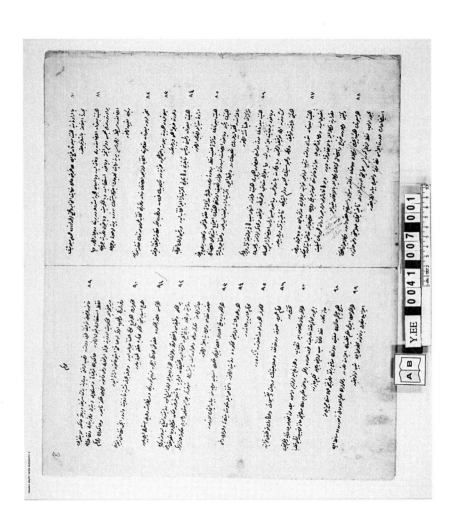

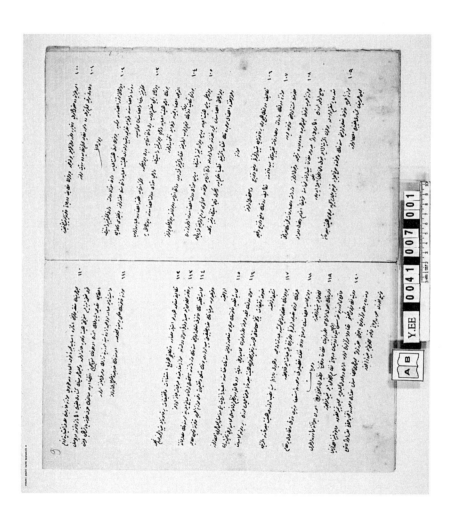

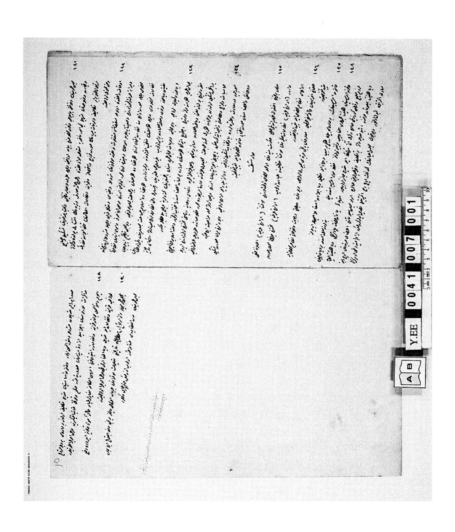

APPENDIX IX

DRAFT CONSTITUTION OF 114 ARTICLES

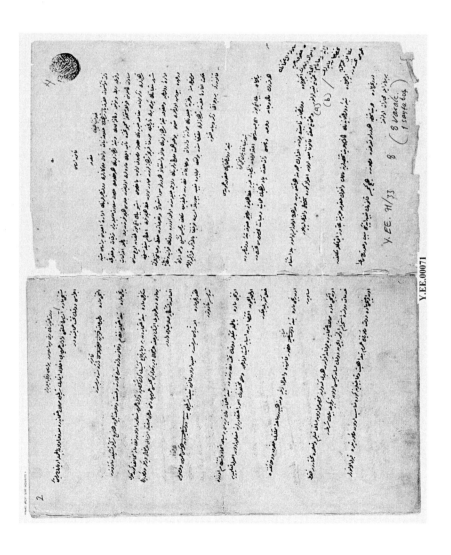

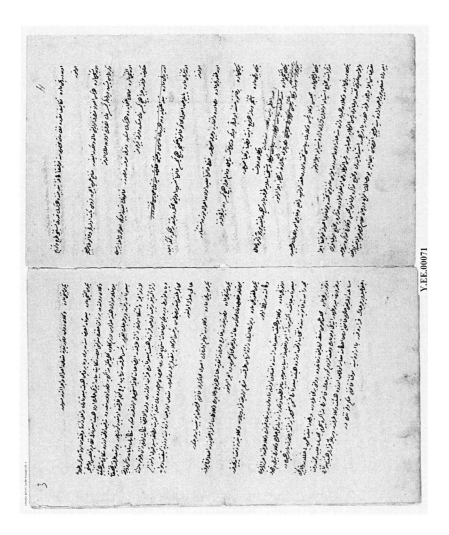

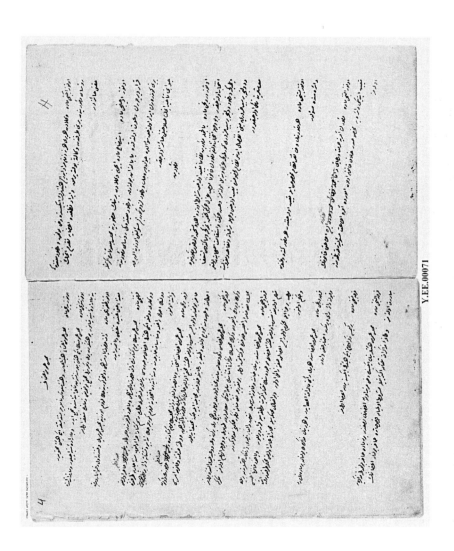

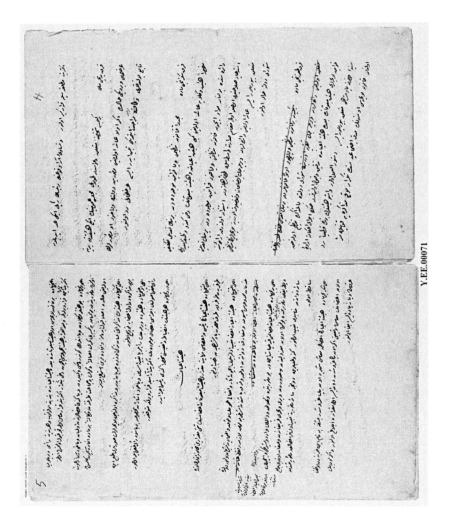

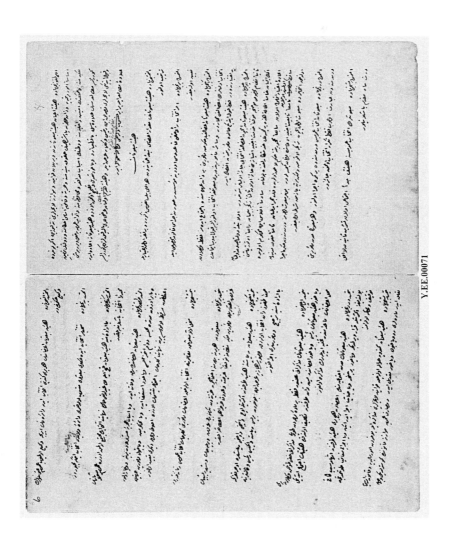

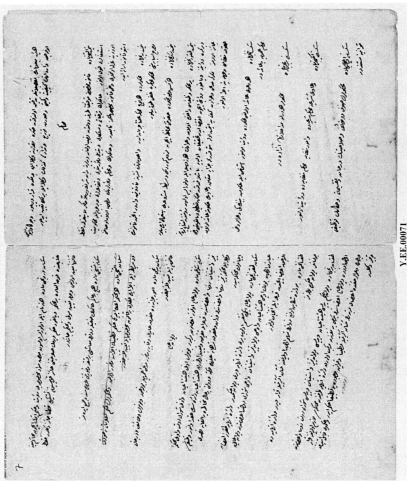

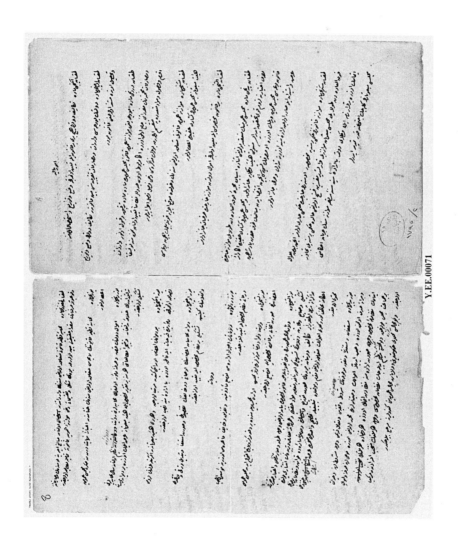

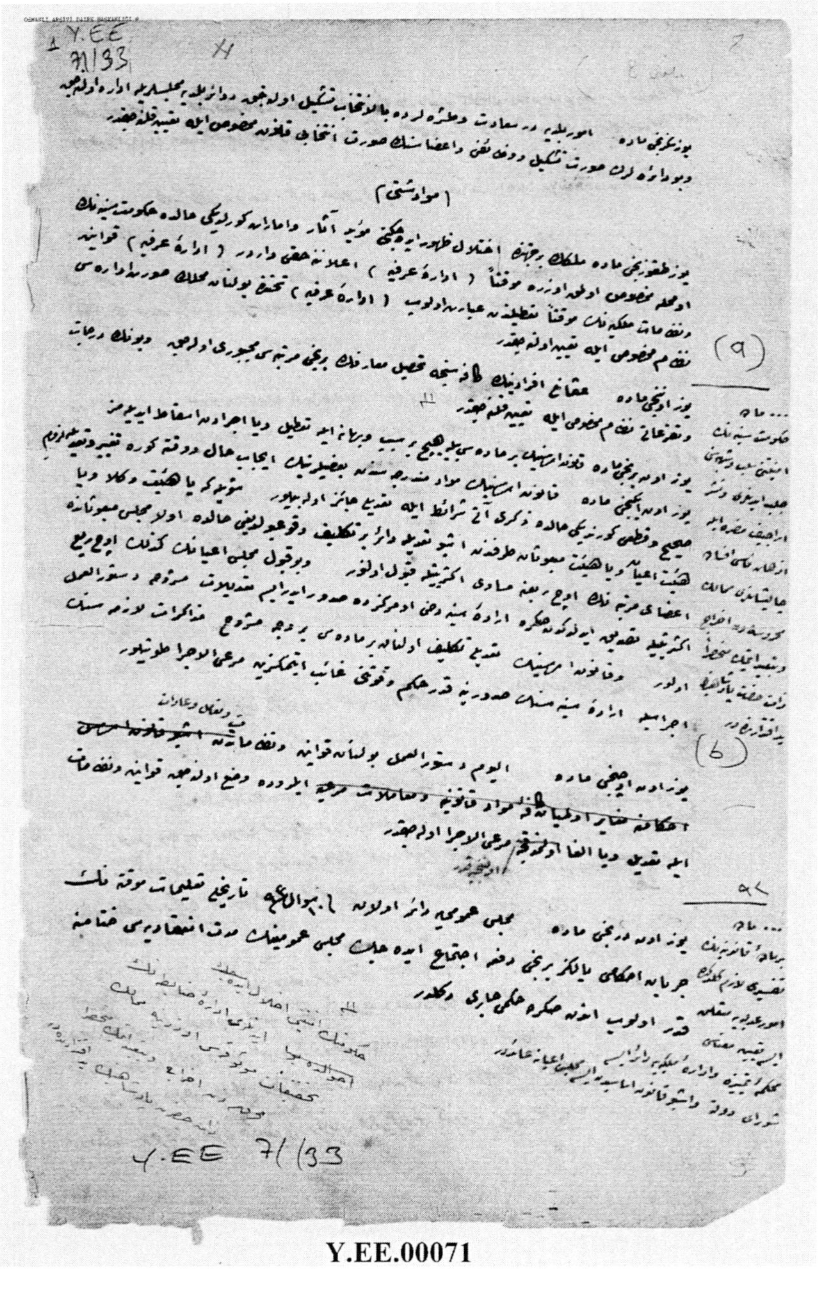

Y.EE.00071

DRAFT CONSTITUTION OF 113 ARTICLES

Y.EE.00071

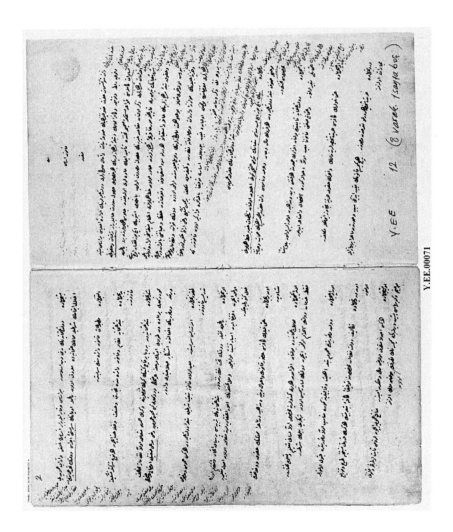

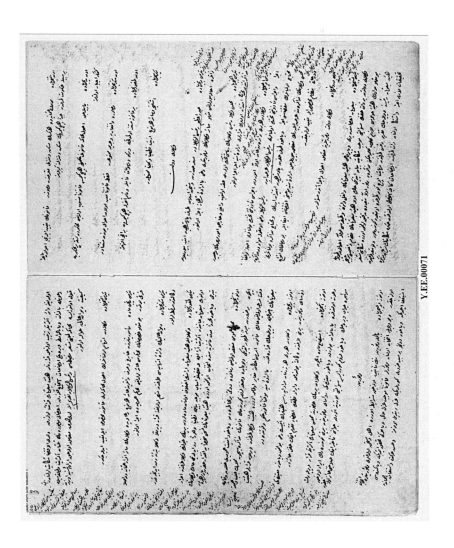

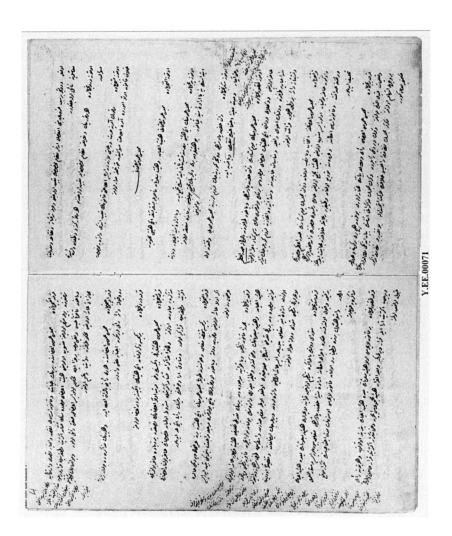

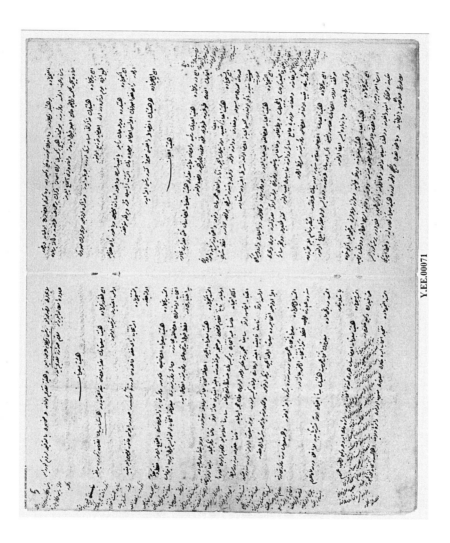

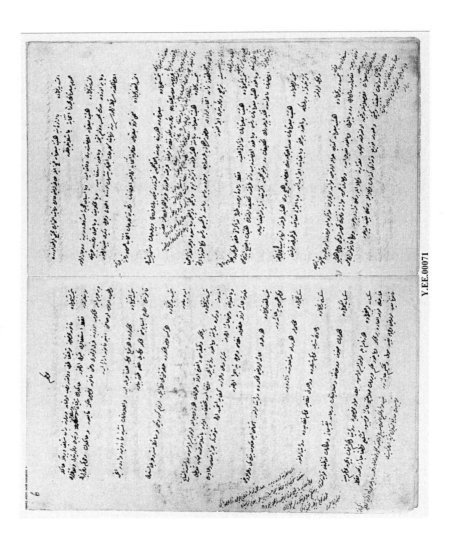

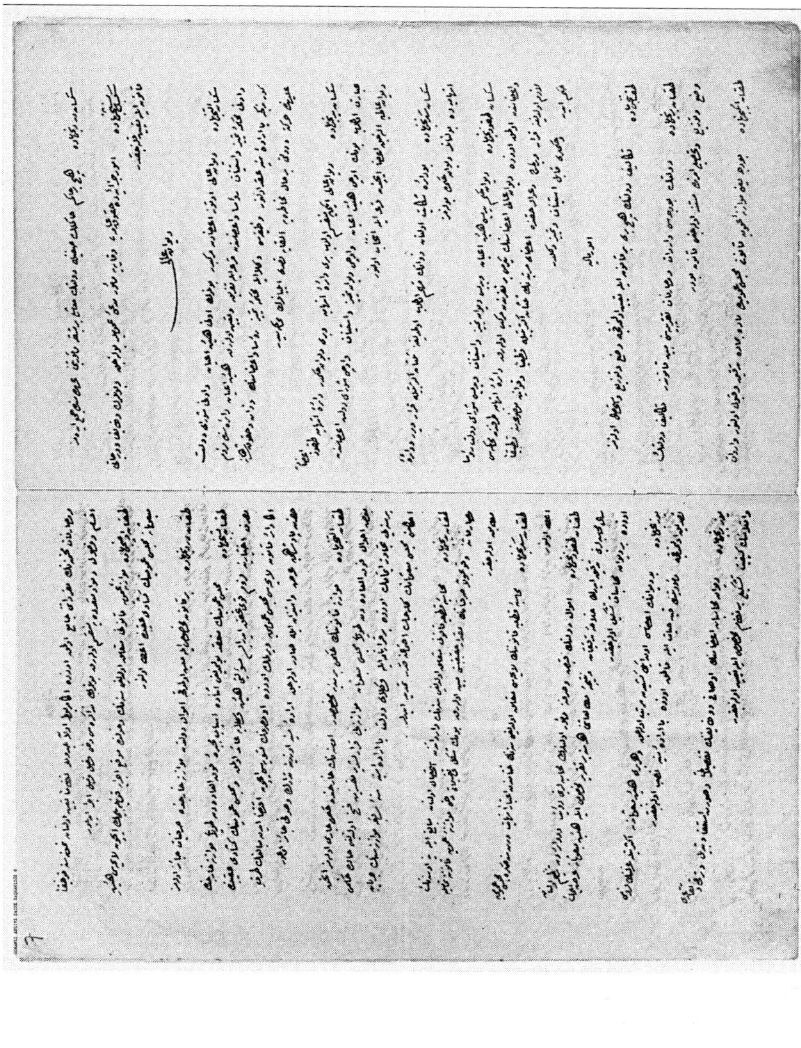

Y.EE.00071

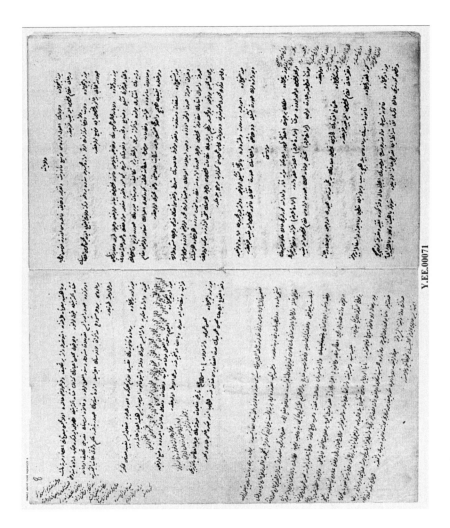

DRAFT CONSTITUTION OF 119 ARTICLES

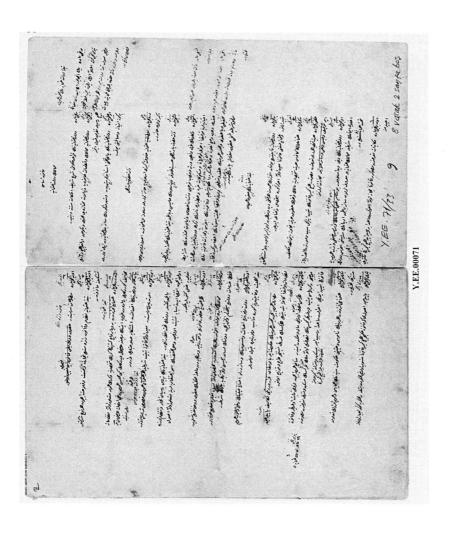

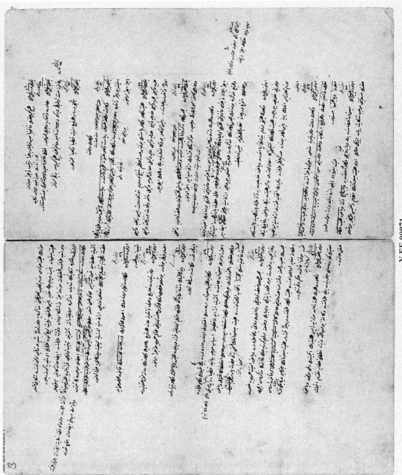

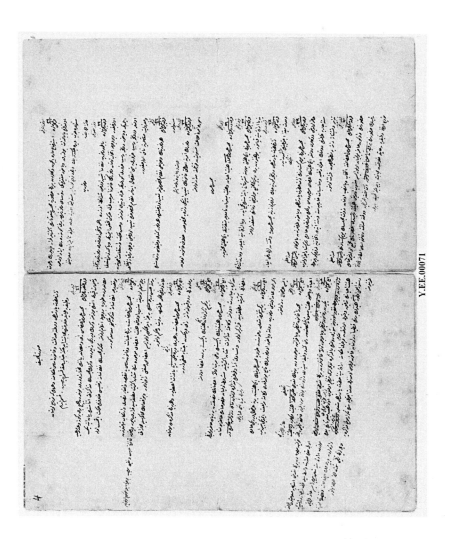

Y.EE.00071

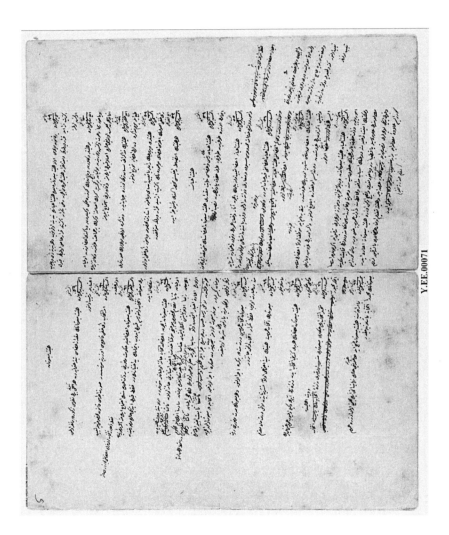

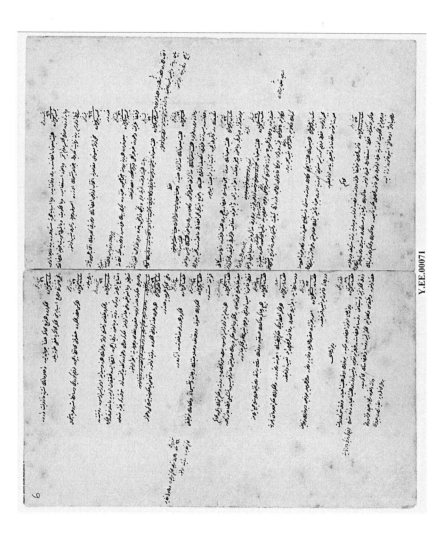

Y.EE.00071

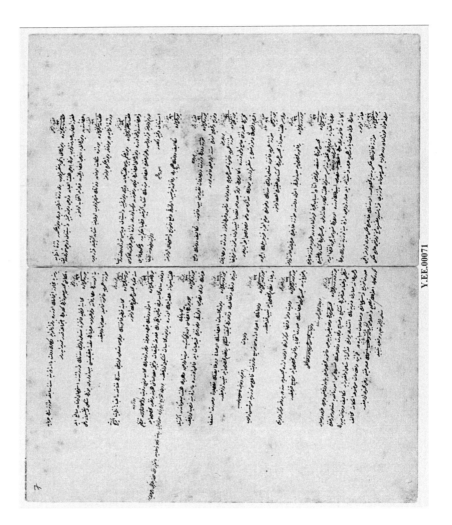

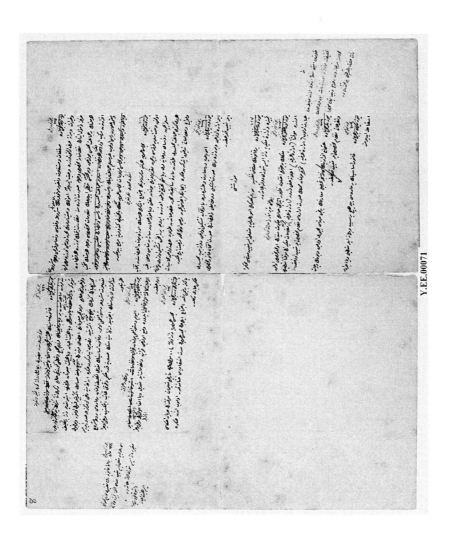

APPENDIX XII

TEXT OF THE ACT OF ENTHRONEMENT
OF ABDÜLAZIZ I

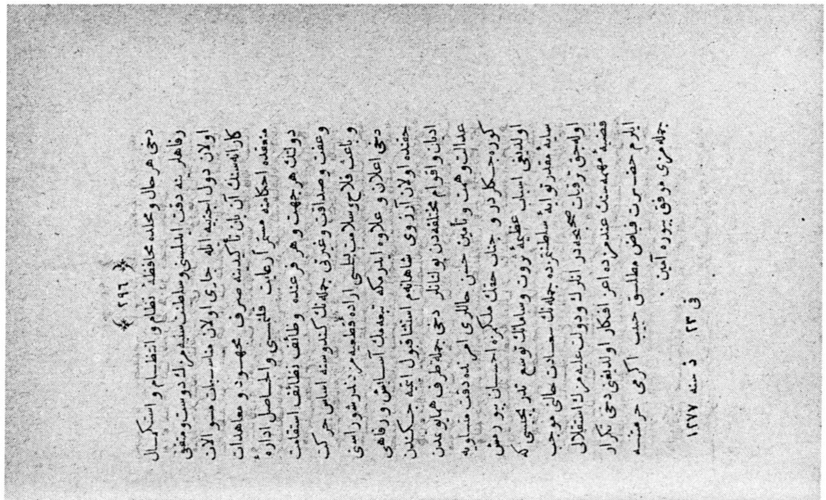

TEXT OF THE ACT OF ENTHRONEMENT
OF MURAD V

۴۰۱

۴۰۲

APPENDIX XIV

TEXT OF THE ACT OF ENTHRONEMENT OF ABDÜLHAMID II

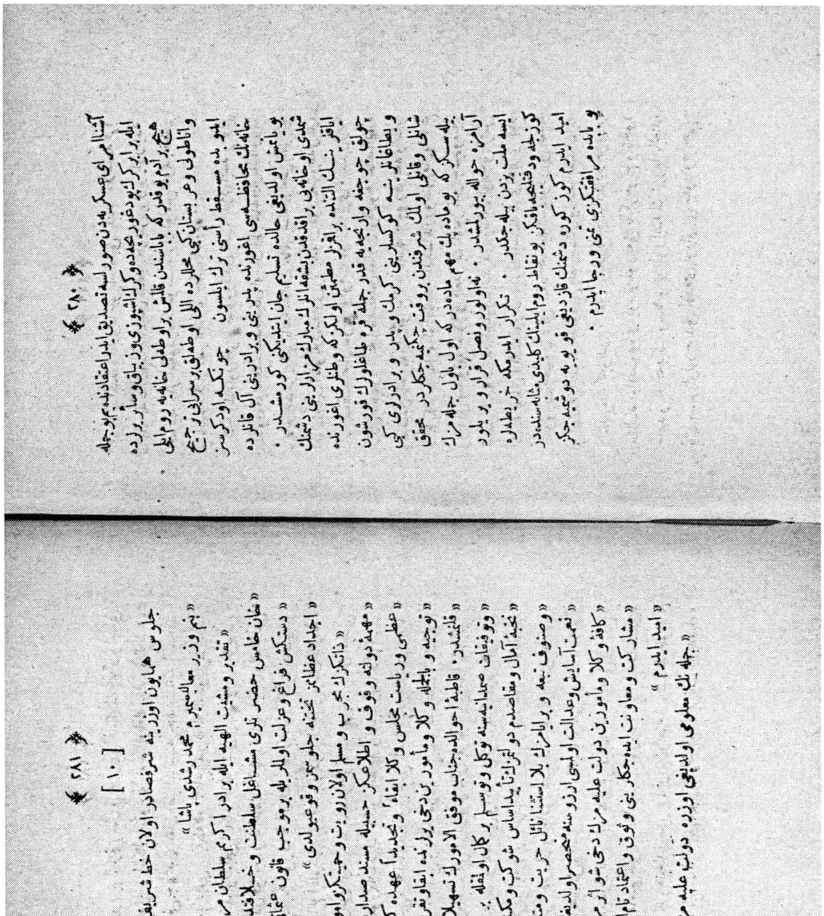

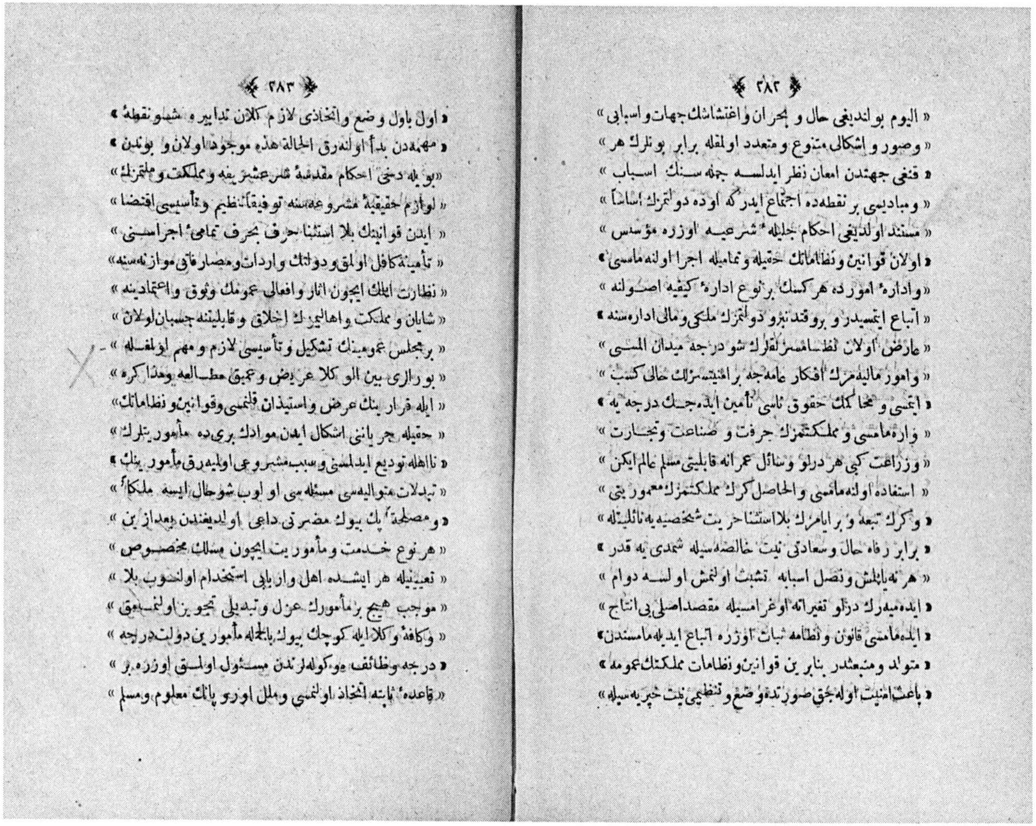

٢٨٢

« اليوم بو انديغی حال و بحران واغتشاشك جهات واسبابی »
« وصور و اشكالی متنوع و متعدد اولمقله برابر بونلرك هر »
« قنغی جهتدن امعان نظر ايدلسه جمله سنك اسباب »
« ومباديسی بر نقطه‌ده اجتماع ايدر كه اوده دولتمزك اساساً »
« مستند اولديغی احكام جليلهٔ شرعيه اوزره مؤسس »
« اولان قوانين ونظاماتك حقيله وتماميله اجرا اولنه‌مامسی »
« واداره‌ٔ اموره هر كسك بر نوع ادارهٔ كيفيه اصولنه »
« اتباع ايتميدر و بو قدنبرو دولتمزك ملكی ومالی اداره‌سنه »
« عارض اولان نظامسزلقلرك شو درجه ميدان المسی »
« وامور ماليه‌مزك افكار عامه‌جه بر امنيتسزلك حالی كسب »
« ايتمسی و محاكمك حقوق ناسی تأمين ايده‌جك درجه‌يه »
« وارمامسی و مملكتمزك حرفت و صناعت وتجارت »
« وزراعت كبی هر درلو وسائل عمرانه قابليتی مسلم عالم ايكن »
« استفاده اولنه‌مامسی والحاصل كرك مملكتمزك معموريتی »
« وكرك تبعه و برايامزك بلا استثنا حريت شخصيه‌يه نائليتله »
« برابر رفاه حال وسعادتی نيت خالصه‌سيله شمدی‌يه قدر »
« هر نه يابلمش ونصل اسبابه تشبث اولنمش اولسه دوام »
« ايده‌ميه‌رك درلو تغيراته اوغرامسيله مقصد اصلی‌يی انتاج »
« ايده‌مامسی قانون ونظامه ثبات اوزره اتباع ايديله‌مامسندن »
« متولد ومنبعثدر بنابرين قوانين ونظامات مملكتك عمومه »
« باعث امنيت اوله‌جق صورتده وضع وتنظيمی نيت خيريه‌سيله »

٢٨٣

« اول باول وضع واتخاذی لازم كلان تدابيره شمو نقطه »
« مهمه‌دن بدأ اولنه‌رق الحالة هذه موجود اولان و بوندن »
« بويله دخی احكام مقدسهٔ شرعشريفه و مملكت وملتمزك »
« لوازم حقيقيهٔ مشروعه‌سنه توفيقاً تنظيم وتأسيسی اقتضا »
« ايدن قوانينك بلا استثنا حرف بحرف تمامیٔ اجراسنی »
« تأمينه كافل اولمق و دولتك واردات ومصارفاتی موازنه‌سنه »
« نظارت ايلك ايچون آثار وافعالی عمومك وثوق واعتمادينه »
« شايان و مملكت واهاليمزك اخلاق و قابليتنه حسبان اولان »
« بر مجلس عموميه‌نك تشكيل وتأسيسی لازم ومهم اولمغله »
« بو رازی بين الوكلا عريض وعميق مطالعه وبعدا كره »
« ايله قرار بنك عرض واستيذان قلنمسی وقوانين ونظاماتك »
« حقيله جريانی اشكال ايدن موادك بريده مأمور يتلرك »
« نااهله توديع ايدلمسی وسبب مشروعی اولميه‌رق مأمور ينك »
« تبدلات متواليه‌سی مسئله‌سی او اوب شوحال ايسه ملكاً »
« ومصلحةً پك بيوك مضرتی داعی اولديغندن بعدازين »
« هر نوع خدمت و مأموريت ايچون مسلك مخصوص »
« تعيينيله هر ايشده اهل واربابی استخدام اولنوب بلا »
« موجب هيچ بر مأمورك عزل وتبديلی تجويز اولنمامق »
« وكافهٔ وكلا ايله كوچك بيوك بالجمله مأمورين دولت درجه »
« درجه وظائف موكوله‌لرندن مسئول اولمق اوزره بر »
« قاعدهٔ ثابته اتخاذ اولنمسی وملل اوزره پاك معلوم ومسلم »

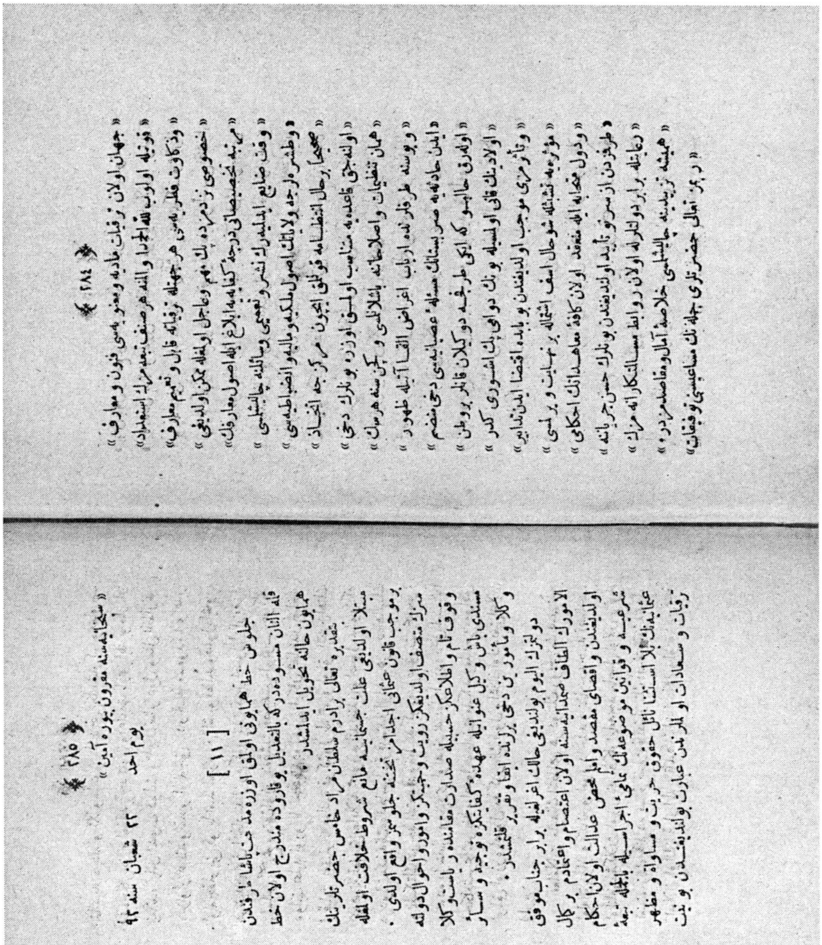

۲۸٤

« جهان اولان ترقیات مادیه و معنویه‌سی فنون و معارف »
« قوتیله اولوب لله الحمد والمنه هر صنف تبعه‌مزك استعداد »
« وذكاوت فطریه‌سی هر جهتله ترقیاته قابل و تعمیم معارف »
« خصوصی نزدمزده پك مهم وعاجل اولمغله ممكن اولدیغی »
« مرتبه تخصیصاتی درجهٔ كفایه‌یه ابلاغ ایله اصول معارفك »
« وقت ضایع ایدلمیه‌رك نشر وتعمیمی وسائلنه چالیشلمسی »
« وطشره‌لرجه ولایاتك اصول ملكیه ومالیه وانضباطیه‌سی »
« صحیحاً برحال انتظامه قونلمق ایچون مركزجه اتخاذ »
« اولنه‌جق قاعده‌یه مناسب اولمسق اوزره بونلرك دخی »
« همان تنظیمات واصلاحاتنه باشلانلمسی و بچن سنه هرسك »
« و بوسنه طرفلرنده ارباب اغراض القا آتیله ظهور »
« ایدن حادثه‌یه صربستانك مسئلهٔ عصیانیه‌سی دخی منضم »
« اولهرق حالبسو كه ایكی طرفجه دوكیلان قانلر بروطن »
« اولادینك قانی اولمسیله بونك دواعی پك اشووری كدر »
« وتأثرمزی موجب اولدیغندن بو بابده اقتضا ایدن تدابیر »
« مؤثره‌یه تشبثله شوحال اسف اشتماله برنهایت ویرلمسی »
« ودول متحابه ایله منعقد اولان كافهٔ معاهداتك احكامی »
« طرفمزدن ازسرنو تأیید اولندیغندن بونلرك حسن جریانه »
« رعایتله برابر دولتلرله اولان روابط مسالمتكارانه‌مزك »
« همیشه تزییدینه چالیشلمسی خلاصهٔ آمال ومقاصدمزدر »
« ربمز تعالی حضرتلری جمله‌نك مساعیسنی توفیقات »

۲۸٥

« سبحانیه‌سنه مقرون بیوره آمین »
یوم احد ۲۲ شعبان سنه ۹۳

[۱۱]

جلوس خط همایونی اولمق اوزره مدحت پاشا طرفندن قلمه آلنان مسوده‌دركه بالتعدیل بوقاروده مندرج اولان خط همایون حالنه تحویل ایدلمشدر .

بتقدیره تعالی برادرم سلطان مراد خامس حضرتلرینك مبتلا اولدیغی علت جسمانیه‌سه مانع شروط خلافت اولمغله برموجب قانون عثمانی اجدادمز تختنه جلوسمز واقع اولدی . مبرك متصف اولدیغكز رویت وجبكز وامور واحوال دولته وقوف تام واطلاعكز حسبیله صدارت مقامنده ر یاست وكلا مسندی باش وكیل عنوانیله عهدهٔ كفایتكزه توجیه و سائر وكلا ومأمورین دخی یرلرنده ابقا وتقریر قلنمشدر .

دولتمزك الیوم بولندیغی حالك اغرلغیله برابر جناب موفق الامورك الطاف صمدانیه‌سنه اولان اعتصام واعتمادم بركمال اولدیغندن واقصای مقصد وامل محض عدالت اولان احكام شرعیه و قوانین موضوعه‌نك تمامیٔ اجراسیله بالجمله تبعهٔ عثمانیه‌نك بلا استثنا نائل حقوق حریت و مساوات و مظهر ترقیات و سعادات اولملرندن عبارت بولندیغندن بو نیت

APPENDIX XV

TEXT OF THE OTTOMAN CONSTITUTION OF 1876

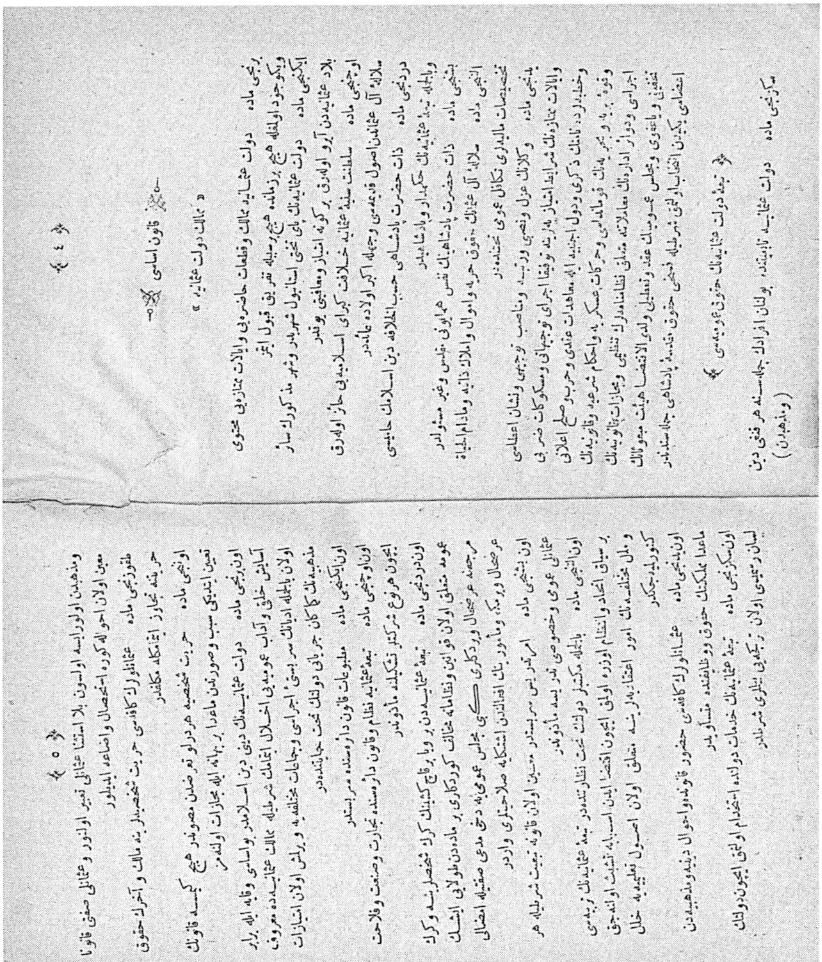

﴿ ٦ ﴾

اون طقوزنجی ماده   دولت مأمورينده عموم تبعه اهليت وقابليتلرينه كوره مناسب
اولان مأموريتلره قبول اولنورلر
يكرمنجی ماده   تكاليف مقرره نظامات مخصوصه سنه توفيقاً كافهٔ تبعه بيننده
هركسك قدرتی نسبتنجه طرح وتوزيع اولنور
يكرمی برنجی ماده   هركس اصولاً متصرف اولديغی مال وملكدن اميندر منافع
عموميه ايچون لزومی ثابت اولمدقجه وقانونی موجبنجه دكر بهاسی پشين ويرلمدكجه
كيمسه نك تصرفنده اولان ملك آلنه مز
يكرمی ايكنجی ماده   ممالك عثمانيه ده هركسك مسكن ومنزلی تعرضدن مصوندر
قانونك تعيين ايلديكی احوالدن ماعدا برسببله حكومت طرفندن جبرا هيچ كيمسه نك
مسكن ومنزلنه كيريله مز
يكرمی اوچنجی ماده   يابيله جق اصول محاكمه قانونی حكمنجه هيچ كيمسه
قانوناً منسوب اولديغی محكمه دن بشقه برمحكمه يه كتمكه اجبار اولنه مز
يكرمی دردنجی ماده   مصادره وانغاريه وجريمه ممنوعدر فقط محاربه اثناسنده
اصولاً تعيين اولنه جق تكاليف واحوال بوندن مستثنادر
يكرمی بشنجی ماده   برقانونه مستند اولمدقجه ويركو ورسومات ناميله ونام آخرله
هيچ كيمسه دن براقچه آلنه مز
يكرمی آلتنجی ماده   اشكنجه وسائر هرنوع اذيت قطعيا وكليا ممنوعدر

﴿ وكلای دولت ﴾

يكرمی يدنجی ماده   مسند صدارت ومشيخت اسلاميه طرف پادشاهيدن امنيت
بيوريلان ذاتلره احاله بيورلديغی مثللو سائر وكلانك مأموريتلری دخی باارادهٔ
شاهانه اجرا اولنور
يكرمی سكزنجی ماده   مجلس وكلا صدر اعظمك رياستی تحتنده اولهرق عقد
اولنوب داخلی وخارجی امور مهمه نك مرجعيدر   مذاكراتندن محتاج استيذان
اولانلرك قرارلری ارادهٔ سنيه ايله اجرا اولنور
يكرمی طقوزنجی ماده   وكلادن هربری دائره سنه عائد اولان اموردن اجراسی
مأذونيتی تحتنده بولنانلری اصولنه توفيقاً اجرا واجراسی مأذونيتی تحتنده اولميانلری
(صدراعظمه)

﴿ ٧ ﴾

صدر اعظمه عرض ايدر   صدر اعظم دخی اومقوله مواددن مذاكره يه محتاج
اولميانلرك مقتضاسنی اجرا و ياخود طرف حضرت پادشاهيدن استيذان ايدرك
ومحتاج مذاكره بولنانلری مجلس وكلانك مذاكره سنه عرض ايليه رك متعلق
بيوريله جق ارادهٔ سنيه موجبنجه اقتضاسنی ايفا ايلر بومصالحك انواع ودرجاتی
نظام مخصوص ايله تعيين اولنه جقدر
اوتوزنجی ماده   وكلای دولت مأموريتلرينه متعلق احوال واجرا آتدن مسؤلدر
اوتوز برنجی ماده   مبعوثان اعضاسندن بری وياخود برقاچی هيئت مبعوثانك
داخل دائرهٔ وظيفه سی اولان احوالدن طولايی وكلای دولتدن برذات حقنده
مسؤليتی موجب شكايت بيان ايتديكی حالده اولا هيئت مبعوثانك نظام داخليسی
موجبنجه بومثللو موادك هيئته حواله سی لازم كلوب كليه جكنی مذاكره يه مأمور
اولان شعبه ده تدقيق اولنمق اوزره شكايتی مشعر هيئت مبعوثان رئيسنه ويريله جك
تقرير رئيس طرفندن نهايت اوچ كون ظرفنده اوشعبه يه كوندريلور وبوشعبه
طرفندن تحقيقات لازمه اجرا واشتكا اولنان ذات طرفندن ايضاحات كافيه استحصال
اولندقدن صكره شكايتك شايان مذاكره اولديغنه دائراً كثريتله ترتيب اولنه جق
قرارنامه هيئت مبعوثانده قرائت اولنه رق ولدی الاقتضا شكايت اولنان ذات
دعوتله بالذات ويا بالواسطه ويره جكی ايضاحات استماع قلنه رق اعضای موجوده نك
ثلثان اكثريت مطلقه سيله قبول اولنور ايسه محاكمه طلبنی مشعر مضبطه سی مقام
صدارته تقديم ايله لدی العرض متعلق اوله جق ارادهٔ سنيه اوزرينه كيفيت ديوان
عالی يه حواله اولنور
اوتوز ايكنجی ماده   وكلادن اتهام اولنانلرك اصول محاكمه لری قانون مخصوص
ايله تعيين ايديله جكدر
اوتوز اوچنجی ماده   مأموريتلرندن خارج وصرف ذاتلرينه عائد هرنوع دعاويده
وكلانك سائر افراد عثمانيه دن اصلا فرقی يوقدر بومثللو خصوصاتك محاكمه سی
عائد اولديغی محاكم عموميه ده اجرا اولنور
اوتوز دردنجی ماده   ديوان عالينك دائرهٔ اتهامی طرفندن متهم اولديغنه قرار
ويريلان وكلا تبرئهٔ ذمت ايدنجيه قدر وكالتدن ساقط اولور
اوتوز بشنجی ماده   وكلا ايله هيئت مبعوثان ارasında اختلاف اولنان ماده لردن
برينك قبولنده وكلا طرفندن اصرار اولنوبده مبعوثان جانبندن اكثريت آرا ايله

﴿ ٨ ﴾

وتفصیلا اسباب موجبه بیانیله قطعیاً ومکرراً رد ایلدیکی حالده وکلانك تبدیلی ویاخود مجدداً مدت قانونیه‌سنده انتخاب اولنمق اوزره هیئت مبعوثانك فسخی منحصراً ید اقتدار حضرت پادشاهیده‌در

اوتوز التنجی ماده. مجلس عمومی منعقد اولمدیغی زمانلرده دولتی بر مخاطره‌دن ویاخود امنیت عمومیه‌یی خللدن وقایه ایچون بر ضرورت مبرمه ظهور ایتدیکی وبوبابده وضعنه لزوم کورینه‌جك قانونك مذاکره‌سیچون مجلسك جلب وجمعنه وقت مساعد اولمدیغی حالده قانون اساسی احکامنه مغایر اولمامق اوزره هیئت وکلا طرفندن ویریلان قرارلر هیئت مبعوثانك اجتماعیله ویریله‌جك قراره قدر باارادهٔ سنیه موقتاً قانون حکم وقوتنده‌در

اوتوز یدنجی ماده وکلادن هربری هرنه‌زمان مراد ایدر ایسه هیئتلرك ایکیسنده دخی بولنمق ویاخود معیتنده‌کی رؤسای مأموریندن برینی طرفندن وکالة بولندیرمق وایراد نطقده اعضایه تقدم ایتمك حقنی حائزدر

اوتوز سکزنجی ماده استیضاح ماده ایچون وکلادن برینك حضورینه مجلس مبعوثانده اکثریتله قرار ویریله‌رك دعوت اولندقده یابالذات بولنه‌رق ویاخود معیتنده‌کی رؤسای مأمورینندن برینی کوندره‌رك ایراد اولنه‌جق سؤاللره جواب ویره‌جك و یاخود لزوم کورر ایسه مسئولیتنی اوزرینه اله‌رق جوابنی تأخیر ایتمك صلاحیتنی حائز اوله‌جقدر

﴿ مأمورین ﴾

اوتوز طقوزنجی ماده بالجمله مأمورین نظاما تعیین اولنه‌جق شرایطا اوزره اهل ومستحق اولدقلری مأموریتلره انتخاب اولنه‌جقدر وبووجهله انتخاب اولنان مأمورلر قانوناً موجب عزل حرکتی تحقق ایتمدکجه ویاکندوسی استعفا ایلمدکجه ویاخود دولتجه برسبب ضروری کورلمدکجه عزل وتبدیل اولنه‌مز وحسن حرکت واستقامت اصحابندن اولانلر ودولتجه برسبب ضروری‌یه مبنی انفصال ایدنلر نظام مخصوصنده تعیین اولنه‌جغی وجهله ترفیاته وتقاعد ومعزولیت معاشلرینه نائل اوله‌جقلردر

قرقنجی ماده هر مأمورینك وظایفی نظام مخصوص ایله تعیین اولنه‌جغندن هر مأمور کندو وظیفه‌سی دائره‌سنده مسؤلدر

(قرق برنجی ماده)

﴿ ٩ ﴾

قرق برنجی ماده مأمورك آمرینه حرمت ورعایتی لازمه‌دن ایسه‌ده اطاعتی قانونك تعیین ایتدیکی دائره‌یه مخصوص‌در خلاف قانون اولان اموردہ آمره اطاعت مسئولیتدن قورتلمغه مدار اوله‌مز

﴿ مجلس عمومی ﴾

قرق ایکنجی ماده مجلس عمومی هیئت اعیان وهیئت مبعوثان ناملریله بشقه بشقه ایکی هیئتی محتویدر

قرق اوچنجی ماده مجلس عمومینك ایکی هیئتی هرسنه تشرین ثانی ابتداسنده تجمع ایدر وباارادهٔ سنیه آچیلور ومارت ابتداسنده ینه باارادهٔ سنیه قپانور بوهیئتلردن بری دیکرینك مجتمع بولنمدیغی زمانده منعقد اوله‌مز

قرق دردنجی ماده ذات حضرت پادشاهی دولتجه کورینه‌جك لزوم اوزرینه مجلس عمومی‌یی وقتندن اول دخی آچار ومدت معینهٔ اجتماعینده تنقیص و یاتمدید ایدر

قرق بشنجی ماده مجلس عمومینك یوم کشادنده ذات حضرت پادشاهی ویاخود طرفلرندن بالوکاله صدر اعظم حاضر اولدیغی ووکلای دولتله ایکی هیئتك اعضای موجوده‌سی برلکده بولندقلری حالده رسم کشاد اجرا اولنوب سنهٔ جاریه ظرفنده دولتك احوال داخلیه ومناسبات خارجیه‌سنه وسنهٔ آتیه‌ده اتخاذینه لزوم کورینه‌جك تدابیر وتشبثاته دائر برنطق همایون قرائت اولنور

قرق التنجی ماده مجلس عمومی اعضالغنه انتخاب ویانصب اولنان ذوات مجلسك یوم کشادنده صدر اعظم حضورنده و اوکون حاضر بولنمیان اولور ایسه منسوب اولدیغی هیئت مجتمع اولدیغی حالده رئیسلری حضورنده ذات حضرت پادشاهی‌یه ووطننه صداقت وقانون اساسی احکامنه وعهده‌سنه تودیع اولنان وظیفه‌یه رعایتله خلافندن مجانبت ایلیه‌جکنه تحلیف ایدیلور

قرق یدنجی ماده مجلس عمومی اعضاسی رأی ومطالعه بیاننده مختار اوله‌رق بونلردن هیچ بری برکونه وعد ووعید وتعلیمات قیدی التنده بولنه‌مز وکرك ویردیکی رأیلردن وکرك مجلسك مذاکراتی اثناسنده بیان ایتدیکی مطالعه‌لردن طولایی بروجهله اتهام اولنه‌مز مکرکه مجلسك نظامنامهٔ داخلیسی خلافنده حرکت ایتمش اوله بوتقدیرجه نظامنامهٔ مذکور حکمنجه معامله کورر

﴾ ١٠ ﴿

قرق سکزنجی ماده مجلس عمومی اعضاسندن برینك خیانت وقانون اساسی یی نقض والغایه تصدی وارتکاب تهمتلرندن بریله متهم اولدیغنه منسوب اولدیغی هیئت اعضای موجوده سنك ثلثان اکثریت مطلقه سیله قرار ویریلور و یاخود قانوناً حبس ونفیی موجب برجزا ایله محکوم اولور ایسه اعضالق صفتی زائل اولور و بو افعالك محاکمه سیله مجازاتی عائد اولدیغی محکمه طرفندن رؤیت وحکم اولنور

قرق طقوزنجی ماده مجلس عمومی اعضاسندن هربری رأینی بالذات اعطا ایدر وهربرینك مذاکره ده بولنان برماده نك ردوقبولنه دائر رأی ویرمکدن اجتنابه حق واردر

اللنجی ماده برکیمسه ذکر اولنان ایکی هیئتك ایکیسنه بردن اعضا اولەمز

اللی برنجی ماده مجلس عمومی هیئتلرینك ایکیسنده دخی مرتب اولان اعضانك نصفندن برزیاده حاضر بولنمدقجه مذاکره یه مبادرت اولنەمز وکافهٔ مذاکرات ثلثان اکثریتیله مشروط اولمیان خصوصاتده حاضر بولنان اعضانك اکثریت مطلقه سیله قرار کیر اولور وتساوئ آرا وقوعنده رئیسك رأیی ایکی عد ایدیلور

اللی ایکنجی ماده برکیمسه شخصنه متعلق دعواسندن طولایی مجلس عمومینك ایکی هیئتندن برینه عرضحال ویردیکی حالده اکر اولا عائد اولدیغی مأمورین دولته ویاخود اومأمورلرك تابع بولندقلری مرجعه مراجعت ایتدیکی تبین ایدر ایسه عرضحالی رد اولنور

اللی اوچنجی ماده مجدداً قانون تنظیمی ویاقوانین موجوده دن برینك تعدیلی تکلیفی هیئت وکلایه عائد اولدیغی کبی هیئت اعیان و هیئت مبعوثانك دخی کندو وظیفهٔ معینه لری دائره سنده بولنان مواد ایچون قانون تنظیمی و یاخود قوانین موجوده دن برینك تعدیلنی استدعایه صلاحیتلری اولمغله اولجه مقام صدارت واسطه سیله طرف شاهانه دن استیذان اولنه رق ارادهٔ سنیه متعلق بیوریلور ایسه عائد اولدیغی دائره لردن ویریله جك ایضاحات وتفصیلات اوزرینه لایحه لرینك تنظیمی شورای دولته حواله اولنور

اللی دردنجی ماده شورای دولتده بالمذاکره تنظیم اولنه جق قوانین لایحه لری هیئت مبعوثانده بعده هیئت اعیانده تدقیق وقبول اولندقدن صکره اجرای احکامنه ارادهٔ سنیهٔ حضرت پادشاهی متعلق بیوریلور ایسه دستور العمل اولور واشبو

(هیئتلرك)

﴾ ١١ ﴿

هیئتلرك برنده قطعیاً رد اولنان قانون لایحه سی اوسنه نك مدت اجتماعیه سنده تکرار موقع مذاکره یه قونیله مز

اللی بشنجی ماده برقانون لایحه سی اولا هیئت مبعوثانده بعده هیئت اعیانده بند بند اوقونوب و هر بندینه رأی و یریلوب اکثریت آرا ایله قرار ویرلدکجه و بعد القرار هیئت مجموعه سی ایچون دخی بتکرار اکثریتله قرار حاصل اولمدقجه قبول اولنمش اولمز

اللی آلتنجی ماده بوهیئتلر وکلادن ویا انلرك کوندره جکی وکیللردن و یاکندی اعضالرندن اولمیان ویاخود رسماً دعوت اولنمش مأمورلرندن بولنمیان هیچ کیمسه یی کرك اصالة وکرك برجماعت طرفندن وکالة برماده افاده سیچون کلمش اولدیغی حالده اصلا قبول ایدەمز وافاده لرینی استماع ایلیه مز

اللی یدنجی ماده هیئتلرك مذاکراتی لسان ترکی اوزره جریان ایدر ومذاکره اولنه جق لایحه لرك صورتلری طبع ایله یوم مذاکره دن اول اعضایه توزیع اولنور

اللی سکزنجی ماده هیئتلرده ویریله جك رأیلر یا تعیین اسامی و یاخود اشارات مخصوصه ویاخود رأی خفی ایله اولور رأی خفی اصولنك اجراسی اعضای موجوده نك اکثریت آراسیله قرار و یرلمکه متوقفدر

اللی طقوزنجی ماده هرهیئتك انضباط داخلیسی منحصراً کندی رئیسی اجرا ایدر

﴾ هیئت اعیان ﴿

آلتمشنجی ماده هیئت اعیانك رئیس واعضاسی نهایت مقداری هیئت مبعوثان اعضاسنك ثلثی مقدارینی تجاوز ایتمامك اوزره طوغریدن طوغری یه طرف حضرت پادشاهیدن نصب اولنور

آلتمش برنجی ماده هیئت اعیانه اعضا تعیین اولنه بیلمك ایچون آثار وافعالی عمومك وثوق و اعتمادینه شایان وامور دولتده خدمات ممدوحه سی مسبوق و متعارف ذواتدن اولمق وقرق یاشندن اشاغی بولنمامق لازمدر

آلتمش ایکنجی ماده هیئت اعیان اعضالغی قیدحیات ایله در بومأموریتلره وکلالق وواليلك واردو مشیرلکی وقاضیعسکرلك وایلچیلك و پطریقلق وخاخام باشیلق مأموریتنده بولنمش اولان معزولیندن و بری و بحری فریقاندن و صفات لازمه یی

﴾ ١٢ ﴿

جامع سائر ذواتدن مناسبلری تعیین اولنور کندو طلبلریله دولتجه سائر مأموریته تعیین اولنانلر اعضالق مأموریتندن ساقط اولور

التمش اوچنجی ماده هیئت اعیانك اعضالق معاشی شهریه اون بیك غروشدر بشقه بر نام ایله خزینه‌دن موظف اولان اعضانك معاش وتعیینی اکر اون بیك غروشدن دون ایسه اول مقداره ابلاغ اولنور و اکر اون بیك غروش وبازیاده ایسه ابقا اولنور

التمش دردنجی ماده هیئت اعیان هیئت مبعوثاندن ویریلان قوانین و موازنه لایحه‌لرینی تدقیق ایله اکر بونلرده اساساً امور دینیه‌یه وذات حضرت پادشاهینك حقوق سنیه‌سنه وحریته و قانون اساسی احکامنه و دولتك تمامیت ملکیه‌سنه وممالکتك امنیت داخلیه‌سنه ووطنك اسباب مدافعه و محافظه‌سنه و آداب عمومیه‌یه خلل ویرر برشی کوررایسه مطالعه‌سنك علاوه‌سیله یاقطعیاً رد ویاخود تعدیل و تصحیح اولنمق اوزره هیئت مبعوثانه اعاده ایدر وقبول ایندیکی لایحه‌لری تصدیق ایله مقام صدارته عرض ایلر و هیئته تقدیم اولنان عرضحاللری بالتدقیق لزوم کورر ایسه علاوهٔ مطالعه ایله برابر مقام صدارته تقدیم ایدر

﴾ هیئت مبعوثان ﴿

التمش بشنجی ماده هیئت مبعوثانك مقدار اعضاسی تبعهٔ عثمانیه‌دن هر اللی بیك نفوس ذکورده بر نفر اولمق اعتباریله ترتیب اولنور

التمش التنجی ماده امر انتخاب رأی خفی قاعده‌سی اوزرینه مؤسسدر صورت اجراسی قانون مخصوص ایله تعیین اولنه‌جقدر

التمش یدنجی ماده هیئت مبعوثان اعضالغیله حکومت مأموریتی برذات عهده‌سنده اجتماع ایده‌مز فقط وکلادن انتخاب اولنانلرك اعضالغی مجازدر وسائر مأموریندن بری مبعوثلغه انتخاب اولنور ایسه قبول ایدوب ایتمامك ید اختیارنده‌در فقط قبول ایتدیکی حالده مأموریتندن انفصال ایدر

التمش سکزنجی ماده هیئت مبعوثان ایچون اعضالغه انتخابی جائز اولمیانلر شونلردر اولا تبعهٔ دولت علیه‌دن اولمیان ثانیاً نظام مخصوصی موجبنجه موقتا خدمت اجنبیه امتیازینی حائز اولان ثالثا ترکجه بیلمیان رابعا اوتوزیاشنی اکمال ایتمیان خامسا حین

(انتخابده)

﴾ ١٣ ﴿

انتخابده برکیمسه‌نك خدمتکارلغنده بولنان سادساً افلاس ایله محکوم اولوبده اعاده اعتبار ایتمامش اولان سابعا سوء احوال ایله مشتهر اولان ثامنا محجوریتنه حکم لاحق اولوبده فك حجر ایدلمیان تاسعا حقوق مدنیه‌دن ساقط اولمش اولان عاشرا تابعیت اجنبیه ادعاسنده بولنان کیمسه‌لردر بونلر مبعوث اوله‌مز درت سنه‌دن صکره اجرا اولنه‌جق انتخابلرده مبعوث اولمق ایچون ترکجه اوقومق وممکن مرتبه یازمق دخی شرط اوله‌جقدر

التمش طقوزنجی ماده مبعوثانك انتخاب عمومیسی درت سنه‌ده برکره اجرا اولنور وهر مبعوثك مدت مأموریتی درت سنه‌دن عبارت اولوب فقط تکرار انتخاب اولنمق جائزدر

یتمشنجی ماده مبعوثلرك انتخاب عمومیسنه هیئتك مبدأ اجتماعی اولان تشرین ثانیدن لااقل درت ماه مقدم باشلانیلور

یتمش برنجی ماده هیئت مبعوثان اعضاسنك هر بری کندینی انتخاب ایدن دائره‌نك ایروجه وکیلی اولمیوب عموم عثمانلولرك وکیلی حکمنده‌در

یتمش ایکنجی ماده منتخبلر انتخاب ایده‌جکلری مبعوثلری منسوب اولدقلری دائرهٔ ولایت اهالیسندن انتخاب ایتمکه مجبوردر

یتمش اوچنجی ماده باارادهٔ سنیه هیئت مبعوثان فسخ ایله طاغیلدیغی حالده نهایت التی ایده مجتمع اولمق اوزره عموم مبعوثانك مجدداً انتخابنه باشلانیله‌جقدر

یتمش دردنجی ماده هیئت مبعوثان اعضاسندن بری وفات ایدر ویا اسباب حجریهٔ مشروعه‌دن برینه دوچار اولور ویا براوزون مدتده مجلسه دوام ایتمز ویاخود استعفا ایدر ویا محکومیت ویا قبول مأموریت جهتیله اعضالقدن ساقط اولورسه یرینه نهایت کله‌جك اجتماعه یتشمك اوزره اصولی وجهله دیکری تعیین اولنور

یتمش بشنجی ماده منحل اولان مبعوثلق مقاملرینه انتخاب اولنه‌جق اعضانك مأموریتی کله‌جك انتخاب عمومی زمانته قدردر

یتمش التنجی ماده مبعوثلردن هر برینه بهرسنه اجتماعیچون خزینه‌دن یکرمی بیك غروش ویریله‌جك وشهریه بشبیك غروش معاش اعتباریله مأمورین ملکیه نظامنه توفیقاً عزیمت و عودت خرجراهی اعطا قلنه‌جقدر

یتمش یدنجی ماده هیئت مبعوثان ریاستنه هیئت طرفندن اکثریتله اوچ وایکنجی واوچنجی ریاستلره اوچرنفرکه جمعاطقوز ذات انتخاب اولنه‌رق حضور شاهانه‌یه

﴾ ١٤ ﴿

عرض ایله بونلردن بریسی ریاسته وایکیسی رئیس وکالتلرینه باارادهٔ سنیه ترجیح ومأمورینلری اجرا قلنور

یتمش سکزنجی ماده هیئت مبعوثانك مذاکراتی علنیدر فقط بر مادهٔ مهمه‌دن طولایی مذاکراتی خفی طوتلمق وکلا جانبندن ویاخود هیئت مبعوثانك اعضاسندن اون بش ذات طرفندن تکلیف اولندقده هیئتك اجتماع ایتدیکی محل اعضانك ماعداسندن تخلیه ایدیله‌رك تکلیفك ردویاقبولیچون اکثریت آرایه مراجعت ایدیلور

یتمش طقوزنجی ماده هیئت مبعوثانك مدت اجتماعیه‌سنده اعضادن هیچ بری هیئت طرفندن اتهامه سبب کافی بولندیغنه اکثریتله قرار وریلمدکجه ویاخود برجنحه ویاجنایت اجرا ایدر ایکن ویا اجرایی متعاقب طوتلمدقجه توقیف ومحاکمه اولنه‌مز

سکساننجی ماده هیئت مبعوثان کندویه حواله اولنه‌جق قوانین لایحه‌لرینی مذاکره ایله بونلردن امور مالیه‌یه وقانون اساسی‌یه تعلق ایدر ماده‌لری رد ویا قبول ویاخود تعدیل ایدر ومصارف عمومیه موازنه قانونده کوسترلدیکی وجهله هیئت مبعوثانده تفصیلاتیله تدقیق اولندقدن صکره مقدارینه وکلا ایله برلکده قرار وریلور وبوکا قارشولق اوله‌جق وارداتك کیفیت وکمیتی وصورت توزیع وتدارکی کذلك وکلا ایله برلکده تعیین ایدیلور

﴾ محاکم ﴿

سکسان برنجی ماده قانون مخصوصنه توفیقاً طرف دولتدن نصب اولنان ویدلرینه برات شریف وریلان حاکملر لاینعزلدر فقط استعفالری قبول اولنور حاکملرك ترقیاتی ومسلکلری وتبدیل مأموریتلری وتقاعدلری وبرجرم ایله محکومیت اوزرینه عزل اولنملری دخی قانون مخصوصی حکمنه تابعدر وحاکملرك ومحاکم مأمورلرینك مطلوب اولان اوصافنی اشبو قانون ارائه ایدر

سکسان ایکنجی ماده محکمه‌لرده هرنوع محاکمه علناً جریان ایدر واعلاماتك نشرینه مأذونیت واردر انجق قانونده مصرح اسبابه مبنی محکمه محاکمه‌یی خفی طوته‌بیلور

سکسان اوچنجی ماده هرکس حضور محکمه‌ده حقوقنی محافظه ایچون لزوم کوردیکی وسائط مشروعه‌یی استعمال ایده‌بیلور

سکسان دردنجی ماده برمحکمه وظیفه‌سی داخلنده اولان دعوانك هرنه وسیله (ایله)

﴾ ١٥ ﴿

ایله اولور ایسه اولسون رؤیتندن امتناع ایده‌مز وبرکره رؤیتنه ویاخود رؤیتی ایچون اقتضا ایدن تحقیقات اولیه‌یه باشلاندقدن صکره تعطیل ویا تعویق دخی جائز اوله‌مز مکرکه مدعی دعوادن کف ید ایتمش اوله شوقدرکه جزایه متعلق دعاویده حکومته عائد اولان حقوق نظامی وجهله ینه اجرا اولنور

سکسان بشنجی ماده هردعوی عائد اولدیغی محکمه‌ده رؤیت اولنور اشخاص ایله حکومت بینینده‌کی دعوالر دخی محاکم عمومیه‌یه عائددر

سکسان التنجی ماده محکمه‌لر هر درلو مداخلاتدن آزاده‌در

سکسان یدنجی ماده دعاوی شرعیه محاکم شرعیه‌ده ودعاوی نظامیه محاکم نظامیه‌ده رؤیت اولنور

سکسان سکزنجی ماده محکمه‌لرك صنوف ووظائف وصلاحیتنك درجات وتقسیماتی وحکامك توظیفی قوانینه مستنددر

سکسان طقوزنجی ماده هرنه نام ایله اولور ایسه اولسون بعض مواد مخصوصه‌یی رؤیت وحکم ایتمك ایچون محاکم معینه خارجنده فوق العاده برمحکمه ویاخود حکم ویرمك صلاحیتنی حائز قومیسیون تشکیلی قطعاً جائز دکلدر فقط قانوناً معین اولدیغی وجهله تعیین مولی وتحکیم جائزدر

طقسانجی ماده هیچ برحاکم حاکملك صفتیله دولتك معاشلی بربشقه مأموریتنی عهده‌سنده جمع ایده‌مز

طقسان برنجی ماده امور جزائیه‌ده حقوق عامه‌یی وقایه‌یه مأمور مدعی عمومیلر بولنه‌جق وبونلرك وظائف ودرجاتی قانون ایله تعیین قلنه‌جقدر

﴾ دیوان عالی ﴿

طقسان ایکنجی ماده دیوان عالی اوتوز اعضادن مرکبدر بونلرك اونی هیئت اعیان واونی شورای دولت واونی محکمهٔ تمییز واستیناف رؤسا واعضاسندن قرعه ایله تفریق وتعیین اولنه‌رق هیئت اعیان دائره‌سنده لزوم کورندکجه باارادهٔ سنیه عقد اولنور وظیفه‌سی وکلا ایله محکمهٔ تمییز رؤسا واعضاسنك وذات وحقوق شاهانه علیهنده حرکته ودولتی برحال مخاطره‌یه القایه تصدی ایلیانلرك محاکمه‌سیدر

طقسان اوچنجی ماده دیوان عالی ایکی‌یه منقسم اولوب بری دائرهٔ اتهامیه وبری

﴿ ١٦ ﴾

دیوان حکمدر دائرهٔ اتهامیه طقوز اعضادن عبارت اولوب بونك اوچی هیئت اعیان و اوچی دیوان تمییز و استیناف واوچی شورای دولت اعضاسندن دیوان عالی‌یه الندجق اعضا ایچندن قرعه ایله انتخاب اولنور

طقسان دردنجی ماده بو دائره شکایت اولنان ذواتك متهم اولوب اولمدیغنه ثلثان اکثریتیله قرار ویرر ودائرهٔ اتهامیه‌ده بولنانلر دیوان حکمده بولنه‌من

طقسان بشنجی ماده دیوان حکم بدیسی هیئت اعیان و یدیسی دیوان تمییز واستیناف ویدیسی شورای دولت رؤسا و اعضاسندن اولمق اوزره دیوان عالی اعضاسنك یکرمی بر نفرندن مرکب اوله‌رق دائرهٔ اتهامیه طرفندن محاکمه‌سی لازم اولدیغنه قرار ویرلمش دعوالر حقنده اعضای مرتبه‌نك ثلثان اکثریتیله قطعیاً وقوانین موضوعه‌سنه تطبیقاً حکم ایدر وحکملری قابل استیناف وتمییز دکلدر

﴿ امور مالیه ﴾

طقسان التنجی ماده تکالیف دولتك هیچ بری بر قانون ایله تعیین اولنمدقجه وضع وتوزیع واستحصال اولنه‌مز

طقسان یدنجی ماده دولتك بودجه‌سی واردات ومصارفات تقریبیه‌سنی مبین قانوندر تکالیف دولتك وضع وتوزیع وتحصیل امرنده مستند اوله‌جغی قانون بودر

طقسان سکزنجی ماده بودجه یعنی موازنهٔ عمومیه قانونی مجلس عمومیده ماده‌بماده تدقیق وقبول اولنور واردات ومصارفات تخمینه‌نك مفرداتنی جامع اولمق اوزره اکا مربوط اولان جدوللر نظاماً تعیین اولنان نمونه‌سنه توفیقاً اقسام وفصول ومواد متعدده‌یه منقسم اوله‌رق بونلرك مذاکره‌سی دخی فصل فصل اجرا ایدیلور

طقسان طقوزنجی ماده موازنهٔ عمومیه قانونی متعلق اولدیغی سنه‌نك دخولنده موقع اجرایه قونیله‌بیلمك ایچون لایحه‌سی هیئت مبعوثانه مجلس عمومینك کشادی عقیبنده اعطا اولنور

یوزنجی ماده بر قانون مخصوص ایله معین اولمدقجه اموال دولتدن موازنه خارجنده صرفیات جائز اوله‌مز

یوز برنجی ماده مجلس عمومینك منعقد بولنمدیغی اثناده اسباب مجبرهٔ فوق العاده‌دن طولایی موازنه خارجنده مصرف اختیارینه لزوم قوی تحقق ایدر ایسه

(مسئولیتی)

﴿ ١٧ ﴾

مسئولیتی هیئت وکلایه عائد اولمق ومجلس عمومینك کشادی عقیبنده اکا دائر قانون لایحه‌سی مجلس عمومی‌یه ویرلمك اوزره اومصرفك تسویه‌سی ایچون اقتضا ایدن مبالغك طرف حضرت پادشاهی‌یه عرض واستیذان ایله صادر اوله‌جق ارادهٔ سنیه اوزرینه تدارك وصرفی جائز اولور

یوز ایکنجی ماده موازنه قانوننك حکمی برسنه‌یه مخصوص اوسنه‌نك خارجنده حکمی جاری اوله‌مز انجق بعض احوال فوق العاده‌دن طولایی مجلس مبعوثان موازنه‌یی قرار لشدیرمقسزین فسخ اولندیغی حالده حکمی برسنه‌یی تجاوز ایتمامك اوزره بر قرارنامه ایله وکلای دولت باارادهٔ سنیه سنهٔ سابقه موازنه‌سنك جریان احکامنی مجلس مبعوثانك کله‌جك اجتماعنه قدر تمدید ایدرلر

یوز اوچنجی ماده محاسبهٔ قطعیه قانونی متعلق اولدیغی سنه‌نك وارداتندن استحصال اولنان مبالغ ایله‌ینه اوسنه‌نك مصارفاتنه وقوع بولان صرفیاتك مقدار حقیقیسنی مبین اوله‌رق بونك شکل وتقسیماتی دخی موازنهٔ عمومیه قانوننه تماماً مطابق اوله‌جقدر

یوز دردنجی ماده محاسبهٔ قطعیه قانوننك لایحه‌سی متعلق اولدیغی سنه‌نك ختامندن اعتباراً نهایت درت سنه صکره مجلس عمومی‌یه اعطا اولنور

یوز بشنجی ماده اموال دولتك قبض وصرفنه مأمور اولنلرك محاسبه‌لرینی رؤیت ودوائردن تنظیم اولنان سال محاسبه‌لرینی تدقیق ایدرك خلاصهٔ تدقیقات ونتیجهٔ مطالعاتنی هرسنه بر تقریر مخصوص ایله هیئت مبعوثانه عرض ایتمك اوزره بر دیوان محاسبات تشکیل اولنه‌جقدر بو دیوان هر اوچ ایده بر کره احوال مالیه‌یی ریاست وکلا واسطه‌سیله باتقریر طرف حضرت پادشاهی‌یه دخی عرض ایدر

یوز التنجی ماده دیوان محاسباتك اعضاسی اون ایکی کشیدن مرتب اوله‌جق وهر بری هیئت مبعوثاندن اکثریتله عزلنك لزومی تصدیق اولنمدقجه مأموریتنده قید حیات ایله قالمق اوزره باارادهٔ سنیه نصب اولنه‌جقدر .

یوز یدنجی ماده دیوان محاسبات اعضاسنك اوصافی ووظایفنك تفصیلاتی وصورت استعفا وتبدیل وترقی وتقاعدی واقلامنك کیفیت تشکیلی بر نظام مخصوص ایله تعیین اولنه‌جقدر

٣

SELECTION OF ARTICLES FROM CONSTITUTIONAL DRAFTS AND THEIR EVOLUTION

THE DEFINITION OF THE OTTOMAN STATE

In the Printed Version of Midhad Pasha's Constitutional Model (Appendix III)

Kanun-ı Cedit ser-levhasıyla Midhad Paşa tarafından tanzim olunan müsvedde Memalik-i Devlet-i Osmaniye

Devlet-i Osmaniye memalik ve kıtaat-ı hazıradan ve eyalat-ı mümtazeden mürekkep olarak hudut-ı muayyene ile mahdut ve usul-ı idaresi şer-i şerife müstenit ve merbuttur.

Memalik-i Devlet-i Osmaniye yekvücut olmakla hiçbir zamanda hiçbir sebeple inkısam kabul etmez ve hududu tağyir edilemez.

In the Draft Constitution Corrected by Safved Pasha (Appendix VIII)

Memalik-i Devlet-i Osmaniye

Madde 1. Devlet-i Osmaniye memalik ve kıtaat-ı hazırayı ve eyalat-ı mümtazeyi muhtevi ve usul-ı idaresi esasen şer-i şerife ahkamına müstenit ve merbuttur.

Madde 2. Memalik-i Devlet-i Osmaniye yekvücut olmakla hiçbir zamanda hiçbir sebeple inkısam kabul etmez.

Madde 3. Devlet-i Osmaniye'nin payitahtı İstanbul şehridir ve şehr-i mezkurun sair bilad-ı Osmaniye'den ayrı olarak bir güne imtiyaz ve muafiyeti yoktur.

In the 119-Article Draft Constitution (Appendix XI)

Memalik-i Devlet-i Osmaniye

Madde 1. Devlet-i Osmaniye'nin kavaid-i hükümeti şer-i şerife ahkamına müstenit ve mebnidir.

Madde 2. Devlet-i Osmaniye memalik ve kıtaat-ı hazırayı ve eyalat-ı mümtazeyi muhtevi ve yekvücut olmakla hiçbir zamanda hiçbir sebeple tefrik kabul etmez.

Madde 3. Devlet-i Osmaniye'nin payitahtı İstanbul şehridir ve şehr-i mezkurun sair bilad-ı Osmaniye'den ayrı olarak bir güne imtiyaz ve muafiyeti yoktur.

In the Ottoman Constitution of 1876 (Appendix XV)

Memalik-i Devlet-i Osmaniye

Madde 1. Devlet-i Osmaniye memalik ve kıtaat-ı hazırayı ve eyalat-ı mümtazeyi muhtevi ve yekvücut olmakla hiçbir zamanda hiçbir sebeple tefrik kabul etmez.

Madde 2. Devlet-i Osmaniye'nin payitahtı İstanbul şehr-idir ve şehr-i mezkurun sair bilad-ı Osmaniye'den ayrı olarak bir gune imtiyaz ve muafiyeti yoktur.

THE DEFINITION OF THE SULTANATE AND THE SULTAN'S PREROGATIVES

In the Printed Version of Midhad Pasha's Constitutional Model

Zat-ı Hazret-i Padişahi ve Hanedan-ı Celili

Saltanat-ı Seniye-i Osmaniye hilafet-i kübra-yı İslamiye'yi haiz olarak sülale-i âl-i Osman'dan ekber ve erşet evlada aittir.

Zat-ı Hazret-i Padişahi haseb-ül hilafe din-i İslam'ın hamisi ve nigehbanı ve kuvve-i berriye ve bahriyenin birinci kumandanıdır.

Vükelanın azl ve nasbı ve düvel-i ecnebiye ile muahedat akdi ve harp ve sulh ilanı ve harekat-ı askeriye ve kaffe-i tedabir-i mülkiyenin ittihaz ve icrası ve mücriminin affı ve Meclis-i Mebusan'ın akd ve feshi zat-ı Hazret-i Padişahi'nin imtiyaz-ı mahsus ve mukaddesidir.

Zat-ı Hazret-i Hilafetpenahi'nin nefs-i hümayunu mukaddes ve her türlü mesuliyetten masun ve mahfuzdur. Muhafaza-ı şan-ı saltanat için muhassas olan tahsisat-ı seniyenin tedariki umum milletin vezaifindendir. Hasb-el-iktiza zam ve tadil edilecek olur ise Meclis-i Mebusan kararı üzere tayin olunur.

Kuvve-i İcraiye

Kuvve-i icraiye münhasıran zat-ı Hazret-i Padişahi'ye aittir. Kaffe-i icraat nam-ı şahaneye olarak vükelası vasıtasıyla ifa olunur. Kuvve-i icraiye münferiden nizam ve kanun yapmaz. Fakat lüzum gördüğü nizamat ve kanunun yapılmasını Şura-yı Devlet'e emreder.

In the Archival Version of Midhad Pasha's Constitutional Model (Appendix IV)

Madde 55. Kuvve-i icraiyenin muvafık-ı kanun olan evamiri mukaddestir. Muhalefet eden kanunen ceza görür.

In the Archival Version of Said Pasha's Constitutional Model (Appendix V)

Kuvve-i hükümet bahsindedir
Kuvve-i hükümetin riyaset ve himayesi hükümdara aittir.

Kuvve-i kanuniye beyanındadır
Kuvve-i kanuniye münferit bir Millet Meclisi'ne tefviz olunmuştur.

Kuvve-i icraiye beyanındadır
Kuvve-i icraiye zat-ı hükümdaride kaimdir.

Zat-ı hükümdarinin vükela vasıtasıyla Millet Meclisi'ne kavanin layıhaları itasına selahiyeti vardır.

Hükümdar kuvve-i askeriyeyi istimal eder fakat kat'a kumanda edemez.

Hükümdar memalikin hiçbir parçasını terk etmeye ve Millet-i Meclisi ihlal etmeye veya Kanun-i Esasi'nin ve kavanin-i sairenin ahkamını tatil etmeye kadir olamaz.

Hükümdar umur-ı devletin ahval-ı umumiyesini her sene bir beyanname-i mahsus ile Millet Meclisi'ne bildirir.

Muahedat akdi hükümdara aittir.

Hükümdar muhafaza-ı devlete nezaret eder. Fakat Millet Meclisi'nin rızası olmadıkça bir muharebeye şüru edemez.

Hükümdarın aff-ı mücazata hakkı vardır. Fakat bu hakkın istimalinden evvel Şura-yı Devlet'in kararı istihsal olunur. Aff-ı umumi icrası bir kanun-ı mahsus suduruna mütevakıftır.

Hükümdar vükelayı nasb ve azl eder. Fakat süferanın ve asakir-i berriye ve bahriye başkumandanlarının ve valilerin ve müddei-i umumilerin ve nizamen birinci derecede sair memurinin azli Meclis-i Vükela ile müzakereye mütevakkıftır.

Kuvve-i adliye beyanındadır
Hükümet-i adliye hükümdar namına olarak icra kılınır.
Politika cünhalarının ve matbuat vasıtasıyla vuku bulan töhmetlerin hakk-ı tetkiki udule aittir.

In the Draft Constitution Corrected by Safved Pasha

Zat-ı Hazret-i Padişahi

Madde 4- Saltanat-ı Seniye-i Osmaniye hilafet-i kübra-yı İslamiye'yi haiz olarak sülale-i âl-i Osman'dan usul-ı kadimesi vechile ekber evlada aittir.

Madde 5. Zat-ı Hazret-i Padişahi haseb-ül hilafe din-i İslam'ın hamisi ve bilcümle tebaa-i Osmaniye'nin hükümdar ve padişahıdır.

Madde 6. Vükelanın azl ve nasbı ve rütbe ve mansıb tevcihi ve nişan itası ve eyalat-ı mümtazenin şerait-i imtiyazelerine tevfikan icra-yı tevcihatı ve meskukat darbı ve hutbelerde nam-ı padişahinin zikri ve düvel-i ecnebiye ile muahedat akdi ve harp ve sulh ilanı ve harekat-ı askeriye ve kaffe-i ahkam-ı şeriye ve kanuniyenin icrası ve mücazat-ı kanuniyenin tadili veya affı ve Meclis-i Umumi'nin akd ve tadili ve lede-l-iktiza Meclis-i Mebusan'ın azası yeniden intihap olunmak şartıyla feshi hukuk-ı mukaddes-i padişahidendir.

In the 119-Article Draft Constitution

Zat-ı Hazret-i Padişahi

Madde 3. Saltanat-ı Seniye-i Osmaniye hilafet-i kübra-yı İslamiye'yi haiz olarak sülale-i âl-i Osman'dan usul-ı kadimesi vechile ekber evlada aittir.

Madde 4. Zat-ı Hazret-i Padişahi haseb-ül hilafe din-i İslam'ın hamisi ve bilcümle tebaa-ı Osmaniye'nin hükümdar ve padişahıdır.

Madde 5. (addition in the margin). Zat-ı Hazret-i Padişahi'nin nefs-i hümayunu mukaddes ve gayri mesuldür.

Madde 6. (addition in the margin). Sülale-i âl-i Osman'ın hukuk, hürriyet ve emval-i zatiye madam-el hayat tahsisat-ı maliyeleri tekafil-i umumi tahtındadır.

Madde 7. Vükelanın azl ve nasbı ve rütbe ve menasıp tevcihi ve nişan itası ve eyalat-ı mümtazenin şerait-i imtiyaziyelerine tevfikan icra-yı tevcihatı ve meskukat darbı ve hutbelerde namının zikri ve düvel-i ecnebiye ile muahedat akdi ve harp ve sulh ilanı ve (kuvve-i berriye ve bahriyenin kumandası)[1] ve harekat-ı askeriye ve ahkam-ı şeriye ve kanuniyenin icrası ve (devair-i idarenin muamelatına müteallik nizamnamelerin tanzimi) ve mücazat-ı kanuniyenin tahfifi veya affı ve Meclis-i Umumi'nin akd ve tatili ve lede-l-iktiza Heyet-i Mebusan'ın azası yeniden intihap olunmak şartıyla feshi hukuk-ı mukaddese-i ~~padişahidendir~~ (padişahi cümlesindendir).

In the Ottoman Constitution

Memalik-i Devlet-i Osmaniye

Madde 3. Saltanat-ı Seniye-i Osmaniye hilafet-i kübra-yı İslamiye'yi haiz olarak sülale-i âl-i Osman'dan usul-ı kadimesi vechile ekber evlada aittir.

Madde 4. Zat-ı Hazret-i Padişahi haseb-ül hilafe din-i İslam'ın hamisi ve bilcümle tebaa-ı Osmaniye'nin hükümdar ve padişahıdır.

Madde 5. (addition in the margin). Zat-ı Hazret-i Padişahi'nin nefs-i hümayunu mukaddes ve gayri mesuldür.

Madde 6. (addition in the margin). Sülale-i âl-i Osman'ın hukuk, hürriyet ve emval ve emlak-i zatiye madam-el hayat tahsisat-ı maliyeleri tekafil-i umumi tahtındadır.

Madde 7. Vükelanın azl ve nasbı ve rütbe ve menasıp tevcihi ve nişan itası ve eyalat-ı mümtazenin şerait-i imtiyaziyelerine tevfikan icra-yı tevcihatı ve meskukat darbı ve hutbelerde namının zikri ve düvel-i ecnebiye ile muahedat akdi ve harp ve sulh ilanı ve kuvve-i berriye ve bahriyenin kumandası ve harekat-ı askeriye ve ahkam-ı şeriye ve kanuniyenin icrası ve devair-i idarenin muamelatına müteallik nizamnamelerin tanzimi ve mücazat-ı kanuniyenin tahfifi veya affı ve Meclis-i Umumi'nin akd ve tatili ve lede-l-iktiza Heyet-i Mebusan'ın azası yeniden intihap olunmak şartıyla feshi hukuk-ı mukaddese-i padişahi cümlesindendir.

---

[1] The parentheses indicate the parts added later.

OTTOMAN SUBJECTHOOD AND THE RIGHTS AND DUTIES OF OTTOMANS

In the Printed Version of Midhad Pasha's Constitutional Model

Tabiiyet-i Osmaniye ve Osmanlıların Hukuk ve Vezaifi

Tabiiyet-i Devlet-i Osmaniye'de bulunan efradın cümlesine bila-istisna Osmanlı tabir olunur.

Osmanlı sıfatı kanunen tayin olunan hususata göre istihsal ve ifade edilir.

Kaffe-i Osmaniyan herhangi kavm ve mezhepten bulunur ise bulunsun hürriyet-i şahsiyelerine malik ve memleketin hukuk ve tekalifinde ve kanun nazarında cümlesi müsavidir.

Lisan-ı Türki devletin lisan-ı resmisidir ve hıdemat-ı devlette istihdam olunmak için devletin lisan-ı resmisini bilmek şarttır.

Mezahip ve edyan-ı muhtelife devletin taht-ı himayesinde olup herkes mensup olduğu din ve mezhebi icrada serbesttir. Fakat bu müsaadeyi su-i istimal ile asayiş ve ahlak-ı umumiyeyi ihlale tasaddi edenler ber-mucib-i kanun ceza göreceklerdir. Herkes kalen ve kalemen beyan-ı efkarda azadedir. Ancak bunu su-i istimal ile asayiş ve ahlak-ı umumiyeyi ihlale tasaddi edenler ber mucib-ı kanun ceza göreceklerdir.

Herkes meşruan mutasarrıf olduğu mal ve mülkünden emindir. Menafi-i umumiye için lüzumu kanunen sabit olmadıkça ve kıymet-i hakikiyesi verilmedikçe kimsenin mülkü zabt olunamaz. Ve kanunun cevazı olmadıkça hiç kimsenin meskeni ve menzili basılamaz.

Matbuat serbesttir. Hukuk ve vezaifi kanun-ı mahsus ile muayyendir.

Tebaa-ı Osmaniye'nin terbiye-i umumiyesi bir siyak-ı intizam ve ittihat üzere olmak için mekatib-i umumiyenin idaresi birleştirilecek ve fakat milel-i muhtelifenin itikat-i mezhebiyelerine asla halel getirilmeyecektir.

Mesarif-i umumiye Meclis-i Mebusan'ın hükümet ile bi-l-ittifak karar verdiği tekalif-i kaffe-i tebaa beyninde herkesin kudret-i maliyesine göre mütesaviyen tarh ve tevzi olunur.

In the Archival Version of Said Pasha's Constitutional Model

Metbuiyet zat-ı hükümdaride kaimdir. Metbuiyet ferağ ve iptal ve ıskat olunabilmekten masundur.

Kanun-ı Esasi ile temin olunan hukuk-ı tebaa bahsindendir

Mevadd-ı siyasiyede ceza-yı idam lağv olunmuştur.

Efrad-ı ahalinin şirket yapmağa ve asayiş ve sükunet üzere ve bila-silah cemiyet akdine ve istida takdimine ve matbuat vasıtasıyla veya sırf aharla beyan-ı efkar etmeğe salahiyetleri vardır. Ve bu salahiyetlerin hududu dahi gayrin hürriyet ve salahiyet ve umumun emniyeti ile mahduttur.

Matbuat kabl-et-tab hükümetin muayenesine arz olunamaz.

Talim ve tedris serbesttir.

Serbest-i talim ve tedris kabiliyet ve adaba muvafakat hususlarında kanunen muayyen olan şeraite tabi ve devletin nezaret ve dikkati tahtında caridir. Devletin nezaret ve dikkati talim ve terbiyeye mahsus tesisatı bila-istisna şamildir.

Umumen emlak taarruzdan masundur. Şu kadar var ki menfaat-ı umumiye için lüzum-ı meşru tebeyyün eylediği halde bir mülkün peşin ve değerli bedel mukabilinde terkini devlet emredebilir.

Müsadere-i emval ve emlak usulü hiçbir vakitte yeniden tesis olunamaz.

Her nevi vergi menafi-i müştereke için mevzudur. Herkes kudreti ve serveti derecesinde vergi verir. Hiçbir vergi hükm-ü kanundan gayri vasıta ile tesis ve tahsil olunamaz.

In the Draft Constitution Corrected by Safved Pasha

Tebaa-i Osmaniye'nin Hukuk-ı Umumiyesi

Madde 7. Devlet-i Osmaniye tabiiyetinde bulunan efradın cümlesine herhangi din ve mezhebden olur ise olsun bila-istisna Osmanlı tabir olunur ve Osmanlı sıfatı kanunen muayyen olan ahvale göre istihsal ve izae edilir.

Madde 8. ~~Osmanlıların~~ (tebaa-ı Devlet-i Osmaniye'nin) kaffesi hürriyet-i şahsiyelerine malik ve aharın hukuk-ı hürriyetine ~~dokunmamak ve şerh ve kanunun tayin ettiği hududa tecavüz etmemekle~~ (tecavüz etmemekle) mükelleftir.[2]

Madde 9. Hürriyet-i şahsiye her türlü taarruzdan masundur. Hiç kimse kanunun tayin ettiği sebep ve suretten ~~ve kanunen mucibi tevfik olan ahvalden ma-ada bir bahane ile tevkif ve haps olunmayacağı gibi nefy ve sair suretle dahi~~ (ma-ada bir bahane ile) mücazat olunamaz.

Madde 10. ~~Devlet-i Osmaniye din-i İslam üzerine müessestir. Bu esasa halel getirmemek ve~~ asayiş-i halkı ve ahlak-ı umumiyeyi ihlal etmemek şartıyla memalik-i Osmaniye'de maruf olan bil-cümle edyanın icrası devletin taht-ı teminindedir.

Madde 12. Matbuat (kavanin-i mevzuası dahilinde) serbesttir. ~~Hukuk ve vezaifi kanun-ı mahsusa ile muayyendir.~~

Madde 13. Tebaa-i Osmaniye nizam ve kanun dairesinde ticaret ve sanat ve ziraat için her nevi şirketler ~~tesisine~~ (teşkiline) mezundur.

Madde 14. ~~Osmanlı efradından~~ tebaa-ı Devlet-i Aliye'den bir veya birkaç kişinin gerek şahıslarına ve gerek umuma müteallik olan nizamata muhalif gördükleri bir maddeden dolayı işin merciine arzuhal verdikleri gibi Meclis-i Umumiye'ye dahi (müddei sıfatıyla) imzalı arzuhal ile beyan-ı hale ve memuriyetin ifalinden iştikaya selahiyetleri ~~olacaktır~~ (vardır).

---

[2] The words scored out indicate the corrections of Safved Pasha, while those in parentheses are the ones he added after corrections.

Madde 15. Emr-i tedris serbesttir. Muayyen olan kanuna tabiyyet şartıyla ~~herkes~~ (tebaa-i Devlet-i Aliye'den herkes) umumi ve hususi tedrise mezundur.

Madde 16. ~~Tebaa-i Osmaniye'nin terbiyesi bir siyak-ı ittihad ve intizam üzere olmak için~~ (iktiza eden esbaba teşebbüs olacak) bil-cümle mektepler devletin taht-ı nezaretinde(dir) bulunacaktır ve her halde milel-i muhtelifenin umur-ı itikadiyelerine müteallik olan usul-i talimiyeye asla halel getirilmeyecektir.

Madde 17. ~~Her Osmanlı~~ Tebaa-i Devlet-i Aliye huzur-ı kanunda ve (umur-ı mezhebiyeden ma-ada) memleketin hukuk ve vezaif ~~meşruasında~~ (nezdinde) müsavidir.

Madde 18. Memalik-i Osmaniye'de bulunan (~~enva-i~~) akvamdan her biri kendilerine mahsus olan lisanı talim ve taallümde muhtardır. Fakat devletin lisan-ı resmisi Türkçe olduğundan hıdemat-ı devlette istihdam olunmak için devletin lisan-ı resmisini bilmek şarttır.

Madde 19. Devlet memuriyetinde ~~asalet ve mensubiyet ve sair türlü izafi haysiyetin dahli olmayıp~~ umum tebaa ehliyet ve ~~liyakatlarına~~ (mahiyetlerine göre) ~~ve nizamen tayin olunacak mesleklerine muvafık olan~~ (münasip olan) memuriyetlere kabul olunurlar.

Madde 20. (Tekalif-i mukarrere nizamat-ı mahsusasına tevfikan) ~~mesarif-i umumiye için Meclis-i Umumi'nin hükümet ile bi-l-ittifak karar verdiği tekalif yapılacak nizamata tevfikan~~ kaffe-i tebaa beyninde herkesin (kudreti nispetinde) ~~kudret-i maliyesine göre bir nispet-i mütesaviyede~~ tarh ve tevzi olunur.

Madde 21. Herkes usulen mutasarrıf olduğu mal ve mülkünden emindir. Menafi-i umumiye için lüzumu sabit olmadıkça (ve kanun mucibince ve değer bahası peşin verilmedikçe kimsenin mekanı alınamaz) ~~ve kıymet-i hakikiyesi peşin verilmedikçe kimsenin mülkü alınamaz ve kanunun cevazı olmadıkça hükümet tarafından cebren hiç kimsenin mezken ve menziline girilemez.~~ (Devlet-i Osmaniye'de herkesin mezken ve menzili taarruzdan masundur ve kanunun…)

Madde 22. (Tebaa-i Osmaniye'den) ~~Osmanlı efradından~~ her birinin namus ve haysiyeti hükümet-i seniyenin himayesi ve umum ~~efradın teavün-i müştereki tahtındadır~~ (the last part was first removed but then reconsidered correct).

Madde 25. Müsadere ve angarya ve cerime ~~külliyen~~ memnudur. (Fakat kanunen muayyen olan ahval bundan müstesnadır) ~~gerek cezai ve gerek sair suretle kimsenin malı zapt olunamaz ve ücretli ve ücretsiz kimse kimseyi cebren işinde kullanamaz.~~ Ve bir kanuna müstenit olmadıkça vergi ve rusumat namıyla ve nam-ı aherle hiç kimseden bir akçe alınamaz.

In the 114-Article Draft Constitution

Tebaa-ı Devlet-i Osmaniye'nin Hukuk-ı Umumiyesi

Birinci madde. Bin iki yüz elli beş senesi (şehr-i şabanının yirmi altıncı günü)[3] ilan olunan Tanzimat-ı Hayriye Hatt-ı Hümayunu mucibince sınıf-ı tebaa-ı Devlet-i Aliye'den her ferdin mal ve can ve ırz ve namusu zat-ı Hazret-i Padişahi'nin himayet ve siyanet-i mahsusası tahtındadır.

---

[3] The parentheses indicate the amendments made on the draft.

Handwritten Amendment in the Margin without any Article Number

Sülale-i âl-i Osman'ın hukuk-ı hürriyetine ve emval ve emlak-ı zatiye ve madam-el hayat tahsisat-ı maliyeleri tekafil-i umumi tahtındadır.

İkinci madde. Devlet-i Osmaniye tabiiyetinde bulunan efradın cümlesine herhangi din ve mezhebden olur ise olsun bila-istisna Osmanlı tabir olunur ve Osmanlı sıfatı kanunen muayyen olan ahvale göre istihsal ve izae edilir.

Üçüncü madde. Tebaa-i Devlet-i Osmaniye'nin kaffesi hürriyet-i şahsiyelerine malik ve aharın hukuk-ı hürriyetine tecavüz etmemekle mükelleftir.

Dördüncü madde. Hürriyet-i şahsiye her türlü taarruzdan masundur. Hiç kimse kanunun tayin ettiği sebep ve suretten ma-ada bir bahane ile mücazat olunamaz.

Beşinci madde. (Devlet-i Osmaniye'nin dini din-i İslam'dır. Bu esası vikaye ile beraber) asayiş-i halkı ve adab-ı umumiyeyi ihlal etmemek şartıyla Memalik-i Osmaniye'de maruf olan bil-cümle edyanın serbesti-i icrası devletin taht-ı himayetindedir.

Altıncı madde. Matbuat ~~kavanin-i mevzuası~~[4] (kanun) dairesinde serbesttir.

Yedinci madde. Tebaa-i Osmaniye nizam ve kanun dairesinde ticaret ve sanat ve felahat için her nevi şirketler teşkiline mezundur.

Dokuzuncu madde. Emr-i tedris serbesttir. Muayyen olan kanuna tabiyet şartıyla ~~tebaa-i Devlet-i Aliye'den herkes~~ (her Osmanlı) umumi ve hususi tedrise mezundur.

Onuncu madde. Bil-cümle mektepler devletin taht-ı nezaretindedir. Tebaa-i Osmaniye'nin terbiyesi bir siyak-ı ittihad ve intizam üzere olmak için iktiza eden esbaba teşebbüs olunacak ve milel-i muhtelifenin umur-ı itikadiyelerine müteallik olan usul-i talimiyeye halel getirilmeyecektir.

Onbirinci madde. Tebaa-i Devlet-i ~~Aliye~~ Osmaniye huzur-ı kanunda ve ahval-ı diniye ve mezhebiyeden ma-ada memleketin hukuk ve vezaifinde müsavidir.

On ikinci madde. Memalik-i Osmaniye'de bulunan efradın her biri kendilerine mahsus olan lisanı talim ve taallümde muhtardır. Fakat hidemat-ı devlette istihdam olunmak için devletin lisan-i resmisi olan Türkçeyi bilmek şarttır.

On üçüncü madde. Devlet memuriyetinde umum tebaa ehliyet ve mahiyetlerine göre münasip olan memuriyetlere kabul olunurlar.

On dördüncü madde. Tekalif-i mukarrere nizamat-ı mahsusasına tevfikan kaffe-i tebaa beyninde herkesin kudreti nispetinde tarh ve tevzi olunur.

On beşinci madde. Herkes usulen mutasarrıf olduğu mal ve mülkünden emindir. Menafi-i umumiye için lüzumu sabit olmadıkça ve kanun mucibince değer bahası peşin verilmedikçe kimsenin tasarrufunda olan mülkü alınamaz.

---

[4] Scored out.

On altıncı madde. Memalik-i Osmaniye'de herkesin mesken ve menzili taarruz-dan masundur. Kanunun tayin eylediği ahvalden ma-ada bir sebeple hükümet tarafından cebren hiç kimsenin mesken ve menziline girilemez.

~~On yedinci madde. Tebaa-i Osmaniye'den her birinin namus ve haysiyeti hükü-met-i seniyenin himayesi tahtındadır.~~

In the 119-Article Draft Constitution

Tebaa-ı Devlet-i Osmaniyenin Hukuk-ı Umumiyesi

~~Birinci madde. Bin iki yüz elli beş senesi şabanının yirmi altıncı günü~~[5] ~~ilan olunan Tanzimat-ı Hayriye Hatt-ı Hümayunu mucibince sınıf-ı tebaa-ı Devlet-i Aliye'den her ferdin mal ve can ve ırz ve namusu zat-ı Hazret-i Padişahi'nin himayet ve siyanet-i mahsusası tahtındadır.~~

Sekizinci madde. Devlet-i Osmaniye tabiiyetinde bulunan efradın cümlesine her-hangi din ve mezhebden olur ise olsun bila-istisna Osmanlı tabir olunur ve Osmanlı sıfatı kanunen muayyen olan ahvale göre istihsal ve izae edilir.

Dokuzuncu madde. Osmanlıların kaffesi hürriyet-i şahsiyelerine malik ve aharın hukuk-ı hürriyetine tecavüz etmemekle mükelleftir.

Onuncu madde. Hürriyet-i şahsiye her türlü taarruzdan masundur. Hiç kimse kanunun tayin ettiği sebep ve suretten ma-ada bir bahane ile ~~tevkif ve haps ve nefy ve saire suretle~~ mücazat olunamaz.

On birinci madde. Devlet-i Osmaniye'nin dini din-i İslam'dır. Bu ~~esasa halel getirmemek~~ (esası vikaye ile beraber) asayiş-i halkı ve adab-ı umumiyeyi ihlal etmemek şartıyla Memalik-i Osmaniye'de maruf olan sair bil-cümle edyanın serbesti-i icrası devletin taht-ı himayetindedir.

On ikinci madde. Matbuat (kanun dairesinde) serbesttir. Hukuk ve vezaifi kanun-ı mahsus ile tayin olunur.

On üçüncü madde. Tebaa-i Osmaniye nizam ve kanun dairesinde ticaret ve sanat ve felahat için her nevi şirketler teşkiline mezundur.

On beşinci madde. Emr-i tedris serbesttir. Muayyen olan kanuna tabiyyet şartıyla ~~her Osmanlı (1) tebaa-i Devlet-i Aliye'den herkes~~ (2)[6] (her Osmanlı) umumi ve hususi tedrise mezundur.

On altıncı madde. Bil-cümle mektepler devletin taht-ı nezaretindedir. Tebaa-i Osmaniye'nin terbiyesi bir siyak-ı ittihad ve intizam üzere olmak için iktiza eden esbaba teşebbüs olunacak ve milel-i muhtelifenin umur-ı itikadiyelerine müteal-lik olan usul-i talimiyeye halel getirilmeyecektir.

---

[5] The parentheses indicate the amendments made on the draft.
[6] They were scored out in this order.

On yedinci madde. ~~Her~~ Osmanlı(ların kaffesi) huzur-ı kanunda ve ~~umur-ı~~ (ahval-ı) diniye ve mezhebiyeden ma-ada memleketin hukuk ve vezaifinde müsavidir.

On sekizinci madde. ~~Memalik-i Osmaniye'de bulunan efradın her biri kendilerine mahsus olan lisanı talim ve taallümde muhtardır.~~ (Tebaa-ı Osmaniye'nin) ~~Fakat~~ hidemat-ı devlette istihdam olunmak için devletin lisan-i resmisi olan Türkçeyi bilmek(leri) şarttır.

On dokuzuncu madde. Devlet memuriyetinde ~~asalet ve mensubiyet ve sair türlü izafi haysiyetin dahi olmayıp~~ umum tebaa ehliyet ve mahiyetlerine göre münasip memuriyetlere kabul olunurlar.

Yirminci madde. ~~Mesarif-i umumiye için Meclis-i Umumi'nin hükümet ile bi-l-ittifak karar verdiği~~ tekalif-i (mukarrere) yapılacak nizamata tevfikan kaffe-i tebaa beyninde herkesin kudreti nispetince tarh ve tevzi olunur.

Yirmi birinci madde. Herkes (usulen) mutasarrıf olduğu mal ve mülkünden emindir. Menafi-i umumiye için lüzumu sabit olmadıkça ve kanun mucibince değer bahası peşin verilmedikçe kimsenin tasarrufunda olan mülk (alınamaz). (Memalik-i Osmaniye'de) herkesin mesken ve menzili taarruzdan masundur. Kanunun tayin eylediği ahvalden ma-ada bir sebeple (hükümet tarafından cebren hiç kimsenin) mesken ve menziline girilemez.

Yirmi ikinci madde. Osmanlı efradından herkesin namus ve haysiyeti hükümet-i seniyenin himayesi ve umum efradın taarruz-ı müşterek-i tahtındadır.

In the Ottoman Constitution

Tebaa-ı Devlet-i Osmaniye'nin Hukuk-ı Umumiyesi

Sekizinci madde. Devlet-i Osmaniye tabiiyetinde bulunan efradın cümlesine herhangi din ve mezhebden olur ise olsun bila-istisna Osmanlı tabir olunur ve Osmanlı sıfatı kanunen muayyen olan ahvale göre istihsal ve izae edilir.

Dokuzuncu madde. Osmanlıların kaffesi hürriyet-i şahsiyelerine malik ve aharın hukuk-ı hürriyetine tecavüz etmemekle mükelleftir.

Onuncu madde. Hürriyet-i şahsiye her türlü taarruzdan masundur. Hiç kimse kanunun tayin ettiği sebep ve suretten ma-ada bir bahane ile mücazat olunamaz.

On birinci madde. Devlet-i Osmaniye'nin dini din-i İslam'dır. Bu esası vikaye ile beraber asayiş-i halkı ve adab-ı umumiyeyi ihlal etmemek şartıyla Memalik-i Osmaniye'de maruf olan sair bil-cümle edyanın serbesti-i icrası devletin taht-ı himayetindedir.

On ikinci madde. Matbuat kanun dairesinde serbesttir.

On üçüncü madde. Tebaa-i Osmaniye nizam ve kanun dairesinde ticaret ve sanat ve felahat için her nevi şirketler teşkiline mezundur.

On beşinci madde. Emr-i tedris serbesttir. Muayyen olan kanuna tabiyyet şartıyla her Osmanlı umumi ve hususi tedrise mezundur.

On altıncı madde. Bil-cümle mektepler devletin taht-ı nezaretindedir. Tebaa-i Osmaniye'nin terbiyesi bir siyak-ı ittihad ve intizam üzere olmak için iktiza eden esbaba teşebbüs olunacak ve milel-i muhtelifenin umur-ı itikadiyelerine müteallik olan usul-i talimiyeye halel getirilmeyecektir.

On yedinci madde. Osmanlıların kaffesi huzur-ı kanunda ve ahval-ı diniye ve mezhebiyeden ma-ada memleketin hukuk ve vezaifinde müsavidir.

On sekizinci madde. Tebaa-ı Osmaniye'nin hıdemat-ı devlette istihdam olunmak için devletin lisan-i resmisi olan Türkçeyi bilmeleri şarttır.

On dokuzuncu madde. Devlet memuriyetinde umum tebaa ehliyet ve kabiliyetlerine göre münasip olan memuriyetlere kabul olunurlar.

Yirminci madde. Tekalif-i mukarrere nizamat-ı mahsusasına tevfikan kaffe-i tebaa beyninde herkesin kudreti nispetince tarh ve tevzi olunur.

Yirmi birinci madde. Herkes usulen mutasarrıf olduğu mal ve mülkünden emindir. Menafi-i umumiye için lüzumu sabit olmadıkça ve kanun mucibince değer bahası peşin verilmedikçe kimsenin tasarrufunda olan mülk alınamaz.

Yirmi ikinci madde. Memalik-i Osmaniye'de herkesin mesken ve menzili taarruzdan masundur. Kanunun tayin eylediği ahvalden gayrı bir sebeple hükümet tarafından cebren hiç kimsenin mesken ve menziline girilemez.

~~Yirmi ikinci madde. Osmanlı efradından herkesin namus ve haysiyeti hükümet-i seniyenin himayesi ve umum efradın taarruz-ı müşterek-i tahtındadır.~~[7]

THE GRAND VIZIERATE AND THE COUNCIL OF MINISTERS

In the Printed Version of Midhad Pasha's Constitutional Model

Sadaret-i mutlaka mesnedi mülgadır. Heyet-i Vükela riyaseti taraf-ı Hazret-i Padişahi'den başvekil namıyla vükeladan birine ihale ve Vükela Heyeti anın reyi ile intihab ve irade-i seniye ile nasb olunur.

Meclis-i Vükela başvekilin riyaseti tahtında akdolunup dahili ve harici kaffe-i umur-ı mühimme ve politikanın merciidir. Müzakeratın kararları irade-i seniye ile icra olunur.

İdare-i devletçe muhill-i emniyet olan ve kanun-ı cedit ahkamına muhalif bulunan icraat-ı umumiyede heyetçe ve her dairenin vezaif-i muayyenesine dair olan ahvalde dahi münferiden vükela mesuldür.

---

[7] This provision does not exist in the final text of the Ottoman Constitution.

In the Archival Version of Said Pasha's Constitutional Model

Vükela ve memurin kendi vazifelerine ait olan hususatça hükümet ve idarenin kaffe-i amalinden mesuldürler.

In the Draft Constitution Corrected by Safved Pasha

Vükela-ı Devlet

Madde 27. (Mesned-i hükümet riyaset-i vükeladır.) ~~Vekalet-i mutlaka unvanı riyaset-i vükela unvanına tahvil olunmuştur.~~ Riyaset-i vükela ve meşihat-i İslamiye taraf-ı padişahiden emniyet buyurulan zatlara ihale buyurulur. Sair vükela reis-i vükelanın (arzıyla memuriyetleri) ~~reyiyle~~ intihab ve ba-irade-i seniye ~~ile nasb~~ icra olunur.

Madde 28. ~~Heyet-i Vükela birinci vükela riyasetinde bulunan sadrazam ikinci Şeyh-ül İslam üçüncü Şura-yı Devlet reisi dördüncü dahiliye vekili beşinci harbiye vekili altıncı bahriye vekili yedinci hariciye vekili sekizinci adliye vekili dokuzuncu maliye vekili onuncu maarif-i umumiye vekili, on birinci nafıa ve ticaret ve ziraat vekili olan zatlardan ibarettir. Reis-i vükela bu vekaletlerden birine deruhte eder.~~

Madde 29. Meclis-i Vükela ~~zikr olunan heyetten mürekkep ve~~ reis-i vükelanın riyaseti tahtında olarak akd olunan dahili ve harici ~~kaffe-i~~ umur-ı mühimmenin merciidir. Müzakeratın kararları irade-i seniye ile icra olur.

Madde 33. Vükela-yı devlet memuriyetlerine müteallik ahval ve icraattan (münferiden? ve meclisçe imzaları tahtında verilen karardan müctemian mesuldür.) ~~ve hususiyle devletçe hıyanet ve Kanun-ı Esasi'yi naks ve ılgaya tasaddi ve her nevi irtikap ve nüfuz-ı memuriyeti sui-i istimal ve emval-ı miriyeyi israf maddelerinden münferiden veya müctemian mesuldur.~~

Madde 39. Meclis-i Umumi münakit olmadığı zamanlarda devleti bir muhataradan veyahut emniyet-i umumiyeyi haleldan vikaye için bir zaruret-i mübrime zuhur ettiği ve bu babda vazına lüzum görünecek kanunun müzakeresi için meclisin celp ve cemine vakit müsait olmadığı halde kaffe-i mesuliyet kendilerine ait olmak ve Kanun-ı Esasi ahkamına mugayir olmamak ~~ve Meclis-i Umumi'nin inikatında tasdik ve kabul olunmaz ise hükm-ü münifesi add olunmak~~ üzere Heyet-i Vükela tarafından (Heyet-i Mebusan'ın ictma?) verilen kararlar muvakkaten kanun hüküm ve kuvvetindedir.

In the 114-Article Draft Constitution

Vükela-yı Devlet

Yirmi ikinci madde. ~~Mesned-i sadaret riyaset-i vükeladır. Riyaset-i vükela~~ (Sadrazam reis-i vükeladır. Mesned-i sadaret) ve meşihat-ı İslamiye taraf-ı padişahiden emniyet buyurulan zatlara ihale ~~buyurulur ve~~ buyrulduğu misillü sair vükela(nın) ~~reis-i vükelanın arzıyla~~ memuriyetleri (dahi) ba-irade-i şahane icra olunur.

Yirmi beşinci madde. Vükela-yı Devlet memuriyetlerine müteallik ahval ve icra-atten mesuldür.

Otuz birinci madde. Meclis-i Umumi münakit olmadığı zamanlarda devleti bir muhataradan veyahut emniyet-i umumiyeyi halelden vikaye için bir zaruret-i mübrime zuhur ettiği ve bu babda vazına lüzum görünecek kanunun müzakeresi için meclisin celp ve cemine vakit müsait olmadığı halde Kanun-ı Esasi ahka-mına mugayir olmamak üzere Heyet-i Vükela tarafından verilen kararlar Heyet-i Mebusan'ın ictimaıyla verilecek karara kadar ba-irade-i seniye muvakkaten kanun hüküm ve kuvvetindedir.

In the 119-Article Draft Constitution

Yirmi yedinci madde. ~~Sadrazam reis-i vükeladır.~~ (Mesned-i sadaret) ~~Vekalet-i mutlaka unvanı riyaset-i vükela unvanına tahvil olunmuştur. Riyaset-i vükela~~ ve (meşihat-i İslamiye taraf-ı padişahiden emniyet buyurulan zatlara ihale ~~buyurulur~~ (buyrulduğu misillü) sair vükelanın (memuriyetleri dahi) ~~intihabı reis-i vükelaya havale buyrularak memuriyetleri~~ (ba-irade-i şahane) ~~ile~~ icra olunur.

Yirmi sekizinci madde. Heyet-i Vükela vükela riyasetinde bulunan sadrazam Şeyh-ül İslam Şura-yı Devlet reisi dahiliye vekili hariciye vekili bahriye vekili harbiye vekili adliye vekili maliye vekili maarif-i umumi vekili nafıa ve ticaret ve ziraat vekili olan zatlardan ibarettir. Reis-i vükela bu vekaletlerden birini deruhte edebilir.

Otuzuncu madde. Vükela devlet memuriyetlerine müteallik ahval ve icraattan ~~ve hususuyla devletçe hıyanet ve Kanun-ı Esasi'yi naks ve ılgaya ve her nevi irtikap ve nüfuz-ı memuriyeti su-i istimal ve emval-i emiriyeyi israf maddelerinden münferiden veya müctemian~~ mesuldur.

Otuz altıncı madde. Meclis-i Umumi münakit olmadığı zamanlarda devleti bir muhataradan veyahut emniyet-i umumiyeyi halelden vikaye için bir zaruret-i mübrime zuhur ettiği ve bu babda vazına lüzum görünecek kanunun müzakeresi için meclisin celp ve cemine vakit müsait olmadığı halde ~~kaffe-i mesuliyet ken-dilerine ait olmak~~ Kanun-ı Esasi ahkamına mugayir olmamak üzere Heyet-i Vükela tarafından verilen kararlar Heyet-i Mebusan'ın ictimaıyla verilecek karara kadar (ba-irade-i seniye) muvakkaten kanun hüküm ve kuvvetindedir.

In the Ottoman Constitution

Yirmi yedinci madde. Mesned-i sadaret ve meşihat-ı İslamiye taraf-ı padişahiden emniyet buyurulan zatlara ihale buyrulduğu misillü sair vükelanın memuriyetleri dahi ba-irade-i şahane icra olunur.

Yirmi sekizinci madde. Meclis-i Vükela sadrazamın riyaseti tahtında olarak akd olunup dahili ve harici umur-ı mühimmenin merciidir. Müzakeratından muhtac-ı istizan olanların kararları irade-i seniye ile icra olunur.

Otuzuncu madde. Vükela devlet memuriyetlerine müteallik ahval ve icraattan mesuldür.

Otuz altıncı madde. Meclis-i Umumi münakit olmadığı zamanlarda devleti bir muhataradan veyahut emniyet-i umumiyeyi halelden vikaye için bir zaruret-i mübrime zuhur ettiği ve bu babda vazına lüzum görünecek kanunun müzakeresi için meclisin celp ve cemine vakit müsait olmadığı halde Kanun-ı Esasi ahkamına mugayir olmamak üzere Heyet-i Vükela tarafından verilen kararlar Heyet-i Mebusan'ın ictimaıyla verilecek karara kadar ba-irade-i seniye muvakkaten kanun hüküm ve kuvvetindedir.

MISCELLANEOUS

In the Printed Version of Midhad Pasha's Constitutional Model

Meclis-i Mebusan

Meclis-i Mebusan devletin tesviye-i düyununu deruhte eder ve lüzumuna göre dahil ve hariçten istikraz akdi ve tahvilat ihracı gibi tedabir-i maliyeyi dahi taraf-ı hükümetten vaki olacak talep üzerine müzakere eyler.

Meclis-i Mebusan'ın esas vezaifi evvela gerek hükümet ve mebusan taraflarından teklif olunan kavanin ve nizamat layıhalarını müzakere, saniyen hükümet ile bi-l-ittifak masarif-i umumiyeyi tayin etmek, salisen varidat-ı umumiyenin suret-i sarf ve istimaline nezaret ile iktizasına göre devairden muhasebat istemek, rabian tekalif-i umumiyenin miktar ve suret-i tevziine hükümetle bi-l-ittifak karar vermek, hamisen kavanin ve nizamat-ı mevzuanın her dairede suret-i cereyanına nezaret edip devlet memurlarından birinin mugayir-i nizam ve kanun, efal ve harekatı suret-i sahihada malum oldukta Şura-yı Devlet'te icra-yı muhakemesini ba-mazbata talep eylemek hususlarından ibarettir.

Şura-yı Devlet

Şura-yı Devlet'in reis ve azası taraf-ı şahaneden azl ve nasb olunur. Şura-yı Devlet evvela kaffe-i kavanin ve nizamat layıhalarını bade-t-tetkik tasdike, saniyen taraf-ı hükümetten kendine havale olunacak umur ve mesalih-i mülkiye hakkında reyini itaya, salisen mülkiye memurları ile adliye memurları beyninde tayin-i vazifeden dolayı zuhura gelen ihtilafatı fasla, rabian metn-i nizamat ve kavaninde arız olacak şübühat-ı hal ve tefsire, hamisen memurin-i devletin memuriyetlerinden dolayı iktiza eden muhakematın icrasına memurdur.

Şura-yı Devlet kuvve-i icraiyenin vezaifine asla müdahale edemez. Fakat kavanin ve nizamatın noksan ve yolsuz bir surette icra olunduğunu tahkik ederse gerek Meclis-i Vükela'ya ve gerek zat-i Hazret-i Padişahi'ye ihtara mezundur.

In the Archival Version of Said Pasha's Constitutional Model (Appendix V)

Ahkamı müstacel olan kavanin Millet Meclisi'nde kabul olunduğu tarihten üç gün ve sair kavanin bir ay sonar neşr olunur.

Neşr-i kavanin için muayyen olan işbu müddetler içinde hükümdar bir kanunun tekrar müzakere edilmesini esbab-ı mucibeyi havi bir beyanname ile Meclis-i

Millet'ten talep edebilir. Meclis dahi müzakere eder. O kanun kati hüküm olur. Ve meclis tarafından hükümdara gönderilir. Bu halde o kanun kavanin-i müstaceleye mahsus olan mühlet içinde neşr edilir.

Hükümdarın tanzim ve tadil-i kavaninde hakk-ı ibtidaisi vardır ve Mebusan-ı Millet Meclisi dahi bu salahiyeti haizdir. Her iki tarafın dahi kuvve-i ibtidaiyesine mebni tanzim edeceği kanun layıhaları için evvel be evvel Şura-yı Devlet'in müzakeresine müracaat kılınır.

Divan-ı Ayan hakkındadır

Ayan kayd-ı hayat ile mansub ve azilden masundurlar.

Divan-ı Ayan'ın müzakeratı umumi değildir.

Divan-ı Ayan Kanun-ı Esasi'nin ve hürriyet-i umumiyenin muhafızıdır.

Divan-ı Ayan'a arz olunmazdan evvel hiçbir kanun neşr olunamaz.

Divan-ı Ayan'ın neşrine muhalefet edeceği kanunlar evvela Kanun-ı Esasi'ye ve diyanete ve ahlaka ve hürriyet-i mezhebiyeye ve hürriyet-i şahsiyeye ve ahalinin huzur-ı kanunda müsavatına ve emlakin taarruzdan masuniyetine ve hükkamın azilden masuniyeti esasına mugayir veyahut bunların ahkamını muhill olacak ve saniyen temamiyet-i mülkü hal-i tehlikede bulunduracak kanunlardır.

Kanun-ı Esasi'ye derç olunamayan ve onun hüsn-ü cereyan ahkamınca lazım olan mevaddin tanzim ve Kanun-ı Esasi'den ahkam-ı muhtelife istinbat olunan maddeler maanisinin izah ve teşrihi hususlarını Divan-ı Ayan kararnamelerle tesviye eder.

Milletçe büyük menfaate ait bir kanun layıhasının esasını Divan-ı Ayan hükümdara hitaben bir beyanname ile vaz edebilir.

Divan-ı Ayan Kanun-ı Esasi'nin tadilatını dahi ber-vech-i meşruh teklif edebilir. Bu teklif eğer hükümdar tarafından kabul olunur ise Divan-ı Ayan'ın bir kararnamesiyle tanzim olunur.

In the Printed Version of Said Pasha's Constitutional Model

Divan-ı Ayan

Sena Kanun-ı Esasi'nin ve hürriyet-i umumiyenin muhafızıdır.

Senaya arz olunmazdan evvel hiçbir kanun neşr olunamaz.

Sena'nın neşrine muhalefet edeceği kanunlar evvela Kanun-ı Esasi'ye ve diyanete ve ahlaka ve hürriyet-i mezhebiyeye ve hürriyet-i şahsiyeye ve ahalinin huzur-ı kanunda müsavatına ve emlakin taarruzdan masuniyetine ve hükkamın azilden masuniyeti esasına mugayir veyahut bunların ahkamını muhill olacak ve saniyen temamiyet-i mülkü hal-i tehlikede bulunduracak kanunlardır.

Kanun-ı Esasi'ye derç olunamayan ve onun hüsn-ü cereyan ahkamınca lazım olan mevaddin tanzim ve Kanun-ı Esasi'den ahkam-ı muhtelife istinbat olunan maddeler maanisinin izah ve teşrihi hususlarını Sena kararnamelerle tesviye eder.

Milletçe büyük menfaate ait bir kanun layıhasının esasını Sena hükümdara hitaben bir beyanname ile vaz edebilir.

Sena Kanun-ı Esasi'nin tadilatını dahi ber-vech-i meşruh teklif edebilir. Bu teklif eğer hükümdar tarafından kabul olunur ise Sena'nın bir kararnamesiyle tanzim olunur.

Mamafih Kanun-ı Esasi'nin mevadd-ı esasiyesince vuku bulacak her nevi tadilat ahalinin ara-yı umumisine arz olunur. Millet Meclisi fesh olunduğu takdirde yeni meclisin içtimaına kadar idare-i hükümetçe muktezi olan hususatta Sena hükümdarın teklifi üzerine teşebbüsat-ı zaruriyeye dahi ibtidar eyler.

In the Draft Constitution Corrected by Safved Pasha

Meclis-i Umumi

Madde 46. Meclis-i Umumi Heyet-i Ayan ve Heyet-i Mebusan namlarıyla başka başka iki heyeti muhtevidir.

Madde 58. Müceddeden kanun tanzimi veya kavanin-i mevcudeden birinin tadili talebi münhasıran Heyet-i Vükela veya Heyet-i Ayan'a veyahut Heyet-i Mebusan'a aittir.

Madde 59. Yeniden bir kanun tanzimi veyahut olan kanunlardan birinin tadili hakkında (böyle bir talep) talep vukuunda (taraf-ı şahaneden bi-l-istizan) layıhası Şura-yı Devlet'te kaleme alınıp evvela Heyet-i Mebusan'da badehu Heyet-i Ayan'da tetkik ve kabul olunduktan ve icra-yı ahkamına irade-i seniye-i Hazret-i Padişahi müteallik olduktan sonra düstur-ül-amel olur ve mezkur heyetlerden birinde katiyen red olunan kanun layıhası o senenin müddet-i ictimaiyesinde mevki-i müzakereye konulamaz.

In the 114-Article Draft Constitution

Kırk sekizinci madde. Müceddeden kanun tanzimi veya kavanin-i mevcudeden birinin tadili teklifi münhasıran Heyet-i Vükela'ya ait olduğu gibi Heyet-i Ayan ve Heyet-i Mebusan'ın dahi kendi vazife-i muayyeneleri dairesinde bulunan mevadd için kanun tanzimi veyahut kavanin-i mevcudeden birinin tadilini istidaya selahiyetleri olmağla evvelce makam-ı sadaret vasıtasıyla taraf-ı Şahane'den istizan olunarak irade-i seniyeye müteallik buyrulur ise ait olduğu dairelerden verilecek izahat ve tafsilat üzerine layıhalarının tanzimi Şura-yı Devlet'e havale olunur.

In the 119-Article Draft Constitution

Kırk beşinci madde. Müceddeden kanun tanzimi veya kavanin-i mevcudeden birinin tadili talebi münhasıran (teklifi) Heyet-i Vükela'ya (ait olduğu gibi) veya Heyet-i Ayan veyahut Heyet-i Mebusan'ın dahi kendi vazife-i muayyeneleri dairesinde bulunan mevadd için kanun tanzimi veyahut (kavanin-i mevcudeden birinin tadilini istidaya selahiyetleri olmağla evvelce makam-ı sadaret vasıtasıyla taraf-ı Şahane'den istizan olunarak irade-i seniyeye müteallik buyrulur ise ait olduğu dairelerden verilecek izahat ve tafsilat üzerine layıhalarının tanzimi Şura-yı Devlet'e havale olunur).

In the Ottoman Constitution

Elli üçüncü madde. Müceddeden kanun tanzimi veya kavanin-i mevcudeden birinin tadili teklifi Heyet-i Vükela'ya ait olduğu gibi Heyet-i Ayan ve Heyet-i
Mebusan'ın dahi kendi vazife-i muayyeneleri dairesinde bulunan mevadd için
kanun tanzimi veya kavanin-i mevcudeden birinin tadilini istidaya selahiyetleri
olmağla evvelce makam-ı sadaret vasıtasıyla taraf-ı Şahane'den istizan olunarak
irade-i seniyeye müteallik buyrulur ise ait olduğu dairelerden verilecek izahat ve
tafsilat üzerine layıhalarının tanzimi Şura-yı Devlet'e havale olunur.

PROVISIONS ON MILITARY POWER, REVOLUTION, AND MARTIAL LAW

In the Archival Version of Said Pasha's Constitutional Model

Kuvve-i askeriye hakkındadır

Kuvve-i askeriye haricen düşmanı def ve dahilen emniyet ve asayişi ve cereyan-ı
kavanini muhafaza için mevzudur.

Dahilen asayişin muhafazasına memur olan kuvve-i askeriye kuvve-i kanuniyenin vaz ettiği kavaid dairesinde olarak ancak hükümet-i meşrua tarafından istimal
olunur.

Muhasara hali ilan olunmasının lüzum ve icabını bir kanun-ı mahsus tayin edeceği misillü bunun şekil ve asarını dahi kanun-ı mezkur tertip eder.

In the Draft Constitution Corrected by Safved Pasha

Mevadd-ı şetta

Madde 125. Mülkün bir cihetinde ihtilal zuhur ettiği halde hükümet-i seniyenin
o mahale mahsus olmak üzere muvakkaten (idare-i örfiye)[8] ilanına hakkı vardır.
(İdare-i örfiye) nizamat-ı mülkiyenin muvakkaten tatilinden ibaret olup (idare-i
örfiye) tahtında bulunan mahalin suret-i idaresi nizam-ı mahsus ile tayin olunacaktır.

In the 114-Article Draft Constitution

Mevadd-ı Şetta

Yüz dokuzuncu madde. Mülkün bir cihetinde ihtilal zuhur edeceğini müeyyed
asar ve emarat görüldüğü halde hükümet-i seniyenin o mahale mahsus olmak
üzere muvakkaten (idare-i örfiye) ilanına hakkı vardır. (İdare-i örfiye) kavanin
ve nizamat-ı mülkiyenin muvakkaten tatilinden ibaret olup (idare-i örfiye) tahtında bulunan mahalin suret-i idaresi nizam-ı mahsus ile tayin olunacaktır.

---

[8] The parentheses are those of Safved Pasha.

Handwritten addition which will appear in the final form of Article 113:

Hükümetin emniyeti ihlal edenleri idare-i zabıtanın tahkikat-ı mevsukası üzerine memalik-i mahruseden ihraç ve tebid etmek münhasıran zat-ı Hazret-i Padişahi'nin yed-i iktidarındadır.

In the 119-Article Draft Constitution

Yüz yedinci madde. Mülkün bir cihetinde ihtilal zuhur ~~ettiği~~ (edeceğini müeyyed asar ve emarat görüldüğü) halde hükümet-i seniyenin o mahale mahsus olmak üzere muvakkaten (idare-i örfiye)[9] ilanına hakkı vardır. (İdare-i örfiye) (kavanin)[10] ve nizamat-ı mülkiyenin muvakkaten tatilinden ibaret olup (idare-i örfiye) tahtında bulunan mahalin suret-i idaresi nizam-ı mahsus ile tayin olunacaktır. Hükümetin emniyeti ihlal ettikleri idare-i zabıtanın tahkikat-ı mevsukası üzerine sabit olanları memalik-i mahruse-i şahaneden ihraç ve tebid etmek münhasıran zat-ı Hazret-i Padişahi'nin yed-i iktidarındadır.

In the Ottoman Constitution

Yüz on üçüncü madde. Mülkün bir cihetinde ihtilal zuhur edeceğini müeyyed asar ve emarat görüldüğü halde hükümet-i seniyenin o mahale mahsus olmak üzere muvakkaten idare-i örfiye ilanına hakkı vardır. İdare-i örfiye kavanin ve nizamat-ı mülkiyenin muvakkaten tatilinden ibaret olup idare-i örfiye tahtında bulunan mahalin suret-i idaresi nizam-ı mahsus ile tayin olunacaktır. Hükümetin emniyeti ihlal ettikleri idare-i zabıtanın tahkikat-ı mevsukası üzerine sabit olanları memalik-i mahruse-i şahaneden ihraç ve tebid etmek zat-ı Hazret-i Padişahi'nin yed-i iktidarındadır.

---

[9] The expression "idare-i örfiye" was put into parentheses by the draftsman or draftsmen.

[10] The parentheses indicate the addition made on the draft.

BIBLIOGRAPHY

ARCHIVES

Ottoman Archives of the Prime Ministry in Istanbul

Section of the Ottoman Ministry of Foreign Affairs

Records of the Ottoman Ministry of Foreign Affairs
vol. HR. d., I, 1256-1342 (1840-1923)

Records of the Ottoman Ministry of Foreign Affairs, Section Legal Affairs
HR. HMŞ. İŞO, vol. I-IV, 1261-1342 (1845-1923)
HR. H, vol. I-II, 1262-1341 (1845-1922)

Records of the Ottoman Ministry of Foreign Affairs, Section Political Affairs
HR. SYS., vol. I-VI, 1845-1922

Records of the Ottoman Ministry of Foreign Affairs, Correspondence Office
HR. MKT, vol. I-III, 1254-1271 (1838-55)

Records of the Ottoman Ministry of Foreign Affairs, Translation Office
HR. TO., vol. I-XXVIII, 1830-1923

Records of the Ottoman Ministry of Foreign Affairs, Ottoman Embassy in Paris
HR. SFR. 04, vol. I-X, 1832-1913

Records of the Ottoman Ministry of Foreign Affairs, Ottoman Embassy in Tehran
HR. SFR. 20, 1256-1341 (1840-1922)

Records of the Ottoman Ministry of Foreign Affairs, Istanbul Committee
HR. IM., vol. II, 1868-1928

Yıldız Palace Collection

Y.A. RES., vol. I, 1293-1308 (1876-90)
YEE. KP., vol. I, 1274-1322 (1857-1904)
YEE, vol. I-III, 1250-1337 (1834-1918)
YEE. d., vol. I, 1293-1328 (1876-1910)
Y. MTV, 1293-1304 (1876-86)
Y.PRK. EŞA, vol. I, 1293-1326 (1876-1908)
Y.PRK. AZJ., vol. I, 1262-1311 (1845-93)
Y.PRK. AZN., vol. I, 1278-1327 (1861-1909)
Y.PRK. HR., vol. I, 1293-1327 (1876-1909)
Y.PRK. UM., vol. I, 1251-1310 (1835-92)
Y.PRK. TKM., vol. I, 1267-1327 (1850-1909)
Y.PRK. ŞH., vol. I, 1293-1327 (1876-1909)

Y.PRK. BŞK., vol. I, 1272-1310 (1855-92)
Y. PRK. A., 1293-1327 (1876-1909)
Y.PRK. DFE., 1277-1326 (1860-1908)
Y. PRK. ŞD., 1289-1330 (1872-1911)
Y.PRK. SGE., 1292-1330 (1875-1911)
Y.PRK. SRN., 1293-1326 (1876-1908)
Y.PRK. DH., 1289-1327 (1872-1909)
Y.PRK. MYD., 1293-1327 (1876-1909)
Y.PRK. MŞ., 1230-1326 (1814-1908)
Y.PRK.M., 1253-1326 (1837-1908)
Y.PRK. TŞF., 1293-1326 (1876-1908)
Y.PRK. NMH., 1284-1327 (1867-1909)

– İrade Section, Dosya Usulü İradeler (İ. DUIT), 1217-1341/1802-1922. The section consists of the thematic classification of *irade*s, imperial orders.

– İrade Section
İrade-i Dahiliye (İ. DH), 1267-96/1850-78.
İrade-i Hariciye (İ. HR), 1267-1309/1850-92.
İradeler, Meclis-i Vala (İ. MVL), 1270-83/1853-67.
İrade-i Şura-i Devlet, (İ. ŞD), 1284-1296/1867-78.
İrade-i Meclis-i Mahsus (İ. MM.S), 1270-1296/1853-78.
Mesail-i Mühimme İradeleri (İ. MSM).

Records of the Library of the Armenian Patriarchate, Istanbul

Adenakro'wt'iwnq Eresp'o'xanagan Ynthano'wr Zho'gho'vo'h'. Bashdonagan Hradarago'wt'iwn. Azkah'in Badriarqaran, G. Bo'lis (Minutes of the National General Assembly. Official Publication. The Armenian Patriarchate of Istanbul), 1860-77.

Public Record Office, London

Foreign Office General Correspondence, Ottoman Empire, 1856-76.
Foreign Office General Correspondence, Embassy of Istanbul, 1856-76.
Foreign Office Confidential Print, 1856-76.

Archives of the French Ministry of Foreign Affairs, La Courneuve, Paris

Série Affaires diverses, 1814-96.
Série Sous-direction des Affaires consulaires et Consulats, 1853-55 & 1856-60.
Série Correspondance politique, Turquie, 1856-77.
Série Mémoires et Documents, Turquie, 1856-76
Série Papiers d'Agents (Chaudordy, Decazes, Montholon, Moüy, Thiers, Thouvenel, Walewski).
Série Protocoles, 1814-1940.

Archives of the Israelite Central Consistory of France

Consistoire central, série Correspondance, 1850-59 & 1859-66
Consistoire central, série Procès verbaux des Délibérations, 1848-71

Archives of the Italian Ministry of Foreign Affairs, Rome

Moscati 6, Serie politica, 1876

Newspapers

Archives israélites: Recueil religieux, moral et littéraire, 1853-77.
Awedaper, 1856.
Journal des Débats, 1876.
Kegho'wni, 1902.
La Turquie, 1876.
Masis, 1856-77.
Orakir G. Bolso'h', 1875.
Revue de Constantinople, 1876.
The Times, 1876, 1877, 1913.

Published Primary Sources

Abdurrahman Şeref. *Tarih Musahabeleri*. İstanbul: Matbaa-i Amire, 1339.
Ahmed Cevded Paşa. *Tarih-i Cevded*. İstanbul: Darü't-Tıbaat'ül Amire, 1288.
Ahmed Lütfi Effendi. *Tarih-i Lütfî*, 8 vol. İstanbul: Sabah Matbaası, 1290-1328 [1873-1912].
Ahmed Midhad Effendi. *Üss-i İnkılab*, 2 vol. İstanbul: Takvim-i Vekayı Matbaası, 1294-95/1877-78.
Ahmed Saib. *Vaka-i Sultan Abdülaziz*. Kahire: Hindiye Matbaası, 1320.
Alboyacıyan, Arşak. "Azkah'in Sahmanatro'wt'iwny o'w ir Dzako'wmy ew Girar'o'wt'iwny." *Yntartzag Oraco'h'c So'wrp P'rgichean Hiwantano'ci Hah'o'c*. Istanbul: Surp Pırgiç, 1910: 76-528.
Ali Haydar Midhad. *The Life of Midhad Pasha. A Record of his Services, Political Reforms, Banishment, and Judicial Murder*. London: John Murray, 1903.
Ali Pasha. *Testament politique* (extrait de la Revue de Paris des 1er avril et 1er Mai 1910). Coulommiers: Imprimerie Paul Brodard, 1910.
Aristarchi Bey. *Législation ottomane ou Recueil des Lois, Règlements, Ordonnances, Traités, Capitulations et Autres Documents Officiels de l'Empire ottoman*. Constantinople: Bureau du Journal Thraky, 1874.
Les Arméniens de Turquie: rapport du Patriarche arménien de Constantinople à la Sublime Porte, traduit de l'arménien par K. S. Achguerd. Paris: Ernest Leroux, 1877.
Asadur, Hrant. *Timasdo'werner*. İstanbul, 1921.
Azkah'in Sahmanatro'wt'iwn Hah'o'c. İstanbul: H. Mühendisyan, 1863.
Berberyan, Avedis. *Badmo'wt'iwn Hah'o'c*. İstanbul: Boğos Kirişyan, 1871.

Calpha, Ambroise. *Dictionnaire de Poche Français-Turc*. Paris: Garnier Frères, 1865.

Çamçyants, Mikayel. *Badmo'wt'iwn Hah'o'c*, 3 vol. (Venedik, 1784-86).

—, *History of Armenia*, tr. Johannes Avdall. Calcutta, 1827.

Campbell, George. *A Handy Book on the Eastern Question. Being a very Recent View of Turkey*. London: John Murray, 1876.

Clician, Vassif Effendi A. *Son Altesse Midhad-Pacha, Grand Vizir*. Paris: Société Anonyme de l'Imprimerie Kugelmann, 1909.

Debré, S. "The Jews of France." *The Jewish Quarterly Review*, vol. 3, no. 3 (April 1891): 367-435.

Deghegakirq Kawar'agan Harsdaharo'wt'eanc. Istanbul: Dbakrutyun Aramyan, 1876.

Dictionary of National Biography: Supplement, edited by Sydney Lee. London: Smith, Elder and Co, 1901.

Düstur, birinci tertib, cüz-i sani (v. 2). İstanbul: Matbaa-i Amire, 1289 [1872].

Dwight, H. G. O. *Christianity in Turkey: A Narrative of the Protestant Reformation in the Armenian Church*. London: J. Nisbet, 1854.

Elliot, Henry George, Sir. *Some Revolutions and Other Diplomatic Experiences*, ed. by his daughter. London: J. Murray, 1922.

Emin, Joseph. *Life and Adventures of Emin Joseph Emin, 1726-1809,* written by himself and edited by his great-great-grand daughter Amy Apcar. Calcutta: Baptist Mission Press, 1918.

Engelhardt, Ed. *Le Droit d'Intervention et la Turquie*. Paris: A. Cotillon, 1880.

—, *La Turquie et le Tanzimat*, 2 vol. Paris: Cotillon, 1882-84.

Fontanier, Victor. *Voyages en Orient, entrepris par ordre du gouvernement français*, 3 vol. Paris: Mongie aîné, 1829-34.

Franco, Moïse. *Essai sur l'Histoire des Israélites de l'Empire ottoman depuis les Origines jusqu'à nos Jours*. Paris: Durlacher, 1897.

Gibb, E. J. W. *A History of Ottoman Poetry*, 6 vol. (London: Luzac, [1900-09]).

Gladstone, W. E. *Bulgarian Horrors and the Question of the East*. London: J. Murray, 1876.

Goodell, William. *Forty Years in the Turkish Empire*. New York: Robert Carter and Brothers, 1876.

La Grande Encyclopédie: Inventaire raisonné des Sciences, des Lettres et des Arts par une Société de Savants et de Gens de Lettres, 31 vol. Paris: Lamiraut, 1885-1902.

Imbert, Paul. *La Rénovation de l'Empire ottoman; affaires de Turquie*. Paris: Perrin, 1909.

Juchereau de Saint-Denys, Antoine de (Bon). *Histoire de l'Empire ottoman depuis 1792 jusqu'en 1844*, 4 vol. Paris: Comptoir des Imprimeurs Réunis, 1844.

Kératry, Emile de. *Mourad V. Prince, Sultan, Prisonnier d'Etat (1840-78) d'après des Témoins de sa Vie*. Paris: Dentu, 1878.

Larousse, Pierre. *Grand Dictionnaire universel du 19ème Siècle: français, historique, géographique, biographique, mythologique, bibliographique, littéraire, artistique, scientifique, etc.*, 17 vol. Paris: Administration du Grand Dictionnaire universel, 1866-77.

Loi constitutive du Département formé sous le nom de Vilayet du Danube. Constantinople: Imprimerie centrale, 1865.

Macler, Frédéric. *Autour de l'Arménie*. Paris: Librairie E. Nourry, 1917.

Mahmud Celaleddin. *Mirat-ı Hakikat*, 3 vol. İstanbul: Matbaa-i Osmaniye, 1326-27.

Martens, G. F. de. *Recueil des Principaux Traités d'Alliance de Paix, de Trêve, de Neutralité, de Commerce, de Limites, d'Echanges, etc.*, 128 vol. Gottingue: Dieterich, 1791-1939.

Mesrovb, Jacob Seth. *History of the Armenians in India from the earliest Times to the Present Day*. Calcutta: Published by the author, 1895.

Milev, Nicholas. "Reshid Pacha et la Réforme ottoman." *Zeitschrift für Osteuropaische Geschichte*, II (1912): 382-98.

Moushegh Yebisgobos (Bishop). *Manche'stri Hah' Kagho'wt'y*. Azk: Boston, 1911.

Moustafa Fazil Pacha. *Lettre adressée au Feu Sultan Abdul Aziz par le Feu Prince Moustafa Fazil*, 1866. Caire: A. Costagliola, 1897.

Nicolaïdes, Demétrius. *Doustour-i Hamidié. Appendice à la Législation ottomane contenant les lois et règlements promulgués à partir de l'année 1874-78*. Constantinople: Journal Thraki, 1878.

Notice biographique sur le Dr. Servicen Effendi, lue devant la S. I. de Médecine dans sa Séance du 3 décembre 1897 par le Dr. V. Torkomian (Extrait de la Gazette médicale d'Orient). Constantinople: Imprimerie A. Christidis, 1898.

Ormanian, Malachia. *L'Eglise arménienne: son Histoire, sa Doctrine, son Régime, sa Discipline, sa Liturgie, sa Littérature, son Présent*. Paris: Ernest Leroux, 1910.

Papers relating to Administrative and Financial Reforms in Turkey, 1858-61. London: Harrison and Sons, 1861.

Prud'homme, M. E. *Constitution Nationale des Arméniens*. Paris: Benjamin Duprat, 1862.

Rodkey, Frederick Stanley. "Lord Palmerston and the Rejuvenation of Turkey, 1830-41." *Journal of Modern History*, vol. 1 (December 1929): pp. 570-93.

Said Paşa. *Said Paşa'nın Hatıratı*, 2 vol. İstanbul: Sabah Matbaası, 1328 [1912].

Saro'wxan. *Hah'gagan Xntirn ew Azkah'in Sahmanatro'wt'iwny T'o'wrqiah'o'wm, 1863-1910*. Tiflis: E'boxa, 1912.

Savvas Pacha. *Etude sur la Théorie du Droit musulman*. 2 vol. Paris: Marchal & Billard, 1892-98.

Schopoff, A. *Les Réformes et la Protection des Chrétiens en Turquie, 1673-1904*. Paris: Librairie Plon, 1904.

Schuyler, Eugene. *Turkistan; Notes of a Journey in Russian Turkistan, Khokand, Bukhara, and Kuldja*. New York: Scribner, Armstrong & Co, 1876.

Sıvacıyan, Mihran H. *Sahmanatro't'iwn Osmanean*. [s.l.]: [s.n.], 1876.

Süleyman Hüsnü Paşa. *Hiss-i İnkılab*. Istanbul: Tanin Matbaası, 1326.

Süleyman Paşazade Sami. *Süleyman Paşa Muhakemesi: 1293 Osmanlı-Rus Muharebesi*. Konstantiniye: Matbaa-i Ebüzziya, 1328 [1912].

Testa, Le Baron I. de. *Recueil des Traités de la Porte ottomane avec les Puissances étrangères depuis le Premier Traité conclu, en 1536, entre Suléyman Ier et François Ier jusqu'à nos Jours, continué par le baron Alfred de Testa et le baron Léopold de Testa*, 11 vol. Paris: Amyot, 1864-1911.

"The Ottoman Constitution, Promulgated the 7th Zilbridje, 1293 (11/23 December, 1876)." *The American Journal of International Law*, vol. 2, no. 4, Supplement: Official Documents (Oct., 1908): 367-87.

Tutundjian, Télémaque. *Pacte politique entre l'Etat ottoman et les Nations non-musulmanes de la Turquie*. Lausanne: Imprimerie G. Vaney-Burnier, 1904.

Türkgeldi, Ali Fuat. *Rical-i Mühimme-i Siyasiye*. İstanbul: [s. n.], 1928.

—, *Mesail-i Mühimme-i Siyasiye*, 3 vol. Ankara: Türk Tarih Kurumu, 1957-66.

Ubicini, A. *Letters on Turkey*, English trans. by Lady Easthope, 2. vol. London: John Murray, 1856.

—, *Etat présent de l'Empire ottoman*. Paris: Librairie militaire de J. Dumaine, 1876.

—, *La Constitution ottomane du 7 Zilhidje 1293 (23 Décembre 1876) expliquée et annotée*. Paris: Cotillon, 1877.

Urquhart, David. *Turkey and Its Resources*. London: Saunders and Otley, 1833.

Viçenyan, Serope (Serviçen). *Paro'h'agan Sgzpo'wnq* (Moral Principles). İstanbul: Mühendisyan, 1851.

Y. A. *Midhad Pacha, La Constitution ottomane et l'Europe*. Paris: Imprimerie Topographique Jean Gainche, 1903.

Young, George. *Corps de Droit ottoman*, 7 vol. Oxford: Clarendon Press, 1905-06.

Zartaryan, Vahan. *H'ishadagaran: Hah' Erewelinero'w Gensakragannery, Lo'wsangarnery, Tzer'akirnery, Kro'wt'iwnnery, 1512-1912*. Istanbul: Zartaryan, 1912?

Printed Works

Abu-Manneh, Butrus. *Studies on Islam and the Ottoman Empire in the 19th Century (1826-1876)*. Istanbul: Isis, 2001.

Ahmed Midhad Effendi. *Üss-i İnkılab*, 2 vol., edited by Tahir Galip Seratlı. İstanbul: Selis Kitapları, 2004.

Aksüt, Ali Kemali. *Sultan Aziz'in Mısır ve Avrupa Seyahati*. Ahmed Sait Oğlu Kitabevi, 1944.

Albers, Pierre & Hedde, René. *Manuel d'Histoire ecclésiastique*, 2 vol. Paris: Librairie Lecoffre, 1939.

Albert, Phyllis Cohen. *The Modernization of French Jewry: Consistory and Community in the Nineteenth Century*. Hanover, New Hampshire: Brandeis University Press, 1977.

Alexander, Larry. *Constitutionalism: Philosophical Foundations*. Cambridge: Cambridge University Press, 2001.

Anagnostopulu, Athanasia. "Tanzimat ve Rum Milletinin Kurumsal Çerçevesi: Patrikhane, Cemaat Kurumları, Eğitim." In *19. Yüzyıl İstanbul'unda Gayrimüslimler*, edited by Pinelopi Sthathis, 1-35. İstanbul: Tarih Vakfı, 1999.

Anderson, Benedict. *Imagined Communities*. London: Verso, 1991.

Anderson, M. S. *The Eastern Question, 1774-1923*. London: Macmillan, 1966.

Anscombe, Frederick. "Continuities in Ottoman Centre-Periphery Relations, 1787-1915." In *The Frontiers of the Ottoman World*, edited by Andrew Peacock, 235-251. Oxford & New York: Oxford University Press, 2009.

Anteby-Yemini, Lisa, Berthomière, William & Sheffer, Gabriel. *Les Diasporas: 200 Ans d'Histoire*. Rennes: PUR, 2005.

Apostolov, Mario. *The Christian-Muslim Frontier: a Zone of Contact, Conflict or Cooperation*. London: Routledge, 2004.

Arberry, A. J. *Religion in the Middle East: Three Religions in Concord and Conflict*, 2 vol. London: Cambridge University Press, 1969.

Ardıç, Nurullah. "Islam, Modernity and the 1876 Constitution." In *The First Ottoman Experiment in Democracy*, edited by Christoph Herzog & Malek Sharif, 89-106. Istanbul: Orient Institut, 2010.

Aristarchi, Yanko. *De Bagdad à Berlin: l'Itinéraire de Yanko Aristarchi Bey, Diplomate ottoman (Correspondance officielle et privée: Berlin, 1854-1892)*, 2 vol. Istanbul: Isis, 2008.

Arjomand, Said Amir (ed.). *Constitutional Politics in the Middle East with Special Reference to Turkey, Irak, Iran and Afghanistan*. Oxford: Hart Publications, 2008.

Artinian, Vartan. *The Armenian Constitutional System in the Ottoman Empire, 1839-1863: a Study of its Historical Development*. Istanbul: [s. n.], 1988.

Aydıngün, İsmail & Dardağan, Esra. "Rethinking the Jewish Communal Apartment in the Ottoman Communal Building." *Middle Eastern Studies*, vol. 42, no. 2 (Mar., 2006): 319-334.

Bailey, Frank Edgar. *British Policy and the Turkish Reform Movement: a Study in Anglo-Turkish Relations, 1826-1853*. Cambridge: Harvard University Press, 1942.

Bardakjian, Kevork. "The Rise of the Armenian Patriarchate of Constantinople". In *Christians and Jews in the Ottoman Empire. The Functioning of a Plural Society: the Central Lands*, vol. 1, edited by Benjamin Braude & Bernard Lewis, 89-100. New York: Holmes & Meier Publishers, 1982.

Barkan, Ömer Lütfi. "Türk Toprak Hukuku Tarihinde Tanzimat ve 1274 (1858) Tarihli Arazi Kanunnamesi." *Tanzimat I*, 321-421. İstanbul: Maarif, 1940).

Barkey, Karen. "In Different Times: Scheduling and Social Control in the Ottoman Empire, 1550 to 1650." *Comparative Studies in Society and History*, vol. 38, no. 3 (Jul., 1996): 460-483.

—, *Empire of Difference: The Ottomans in Comparative Perspective*. Cambridge: Cambridge University Press, 2008.

Barsoumian, Hagop. "The Dual Role of the Armenian *Amira* Class within the Ottoman Government and the Armenian *Millet* (1750-1850)." In *Christians and Jews in the Ottoman Empire. The Functioning of a Plural Society: the Central Lands*, vol. 1, edited by Benjamin Braude & Bernard Lewis, 171-184. New York: Holmes & Meier Publishers, 1982.

Başbakanlık Osmanlı Arşivi Rehberi. İstanbul: Başbakanlık Devlet Arşivleri Genel Müdürlüğü, 2000.

Batwagan-Toufanian, Saténig. "Le Piège de l'Orgueil, la Constitution d'un Etat de droit en Arménie." Unpublished PhD dissertation, Paris: Ecole des Hautes Etudes en Sciences sociales, 2013.

Baykal, Bekir Sıtkı. "Midhad Paşa'nın Gizli Bir Siyasi Teşebbüsü." In *III. Türk Tarih Kongresi, Ankara, 15-20 Kasım 1943*, 470-477. Ankara: Türk Tarih Kurumu, 1948.

Baysun, Cavid. "Mustafa Reşid Paşa." In *Tanzimat I*, 723-46. İstanbul: Maarif, 1940.

Bejarano, Margalit. "Constitutional Documents of two Sephardic Communities in Latin America (Argentina and Cuba)." *Jewish Political Studies Review*, vol. 8, no. 3-4 (Fall 1996): 127-148.

Bellamy, Richard & Castiglione, Dario (eds.). *Constitutionalism in Transformation: European and Theoretical Perspectives*. Oxford: Cambridge: Blackwell, 1996.

Benbassa, Esther. *Un Grand Rabbin sépharade en Politique 1892-1923*. Paris: Presses du CNRS, 1990.

Berkes, Niyazi. *The Development of Secularism in Turkey*. London: Hurst, 1998.

Bernard-Griffiths, Simone. "Autour de la Révolution d'Edgar Quinet. Les Enjeux du Débat Religion-Révolution dans l'Historiographie d'un Républicain désenchanté." *Archives de Sciences sociales des Religions*, vol. 66, no. 1 (1988): 53-64.

Beydilli, Kemal. "Kabakçı İsyanı Akabinde hazırlanan Hüccet-i Şeriyye." *Türk Kültürü İncelemeleri Dergisi*, no. 4 (2001): 33-48.

Beylérian, A. "Krikor Odian (1834-1887): Un Haut Fonctionnaire ottoman, Homme des Missions secrètes." *Revue du Monde arménien*, vol. 1 (1994): 45-86.

Boissel, Jean. "Un Diplomate du XIXème Siècle, Défenseur de l'Empire ottoman: Prosper Bourée." *Revue d'Histoire diplomatique*, 87 (Janvier-Juin 1973): 115-138.

Bournoutian, George A. *Russia and the Armenians of Transcaucasia, 1797-1889: a Documentary Record*. California: Mazda Publishers, 1998.

—, *A Concise History of the Armenian People (From Ancient Times to the Present)*. Costa Mesa, Calif: Mazda Publishers, 2003.

Bowen, H. "Ali Pasha Muhammad Amin." In *The Encyclopaedia of Islam*, new edition, vol. 1. Leiden: Brill, 1986: 396-398.

Braude, Benjamin. "Foundation Myths of the *Millet* System." In *Christians and Jews in the Ottoman Empire. The Functioning of a Plural Society: the Central Lands*, vol. 1, edited by Benjamin Braude & Bernard Lewis, 69-88. New York: Holmes & Meier Publishers, 1982.

Bridges, Peter. "Eugene Schuyler, the Only Diplomatist." *Diplomacy and Statecraft*, 16 (2005): 13-22.

Burke, Peter. "Cultures of Translation in Early Modern Europe." In *Cultural Translation in Early Modern Europe*, edited by Peter Burke & R. Po-Chia Hsia, 7-38. Cambridge University Press, 2007.

—, "Translations into Latin in Early Modern Europe". In *Cultural Translation in Early Modern Europe*, edited by Peter Burke & R. Po-Chia Hsia, 65-80. Cambridge University Press, 2007.

—, *Cultural Hybridity*. Cambridge: Polity Press, 2009.

Buzpınar, Ş. Tufan. "The Question of Caliphate under the Last Ottoman Sultans." In *Ottoman Reform and Muslim Regeneration: Studies in honour of Butrus Abu-Manneh*, edited by Itzchak Weismann & Fruma Zachs, 17-36. London: Tauris, 2005.

Callinicos, Alex. *Making History: Agency, Structure, and Change in Social Theory*. Chicago, Illinois: Haymarket Books, 2009.

Carlsnaes, Walter. "The Agency-Structure Problem in Foreign Policy Analysis." *International Studies Quarterly*, vol. 36, no. 3 (Sep., 1992): 245-270.

Castells, Manuel. *The Rise of the Network Society*. Oxford: Blackwell Publishers, 1998.

Cevded Paşa. *Tezakir*, 4 vol. Ankara: Türk Tarih Kurumu, 1991.

Chouraqui, André. *Cent Ans d'Histoire: L'Alliance Israélite Universelle et la Renaissance juive contemporaine*. Paris: Presses universitaires de France, 1965.

Clay, C. G. A. *Gold for the Sultan: Western Bankers and Ottoman Finance, 1856-1881: a Contribution to Ottoman and to International Financial History*. London, New York: Tauris, 2000.

Cohen, Robin. *Global Diaporas: An Introduction*. London: University of Warwick, 1997.

Cololyan, Hagop. *Bo'lis ew ir Tery*, 4 vol. Beyrut: Mesrob, 1965-88.

Czygan, Christiane. "Reflections on Justice: A Young Ottoman View of the Tanzimat." *Middle Eastern Studies*, vol. 46, no. 6 (November 2010): 943-956.

Çadırcı, Musa. *Tanzimat Döneminde Anadolu Kentlerinin Sosyal ve Ekonomik Yapısı*. Ankara: Türk Tarih Kurumu, 1997.

Çağlar, Burhan. *İngiliz Said Paşa ve Günlüğü (Jurnal)*. İstanbul: Arı Sanat Yayınevi, 2010.

Çakır, Coşkun. *Tanzimat Dönemi Osmanlı Maliyesi*. İstanbul: Küre, 2001.

Çelik, Mehmet. "Tanzimat in the Balkans: Midhad Pasha's Governorship in the Danube Province (Tuna Vilayeti), 1864-1868." Unpublished MA Thesis, Bilkent University, 2007.

Çizakça, Murat. *A Comparative Evolution of Business Partnerships*. Leiden: Brill, 1996.

Davison, Roderic. *Reform in the Ottoman Empire, 1856-1876*. Princeton University Press, 1963.

—, "The *Millets* as Agents of Change in the Nineteenth-Century Ottoman Empire." In *Christians and Jews in the Ottoman Empire. The Functioning of a Plural Society: the Central Lands*, vol. 1, edited by Benjamin Braude & Bernard Lewis, 339-368. New York: Holmes & Meier Publishers, 1982: 319-37.

—, *Essays in Ottoman and Turkish History, 1774-1923: The Impact of the West*. Austin: Texas University Press, 1990.

—, *Nineteenth Century Ottoman Diplomacy and Reforms*. Istanbul: Isis, 1999.

Delanty, Gerard & Rumford, Chris. *Rethinking Europe: Social Theory and the Implications of Europeanization*. New York: Routledge, 2005.

Demirel, Fatmagül. *Adliye Nezareti: Kuruluşu ve Faaliyetleri (1876-1914)*. İstanbul: Boğaziçi Üniversitesi Yayınevi, 2007.

Deringil, Selim. *The Well-Protected Domains: Ideology and the Legitimation of Power in the Ottoman Empire, 1876-1909*. London: Tauris, 1999.

Der Minassian, Anahide. *Ermeni Kültürü ve Modernleşme*, trans. Sosi Dolanoğlu. İstanbul: Aras Yayıncılık, 2006.

—, "Etat national et Diaspora: le Cas arménien." In *Arméniens et Grecs en Diaspora: Approches comparatives*, edited by Michel Bruneau et al., 43-58. Athènes: Ecole française d'Athènes, 2007.

Devereux, Robert. *The First Ottoman Constitutional Period: a Study of the Midhad Constitution and Parliament*. Baltimore: The Johns Hopkins Press, 1963.

Dumont, Paul. "La Période des Tanzimat." In *Histoire de l'Empire Ottoman*, sous la direction de Robert Mantran, 459-522. Paris: Fayard, 1989.

Dustur: A Survey of the Constitutions of the Arab and Muslim States. Leiden: Brill, 1966.

Eire, Carlos M. N. "Early Modern Catholic Piety in Translation." In *Cultural Translation in Early Modern Europe*, edited by Peter Burke & R. Po-Chia Hsia, 83-100. Cambridge University Press, 2007.

Eisenstadt, S. N. "Multiples Modernities." *Deadalus* 129 (Winter 2000): 1-29.

Ekinci, Cevat (ed.). *Gökkube Altında Birlikte Yaşamak: Belgelerin Diliyle Osmanlı Hoşgörüsü*. Ankara: Başbakanlık Devlet Arşivleri, 2006.

Eldem, Edhem. *A History of the Ottoman Bank*. Istanbul: Ottoman Bank Historical Research Center, 1999.

—, "Istanbul: from Imperial to Peripheralized Capital." In *The Ottoman City between East and West: Aleppo, Izmir and Istanbul*, edited by Edhem Eldem, Daniel Goffman & Bruce Masters, 135-227. Cambridge University Press, 2001.

Eriksson, T. E. *Libri Armeniaci Bibliothecae Universitatis Helsingiensis*, 1951.

Evtuhov, Catherine & Kotkin, Stephen (eds.). *The Cultural Gradient: The Transmission of Ideas in Europe, 1789-1991*. Oxford: Rowman & Littlefield, 2003.

Exertzoglu, Haris. "The Development of a Greek Ottoman Bourgeoisie: Investment Patterns in the Ottoman Empire, 1850-1914." In *Ottoman Greeks in the Age of Nationalism: Politics, Economy, and Society in the Nineteenth Century*, edited by Dimitri Gondicas and Charles Issawi, 89-107. Princeton & New Jersey: Darwin Press, 1999.

Fadeeva, I. L. *Osmanskaya Imperiya i Anglo-Turetskie Otnoskeniya v Seredine XIX v*. Moskow: Nauka, 1982.

Fairclough, Norman. *Discourse and Social Change*. Cambridge: Polity Press, 2007.

Faist, Thomas. "The Border-Crossing Expansion of Social Space: Concepts, Questions and Topics." In *Transnational Social Spaces: Agents, Networks and Institutions*, edited by Thomas Faist & Eyüp Özveren, 2-34. Aldershot: Ashgate, 2004.

Feldman, Eliyahu. "The Question of Jewish Emancipation in the Ottoman Empire and the Danubian Principalities after the Crimean War." Reprinted from *Jewish Social Studies*, vol. 41, no. 1 (Winter 1979): 41-74.

Ferguson, Niall. *The World's Banker: The History of the House of Rothschild*. Weidenfeld & Nicolson: London, 1998.

Findley, Carter Vaughn. *Bureaucratic Reform in the Ottoman Empire: the Sublime Porte, 1789-1922*. Princeton, N. J.: Princeton University Press, 1980.

—, "The Acid Test of Ottomanism: the Acceptance of non-Muslims in the late Ottoman Bureaucracy." In *Christians and Jews in the Ottoman Empire. The Functioning of a Plural Society: the Central Lands,* vol. 1, edited by Benjamin Braude & Bernard Lewis, 339-368. New York: Holmes & Meier Publishers, 1982.

—, *Ottoman Civil Officialdon: a Social History*. Princeton, New Jersey: Princeton University Press, 1989.

—, "Political Culture and the Great Households." In *The Cambridge History of Turkey: The Later Ottoman Empire, 1603-1839*, v. 3, edited by Suraiya Faroqhi, 65-80. Cambridge: Cambridge University Press, 2006.

—, "The Tanzimat." In *The Cambridge History of Turkey: Turkey in the Modern World*, v. 4, edited by Reşat Kasaba, 11-37. Cambridge: Cambridge University Press, 2008.

Finkel, Caroline. *Osman's Dream: The Story of the Ottoman Empire, 1300-1923*. New York: Basic Books, 2006.

Foucault, Michel. *L'Ordre du Discours: Leçon inaugurale au Collège de France prononcée le 2 décembre 1970*. Paris: Gallimard, 1971.

Frangakis-Syrett, Elena. "The Economic Activities of the Greek Community of Izmir in the Second Half of the Nineteenth and Early Twentieth Centuries." In *Ottoman Greeks in the Age of Nationalism: Politics, Economy, and Society in the Nineteenth Century*, edited by Dimitri Gondicas and Charles Issawi, 17-44. Princeton & New Jersey: Darwin Press, 1999.

Frazee, Charles. *Catholics and Sultans: The Church and the Ottoman Empire*. London: Cambridge University Press, 1983.

Frenette, Derek Angus. "L'Alliance Israélite Universelle and the Politics of Modern Jewish Education in Bagdad, 1864-1914." Unpublished MA Thesis, Simon Fraser University, 2005.

Galante, Abraham. *Documents officiels turcs concernant les Juifs de Turquie: recueil de 114 lois, règlements, firmans, bérats, ordres et décisions de tribunaux*. Istanbul: Haim, Rozio, 1931.

—, *Histoire des Juifs d'Anatolie, Les Juifs d'Izmir (Smyrne)*, 2 vol. Istanbul: Babok, 1937-39.

—, *Histoire des Juifs de Turquie*, 9 vol. Istanbul: Editions Isis, [1985].

Gazmararyan, M. *Kriko'r Odeani Ko'harnery*, v. 2. İstanbul: Der Sahakyan, 1931.

Gellner, Ernest. *Nations and Nationalism*. Oxford: Blackwell Publishers, 1997.

Genieys, William & Smyrl, Marc. *Elites, Ideas, and the Evolution of Public Policy*. New York: Palgrave, 2008.

George, Joan. *Merchants in Exile: The Armenians in Manchester, England, 1835-1935*. Princeton and London: Gomidas Institute, 2002.

Georgeon, François. *Abdülhamid II: le Sultan Calife, 1876-1909*. Paris: Fayard, 2003.

Geyer, Michael & Bright, Charles. "World History in a Global Age." *The American Historical Review* 100 (1995): 1034-1060.

Ghougassian, Vazken. "The Quest for Enlightenment and Liberation: The Case of the Armenian Community of India in the Late Eighteenth Century." In *Enlightenment and Diaspora: the Armenian and Jewish Cases*, edited by Richard G. Hovannisian & David N. Myers, 241-264. Atlanta, Georgia: Scholars Press, 1999.

Gleason, J. H. *The Genesis of Russophobia in Great Britain*. Cambridge: Harvard University Press, 1950.

Goffman, Daniel. *The Ottoman Empire and Early Modern Europe*. Cambridge: Cambridge University Press, 2002.

Goldie, Mark & Wokler, Robert (eds.). *The Cambridge History of Eigtheenth-Century Political Thought*. Cambridge: Cambridge University Press, 2006.

Gooday, Graeme J. N. & Low, Morris F. "Technology Transfer and Cultural Exchange: Western Scientists and Engineers Encounter Late Tokugawa and Meiji Japan." *Osiris*, 2nd Series, vol. 13, Beyond Joseph Needham: Science, Technology, and Medicine in East and Southeast Asia (1998): 99-128.

Gordon, Scott. *Controlling the State. Constitutionalism from Ancient Athens to Today*. Cambridge; London: Harvard University Press, 1999.

Göçek, Fatma Müge. *Rise of the Bourgeoisie, Demise of Empire: Ottoman Westernization and Social Change*. New York: Oxford University Press, 1996.

Greenwood, Keith M. *Robert College: the American Founders*. Istanbul: Boğaziçi University Press, 2000.

Gürdoğan, Burhan. "İkinci Meşrutiyet Devrinde Anayasa Değişiklikleri." *Ankara Üniversitesi Hukuk Fakültesi Dergisi*, vol, 16, no. 1-4 (1959): 91-105.

Hacker, Joseph R. "Ottoman Policy toward the Jews and Jewish Attitudes toward the Ottomans during the Fifteenth Century." In *Christians and Jews in the Ottoman Empire*, vol. 1, edited by Benjamin Braude & Bernard Lewis, 117-126. New York: Holmes & Meier Publishers, 1982.

Hanioğlu, Şükrü. *A Brief History of the Late Ottoman Empire*. Princeton University Press, 2008.

Hartmann, Elke. "The 'Loyal Nation' and Its Deputies: The Armenians in the First Ottoman Parliament." In *The First Ottoman Experiment in Democracy*, edited by Christoph Herzog & Malek Sharif, 187-222. Istanbul: Orient Institut, 2010.

Herlihy, Patricia. "Eugene Schuyler and the Bulgarian Constitution of 1876." In *Russia, Europe, and the Rule of Law*, edited by Ferdinand Feldbrugge, 165-184. Leiden & Boston: Martinus Nijhoff Publishers, 2007.

Horowitz, Richard S. "International Law and State Transformation in China, Siam, and the Ottoman Empire during the Nineteenth Century." *Journal of World History*, vol. 15, no. 4 (Dec., 2004): 445-486.

Hourani, Albert Habib. *Arabic Thought in the Liberal Age*, 2nd imp. Oxford: Oxford University Press, 1969.

Hurewitz, J. C. *Diplomacy in the Near and Middle East: A Documentary Record, 1535-1956*, 2 vol. New Jersey: Van Nostrand, 1956.

—, "Ottoman Diplomacy and the European State System." *Middle East Journal*, vol. 15, no. 2 (Spring 1961): 141-152.

—, *The Middle East and North Africa in World Politics: a Documentary Record*, 2 vol. (New Haven: Yale University Press, 1975).

Hussin, Iza. "Misreading and Mobility in Constitutional Texts: A Nineteenth-Century Case." *Indiana Journal of Global Legal Studies*, vol. 21 # 1 (Winter 2014): 145-158.

Işın, Ekrem. *İstanbul'da Gündelik Hayat*. İstanbul: İletişim Yayınları, 1995.

İlhan, M. Mehdi. "An Overview of the Ottoman Archival Documents and Chronicles." *Ankara Üniversitesi Dil ve Tarih Coğrafya Fakültesi Tarih Bölümü Tarih Araştırmaları Dergisi*, vol 27, no. 44 (2008): 21-40.

İnalcık, Halil. "Osmanlı Hukukuna Giriş: Örfi-Sultani Hukuk ve Fatih'in Kanunları." *Ankara Üniversitesi Siyasal Bilgiler Fakültesi Dergisi*, vol. 13, no. 2 (1958): 102-126.

—, "The Nature of Traditional Society: Turkey." In *Political Modernisation in Japan and Turkey*, edited by Robert E. Ward & Dankwart A. Rustow, 42-63. Princeton: Princeton University Press, 1964.

—, "Centralization and Decentralization in Ottoman Administration". In *Studies in Eighteenth Century Islamic Society*, edited by Thomas Naff and Roger Owen, 27-53. Carbondale: Southern Illinois University Press, 1977.

Israel, Jonathan I. *Radical Enlightenment: Philosophy and the Making of Modernity, 1650-1750*. Oxford: Oxford University Press, 2002.

Issawi, Charles. "Population and Resources in the Ottoman Empire and Iran." In *Studies in Eighteenth Century Islamic History*, edited by Thomas Naff and Roger Owen, 152-164. Carbondale: Southern Illinois University Press, 1977.

—, *The Economic History of Turkey, 1800-1914*. Chicago: University of Chicago Press, 1980.

—, "Introduction." In *Ottoman Greeks in the Age of Nationalism: Politics, Economy, and Society in the Nineteenth Century*, edited by Dimitri Gondicas & Charles Issawi, 1-16. Princeton & New Jersey: Darwin Press, 1999.

Jensen, R. J. "Eugene Schuyler and the Balkan Crisis." *Diplomatic History*, vol. 5, no. 1 (Winter 1981): 23-39.

Jones, Raymond A. *The British Diplomatic Service, 1815-1914*. Gerrards Cross: Colin Smythe, 1983.

Kabadayı, Mustafa Erdem. "The Sharp Rise and the Sudden Fall of an Ottoman Entrepreneur: the Case of Mkrdich Cezayirliyan." In *Merchants in the Ottoman Empire*, edited by Suraiya Faroqhi & Gilles Veinstein, 281-299. Paris: Peeters, 2008.

Kafadar, Cemal. "Yeniçeri-Esnaf Relations: Solidarity and Conflict." Unpublished MA Thesis, McGill University, 1981.

—, "Janissaries and other Riffraff of Ottoman Istanbul: Rebels without a Cause?" *International Journal of Turkish Studies*, vol. 12, nos. 1 & 2 (2007): 113-134.

Kansu, Aykut. *Politics in Post-Revolutionary Turkey, 1908-1913*. Leiden: Brill, 2000.

Kaplan, Mehmet. *Namık Kemal: Hayatı ve Eserleri*. Istanbul: İbrahim Horoz Basımevi, 1948.

Kara, İsmail. *İslamcıların Siyasi Görüşleri*. İstanbul: Dergah Yayınları, 2001.

Karaca, Filiz. *Osmanlı Anayasası: Kanun-ı Esasi*. İstanbul: Doğu Kütüphanesi, 2009.

Karateke, Hakan T. "Who is the Next Ottoman Sultan? Attempts to Change the Rule of Succession during the Nineteenth Century." In *Ottoman Reform and Muslim Regeneration: Studies in honour of Butrus Abu-Manneh*, edited by Itzchak Weismann & Fruma Zachs, 37-53. London: Tauris, 2005.

Karpat, Kemal H. "*Millet*s and Nationality: The Roots of the Incongruity of Nation and State in the Post-Ottoman Era." In *Christians and Jews in the Ottoman Empire. The Functioning of a Plural Society: the Central Lands*, vol. 1, edited by Benjamin Braude & Bernard Lewis, 141-169. New York: Holmes & Meier Publishers, 1982.

Karpat, Kemal & Zens, Robert, W. *Ottoman Borderlands: Issues, Personalities and Political Changes*. Madison: University of Winsconsin, 2003.

Kasaba, Reşat. *The Ottoman Empire and the World Economy: The Nineteenth Century*. Albany: State University of New York Press, 1988.

—, "Economic Foundations of a Civil Society: Greeks in the Trade of Western Anatolia, 1840-1876." In *Ottoman Greeks in the Age of Nationalism: Politics, Economy, and Society in the Nineteenth Century*, edited by Dimitri Gondicas & Charles Issawi, 77-87. Princeton & New Jersey: Darwin Press, 1999.

Kaynar, Reşat. *Mustafa Reşid Paşa ve Tanzimat*. Ankara: Türk Tarih Kurumu, 1954.

Khaçadıryan, Boğos. *O'ro'kah't' P'ar'ac, T'arkmano'wt'iwny Kraparic & Dzano't'akro'wt'o'wnnery Panasiragan Kido'wt'o'wnneri Do'gdo'r, Pro'feso'r Bo'gho's Xach'adrh'ani*. Yerevan: Hayasdan, 2002.

Kılıç, Selda Kaya. "1876 Kanun-ı Esasi'nin Hazırlanması ve Meclis-i Mebusan'ın Toplanması." Unpublished Master's Thesis, Ankara Üniversitesi Sosyal Bilimler Enstitüsü: Ankara, 1991.

—, "1876 Anayasası'nın Bilinmeyen İki Tasarısı." *OTAM* (Ankara Üniversitesi Osmanlı Tarihi Araştırma Merkezi Dergisi), 4 (1993): 557-635.

—, *Osmanlı Devleti'nde Meşrutiyet'e Geçiş: İlk Anayasa'nın Hazırlanması*. Ankara: Berikan Yayınevi, 2010.

Kili, Suna. *Osmanlı ve Türk Anayasaları*. İstanbul: Boğaziçi Üniversitesi Yayınları, 1980.

Kili, Suna & Gözübüyük, Şeref. *Türk Anayasa Metinleri: Sened-i İttifak'tan Günümüze*. Anakara: İş Bankası Kültür Yayınları, 1985.

Kirakossian, Arman J. *British Diplomacy and the Armenian Question, from 1830s to 1914*. Princeton & London: Gomidas Institute Books, 2003.

Khoury, Dina Rizk. "The Ottoman Centre versus Provincial Power-Holders." In *The Cambridge History of Turkey: the Later Ottoman Empire, 1603-1839*, v. 3, edited by Suraiya Faroqhi, 135-156. Cambridge: Cambridge University Press, 2006.

Koçunyan (Beşiryan), Aylin. "Hopes of Secularization in the Ottoman Empire: The Armenian National Constitution and the Newspaper *Masis*, 1856-1863." MA Thesis, Istanbul: Boğaziçi University, 2007.

—, "Negotiating the Ottoman Constitution, 1856-1876." PhD dissertation, Florence: European University Institute, 2013.

—, "The Transcultural Dimension of the Ottoman Constitution." In *Well-Connected Domains: towards an Entangled Ottoman History*, edited by Pascal Firges, Tobias Graf, Christian Roth and Gülay Tulasoğlu, 235-258. Leiden: Brill, 2014.

—, "Long Live Sultan Abdulaziz, Long Live the Nation, Long Live the Constitution!" In *Constitutionalism, Legitimacy and Power: Nineteenth-Century Experiences*, edited by Kelly Grotke and Markus Prutsch, 189-210. Oxford: Oxford University Press, 2014.

—, "The *Millet* System and the Challenge of Other Confessional Models, 1856-1865." *Ab Imperio*, 1/2017: 59-85.

Kolb, Deborah M. "Negotiation Theory through the Looking Glass of Gender." In *ICAR (Institute for Conflict Analysis & Resolution) Working Papers.* George Mason University, 1994): 1-32.

Köksal, Yonca. "Imperial Center and Local Groups: Tanzimat Reforms in the Provinces of Edirne and Ankara." *New Perspectives on Turkey,* 27 (Fall 2002): 107-138.

Kramer, Roderick M. & Messick, David M (eds.). *Negotiation as a Social Process.* Thousand Oaks: Sage Publications, 1995.

Krikorian, Mesrob K. *Armenians in the Service of the Ottoman Empire, 1860-1908.* London: Routledge, 1977.

Kuneralp, Sinan. "Bir Osmanlı Diplomatı Kostaki Musurus Pasha, 1807-1891." *Belleten,* vol. 34, no. 135 (July 1970): 421-435.

—, "Les Grecs en Stambouline: Diplomates ottomans d'Origine grecque." In *Le différend gréco-turc,* edited by Semih Vaner, 41-46. Paris: L'Harmattan, 1988.

—, *Son Dönem Osmanlı Erkan ve Ricali, 1839-1922.* Istanbul: Isis, 1999.

Kuntay, Mithat Cemal. *Namık Kemal: Devrinin İnsanları ve Olayları Arasında,* 2 vol. İstanbul: Maarif Basımevi, 1944-56.

Kurkjian, V. M. *A History of Armenia.* New York: AGBU, 1958.

Ladeur, Karl-Heinz. "The Myth of the Neutral State and the Individualisation of Religion: the Relationship between State and Religion in the Face of Fundamentalism." In *Constitutional Secularism in an Age of Religious Revival,* edited by Susanna Mancini & Michel Rosenfeld, 33-53. Oxford: Oxford University Press, 2014.

Lane, Jan-Erik. *Constitutions and Political Theory.* New York: Manchester University Press, 1996.

Levy, Avigdor. *The Sephardim in the Ottoman Empire.* Princeton, NJ: The Darwin Press, 1992.

—, "Introduction." In *The Jews of the Ottoman Empire,* edited by Levy, 1-150. Princeton, New Jersey: Darwin Press, 1994.

Lewis, Bernard. "Turkey." In *Dustur: a Survey of the Constitutions of the Arab and Muslim States,* 6-24. Leiden: Brill, 1966.

—, *The Emergence of Modern Turkey,* 2nd ed. London: Oxford University Press, 1968.

—, *Islam in History: Ideas, People, and Events in the Middle East.* Illinois: Open Court, 2001.

Lynch, H. F. B. *Armenia: Travels and Studies,* 2 vol. Beirut: Khayats, 1965.

Mahmud Celaleddin Paşa. *Mirat-ı Hakikat,* 2 vol., edited by İ. Miroğlu et al. İstanbul: Tercüman Gazetesi, 1979.

Mantran, Robert. "Les Débuts de la Question d'Orient (1774-1839)." In *Histoire de l'Empire Ottoman,* sous la direction de Robert Mantran, 421-458. Paris: Fayard, 1989.

Ma'oz, Moshe. "Changing Relations between Jews, Muslims, and Christians during the Nineteenth Century, with Special Reference to Ottoman Syria and Palestine." In *Jews, Turks, Ottomans: a Shared History, Fifteenth through the Twentieth Century,* edited by Avigdor Levy, 108-118. Syracuse, New York: Syracuse University Press, 2002.

Mardin, Şerif. *The Genesis of Young Ottoman Thought: A Study in the Modernization of Turkish Political Ideas*. Syracuse, NY: Syracuse University Press, 2000.

Martucci, Roberto (ed.). *Constitution & Révolution aux États-Unis d'Amérique et en Europe (1776/1815)*. Macerata: Laboratorio di storia costituzionale, 1995.

Masayuki, Ueno. "The First Draft of the Armenian *Millet* Constitution." *AJAMES* (Annals of Japan Association for Middle East Studies), no. 23-1 (2007): 213-251.

Mehmet Süreyya. S*icill-i Osmani*, 6 vol. Istanbul: Tarih Vakfı Yurt Yayınları, 1996.

Meijer, Roel. "Introduction." In *Cosmopolitanism, Identity and Authenticity in the Middle East*, edited by Roel Meijer, 1-11. Surrey: Curzon, 1999.

Midhad Paşa. *Tabsıra-i İbret*, vol. 1 of *Midhad Paşanın Hatıraları*. ed. Osman Selim Kocahanoğlu. Istanbul: Temel Yayınları, 1997.

—, *Mirat-ı Hayret*, vol. 2 of *Midhad Paşanın hatıraları*, ed. Osman Selim Kocahanoğlu. İstanbul: Temel Yayınları, 1997.

Morehouse, Barbara J. "Theoretical Approaches to Border Spaces and Identities." In *Challenged Borderlands: Transcending Political and Cultural Boundaries*, edited by Vera Pavlakovitch-Kochi, Barbara J. Morehouse & Doris Wastl-Walter, 19-40. Adershot: Ahgate, 2004.

Mouradian, Claire. "Une Emule de l'Alliance: l'Union générale arménienne de Bienfaisance." In *Histoire de l'Alliance israélite universelle, de 1860 à nos Jours*, edited by André Kaspi, 64-67. Paris: Armand Colin, 2010.

Nalbandian, Louise. *The Armenian Revolutionary Movement*. Berkeley: University of California Press, 1963.

Ninth Mediterranean Research Meeting, Florence & Montecatini Terme, 12-15 March 2008, organised by the Mediterranean Program of the Robert Schuman Centre for Advanced Studies at the European University Institute. Workshop no. 12 on *Secularisation, Secularism, Secular: Democracy and Religious Minorities* organised by Sandrine Bertaux and Murat Akan.

Ocak, Ahmed Yaşar. "Islam in the Ottoman Empire: A Sociological Framework for a New Interpretation". In *Ottoman Borderlands: Issues, Personalities and Political Changes*, edited by Kemal H. Karpat & Robert W. Zens, 183-197. Madison: University of Wisconsin Press, 2003.

Ortaylı, İlber. *Studies on Ottoman Transformation*. Istanbul: Isis Press, 1994.

Pakalın, Mehmed Zeki. *Son Sadrazamlar ve Başvekiller*, 5 vol. İstanbul: İstanbul: Ahmed Said Matbaası, 1940-48.

Palmer, R. R. *Age of the Democratic Revolution: A Political History of Europe and America, 1760-1800*. Princeton: Princeton University Press, 1959.

Pamuk, Şevket. *The Ottoman Empire and European Capitalism, 1820-1913: Trade, Investment and Production*. Cambridge: Cambridge University Press, 1987.

—, *A Monetary History of the Ottoman Empire*. Cambridge: Cambridge University Press, 2000.

Pamukciyan, Kevork. *Biyografileriyle Ermeniler*. İstanbul: Aras Yayıncılık, 2003.

Papadopoullos, Th. H. *The History of the Greek Church and People under Turkish Domination*. Brussels: Bibliotheca Graeca Aevi Posterioris, 1952.

Pasquier, Marcel du. "Edgar Quinet et la Pensée protestante en Suisse romande: Ernest Naville, Charles Secrétan, Amiel, Merle d'Aubigné, Ferdinand Buisson." *Revue de théologie et de philosophie*, vol. 8, no. 1 (1958): 1-13.

Pastermadjian, H. *Histoire de l'Arménie depuis les origines jusqu'au Traité de Lausanne*. Paris: Librairie orientale H. Samuelian, 1964.

Pavlakovitch-Kochi, Vera, Morehouse, Barbara J. and Wastl-Walter, Doris (eds.). "Introduction: Perspectives on Borderlands." In *Challenged Borderlands: Transcending Political and Cultural Boundaries*, 3-12. Adershot: Ahgate, 2004.

Paz, Moria. "A Non-Territorial Ethnic Network and the Making of Human Rights Law: the Case of the Alliance Israélite Universelle." *International Journal of Human Rights Law*, vol. 41:1 (2009-2010): 1-24.

Peacock, A.C.S. "Introduction: The Ottoman Empire and Its Frontiers." In *The Frontiers of the Ottoman World*, edited by A.C.S. Peacock, 1-27. Oxford & New York: Oxford University Press, 2009.

Petmezas, Socrates D. "The Formation of Early Hellenic Nationalism and the Special Symbolic and Material Interests of the New Radical Republican Intelligentsia (ca. 1790-1830)." *Historein*, I (1999): 51-74.

Philliou, Christine. "Communities on the Verge: Unravelling the Phanariot Ascendency in Ottoman Governance." *Comparative Studies in Society and History*, vol. 51, no. 1 (2009): 151-181.

Pirie, Fernanda & Scheele, Judith (eds). *Legalism: Justice and Community*. Oxford: Oxford University Press, 2014.

Pocock, J. G. A. *Politics, Language and Time: Essays on Political Thought and History*. New York: Atheneum, 1973.

—, *Virtue, Commerce and History: Essays on Political Thought and History, Chiefly in the Eighteenth Century*. Cambridge: Cambridge University Press, 1985.

—, *The Machiavellian Moment: Florentine Political Thought and the Atlantic Republican Tradition*. Princeton, N.J.: Princeton University Press, 2003.

Preuss, Ulrich Klaus. *Constitutional Revolution: the Link between Constitutionalism and Progress*, translated by Deborah Lucas Schneider. N.J.: Humanities Press, 1995.

Prousis, Theophilus C. *British Consular Reports from the Ottoman Levant in an Age of Upheaval, 1815-1830*. Istanbul: Isis Press, 2008.

Pundeff, Marin V. *Bulgaria in American Perspective: Political and Cultural Issues*. Boulder, CO: Columbia University Press, 1994.

Quataert, Donald. "Ottoman Reform and Agriculture in Anatolia, 1876-1908." Unpublished PhD dissertation, Los Angeles: University of California, 1973.

—, *The Ottoman Empire, 1700-1922*. Cambridge University Press, 2000.

Rials, Stéphane. *Révolution et contre-révolution au XIXe siècle*. Paris: Diffusion Université Culture, Albatros, 1987.

Rodrigue, Aron. "The Beginnings of Westernisation and Community Reform among Istanbul's Jewry, 1854-1865." In *The Jews of the Ottoman Empire*, edited by Avigdor Levy, 1-150. Princeton, New Jersey: Darwin Press, 1994.

Rosenberg, Ralph P. "Eugene Schuyler's Doctor of Philosophy Degree: a Theory concerning the Dissertation." *The Journal of Higher Education*, vol. 33, no. 7 (October 1962): 381-386.

Rubin, Avi. "Legal Borrowing and its Impact on Ottoman Legal Culture in the Late Nineteenth Century." *Continuity and Change* 22 (2), 2007: 279-303.

—, *Ottoman Nizamiye Courts: Law and Modernity*. New York: Palgrave, 2011.

Saideman, M. S. *The Ties that Divide: Ethnic Politics, Foreign Policy, and International Politics*. New York: Columbia University Press, 2001.

Seton-Watson, R. W. *Disraeli, Gladstone and the Eastern Question*. London: Frank Cass, 1962.

Shain, Yossi. *Kinship & Diasporas in International Affairs*. Ann Arbor: University of Michigan, 2007.

Shaw, S. "The Nineteenth Century Ottoman Tax Reforms and Revenue System." *International Journal of Middle Eastern Studies*, vol. 6, no. 4 (Oct., 1975): 421-459.

—, *The Jews of the Ottoman Empire and the Turkish Republic*. Basingstoke: Macmillan, 1991.

Shaw, Stanford J. and Shaw, Ezel Kural. *History of the Ottoman Empire and Modern Turkey: Reform, Revolution and Republic. The Rise of Modern Turkey, 1808-1975*, v. 2. Cambridge: Cambridge University Press, 2002.

Sheffer, Gabriel. "The Politics of Ethno-National Diasporas." In *Les Diasporas: 200 Ans d'Histoire*, edited by Lisa Anteby-Yemini, William Berthomière & Gabriel Sheffer, 125-135. Rennes: PUR, 2005.

Sheremet, V. I. *Osmanskaya Imperiya i Zapadnaya Yevropa. Vtoraya Tret' XIX v.* Moscow: Nauka, 1986.

Schroeter, Daniel J. "The Changing Relationship between the Jews of the Arab Middle East and the Ottoman State in the Nineteenth Century." In *Jews, Turks, Ottomans: a Shared History, Fifteenth through the Twentieth Century*, edited by Avigdor Levy, 88-107. Syracuse, New York: Syracuse University Press, 2002.

Smith, Tony. *Foreign Attachments: The Power of Ethnic Groups in the Making of the American Foreign Policy*. Cambridge: Harvard University Press, 2000.

Sohrabi, Nader. "Global Waves, Local Actors: What the Young Turks Knew about Other Revolutions and Why It Mattered?" *Comparative Studies in Society and History* 44 (1), 2002: 45-79.

Stamatopoulos, Dimitrios. "From *Millet*s to Minorities in the 19th-Century Ottoman Empire: an Ambiguous Modernization." In *Citizenship in Historical Perspective*, edited by S. G. Ellis, G. Halfadanarson & A.K. Isaacs, 253-273. Pisa: Edizioni Plus, 2006.

Stepanyan, Hasmik A. *Hah'adar'T'o'wrqeren Krqeri & Hah'adar'T'o'wrqeren Barperagan Mamo'wli Madenakido'wt'iwn, 1727-1968*. Istanbul: Turkuaz Yayınları, 2005.

Strauss, Johann. "The *Millet*s and the Ottoman Language: the Contribution of Ottoman Greeks to Ottoman Letters (19th-20th Centuries)." *Die Welt des Islams*, New Series, vol. 35, Issue 2 (Nov., 1995): 189-249.

—, "Who Red What in the Ottoman Empire (19th-20th centuries)?" *Arabic Middle Eastern Literatures*, vol. 6, no. 1, 2003: 39-76.

—, "A Constitution for a Multilingual Empire: Translations of the *Kanun-i Esasi* and Other Texts into Minority Languages." In *The First Ottoman Experiment in Democracy*, edited by Christoph Herzog & Malek Sharif, 21-51. Istanbul: Orient-Institut, 2010.

Şehsuvaroğlu, Y. Haluk. *Sultan Aziz, Hususi, Siyasi Hayatı, Devri*. İstanbul: Hilmi Kitabevi, 1949.

Şeni, Nora. "The Camondos and Their Imprint on 19th-Century Istanbul." *International Journal of Middle East Studies* 26 (1994): 663-675.

Şeni, Nora & Le Tarnec, Sophie. *Les Camondo ou l'Eclipse d'une Fortune*. Actes du Sud, 1997.

Şentürk, M. Hüdai. *Osmanlı Devleti'nde Bulgar Meselesi, 1850-1875*. Ankara: Türk Tarih Kurumu, 1992.

Tanör, Bülent. *Osmanlı-Türk Anayasal Gelişmeler*. İstanbul: Afa Yayınları, 1996.

Tansel, Fevziye Abdullah. *Hususi Mektuplarına Göre Namık Kemal ve Abdülhak Hamid*. Ankara: [s. n.], 1949.

Tcholakian, Hovannes. *L'Eglise Arménienne catholique en Turquie*. İstanbul: Ohan Matbaacılık, 1998.

Temperley, Harold. "The Last Phase of Stratford de Redcliffe, 1855-1858." *English Historical Review*, 47: 186 (April 1932): 216-259.

—, "British Policy towards Parliamentary Rule and Constitutionalism in Turkey (1830-1914)." *Cambridge Historical Journal*, Vol. 4, no. 2 (1933): 156-191.

Theis, Laurent. *Guizot: La Traversée d'un Siècle*. Paris: CNRS, 2014. Kindle edition.

Tezcan, Baki. *The Second Ottoman Empire*. Cambridge: Cambridge University Press, 2010.

Todorova, Maria. *Angliya, Rossiya i Tanzimat*. Moscow: Nauka, 1983.

—, *Imagining the Balkans*. New York: Oxford University Press, 1997.

Torfing, Jacob. *New Theories of Discourse: Laclau, Mouffe and Zizek*. Oxford: Blackwell, 1999.

Tölölyan, Khachig. "Restoring the Logic of the Sedentary to Diaspora Studies." In *Les Diasporas: 200 Ans d'Histoire*, edited by Lisa Anteby-Yemini, William Berthomière & Gabriel Sheffer, 137-148. Rennes: PUR, 2005.

Trivellato, Francesca. *The Familiarity of Strangers: the Sephardic Diaspora, Livorno, and Cross-Cultural Trade in the Early Modern Period*. New Heaven & London: Yale University Press, 2009.

Tunaya, Tarık Zafer. "Midhad Paşa'nın Anayasa Tasarısı: Kanun-ı Cedid." In *Tanzimat'tan Cumhuriyet'e Türkiye Ansiklopedisi*, edited by Murat Belge, 30-34. İstanbul: İletişim Yayınları, 1985.

—, *Türkiye'de Siyasal Gelişmeler, 1876-1938: Kanun-ı Esasi ve Meşrutiyet Dönemi, 1876-1918*, v. 1. İstanbul: İstanbul Bilgi Üniversitesi Yayınları, 2003.

Türkmen, Zekeriya. "31 Mart Olayı'ndan sonra Yıldız Evrakı Tedkik Komisyonu'nun Kuruluşu, Faaliyetleri ve Yıldız Sarayı'nın Araştırılması." In *XIII. Türk Tarih Kongresi, Ankara, 4-8 Ekim 1999. Kongreye Sunulan Bildiriler*, v. 3, 559-577. Ankara: Türk Tarih Kurumu, 2002.

Uzunçarşılı, İ. Hakkı. *Midhad Paşa ve Taif Mahkumları*. Ankara: Türk Tarih Kurumu, 1970.

Velidedeoğlu, Hıfzı Veldet. "Kanunlaştırma Hareketleri ve Tanzimat." In *Tanzimat I*, 139-209. İstanbul: Maarif, 1940.

Vernon, James (ed.). *Re-reading the Constitution: New Narratives in the Political History of England's Long Nineteenth-Century*. New York: Cambridge University Press, 1996.

Wallerstein, Immanuel. *The Modern World-System III: The Second Era of Great Expansion of the Capitalist World-Economy, 1730-1840s*. San Diego: Academic Press, 1989.

Waterfield, G. *Layard of Nineveh*. London: J. Murray, 1963.

Waugh, Evelyn. *When the Going was Good*. London: Duckworth, 1945.

Webster, Charles K. *The Foreign Policy of Palmerston*. London, 1969.

Weiker, Walter F. "The Ottoman Bureaucracy: Modernisation and Reform." *Administrative Science Quarterly*, vol. 13, no. 3, Special issue on Organisations and Social Development (Dec. 1968): 451-470.

Wight, Colin. "State Agency: Social Action without Human Activity?" *Review of International Studies*, vol. 30, no. 2 (April 2004): 269-280.

Wright, Vincent. "La Loi de Sûreté générale de 1858." *Revue d'Histoire moderne et contemporaine*, vol. 16, no. 3 (July-September 1969): 414-430.

Yaycıoğlu, Ali. "Sened-i İttifak (1808): Osmanlı İmparatorluğu'nda Bir Ortaklık ve Entegrasyon Denemesi". In *Nizam-ı Kadim'den Nizam-ı Cedid'e III. Selim ve Dönemi*, edited by Seyfi Kenan, 667-709. Istanbul: ISAM, 2010.

Yılmaz, Hüseyin. "Osmanlı Devleti'nde Batılılaşma Öncesi Meşrutiyetçi Gelişmeler." *Divan*, vol. 13, no. 24 (2008): 1-30.

Zarinebaf, Fariba. "From Istanbul to Tabriz: Modernity and Constitutionalism in the Ottoman Empire and Iran." *Comparative Studies of South Asia, Africa and the Middle East*. vol. 28, no. 1 (2008): 154-169.

Zubaida, Sami. "Cosmopolitanism and the Middle East." In *Cosmopolitanism, Identity and Authenticity in the Middle East*, edited by Roel Meijer, 15-33. Surrey: Curzon, 1999.

Zürcher, Erik J. *Turkey: A Modern History*. London: I. B. Tauris, 1998.

INDEX

PRINTED ON PERMANENT PAPER • IMPRIME SUR PAPIER PERMANENT • GEDRUKT OP DUURZAAM PAPIER - ISO 9706

N.V. PEETERS S.A., WAROTSTRAAT 50, B-3020 HERENT